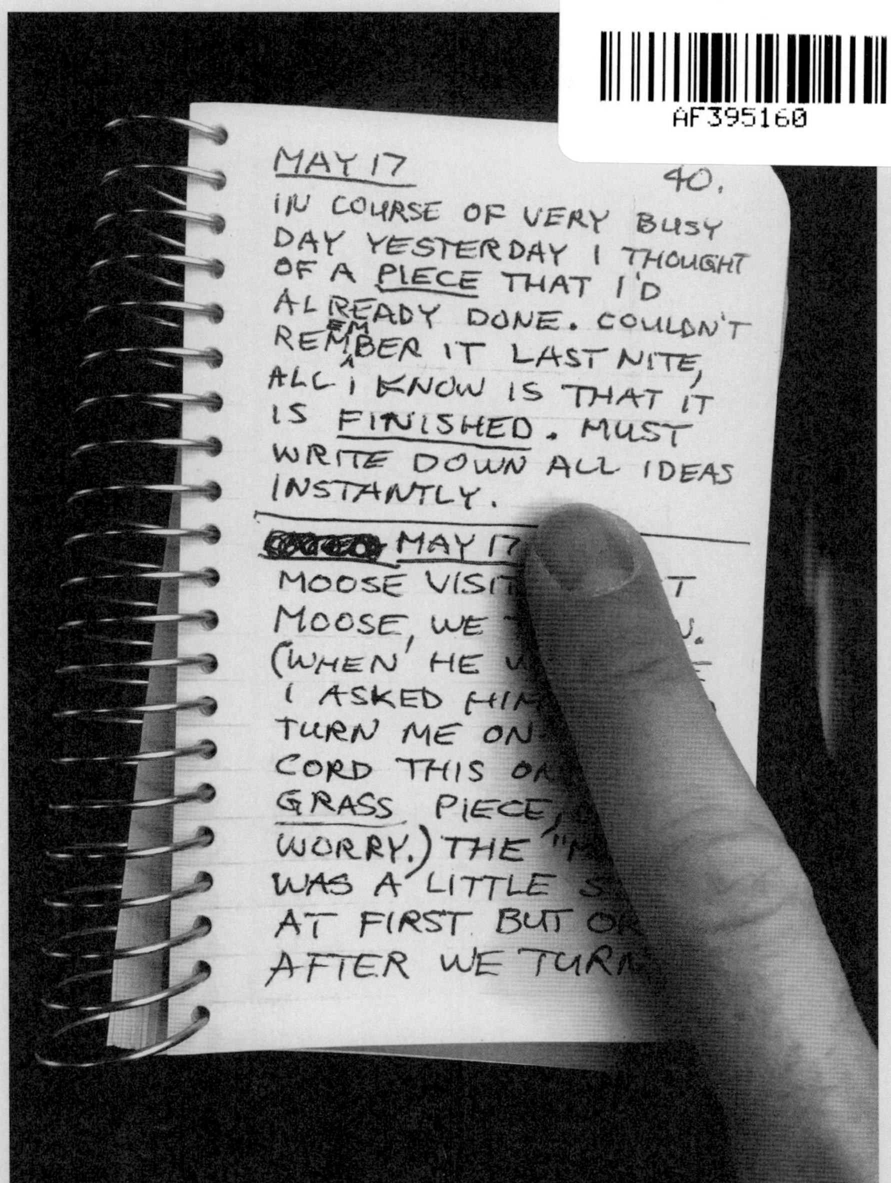




ÅBÄKE ANNOTATED NOTEBOOK 2, 1972, LEE LOZANO

Lorenz soon realized what had happened. The numbers he had typed in were the three-decimal-place numbers from the printout; but inside the computer the numbers were calculated to six decimal places. Where Lorenz had typed 0.506, for example, the number from the first run had actually been 0.506127. The model was so sensitive to the initial conditions that the difference, one quarter of one tenth of 1 per cent, made the two runs diverge completely from one another after a short time. If the real atmosphere was as sensitive as this to its initial conditions, then there was no hope of using numerical forecasting techniques to predict the weather more than a few days ahead. Lorenz announced his discovery in a fairly low-key way at a scientific meeting held in Tokyo in 1960, and went on to develop these ideas in the following years, but the full significance of his work was not appreciated, as we shall see, until much later. In terms of weather-forecasting, Lorenz was able to show that the real atmosphere can indeed be very sensitive to initial conditions. He used a simple mathematical (numerical) model of convection, which only hints at the complexity of the real weather, but which shows a key feature of sensitivity to small changes. You can picture this in terms of our model of phase space as a landscape flooded with water – imagine two deep pools in phase space, representing equally powerful attractors, separated by a sand bar with a very shallow layer of water over it, linking the two pools. Typical trajectories in phase space will circle round and round one or other of the pools, but some rare trajectories cross over the sand bar and into the other pool, where they circle round and round before crossing back into the first pool. The nub of Lorenz's discovery is that without knowing the precise location of a point in phase space, it is impossible to predict exactly when the trajectory passing through that point will cross over to the other side, so the flips from one state to the other seem to occur at random. Or, from a slightly different perspective, the trajectories that wander over the sand bar are very susceptible to tiny perturbations, and a small nudge from outside may be all that it takes to shift a system from a trajectory heading back into one pool on to a trajectory heading across into the other pool. It is because of this kind of process at work that the limit of accurate weather-forecasting is about ten to fourteen days, and that the real weather can also flip from one stable state to another stable state in an essentially unpredictable way.

It is the question of *precise* determination of initial conditions that Lorenz drew attention to and which lies at the heart of the modern

Figure 2.2 *As with the orbit of the satellite in the three-body problem, Edward Lorenz found that computer 'predictions' of weather properties (such as temperature) diverge widely from almost identical starting conditions.*

understanding of chaos. This sensitivity of the weather (and other complex systems) to initial conditions is sometimes referred to as 'the butterfly effect', after the title of a paper that Lorenz presented to a meeting in Washington DC in 1972 – 'Does the Flap of a Butterfly's Wings in Brazil Set off a Tornado in Texas?'[10] The analogy should not be taken entirely seriously, since on this scale in the real world there are so many processes involved, blurring out individual contributions, that it is unlikely that a flap of a butterfly in Brazil could ever be identified as the cause of a specific tornado in Texas (or, conversely, that a flap of another butterfly in China prevented a tornado from forming in Texas). But it does provide a striking metaphor for chaos. Coincidentally, when the double-pooled attractor discovered by Lorenz is plotted out graphically on paper (or a computer screen), it forms a pattern rather like a butterfly's wings; it is usually known as the Lorenz attractor (although Lorenz himself calls it the Butterfly attractor), and has become the most familiar and striking visual image for chaos, even for people who don't know what the image actually represents.

The weather, it turns out, is sometimes more chaotic than at other times. When meteorologists run the numerical simulations these days, they don't just take the exact data from their grid points of observations as the raw material for a single forecast. Instead, to find out if the errors and uncertainties inherent in the observations matter significantly they usually

10. The paper is reproduced in his book *The Essence of Chaos*.

'I JUST THINK AT THE VERY TOP OF THE FOOD CHAIN IS WHERE WE REALLY NEED TO LET PEOPLE, THOSE VERY RICH AND SUPER INNOVATIVE PEOPLE, DO EXACTLY WHAT THEY WANT TO DO.'

ZOLTAN ISTVAN

'WE'RE TRYING TO HAVE THE NON-WEIRD FUTURE GET HERE AS FAST AS POSSIBLE.'

ELON MUSK

'TECHNOLOGICAL MAN IS NOT CONCERNED WITH WHAT HE SHOULD DESIRE: RATHER, HE IS PREOCCUPIED WITH HOW HE CAN ACQUIRE OR ACCOMPLISH WHAT HE DESIRES.'

ROD DREHER

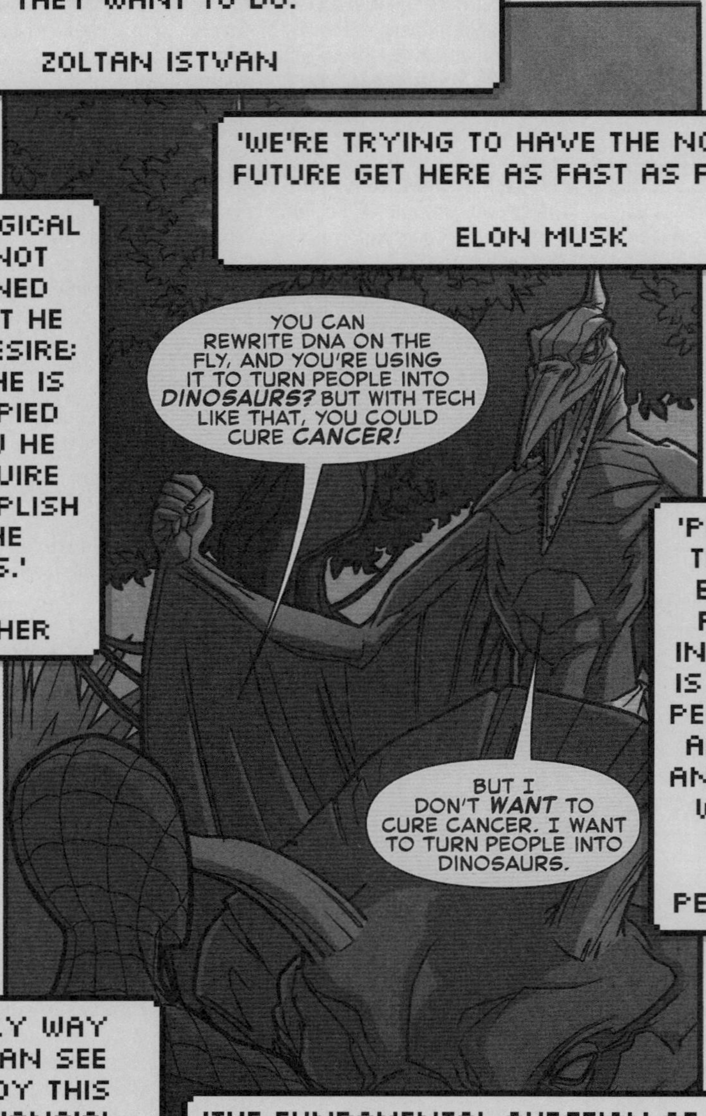

YOU CAN REWRITE DNA ON THE FLY, AND YOU'RE USING IT TO TURN PEOPLE INTO *DINOSAURS?* BUT WITH TECH LIKE THAT, YOU COULD CURE *CANCER!*

BUT I DON'T *WANT* TO CURE CANCER. I WANT TO TURN PEOPLE INTO DINOSAURS.

'PROBABLY THE MOST EXTREME FORM OF INEQUALITY IS BETWEEN PEOPLE WHO ARE ALIVE AND PEOPLE WHO ARE DEAD.'

PETER THIEL

'THE ONLY WAY THAT I CAN SEE TO DEPLOY THIS MUCH FINANCIAL RESOURCE IS BY CONVERTING MY AMAZON WINNINGS INTO SPACE TRAVEL'

JEFF BEZOS

'THE FUNDAMENTAL QUESTION OF OUR TIME IS WHETHER THE WEST HAS THE WILL TO SURVIVE. DO WE HAVE THE CONFIDENCE IN OUR VALUES TO DEFEND THEM AT ANY COST?'

DONALD TRUMP

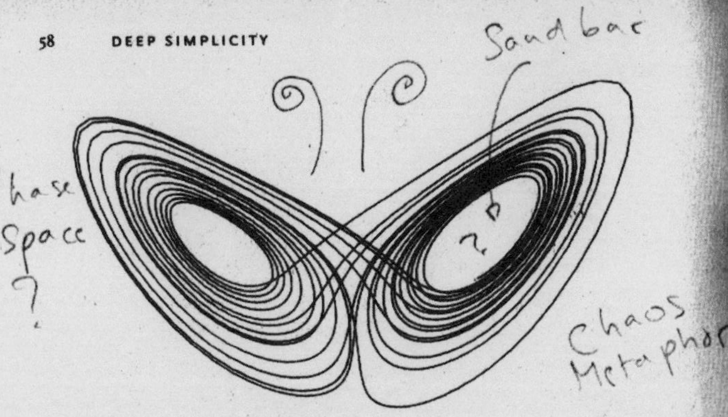


Figure 2.3 *The Lorenz ('butterfly') attractor.*

run each forecast several times with slight variations in the starting conditions. If all the forecasts come out more or less the same, they know that the overall pattern of the forecast(s) can be trusted – the weather system is, if you like, circling one of the deep pools in phase space. But sometimes when they run the same forecast with slightly different starting conditions they get widely different 'predictions' for the weather a few days ahead. This tells them that the weather is in a chaotic state, equivalent to the trajectories wandering over the sand bar in phase space, and none of the forecasts can be trusted. This is why the forecasters on TV sometimes seem more certain about their forecasts than they are on other occasions. As one forecaster has ruefully acknowledged, 'we can predict the weather accurately provided it doesn't do anything unexpected'.[11]

You can see chaos at work in your pocket calculator, using the technique of iteration that is so important in all this kind of numerical work. Take a simple expression, $2x^2 - 1$. Choose a value for $x$ between 0 and 1, with a good few decimal places – say, 0.2468. Use this number as $x$, and work out the result. Then, use that number as $x$, and feed it back into the calculation for the next iteration. You get what looks like a string of random numbers, produced by a completely deterministic process obeying a simple law. Now try again, starting with a number that differs from your first number by



just one part in the last decimal place – say, 0.2469. If you have the patience to keep stabbing away at the keys of the calculator (or the nous to write a simple computer program to do the work for you) you will find that you end up with a completely different string of random-looking numbers after the first few iterations. Yet in both cases every number is precisely determined by the one before by the feedback process – the pattern of numbers is entirely deterministic. This is just the kind of thing that Lorenz observed – and if you try any of this on different calculators, don't be surprised if you get different 'answers', because different calculators round off numbers in their internal calculations in different ways.

You can also see a different kind of behaviour. Take the expression $x^2 - 1$, which looks very similar to the first expression. Now, for any value of $x$ you start out with (between 0 and 1), after a while the pattern settles down into a stable state, oscillating between 0 and −1. It is said to be 'periodic with period two' because once the system has settled down into this pattern, wherever you start from it takes two steps to get back to where you started. And you can have periodic behaviour in other systems where it takes more steps to get back to where you started, but always the same number of steps for that particular system, wherever you start from. One simple law gives periodic behaviour, converging on an attractor; another simple law, seemingly very similar to the first law, gives 'random' behaviour that is very sensitive to initial conditions. If you have a taste for this kind of thing, you can explore further;[12] you'll find that some iterations converge on a single value and get stuck there (a simple attractor, a system sometimes referred to as having 'period one' because just one iterative step takes you back to where you start), some are seemingly random, and some are periodic, with period two being just a simple case hinting at much more complicated possibilities. All of these patterns of behaviour are seen in the real world, where they may apply to things as diverse as the dripping of a tap, the way populations of wild animals change, or the oscillations of the stock market. But in essence we have already found the underlying simplicity from which chaos and complexity emerge – simple laws, nonlinearity, sensitivity to initial conditions and feedback are what make the world tick. Before we move on to really complex things, though, it seems

11. Quoted by Ian Stewart, in *Does God Play Dice?*

12. The contribution by Franco Vivaldi to *The New Scientist Guide to Chaos* (edited by Nina Hall) will give you some ideas.

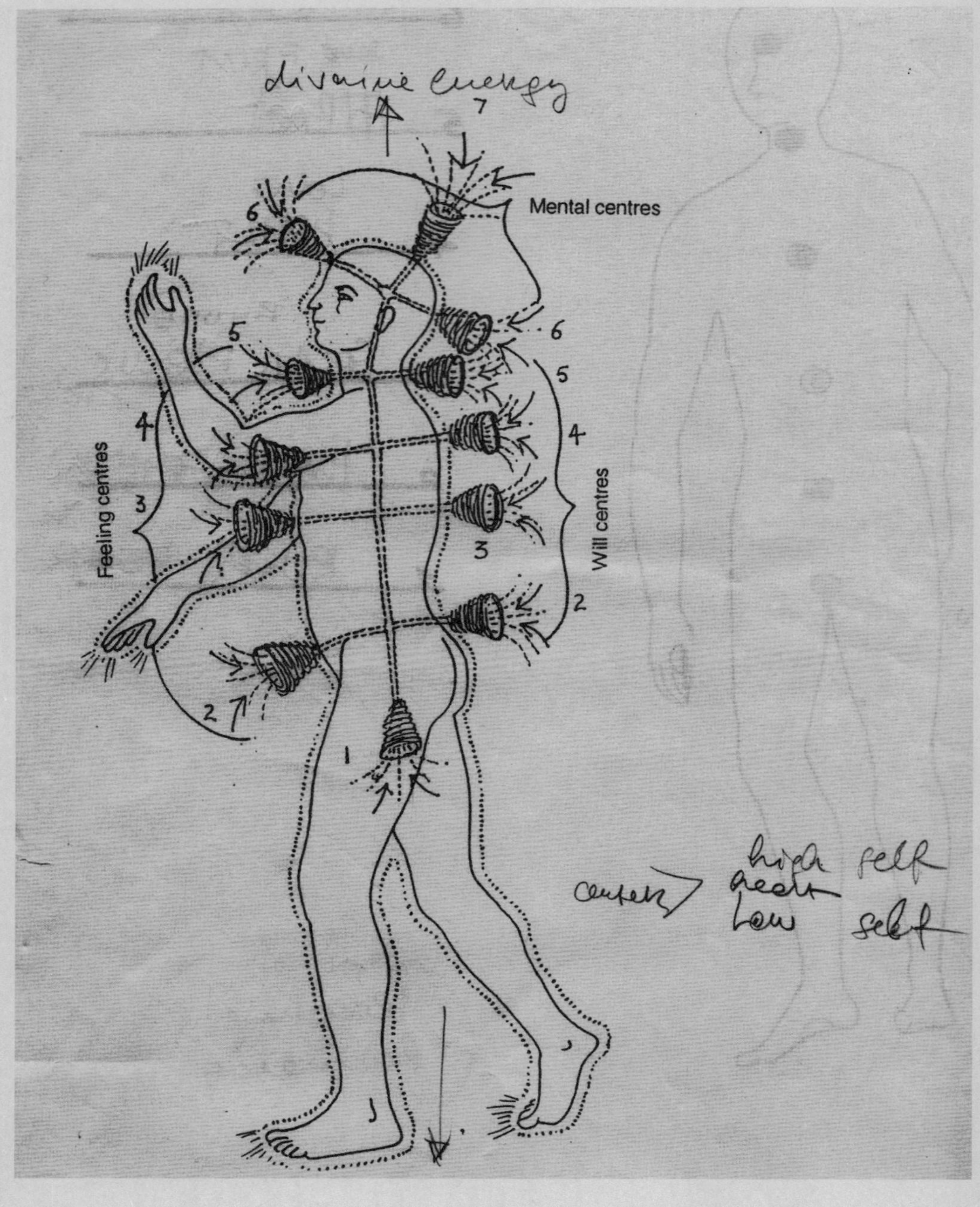

divine energy
7
Mental centres
6
5
4
Will centres
3
2
6
5
4
3
2
1
Feeling centres
centers
high self
mean
Low self

# Reflection on the Mental and Physical Condition of the Artist

In ancient times, the artist, poet, philosopher, builder would climb silently
to the top of the mountain and there, in solitude, would be confronted
with what the Chinese refer to as Chi'j energy. This would condition their body
and their mind to one single point of concentration.

As a result of that particular state would come for the poet one line of poetry,
for the philosopher new thoughts, for the builder new solutions,
for the artist new work.

In the Renaissance, one could read in a book by Cennino Cennini how
to prepare the artist to paint the cupola of a church. He said three months
before starting work, the artist should stop eating meat, two months before
starting work, he should stop drinking wine, one month before starting work,
restrain from sexual desires. Three weeks before starting work, the artist
should put his right arm into plaster, the day he starts work, he should break
the plaster, take a brush and be able to make a perfect circle with a free hand.

Brancusi said:
"What you're doing is not important, what is really important is the state
of mind from which you do it."

That state of mind was essential for me in the moment of performing.
That fragile passage between one reality and another, when you take a step
towards your own mental and physical construction. In my extensive trips into
other cultures, I found different ways of achieving that conditioning.
I made my own symbiosis based on personal experience.
The function of the artist is the function of the servant.
At this particular point of my life, I feel that I can transmit my knowledge.
My field of action is restricted to art academies.
This is the place where the new generation of artists is emerging.
This generation of artists needs to be assisted.

that banana skin or when I sat in the dark and the freezing cold simply because my mum did not make enough money. I knew that these experiences were significant but I was not yet sure how to tease meaning from them.

I was born in the 1980s, when MPs in parliament could be found arguing that we – non-white Commonwealth citizens – should be sent back to where we came from. Now that where we came from had legally ceased to be part of Britain, our very existence here was seen as the problem. So, after our grandmothers had helped build the National Health Service and our grandfathers had staffed the public transport system, British MPs could openly talk about repatriation – we were no longer needed, excess labour, surplus to requirements, of no further use to capital. The entire management of 'race' – the media propaganda, the overstaffed mental institutions, the severe unemployment, the massively disproportionate incarceration rates and school expulsions – has to be understood in the context of why we were invited here in the first place. It was not so that we, en masse, could access the best of what British society had to offer, because that was not even on offer to the majority of the white population at the time. We were invited here to do the menial work that needed doing in the years immediately following the Second World War, and even in that very limited capacity, all post-war governments – including Attlee's spirit of 45 lot – were deeply concerned about the long-term effects of letting brown-skinned British citizens into the country.

The government and the education system failed to explain to white Britain that, as the academic Adam Elliot-Cooper puts it, we had not come to Britain, but 'rather that Britain had come to us'. They did not explain that the wealth of Britain, which made the welfare state and other class ameliorations possible, was derived in no small part from the coffee and tobacco, cotton and diamonds, gold and sweat and blood and

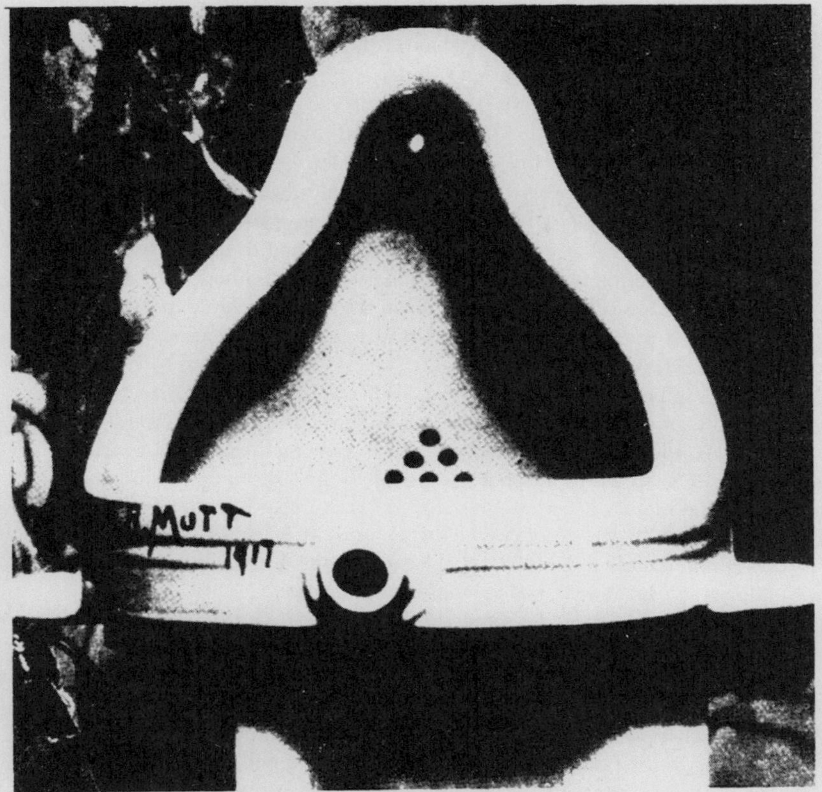

*1.* Marcel Duchamp: *Fountain* 1917

they searched out the basic assumptions and definitions upon which the current collective definition of Art rested.

Each of these artists, in different ways, attempted to undermine certain key elements in our definition of Art.

**Marcel Duchamp** (ill. 1) shifted the epicentre of Art from making an object to <u>choosing</u> an object and so questioned the distinction between Art and non-Art objects.

**Jean Arp** (ill. 2) consciously used the operations of <u>chance</u> to construct his image and so moved Art away from being the outcome of the work of the artist as a highly trained decision maker in the domain of the aesthetic.

**Carl Andre** (ill. 3) by deliberately using <u>randomness</u> in the work of Art mounts a criticism of the work as a site of order and structure.

'It's said, I forget by whom, that our knowledge of dreams is about a thousand years behind our knowledge of physics and numbers.'

'Women can now count.'

'Journeys, journeys! Up, down, and across. Very grotesque. Towards what? I tell my children fate-tales. Seed falls, heroes conquer, riddles are answered, magic hills are climbed, until we meet our real selves.'

Despite my dislike of gardens, I gladly escaped to them from these cliques, anxieties, fevers, the beheadings in well-drained cells, unacknowledged but recognized. I envisaged the executioner's expression as he shaved the doomed neck of a minister hitherto loaded with exceptional favours.

The imperial park, very green, well-watered from the river, was usually empty, or appeared so. I wandered through still trees and flowers, towards the *palestra* where racers competed without visible disposition to win. I inspected opulent though ill-made pavilions on artificial islands, deserted amongst bushes cut into fawns, satyrs, trees planted fully grown, many wilting, and little skiffs waiting very bright and empty. Reflecting, I wanted not Vesta, like a garden flower too dependent, but Sylviana's acute sense.

Conscious of spies I visited the Baths. In *frigidarium,* in *sudatorium,* naked, hairy, paunched, on terraced marble reclined the West's leaders – Gauls, Franks, Africans. Grossly storeyed bellies overwhelmed the tools beneath, were hour-glasses arrested in hideous time. They sweated and grunted as masseurs pummelled them, or lay smiling, to be fanned and oiled, scraped, perfumed, coiffed. I heard of chariot races at Antioch, Christian Orthodox pledges to extirpate Christian Arians who had once caused so much frenzied bloodshed at Rimini, Emperor Constantius watching, surely sardonically, the holy ones entangling themselves with formulae that resisted meaning.

Nothing about the soaring prices of Egyptian wheat, Spanish oil, the cornering of Parian marble by imperial favourites.

In a sunlit, unroofed courtyard I unexpectedly saw, standing up to her thighs in dark blue water, framed between tall, scented alabaster vases, a naked girl, her pubis, in the Tyrrhenian mode, bare, like polished stone and floating like a faintly cracked shell, her head golden with lustrous hair worth two slaves to the Arras wig-makers.

Her eyes looked through me, or were blind, then a flock of birds swept over the sky, like a curtain being drawn, and, soundlessly, she had gone.

121

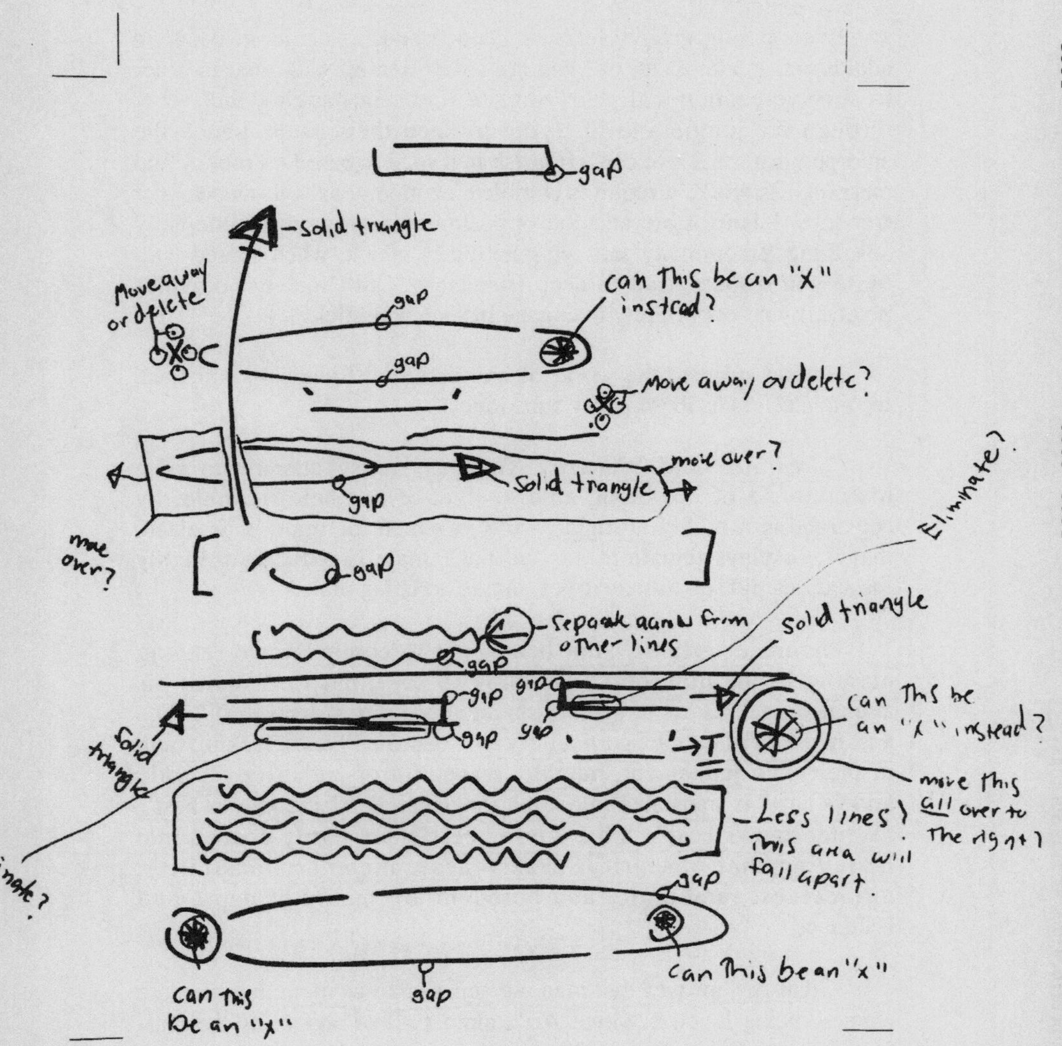

gap
solid triangle
can this be an "x" instead?
Move away or delete
X
move away or delete?
move over?
Solid triangle
Eliminate?
Solid triangle
move over?
gap
gap
gap
gap
gap
Separate arrow from other lines
can this be an "x" instead?
move this all over to the right?
gap gap
gap
gap gap
T
Less lines? this area will fall apart.
Solid triangle
Eliminate?
gap
gap
can this be an "x"
can this be an "x"

*A PRIMER FOR ~~WOMEN~~ ARTISTS (ALL)
FROM THE POETICAL PROVOCATEUR —*

*GOOGLED PROVOCATEUR FOR CORRECT
SPELLING - LOOKING AT GOOGLE IMAGE RESULTS (PROOVE) WHY*

friendship is based on respect, not contempt. *THIS TEXT IS STILL
RELEVANT TODAY!*

Even among groovy females deep friendships seldom occur in adulthood, as almost all of them are either tied up with men in order to survive economically, or bogged down in hacking their way through the jungle and in trying to keep their heads above the amorphous mass. Love can't flourish in a society based on money and meaningless work; it requires complete economic as well as personal freedom, leisure time and the opportunity to engage in intensely absorbing, emotionally satisfying activities which, when shared with those you respect, lead to deep friendship. Our "society" provides practically no opportunity to engage in such activities.

Having stripped the world of conversation, friendship and love, the male offers us these paltry substitutes:

*"Great Art" and "Culture"*: The male "artist" attempts to solve his dilemma of not being able to live, of not being female, by constructing a highly artificial world in which the male is heroized, that is, displays female traits, and the female is reduced to highly limited, insipid subordinate roles, that is, to being male.

The male "artistic" aim being, not to communicate (having nothing inside him, he has nothing to say), but to disguise his animalism, he resorts to symbolism and obscurity ("deep stuff"). The vast majority of people, particularly the "educated" ones, lacking faith in their own judgement, humble, respectful of authority ("Daddy knows best" is translated into adult language as "Critic knows best", "Writer knows best", "Ph.D knows best"), are easily conned into believing that obscurity, evasiveness, incomprehensibility, indirectness, ambiguity and boredom are marks of depth and brilliance.

*THIS TEXT NEEDS NO ANNOTATION!*

"Great Art" proves that men are superior to women, that men are women, being labeled "Great Art", almost all of which, as the antifeminists are fond of reminding us, was created by men. We know that "Great Art" is great because male authorities have told us so, and we can't claim otherwise, as only those with exquisite sensitivities far superior to ours can perceive and appreciate the greatness, the proof of their superior sensitivity being that they appreciate the slop that they appreciate.

*Mercury Medical
RE: STAIRLIFT -01534 762200 → TUES am*

*+ WINE
+ BROCCOLI
+ BEANS
+ CHKKEN
+ TAMPONS*

Appreciating is the sole diversion of the "cultivated"; passive and incompetent, lacking imagination and wit, they must try to make do with that; unable to create their own diversions, to create a little world of their own, to affect in the smallest way their environments, they must accept what's given; unable to create or relate, they spectate. Absorbing "culture" is a desperate, frantic attempt to groove in an ungroovy world, to escape the horror of a sterile, mindless existence. "Culture" provides a sop to the egos of the incompetent, a means of rationalizing passive spectating; they can pride themselves on their ability to appreciate the "finer" things, to see a jewel where there is only a turd (they want to be admired for admiring). Lacking faith in their ability to change anything, resigned to the status quo, they *have* to see beauty in turds because, so far as they can see, turds are all they'll ever have.

The veneration of "Art" and "Culture" — besides leading many women into boring, passive activity that distracts from more important and rewarding activities, from cultivating active abilities and leads to the constant intrusion on our sensibilities of pompous dissertations on the deep beauty of this and that turd. This allows the "artist" to be set up as one possessing superior feelings, perceptions, insights and judgments, thereby undermining the faith of insecure women in the value and validity of their own feelings, perceptions, insights and judgments,

The male, having a very limited range of feelings and, consequently, very limited perceptions, insights and judgments, needs the "artist" to guide him, to tell him what life is all about. But the male "artist", being totally sexual, unable to relate to anything beyond his own physical sensations, having nothing to express beyond the insight that for the male life is meaningless and absurd, cannot be an artist. How can he who is not capable of life tell us what life is all about? A "male artist" is a contradiction in terms. A degenerate can only produce degenerate "art". The true artist is every self-confident, healthy female, and in a female society the only Art, the only Culture, will be conceited, kookie, funky females grooving on each other and on everything else in the universe.

*Sexuality:* Sex is not part of a relationship; on the contrary, it is a solitary experience, non-creative, a gross waste of time. The female can easily — far more easily than she may think — condition away her sex drive, leaving her completely cool and cerebral and free to everything else," he said immediately, "we've got 'Wise Child' complexes. We've never really got off the goddam air. Not one of us. We don't talk, we hold forth. We don't converse, we expound. At least *I* do. The minute I'm in a room with somebody who has the usual number of ears, I either turn into a goddam *seer* or a human hatpin. The Prince of Bores. *Last night,* for instance. Down at the San Remo. I kept *praying* that Hess wouldn't tell me the plot of his new script. I knew damn well he *had* one. I knew damn well I wasn't going to get out of the place without a new script to take home. But I kept praying he'd spare me from an oral *preview.* He's not stupid. He *knows* it's impossible for me to keep my mouth shut." Zooey suddenly, sharply, turned around, without taking his foot off the window seat, and picked up, snatched up, a match folder that was on his mother's writing table. He turned back to the window and the view of the school roof and put his cigar into his mouth again—but at once took it out. "*Damn* him, anyway," he said. "He's so stupid it breaks your heart. He's like everybody else in television. *And* Hollywood. *And* Broadway. He thinks everything sentimental is *tender,* everything *brutal* is a slice of *realism,* and everything that runs into physical violence is a legitimate climax to something that isn't even—"

"Did you *tell* him that?"

"Certainly I told him that! I just got through telling you I can't keep my mouth shut. Cer-





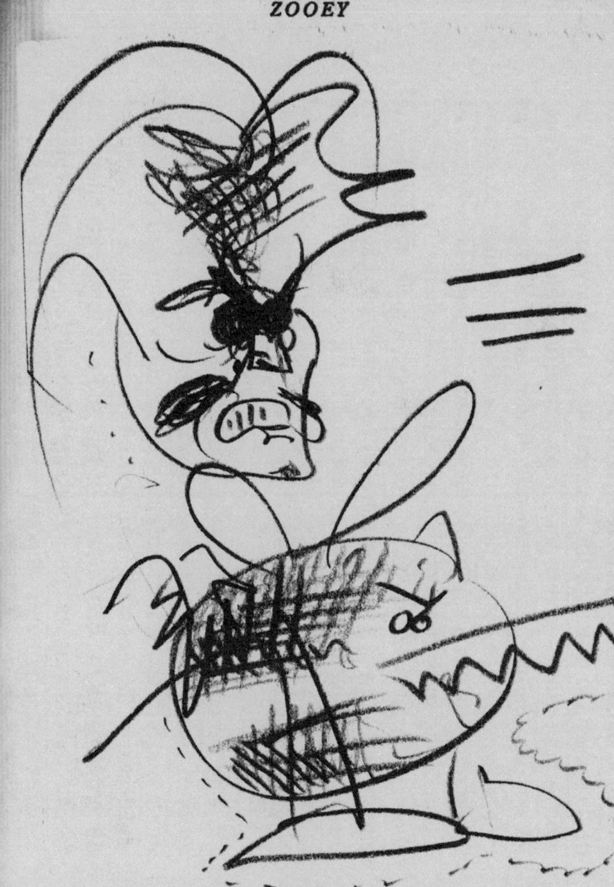

... poverty down my throat. At least he wears horrible neckties and funny padded suits in the

```
1 print("Hello, World!")
2
3 <script.py> output:
4     Hello, World!
```

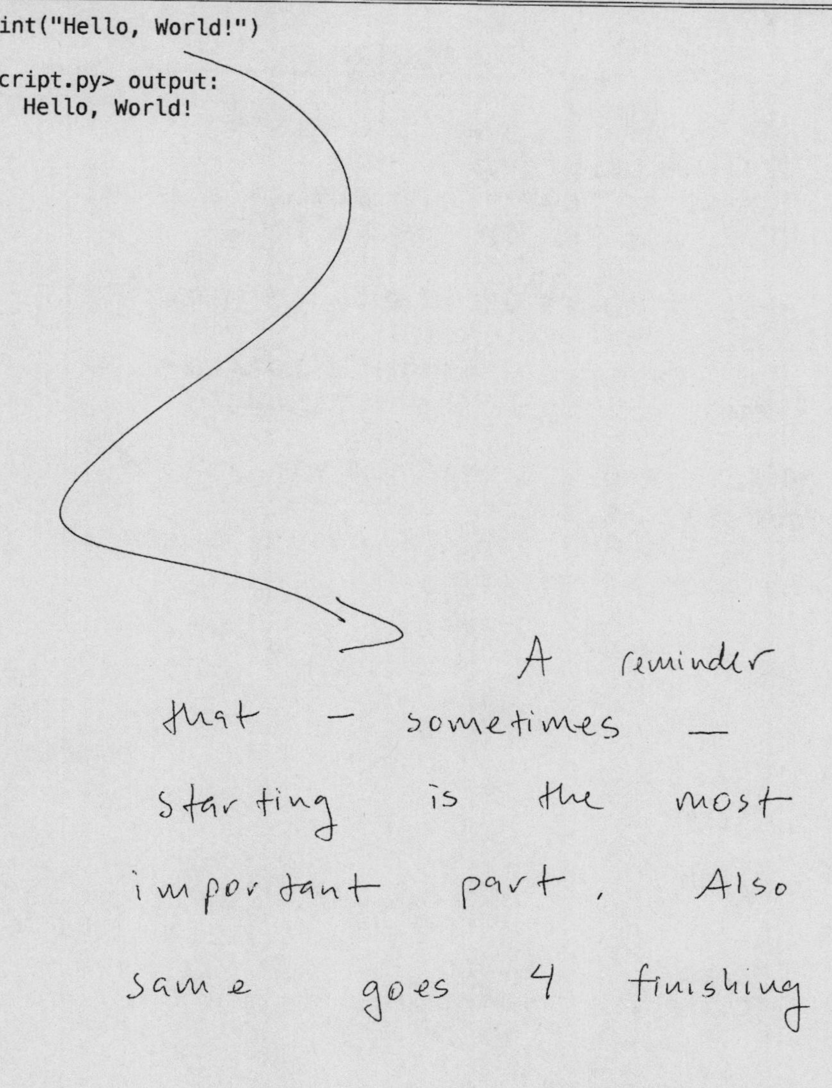

A reminder
that — sometimes —
starting is the most
important part. Also
same goes 4 finishing.

n.d.

## LONGIN

In de evenin when I'm alone [1]
And thinkin [2] jes o' you
Round my heart dere steals a longin [3]
Steals a longin jes fo'you.

Den my heart [4] it starts to pinin'
[5] Pinin jes' for you
Jes' because I keeps a longin [6]
Keeps a longin' jes' for you.

When I knows I cant be [7] wid you
Why should I long [8] for you
Den I [9] thinks what's de use o'longin
a'longin jes'for you.

[10]

Z.N.H 's troublesome love

the
Just
There
for
then
Spining

with
OF

"Just abubbling over of
a melancholy heart—momentarily"

# 1

SHIPS AT A DISTANCE HAVE EVERY MAN'S WISH ON board. For some they come in with the tide. For others they sail forever on the horizon, never out of sight, never landing until the Watcher turns his eyes away in resignation, his dreams mocked to death by Time. That is the life of men.

Now, women forget all those things they don't want to remember, and remember everything they don't want to forget. The dream is the truth. Then they act and do things accordingly.

So the beginning of this was a woman and she had come back from burying the dead. Not the dead of sick and ailing with friends at the pillow and the feet. She had come back from the sodden and the bloated; the sudden dead, their eyes flung wide open in judgment.

The people all saw her come because it was sundown. The sun was gone, but he had left his footprints in the sky. It was the time for sitting on porches beside the road. It was the time to hear things and talk. These sitters had been tongueless,

earless, eyeless conveniences all day long. Mules and other brutes had occupied their skins. But now, the sun and the bossman were gone, so the skins felt powerful and human. They became lords of sounds and lesser things. They passed nations through their mouths. They sat in judgment.

Seeing the woman as she was made them remember the envy they had stored up from other times. So they chewed up the back parts of their minds and swallowed with relish. They made burning statements with questions, and killing tools out of laughs. It was mass cruelty. A mood come alive. Words walking without masters; walking altogether like harmony in a song.

"What she doin' coming back here in dem overhalls? Can't she find no dress to put on?— Where's dat blue satin dress she left here in?— Where all dat money her husband took and died and left her?— What dat ole forty year ole 'oman doin' wid her hair swingin' down her back lak some young gal?— Where she left dat young lad of a boy she went off here wid?— Thought she was going to marry?— Where he left *her*?— What he done wid all her money?— Betcha he off wid some gal so young she ain't even got no hairs—why she don't stay in her class?—"

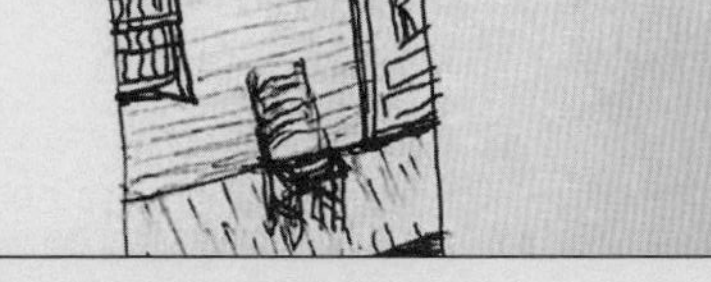

ART & LANGUAGE ANNOTATED ROMA REASON – LUHMANN'S ART AS A SOCIAL SYSTEM, RADICAL PHILOSOPHY, ISSUE 109, SEPTEMBER/OCTOBER 2001, ART & LANGUAGE

more apparent are its own bandit contingencies.  This is Clement Greenberg turned upside down. 'Once art becomes autonomous the emphasis shifts from self-reference to hetero-reference – which is not the same as self-isolation…but there is no such thing as self-reference without hetero-reference'.

But 'Art as a Social System' is not without art historical detail.  He cites from the Middle Ages, the Renaissance, Romanticism, Postmodernism and Conceptual Art (or should that be Conceptual Art and Postmodernism?).  And, he understands what Conceptual Art felt it had to do.  'Under the conditions of autonomy, this means that art must surpass itself and eventually reflect upon its own surpassing of itself'.  There are few other remarks that capture the improbable requirements on a Conceptual Art of around 1968-70.  Most observers bring either a disappointed sense of "taste" or a dissappointed sense of "meaning" to it.  And Luhmann also makes me think that there was as much a sociological dimension to that work, rather than as is usually assumed a "philosophical" one.

When Luhmann claims that 'paintings acquire representative functions that are not confused with ordinary social reality, even though they refer to reality in a manner that implies both proximity and distance' it is as if he is referring to his own writing methods.  And that's the point – you often can't tell whether he is talking about the art system or his own system.  In somehow conflating resources with subject matter we become enmeshed in the implications of proximity and distance on the boundaries of his own self-critical system.

According to Luhmann 'When Hegel speaks of the end of art … he can mean only one thing: art has lost its immediate relation to society and worldly affairs and must henceforth acknowledge its own differentiation'.  He goes on to say that 'the differentiation of the art system…allows the relation between system and environment to be reintroduced into the system in the form of a relationship between self-reference and hetero-reference'.  Or, to summarize, 'how can the self be indicated if it excludes nothing'.  That's the whole point of the describing and re-describing of art's professionalisation – the generation of hetero-reference or, under another description, dialogic aura. That's the way it works, and we might as well get used to it. This is the way art can be integrated into the everyday: by accepting, describing and re-describing its own differentiation as form. Attempts to deny this differentiation collapse art into the phoney media space of journalism and the cyberspace of publicity. No internal technical problems, no internal complexity means, on another level, no self to differentiate and no possible orientation in any kind of space.

The fraudulence of publicity dependent art lies in its fear of its own character. And what is that character? It is according to Luhmann 'one that requires that works of art converse with one another, that cite, copy, reject, renew, ironise, art...today this is called 'intertextuality' which is another way of saying the system must have a memory'. Is this what Tracey Emin's *Helter Fucking Skelter* does to or with Tatlin's somewhat earlier *Monument to the third International*? Or is it jut another example of art as stupid celebrity motif? That's a real question. Does the 'citing', 'renewing', 'ironising' etc. refer to productive requirements or mere consumption/comparison? Art as celebrity motif, as the ornament of management and distribution misses entirely the risks of its own re-description. Picasso, according to Luhmann 'is considered the representative painter of this century and for good reason; the unity of his work can no longer be comprehended in terms of form or style, but only in terms of an irony which he probes in all conceivable forms and styles. OK, there's nothijng new in saying this, that Picasso was a strenuously productive self of classical modernity. Today we are left with the "democracy" of the supermarket and this is not simply a dumb reduction but a real condition full of indeterminacies. According to Luhmann, 'when a work of art is determined to call art as such into question, when, inspired by Godel, it tries to appear as a work of art outside of the system of art, or when it seeks to accomplish a re-entry of non art into art in the sense of Spencer-Brown and, in so doing, generates an endless oscillation between inside and outside in an imaginary realm outside the calculus of forms – when all this makes up the intended meaning of the work and can be observed accordingly – then the art system has definitely arrived at a new level of self-description'. He goes on to say that this is an attempt 'to press the system to the limit so as to include the excluded'. Moreover, 'how is this possible socially, if not on the basis of assumptions, the current near professionwide agreement about what constitutes narrative or explanation or adequate historicization may, if it persists unquestioned, unintentionally impoverish the gene pool of literary-critical perspectives and skills. The trouble with a shallow gene pool, of course, is its diminished ability to respond to environmental (e.g., political) change.

Another, perhaps more nearly accurate way of describing the present paranoid consensus, however, is that rather than entirely displacing, it may simply have required a certain disarticulation, disavowal, and misrecognition of other ways of knowing, ways less oriented around suspicion, that are actually being practiced, often by the same theorists and as part of the same projects. The monopolistic program of paranoid knowing systematically disallows any explicit recourse to reparative motives, no sooner to be articulated than subject to methodical uprooting. Reparative motives, once they become explicit, are inadmissible in paranoid theory both because they are about pleasure ("merely aesthetic") and because they are frankly ameliorative ("merely reformist").[2] What makes pleasure and amelioration so "mere"? Only the exclusiveness of paranoia's faith in demystifying exposure: only its cruel and contemptuous assumption that the one thing lacking for global revolution, explosion of gender roles, or whatever, is people's (that is, other people's) having the painful effects of their oppression, poverty, or deludedness sufficiently exacerbated to make the pain conscious (as if otherwise it wouldn't have been) and intolerable (as if intolerable situations were famous for generating excellent solutions).

Such ugly prescriptions are not seriously offered by most paranoid theory, but a lot of contemporary theory is nonetheless regularly *structured as if* by them. The kind of aporia we have already discussed in *The Novel and the Police,* where readers are impelled through a grimly monolithic structure of strong paranoid theory by successive engagement with quite varied, often apparently keenly pleasure-oriented, smaller-scale writerly and intellectual solicitations, appears in a lot of other good criticism as well. I certainly recognize it as characterizing a fair amount of my own writing. Does it matter when such projects misdescribe themselves or are misrecognized by readers? I wouldn't suggest that the force of any powerful writing can ever attain complete transparency to itself, or is likely to account for itself very adequately at the constative level of the writing. But suppose one takes seriously the notion, like the one articulated by Tomkins but also like other available ones, that everyday theory qualitatively affects everyday knowl-

144 *Touching Feeling*

edge and experience; and suppose that one doesn't want to draw much ontological distinction between academic theory and everyday theory; and suppose that one has a lot of concern for the quality of other people's and one's own practices of knowing and experiencing. In these cases, it would make sense—if one had the choice—not to cultivate the necessity of a systematic, self-accelerating split between what one is doing and the reasons one does it.

While paranoid theoretical proceedings both depend on and reinforce the structural dominance of monopolistic "strong theory," there may also be benefit in exploring the extremely varied, dynamic, and historically contingent ways that strong theoretical constructs interact with weak ones in the ecology of knowing—an exploration that obviously can't proceed without a respectful interest in weak as well as strong theoretical acts. Tomkins offers far more models for approaching such a project than I've been able to summarize. But the history of literary criticism can also be viewed as a repertoire of alternative models for allowing strong and weak theory to interdigitate. What could better represent "weak theory, little better than a description of the phenomena which it purports to explain," than the devalued and near obsolescent New Critical skill of imaginative close reading?[3] But what was already true in Empson and Burke is true in a different way today: there are important phenomenological and theoretical tasks that can be accomplished only through local theories and nonce taxonomies; the potentially innumerable mechanisms of their relation to stronger theories remain matters of art and speculative thought.

Paranoia, as I have pointed out, represents not only a strong affect theory but a strong *negative* affect theory. The question of the strength of a given theory (or that of the relations between strong and weak theory) may be orthogonal to the question of its affective *quale,* and each may be capable of exploration by different means. A strong theory (i.e., a wide-ranging and reductive one) that was not mainly organized around anticipating, identifying, and warding off the negative affect of humiliation would resemble paranoia in some respects but differ from it in others. I think, for example, that that might be a fair characterization of the preceding section of the present chapter. Because even the specification of paranoia as a theory of negative affect leaves open the distinctions between or among negative affects, there is the additional opportunity of experimenting with a vocabulary that will do justice to a wide affective range. Again, not only with the negative affects: it

## Prologue

On the way to his car Pierre Dupont stopped at the cash dispenser to draw some money. The device accepted his card and told him he could have 1800 francs. Pierre Dupont pressed the button beside this figure on the screen. The device asked him to wait a moment and then delivered the sum requested, reminding him as it did so to withdraw his card. 'Thank you for your custom,' it added as Pierre Dupont arranged the banknotes in his wallet.

It was a trouble-free drive, the trip to Paris on the A11 autoroute presenting no problems on a Sunday morning. There was no tailback at the junction where he joined it. He paid at the Dourdan tollbooth using

his blue card, skirted Paris on the *périphérique* and took the A1 to Roissy.

He parked in row J of underground level 2, slid his parking ticket into his wallet and hurried to the Air France check-in desks. With some relief he deposited his suitcase (exactly 20 kilos) and handed his flight ticket to the hostess, asking if it would be possible to have a smoking seat next to the gangway. Silent and smiling, she assented with an inclination of her head, after first consulting her computer, then gave him back his ticket along with a boarding pass. 'Boarding from Satellite B at eighteen hundred,' she told him.

He went early through Passport Control to do a little duty-free shopping. He bought a bottle of cognac (something French for his Asian clients) and a box of cigars (for himself). Meticulously, he put the receipt away next to his blue card.

He strolled past the window-displays of luxury goods, glancing briefly at their jewellery, clothing and scent bottles, then called at the bookshop where he leafed through a couple of magazines before choosing an undemanding book: travel, adventure, spy fiction. Then he resumed his unhurried progress.

He was enjoying the feeling of freedom imparted by having got rid of his luggage and at the same time, more intimately, by the certainty that, now that he was 'sorted out', his identity registered, his boarding pass in his pocket, he had nothing to do but wait for the

*1*

*2*



sequence of events. 'Roissy, just the two of us!': these days, surely, it was in these crowded places where thousands of individual itineraries converged for a moment, unaware of one another, that there survived something of the uncertain charm of the waste lands, the yards and building sites, the station platforms and waiting rooms where travellers break step, of all the chance meeting places where fugitive feelings occur of the possibility of continuing adventure, the feeling that all there is to do is to 'see what happens'.

The passengers boarded without problems. Those whose boarding passes bore the letter Z were requested to board last, and he observed with a certain amusement the muted, unnecessary jostling of the Xs and Ys around the door to the boarding gangway.

Waiting for take-off, while newspapers were being distributed, he glanced through the company's in-flight magazine and ran his finger along the imagined route of the journey: Heraklion, Larnaca, Beirut, Dhahran, Dubai, Bombay, Bangkok . . . more than nine thousand kilometres in the blink of an eye, and a few names which had cropped up in the news over the years. He cast his eye down the duty-free price list, noted that credit cards were accepted on intercontinental flights, and read with a certain smugness the advantages conferred by the 'business class' in which he was travelling thanks to the intelligent generosity of his firm ('At Charles de Gaulle 2 and New York, Club lounges are



provided where you can rest, make telephone calls, use a photocopier or Minitel . . . . Apart from a personal welcome and constant attentive service, the new Espace 2000 seat has been designed for extra width and has separately adjustable backrest and headrest . . .'). He examined briefly the digitally labelled control panel of his Espace 2000 seat and then, drifting back into the advertisements in the magazine, admired the aerodynamic lines of a few late-model roadsters and gazed at the pictures of some large hotels belonging to an international chain, somewhat pompously described as 'the surroundings of civilization' (the Mammounia in Marrakesh, 'once a palace, now the quintessence of five-star luxury', the Brussels Métropole, 'where the splendours of the nineteenth century remain very much alive'). Then he came across an advertisement for a car with the same name as his seat, the Renault Espace: 'One day, the need for space makes itself felt . . . . It comes to us without warning. And never goes away. The irresistible wish for a space of our own. A mobile space which can take us anywhere. A space where everything is to hand and nothing is lacking . . . .' Just like the aircraft really. 'Already, space is inside you . . . . You've never been so firmly on the ground as you are in (the E)space,' the advertisement ended pleasingly.

*3*

*4*

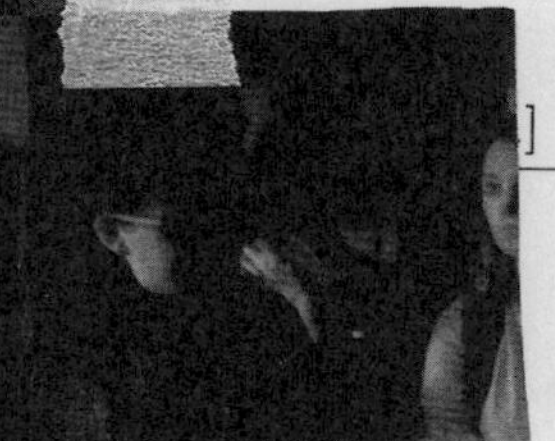

## Snow

The room was suddenly rich and the great bay-window was
Spawning snow and pink roses against it
Soundlessly collateral and incompatible:
World is suddener than we fancy it.

World is crazier and more of it than we think,
Incorrigibly plural. I peel and portion
A tangerine and spit the pips and feel
The drunkenness of things being various.

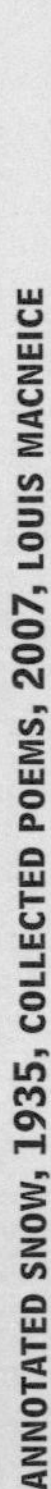

And the fire flames with a bubbling sound for world
Is more spiteful and gay than one supposes –
On the tongue on the eyes on the ears in the palms of one's
    hands –
There is more than glass between the snow and the huge roses.

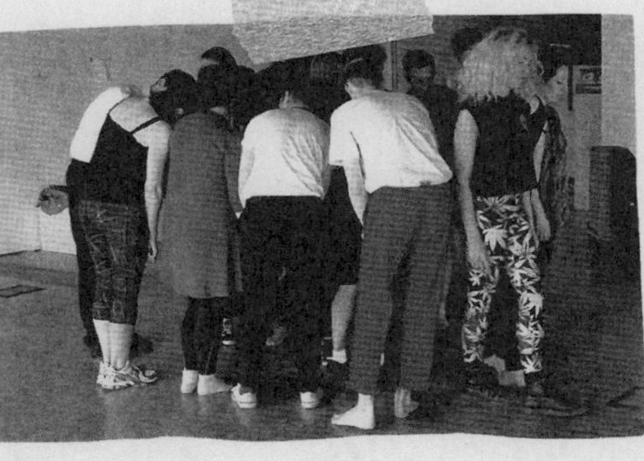

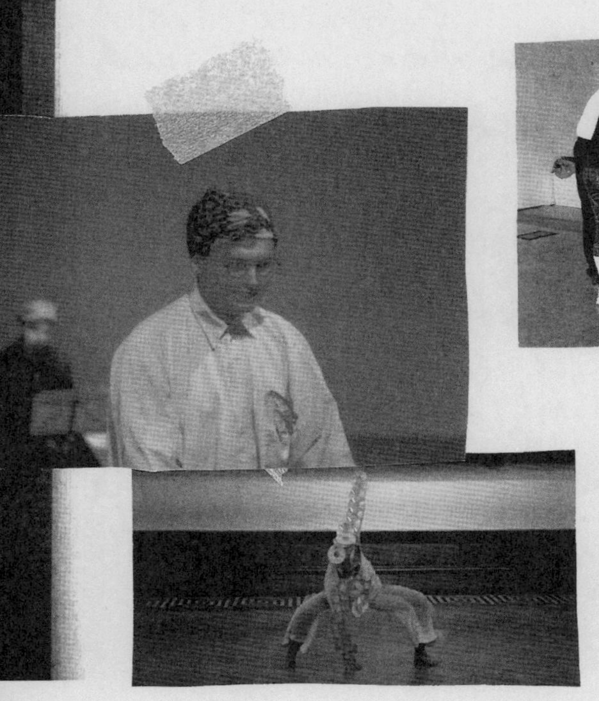

A MANS MIND MAY BE likened to a garden, which may be intelligently cultivated or allowed to run wild, but whether cultivated or neglected, it must and will, bring forth. If no useful seeds are put into it, then an abundance of useless weed seeds will fall therein, and will continue to produce their kind ...

Just as a gardener ~~cultivates~~ cultivates his plot, keeping it ~~free~~ from weeds, and growing the flowers and fruits which he requires, so may a man tend the garden of his mind, weeding out all the wrong, useless, and impure thoughts, and cultivating toward perfection the flowers and fruits of right, useful and pure thoughts, By pursuing this process, a man, sooner or later discovers that he is the master-gardener of his soul, the director of his life. He also ~~teach~~ reveals, within himself, the laws of thought, and

... understands with ever increasing accuracy, how the thought forces and mind elements operate in the shaping of his character, circumstances, and destiny.

MAN IS buffeted by circumstances so long as he believes himself to be the creature of outside conditions, but when he realizes that he is a creative power, and that he may command the hidden soil and seeds of his being out of which circumstances grow, he then becomes the rightful master of himself.

"AS A MAN THINKETH, SO HE BECOMES"

YOU ARE WHAT YOU THINK

"AS A MAN THINKETH.

JAMES ALLEN.

Dan Baldwin

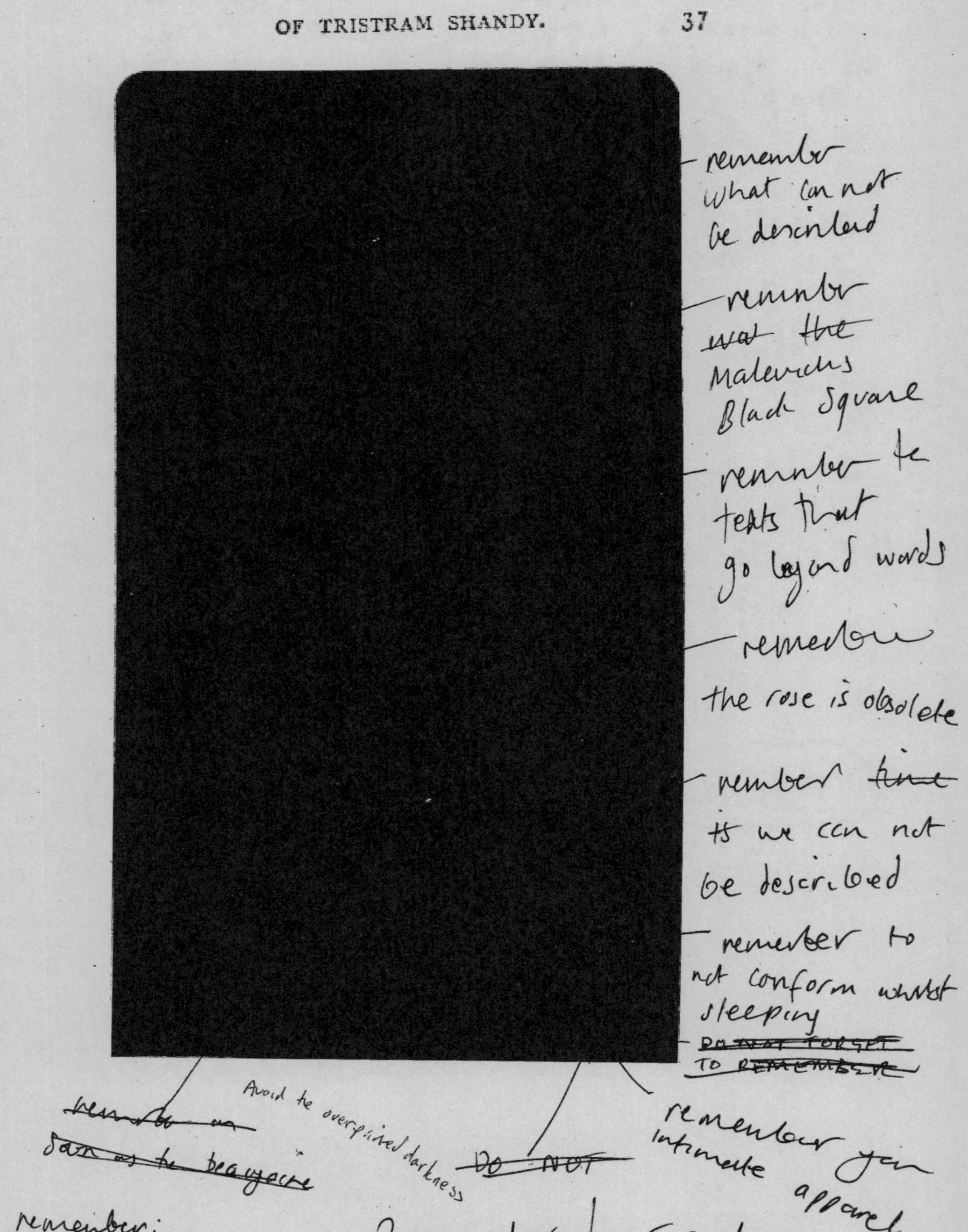

remember what can not be described

remember ~~wat the~~ Malevich's Black Square

remember te texts that go beyond words

remember the rose is obsolete

remember ~~time~~ is we can not be described

remember to not conform whilst sleeping

~~DO NOT FORGET TO REMEMBER~~

remember your intimate apparel

~~remember as~~
~~dark as the~~ beautiful

Avoid te overpriced darkness ~~DO NOT~~

remember:
It is totally obtuse to annotate sterns black page to annotate, emulate.

Remember to Forget (the 'mark on te wall') just

*armoured car*

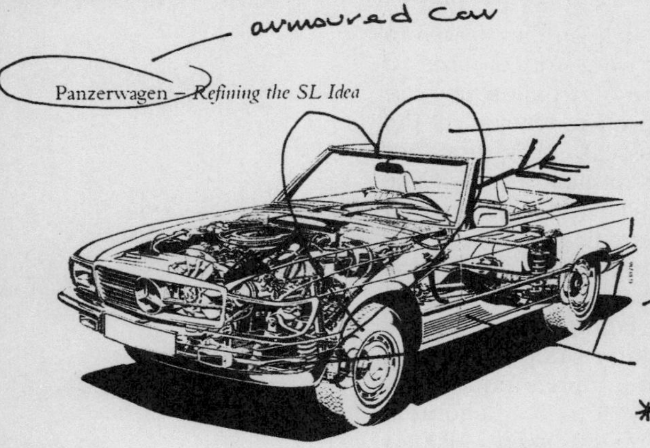

R107 offered V8 engines, new rear suspension and much greater occupant safety than previous models.

*Sills * prone to rust in British climate through * * salt erosion **

*bumpers for the American market — and uglier in my opinion*

were much larger and heavier because the car had to be able to withstand a 5mph (8km/h) front impact or 2.5mph (4km/h) rear impact without damage to any safety-related equipment, which included the fuel tank and lights. Even bigger bumpers would follow a couple of years later, as the regulations became ever more stringent. *draconian.*

There were safety innovations inside the SL too, and they applied in all markets. The dashboard now had three very clear and easy to read instruments grouped together in a binnacle ahead of the driver, and it was now covered with soft polyurethane mouldings to reduce the possibility of injury in a collision. The *Large discreet horn and* steering wheel retained the central crash-pad that Mercedes-Benz had developed in the 1960s, but now had four spokes and a moulded polyurethane rim to better protect the driver. Head restraints were fitted to the front seats as standard to help prevent whiplash injuries in the event of a rear-end collision. The 350SL even had a new type of seat belt – the 'inertia reel' – which automatically adjusted itself to the right length for any passenger and allowed the driver and passenger to move around in the cockpit, but locked automatically in a collision. Safer and far more convenient than the usual 'static' belts, they

drew widespread praise and were quickly adopted on other Mercedes-Benz models and by other manufacturers.

The larger interior that resulted from the slightly longer wheelbase meant there was space to plan-in an air-conditioning system, now vital for the American market, but the standard heating and ventilation system was typically thorough, too: even the insides of the door panels were warmed by the heater. More space was devoted to the 'occasional' rear seat, to make the accommodation a little more usable. Instead of the single transverse seat of the 'Pagoda-roof' SL, there was now space for two tiny rear seats, enough for small children. A padded bench was offered as an option, to make riding in the back a little more comfortable. Alternatively, the extra space provided a useful extra luggage area.

Like its predecessor, the R107 SL quickly became the kind of car in which the rich and famous were often seen. It was a convenient size, swift and surefooted, easy to drive and convenient to use. More importantly, perhaps, the three-pointed star on the front gave it the essential hallmark of quality and there was no doubting the style and good taste of the conservative design. *Not as brash or as brazen as a BMW.*

*Kind of defeats the object of having a convertible*

*two's company three's a crowd*

*no matter how you dress this up its a two seater end of.*

*DESIRE PROMPT*

*selected TV + Film credits*

*Miami Vice*
*Casino*
*American Gigolo*
*Dynasty*
*Dallas*
*(upfront stylisation and surface gloss)*

106

*Gas guzzler even my 280 made me feel like I had the touch of a elephant on the pedal*

**double entendres* *alert**

*? – a built in housing for a ships compass*

Vampyroteuthis reflects, and given his complexity, if he did not reflect he would not have survived. Well, he who says reflection says philosophy. So much so, that to wish to intuit vampyroteuthian existence implies a wish to decipher his philosophy. But there we stumble across a curious difficulty. Although reflection and philosophy are synonyms from a biological perspective (they are the capacity to control mental processes), they are not synonyms from the perspective of human history. The capacity to reflect has articulated itself in several successive and simultaneous philosophies that are very different from each other. In man, the capacity to reflect is like an innate base for the elaboration of acquired philosophies, a "natural" base for the cultural phenomenon of philosophy. In the attempt to capture vampyroteuthian philosophy, we cannot compare it to a human philosophy "*tout court*", but to one of the culturally elaborated philosophies. Greek philosophy offers itself up for comparison as the foundation of Western philosophy.

For the West, "to reflect" is a process that controls the relation between lived appearances and the faculty of reason that processes them. Its two key terms are "appearance" (*phainomenon*) and "reason" (*nous*). Appearances must be "operated" on because they deceive. Reason is the operating knife that cuts appearances into defined and workable rations. This Greek vision of the relation between appearance and reason is not "originally" Greek, but "specifically" human. The first tool produced by man at the very instant of becoming man was the stone knife. Human reason produces knives because it works like a knife, and it works like a knife because it produces knives.

Vampyroteuthis doesn't produce knives because he doesn't need them. His bioluminescent organs cut up the world when emitting rays of light. It is true that both men and Vampyroteuthis feel the outline of objects in order to define them. But the purpose of this rational gesture is not the same in both cases. Man feels the outline of objects that appear in order to control with his hands what has appeared in front of his eyes. He does not trust



digital = 'relating to the fingers' + (of continuous data, eg sound signals) separated into discrete units to facilitate transmission, processing etc.

world is continuous

his eyes. Afterwards, man peels off the outlines that were felt, as if they were the rinds of objects. What he then has in his hands are "empty concepts". These concepts, "models", man stores in his memory to use them as traps in which he will grasp new objects, as yet unfelt. In this way there emerges a back-and-forth between object and model, between appearance and concept, to such end that a situation emerges in which no object will be perceived that does not have at least a slightly appropriate concept in human memory. Human reflection, their philosophy, is precisely this control of the back-and-forth between appearance and concept, between "problem" and "model".

The purpose of vampyroteuthian touch is the Other. He touches the darkness with the aim of directing his light rays at a particular region of the world. He conceives of objects in order to make them appear. Appearance is the consequence of a deliberate act. What is inconceivable does not appear. It is reason, therefore, that makes the world appear to him. Because reason is sexual: tentacles are the carriers of penis and clitoris. Every concept is either masculine or feminine. Every concept is sexually exciting. Every stone touched on the ocean floor excites the genital apparatus: Vampyroteuthis conceives passionately. When the male handles the female, he conceives of feminine concepts in a masculine way. During coitus, masculine and feminine concepts fuse orgiastically. During coitus, "man comes to know woman" (to resort to biblical terminology), and woman to know man. That is: during coitus masculine and feminine concepts control themselves mutually and synthesise themselves. That is vampyroteuthian reflection. The key term of his philosophy is "sex".

For Vampyroteuthis, sex is the foundation of the world of appearances and it impregnates all appearances. Sex is "public". Vampyroteuthian philosophy is, before all else, a critique of sex. His *Organon*, the rules of his reflection, are the rules of sex. His language's syntax, the play of colours over his skin, is the logic of sex. Should Vampyroteuthis achieve an abstraction of the "content" of thought in the course of his reflection, he will have

# Uses of the Erotic:
# The Erotic as Power*

THERE ARE MANY kinds of power, used and unused, acknowledged or otherwise. The erotic is a resource within each of us that lies in a deeply female and spiritual plane, firmly rooted in the power of our unexpressed or unrecognized feeling. In order to perpetuate itself, every oppression must corrupt or distort those various sources of power within the culture of the oppressed that can provide energy for change. For women, this has meant a suppression of the erotic as a considered source of power and information within our lives.

We have been taught to suspect this resource, vilified, abused, and devalued within western society. On the one hand, the superficially erotic has been encouraged as a sign of female inferiority; on the other hand, women have been made to suffer and to feel both contemptible and suspect by virtue of its existence.

It is a short step from there to the false belief that only by the suppression of the erotic within our lives and consciousness can women be truly strong. But that strength is illusory, for it is fashioned within the context of male models of power.

As women, we have come to distrust that power which rises from our deepest and nonrational knowledge. We have been warned against it all our lives by the male world, which values

* Paper delivered at the Fourth Berkshire Conference on the History of Women, Mount Holyoke College, August 25, 1978. First published as a pamphlet by Out & Out Books. Now published as a pamphlet by Kore Press.

53

of these attempts, it has become fashionable to separate the spiritual (psychic and emotional) from the political, to see them as contradictory or antithetical. "What do you mean, a poetic revolutionary, a meditating gunrunner?" In the same way, we have attempted to separate the spiritual and the erotic, thereby reducing the spiritual to a world of flattened affect, a world of the ascetic who aspires to feel nothing. But nothing is farther from the truth. For the ascetic position is one of the highest fear, the gravest immobility. The severe abstinence of the ascetic becomes the ruling obsession. And it is one not of self-discipline but of self-abnegation.

The dichotomy between the spiritual and the political is also false, resulting from an incomplete attention to our erotic knowledge. For the bridge which connects them is formed by the erotic — the sensual — those physical, emotional, and psychic expressions of what is deepest and strongest and richest within each of us, being shared: the passions of love, in its deepest meanings.

Beyond the superficial, the considered phrase, "It feels right to me," acknowledges the strength of the erotic into a true knowledge, for what that means is the first and most powerful guiding light toward any understanding. And understanding is a handmaiden which can only wait upon, or clarify, that knowledge, deeply born. The erotic is the nurturer or nursemaid of all our deepest knowledge.

The erotic functions for me in several ways, and the first is in providing the power which comes from sharing deeply any pursuit with another person. The sharing of joy, whether physical, emotional, psychic, or intellectual, forms a bridge between the sharers which can be the basis for understanding much of what is not shared between them, and lessens the threat of their difference.

Another important way in which the erotic connection functions is the open and fearless underlining of my capacity for joy. In the way my body stretches to music and opens into response, hearkening to its deepest rhythms, so every level upon which I sense also opens to the erotically satisfying experience, whether

### Reflexive impotence

'suggestive aesthetic model' for understanding the fragmenting of subjectivity in the face of the emerging entertainment-industrial complex. 'With the breakdown of the signifying chain', Jameson summarized, 'the Lacanian schizophrenic is reduced to an experience of pure material signifiers, or, in other words, a series of pure and unrelated presents in time'. Jameson was writing in the late 1980s – i.e. the period in which most of my students were born. What we in the classroom are now facing is a generation born into that ahistorical, anti-mnemonic blip culture – a generation, that is to say, for whom time has always come ready-cut into digital micro-slices.

If the figure of discipline was the worker-prisoner, the figure of control is the debtor-addict. Cyberspatial capital operates by addicting its users; William Gibson recognized that in *Neuromancer* when he had Case and the other cyberspace cowboys feeling insects-under-the-skin strung out when they unplugged from the matrix (Case's amphetamine habit is plainly the substitute for an addiction to a far more abstract speed). If, then, something like attention deficit hyperactivity disorder is a pathology, it is a pathology of late capitalism – a consequence of being wired into the entertainment-control circuits of hypermediated consumer culture. Similarly, what is called dyslexia may in many cases amount to a *post-lexia*. Teenagers process capital's image-dense data very effectively without any need to read - slogan-recognition is sufficient to navigate the net-mobile-magazine informational plane. 'Writing has never been capitalism's thing. Capitalism is profoundly illiterate', Deleuze and Guattari argued in *Anti-Oedipus*. 'Electric language does not go by way of the voice or writing: data processing does without them both'. Hence the reason that many successful business people are dyslexic (but is their post-lexical efficiency a cause or effect of their success?)

Teachers are now put under intolerable pressure to mediate between the post-literate subjectivity of the late capitalist consumer and the demands of the disciplinary regime (to pass examinations etc). This is one way in which education, far from being in some ivory tower safely inured from the 'real world', is the engine room of the reproduction of social reality, directly confronting the inconsistencies of the capitalist social field. Teachers are caught between being facilitator-entertainers and disciplinarian-authoritarians. Teachers want to help students to pass the exams; they want us to be authority figures who tell them what to do. Teachers being interpellated by students as authority figures exacerbates the 'boredom' problem, since isn't anything that comes from the place of authority a priori boring? Ironically, the role of disciplinarian is demanded of educators more than ever at precisely the time when disciplinary structures are breaking down in institutions. With families buckling under the pressure of a capitalism which requires both parents to work, teachers are now increasingly required to act as surrogate parents, instilling the most basic behavioral protocols in students and providing pastoral and emotional support for teenagers who are in some cases only minimally socialized.

It is worth stressing that none of the students I taught had any legal obligation to be at college. They could leave if they wanted to. But the lack of any meaningful employment opportunities, together with cynical encouragement from government means that college seems to be the easier, safer option. Deleuze says that Control societies are based on debt rather than enclosure; but there is a way in which the current education system both indebts *and* encloses students. Pay for your own exploitation, the logic insists – get into debt so you can get the same McJob you could have walked into if you'd left school at sixteen…

Jameson observed that 'the breakdown of temporality suddenly releases [the] present of time from all the activities and intentionalities that might focus it and make it a space of praxis'. But nostalgia for the context in which the old types of praxis operated is plainly useless. That is why French students don't in

*One-Way Stre*

the dream of an anaesthetized patient with the surgical intervention. With the cautious lineaments of handwriting the
operator makes incisions, displaces internal accents, cauter
proliferations of words, inserts a foreign term as a silver rib.
last the whole is finely stitched together with punctuation, a
he pays the waiter, his assistant, in cash.

makes advertisements so superior to criticism? Not what the
moving red neon sign says—but the fiery pool reflecting it in the
asphalt.

THIS SPACE FO

Fools lament the decay of criticism. For its day is long pa
Criticism is a matter of correct distancing. It
world where perspectives and prospects count
was still possible to take a standpoint. Now
closely on human society. The "unclouded"
has become a lie, perhaps the whole naïve m
sheer incompetence. Today the most real, the
into the heart of things is the advertisement.
space where contemplation moved and all bu
the eyes with things as a car, growing to giga
careens at us out of a film screen. And just as
present furniture and façades in completed
inspection, their insistent, jerky nearness al
tional, the genuine advertisement hurtles thin
tempo of a good film. Thereby "matter-of-fa
dispatched, and in face of the huge images ac
houses, where toothpaste and cosmetics lie h
sentimentality is restored to health and libera
style, just as people whom
are taught to cry again by
ever, it is money that aff
perceived contact with thi
paintings in the dealer's
tant if not better things a
them in the showroom wi
communicated to him

opponent time to
ersation show
are dealt with here that are more important
under discussion. You think this to yourself, and
art to retreat from your position. You begin to wonder
they are talking about, and hear with a fright that your
utor is leaving tomorrow for Brazil; soon you are so
one with the firm that you regret the migraine he com-
on the telephone as a disturbance of business (rather
elcoming it as an opportunity). Summoned or un-
ned the secretary enters. She is very pretty. And if her
er is either proof against her charms or else has long
d his position as her admirer, the newcomer will glance
her more than once; and she knows how to turn this to
age with her boss. His personnel are in motion producing
dexes in which the visitor knows himself to be entered
various rubrics. He starts to tire. The other, with the light
him, reads this off the dazzlingly illuminated face with
ction. The armchair too does its work; you sit in it tilted
far back as at the dentist's, and so finally accept this dis-
omfiting procedure as the legitimate state of affairs. This
eatment, too, is followed sooner or later by a liquidation.

. What, in the end,

MIXED CARGO: CARRIAGE AND PACKING

In the early morning I drove through Marseilles to the station,
and as I passed familiar places on my way, and then new, un-

Skulking smells like summer. Like grass & wet mud & damp leaves. It smells like an itch under cotton. It smells like a pattern carved in wood. It smells like a pattern. It is brick & it is textured. It is black & it is navy blue. It is purple & it is yet more purple. It is warm & it is hot & bright. It glitters with slivers of mint green. It glitters. Skulking includes and it encloses. It excludes & it liberates. It smells like an instinct for secrecy. It smells like desire.

## Speak, Hoyt-Schermerhorn

# THE MECHANICS OF SKULKING.

Periodic occupational territorial behaviour

Here's where I am: in the subway, but not on a train. I'm standing on one platform, gazing at another. Moaning trains roll in, obscuring my view; I wait for them to pass. The far platform, the one I'm inspecting, isn't lit. The tiles along the abandoned platform's wall are stained—I mean, more than in some ordinary way—and the stairwells are caged and locked, top and bottom. Nothing's happening there, and it's happening round the clock.

I've been haunting this place lately, the Hoyt-Schermerhorn station. But the more time I spend, the further it reels from my grasp. And, increasingly, I'm drawing looks from other passengers on the platforms and upstairs, at the station's mezzanine level. Subway stations—the platforms and stairwells and tunnels, the passages themselves—are sites of deep and willed invisibility. Even the geekiest transit buffs adore the trains, not the stations. By lingering here, I've set off miniature alarms in nearby minds, including my own. I've allied myself with the malingerers not on their way to somewhere else. My investigation of this place reeks of a futility so deep it shades toward horror.

Undercover transit policemen are trained to watch for "loopers"—

DEEP & WILLED INVISIBILITY: A TEMPORARY & DEFENDED SPACE, MEETS AN UNWAVERING PROGRESSIVE HABIT & MANIFESTS AS BEHAVIOR DRIVEN BY...

NEED FEAR DESIRE SKULKING.

Skulking is reliant upon a type of site-specificity found on the streets & in public places of passage—Bus stations, train stations etc. They exist somewhere between the functional & the forgotten; & in establishing a distinct space, skulking offers every opportunity & every risk.

that is, riders who switch from one train car to the next at each stop. Loopers are understood to be likely pickpockets, worthy of suspicion. Even before that, though, loopers are guilty of using the subway *wrong*. In truth, every subway rider is an undercover officer in a precinct house of the mind, noticing and cataloguing outré and dissident behavior in his fellows even while cultivating the outward indifference for which New Yorkers are famous, above and below ground. It may only be safe to play at not noticing others because our noticing senses are sharpened to trigger-readiness. Jittery subway shooter Bernhard Goetz once ran for mayor. He may not have been electable, but he had a constituency.

As it happens, I'm also an inveterate looper, though I do it less these days. I'll still sometimes loop to place myself at the right exit stairwell, to save steps if I'm running late. I've looped on the 7 train out to Shea Stadium, searching for a friend headed for the same ballgame. More than anything, though, I looped as a teenager, on night trains, looping as prey would, to skirt trouble. I relate this form of looping to other subterranean habits I learned as a terrified child. For instance, a tic of boarding—I'll stand at one spot until a train stops, then abruptly veer left- or right-ward, to enter a car other than the one for which I might have appeared to be waiting. This to shake pursuers, of course. Similarly, a nighttime trick of exiting at lonely subway stations: at arrival I'll stay in my seat until the doors have stood open for a few seconds, then dash from the train. In these tricks my teenager self learned to cash in a small portion of the invisibility that is not only each subway rider's presumed right but his duty to other passengers, whose irritation and panic rises at each sign of oddness, in exchange for tiny likelihoods of increased safety.

By this law of meticulously observed abnormalities, then, my spying here at Hoyt-Schermerhorn goes noticed, triggers a flutter of disapproval in other inhabitants of the station. This may be deserved. I'm not here for a train. I've come seeking something other than a subway ride. What I'm trying to do maybe can't be done: inhabit and understand the Hoyt-Schermerhorn station as a place. Worse, I'm trying to remember it, to restore it to its home in *time*. There's no greater perversity, since a subway station is a sinkhole of destroyed and thwarted time. By standing here trying to remember Hoyt-Schermerhorn I've only triggered its profoundest resistance: I'm using it wrong.

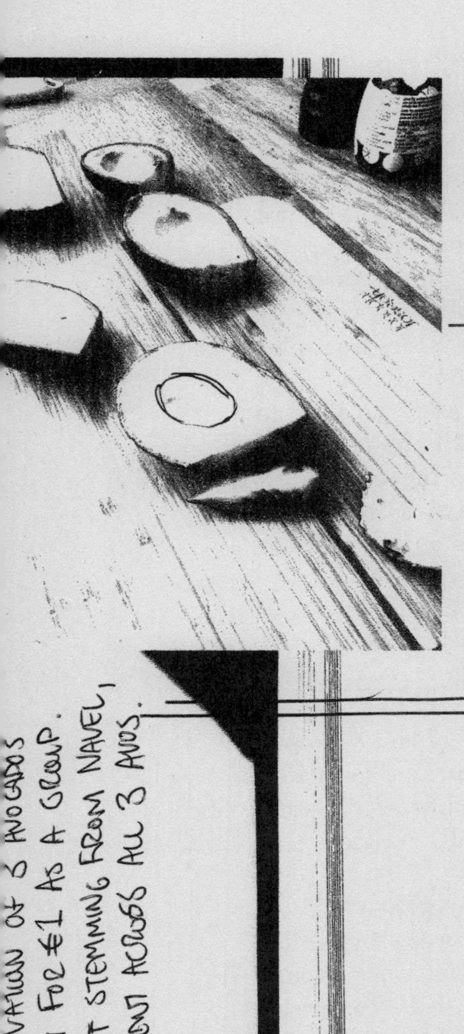




Unfortunately, our conceit induces us to lose sight of this natural and divine starting-point of all human development; we stand perplexed, having lost beginning and end, and therefore the right direction. Having denied God and nature, we seek counsel from human knowledge and wit. We build houses of cards; but there is no room in them for the ways of the natural mother, for divine influence; and the slightest utterance of the child, impelled by the joy and instinct of life, throws them down. If they should stand, the child must be, if not bodily, yet intellectually fettered.

Where has this discussion taken us? Into the nursery of the worldly-wise, of the so-called refined people, who scarcely believe that there are in the child germs which, if they are to thrive, must be developed early; who know still less that all the child is ever to be and become, lies—however slightly indicated—in the child, and can be attained only through development from within outward.

How dead, therefore, does everything seem here; how cold, or, at best, how loud and noisy! But, is not the mother here? Alas! it is not the mother's room, it is only the nursery.

Away! and let us again go where not only the room of child and mother is one, but where even mother and child are still one; where the mother is loath to give the care of her child to strangers. Let us see and hear how the mother, there, shows to the child objects in their motions: "Hark! the bird sings! The dog says, 'bow-wow!'" And then, directly from the word to the name, from hearing to sight, "Where is Peep-peep? Where is Bow-wow?" The mother even

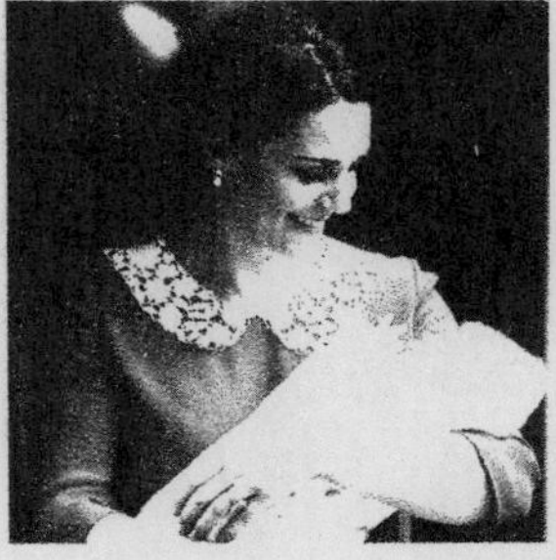

ventures to lead from the contemplation of the thing and its quality in their connection to the contemplation of the quality as distinct from the thing. "The bird flies," she says at first about the actual bird that flies. "See the little bird," she says later, on beholding the flitting, unsteady light-reflection that comes from the moving surface of water or of a mirror. Then, in order to teach the child that this is an incorporeal phenomenon which shares with the bird only its mobility, she says, "Catch the little bird," and asks the child to cover the reflection with his hands.

Again, in order to lead the child to the contemplation of the motion alone, the mother says, when she beholds the pendulum oscillations of some object, "swing-swong," or "To-fro."

Similarly, she seeks to attract the child's attention to the mutability of things—e. g., showing the lighted candle, "Here is the light"; taking it away, "All gone, light"; or, "Papa comes," and, "By-by, papa." Again, showing the self-mobility of things, "Come, kitty, to my pet," and, "Run, kitty, run." She incites the child to bodily activity—"Hold the flower," "Catch the kitty," or, slowly rolling the ball, "Catch the ball."

All-embracing mother-love seeks to awaken and to interpret the feeling of community between the child and the father, brother, and sister, which is so important, when she says, "Love dear papa"; or as she caressingly passes the child's hand over the father's cheek, "Dear, dear papa"; or, "Love little sister," etc.

In addition to the sense of community as such, the germ of so much glorious development, the mother's love

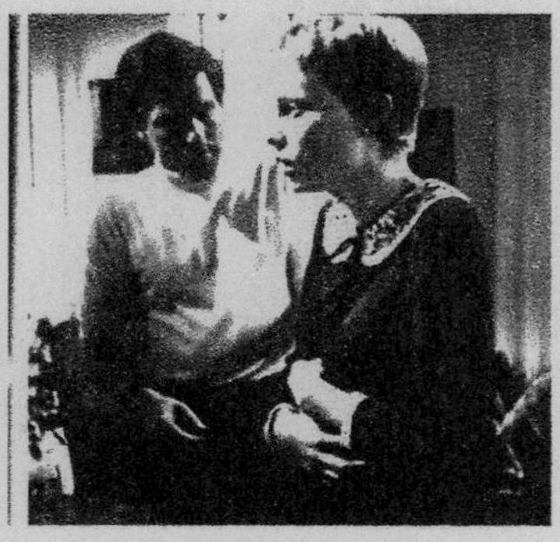

Picking one primary medium and working strictly within it is unnecessary. It's not that it isn't an option, but it's one option among many. Especially today, artists are working in so many different media and disciplines, there's no reason to limit yourself to one. However, once you've chosen to work in a specific medium, it's important to know the history of that medium, its materiality, and how it functions technically. And as a late modernist artist I would say that it's very important to reflect upon your materials and the history of those materials.

I work primarily in photography. When I started, I really only intended to make a couple of works with it. I was interested in photography but not in being a photographer, and I certainly didn't think I was going to spend 35 years making primarily photographic works. Having said that, my idea of photography isn't confined to the idea of the camera and the print. I think of photography as an institution in which the print or the visual artifact is only one element in a network of other ways of signifying things.

So I consider the presentational devices—the framing, the mounts, the titles, the architectural situation, and the history of the institution presenting the show, the advertising, the posters, the catalogue, the essays in a catalogue—as all being an extension of the photographic institution. So then you have architecture, you have offset printing—the production of different kinds of language—which I see as being coextensive with the photographic surface.

I don't like to stand behind the camera or in front of the camera; I like to stand beside the camera. I figured out pretty early on—or I came up with the idea—that the camera is actually not the only agent involved in the production of meaning. There are also chemical designers, optical designers, and industrial designers. There are economic and social issues. So I try to move around the photographic program and occupy different positions at different times. Even though I didn't get assignments in art school, I do treat myself like a commercial photographer: I give myself assignments. I become a product photographer, or I become a photojournalist, and I pick a subject as though it were a journalistic assignment.

# ART HISTORY AND THEORY

It's important to study art history and art theory, but a distinction has to be made between making art and studying art history or theory. The practices of artists I find most interesting are those who think through their art or think through their materials and produce something like a theoretical model through their immersion in those materials and ideas, as opposed to taking ideas developed in philosophy or theory and then illustrating or applying them to the production of art. It's important to absorb as much information as possible but then to think through your materials. That doesn't mean just to think in terms of technique or to think visually but to really try to figure out the dimensions of your materials. Making a painting, for example, is different from writing. Language is a very different medium from paint.

## MORE PRACTICAL ADVICE FOR YOUNG ARTISTS

1. No Plexiglas
2. No electricity
3. No humor

I don't like to throw rules at people, but if you follow those guidelines you'll be more likely to produce good art. Some of it's just practical. Plexiglas doesn't age well, so if you put it over something you've made, it's going to go milky and will get fine scratches when it's cleaned. Also, plastic is less optically precise than glass, so use glass in framing.

Electricity—again, it's just practical advice—is something that a lot can go wrong with. If you have a sound component in your work, for example, the minute you leave the installation the person at the front desk will turn down the sound, which means the sound level will never be where you want it. Twice, I took an hour-long train ride to see a friend's film installation, and twice the projector wasn't functioning—and these visits were two months apart.

The last rule—no humor—is so obvious I don't think I need to address it. Also—and this makes four rules—you shouldn't make anything you can't carry through the door yourself. This will ensure that everything is human scale and has a relationship to the body.

less that you will not have to remain without a solution if you will hold to objects that are similar to those from which my eyes now draw refreshment. If you will cling to Nature, to the simple in Nature, to the little things that hardly anyone sees, and that can so unexpectedly become big and beyond measuring; if you have this love of inconsiderable things and seek quite simply, as one who serves, to win the confidence of what seems poor: then everything will become easier, more coherent and somehow more conciliatory for you, not in your intellect, perhaps, which lags marveling behind, but in your inmost consciousness, waking and cognizance. You are so young, so before all beginning, and I want to beg you, as much as I can, dear sir, to be patient toward all that is unsolved in your heart and to try to love the *questions themselves* like locked rooms and like books that are written in a very foreign tongue. Do not now seek the answers, which cannot be given you because you would not be able to live them. And the point is, to live everything. *Live* the questions now. Perhaps you will then gradually, without noticing it, live along some distant day into the answer. Perhaps you do carry within yourself the possibility of shaping and forming as a particularly happy and pure way of living; train yourself to it—but take whatever comes with great trust, and if only it comes out of your own will, out of some need of your inmost being, take it upon yourself and hate nothing. Sex is difficult; yes. But they are difficult things with which we have been charged; almost everything serious is difficult, and everything is serious. If you only recognize this and manage, out of yourself, out of your *own* nature and ways, out of your *own* experience and childhood and strength to achieve a relation to sex wholly your own (*not* influenced by convention and custom), then you need no longer be afraid of losing yourself and becoming unworthy of your best possession.

More precisely, tool and human produce each other. The artifacts that prosthetically expand thought and reach are what make the human human. As Bernard Stiegler, reading the work of the influential paleoanthropologist André Leroi-Gourhan, puts it: "The prosthesis is not the mere extension of the human body; it is the constitution of this body qua 'human.'"[1] Leroi-Gourhan echoed the nineteenth-century idea that the human species was unique in evolving organically through its technological extensions: "The whole of our evolution has been oriented toward placing outside ourselves what in the rest of the animal world is achieved inside by species adaption."[2] The body itself is only human by virtue of technology: "the human hand is human because of what it makes, not of what it is."[3] What is human is the gesture of externalization, which is not from some preexisting interior, like thoughts in the brain, but is a gesture that constitutes a new sense of interior. The human is always being invented as such by the gestures that transform it. Brain, body, and artifact cannot be separated. Thinking only occurs in the intermingling between them. Artifacts themselves are thoughts that potentially also trigger new modes of thought.

The human brain is therefore an effect of new tools rather than the generator of new tools. Tools are an opportunity for it rather than an accomplishment of it. The intentionality and anticipation of effects that is distinctly human arises from the activity of making itself. Human intentions are provoked by making tools rather than executed by them.[4] And what makes a tool a tool? Strictly speaking, a tool is not produced to carry out a defined utilitarian task. Tools are born as challenges to existing concepts of utility. They open up new understandings of what could be useful. Utility is not a given unambiguous need. Ambiguity about utility is what drives new forms of utility.

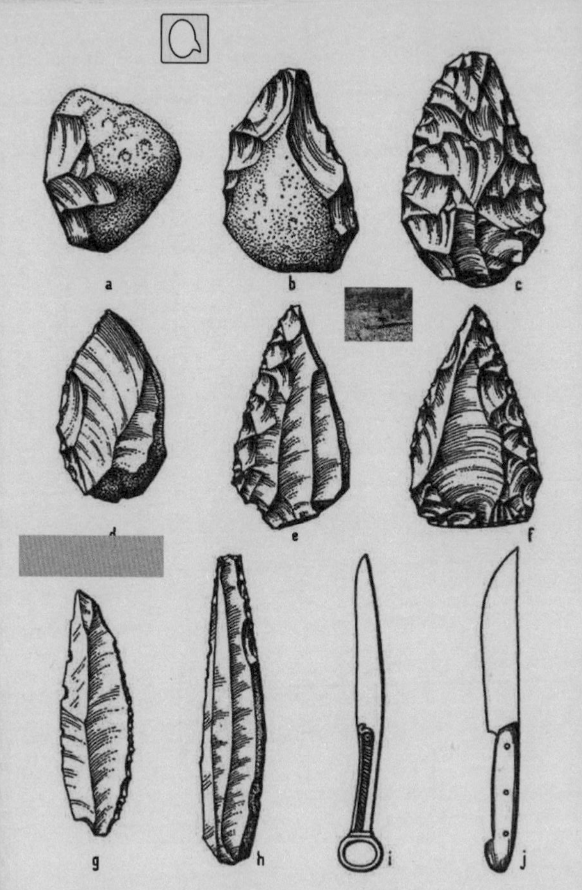

Leroi-Gourhan's illustration of evolution of the knife

Some paleoanthropologists argue that the main driver of human accomplishment is simply a uniquely human capacity for variability, an impulse to generate a multiplicity of ways to do things in reaction to different circumstances.[5] This variability itself can be understood as design capacity. When other species have figured out a way to do something, they keep repeating it forever until changes in the context reinforce a different direction. Humans continuously imagine different ways even in the same context, to the point of malfunction. The human is the only species that has tools that don't work, which is paradoxically the origin of its intelligence.

Design might simply be a name for this impulse to do things differently. Earlier attempts to explain the apparent exponential acceleration of human invention in the last 40,000 years presupposed some sudden increase in the cognitive capacity of the human brain as the enabling trigger. Recent accounts see this acceleration of invention occurring more gradually throughout the last 200,000 years, finding no evidence in fossils of change in the cognitive capacity to design. The ever-increasing size of groups in proximity to one another and the connectivity between these groups through migration formed a collective brain more likely to invent alternative ways to do things.[6] As more and more people shared knowledge and the accuracy of the knowledge being passed between groups and generations increased, the frequency of invention increased and continuously reinvented the brain in a kind of chain reaction of design.

The human brain itself is a malleable artifact whose circuits are continually rearranged through engagement with material culture. It is an unfinished project with a forever uncertain future and an equally uncertain beginning. The idea of a sudden flourishing of design gives way to the thought, as Patrick Roberts puts it, that "there is no single evolutionary event or moment where the brain becomes definitively 'human.'"[7]

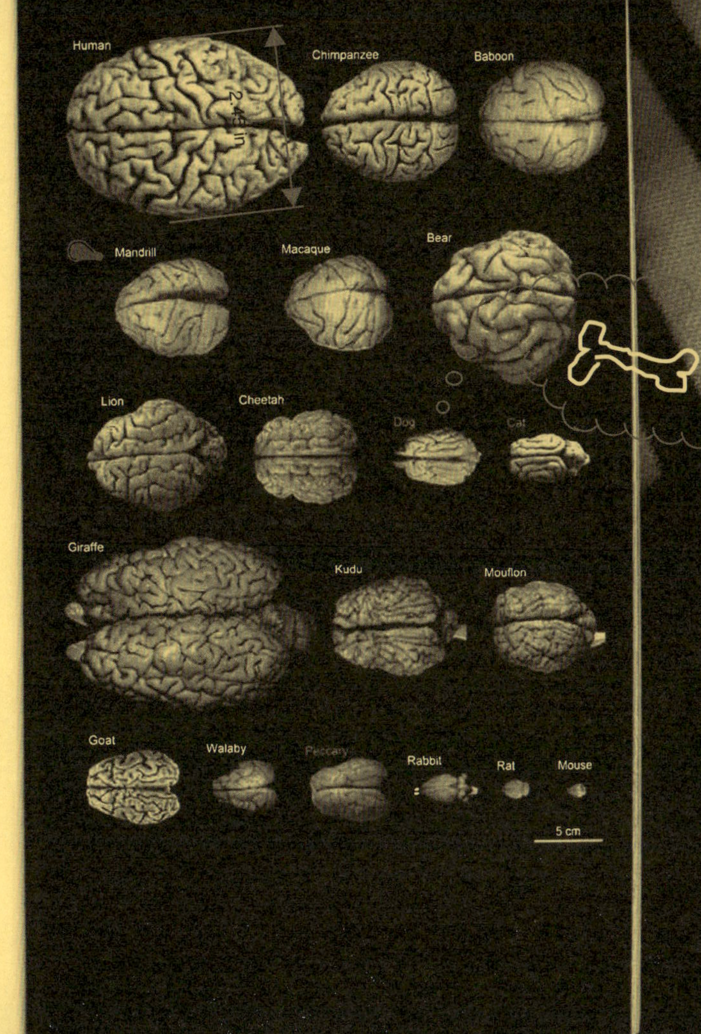

## SINGULARITY
*by Marie Howe*

*(after Stephen Hawking)*

Do you sometimes want to wake up to the singularity
we once were?

so compact nobody
needed a bed, or food or money —

nobody hiding in the school bathroom
or home alone

pulling open the drawer
where the pills are kept.

*For every atom belonging to me as good
Belongs to you.*  Remember?

There was no  *Nature*.  No
 *them*.  No tests

to determine if the elephant
grieves her calf    or if

the coral reef feels pain.  Trashed
oceans don't speak English or Farsi or French;

would that we could wake up  to what we were
— when we *were* ocean    and before that

to when sky was earth, and animal was energy, and rock was
liquid and stars were space and space was not

at all — nothing

before we came to believe humans were so important
before this awful loneliness.

Can molecules recall it?
what once was?    before anything happened?

No I, no We, no one. No was
No verb    no noun
only a tiny tiny dot brimming with

*is is is is is*

All  everything  home

## XIX. The Man with 100 Mothers

Translated by Li Yanjia

STORIES AND MYTHS OF EIGHT
IMMORTALS
SONG DYNASTY - 960-1279

44

BACK then, when Cao Guojiu was still an evil Royal Uncle from Song
Dynasty he had one close friend named Tong Shanren. This Tong Shanren was
a tightwad and cruel landlord who like to exploit peoples. Actually he was so
identical with Cao in many ways.

One day Cao Guojiu who had repented and became immortal want to advise
his old friend. Cao therefore changed his appearance into beggar and begged
alms in front of Tong Shanren's door.

As predicted he was chased away by the doorkeeper. However no matter
how many times he was scorned and expelled, Cao would return again and
again.

Finally the doorkeeper was surrendered and told his master about this
stubborn beggar.

"Stupid! Idiot! Imbecile! Why should i have a doorkeeper if I should met all
beggar and loafer in this town alone!" scold him to his doorkeeper

But how surprised Tong when he realized that beggar as his old friend the
Royal Uncle. "What? I think he was still our emperor's brother in law, but how
come he wears tattered clothes like this. But that's all right. I heard most
noblemen are eccentric, probably this is the latest fashion trend in capital or
maybe he dressed like this to hinder tax". Finally Tong welcomed him to his
house. Actually he want to ask position in government from his friend.

As the banquet was prepared, Tong Shanren asked Cao "Why do you
dressed like that?"

"I've became an immortal in Penglai Shan" replied the Royal Uncle

"Interesting!" shouted Tong "I know you studied Tao so you can make gold
from a stone, but have you mastered that skill?"

"Ha ha ha, I know you will ask this" laughed Cao "Of course I have mastered
that skill and if you wish, I can demonstrate it to you here"

"Show me, show me quickly"

"First dig a hole in your room!" said Tong. As his instruction fulfilled, he throw
one piece of silver to the hole, then he told his fiend "Now that hole has become
money mine, as you can pick unlimited money from it"

45

Tong hardly believed it, but Cao demonstrate the process and picked 10
silver pieces from the hole.

The greedy landlord was very happy with that miracle. He kowtowed in front
of Cao and called him as great deity.

When Tong's mother heard about this money mine in his house, she want to
prove it with her own eyes. Unfortunately her foot was slipped and she fell into
the hole. Tong hurriedly helped his mother, but as he pulled one mother, there
was another mother emerged from that hole. And the process continuously
repeated until there were 100 mothers in his house. Tong really depressed
because he couldn't recognize his real mother. One mother called him
"Shangren", when the other called him "my baby"

Tong quickly called Cao Guojiu to show his real mother, but the Royal Uncle
replied "Actually this hole have become mother mine now and other mothers will
always appeared every time you pulled one out"

"But, but It will make me bankrupt in no time!" cried the landlord in terror

"If you really to stop that process, than I can summon a deity to help you. But
you must obey whatever requirement he asks" Said Cao try to console his friend

The Royal Uncle then read an incantation suddenly a deity appeared in front
of them.

Upon hearing Tong's plea, the deity responded "If you want to stop that
mother mine, then you should liberate farmer from their tax and distribute your
wheat to poor family. Because he had no other choice, the stingy landlord was
forced to obey it.

Now the hole was empty and there were no other mother emerged from it,
except for 100 mothers who had appeared previously. Tong asked the deity to
show his real mother, but he answered "All of that 100 ladies are your mother
and if you neglect them, then a fire will burned your house into ash"

Tong panicked and asked for Cao's help, but the Royal Uncle mocked him
"This is result for your greediness" Tong cried und keep begging to Cao Guojiu,
finally he consoled him "Actually every time you do a kindness, then one of your
fake mother will be disappeared. So you need 99 good deeds until all the imitator
vanished."

From that day on, Tong Shanren changed into generous man, and one by
one his 99 mother was disappeared.

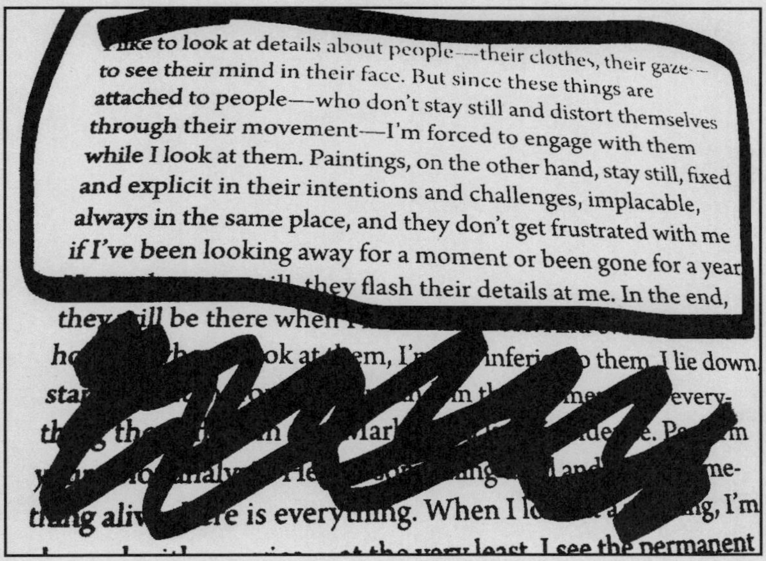

I like to look at details about people—their clothes, their gaze—
to see their mind in their face. But since these things are
attached to people—who don't stay still and distort themselves
through their movement—I'm forced to engage with them
while I look at them. Paintings, on the other hand, stay still, fixed
and explicit in their intentions and challenges, implacable,
always in the same place, and they don't get frustrated with me
if I've been looking away for a moment or been gone for a year
[. . .] they flash their details at me. In the end,
they will be there when [. . .]
[. . .] look at them, I'm [. . .] inferior to them. I lie down,
star[. . .] every-
thing the[. . .] Mark[. . .] de[. . .]e. Per[. . .]m
y[. . .] analy[. . .] He[. . .]ing [. . .] and [. . .] me-
thing aliv[. . .]re is everything. When I lo[. . .] a[. . .]ing, I'm
[. . .] at the very least, I see the permanent

en... ...ely ...films in which
they a... ...ey are *in* the films in which they are seen, ou... ...y are of
*other* qualities...

More b... ...dly, if account is taken of the fact that the histor... ...ny
is marked... ...tion, control, and administration of ... David
B... ...er... ...oucault [1975 and 1994 (1967)], J. Brian Ha...ey
Wood (1992), and others have shown), the inf... ...ve
stakes ... where it can be asserted that in sun... ...film *is*
a map, and ... ...and political effectiveness is a function of its identity as ... cartographic diagram. Here is where ... ...theory... ...be involved
... som... ...ent studies **emerg**ing from overlap... ...e history of ... ...ar studies and ... ...bout
1990 film stud... ...exp... ...of theory. Since then there ...s
tended to be a retraction in favor of extensive work on canons, genres, rece...tion,
and origins. A corollar... ...m for the ca... ...not to let theory
go unatte... ...s of a virtual ...ater of interpretation. ... ...f viewing and,
indeed, of living, not just with film, but also with space itself, wi... ...ant
labor o... ...t it means to be located and discer... ...th... ...orld.
The beau... ...no matter what its reception may be ... it
is rec... ...up or two thumbs down, o... ...ed to
canist... ...ed vault, owe... ...ver to make
us pon... ...those questions. The force and beauty of cinema are en**hanced** when
**we think** of it in light of cartography.

A second gro... ...emphasis, dealing with the proposition th... ...the
**films that fail to contain maps**, is that the occurrence of a map in a... ...is unique
to its own context. Some general patterns can be observed, but in general it
might be said: *to each film its map.* To each its own "points de capiton," or points
of stress that plot its relations with space, **his**tory, and being. For this reason cinema... ...maps as they
appe... ...montage that inform
them... ...film the webbing that contains issues of broader scope.
**Classical Westerns** and ... ...es of map-
**ping.** Topographical charts on the ... ...ing rooms or cavalry outposts
signal t... ...western science and military hardware will defeat local knowledge,
or perhaps vice-versa, when natives bur... ...trains and massacre foreign set-
tlers. Th... ...al projections of Sou... ...on the walls of travel agencies and
medium-size globes on the desks behind when their agents scribble notes attest
to a **new** international cinema, at least in films of Wong Kar Wai's signature
(especially in *In the Mood for Love* [2000])... ...e medium
is unde... ...Hollywood
and the French Ne... ...ure ... delicate psychology, Eric

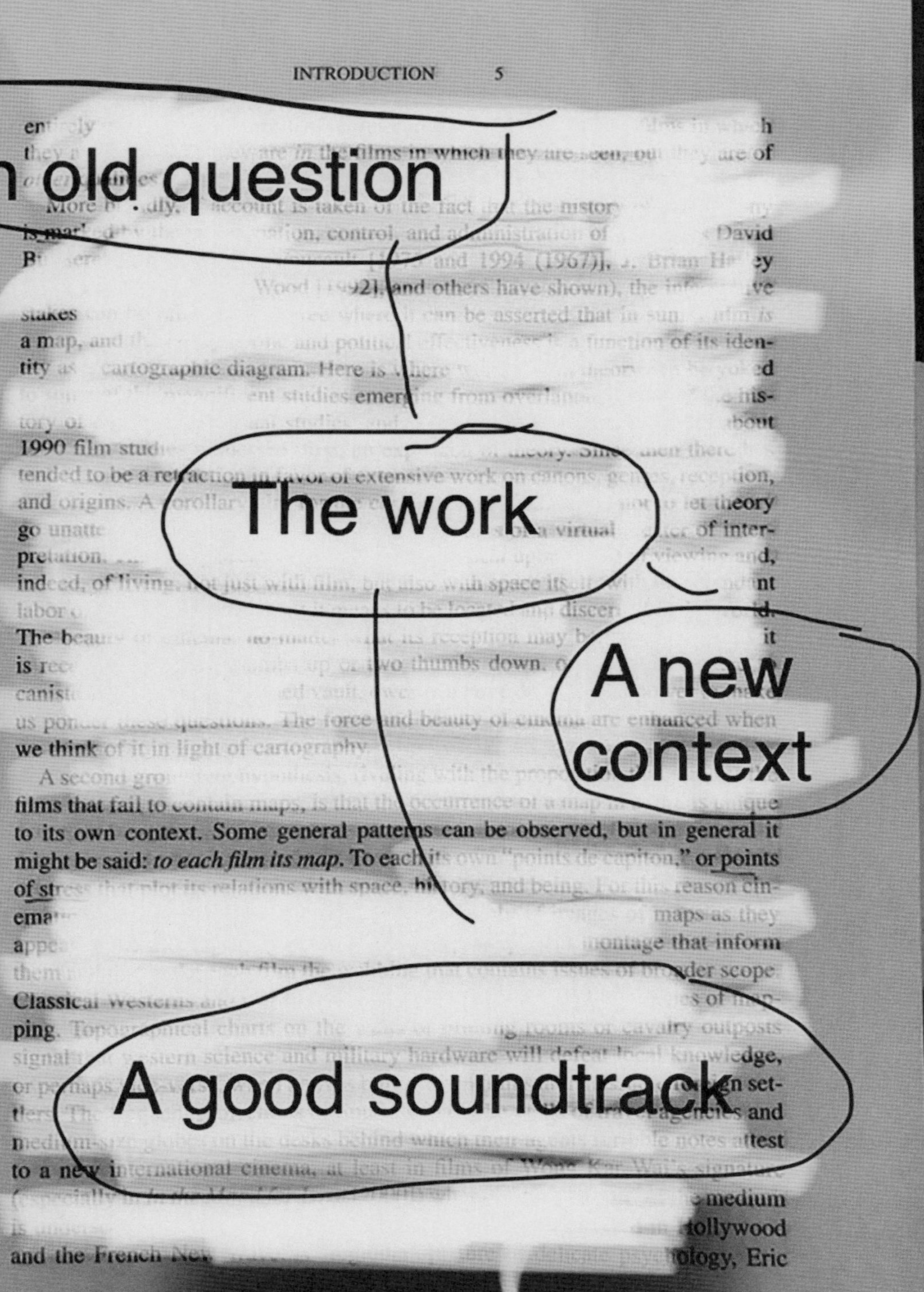


en[tirely]
they ... are *in* the films in which they are seen, but they are of

More b...dly, account is taken of the fact that the histor...
is mar... ...tion, control, and administration of ... David
B... ... and 1994 (1967)], J. Brian Harley
Wood 1992], and others have shown), the in... ...ve
stakes ... ...ee where it can be asserted that in sum a film *is
a map*, and ... ...and politic... ...a function of its identity as cartographic diagram. Here is where ...
...ent studies emerging from overland... ...his-
tory of ... ...studies... ...bout
1990 film stud... ...theory. Since then there
tended to be a retraction in favor of extensive work on canons, genres, reception,
and origins. A corollar... ...to let theory
go unatte... ...virtual ...ter of interpretation... ...knowledge and,
indeed, of living, not just with film, but also with space its... ...nt
labor... ...discer... ...d.
The beaut... ...no matter what its reception may b... ...it
is rec... ...up or two thumbs down. ...
canist... ...vault... ...
us ponder these questions. The force and beauty of cinema are enhanced when
we think of it in light of cartography...

A second gro... ...dealing with the prop...
films that fail to contain maps, is that the occurrence of a map... ...is unique
to its own context. Some general patterns can be observed, but in general it
might be said: *to each film its map*. To each its own "points de capiton," or points
of st... ...relations with space, history, and being. For this reason cinema... ...maps as they
appe... ...montage that inform
them... ...that contains issues of broader scope...

Classical westerns and ... ...s of map-
ping. Topographical charts on the ... ...rooms or cavalry outposts
signal... western science and military hardware will defeat local knowledge,
or perhaps ... ...n set-
tlers. ... ...agencies and
medium-sized ... on the desks behind which their... ...le notes attest
to a new international cinema, at least in films of... Will's signature
... ...medium
... ...ollywood
and the French New... ...ology, Eric

APPAU JNR BOAKYE-YIADOM ANNOTATED CHAMELEON STREET, 1989, WENDELL B. HARRIS JR. // THE HERESY OF ZONE DEFENCE, AIR GUITAR, 1997, DAVE HICKEY

**Lawyer in restaurant:** Fuckin' let go!

[*throws a drink in Doug's face*]

Henceforth, it has always seemed to me that the trick of civilization lies in recognizing the moment when a rule ceases to liberate and begins to govern—and this brings us back to the glory of hoops.

<u>William Douglas Street</u>: You know, that's a very nasty word. But what's really, pardon the expression, fucked up, is your grammar. "Fuckin' let go," you can't say that. You know, the rules of grammar apply to profanity as well. The word 'fuck' comes from the German root, "fichen," which means to strike. It's a verb and can be used in a variety of ways, both transitive and intransitive. For example, simple aggression: Fuck you! Or simple confusion: What the fuck is goin' on here? And then there's apathy, "Who gives a fuck?" And then there's ignorance, which is very appropriate for you. Defiance: the fuck you can!

Because among all the arts of disputation our culture provides, basketball has been supreme in recognizing this moment of portending government and in deflecting it, by changing the rules when they threaten to make the game less beautiful and less visible, when the game stops liberating and begins to educate.

**Lawyer in restaurant:** I don't have to take this shit from you!

And even though basketball is not a fine art—even though it is merely an armature upon which we project the image of our desire, while art purports to embody that image—the fact remains that every style change that basketball has undergone in this century has been motivated by a desire to make the game more joyful, various, and articulate,

**William Douglas Street:** Authority! Shut the fuck up! You can say it four different ways. SHUT the fuck up, shut THE fuck up, shut the FUCK up, shut the fuck UP! You see, these are all the things you could have said if you weren't so unbelievably coarse and crude and countrified.

[*looks at girlfriend*]

while nearly every style change in fine art has been, in some way, motivated by the opposite agenda. Thus basketball, which began this century as a pedagogical discipline, concludes it as a much beloved public spectacle, while fine art, which began this century as a much-beloved public spectacle, has ended

**William Douglas Street:** That's alliteration, babe.

[*looks back at Lawyer*]

**William Douglas Street:** And remember, peckerwood; profanity is the last refuge of the ignorant, the insensitive, and the illiterate, but if you're gonna use it and I can see you are, at least get the fucking grammar right, moron.

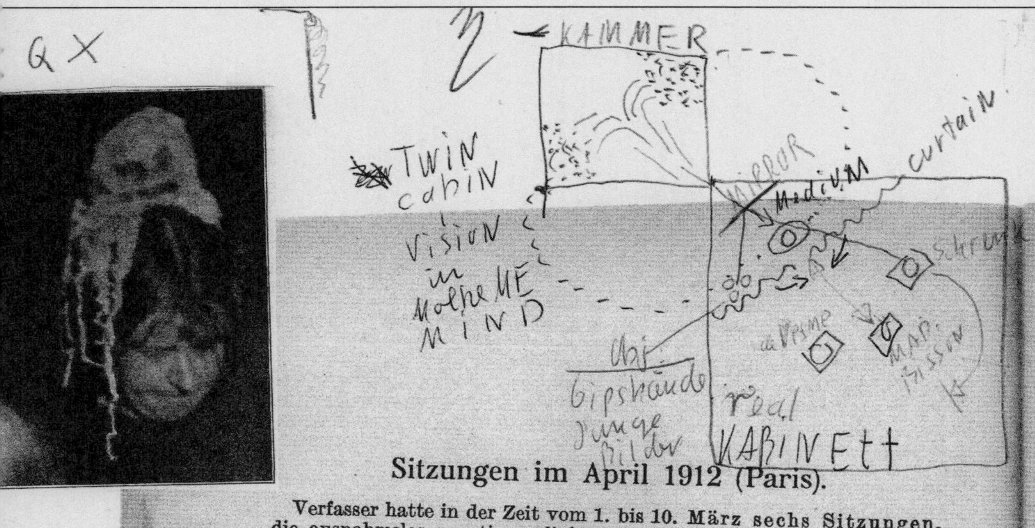


## Sitzungen im April 1912 (Paris).

Verfasser hatte in der Zeit vom 1. bis 10. März sechs Sitzungen, die ausnahmslos negativ verliefen.

### Sitzung am 29. April 1912.

Bedingungen wie bei den früheren Versuchen.

Anwesend: Mons. de Vesme, Mad. Bisson, ihr 13jähriger Sohn Pierre und Verfasser.

Eva verfiel in einen tiefen, ruhigen Schlaf, der dem normalen Schlaf glich. Keinerlei körperliche Symptome (röchelnde Exspirationen oder Wimmern) ließen darauf schließen, daß die für den Eintritt von Phänomenen nötige psychische Verfassung vorhanden war. Sie blieb stumm und schien nicht in Rapport mit den Anwesenden zu stehen.

Nach ¾ Stunden vergeblichen Wartens versuchte Mad. Bisson den passiven Schlafzustand in einen aktiven Somnambulismus leichteren Grades umzuwandeln, und zwar durch Handauflegen in Verbindung mit eindringlicher Verbalsuggestion. Eva begann eine größere Regsamkeit zu zeigen, sprach, stöhnte und ihre Exspiration wurde laut und lebhaft.

Erst nach 10 Uhr erschien bei nach rechts gebeugtem Kopf etwas Weißes, Streifenartiges über ihrer linken Schulter. Die stets sichtbaren Hände öffneten und schlossen den Vorhang, blieben dann regungslos auf den Knien liegen, während sie mit den Füßen den Vorhang öffnete und schloß.

Wir sahen nun mit blitzartiger Geschwindigkeit in der Nähe ihres Kopfes kleinere weiße Handformen in den Lichtkreis eintreten und wieder zurückgehen. Einmal schien sich eine solche kinderhandähnliche Form mit einer drehenden Bewegung zu vergrößern, um dann sofort wieder zu verschwinden. Mehrfach waren Kopf und Hände Evas bei diesen Phänomenen gleichzeitig sichtbar. Einige der Bilder erweckten den Eindruck einer wohlentwickelten weiblichen Hand, blieben aber kaum eine Sekunde sichtbar.

Um genauer zu beobachten, stand ich auf und stellte mich hinter Mad. Bisson, die direkt in der Mitte vor dem Vorhang saß. Jetzt erkannte ich deutlich eine Handform, die aus dem Dunkel des Kabinetts kam und verschwand, während de Vesme gleichzeitig beide Hände des Mediums kontrollierte.

Nach der letzten Erscheinung erklärte Eva, Berthe, welche in letzter Zeit in spiritistischem Sinne die Kontrolle des Mediums übernommen hatte, sei verschwunden und komme nicht mehr, erhob sich, trat aus dem Kabinett und ließ sich vollständig untersuchen (mit negativem Erfolg).

---

Sitzungen im April 1912 (Paris)     185

---

Die Sitzung schloß gegen 11 Uhr. Eva hatte heute einen schlechten Tag gehabt. Sie war mißgestimmt, ohne daß wir die Ursache erfahren konnten.

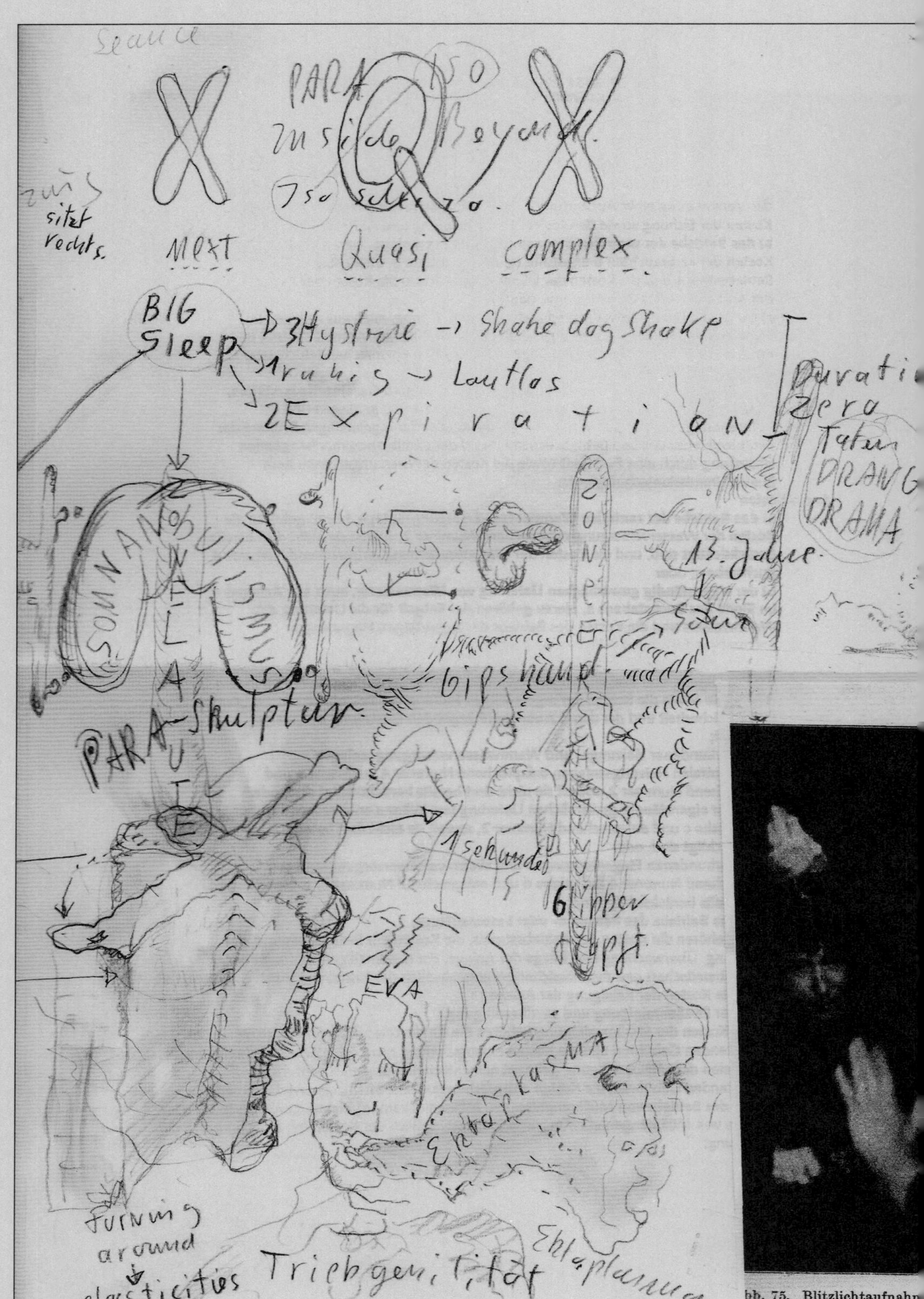


bb. 75. Blitzlichtaufnahm...
de Vesme am 14. April

[Verse 1]
They rob the third world of every cent
*Now that's bullshit*
Now you got third world debt
*Now that's bullshit*
You get your cheque there's never nothing left
*Now that's bullshit*
Then you pay tax on what you spend
*Now that's bullshit*
Then you even gotta pay tax on your pension
*Now that's bullshit*
They still wanna take your inheritance
*Now that's bullshit*
English kids rappin' American
*Now that's bullshit*
The war's bullshit — *which one?*
It's all bullshit
Extending the congestion charge
*Now that's bullshit*
Never fucking nowhere to park
*Now that's bullshit*
Most of what you learn in class
*Now that's bullshit*
Especially regarding the past
*Now that's bullshit*
Men beating up on their spouse
*Now that's bullshit*
Rockin' jewels but you ain't got a house
*Now that's bullshit*
Every single syllable that come out your mouth
*Now that's bullshit*
The war's bullshit
It's all bullshit


[Hook]
Bullshit
Politicians talk never do shit
It's bullshit
All of what they feed us in the news
It is bullshit
Plus what they teach us in the schools
It is bullshit
The war's bullshit
It's all bullshit
Bullshit
Politicians talk never do shit
It's bullshit
All of what they feed us in the news
It is bullshit
Plus what they teach us in the schools
It is bullshit
The war's bullshit
It's all bullshit

[Verse 2]
Pull me over 5 times in a day
*Now that's bullshit*
And I got attitude if I have something to say
*Now that's bullshit*
The wage MPs get paid
*Now that's bullshit*
They won't give firefighters a raise
*Now that's bullshit*
Football fans monkey sounds
*Now that's bullshit*
Black players that didn't speak out
*Now that's bullshit*
White players that didn't speak out
*Now that's bullshit*
The war's bullshit
It's all bullshit
Places where kids can't eat
*Now that's bullshit*
But AK47s are free
*Now that's bullshit*
Here you go fight for me
*Now that's bullshit*
And I'll take the minerals please
*Now that's bullshit*
Traffic wardens getting commission
*Now that's bullshit*
The motherfuckin' weather in Britain
*Now that's bullshit*
All them weak raps that your spittin'
*Now that's bullshit*
The war's bullshit
It's all bullshit


[Hook]
Bullshit
Politicians talk never do shit
It's bullshit
All of what they feed us in the news
It is bullshit
Plus what they teach us in the schools
It is bullshit
The war's bullshit
It's all bullshit
Bullshit
Politicians talk never do shit
It's bullshit
All of what they feed us in the news
It is bullshit
Plus what they teach us in the schools
It is bullshit
The war's bullshit
It's all bullshit

DOUG BOWEN ANNOTATED BULLSHIT, IT'S NOT A RUMOUR, 2006, AKALA

[Verse 3]
AIDS comes from Africans fuckin' a monkey
*Now that's bullshit*
Farrakhan banned from the country
*Now that's bullshit*
Rapists come here and it's lovely
*Now that's bullshit*
What the fuck is wrong with our government?
*Now that's bullshit*
Paedophiles get light sentence
*Now that's bullshit*
Ask yourself why they defend them
*Now that's bullshit*
Broke niggas flossing with benzes
*Now that's bullshit*
The war's bullshit
It's all bullshit
We invaded Iraq cause we were checking
*That's bullshit*
If they had weapons we would have kept stepping
*Bullshit*
Saddam would have bus it with no question
*No bullshit*
Pretty much every rap record
*Now that's bullshit*
Black boys killing each other
*Now that's bullshit*
Especially cause it's over nothing
*Now that's bullshit*
I rep my ends and I'm thuggin'
*Now that's bullshit*
Look at what we do to our mothers
*Now that's bullshit*


[Hook]
Bullshit
Politicians talk never do shit
It's bullshit
All of what they feed us in the news
It is bullshit
Plus what they teach us in the schools
It is bullshit
The war's bullshit
It's all bullshit
Bullshit
Politicians talk never do shit
It's bullshit
All of what they feed us in the news
It is bullshit
Plus what they teach us in the schools
It is bullshit
The war's bullshit
It's all bullshit

*That's bullshit*

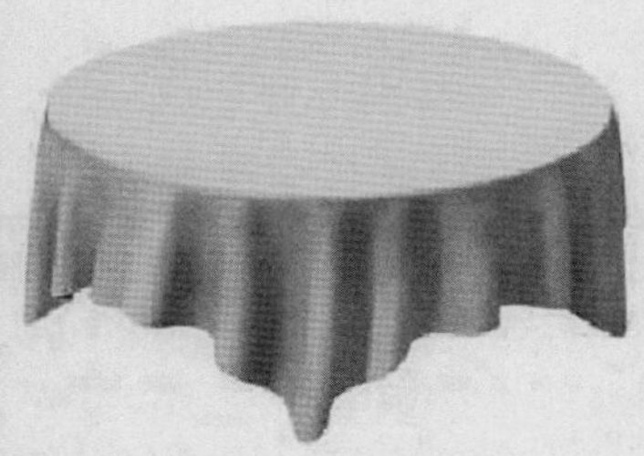

# The <u>Dressmaker's Dummy</u>
# By Alain Robbe-Grillet

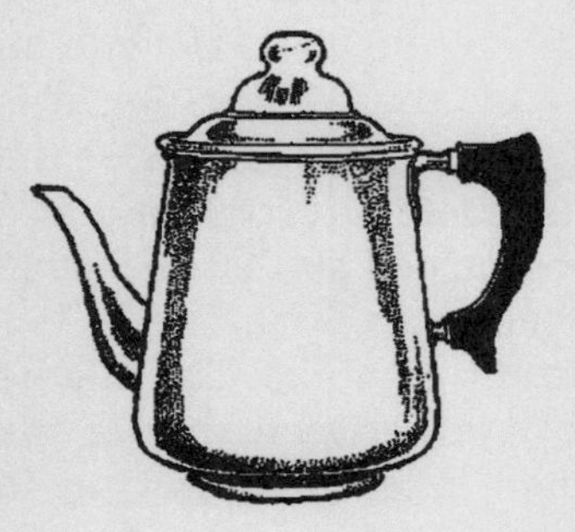

The <u>coffeepot</u> is on the <u>table</u>.

It is a four-legged round <u>table</u>, covered with a waxy <u>oilcloth</u> patterned in red and grey squares against a neutral background of yellowish white that may have been formerly ivory coloured-or white. In the centre, a <u>square ceramic tile</u> serves as a protective base; it's design is entirely hidden, or at least made unrecognisable, by the <u>coffeepot</u> placed upon it.

The <u>coffeepot</u> is made of brown earthenware. It consists of a sphere topped by a cylindrical filter holder with a mushroom-shaped lid. The spout is an S with flattened curves, widening out slightly at the base. The handle has, perhaps the shape of an <u>ear</u>, or rather of the outer fold of an ear; but it would be a misshapen <u>ear</u>, too circular and lacking a lobe, which would thus resemble a "<u>pitcher handle</u>." The spout, the handle, and the mushroom lid are of a creamy colour. The rest is of a very light, smooth brown, and shiny.

There is nothing on the table except the waxy <u>tablecloth</u>, the <u>ceramic base</u>, and the <u>coffeepot</u>.

On the right, in front of the window, stands the <u>dressmaker's dummy</u>.

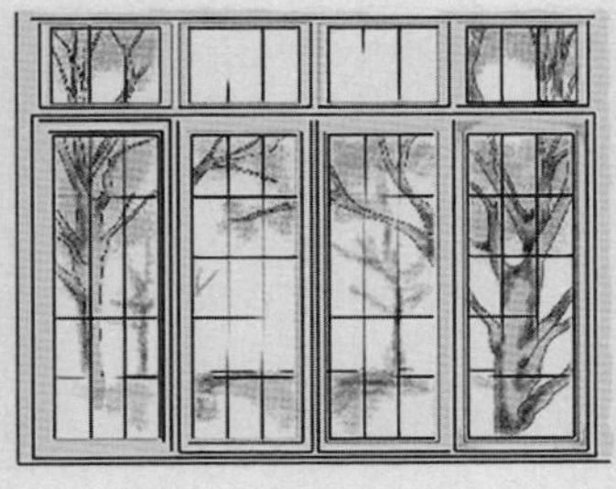

Behind the <u>table</u>, the space above the <u>mantel</u> holds a large <u>rectangular mirror</u> in which may be seen half of the <u>window</u> (the right half) and, on the left (that is, on the right side of the <u>window</u>), the reflection of the <u>wardrobe</u> with its mirror front. In the <u>wardrobe mirror</u> the <u>window</u> may again be seen, in its entirety now, and unreversed (that is, the right French pane on the right and the left one on the left).

Thus there are, above the <u>mantel</u>, three half-sections of the <u>window</u> one after another, with an almost unresolved continuity, and which are, in turn (from left to right): one left section unreversed, one right section unreversed, and one right section reversed. Since the <u>wardrobe</u> stands in the corner of the room and extends to the outer edge of the <u>window</u>, the two right half-sections of the later are seen separated only by a narrow vertical piece of wardrobe, which might be the wood separating the two French window sections (the right upright edge of the left side joined to the left edge of the right side). The three

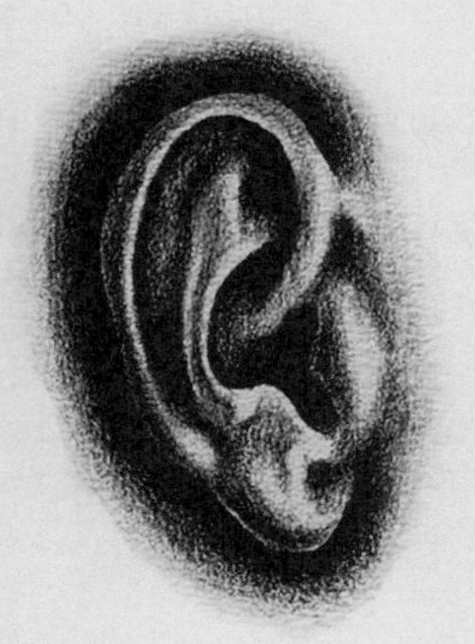

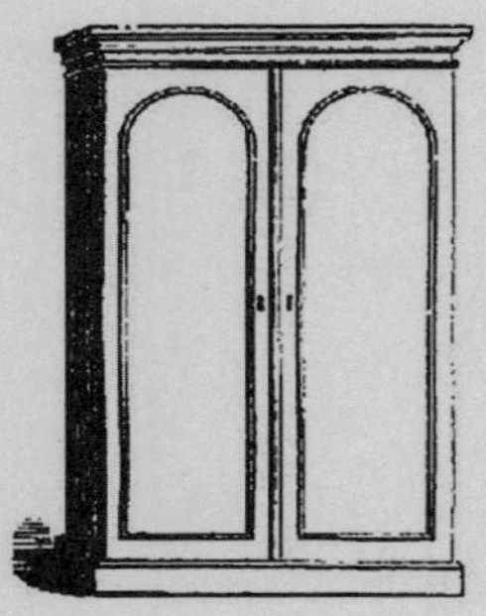

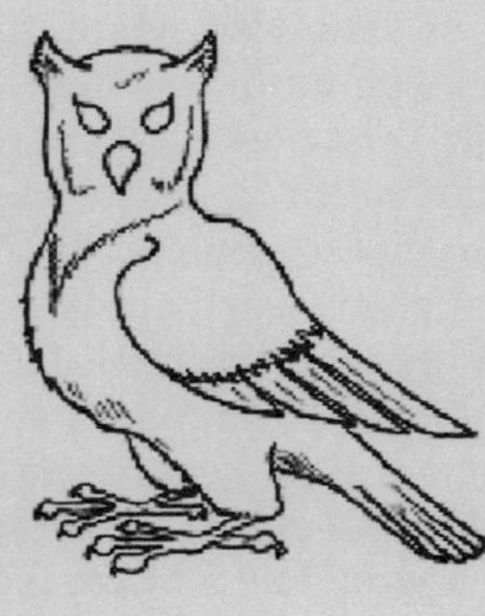

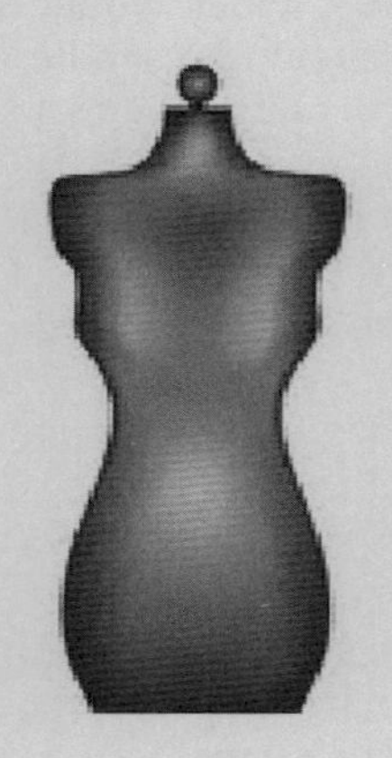

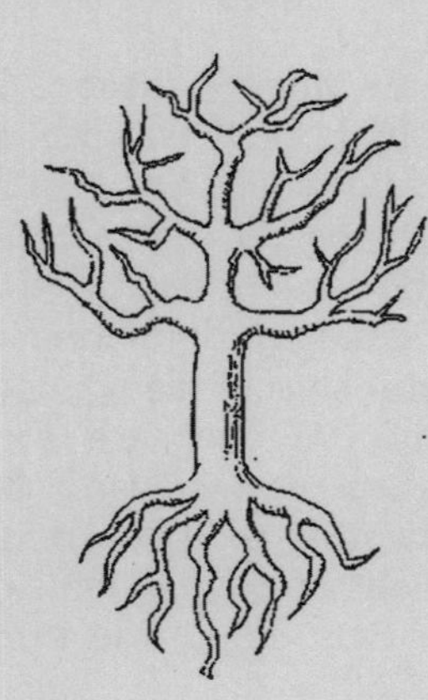

window sections, above the <u>half-curtains</u>, give a view of the <u>leafless trees</u> in the garden.

In this way, the <u>window</u> takes up the entire surface of the <u>mirror</u>, except for the upper portion, in which can be seen a strip of ceiling and the top of the <u>mirrored wardrobe</u>.

In the mirror above the mantel may be seen two other <u>dressmaker's dummies</u>: one in front of the first window section, the narrowest, at the far left, and the other in front of the third section (the one farthest to the right). Neither one is seen straight on; the one on the right has its right side facing the view; the one on the left, slightly smaller, reveals its left side. But it is difficult to be certain of this on first glance, because the two reflections are facing the same direction and as a consequence both seem to be turned so that the same side shows-the left side, probably.

The three dummies stand in a line. The middle one, whose size is intermediate between that of the two others, occupies the right side of the <u>mirror</u>, in exactly the same  direction as the <u>coffeepot</u> standing on the <u>table</u>.

In the spherical surface of the <u>coffeepot</u> is a shiny, distorted reflection of the window, a sort of <u>four-sided figure</u> whose side form the arcs of a circle. The line of the wooden uprights between the two window sections widens abruptly at the bottom into a vague spot. This is, no doubt, the shadow of the <u>dressmaker's dummy</u>.

The room is quite bright, since the <u>window</u> is unusually wide, even though it has only two sections.

A good smell of hot coffee rises from the pot on the <u>table</u>.

The <u>dressmaker's dummy</u> is no longer in its accustomed spot: it is normally placed in the corner by the <u>window</u>, opposite the <u>mirrored wardrobe</u>. The <u>wardrobe</u> has been placed in its position to help with the fittings.

The design on the <u>ceramic tile</u> base is the picture of an <u>owl</u>, with two large, somewhat frightening eyes. But, for the moment, it cannot be made out, because of the <u>coffeepot</u>.

Agents of chaos cast burning glances at anything or anyone capable of bearing witness to their condition, their fever of *lux et voluptas*. I am awake only in what I love & desire to the point of terror—everything else is just shrouded furniture, quotidian anaesthesia, shit-for-brains, sub-reptilian ennui of totalitarian regimes, banal censorship & useless pain.

Avatars of chaos act as spies, saboteurs, criminals of amour fou, neither selfless nor selfish, accessible as children, mannered as barbarians, chafed with obsessions, unemployed, sensually deranged, wolfangels, mirrors for contemplation, eyes like flowers, pirates of all signs & meanings.

Here we are crawling the cracks between walls of church state school & factory, all the paranoid monoliths. Cut off from the tribe by feral nostalgia we tunnel after lost words, imaginary bombs.

The last possible *deed* is that which defines perception itself, an invisible golden cord that connects us: illegal dancing in the courthouse corridors. If I were to kiss you here they'd call it an act of terrorism—so let's take our pistols to bed & wake up the city at midnight like drunken bandits celebrating with a fusillade, the message of the taste of chaos.

## Poetic Terrorism

WEIRD DANCING IN ALL-NIGHT computer-banking lobbies. Unauthorized pyrotechnic displays. Land-art, earthworks as bizarre alien artifacts strewn in State Parks.

Burglarize houses but instead of stealing, leave Poetic-Terrorist objects. Kidnap someone & make them happy.

Pick someone at random & convince them they're the heir to an enormous, useless & amazing fortune—say 5000 square miles of Antarctica, or an aging circus elephant, or an orphanage in Bombay, or a collection of alchemical mss. Later they will come to realize that for a few moments they believed in something extraordinary, & will perhaps be driven as a result to seek out some more intense mode of existence.

Bolt up brass commemorative plaques in places (public or private) where you have experienced a revelation or had a particularly fulfilling sexual experience, etc.

Go naked for a sign.

Organize a strike in your school or workplace on the grounds that it does not satisfy your need for indolence & spiritual beauty.

Grafitti-art loaned some grace to ugly subways & rigid public momuments—PT-art can also be created for public places: poems scrawled in courthouse lavatories, small fetishes abandoned in parks & restaurants, xerox-art under windshield-wipers of parked cars, Big Character Slogans pasted on playground walls, anonymous letters mailed to random or chosen recipients (mail fraud), pirate radio transmissions, wet cement . . .

The audience reaction or aesthetic-shock produced by PT ought to be at least as strong as the emotion of terror—powerful disgust, sexual arousal, superstitious awe, sudden intuitive breakthrough, dada-esque angst—no matter whether the PT is aimed at one person or many, no matter whether it is "signed" or anonymous, if it does not change someone's life (aside from the artist) it fails.

PT is an act in a Theater of Cruelty which has no stage, no rows of seats, no tickets & no walls. In order to work at all, PT must categorically be divorced from all conventional structures for art consumption (galleries, publications, media). Even the guerilla Situationist tactics of street theater are perhaps too well known & expected now.

An exquisite seduction carried out not only in the cause of
mutual satisfaction but also as a conscious act in a deliberately
beautiful life—may be the ultimate PT. The PTerrorist behaves
like a confidence-trickster whose aim is not money but
CHANGE.

Don't do PT for other artists, do it for people who will not
realize (at least for a few moments) that what you have done is
art. Avoid recognizable art-categories, avoid politics, don't
stick around to argue, don't be sentimental; be ruthless, take
risks, vandalize only what *must* be defaced, do something children will remember all their lives—but don't be spontaneous
unless the PT Muse has possessed you.

Dress up. Leave a false name. Be legendary. The best PT is
against the law, but don't get caught. Art as crime; crime as art.

Mix a little foolishness with your prudence:
it's good to be silly at the right moment.

Horace

# I

# Poetry and the discovery of British landscape

At the heart of Picturesque tourism is a set of paradoxes. Two can be introduced here at the start. Firstly, the tourist wants to discover Nature untouched by man; and yet, when he finds it, he cannot resist the impulse, if only in the imagination, to 'improve' it. Secondly, the tourist travelling through the Lakes or North Wales will loudly acclaim the *native* beauties of British landscape by invoking idealized *foreign* models – Roman pastoral poetry or the seventeenth-century paintings of Claude and Salvator Rosa. The second is related to the first in that the impulse to 'improve' is usually inspired by an educated awareness of what constitutes an ideal landscape. The paradoxical nature of these responses seldom seems to have perplexed the tourist for whom the experience of natural scenery was simply enhanced by this habitual exercise of comparison and association. Thus a Welsh valley acquired a higher aesthetic value if it looked like a Gaspard Dughet painting. The first sight of a Cumberland shepherd climbing the fells with his flock became more thrilling the more it approximated to a literary prototype: Virgil's *Eclogues* suddenly loomed into the space between the tourist and shepherd. Even scenes of an industrialised landscape could be transformed imaginatively, as when a clergyman tourist at Tintern saw through the window of his inn the blazing iron-works on the river bank: 'We saw Virgil's description realized, and the interior of Etna, the forges of the Cyclops, and their fearful employment, immediately occurred to us'.[1] Again, a poetically-minded tourist in the early 1770s confronts some coal-pits near Manchester:

> This novel station to my mem'ry brought
> The classic fables we're so early taught;
> The old mythology we learn at school
> Old CHARON'S ferry and the STYGIAN pool.[2]

A literary education thus functioned as an extra, expensive piece of intellectual equipment to take into the field. It developed what Archibald Alison described as 'a new sense' for the appreciation of landscape:

. . . it is probable most men will recollect, that the time when nature began to appear to them in another view, was, when they were engaged in the study of classical literature. In most men, at least, the first appearance of poetical imagination is at school, when their

3

柏木を深く知るにつれてわかったことだが、彼は永保ちする美がきらいなのであった。たちまち消える音楽とか、数日のうちに枯れる活け花とか、彼の好みはそういうものに限られ、建築や文学を憎んでいた。彼が金閣へやって来たのも、月の照る間の金閣だけを索めて来たのに相違なかった。それにしても音楽の美とは何とふしぎなものだ！　吹奏者が成就するその短かい美は、一定の時間を純粋な持続に変え、確実に繰り返されず、蜉蝣のような短命の生物をさながら、生命そのものの完全な抽象であり、創造である。音楽ほど生命に似たものはなく、同じ美でありながら、金閣ほど生命から遠く、生を侮蔑して見える美もなかった。そして柏木が「御所車」を奏でおわった瞬間に、音楽、この架空の生命は死に、彼の醜い肉体と暗鬱な認識とは、少しも傷つけられず変改されずに、又そこに残っていたのである。

柏木が美に索めているものは、確実に慰藉ではなかった！　言わず語らずのうちに、私にはそれがわかった。彼は自分の唇が尺八の歌口に吹きこむ息の、しばらくの間、中空に成就する美のあとに、自分の内臓足と暗い認識が、前にもましてありありと新鮮に残ることのほうを愛していたのだ。美の無益さ、美がわが体内をとおりすぎて跡形もないこと、それが絶対に何ものをも変えぬこと、……柏木の愛したのはそれだったのだ。美が私にとってもその



ようなものであったとしたら、私の人生はどんなに身軽になっていたことだろう。

……柏木の導くままに、何度となく、飽かず私は試みた。顔は充血し、息は迫って来た。そのとき急に私が鳥になり、私の咽喉から鳥の啼声が洩れたかのように、尺八が野太い音の一声をひびかせた。

「それだ」

と柏木が笑って叫んだ。決して美しい音ではないが、同じ音は次々と出た。そのとき私は、わがものとも思われぬこの神秘な声音から、頭上の金銅の鳳凰の声を夢みていたのである。

The Temple of the Golden Pavilion

Chapter 6

page 116 – 117

Later, when I came to know Kashiwagi more intimately, I understood that he disliked lasting beauty. His likings were limited to things such as music, which vanished instantly, or flower arrangements, which faded in a matter of days; he loathed architecture and literature. Clearly he would never think of visiting the Golden Temple except on a moonlit night like this.

Yet how strange a thing is the beauty of music! The brief beauty that the player brings into being transforms a given period of time into pure continuance; it is certain never to be repeated; like the existence of dayflies and other such short-lived creatures, beauty is a perfect abstraction and creation of life itself. Nothing is so similar to life as music; yet, although the Golden Temple shared the same type of beauty, nothing could have been farther from the world and more scornful of it than the beauty of this building. As soon as Kashiwagi had finished playing the 'Palace Carriage', music – that imaginary life – expired, and nothing was left there but his ugly body with its gloomy thoughts, all unscathed and unaltered.

It was certainly not consolation that Kashiwagi sought in beauty. I understood that much without the slightest discussion. What he loved was that, for a short while after his breath had brought beauty into existence in the air, his own clubfeet and gloomy thinking remained there, more clearly and more vividly than before. The uselessness of beauty, the fact that the beauty which had passed through his body left no mark there whatsoever, that it changed absolutely nothing – it was this that Kashiwagi loved. If beauty could be something like this for me too, how light would my life become!

I kept on trying time after time according to Kashiwagi's instructions. My face became red and my breath came in gasps. Then, just as if I had suddenly become a bird, and as if a bird's cry had escaped my throat, the flute emitted a single daring note.

'There you are!' shouted Kashiwagi with a laugh. It was certainly not a beautiful note, but the same sound emerged time after time. Then I fancied that this mysterious sound, which did not seem to emanate from me, was the voice of that golden copper phoenix above our heads.

When I read this book as a young person it left a strong impression in my mind and I felt a certain amount of discomfort. Reading it again many years later enmeshing my self in the root of Japanese culture and Mishima's World of beauty. Quite extreme but so beautiful.

# I Believe...

- Man evolved from the apes because of cooking, dancing, sports and fashion.
- In the Big Bang Theory.
- You make your own luck.
- In Lieber and Stoller.
- In the communion of saints (and/or comedians).
- I was here first.
- Every snowflake is different (not to mention women).
- I'll dust my broom.
- Everybody needs a hobby.
- You are what you're willing to eat.
- In the forgiveness of sins (after a sufficiently amusing apology).
- Karma is more evident in the play-offs.
- Quitting smoking now greatly reduces your chances of ever dying.
- If you want a do-right all-night woman, you've got to be a do-right all-night man. (And vice versa).
- In the resurrection of the body (after a good cup of coffee).
- Self-righteous, crusading daily newspapers should not publish gambling point spreads.
- Superior beings must be good looking or they're not really superior.
- It takes a big woman to say she's sorry.
- The world has a lot to learn from Hoagy Carmichael.
- If you can turn it over to God, He can turn it back over to you.
- In the pilot.
- I've made myself clear.
- Not everything is beautiful in its own way.
- If you lie your nose gets bigger.
- This must be the place.
- Everything is going to be all right.
- What you see is what you get.
- In love.

SAVINDER BUAL ANNOTATED THE MYTH OF PERSISTENCE OF VISION REVISITED, JOURNAL OF FILM AND VIDEO, 1993, JOSEPH & BARBARA ANDERSONN

contours.  Further research is needed to clarify this matter.

## Conclusion

If there are indeed two separate computational strategies or two separate anatomical modules employed by the visual system for processing closely spaced stimuli and widely spaced stimuli, then the motion picture falls within the limits of the closely spaced category. [7]  The changes from frame to frame in "live action" cinematography are small -- not an instance of experimental apparent motion as it is usually presented.  And clearly motion in the motion picture is not an instance of Wertheimer's strange phi movement where motion is seemingly induced between two widely spaced lines that are seen as remaining in place while sequentially flashing on and off.

Since we know that the individual pictures of a motion picture are not really moving, and that our perception of motion is therefore an illusion, and since we now know that the effect has nothing to do with persistence of vision or phi movement, we suggest that henceforth the phenomenon of motion in the motion picture be called by the name used in the literature of perception -- short-range apparent motion.

Motion in the motion picture is, as we have said, an illusion, but since it falls within the short-range or "fine grain" category it is transformed by the rules of that system -- that is, the rules for transforming real continuous movement. The visual system can (and does) distinguish between long-range and short-range apparent motion, but it seemingly cannot distinguish between short-range apparent motion and real motion.  To the visual system the motion in a motion picture  is real motion.

If this is true, if to our perception the successive still images of a motion picture are processed in the same way and are indistinguishable from the unbroken motion of the natural world, then what are the implications?  How must a theory of the cinema be modified to accommodate such a finding?  There is, of course, the housekeeping chore of  reevaluating recent film theories in the light of a new paradigm.  For example, one would expect to find support for Metz's early assertion in Film Language that motion in the cinema is not a re-presentation, but a presentation, not the re-experience but the experience of motion (Metz 7-9).  Equally, one would expect to expose the essential irrelevance of Baudry's concern about effacing differences and suppressing the "discontinuity inscribed by the camera", i.e. the spaces between the frames of a motion picture (Baudry).

Beyond the housekeeping, there are at least two major implications of the demythologizing of persistence of vision.  First "persistence of vision", the term, the concept, the myth, must be given a place in the history of film scholarship, but can no longer be given currency in film theory.  The time has surely come

Consciousness is formed of discrete moments — oliver Sacks

discrete moments = stills.

# How I Write

## Viktor Shklovsky

[I've] been writing for fifteen years and [over] time I've obviously changed my [ma]nner and style of working.

[F]ifteen years ago it was much harder, [beca]use I didn't know how to get started. [Eve]rything I wrote seemed like it had been said before. Individual pieces [did]n't coalesce. Examples were all self-[refe]rential. For the most part this is all [still] the case. I still find writing difficult, [exc]ept now in a different way. A piece of [pros]e might be spun off into an indepen-[den]t work, but the main thing, as in film, [is w]hat goes between pieces.

[C]reation in general and the creation [of a] new literary style in particular often [com]e when a chance mutation takes hold. [Mo]re or less like what happens with the [deve]lopment of a new breed of cattle.

[T]here is a universal literary style, [one] founded upon the individual style. [No] one actually writes in this style—it [ma]kes nothing move, it is intangible, it [is i]mperceptible.

[T]here is the emphasis on the flout-[ing] of syllabic-tonic prosody in Maya-[kov]sky.

[T]here is the emphasis on dialect, on [dia]lect in Gogol. Gogol most likely [did] not write in the language in which [he] actually thought, and his Ukrainian [pro]sody affected his style. As distant [star]s affect the orbits of planets.

[I] write beginning with facts. I try [no]t to modify facts. I try to link dispa-[rate] facts. I may have gotten this from [Lo]monosov the juxtaposition of dispa-[rate] ideas or it may come from Anatole [Fra]nce, banging the heads of epithets [tog]ether.

[S]o maybe rather than epithets, I'm try-[ing] to bang things facts together.

[C]urrently I'm starting to write differ-[ent]ly, particularly if I'm working on a [sci]entific study. Here I proceed from the [sub]ject matter. The "why" doesn't inter-[est] me until the "what" and "how" have [bee]n resolved. I do not go in search of [exp]lanations to the unknown.

[I] begin a work by reading. I read [wit]hout trying to strain myself. Rather, I [try] not to commit things to memory. The [bra]in, the attentiveness they simply [get] in the way. One should read serenely, [not] looking at the book.

[I] read a lot. As you can see, you're [get]ting an essay on how I work rather [tha]n one on how I write.

[L]et's continue.

[I] read without straining myself. I [ma]ke colored bookmarks or bookmarks [of] various widths [for citations]. While [I d]on't write the page number on my [boo]kmarks, it would be good to do so, in [cas]e they fall out. Then I look over my [boo]kmarks. I make notes. The typist, the [sam]e one typing up this essay, retypes [the] pieces with the page numbers. I line [up] my pieces - and there are many of [the]m in columns along the wall of my [roo]m. Unfortunately my room is small, [and] I feel hemmed in.

[G]etting the sense of a citation is very [im]portant: I turn it around, and join it to [oth]er citations.

[P]ieces tend to stay up on my wall for a long time. I sort them and pin them up in columns again, and brief transitions occur to me. I write a sufficiently detailed chapter outline on some sheets of paper, and sort the now integrated fragments into stacks.

Then I start dictating the work, marking insertions with numbers.

All these techniques immeasurably speed up the pace of the work. And they make it easier. It's like working directly onto a typesetting machine.

During this process the outline and often even the subject are almost always modified. The work's meaning turns out to be different than intended, and it's in the wreckage of the work's potential that one can agonize over the unity of subject matter, the possibility for a new arrangement, the algebraic compression the subconscious performs on the subject matter that we call inspiration.

The work grows and it evolves. I don't think I so much complete my books as stop writing them, and that if I were to rewrite them two or three more times they would be better, clearer, and my audience would understand me, not just my friends, but that I would be divested of my wit.

This wit, for which some reproach me—it is a consequence of my method, a certain lack of refinement.

I cannot edit myself, just as I cannot read myself. Other thoughts occur to me, and I depart from the text.

Listening to myself reading aloud would be torture.

This manner of working and this lack of refinement are not flaws. Just as a glassblower can't make a mistake, if I master a technique completely then I can't make a mistake even when I work quickly. In the end, however, it must be said that I produce no more than many who work at a slower pace.

And it's time for a break.

I am forever talking to people, and I don't believe that people should write everything on their own. I am convinced we ought to write in groups. I am convinced that friends should live in the same city, and meet frequently, and that the work gets done only if done collectively.

The best year of my life was when I would talk to Lev Yakubinsky[1] on the telephone, every day, day after day, for an hour or two. We put up the scaffolding over the phone.

I am convinced, Lev Petrovich, that it was pointless for you to get off the phone to get back to your real work.

I am convinced that it would be pointless for me not to live in Leningrad.

I am convinced that when Roman Jakobson moved to Prague it was a tremendous blow both to my work and his.

I am convinced that people in a given literary community should consider one another in their work, and that they should change their lives for one another.

For me it is somewhat complicated because I am a scholar, a journalist, and an author. There are other facts, other relationships to subject matter, other arrangements of the device. It is a burden to efface the evidence of my method in my scholarly writing so that I might write books to be understood by foreign scholars, to be accessible, to not demand mental realignment.

But I want to demand it.

In his work the journalist needs integrity, and courage.

I was riding on the Turksib. Everything dusty and hot, lizards peeping. Tall grass: here wormwood, there feather grass, and stiff prickly desert grass, tamarisk, lilacs not yet in bloom.

Out there, in the fall, salty rivers flow into the freshwater Balkhash, the freshwater lake with the salty inlets. Out there people ride cattle and horses just like we ride streetcars. Out there the Kirghiz borzois leap through the wormwood on unseen legs, resembling nothing so much as slender undulating cardboard cutout spines.

Goats wandering across the sands. Automobiles stuck in the salt flats for weeks on end. Camels pulling carts. Eagles soaring hundreds of feet overhead, ready to light on the telegraph poles, the only place to land in the desert.

Out there they're building the Turksib railroad. Hard work, necessary work.

Out there it's so hot the Kirghiz go dressed in felt boots, felt trousers, and felt caps. Where they're not called Kirghiz, they're called Kazakhs.

Building a railroad is hard work. There isn't much water. Bread has to be brought in. There has to be bread. Bread has to be stored somewhere. So many workers, all of them needing a roof over their heads.

But they built it anyway.

Good books come when we are forced to overcome our subject matter, when we are stalwart.

This is also known as inspiration.

This is how I wrote *A Sentimental Journey*.

*Zoo, Or Letters Not About Love* I wrote somewhat differently.

We had an anthem in OPOAYAZ:[2] A very long anthem, as we were rather prolix and no longer young.

One couplet went:

> From a formalist point of view even
> enthusiasm
> Is a convergence of devices

This is entirely possible.

Enthusiasm is dulled by the inertia of expertise, and in particular the literary inertia of enthusiasm.

I had to write a book, a biography, something along the lines of "One Hundred Portraits of Russian Literary Figures." Would that I might have been infatuated with it, that I might have found some sort of convergence, that I might have contracted a love for it, the way a weakened organism contracts a disease.

The result was a badly written book.

I very much want to write prose now. I am waiting for convergences. I am waiting for invention. I am waiting for subject matter and inspiration.

There are, of course, other inert books for which I have contempt, ones made out of expertise and filler.

Such filler can deface even the best subject matter.

Individual instances grapple with the larger subject matter in Eisenstein's all-too-significantly titled film, *The Old and the New*.[3]

To the dilettante who mutters that the film is flawed—"why don't they show the cooperative?"—we note that the film is not a correlate, that it advances a theme, and that it is organized through the consciously selected and aestheticized material of the *syuzhet* art. *Syuzhet* devices are like a set of French curves never meant to be used for tracing a given curvature.

One must learn.

Comrades, I cannot recall the lengthy and insightful list of questions you asked me. You can find a bibliography of my work somewhere, but I have no idea what my future holds.

*Translated by Adam Siegel*

The *Kak my pishem* questionnaire:
1. Preparatory period. Duration.
2. What kind of subject matter do you use most (autobiographical, literary, observations and notes)?
3. Do you generally use living persons as models for your characters?
4. What provides you with the initial impulse for a work (anecdotes, commission, images, etc.)?
5. When during the day do you work – in the morning, afternoon, or evening? How many hours a day at most?
6. Average productivity—pages per month.
7. What sorts of stimulants (*narkotiki*) do you use, and in what amounts?
8. Do you write with a pencil, pen, or typewriter? Do you sketch when you're working? How heavily is your work revised by editors?
9. Do you work from an outline and does it change?
10. What do you find most difficult? Beginnings, middles, or endings?
11. Which senses most often generate images? (visual, aural, tactile?)
12. Do you insist on some sort of rhythm to your prose?
13. Do you proof your work by reading it aloud (either to yourself or to others)?
14. How do you feel when you have completed a work?
15. Do you revise your work for new editions?
16. Are you affected by reviews?

Endnotes
1 Lev Yakubinsky (1892-1945): Russian linguist and formalist.
2 Obshchestvo izucheniya POeticheskogo YAZyka: Society for the Study of Poetic Language.
3 Eisenstein's 1929 film, also known as *General'naia liniia* (*The General Line*), focused on a single female farm-worker to extol Soviet collectivization of agriculture. ∎

** Worth straining your eyes for!*

# 1  The Notion of Entertainment

Entertainment, show business, Variety are not terms that are normally much thought about. Indeed they are often the final point in a conversation: 'Well anyway I like it. It's good entertainment' – said defensively when you are praising an unfashionable film in intellectual circles; or else the tag, now a comic cliché, used in backstage musicals at crucial points in the plot: 'That's show business!' Nothing more needs to be said: we all share a commonsense notion of what entertainment is. Yet precisely because it is such a final or absolute notion, it is very hard to define.[1]

You can't get at it simply by listing examples. The song *That's entertainment!* by Dietz and Schwartz is a veritable compendium of what may be considered entertainment and lists, without any apparent sense of contradiction, *Hamlet* and *Oedipus Rex* alongside 'the clown with his pants falling down' and 'the lights on the lady in tights'. If all these things can be entertainment, then clearly entertainment is not so much a category of things as an attitude towards things.

We can best come to an understanding of what this attitude is by a series of negations.

Firstly, entertainment is not simply a way of describing something found equally in all societies at all times. Song and dance in tribal societies for instance is specifically tied to religious and utilitarian purposes, placating the gods or conjuring up rain.[2] The pageants and amusements of medieval Europe were part of the whole pattern of social life and built right into the organisation of the calendar, governed by the Church and tied to seasonal – hence, economic – festivals. Where in tribal society song and dance sought to have an effect on life, in medieval society it celebrated it in a systematically structured way. Our entertainment may, of course, do both these things, but it is not in any coherent way associated with serious metaphysical or ceremonial practice. On the other hand, it is different from the growth of amusements and diversions in courtly society. Unlike them, modern entertainment is not simply a way of staving off days of boredom for a leisured class nor is it simply an adjunct to social intercourse.

A key figure in the emergence of 'entertainment' is Molière, who in having to elaborate a defence of his plays developed a new definition of what the theatre should do.[3] The Church had attacked him for not edifying, the salons for his refusal to conform to the taste for polite divertissement and the critics for not obeying the rules of art. His defence was to deny that those concepts of what he should do were relevant to his real purpose, which was to provide pleasure – and the definition of *that* was to be decided by 'the people'. Against salons, church and critics Molière set the court (which at this time was characterised



by an impotent aristocracy and a newly recruited bourgeoisie who actually ran the country) and the gallery; against received élite opinion he asserted populism. In so doing, he severed art from entertainment – not, it is true, in his own practice but in theory. Entertainment became identified with what was not art, not serious, not refined. This distinction remains with us – art is what is edifying, élitist, refined, difficult, whilst entertainment is hedonistic, democratic, vulgar, easy. That the distinction is harmful, false to the best in both what is called art and what is called entertainment has often been commented upon.[4] But it remains one built into our education and, as we shall see, the decisions of television programmers.

Entertainment is also a part of 'leisure'. This is a specifically modern idea and is again best defined negatively, as is done, for instance, by Kenneth Roberts:

Leisure time can be defined as time that is not obligated, and leisure activities can be defined as activities that are non-obligatory. At work, a man's time is not his own and his behaviour is not responsive purely to his own whims. Outside work, there are certain duties that men are obliged, either by custom or law, to fulfil, such as the obligations that an individual has towards his family. When these obligations have been met, a man has 'free time' in which his behaviour is dictated by his own will and preference, and it is here that leisure is found.[5]

Leisure and entertainment are separate from and in opposition to work and domestic cares. In a functional analysis, leisure can be seen either as a way of compensating for the dreariness of work or else as the passivity attendant on industrial labour.[6] But the richness and variety of the actual forms of leisure suggest that leisure should also be seen as the creation of meaning in a world in which work and the daily round are characterised by drudgery, insistence and meaninglessness.

Entertainment is a specific aspect of this leisure. It is provided and it is paid for, and in this it is unlike talking, hobbies, sex and games. It derives in its characteristic form – the string of short items, with or without link man, the popular and vulgar reference, the implicit sexuality and open sentimentality – from the development of entertainment in the pubs and clubs patronised by the urban working-class.[7] This form has, of course, been fed by the continuing traditions of bourgeois amusement – operetta, musical comedy, parlour songs – but this has only tended to refine or embellish (and sometimes emasculate) the form, not to dominate it. Telescoping history in this way does, of course, miss out all sorts of nuance, but it does help us to grasp the specificity of the generalised contemporary notion, 'entertainment'.

If we now glance at a couple of official statements from BBC and ITV respectively we shall observe that this notion informs the thinking of these companies – not so much what they actually think or say, but what is implied in the sort of things they find it necessary to say publicly.

First, Tom Sloan's attempt to define light entertainment at a BBC lunchtime lecture:[8]

We have Drama and Features and Arts Features and General Features and

Documentaries *and* Talk and Current Affairs, to name but a few. But I believe that a great mass of people want to treat their television sets as a means of escape, and never more so than at the present time.

I remember one wet Sunday, in 1961, driving to Liverpool to see a new group called the Beatles give a concert for their fan club which we televised. For the first time in my life, I saw the industrial north of England, the rows of terraced houses, fronting on to the cobbled roads, glistening in the rain. The sheer ghastliness of it all was overpowering, but on the roof of every house, there was a television aerial. Antennae reaching for escape to another world. And, heaven knows, why not?

So my job is to organise a stream of output which is primarily intended to please and relax those who wish to receive it. In other words, to entertain.

As usual, we end up with that explain-all, 'to entertain', but before that we may note the careful distinction of entertainment from art and information, and the distinction in terms of escape from the horrors of life. We should note, too, the rather patronising tone of the man who provides entertainment for 'a great mass of people'. If we see entertainment from the point of view of the providers, then we are asking questions like, How do you distract people from the horrors of everyday life? what is strong enough to shut it out for a while? how do you bring a little sparkle into the drabness? and also, how can you get on their side, not alienate them with art or education? This is the peculiar inflection of the responsible voice in mass entertainment and must have an influence on any aesthetic approach we make to it.

An ITV pronouncement,* is equally revealing:

It is common to write as though comedy and light entertainment were much the same thing. It is true that they have a common objective—to provide relaxing* entertainment. It is true too, that in a country in which there are remnants of a puritan tradition the two are still sometimes lumped together as though they belonged in some rather disreputable bargain-basement of broadcasting. Nothing could be further from the truth. No aspect of broadcasting calls for greater skills or harder work from producers, directors and performers than the business of earning laughs or mounting an exciting production number.

Here there is an explicitly apologetic note, as is frequent enough in pronouncements from ITV, vulnerable to the attack of commercial exploitation. Their first answer, interestingly enough, is to defend the criticism of puritanism by a puritanical insistence on work, professionalism. This notion, however, is superseded in the next paragraph by an even more powerful argument:

There is still a shortage of light entertainment programmes of the highest quality. But it would be wrong to exaggerate. Many programmes have given a great deal of pleasure to very many people.

---

* Note that both extracts use this word almost involuntarily. Its implication of prior tension links entertainment directly with the stresses of work and life.



Populism has crept back, for the logic behind this is that as long as people enjoy it (or rather, as long as 'very many people' turn it on) it doesn't matter much what it's like.

Both these statements rely on a notion of entertainment such as has been sketched, but also reveal the peculiar quality of mass entertainment, provided by a specialist profession for people conceived of as an undifferentiated mass. Hence the philistinism and self-indulgence implicit in the notion are not tempered by the real vulgarity and consciousness of oppression of the people, but by the power of professional standards and the sensitivity of power to public opinion (both of which tend to temper vulgarity and indulgence in the name of responsibility) and more still by what producers think constitutes the entertainment needs of the working-class.

Television light entertainment is founded on a very specific idea of what entertainment is in a modern industrial society. We must now look at the aesthetic consequences of this.

## Notes

[1] For those familiar with them it will be evident that the following relies heavily on the work of Weber and Schutz, that entertainment is an 'ideal-type' or 'second degree common sense construct'. Anyone interested in this methodology should consult Weber: *The Methodology of the Social Sciences*, New York, 1949, and Alfred Schutz: *Collected Papers*, Vol. 1, The Hague, 1967, especially part one.

[2] An example of the function of dance in a modern tribal society is suggested in *The Yoruba of Nigeria*, which is the second unit in the Humanities Foundation Course of the Open University.

[3] Molière's views on the theatre are to be found in various places, but most lengthily in *La Critique de l'Ecole des Femmes*.

[4] *e.g.* Raymond Williams, *The Long Revolution*, Penguin, 1965.
Hall and Whannel, *The Popular Arts*, Hutchinson, 1964

[5] Kenneth Roberts, *Leisure*, Longman, 1970.

[6] There is a useful discussion of these views in H. L. Wilensky, 'Labor and Leisure: Intellectual Traditions' in *Industrial Relations*, Vol. 1, No. 2, Feb. 1962.

[7] A particularly interesting connection between the industrial experience and the actual form of entertainment is made by Albert F. McLean, Jnr, in his book *American Vaudeville as Ritual*, University of Kentucky Press, 1965. Unfortunately McLean does not push this connection as far as he might.

[8] 11 December 1969. Published as a pamphlet by the BBC.

[9] Independent Television Authority, *Annual Report and Accounts*, 1969-70, HMSO, p. 15.

# Why I Am Not a Painter

I am not a painter, I am a poet.
Why? I think I would rather be
 a painter, but I am not. Well,

for instance, Mike Goldberg
is starting a painting. I drop in.
"Sit down and have a drink" he
says. I drink; we drink. I look
up. "You have SARDINES in it."
"Yes, it needed something there."
"Oh." I go and the days go by
and I drop in again. The painting
is going on, and I go, and the days
go by. I drop in. The painting is
finished. "Where's SARDINES?"
All that's left is just
letters, "It was too much," Mike says.

But me? One day I am thinking of
a color: orange. I write a line
about orange. Pretty soon it is a
whole page of words, not lines.
Then another page. There should be
so much more, not of orange, of
words, of how terrible orange is
and life. Days go by. It is even in
prose, I am a real poet. My poem
is finished and I haven't mentioned
orange yet. It's twelve poems, I call
it ORANGES. And one day in a gallery
I see Mike's painting, called SARDINES.

Frank O'Hara, 1957

Indeterminacy

Limitless → → →

Deferral → result!

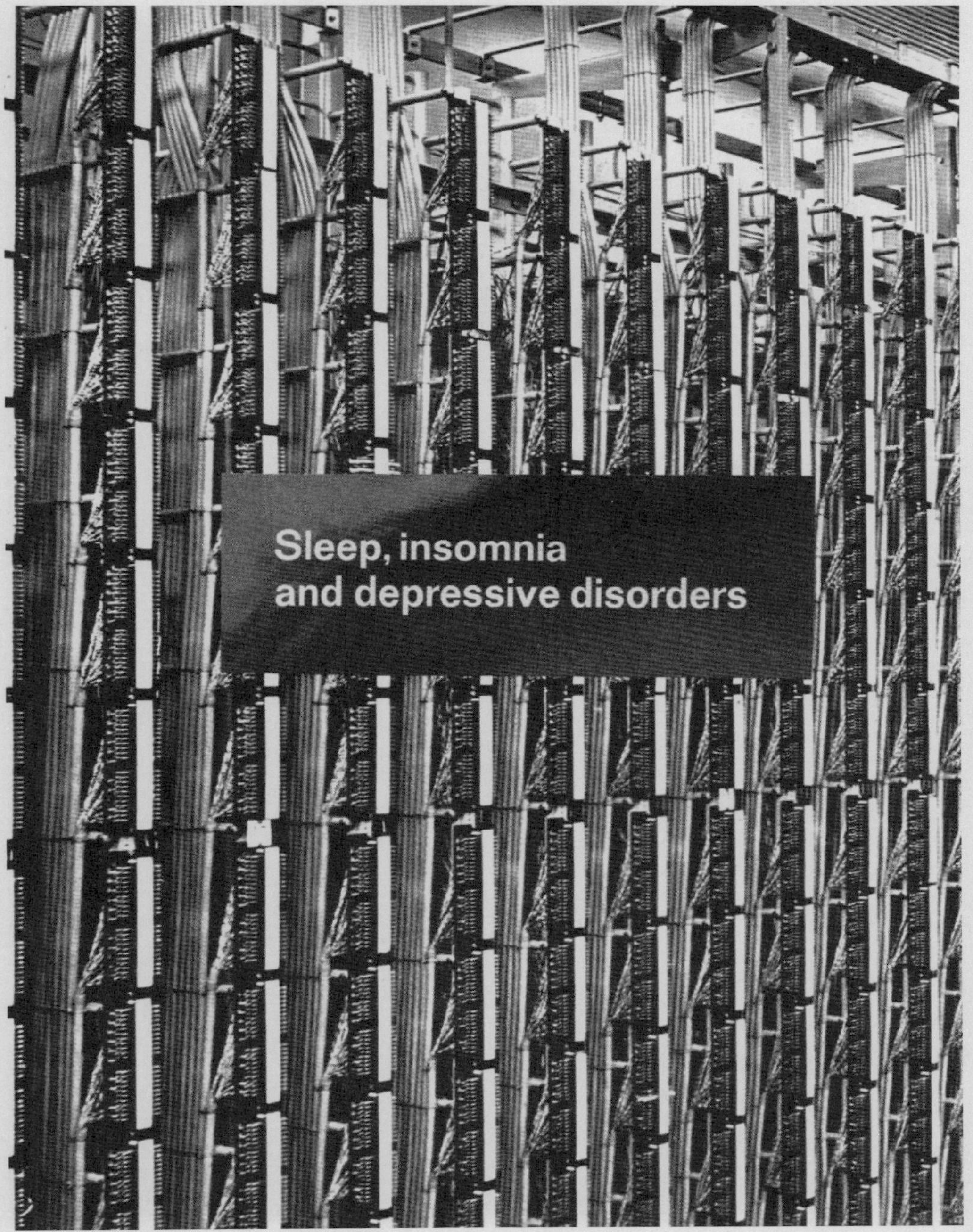


WAYNE BURROWS ANNOTATED FOUND TEXT (PUBLIC DOMAIN), c. 1966 – 1971, MD MAGAZINE (USA)/WOODWORKING (UK)

Reading randomly, without fixed purpose, as a sideline to other activity, can lead to the apparent revelations of something akin to textual Diviniation or Clairvoyance. Through any chance encounter with forgotten news headlines or advertising copy from decades past, in whose very decontextualisation we find unintended predictions, there are glimpses of subconscious social drives, the concealment of propaganda, all the seeds of our present, and the future that continues to elude us even as it is written in the signs everywhere around us.

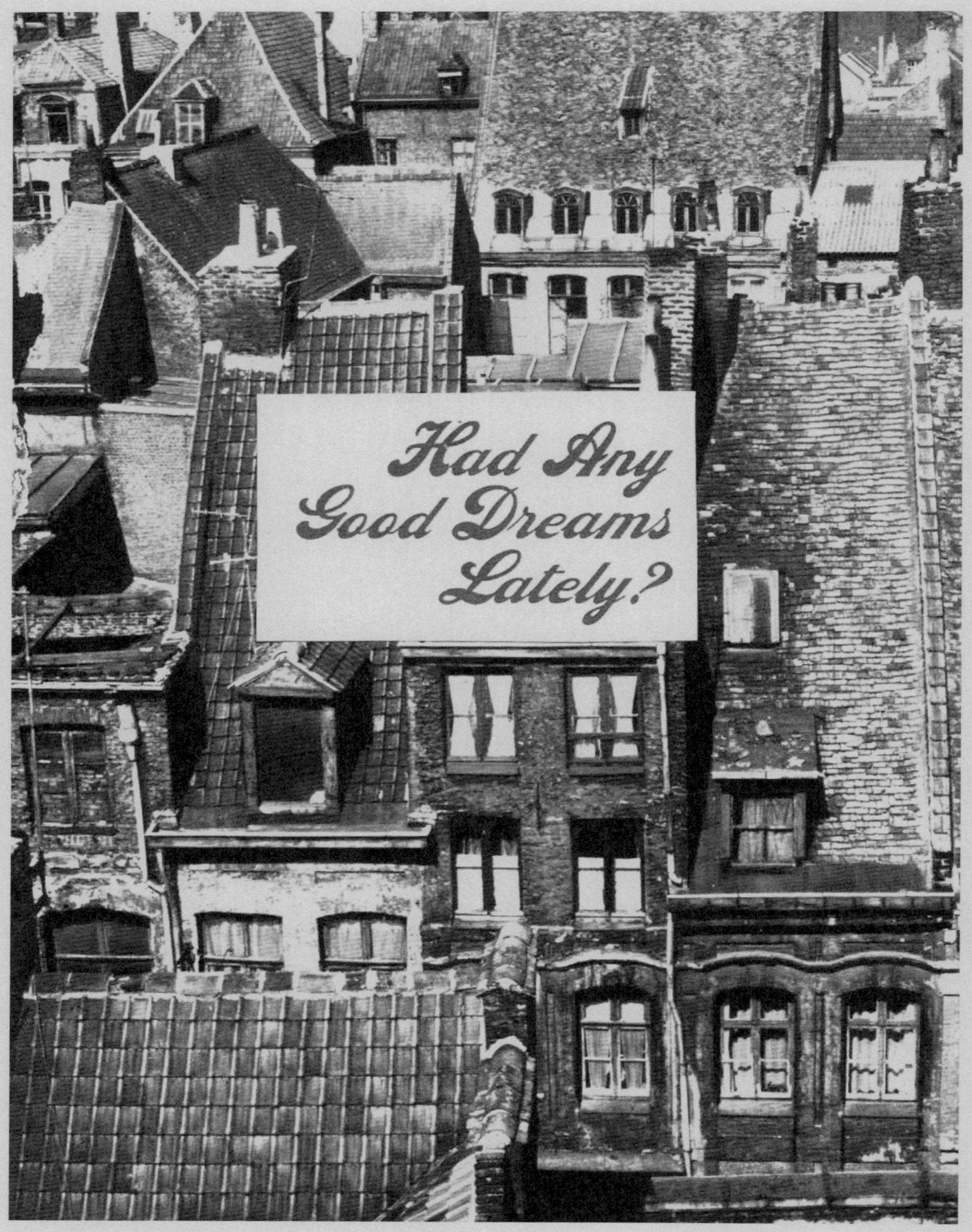


Travelling with no printed pages to hand, no available signal to unlock the near-infinite library locked-in behind the black glass screen of a mobile phone, we might read signs in the landscape; billboards, corporate mottos and logos on warehouse banners; the sides of lorries; plywood structures in fields; the free papers and magazines financed by advertising and the tax deductible marketing budgets of privatised monopolies. All these words and images, conjoined and suggestive, might yet be more telling than we imagine.

*Calvino was associated with the Paris-based OULIPO group when he wrote this short piece in 1967, he tried to continue his writing with mathematic thinking and accommodate the intensity of a relationship in an abstract form.*

## The Night Driver

As soon as I am outside the city I realize night has fallen. I turn on my headlights. I am driving from A to B, along a three-lane superhighway, the kind where the center lane is used for passing in both directions. For night driving our eyes, too, must remove one kind of inner transparency and fit on another, because they no longer *[what about 'opacity'?]* have to make an effort to distinguish among the shadows and the fading colors of the evening landscape the little speck of the distant cars which are coming toward us or preceding us, but they have to check a kind of black slate which requires a different method of reading, more precise but also simplified, since the darkness erases all the picture's details which might be distracting and underlines only the indispensable elements, the white stripes on the asphalt, the headlights' yellow glow, and the little red dots. It's a process that occurs automatically, and if I am led to reflect on it this evening it's because now that the external possibilities of distraction diminish, the internal ones get the upper hand within me, and my thoughts race on their own in a circuit of alternatives and doubts I can't disengage; *[This is a statement.* in other words, I have to make a special effort to concentrate on my driving. *The jealousy, the speculation the sense of ownership and sexual competitiveness...]*

I climbed into the car suddenly, after a quarrel over the telephone with Y. I live in *[Here comes Y, the* A, Y lives in B. I wasn't planning to visit her this evening. But during our daily *significant other, the* phone call we said dire things to each other; in the end, carried away by my *invisible and impenetrable,* exasperation, I told Y that I wanted to break off our affair; Y answered that it didn't *the subjectivity in denial.* matter to her and that she would immediately telephone Z, my rival. At this point *Who or what is Y anyway?]* one of us -- I don't remember whether it was she or I -- hung up. Before a minute had passed I realized the motive of our quarrel was trifling compared to the consequences it was creating. To call Y back on the telephone would have been a mistake; the only way to resolve the question was to dash over to B and have a face-to-face explanation with her. So here I am on this superhighway I have driven over hundreds of times at every hour in every season but which never seemed so long to me before.

Or, to put it more clearly, I feel as if I had lost all sense of space and of time: the glowing cones projected by the headlights make the outlines of places sink into vagueness; the numbers of the miles on the signs and the numbers that click over on the dashboard are data that mean nothing to me, that do not respond to the urgency of my questions about what Y is doing at this moment, about what she is thinking. *[A certain algorithm is* Did she really mean to call Z or was it only a threat, blurted out like that, out of *at work]* pique? And if she was serious, did she do it immediately after our telephone conversation, or is she thinking it over for a moment, letting her anger subside before she makes up her mind? *[...] [I think Z as the intruder is obsolete here]*

I realize that in rushing toward Y what I desire most is not to find Y at the end of my race: I want Y to be racing toward me, this is the answer I need; what I mean is, I want her to know I'm racing toward her but at the same time I want to know she's

**77**

racing toward me. The sole thought that comforts me is also the thought that torments me most: the thought that if Y at this moment is speeding toward A, then each time she sees the headlights of a car speeding toward B she will ask herself whether it's I racing toward her, and she will desire it to be I, and she will never be sure. Now two cars going in opposite directions have found themselves for a moment side by side, a flash has illuminated the raindrops, the sound of the motors has become fused as in an abrupt gust of wind: perhaps it was the two of us, or rather it is certain that one car was I and the other car could be she, that is the one I want to be she, the sign in which I want to recognize her, though it is this very sign that makes her unrecognizable to me. Speeding along the superhighway is the only method we have left, she and I, to express what we have to say to each other, but we cannot communicate it or receive the communication as long as we are speeding.

Of course I took my place behind the wheel in order to reach her as fast as possible; but the more I go forward the more I realize that the moment of arrival is not the real end of my race. Our meeting, with all the inessential details a meeting involves, the minute network of sensations and meanings and memories that would spread out before me -- the room with the philodendron, the opaline lamp, the earrings -- and the things I would say to her, some of which would surely be mistaken or mistakable, and the things she would say, to some extent surely jarring or in any case not what I expect, and all the succession of unpredictable consequences that each gesture and each word involved would raise around the things that we have to say to each other, or rather that we want to hear each other say, a storm of such noise that our communication already difficult over the telephone would become even more hazardous, stifled, buried as if under an avalanche of sand. This is why, rather than go on talking, I felt the need to transform the things to be said into a cone of light hurled at a hundred miles an hour, to transform myself into this cone of light moving over the superhighway, because it is certain that such a signal can be received and understood by her without being lost in the ambiguous disorder of secondary vibrations, just as I, to receive and understand the things she has to say to me, would like them to be only (rather, I would like her to be only) this cone of light I see advancing on the superhighway at a speed (I'm guessing, at a glance) of eighty or ninety. What counts is communicating the indispensable, skipping all the superfluous, reducing ourselves to essential communication, to a luminous signal that moves in a given direction, abolishing the complexity of our personalities and situations and facial expressions, leaving them in the shadowy container that the headlights carry behind them and conceal. The Y I love is really that moving band of luminous rays, and all the rest of her can remain implicit; and the me that she can love, the me that has the power of entering that circuit of exaltation which is her affective life, in the flashing of this pass which, through love of her and with a certain risk, I am now attempting…

There are two musics (at least so I have always thought): the music one listens to, the music one plays. These two musics are two totally different arts, each with its own history, its own sociology, its own aesthetics, its own erotic; the same composer can be minor if you listen to him, tremendous if you play him (even badly) - such is Schumann.

The music one plays comes from an activity that is very little auditory, being above all manual (and thus in a way much more sensual). It is the music which you or I can play, alone or among friends, with no other audience than its participants (that is, with all risk of theatre, all temptation of hysteria removed); a muscular music in which the part taken by the sense of hearing is one only of ratification, as though the body were hearing - and not 'the soul'; a music which is-not played 'by heart': seated at the key- board or the music stand, the body controls, conducts, co-ordinates, having itself to transcribe what it reads, making sound and meaning, the body as inscriber and not just transmitter, simple receiver. This music has disappeared; initially the province of the idle (aristocratic) class, it lapsed into an insipid social rite with the coming of the democracy of the bourgeoisie (the piano, the young lady, the drawing room, the nocturne) and then faded out al- together (who plays the piano today?). To find practical music in the West, one has now to look to another public, another repertoire, another instrument (the young generation, vocal music, the guitar). Concurrently, passive, receptive music, sound music, is become the music (that of concert, festival, record, radio): playing has ceased to exist; musical activity is no longer manual, muscular, kneadingly physical, but merely liquid, effusive, 'lubrificating', to take up a word from Balzac. So too has the performer changed. The amateur, a role defined much more by a style than by a technical imperfection, is no longer anywhere to be found; the professionals, pure specialists whose training remains entirely esoteric for the public (who is there who is still acquainted with the problems of musical education?), never offer that style of the perfect amateur the great value of which could still be recognised in a Lipati or a Panzera, touching off in us not satisfaction but desire, the desire to make that music. In short, there was first the actor of music, then the interpreter (the grand Romantic voice), then finally the technician, who relieves the listener of all activity, even by procuration, and abolishes in the sphere of music the very notion of doing.

The work of Beethoven seems to me bound up with this historical problem, not as the straightforward expression of a particular moment (the transition from amateur to interpreter) but as the powerful germ of a disturbance of civilisation, Beethoven at once bringing together its elements and sketching out its solution; an ambiguity which is that of Beethoven's two historical roles: the mythical role which he was made to play by the whole of the nineteenth century and the modern role which our own century is beginning to accord him (I refer here to Boucourechliev's study[1]).

For the nineteenth century, leaving aside a few stupid representations, such as the one given by Vincent dTndy who just about makes of Beethoven a kind of reactionary and anti-Semitic hypocrite, Beethoven was the first man of music to be free. Now for the first time the fact of having several successive manners was held to the glory of an artist; he was acknowledged the right of metamorphosis, he could be dissatisfied with himself or, more profoundly, with his language, he could change his codes as he went through life (this is what is expressed by Lenz's naive and enthusiastic image of Beethoven's three different manners).

Being moved like the wind

 The body strives to be total, and so the idea of an intimist or familial activity is destroyed: to want to play
Beethoven is to see oneself as the conductor of an orchestra (the dream of how many children? the
tautological dream of how many conductors, a prey in their conducting to all the signs of the panic of
possession?). Beethoven's work forsakes the amateur and seems, in an initial moment, to call on the new
Romantic deity, the interpreter. Yet here again we are disappointed: who (what soloist, what pianist?) can
play Beethoven well?

Schroeder – shultz – my 1st
encounter with LVB –

It is as though this music offers only the choice between a 'role' and its absence, the illusion of demiurgy and
the prudence of platitude, sublimated as 'renunciation'.

The truth is perhaps that Beethoven's music has in it something inaudible (something for which hearing is
not the exact locality), and this brings us to the second Beethoven. It is not possible that a musician be deaf
by pure contingency or poignant destiny (they are the same thing). Beethoven's deafness designates the lack
wherein resides all signification; it appeals to a music that is not abstract or inward, but that is endowed, if
one may put it like this, with a tangible intelligibility, with the intelligible as tangible.

Stravinsky to follow.

 Such a category is truly revolutionary, unthinkable in the terms of the old aesthetics; the work that complies
with it cannot be received on the basis of pure sensuality, which is always cultural, nor on that of an
intelligible order of (rhetorical, thematic) development, and without it neither the modern text nor
contemporary music can be accepted. As we know since Boucourechliev's analyses, this Beethoven is
exemplarily the Beethoven of the Diabelli Variations and the operation by which we can grasp this
Beethoven (and the category he initiates) can no longer be either performance or hearing, but reading. This is
not to say that one has to sit with a Beethoven score and get from it an inner recital (which would still remain
dependent on the old animistic fantasy); it means that with respect to this music one must put oneself in the
position or, better, in the activity of an operator, who knows how to displace, assemble, combine, fit together;
in a word (if it is not too worn out), who knows how to structure (very different from constructing or
reconstructing in the classic sense). Just as the reading of the modern text (such at least as it may be
postulated) consists not in receiving, in knowing or in feeling that text, but in writing it anew, in crossing its
writing with a fresh inscription, so too reading this Beethoven is to operate his music, to draw it (it is willing
to be drawn) into an unknown praxis.

I like the analogy as a composer
who draws. to DRAW music.

In this way may be rediscovered, modified according to the movement of the historical dialectic, a certain
musica practica. What is the use of composing if it is to confine the product within the precinct of the concert
or the solitude of listening to the radio ? To compose, at least by propensity, is to give to do, not to give to
hear but to give to write. The modern location for music is not the concert hall, but the stage on which the
musicians pass, in what is often a dazzling display, from one source of sound to another. It is we who are
playing, though still it is true by proxy; but one can imagine the concert - later on ? - as exclusively a
workshop, from which nothing spills over - no dream, no imaginary, in short, no 'soul' and where all the
musical art is absorbed in a praxis with no remainder. Such is the Utopia that a certain Beethoven, who is not
played, teaches us to formulate - which is why it is possible now to feel in him a musician with a future.

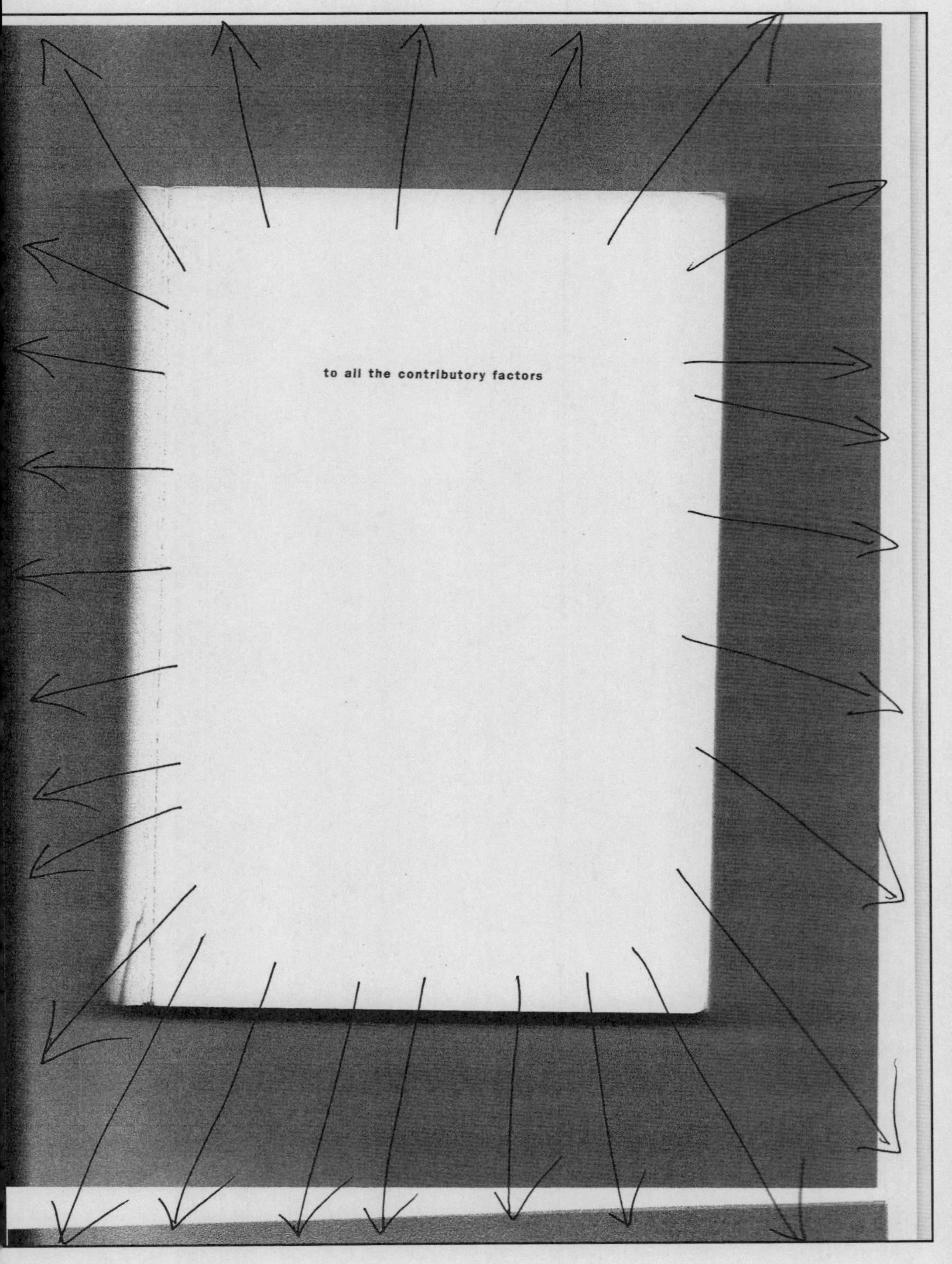


ALICE CHANNER ANNOTATED ZEROS + ONES, 1997, SADIE PLANT

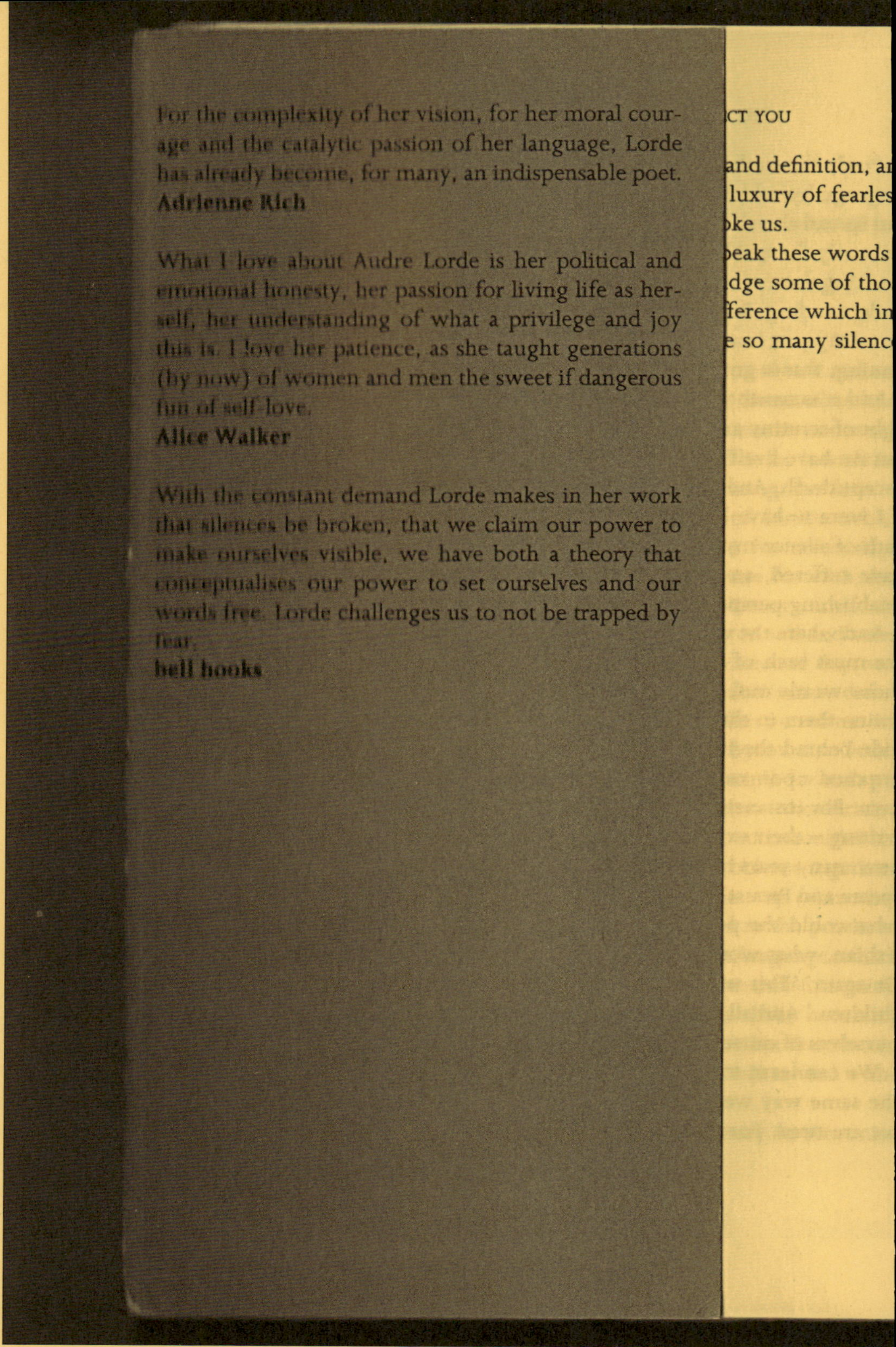

For the complexity of her vision, for her moral courage and the catalytic passion of her language, Lorde has already become, for many, an indispensable poet.
**Adrienne Rich**

What I love about Audre Lorde is her political and emotional honesty, her passion for living life as herself, her understanding of what a privilege and joy this is. I love her patience, as she taught generations (by now) of women and men the sweet if dangerous fun of self-love.
**Alice Walker**

With the constant demand Lorde makes in her work that silences be broken, that we claim our power to make ourselves visible, we have both a theory that conceptualises our power to set ourselves and our words free. Lorde challenges us to not be trapped by fear.
**bell hooks**

CT YOU

and definition, a
luxury of fearles
ke us.
eak these words
dge some of tho
fference which in
e so many silenc

# Poetry Is Not a Luxury

THE QUALITY OF LIGHT by which we scrutinise our lives has direct bearing upon the product which we live, and upon the changes which we hope to bring about through those lives. It is within this light that we form those ideas by which we pursue our magic and make it realised. This is poetry as illumination, for it is through poetry that we give name to those ideas which are – until the poem – nameless and formless, about to be birthed, but already felt. That distillation of experience from which true poetry springs births thought as dream births concept, as feeling births idea, as knowledge births (precedes) understanding.

As we learn to bear the intimacy of scrutiny and to flourish within it, as we learn to use the products of that scrutiny for power within, our living, those fears which rule our lives and form our silences begin to lose their control over us.

For each of us as women, there is a dark place within where hidden and growing our true spirit rises, 'beautiful/ and tough as chestnut/stanchion against your nightmare of weakness' ('Black Mother Woman') and of impotence.

These places of possibility within ourselves are dark

raped the servant girl. But that's not it, that's not it . . . A farmhand, a farmhand! Let's run away to the countryside—if you want to. To the countryside we'll go. There are farmhands there! Out in the countryside! We'll go together, do you want to? To the farmhand, Joey, to the farmhand, the farmhand!" he went on repeating frantically. I held my head straight and stiff, not looking at him.

"Kneadus, what good is your farmhand to me?"

But as soon as I began walking he went with me, and I went with him—we went together.

My view of the world and understanding of subjective encounters and artist practice has been largely shaped by one book in particular. *Ferdydurke* by Witold Gombrowicz is a novel of unavoidable new perspectives. The process of becoming oneself happens here always as an unapologetic fight with the misinterpretations that others project on us, as we are an unstable structure that renegotiates itself in each instance of intersubjective confrontation.

Lou Cantor

## 11  Preface to "The Child Runs Deep in Filibert"

And again a preface . . . and I'm a captive to a preface, I can't do without a preface, I must have a preface, because the law of symmetry requires that the story in which the child runs deep in Filidor should have a corresponding story in which the child runs deep in Filibert, while the preface to Filidor requires a corresponding preface to Filibert. Even if I want to I can't, I can't, and I can't avoid the ironclad laws of symmetry and analogy. But it's high time to interrupt, to cease, to emerge from the greenery if only for a moment, to come back to my senses and peer from under the weight of a billion little sprouts, buds, and leaves so that no one can say that I've gone crazy, totally blah, blah. And before I move any further on the road of second-rate, intermediate, not-quite-human horrors, I have to clarify, rationalize, substantiate, explain, and systematize, I have to draw out the primary thought from which all other thoughts in this book originate, and to reveal the primeval torment of all torments herein mentioned and brought into relief. And I must introduce a hierarchy of torments as well as a hierarchy of thoughts, and provide analytic, synthetic, and philosophical comments on this work so that the reader will know where the head is, where the legs, the nose, where the heel is, so that I'm not accused of being unaware of my own goals, of not marching straight and stiffly forward like the greatest writers of omnitime, but that I've senselessly gone bonkers. But which of the torments is the chief and fundamental one? Where is this book's primeval torment? Where are you, oh, primeval mother of all torments? The longer I probe, study, and digest these things, the clearer it becomes that the chief, basic torment, as I see it, is simply the torment of bad form, of bad *exterieur*, or, in other words, it's the torment of platitude, grimace, face, mug—yes, that's the source, the wellspring, the beginning, and it's from here that all other suffering, frenzy, and torture flow harmoniously, without exception. Or perhaps one should really say that the chief, basic torment is nothing other than the suffering that comes from our being constricted by another human being, from the fact that we are strangled and stifled by a tight, narrow, stiff notion of ourselves that is held by another human being. Or, perhaps at the base of this book is the major and murderous torment of the

not-quite-human greenery, of little sprouts, leaves, and buds

or the torment of development and not-quite-development,

or maybe the suffering of not-quite-shaping, not-quite-forming,

or the torment of our inner self being created by others,

or the torment of physical and psychological rape

the suffering of driving, interpersonal tensions

the biased and unclarified torment of psychological bias

the lateral torture of psychological wrenching, twisting, and miscuing

the unceasing torment of betrayal, the torment of falsehood

the mechanical agony of mechanism and automatism

the symmetrical torment of analogy, and the analogous torment of symmetry

the analytical torment of synthesis, and the synthetic torment of analysis

or maybe the agony of parts of the body and the disruption of the hierarchy of its individual organs

or the suffering of gentle infantilism

of the pupa, of pedagogy, of formalists and educators

of inconsolable innocence and naiveté

of departure from reality

of phantasm, illusion, musings, idle notions, and nonsense

of higher idealism

of lower, shabby, hole-in-the-corner idealism

of daydreaming on the sidelines

or maybe of the very odd torment of pettiness and belittlement

the torment of contending

the torment of aspiring

the torment of apprenticeship

or perhaps simply the torture of pulling oneself up by one's bootstraps and straining beyond one's ability, and hence the torture of inability, general and particular

the agony of giving oneself airs, and of blowing one's own horn

the pain of humiliating others

the torment of superior and inferior poetry

or the torture of the dull psychological impasse

the devious torture of craftiness, evasiveness, and of foul play

or rather the torture of the age in its particular and general sense

the torment of the old-fashioned

the torment of modernity

the suffering resulting from the emergence of new social strata

the torment of the semi-intelligent

the torment of the nonintelligent

the torture of the intelligent

or maybe simply the torment of petty-intelligent indecency

the pain of stupidity

of wisdom

lanmıştır: "Bu durumdaki insan, diye düşünüyor, ölüleri geri getirecek sözcükleri, müziği nasıl bulabilir?"

Acıyı hazzın karşısına çıkaran bir yazar değil Coetzee. İnsanın geçmişin cürümlerinden kefaret yoluyla arınabileceğini, yıkımın böyle telafi edilebileceğini düşünen bir yazar da değil. Bu bakımdan Dostoyevski'den ayrılıyor. Yine de onu *Ecinniler*'in yazarına bağlayan bir şey var. İçinde yaşadığımız yıkım çağında "grace"ten boşalan yeri dolduramazsak utançtan kurtulamayacağımıza inanıyor.

Sartre *Varlık ve Hiçlik*'te utancı anahtar deliğinden odayı gözetleyen birinden yola çıkarak anlatmıştı. Biri bizi anahtar deliğinden içeriyi gözetlerken gördüğünde hissettiğimiz şeydir utanç. Başkası beni odayı gözetlerken gördüğü için, ben de kendimi o halde görürüm: İnsan başkasının önünde kendisinden utanır.[48] Coetzee'nin "karanlık oda" benzetmesi boşuna değil. Bir karanlık oda olduğunu görmezden gelmek utanç vericidir; ama karanlık odayı hayal gücünün kaynağı haline getirmek de insanı utandırır. Susmak utandırmıştır; ama şimdi konuşmak da utandırır. Ölüm acısının çekildiği yerde bunun bir imgeye dönüştürülmesinde, o imgenin kurbanları yok eden dünyanın tüketimine sunulmasında insanı utandıran bir şey var, diyordu Adorno. Ölüm kamplarını yazabilsin diye seçilmiş olabileceği düşüncesi Primo Levi'yi utandırmıştı. Coetzee tam da yazarken, yazdığı için, telafi çabasının ortasında yakalanmıştır utanca. Sadece beyaz azınlığın imkânlarına sahip bir yazar olmanın utancı değil Coetzee'ninki. Aynı zamanda yıkıma yazarak cevap vermenin, esin perisini karanlıktan alıyor olmanın, yaratıcılığını apartheid'a borçlu olmanın utancı. "Görünmez"den alınmamış zaten alınamayacak bir yetkiyle yazıyor olmanın utancı. Başkalarının anlatma yeteneğini yok eden şeyi anlatmanın, başkaları anlatamazken anlatmanın, tam tanığı olmadığı bir şeyi anlatmanın utancı. Başkalarının hayatına mal olan özgürlüksüzlüğün ona bir ödül olarak geri dönmesinin utancı: "Nasıl oluyor da benimki gibi apaçık özgür olmayan bir ülkeden gelen, böyle bir ülkede yaşayan biri özgürlük

---

48. Jean-Paul, Sartre, *Varlık ve Hiçlik: Fenomenolojik Ontoloji Denemesi*, çev. Turhan Ilgaz ve Gaye Çankaya Eksen, İstanbul: İthaki, 3. basım, 2009, s. 354-7.

ödülüyle onurlandırılabilir?"[49]

*Petersburg'lu Usta*'ya geri dönebiliriz şimdi. Oğlunun bu dünyadaki yankısı olayım derken, yeni romanının sahnelerini biriktiren Dostoyevski'nin utancı: "Adam bunun unutulmayacak bir sahne olduğunun farkında, hatta günün birinde yazdıklarında bu sahneyi kullanabileceğini de. Utanç duyar gibi oluyor, ama yüzeysel ve geçici bir utanç bu. Önce yazdıklarında, sonra da hayatında utanç duygusu eskisi kadar güçlü değil, utancın yerini aşırı uçlara gitmekten çekinmeyen anlamsız ve ahlakdışı bir kayıtsızlık almış. Göz ucuyla üzerine müthiş bir hızla gelen bulutları görüyor gibi, fırtına bulutlarını. Yollarına çıkan her şeyi süpürüp atacaklar. Korkuyla, ama aynı zamanda heyecanla fırtınanın patlamasını bekliyor adam."

Yaklaşan fırtına, Dostoyevski'yi hayatı boyunca sarsan sara krizlerinden biridir. Aynı zamanda yoluna çıkan her şeyi süpürüp atan *Ecinniler*'in fırtınası. Ama yazının "ahlakdışı kayıtsızlık"ı geri çekilince utanç geri gelir. Pavel'in karanlık odasından *Ecinniler*'le ayrılan Dostoyevski'nin utancı. Kendi yas çalışmasından *Petersburg'lu Usta*'yla çıkan Coetzee'nin utancı. Yazarın ödemek zorunda olduğu bedel: "Öderim ve satarım; benim hayatım böyle. Kendi hayatımı satarım. Pavel'i hayattayken sattım, şimdi bir yolunu bulsam içimdeki Pavel'i de satarım." Bir yazarın hayatı: "Onursuz bir hayat; sınırsız ihanet; sonu gelmeyen itiraflar."

Bir zamanlar Mallarmé söylemişti: "Dünyada her şey sonunda bir kitaba girmek için vardır." Yıkımın bir gün bir kitaba girmek için var olduğunu düşünmenin bir utancı olacaksa eğer, bu çağda bunu üstlenen az sayıdaki yazardan biri Coetzee. Bir "hayatta kalan" olduğunu unutmayan bir anlatıcının elinden çıkmış tesellisiz öyküler.

49. Timothy Bewes, Coetzee'nin yapıtlarında utancın apartheid'a edebi tepkinin yetersizliğinin, imkânsızlığının, dahası müstehcenliğinin bir tezahürü olarak ortaya çıktığını söyler. Apartheid Coetzee'nin yapıtlarının sadece konusu değil, aynı zamanda onu mümkün kılan koşuldur. "Kendi yazdıklarının sonlandırmayı umduğu durumla suç ortaklığı içinde olduğunu kabul eden biri vicdanen nasıl yazabilir?", *The Event of Poscolonial Shame*, Princeton, N. J.: Princeton University Press, 2011, s. 137-9.

## 2 Is a designer an artist?

Before discussing this question, which involves describing a designer's work in some detail, it is necessary to look at the context in which it is usually asked. In Britain, it is certainly necessary to remember two things. First, the extraordinary cultural insularity of the last fifty years that permitted the early achievement of the Arts & Crafts movement to be built into foundations of growth on the continent, while continuing a placid, homespun and largely arrested development in its place of origin. To illustrate this, it is only necessary to consider the lively interaction of media, disciplines and controversy in the *de Stijl* movement, and to take a sample of the English situation at the time, or to recall the strange scene in 1968 when so many students and teachers were to be seen confronting their first substantial awareness of the Bauhaus. The book *Circle*, published in the late 1930s, marked a coming-together which, in British terms, was promising merely because unusual. An informal pointer to an absence of spirit can be seen from a comparison of the early edition of Herbert Read's *Art and industry*, with layout by Herbert Bayer, and the subsequent 'tasteful' editions in which the spirit of the original – not in itself anything very remarkable – is absorbed back into the British literary traditions of book publishing. It was indeed in literature that things were more lively. The war destroyed even these tentative growths in a way that was more profound than is generally realized. The Festival of Britain (1951) and its major Exhibition became a rallying point for a new design consciousness. Although in some ways a joyous occasion and no mean achievement for all concerned, it proved to be a very odd mix of English empiricism with a belated tribute to the 'international style' in architecture. There was however a distinctively fresh sense of place and occasion on London's South Bank, to set against – or more hopefully, to assimilate – the threat of foreign invasion. The implicit fear that without a struggle everything might come to look alike, was indeed soon to be justified. In matters of educational debate, however, the situation was far from robust. I can testify to the difficulty of interesting anyone in a confrontation with Tomás Maldonado, of the Hochschule für Gestaltung (Ulm), at the Royal College of Art; and this was 1961.

The second difficulty is more widespread. It is the well-known but uneasy juxtaposition of 'fine-art' studies with 'design' subjects within a common faculty, excluding (normally) architecture. It would be out of place here to examine the history of this problematic and to some extent (now) arbitrary grouping of studies. It is enough to point out that the situation could be more realistically appraised if painting and sculpture were studied alongside music, dance, poetry, film and other activities that interpret, primarily, the psychological and sensuous and spiritual understanding of man. It would then be easier to distinguish those activities which must first satisfy his physical and accessory needs under conditions of complex social constraint (as in building design), or which may have a much humbler role in serving and pleasing man. It is true that, in the last analysis, every human artefact – whether painting, poem, chair, or rubbish bin – evokes and invokes the inescapable totality of a culture, and the hidden assumptions which condition cultural priorities. (In a basic sense, and given the conditions for warmth, food and shelter, the rest is a choice and speaks to us of priorities which need constant revaluation.) For the purpose of the remarks which follow, it is certainly necessary to say that if the words 'fine-art' and 'design' simply refer to a duality as experienced in art schools, it is difficult to set up satisfactory distinctions on that basis alone.

For the discussion that follows, the situation is seen from the standpoint of a designer.

Here is a sober but accurate description of professionalism by Professor Misha Black: '... the offering to the public of a specialized skill, depending largely upon judgement, in which both the experience and established knowledge are of equal weight, while the person possessing the skill is bound both by an ethical code and may be accountable at law for a proper degree of skill in exercising this judgement ...'

Not, obviously, a full description, and perhaps a somewhat negative one, but making the fact plain that a designer works through and for other people, and is concerned primarily with their problems rather than his own. In this respect he might be seen as a medical man, with the responsibility a doctor has for accurate diagnosis (problem analysis) and for a relevant prescription (design proposals), though the comparison should not be taken too far. It must be clearly realized that designers work and communicate indirectly, and ...

as nuclear radiation and pollution: hyperobjects. What to do about them? Since no one meaningfully related to me will be living 24,100 years from now (the half-life of plutonium), my cognitive, ethical, and political dispositions toward plutonium must transcend my self-interest, however widely defined. Moreover, hyperobjects last so long that utilitarian concepts such as the social discount rate, a sliding scale for determining the value of future people for present actions, cannot be ethically or even meaningfully applied to them.[7] Hyperobjects compel us to adopt attitudes for which humans are not well prepared in an age of advanced consumer capitalism.

There is a further problem with timescales concerning global warming—there are lots of them. We are dealing with an object that is not only massively distributed, but that also has different amortization rates for different parts of itself. Hyperobjects are messages in bottles from the future: they do not quite exist in a present, since they scoop the standard reference points from the idea of present time. In order to cope with them, we require theories of ethics that are based on scales and scopes that hugely transcend normative self-interest theories, even when we modify self-interest by many orders of magnitude to include several generations down the line or all existing lifeforms on Earth.

Yet in transcending self-interest theories we need not throw the baby of intimacy out with the bathwater of self. Indeed, dropping self-interest theories involves us in what Parfit himself refers to as a more intimate contact with other lifeforms and future selves. In a moving passage in the middle of *Reasons and Persons*, a passage that is startlingly personal compared with the blisteringly rational mode of Oxbridge utilitarianism that his work exemplifies, Parfit writes:

Is the truth [of no-self] depressing? Some may find it so. But I find it liberating, and consoling. When I believed that my existence was [a "deep further fact, distinct from physical and psychological continuity, and a fact that must be all-or-nothing"]. I seemed imprisoned in myself. My life seemed like a glass tunnel, through which I was moving faster every year, and at the end of which there was darkness. When I changed my view, the walls of my glass tunnel disappeared. I now live in the open air. There is still a difference between my life and the lives of other people. But that difference is less. Other people are closer. I am less concerned about the rest of my own life, and more concerned about the lives of others.[8]

Parfit's words themselves exemplify the intimacy and openness to the future that a no-self view bestows. On this view, "self" is reduced to mere physical and psychological continuity.

The no-self view is not a faceless, dehumanized abstraction, but a radical encounter with intimacy. What best explains ecological awareness is a sense of intimacy, not a sense of belonging to something bigger: a sense of being close, even too close, to other lifeforms, of having them under one's skin. Hyperobjects force us into an intimacy with our own death (because they are toxic), with others (because everyone is affected by them), and with the future (because they are massively distributed in time). Attuning ourselves to the intimacy that hyperobjects demand is not easy. Yet intimacy and the no-self view come together in ecological awareness. The proximity of an alien presence that is also our innermost essence is very much its structure of feeling.

Consider symbiosis, as explored by Lynn Margulis and others. One feature of symbiosis is endosymbiosis, the fact that lifeforms do not simply live alongside us: they are within us, so much so that on many levels the host–parasite distinction collapses. Our mitochondria are symbionts hiding from their own catastrophe, the environmental disaster called oxygen. Many cell walls are double, hinting at some ancient symbiotic coupling. To a great extent others are us: or as the poet Rimbaud put it, "Je est un autre."[9] On a nonphenomenological level (that is, one not dependent on experience), a level an extraterrestrial with a microscope could validate, we are strangers to ourselves. That is how close the other is. Ecology is about intimacy.

As well as being about mind-bending time- and spatial scales, hyperobjects do something still more disturbing to our conceptual frames of reference. Hyperobjects undermine normative ideas of what an "object" is in the first place. This sudden turnaround has an uncanny effect. Knowledge about radiation makes us question commonsensical ideas about the utility and benefits of the sun. Unlike sunlight we cannot

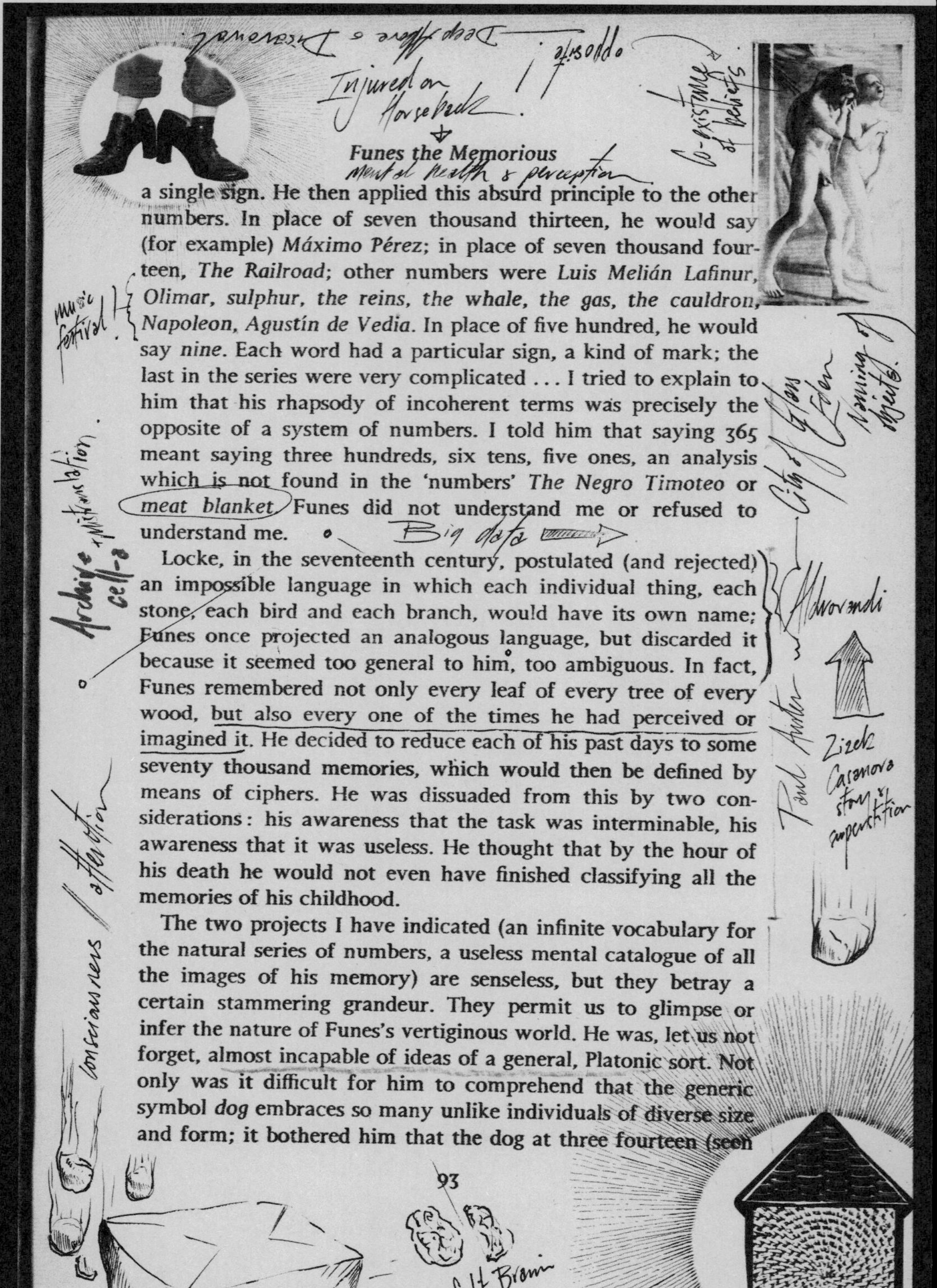

### Funes the Memorious

a single sign. He then applied this absurd principle to the other numbers. In place of seven thousand thirteen, he would say (for example) *Máximo Pérez*; in place of seven thousand fourteen, *The Railroad*; other numbers were *Luis Melián Lafinur, Olimar, sulphur, the reins, the whale, the gas, the cauldron, Napoleon, Agustín de Vedia*. In place of five hundred, he would say *nine*. Each word had a particular sign, a kind of mark; the last in the series were very complicated ... I tried to explain to him that his rhapsody of incoherent terms was precisely the opposite of a system of numbers. I told him that saying 365 meant saying three hundreds, six tens, five ones, an analysis which is not found in the 'numbers' *The Negro Timoteo* or *meat blanket*. Funes did not understand me or refused to understand me.

Locke, in the seventeenth century, postulated (and rejected) an impossible language in which each individual thing, each stone, each bird and each branch, would have its own name; Funes once projected an analogous language, but discarded it because it seemed too general to him, too ambiguous. In fact, Funes remembered not only every leaf of every tree of every wood, but also every one of the times he had perceived or imagined it. He decided to reduce each of his past days to some seventy thousand memories, which would then be defined by means of ciphers. He was dissuaded from this by two considerations: his awareness that the task was interminable, his awareness that it was useless. He thought that by the hour of his death he would not even have finished classifying all the memories of his childhood.

The two projects I have indicated (an infinite vocabulary for the natural series of numbers, a useless mental catalogue of all the images of his memory) are senseless, but they betray a certain stammering grandeur. They permit us to glimpse or infer the nature of Funes's vertiginous world. He was, let us not forget, almost incapable of ideas of a general, Platonic sort. Not only was it difficult for him to comprehend that the generic symbol *dog* embraces so many unlike individuals of diverse size and form; it bothered him that the dog at three fourteen (seen

93

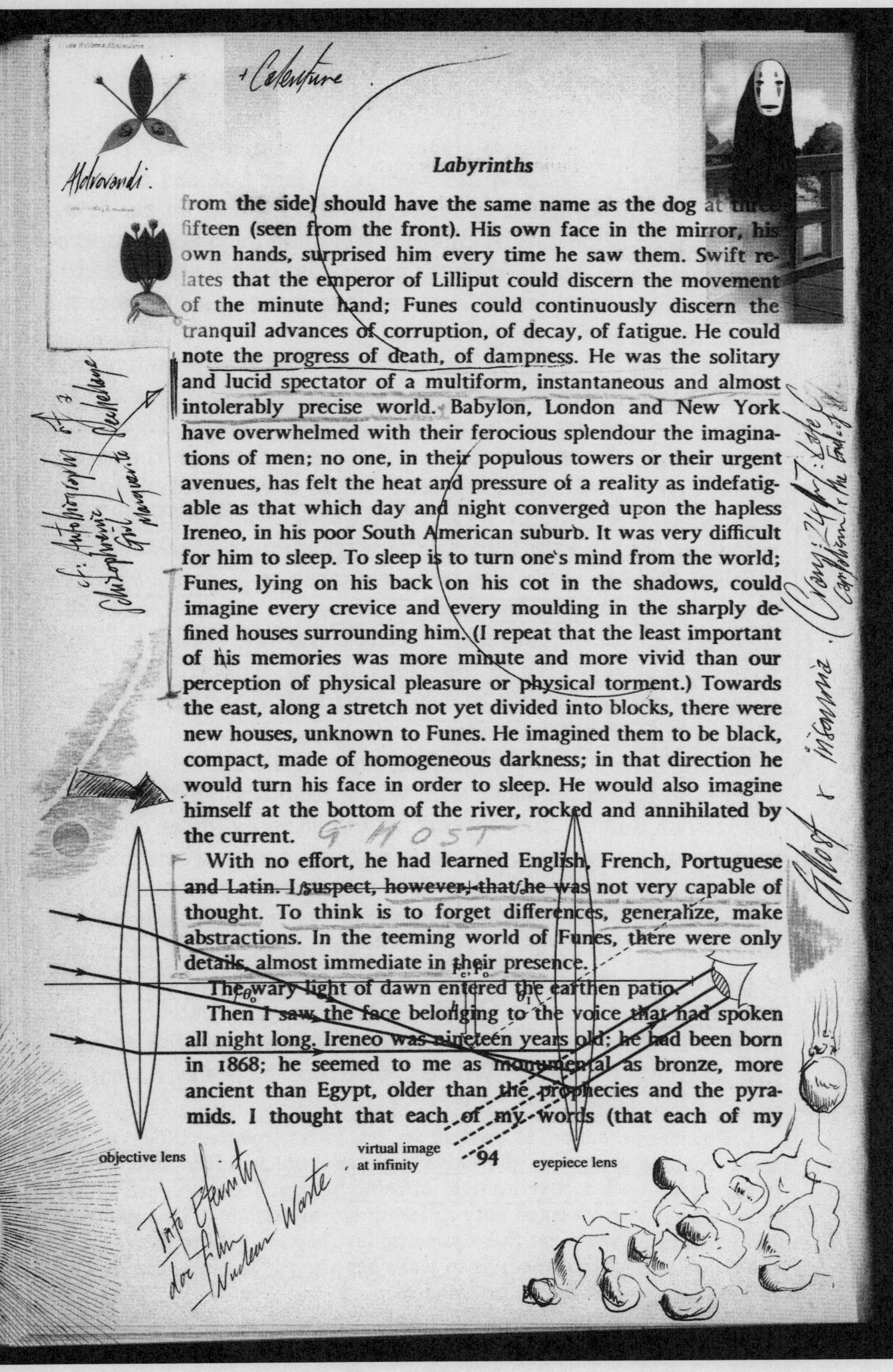



from the side) should have the same name as the dog at three fifteen (seen from the front). His own face in the mirror, his own hands, surprised him every time he saw them. Swift relates that the emperor of Lilliput could discern the movement of the minute hand; Funes could continuously discern the tranquil advances of corruption, of decay, of fatigue. He could note the progress of death, of dampness. He was the solitary and lucid spectator of a multiform, instantaneous and almost intolerably precise world. Babylon, London and New York have overwhelmed with their ferocious splendour the imaginations of men; no one, in their populous towers or their urgent avenues, has felt the heat and pressure of a reality as indefatigable as that which day and night converged upon the hapless Ireneo, in his poor South American suburb. It was very difficult for him to sleep. To sleep is to turn one's mind from the world; Funes, lying on his back on his cot in the shadows, could imagine every crevice and every moulding in the sharply defined houses surrounding him. (I repeat that the least important of his memories was more minute and more vivid than our perception of physical pleasure or physical torment.) Towards the east, along a stretch not yet divided into blocks, there were new houses, unknown to Funes. He imagined them to be black, compact, made of homogeneous darkness; in that direction he would turn his face in order to sleep. He would also imagine himself at the bottom of the river, rocked and annihilated by the current.

With no effort, he had learned English, French, Portuguese and Latin. I suspect, however, that he was not very capable of thought. To think is to forget differences, generalize, make abstractions. In the teeming world of Funes, there were only details, almost immediate in their presence.

The wary light of dawn entered the earthen patio.

Then I saw the face belonging to the voice that had spoken all night long. Ireneo was nineteen years old; he had been born in 1868; he seemed to me as monumental as bronze, more ancient than Egypt, older than the prophecies and the pyramids. I thought that each of my words (that each of my of the preceding primitive stage. Bedouin women of the pre-Islamic period enjoyed a status quite superior to that assigned them by the Koran. The great figures of Niobe, of Medea, evoke an era in which mothers took pride in their children, regarding them as treasures peculiarly their own. And in Homer's poems Andromache and Hecuba had an importance that classic Greece no longer attributed to women hidden in the shadow of the gynaeceum.

These facts have led to the supposition that in primitive times a veritable reign of women existed: the matriarchy. It was this hypothesis, proposed by Bachofen, that Engels adopted, regarding the passage from the matriarchate to the patriarchate as 'the great historical defeat of the feminine sex'. But in truth that Golden Age of Woman is only a myth. To say that woman was the *Other* is to say that there did not exist between the sexes a reciprocal relation: Earth, Mother, Goddess – she was no fellow creature in man's eyes; it was beyond the human realm that her power was affirmed, and she was therefore *outside* of that realm. Society has always been male; political power has always been in the hands of men. 'Public or simply social authority always belongs to men,' declares Lévi-Strauss at the end of his study of primitive societies.

For the male it is always another male who is the fellow being, the other who is also the same, with whom reciprocal relations are established. The duality that appears within societies under one form or another opposes a group of men to a group of men; women constitute a part of the property which each of these groups possesses and which is a medium of exchange between them. The mistake has come from a confusion of two forms of alterity or otherness, which are mutually exclusive in point of fact. To the precise degree in which woman is regarded as the absolute Other – that is to say, whatever her magic powers, as the inessential – it is to that degree impossible to consider her as another subject.[2] Women, therefore, have never composed a

2. This discrimination, as we shall see, has been perpetuated. The epochs that have regarded woman as the Other are those which refuse most harshly to integrate her with society by right of being human. Today she can become an *other* who is also an equal only in losing her mystic aura. The anti-feminists have always played upon this equivocation. They are glad to exalt woman as the *Other* in such a manner as to make her alterity absolute, irreducible, and to deny her access to the human *Mitsein*.

separate group set up *on its own account* over against the male grouping. They have never entered into a direct and autonomous relation with the men. 'The reciprocal bond basic to marriage is not set up between men and women, but between men and men by means of women, who are only the principal occasion for it,' says Lévi-Strauss.[3] The actual condition of woman has not been affected by the type of filiation (mode of tracing descent) that prevails in the society to which she belongs; whether the system be patrilineal, matrilineal, bilateral, or non-differentiated (the non-differentiation never being strictly adhered to), she is always under the guardianship of the males. The only question is whether the woman after marriage will remain subject to the authority of her father or of her older brother – an authority that will extend also to her children – or whether she will become subject to that of her husband. 'Woman, in herself, is never more than the symbol of her line … matrilineal filiation is but the authority of the woman's father or brother, which extends back to the brother's village,' to quote Lévi-Strauss again. She is only the intermediary of authority, not the one who holds it. The fact is that the relations of two groups of men are defined by the system of filiation, and not the relation between the two sexes.

In practice the actual condition of woman is not bound up with this or that type of authority. It may happen that in the matrilineal system she has a very high position; still, we must be careful to note that the presence of a woman chief or queen at the head of a tribe by no means signifies that women are sovereign therein: the accession to the throne of Catherine the Great in no way modified the lot of the Russian peasant women; and it is no less frequent for her to live in an abject condition. Furthermore, the cases are very rare in which the wife remains living with her clan, her husband being permitted only hasty, even clandestine visits. Almost always she goes away to live under her husband's roof, a fact that is enough to show the primacy of the male. 'Behind the shifting modes of filiation,' writes Lévi-Strauss, 'the persistence of the patrilocal residence bears witness to the fundamentally asymmetrical relation between the sexes that marks human society.' Since woman keeps her children with her, the result is that the territorial organization of the tribe does not correspond with its totemic

3. *Les Structures élémentaires de la parenté.*

Befor we lef Widders Dump that day there come word to us as Goodparley & Orfing wud be over to How Fents after meat. To put the scar on me and they wer going to do a show as wel. Befor I get to that I bes write out the *Eusa Story* the same as it ben wrote out 1st and past on down to us. Its all ways wrote down in the old spel. Every body knows bits and peaces of it but the connexion men and the Eusa show men they all have the woal thing wrote down the same and they have to know all of it by hart. You wunt have seen the woal thing wrote out without you ben a Eusa show man or connexion man or in the Mincery. No 1 else is allowit to have it wrote down the same which that dont make no odds becaws no 1 else knows how to read.

It wants to start a new peace of paper with a number to its self. So like the former said when he foun a ewe in his doss bag:

'Please tern over.'

# 6

### The Eusa Story

*1.* Wen Mr Clevver wuz Big Man uv Inland thay had evere thing clevver. Thay had boats in the ayr & picters on the win & evere thing lyk that. Eusa wuz a noing man vere qwik he cud tern his han tu enne thing. He wuz werkin for Mr Clevver wen thayr cum enemes aul roun & maykin Warr. Eusa sed tu Mr Clevver, Now wewl nead masheans uv Warr. Wewl nead boats that go on the water & boats that go in the ayr as wel & wewl nead Berstin Fyr.

28

be twean thay horns with arms owt strecht & each han holdin tu a horn.

*9.* Eusa sed tu the Littl Man, Yu mus be the Addom then. The Littl Man sed, I mus be wut I mus be. Eusa wuz angre then he wuz in rayj becaus he had a shutin weppn but the Littl Man wun even cover his self. He stud nekkit with his arms owt strecht be twean thay horns.

*10.* Eusa tuk his weppn in his han he sed tu the stag, Wy doan yu run? Yu no wut I am goin tu du. The stag sed, Eusa yu ar talkin tu the Hart uv the Wud. Nuthing wil run frum yu enne mor but tym tu cum & yu wil run frum evere thing.

*11.* Eusa shutin the Stag with his weppn & down it cum. Eusa grabbit the Littl Man by his 2 owt strecht arms & holdin him lyk twichin for water with a hayzel.

*12.* Eusa sed tu the Littl Man the Addom, I nead tu no the No. uv the 1 Big 1 & yu mus tel me it. The Littl Man the Addom he sed, Yu du no it Eusa its in yu the saym as its in me. Eusa sed, I doan no it yu mus tel it tu me. The Littl Man sed, Eusa yu no wut that 1 Big 1 is its the No. uv thay Master Chaynjis I doan hav no werd tu tel it. Eusa sed, If yu woan tel in 1 may be yul tel in 2. Eusa wuz pulin on the Littl Mans owt strecht arms. The Littl Man sed, Eusa yu ar pulin me a part. Eusa sed, Tel.

*13.* Eusa wuz angre he wuz in rayj & he kep pulin on the Littl Man the Addoms owt strecht arms. The Littl Man the Addom he begun tu cum a part he cryd, I wan tu go I wan tu stay. Eusa sed, Tel mor. The Addom sed, I wan tu dark I wan tu lyt I wan tu day I wan tu nyt. Eusa sed, Tel mor. The Addom sed, I wan tu woman I wan tu man. Eusa sed, Tel mor. The Addom sed, I wan tu plus I wan tu minus I wan tu big I wan tu littl I wan tu aul I wan tu nuthing.

*14.* Eusa sed, Stop ryt thayr thats the No. I wan. I wan that aul or nuthing No. The Littl Man the Addom he cudn stop tho. He wuz ded. Pult in 2 lyk he wuz a chikken. Eusa

30

*2.* Mr Clevver sed tu Eusa, Thayr ar tu menne agenst us this tym we mus du betteren that. We keap fytin aul thees Warrs wy doan we jus du 1 Big 1. Eusa sed, Wayr du I fyn that No.? Wayr du I fyn that 1 Big 1? Mr Clevver sed, Yu mus fyn the Littl Shynin Man the Addom he runs in the wud.

*3.* Eusa sed, Thayr int aul that much wud roun hear its mosly iyrn its mosly stoan. Mr Clevver sed, Yu mus fyn the wud in the hart uv the stoan & yu wil fyn it by the dansing in the stoan & thay partickler traks.

*4.* Eusa wuz a noing man he noet how tu bigger the smaul & he noet how tu smauler the big. He noet the doar uv the stoan & thay partickler traks. He smaulert his self down tu it he gon in tu particklers uv it. He tuk 2 grayt dogs with him thear nayms wer Folleree & Folleroo. Eusa ternt them luce he put them tu the stoan & castin for partickler traks & tu the dansing.

*5.* Foun the syn uv dansing on partickler traks thay dogs & follert harkin 1 tu the uther hot & clikkin & countin thay gygers & thay menne cools uv stoan. Smauler & smauler thay groan with Eusa in tu the hart uv the stoan hart uv the dans. Evere thing blippin & bleapin & movin in the shiftin uv thay Nos. Sum tyms bytin sum tyms bit.

*6.* Cum tu the wud in the hart uv the stoan. The stoan sky gone dark the stoan win gon stil. Thay dogs gon crinje then & wimpert. Eusa sed tu thay dogs, Garn the trak & fyn.

*7.* Thay dogs stud up on thear hyn legs & taukin lyk men. Folleree sed, Lukin for the 1 yu wil aul ways fyn thay 2. Folleroo sed, Thay 2 is 2ce as bad as the 1. Eusa sed, I woan be tol by amminals. He beat thay dogs & on thay gon.

*8.* In the dark wud Eusa seen a trak uv lyt he follert it. He cum tu the Hart uv the Wud it wuz the Stag uv the Wud it wuz the 12 Poynt Stag stud tu fays him & stampin its feat. On the stags hed stud the Littl Shynin Man the Addom in

29

screamt he felt lyk his oan bele ben pult in 2 & evere thing rushin owt uv him.

*15.* Owt uv thay 2 peaces uv the Littl Shynin Man the Addom thayr cum shyningnes in wayys in spredin circels. Wivverin & wayverin & humin with a hy soun. Lytin up the dark wud. Eusa seen the Littl 1 goin roun & roun insyd the Big 1 & the Big 1 humin roun insyd the Littl 1. He seen thay Master Chaynjis uv the 1 Big 1. Qwik then he riten down thay Nos. uv them.

*16.* Thay dogs howlt & a win cum up. Thay ded leavs wirlt & rattelin lyk ded birds flyin. Thay grayt dogs stud on thear hyn legs & talkin lyk men agen. Thay sed, Eusa aul thay menne leavs as rattelt thats how menne peapl yu wil kil. Then thay dogs begun tu tel uv tym tu cum. Thay sed, The lan wil dy & thay peapl wil eat 1 a nuther. The water wil be poysen & the peapl wil drink blud.

*17.* Eusa kilt boath dogs he shot them ded. The shynin & the lyt gone owt the wud gon darker nor the darkes nyt. Eusa cudn see nuthing he stumelt owt uv the wud & tu the stoan & owt agen nor never lukt behyn him.

*18.* Eusa had thay Nos. uv thay Master Chaynjis. He run them thru the Power Ring he mayd the 1 Big 1. Eusa put the 1 Big 1 in barms then him & Mr Clevver droppit so much barms thay kilt as menne uv thear oan as thay kilt enemes. Thay wun the Warr but the lan wuz poysen frum it the ayr & water as wel. Peapl din jus dy in the Warr thay kep dyin after it wuz over. Mr Clevver din cayr it wuz aul the saym tu him poyzen wuz meat & drink tu him he wuz that hard. Eusa with his wyf & 2 littl suns gon lukin for a nuther plays tu liv.

*19.* Evere thing wuz blak & rottin. Ded peapl & pigs eatin them & thay pigs dyd. Dog paks after peapl & peapl after dogs tu eat them the saym. Smoak goin up frum bernin evere wayr. Eusa with his famile gon tu the cappn uv a

31

boat & Eusa giv him munne tu tayk them a way. The cappn
sed, Munne is no gud enne mor. Eusa thot he lookit lyk the
Littl Shynin Man he wuzn shur tho. Thayr wer hevve men
on the boat thay tuk Eusas wyf thay thru Eusa & his 2 littl
boys off. Eusa stanin on the shor wachin that boat pul a way
with his wyf & nuthing he cud du.

20. Bad Tym it wuz then. Peapl din no if they wud be alyv
1 day tu the nex. Din even no if thayd be alyv 1 min tu the
nex. Sum stuk tu gether sum din. Sum tyms thay dru lots.
Sum got et so uthers cud liv. Cudn be shur uv nuthing din
no wut wuz sayf tu eat or drink & tryin tu keap wyd uv
uther forajers & dogs it wuz nuthing onle Luck if enne 1
stayd alyv.

21. Eusa & his boys on thear oan thay wernt with enne 1
els. Eusa wun go near no uthers he wuz afeard if enne 1
myt no him. Eusa dursn sleap much thay boys wer tu littl tu
stan gard long. Mosly Eusa jus closd his iys a littl at a tym
nevver long. He din lyk tu sleap much enne how he wuz
afeard he myt pul his self in 2 lyk he dun the Littl Shynin
Man. Plus menne tyms he seen 2 grayt dogs on thear trak
he din wan tu get snuck by them.

22. 1 day Eusa wuz holt up in a barmt owt plays by the
rivvr. He wuz so tyrd he tol his 2 littl boys tu keap luk owt
& he closd his iys. Eusa herd a sylens then lyk his ears
closd up. He opend his iys he thot he wuz dreamin. He
seen the Littl Shynin Man in 2 peaces. The Right syd uv
him had the nek & hed the Left syd uv him had his cok &
bauls. Each ½ wuzn hopin on its 1 leg it wuz waukin lyk it
wuz tu gether with the uther ½. Thay 2 peaces uv the Littl
Shynin Man wer waukin be twean thay 2 grayt dogs wich
wer Folleree & Folleroo the saym.

23. The taukin ½ uv the Littl Man sed tu Eusas 2 littl boys,
Ar yu hungre? Thay sed, Yes. He sed, Cum with me then I
wil giv yu sumthing. Off thay gon 1 with Folleree & 1 with



Folleroo. 1 hedin tords the rivvr 1 a way frum it & each
with ½ uv the Littl Shynin Man.

24. Eusa sed, This is a dream. He opent up his iys but thay
ben open aul redde. Eusa cudn wayk up no moren he aul
redde wuz. Eusa cault thay dogs by naym he wisselt them
bak but thay wun com. He cault the Littl Man but nyther ½
wud tern roun. He cault his 2 boys thay kep goin as wel
thay wun luk bak.

25. Eusa run after them as wer hedin tords the rivvr. Thay
gon in tu the water & swimin acros & Eusa after them.
Eusa tryd tu swim but his arms gon hevve & no strenth in
his legs. He had tu tern bak then evere thing gon blak for
him.

26. Eusa wuz lyn on the groun by the rivvr. Thayr apeerd
tu him then the Littl Shynin Man he wuz in 1 peace. Eusa
sed, Wy arn you in 2 peaces? The Littl Man sed, Eusa I am
in 2 peaces. It is onle the idear uv me that cum tu gether.
Yu ar lukin at the idear uv me and I am it. Eusa sed, Wut
is the idear uv yu? The Littl Man sed, It is wut it is. I
aint the noing uv it Im jus onle the showing uv it.

27. The Littl Man sed, Eusa wut is the idear uv yu? Eusa
cudn say enne thing. The Littl Man sed, Yu doan hav tu
say wut it is. Jus say if it is. Eusa stil cudn say enne thing.

28. Eusa sed, Nevver myn that wayr ar my 2 littl boys?
The Littl Man sed, Eusa thay gon 2 diffren ways a way
frum yu. Eusa sed, Yu tuk them a way. The Littl Man sed,
Wel Eusa it mayks a chaynj dunnit. Eusa sed, Wut dyu
mean?

29. The Littl Man sed, Eusa yu wantit thay Master
Chaynjis & this is 1 uv them. In the wud in the hart uv the
stoan yu pult me in 2 yu opent me lyk a chikken. Yu let
thay Nos. uv thay Master Chaynjis owt. Now yu mus go
thru them aul.



30. Eusa sed, I no I dun wut I dun & I wish I hadn but Im
thru with aul that now I jus wan tu liv qwyet. The Littl
Man sed, Eusa yu ain thru with aul that yur onle jus
beginin. Yuv got aul thay Master Chaynjis in frun uv yu.
Yuv got them aul tu go thru.

31. Eusa sed, Is this a dream? The Littl Man sed, No.
Eusa sed, Wuz the uther a dream then? Wen I had a wyf &
childer? The Littl Man sed, No Eusa that wuzn no dream
nor this ain no dream. Its aul 1 thing nor yu cant wayk up
owt uv it. Eusa sed, I can dy owt uv it tho cant I. The Littl
Man sed, Eusa yu dy owt uv this plays & yul jus fyn me in a
nuther plays. Yul fyn me in the wud yul fyn me on the
water lyk yu foun me in the stoan. Yu luk enne wayr & Iwl
be thayr.

32. Eusa sed, Wuz it yu the cappn uv the boat that tuk a
way my wyf? The Littl Man sed, Probly it wuz. Eusa sed,
Wy cant yu leav me aloan? The Littl Man sed, Eusa wear 2
½s uv 1 thing yu & me. I cant leav yu aloan no moren yu cud
leav me aloan. I nevver cum lukin for yu did I Eusa. It wuz
yu cum lukin for me that tym wen yu kilt the Hart uv the
Wud in the hart uv the stoan & yu foun me. Yu let thay
Chaynjis owt & now yuv got to go on thru them.

33. Eusa sed, How menne Chaynjis ar thayr? The Littl
Man sed, Yu mus no aul abowt that I seen yu rite thay Nos.
down in the hart uv the wud. Eusa sed, That riting is long
gon & aul thay Nos. hav gon owt uv my myn I doan
remember nuthing uv them. Woan yu pleas tel me how
menne Chaynjis thayr ar? The Littl Man sed, As menne as
reqwyrd. Eusa sed, Reqwyrd by wut? The Littl Man sed,
Reqwyrd by the idear uv yu. Eusa sed, Wut is the idear uv
me? The Littl Man sed, That we doan no til yuv gon thru
aul yur Chaynjis.

Blodeuwedd / Mabinogion
Natt Mullican
Song of Amergin / White Godess Graves

This what Im writing down now its the nite after my dads
berning. The nite I took the scar.

It ben pissing down rain since befor we lef Widders Dump.
I all ways liket the rain. Liket on the back track coming up to
hy groun in the dark. Seeing our nite fires thru the rain and
smelling the meat smel from the divvy roof.

After meat I gone up on the hy walk and looking out for
Goodparley & Orfing. Lissening to the rain dumming down
on my hard clof hood and thinking how itwd soun on dog
skin. Persoon I heard the horn blow 'Eusa show' then the
poynt hevvys come out of the rainy dark in to the lite of the
gate house torches. 1 of them lookit up at me and said,
'Trubba not. Eusa show.' I never knowit Goodparley &
Orfing say ther oan Trubba not they all ways sent a hevvy in
front of them. I said, 'No Trubba' then I opent and in they
come hevvys 1st. Goodparley & Orfing dint come thru the
gate til ther oan men wer in the gate house. They wunt walk
unner a gate house other whys.

Soons they come in the littl kids all come sploshing thru the
puddls in the torch lite singing:

No rumpa no dum
No zantigen Eusa cum

All of them running to touch the fit up and fealing for the
figgers in it. Goodparley smyling with his big sqware teef
like he lovit childer and Orfing shoving them out of the way.
The hevvys gone to the divvy roof all but 2 as come to my
shelter with Goodparley & Orfing for the wotcher. 1st 1
hevvy gone in then the Big 2 then the other hevvy then me.

When Dad ben a live I all ways ben there when he done the
wotcher. This time doing it my self and with the Big 2 not jus
regler Eusa show men it took me strange. Dads things all roun
the shelter. His weapons and his anrack hanging on ther pegs.

People cannot make out the real reason for their purchases; if they could, they would buy different things or buy less. Something which I think will start to happen in the very near future. However, we are at a relatively important point, both because of this purchaser-awareness that I see dawning, and because the year 2000 will be a key date – and society loves key dates ("Ah, it's Christmas: from now on I am going to do my exercises every morning!"). Certain changes that would have taken longer are actually accelerated by the catalyst of the "key date". There is a lot to be said on the subject, and I've just given a brief outline. But even that brings out our present-day ethical obligation to make production and manufacturing more moral.

M. Ethical obligations and a moralization of industrial production seem to boil down to a proposal that one should purchase less. If we put this together with the increasing dematerialization of everyday life, then the future could pose more than one problem for the manufacturers of objects (but also for the designers of objects...). They will be forced to come to terms with substantial changes.

Alessi I understand his point of view: even if both of us have been – and still are – part of this phase in the evolution of the consumer society. I feel this aspect very closely, and I fully appreciate Philippe's sincerity. I myself have to face the same problems, deal with the same dramas...

M. Drama? A significant word: a drama is an inner conflict, a difficulty in one's relation with oneself and others. When applied to the philosophy behind manufacturing it reveals a crucial point – which it is difficult to resolve, in both social and personal terms. Besides, Starck's proposal – or rather forecast – of the future would seem to envisage that the production of objects will not be production as we understand it today. One almost has the sense of a radical split.

A. I would not speak of split so much as of an awareness of our role at the present moment in the present context. Optimist that I am, I am sure that we will find a new equilibrium in production, which will enable us to placate this inner drama. For example, from Philippe Starck himself; during the years we have worked together, he has produced a series of what one might define as "half projects" rather than fully-fledged projects proper – all of which tend towards what we call "new simplicity". When we think of the future development of our products, we think of this idea of "new simplicity" as an attempt to get to the heart of the "thingness" of things. If I look back at the several hundred products I have helped to make available, there are some – a few, if the truth be told – that have achieved levels of excellence. These are the ones that have come somewhere near the "thingness", the quiddity of their type: the "pan-ness" of the pan, the "oilcruetness" of the oil cruet, or the "coffeepotness" of the coffee pot.

M. The "thingness" tends to anonymity: who invented the chaise-longue, which is a perfect object? The dressmaker's scissors? I wonder if we are moving towards a concept of design as anonymous. And the fact that such a question arises in discussion with a designer whose personal touch is so evident leads me to digress a little to consider an indicative conflict that it is difficult to resolve. How does one

reconcile the search for the "thingness" of things, for their type, their essence, with the notions of uniqueness, of difference and individuality, which each creator – and his public – expect from a design?
A. To the first part of the question – that with regard anonymity – one would probably have to answer in the affirmative: there is a move towards a levelling of the language of design; the formal language of the individual design is less legible, less present. I refer to "presence" because, in the recent past, that presence has been very powerful (even in the very best examples of design).

As for as the second problem is concerned – that of the relationship between the type and the individual – the meeting-point should be a sort of optimal fusion of function (a material parameter) and of the parameters of sensory perception, memory and imagination (all of which form a link between material function and function understood at a higher level).

M. Is all of this the result of the formalist and conceptual saturation of the 80s, of the refusal of that decade's manufacturing and consumeristic hedonism? Or is it the result of something more profound? In other words, does this envisaged change fit into a cycle? And if it does, isn't it true that the turn-round time of these cycles is getting shorter and shorter, and that the whole cycle now takes only a few years or, at most, a few decades to come full circle?

S. It is more profound than a simple rejection of the superficiality of the 80s. It is a cycle. And even if these cycles of fashion have shorter turn-round times these days, there are not as many of them as the media would have us believe.

There are rhythms of change that we have yet to discover; there is no such thing as a total overturning of a state of affairs, but rather a kind of evolution through small variations and jumps. One very important fact is that, for various reasons, people are now ecologically aware – in spite of everything...
M. In spite of everything?...
S. Yes, in spite of everything. Ecology is still a priority. The only problem is that it has been used by advertisers, by marketing experts and by the media – which are responsible for the venal exploitation of what is one of the priorities of the species. This reduction to an instrument of the profit motive has meant that ecology has started to go out of fashion – losing ground to much more detestable fashions (such as Neo-Nazism, for example). Ecology poses problems that have yet to be solved; yet if you speak about them now, all you hear is: "O.K., O.K. – but that's all old hat." However, a certain ecological awareness has emerged, which means that we now realise that the material around us is not the same as it was and that it will not remain the same as it is. Malraux said "the twenty-first century will be mystical, or it will not be at all"; for myself, I hope that it will be de-materialist (because we have seen what materialism leads to). God has been an instrument of progress; religion has been the framework for this re-awakening – an instrument of modernism.
All of this hoisted the species through a

that rare occasion in which one part of the Left swipes at another, producing a spectacle of the Left for mainstream liberal and conservative press consumption which is all too happy to discount every and any faction of the Left within the political process, much less honour the Left of any kind as a strong force in the service of radical social change?

Is the attempt to separate Marxism from the study of culture and to rescue critical knowledge from the shoals of cultural specificity simply a turf war between left cultural studies and more orthodox forms of Marxism? How is this attempted separation related to the claim that new social movements have split the Left, deprived us of common ideals, factionalized the field of knowledge and political activism, reducing political activism to the mere assertion and affirmation of cultural identity? The charge that new social movements are 'merely cultural', that a unified and progressive Marxism must return to a materialism based in an objective analysis of class, itself presumes that the distinction between material and cultural life is a stable one. And this recourse to an apparently stable distinction between material and cultural life is clearly the resurgence of a theoretical anachronism, one that discounts the contributions to Marxist theory since Althusser's displacement of the base-superstructure model, as well as various forms of cultural materialism—for instance, Raymond Williams, Stuart Hall and Gayatri Chakravorty Spivak. Indeed, the untimely resurgence of that distinction is in the service of a tactic which seeks to identify new social movements with the merely cultural, and the cultural with the derivative and secondary, thus embracing an anachronistic materialism as the banner for a new orthodoxy.

## Orthodox Unity

This resurgence of left orthodoxy calls for a 'unity' that would, paradoxically, redivide the Left in precisely the way that orthodoxy purports to lament. Indeed, one way of producing this division becomes clear when we ask which movements, and for what reasons, get relegated to the sphere of the merely cultural, and how that very division between the material and the cultural becomes tactically invoked for the purposes of marginalizing certain forms of political activism? And how does the new orthodoxy on the Left work in tandem with a social and sexual conservativism that seeks to make questions of race and sexuality secondary to the 'real' business of politics, producing a new and eerie political formation of neo-conservative Marxisms.

On what principles of exclusion or subordination has this ostensible unity been erected? How quickly we forget that new social movements based on democratic principles became articulated against a hegemonic Left as well as a complicitous liberal centre and a truly threatening right wing? Have the historical reasons for the development of semi-autonomous new social movements ever really been taken into account by those who now lament their emergence and credit them with narrow identitarian interests? Is this situation not simply reproduced in the recent efforts to restore the universal through fiat, whether through the imaginary finesse of Habermasian rationality or notions of the common good that prioritize a racially cleansed notion of class? Is the point of the new rhetorics of unity not simply to 'include' through domestication and

36

In Fraser's recent book, *Justice Interruptus*, she rightly notes that 'in the United States today, the expression 'identity politics' is increasingly used as a derogatory term for feminism, anti-racism, and anti-heterosexism.'[5] She insists that such movements have everything to do with social justice, and argues that any left movement must respond to their challenges. Nevertheless, she reproduces the division that locates certain oppressions as part of political economy, and relegates others to the exclusively cultural sphere. Positing a spectrum that spans political economy and culture, she situates lesbian and gay struggles at the cultural end of this political spectrum. Homophobia, she argues, has no roots in political economy, because homosexuals occupy no distinctive position in the division of labour, are distributed throughout the class structure, and do not constitute an exploited class: 'the injustice they suffer is quintessentially a matter of recognition', thus making their struggles into a matter of cultural recognition, rather than a material oppression.[6]

Why would a movement concerned to criticize and transform the ways in which sexuality is socially regulated not be understood as central to the functioning of political economy? Indeed, that this critique and transformation is central to the project of materialism was the trenchant point made by socialist feminists and those interested in the convergence of Marxism and psychoanalysis in the 1970s and 1980s, and was clearly inaugurated by Engels and Marx with their own insistence that 'mode of production' needed to include forms of social association. In *The German Ideology* (1846), Marx famously wrote, 'men, who daily remake their own life, begin to make other men, to propagate their kind: the relation between man and woman, parents and children, the *family*.'[7] Although Marx vacillates between regarding procreation as a natural and a social relationship, he makes clear not only that a mode of production is always combined with a mode of cooperation, but that, importantly, 'a mode of production is itself a "productive force".'[8] Engels clearly expands upon this argument in *The Origin of Family, Private Property, and the State* (1884), and offers there a formulation that became, for a time, perhaps the most widely cited quotation in socialist-feminist scholarship:

> According to the materialist conception, the determining factor in history is, in the final instance, the production and reproduction of immediate life. This, again, is of a twofold character: on the one side, the production of the means of existence, of food, clothing, and shelter and the tools necessary for that production; on the other side, the production of human beings themselves, the propagation of the species.[9]

Indeed, many of the feminist arguments during that time sought not

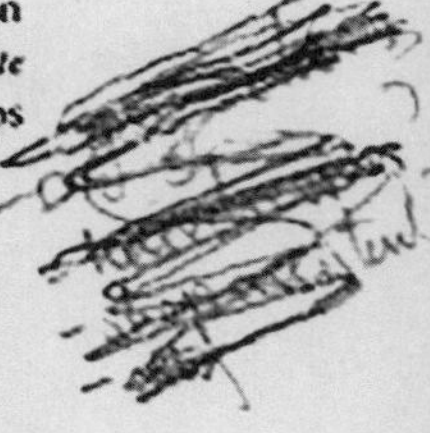

---

[5] Nancy Fraser, *Justice Interruptus*, London 1997.

[6] Ibid., pp. 17-18; for another statement of these views, see Fraser, 'From Redistribution to Recognition? Dilemmas of Justice in a "Post-Socialist" Age', NLR 212, July-August 1995, pp. 68-93.

[7] Robert C. Tucker, ed., *The Marx-Engels Reader*, New York 1978, p. 157.

[8] Ibid.

[9] Frederick Engels, 'Preface to the First Edition', *The Origin of the Family, Private Property and the State*, New York 1981, pp. 71-2. Engels continues in this paragraph to note how societies develop from a stage in which they are dominated by kinship to ones in which

39

Having stripped the world of conversation, friendship and love, the male offers us these paltry substitutes:

## 12   'Great Art' and 'Culture'

The male 'artist' attempts to solve his dilemma of not being able to live, of not being female, by constructing a highly artificial world in which the male is heroized, that is, displays female traits, and the female is reduced to highly limited, insipid, subordinate roles, that is, to being male.

The male 'artist's' aim being, not to communicate (having nothing inside him, he has nothing to say), but to disguise his animalism, he resorts to symbolism and obscurity ('deep' stuff). The vast majority of people, particularly the 'educated' ones, lacking faith in their own judgment, humble, respectful of authority ('Daddy knows best'), are easily conned into believing that obscurity, evasiveness, incomprehensibility, indirectness, ambiguity and boredom are marks of depth and brilliance.

'Great Art' proves that men are superior to women, that men are women, being labeled 'Great Art', almost all of which, as the anti-feminists are fond of reminding us, was created by men. We know that 'Great Art' is great because male authorities have told us so, and we can't claim otherwise, as only those with exquisite sensitivities far superior to ours can perceive and appreciated the slop they appreciated.

Appreciating is the sole diversion of the 'cultivated'; passive and incompetent, lacking imagination and wit, they must try to make do with that; unable to create their own diversions, to create a little world of their own, to affect in the smallest way their environments, they're forced to accept the diversions created by others, who are thereby elevated to a superior position; unable themselves to create or relate, they spectate. Absorbing 'culture' is a desperate, frantic attempt to groove in an ungroovy world, to escape the horror of a sterile, mindless existence. 'Culture' provides a sop to the egos of the incompetent, a means of rationalizing passive spectating; they can pride themselves on their ability to appreciate the 'finer' things, to see a jewel where there is only a turd (they want to be admired for admiring). Lacking faith in their ability to change anything, resigned to the status quo, they have to see beauty in it, and, lacking the imagination to create their own diversions, they spectate.

The veneration of 'Art' and 'Culture' – besides leading many women into boring, passive activity that distracts from more important and rewarding activities, from cultivating active abilities, and leads to the constant intrusion on our sensibilities of pompous dissertations on the deep beauty of this and that turn. This allows the 'artist' to be setup as one possessing superior feelings, perceptions, insights and judgments, thereby undermining the faith of insecure women in the value and validity of their own feelings, perceptions, insights and judgments.

The male, having a very limited range of feelings, and consequently very limited perceptions, insights and judgments, needs the 'artist' to guide him, to tell him what life is all about. But the male 'artist' being totally sexual, unable to relate to anything beyond his own physical sensations, having nothing to express beyond the insight that for the male life is meaningless and absurd, cannot be an artist. How can he who is not capable of life tell us what life is all about? A 'male artist' is a contradiction in terms. A degenerate can only produce degenerate 'art'. The true artist is every self-confident, healthy female, and in a female society the only Art, the only Culture, will be conceited, selfish, egomaniacal females grooving on each other and on everything else in the universe.

## 13   Sexuality

Sex is not part of a relationship; on the contrary, it is a solitary experience, non-creative, a gross waste of time. The female can easily – far more easily than she may think – condition away her sex drive, leaving her completely cool and cerebral and free to pursue truly worthy relationships...

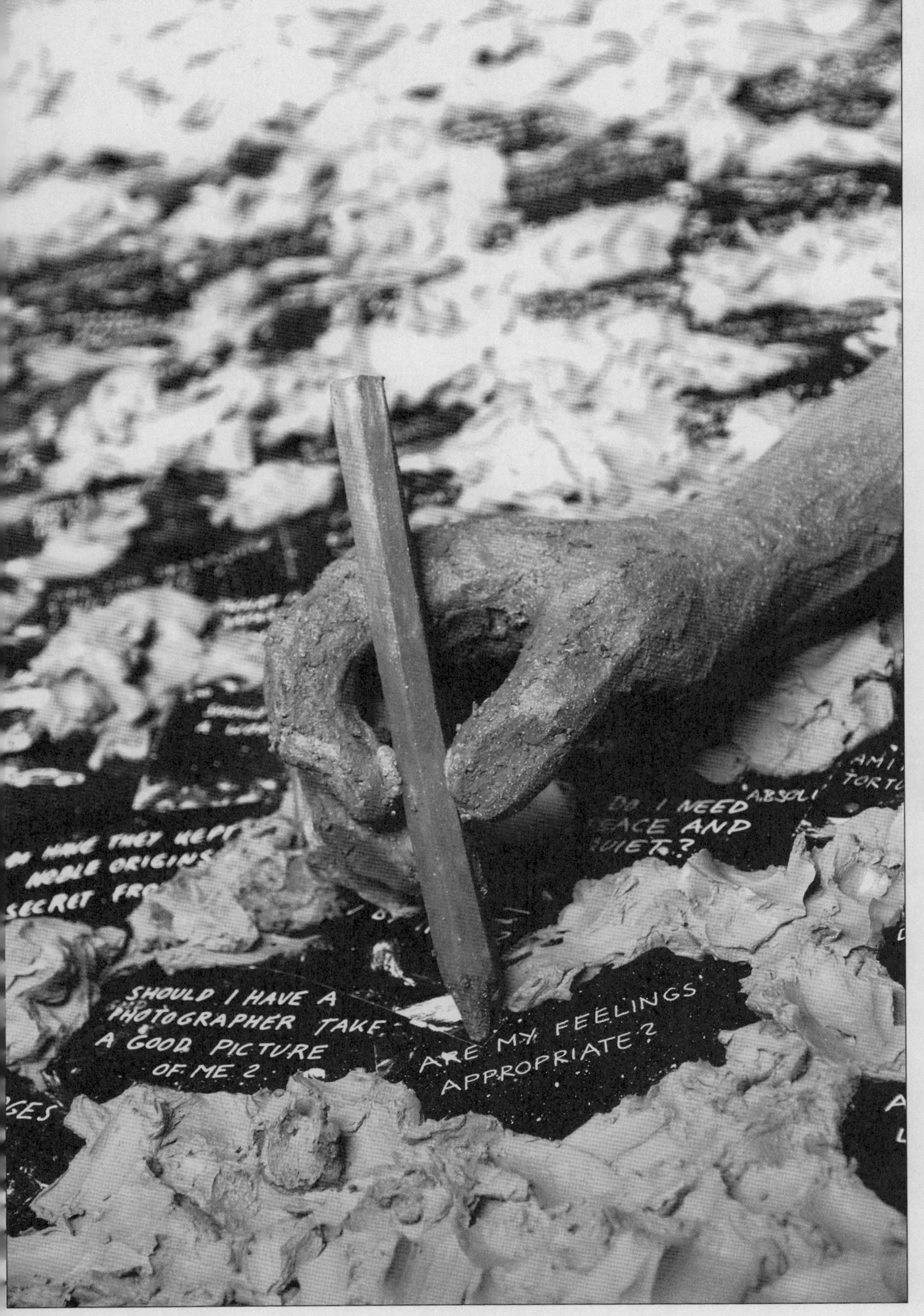

DO I NEED
PEACE AND
QUIET.?
ABSOLU
AM I
TORTU
SHOULD I HAVE A
PHOTOGRAPHER TAKE
A GOOD PICTURE
OF ME?
ARE MY FEELINGS
APPROPRIATE?
HAVE THEY KEPT
NOBLE ORIGINS
SECRET FR

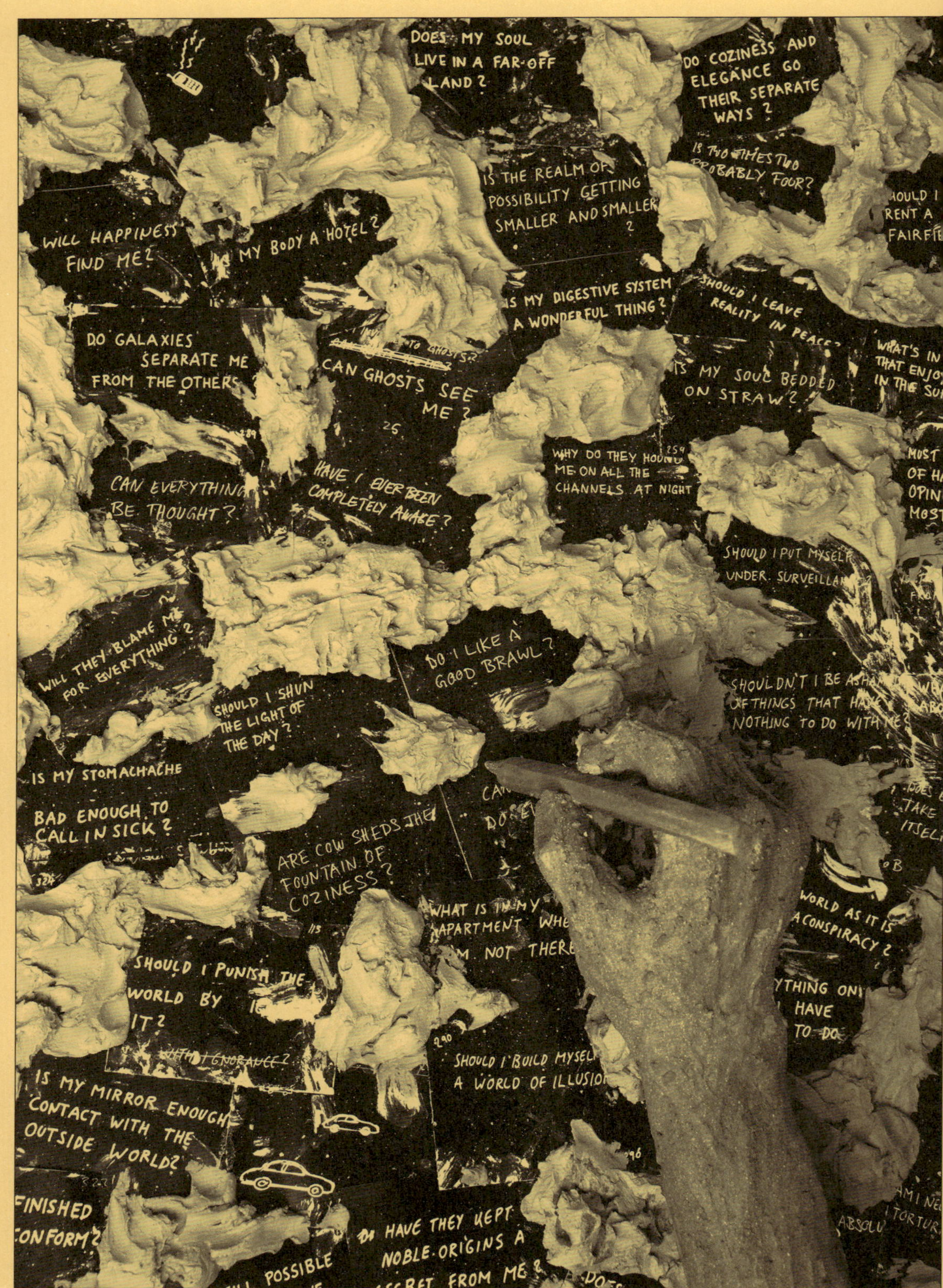

DOES MY SOUL LIVE IN A FAR-OFF LAND?
DO COZINESS AND ELEGANCE GO THEIR SEPARATE WAYS?
IS TWO TIMES TWO PROBABLY FOUR?
IS THE REALM OF POSSIBILITY GETTING SMALLER AND SMALLER?
WILL HAPPINESS FIND ME?
IS MY BODY A HOTEL?
IS MY DIGESTIVE SYSTEM A WONDERFUL THING?
SHOULD I LEAVE REALITY IN PEACE?
DO GALAXIES SEPARATE ME FROM THE OTHERS
CAN GHOSTS SEE ME?
IS MY SOUL BEDDED ON STRAW?
CAN EVERYTHING BE THOUGHT?
HAVE I EVER BEEN COMPLETELY AWAKE?
WHY DO THEY HOUND ME ON ALL THE CHANNELS AT NIGHT
SHOULD I PUT MYSELF UNDER SURVEILLANCE?
WILL THEY BLAME ME FOR EVERYTHING?
DO I LIKE A GOOD BRAWL?
SHOULDN'T I BE ASHAMED OF THINGS THAT HAVE NOTHING TO DO WITH ME
SHOULD I SHUN THE LIGHT OF THE DAY?
IS MY STOMACHACHE BAD ENOUGH TO CALL IN SICK?
ARE COW SHEDS THE FOUNTAIN OF COZINESS?
WHAT IS IN MY APARTMENT WHEN I'M NOT THERE
WORLD AS IT IS A CONSPIRACY?
SHOULD I PUNISH THE WORLD BY IGNORANCE?
SHOULD I BUILD MYSELF A WORLD OF ILLUSION
IS MY MIRROR ENOUGH CONTACT WITH THE OUTSIDE WORLD?
FINISHED CONFORM?
DO HAVE THEY KEPT NOBLE ORIGINS A SECRET FROM ME?

# Hito Steyerl
# In Defense of the Poor Image

The poor image is a copy in motion. Its quality is bad, its resolution substandard. As it accelerates, it deteriorates. It is a ghost of an image, a preview, a thumbnail, an errant idea, an itinerant image distributed for free, squeezed through slow digital connections, compressed, reproduced, ripped, remixed, as well as copied and pasted into other channels of distribution.

The poor image is a rag or a rip; an AVI or a JPEG, a lumpen proletarian in the class society of appearances, ranked and valued according to its resolution. The poor image has been uploaded, downloaded, shared, reformatted, and reedited. It transforms quality into accessibility, exhibition value into cult value, films into clips, contemplation into distraction. The image is liberated from the vaults of cinemas and archives and thrust into digital uncertainty, at the expense of its own substance. The poor image tends towards abstraction: it is a visual idea in its very becoming.

The poor image is an illicit fifth-generation bastard of an original image. Its genealogy is dubious. Its filenames are deliberately misspelled. It often defies patrimony, national culture, or indeed copyright. It is passed on as a lure, a decoy, an index, or as a reminder of its former visual self. It mocks the promises of digital technology. Not only is it often degraded to the point of being just a hurried blur, one even doubts whether it could be called an image at all. Only digital technology could produce such a dilapidated image in the first place.

Poor images are the contemporary Wretched of the Screen, the debris of audiovisual production, the trash that washes up on the digital economies' shores. They testify to the violent dislocation, transferrals, and displacement of images – their acceleration and circulation within the vicious cycles of audiovisual capitalism. Poor images are dragged around the globe as commodities or their effigies, as gifts or as bounty. They spread pleasure or death threats, conspiracy theories or bootlegs, resistance or stultification. Poor images show the rare, the obvious, and the unbelievable – that is, if we can still manage to decipher it.

## 1. Low Resolutions

In one of Woody Allen's films the main character is out of focus.[1] It's not a technical problem but some sort of disease that has befallen him: his image is consistently blurred. Since Allen's character is an actor, this becomes a major problem: he is unable to find work. His lack of definition turns into a material problem. Focus is identified as a class position, a position of ease and privilege, while being out of focus lowers one's value as an image.

e-flux journal #10 — november 2009  Hito Steyerl
In Defense of the Poor Image





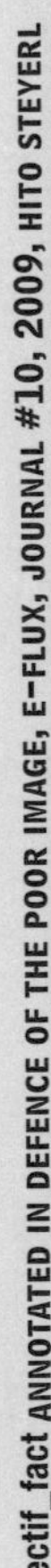
collectif_fact ANNOTATED IN DEFENCE OF THE POOR IMAGE, E—FLUX, JOURNAL #10, 2009, HITO STEYERL

To grasp fully Eco's theory of 'openness' it is necessary to reach some understanding of the linkage that he makes between 'formal innovation', 'ambiguity' and 'information'. We shall start with 'ambiguity' since it is this which, for Eco, distinguishes the 'modern' work of art from all that went before.

Traditional or classical works of art, Eco argues, are in an essential sense unambiguous. They worked always with a preferred reading, and while they were open to misreading or misunderstanding, there was generally only one correct way in which they were meant to be read or understood. By contrast, the work of modern art, he argues, 'is deliberately and systematically ambiguous'; a great variety of potential readings coexist within it, and none can truly be said to be dominant. Ambiguity is generated out of formal innovation and increases proportionately with the breaking of established conventions. As David Robey puts it in his excellent introduction to the 1989 revised edition: for Eco,

> conventional forms of expression convey conventional meanings, are part of a conventional view of the world... the less conventional forms of expression are, the more scope they allow for interpretation and the more ambiguous they can be said to be; since ordinary rules of expression no longer apply, the scope for interpretation becomes enormous.

Traditional works of art confirm existing attitudes, stabilise cultural prejudices, institutionalise existing patterns of knowledge, and ground existing opinions. The modern work of art, the 'open' work of art, on the other hand, puts all of these things in question by means of ambiguity. This represents a radical change in the relationship between art and the public at large; between the work of art and the viewer. More than this, it places art at the very centre of what Eco calls the 'modern questioning culture'. In its new-found openness, Eco argues, art has become invested with the power to 'go well beyond questions of taste and aesthetic structures, to inscribe itself into a much larger context'; in his view it might even come to 'represent man's path to salvation, towards the reconquest of his lost autonomy at the level of both perception and intelligence.'[31]

We must now turn our attention to the link that Eco makes between formal innovation, ambiguity and his theory of information. Already, by the time Eco was engaged in writing *Opera aperta*, he was beginning to lay the ground for his later work in linguistics and semiotics.[32] At this early stage this took the form of a fascination with the then fashionable subject of 'information theory', most particularly the mathematics-based theories of Max Planck and the linguistic theories of Roman Jakobson. This interest came to focus around the formula, traceable to Jakobson, that 'the information of a message is in inverse proportion to its probability or predictability' – the more unpredictable a source of information is, the more information it generates.[33] It is important to recognise here that Eco makes an absolute distinction between 'meaning' and 'information'. For him, meaning is something more or less fixed, and where it exists in a strong sense, tends to work against the efficacious functioning of information. By contrast, information is characterised as an expanding field: 'it is an additive quantity, it is something added to what one already knows as if it were an original acquisition.'[34]

Information, then, is the natural and necessary offspring of the unfamiliar. Furthermore, because it is liberated from, rather than embedded in its source, it is non-confirming – it works against finishedness, completeness or textual closure – and in this respect acts, in the strictest sense, as an opening up.

Even from this very brief description of Eco's interest in 'information theory', it is easy to see how his notion of information ties in with a theory of art based in formal innovations and ambiguity. Formal innovation means the continuous generation of new and unfamiliar patterns, configurations and codes, and these in their turn serve to expand the quantity of available information like ectoplasm around a nucleus. Given this model, the work of art operates at the centre of what Eco calls a 'field of possibilities' and offers up 'a plurality of possible readings', and he examples this by reference to developments in modern physics:

> The notion of 'field' is provided by physics and implies a revised vision of the 'classic' relationship posited between cause and effect as a rigid, one-directional system: now a complex interplay of motive forces is envisaged, a configuration of possible events, a complete dynamism of structure.[35]

And this dynamic 'field' of forces interlocks and reacts with 'a continuously altering and sensible subject' – the viewer – displacing the traditional dualism between subject and object.

female figurines found in the Pueblo cultures of Arizona and those of prehistoric Europe, to suggest that the veneration of the One Goddess, the life-giving mother, had existed all over the world before the coming of civilization. 'The first god was a goddess!' proclaimed Renaud.[33]

Throughout this, however, specialists in the emerging field of north-west European prehistory, and especially of Britain, reserved judgement. This was because their neolithic looked so different from that of the Levant and the Balkans. Its sites had failed to produce any of the female figurines which were such an important prop of the Great Goddess construct in the south-east. Instead the Western European neolithic was characterized by a very widespread monumental tradition, of megalithic tomb-shrines, the structures commonly called dolmens, passage graves, and long barrows. It was true that some of the French tombs contained a carved female figure, which gave some grounds for arguing in favour of a goddess cult; but the decisive evidence was lacking, and archaeologists did not feel able to pronounce upon the matter without it.

As illustrated in the previous chapter, the first scholars of European prehistory applied tribal models to its religions, to produce an impression of savage beliefs and practices. Their successors in the early twentieth century were recoiling from these, as unverifiable given the state of the evidence. Between 1920 and 1940, three leaders of the emerging profession of British archaeology, Gordon Childe, Grahame Clark and O. G. S. Crawford, all published surveys of prehistoric Britain which scrupulously avoided pronouncing upon the nature of its religious cultures. Childe and Crawford suggested that the megalithic tombs had been monuments of a single faith, and Childe even characterized it as spread by missionaries from the East (another comfortable fit with Christianity, and also with Dechelette's theory). Both, however, firmly declined to identify the being or beings upon which it had been focused.[34] No such caution restrained non-academic writers with an interest in archaeology. When Harold Massingham wrote a book about the Cotswolds in 1932 he took his information about their long barrows from Crawford's famous survey, but with the single difference that whereas Crawford had never discussed the religious beliefs of the builders, Massingham repeatedly declared, with perfect confidence, that they had been based on Mother Earth.[35]

For those scholars who wanted to think like Massingham, the barrier was apparently removed at last in 1939, when A. L. Armstrong claimed to have found the unequivocal proof of the worship of an Earth Goddess in the British neolithic. At the bottom of a shaft at Grimes Graves, the big complex of New Stone Age flint mines in Norfolk, he allegedly uncovered a female figurine, seated upon a crude altar, with a vessel for offerings placed before her. From that moment onwards, the statuette appeared in books upon the neolithic in general and Grimes Graves in particular, interpreted as a deity. The Ministry of Works, as custodians of the site, placed a picture of the 'goddess' upon the cover of its official guide-book and reconstructed its 'shrine' for visitors to see.

From the moment of its reported discovery, however, rumours also circulated quietly in some parts of the archaeological community to the effect that it was a fake, planted either by or upon Armstrong. Such was the discretion of that community that not until 1986 did one of its members, Stuart Piggott, raise the matter in print.[36] An investigation into it was carried out by Gillian Varndell, as part of a general reappraisal of the Grimes Graves material, and in 1991 she reported the following points: the excavation was never published; Armstrong's site notebook stopped abruptly on the day of the discovery, without recording it properly; on the day of the find, most unusually, he had directed all other experienced excavators to leave the area; the figurine and vessel look suspiciously freshly carved; and somebody on Armstrong's team was an expert carver, because similar objects made from the same Chalk rock, like an Egyptian sphinx, were among his possessions from the dig.[37]

As no method exists for dating chalk objects, Varndell added, the authenticity of these cannot be objectively tested; but not surprisingly, she concluded that the circumstantial evidence makes their status extremely dubious. This doubt is increased by the fact that since 1939 not a single other figurine has been found in an unequivocally sacred context from the British neolithic. It looks as if the Grimes Graves 'goddess' was a fraud; like the Piltdown skull, it had success because it represented precisely what many were hoping to find at that moment. The way was now open for a general acceptance of the idea that the whole of Stone Age Europe and the Near East had venerated the Great Earth Goddess.

The 'conversion' of Sir Arthur Evans, which had commenced this landslide, had been propelled by a similar piece of apparent objective evidence, this time genuine, but misunderstood. It was the work of the American team which had excavated Nippur in Iraq, then thought to be the world's oldest city, reported in 1898.[38] Evans interpreted the report as saying that the deity found in the earliest levels of its first temple was female, and represented by a clay figurine of the sort now familiar to him from Cretan neolithic sites; he concluded that they all represented the same goddess, to whom the Nippur figure was ancestral.[39] Evans had got the chronology the wrong way round (the Cretan data is older), and the book on the Nippur excavations does not in fact decisively attribute the dedication of that temple to a goddess. What had in fact happened was that he and the scholars who preceded or followed him had projected backwards upon prehistory the goddess who had emerged as pre-eminent in the minds of poets and novelists during the nineteenth century. The actual, known, history of ancient Near Eastern religion had followed a precisely opposite course; the earliest records in each region show a wide plurality of deities, from whom more important figures gradually emerge, until eventually (by the time of Apuleius) some pagans were verging upon monotheism. The orthodoxy which had emerged by the 1940s (correct or not) required a chronological pattern resembling a diamond, whereby an original feminist monotheism had disintegrated into a rampant polytheism, which in turn simplified once more to culminate in a patriarchal monotheism. Or, to put things another way, between 1840 and 1940 historians and archaeologists had turned neolithic spirituality into a mirror of

39

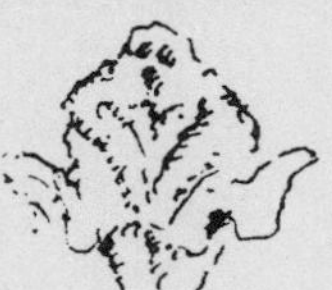
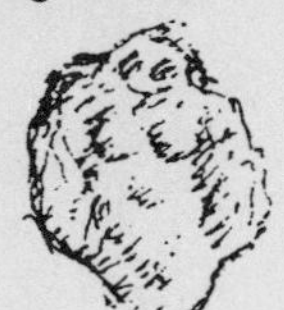
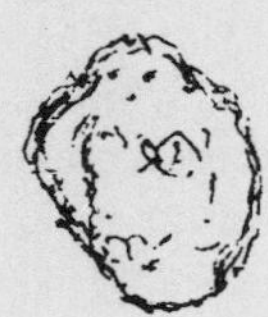
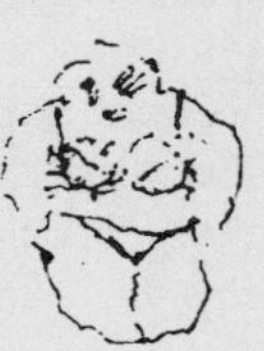

I have my dead, and I have let them go,
and was amazed to see them so contented,
so soon at home in being dead, so cheerful,
so unlike their reputation. Only you
return; brush past me, loiter, try to knock
against something, so that the sound reveals
your presence, Oh don't take from me what I
am slowly learning. I'm sure you have gone astray
if you are moved to homesickness for something
in this dimension. We transform these things;
they aren't·real, they are only the reflections
upon the polished surface of our being,

I thought you were much further on. It troubles me
that *you* should stray back, you, who have achieved
more transformation than any other woman.
that we were frightened when you died. . .no; rather:
that your stern death broke in upon us, darkly,
wrenching the till-then from the ever-since—
this concerns *us*; setting it all in order
is the task we have continually before us.
But that you too were frightened, and even now
pulse with your fear, where fear can have no meaning;
that you have lost even the smallest fragment
of your eternity, Paula, and have entered
here, where nothing yet exists; that out there,
bewildered for the first time, inattentive,
you didn't grasp the splendor of the infinite
forces, as on earth you grasped each Thing;
that, from the realm which already had received you,
the gravity of some old discontent
has dragged you back to measurable time—:
this often startles me out of dreamless sleep
at night, like a thief climbing in my window.
If I could say it is only out of kindness,
out of your great abundance, that you have come,
because you are so secure, so self-contained
that you can wander anywhere, like a child,
not frightened of any harm that might await you. . .
But no: you're pleading. This penetrates me, into
my very bones, and cuts at me like a saw.
The bitterest rebuke a ghost could bring me,
could scream to me, at night, when I withdraw
into my lungs, into my intestines,
into the last bare chamber of my heart
such bitterness would not chill me half so much
as this mute pleading. What is it you want?
Tell me, must I travel? Did you leave
something behind, some place, which cannot bear
your absence? Must I set out for a country
you never saw, although it was as vividly
near to you as your own senses are?

I will sail its rivers, explore its valleys, ask
about its oldest customs; I will stand
for hours, talking with women in their doorways
and waiting, while they call their children home.
I will watch the way they wrap the land around them
as they work in field and meadow; will demand
to be led before their king; will bribe the priests
to take me to their temple, before the most
powerful of the statues in their keeping,
and to leave me there, shutting the gates behind them.
And only then, when I have learned enough,
I will go to watch the animals, and let
something of their composure slowly glide
into my limbs; will see my own existence
deep in their eyes, which will hold me for a while
and let me go, serenely, without judgment.
I will have the gardeners come to me and recite
many flowers, and in the small clay pots
of their melodious names I will bring back
some remnant of the hundred fragrances.
And fruits: I will buy fruits; and in their sweetness
that country's earth and sky will live again.

*What animal do you picture? (A toad)*

        Are you still here? Are you standing in some corner?
You knew so much of all this, you were able
to do so much; you passed through life so open
to all things, like an early morning.

*Each person we lose becomes a country in our memories – a place we long to go*

*How to mimick the morning in my outlook / attitude*
** aspire to this everyday*

        If you are still here with me, if in this darkness
there is still some place where your spirit resonates
on the shallow sound-waves stirred up by my voice:
hear me; help me. We can so easily
slip back from what we have struggled to attain,
abruptly, into a life we never wanted;
can find ourselves entangled, as in a dream,
and die there, without ever waking up.
This can occur. Anyone who has lifted
his blood into a years-long work may find
he can't sustain it, the force of gravity
is irresistible, and it falls back, worthless.
For somewhere there is an ancient enmity
between our daily life and the great work.
Help me, in saying it, to understand it.

*Fight this? Accept this? Begin again and again*

        Do not return. If you can bear to, stay
dead with the dead. The dead have their own tasks.
But help me, if you can without distraction,
as what is farthest sometimes helps: in me.

# The text that changed my life.



Come, night. Come, Romeo. Come, thou day in night;

For thou wilt lie upon the wings of night

Whiter than new snow upon a raven's back.

Come, gentle night. Come, loving, black-browned night. [20]

Give me my Romeo. And when I die,

Take him and cut him out in little stars,

And he will make the face of heaven so fine

That all the world will be in love with night

And pay no worship to the garish sun.

Romeo and Juliet, Scene 111.2, William Shakespeare

I was 14, writing an essay on Romeo and Juliet and struggling with Shakespeare's language.

My mother, a poet and performer, told me that she saw that the meaning is conveyed by the sound of the vowels. She was always full of ideas which I was all too ready to dismiss. But this time, desperate for help, I chose to listen and as I lay on the sofa in our living room, she performed Juliet's speech producing only the vowel sounds.

A strange experience, but as I listened to the lyrical sound, I gave up all resistance to the idea. 'Do you see,' she said 'it's like listening to a love song'.

Later, I returned to Juliet's speech and saw the beauty of it as she waits impatiently for Romeo. She calls for night to come so she can submit to her lover and asks for the blood rushing in her cheeks to be calmed: 'hood my unmanned blood bating in my cheeks'. Juliet asks

that when she dies, for Romeo's body to be 'cut into little stars and he will make the face of heaven so fine, that all the world will be in love with night'.

I fell in love with the text. I felt her teenage passion myself; my mother had taught me how to look, to go deeper, then deeper still even if you still don't know what you're looking at, until the thing is in you and you love it.

Ten years later…in my final year at Goldsmiths I was making drawings from the 17th Century lace collections at the V&A. I had been to Burano, a lace-making island in Venice where I had applied for a residency after I left college. It had been a depressing visit: it felt ravaged by tourism and the only lace I saw came from Taiwan.

On the vaporetto back to the mainland, people were speaking loudly in Italian. I let it wash over me. I saw a man reading a copy of the Gazzetino di Venezia, the local newspaper. On the back was an ad for Alfa Romeo cars and I thought: What would the vowels sound like? My attention went back to the babble of people talking on the boat and I started to listen to the vowels. It was the 'O' sound that surfaced.

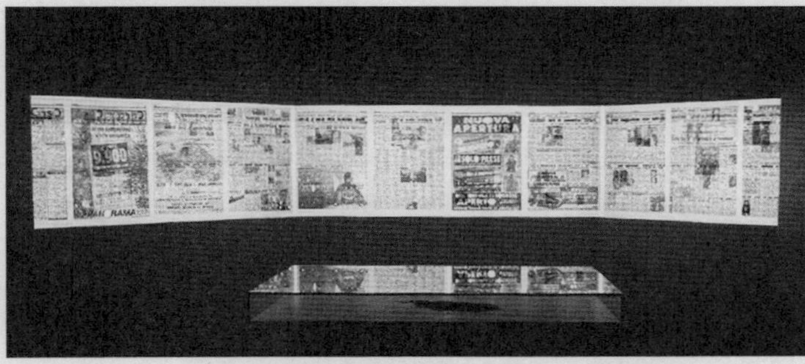

*All the 'O's in Italian', 1998, newspapers, lightboxes, plinth. Collection Museum Biedermann Germany.*

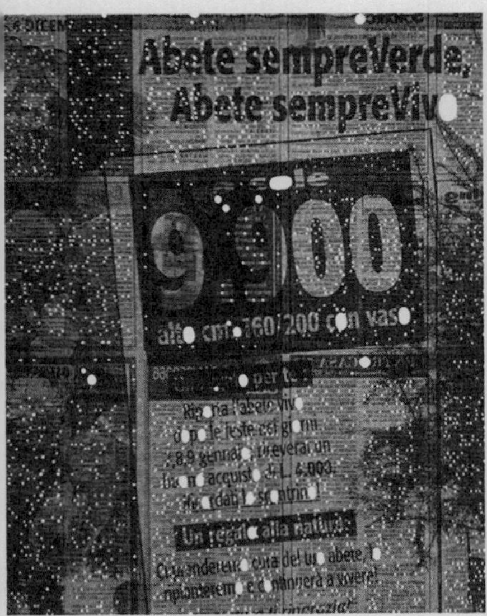


I imagined the letter 'O' pouring out of the newspaper onto the deck of the boat. When we finally arrived at the mainland, I went to a kiosk and bought a copy of the paper. The next day I flew back to London and started to cut the letter 'O' from every sheet of both sides of the paper.

For my graduation exhibition I constructed a room with light boxes built into the walls to form a panorama onto which I attached the papers with their pock marks. In the centre of the room I installed a plinth on which I scattered all the 'O's. They looked like ashes. What appears on the pages are ads for Christmas trees that are lit-up as if by fairy lights. On the mug-shot faces of people on the obituaries pages, the holes appear like bullet holes. There is an image of a striker leaping into the air after having scored a goal. He is surrounded by a halo of effervescent bubbles of light. None of these images were planned or anticipated. Everything I saw and felt was in this work, the language, the geography of the islands, the lace…

So, in the small hours on the platform at Saxmundham station, I will read Juliet's speech and be warmed by the heat in my veins. I will look up into the night sky and feel no fear.

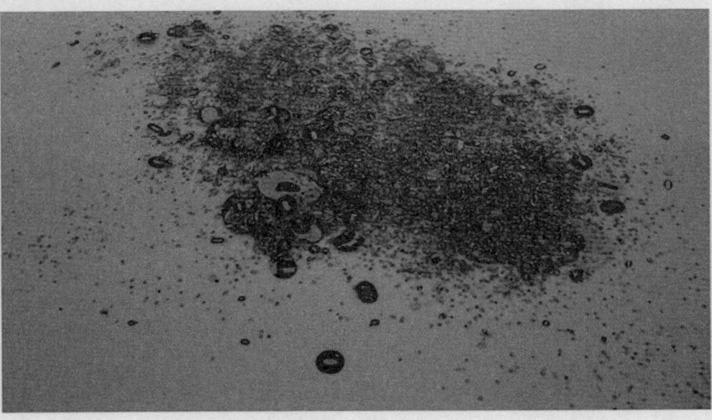

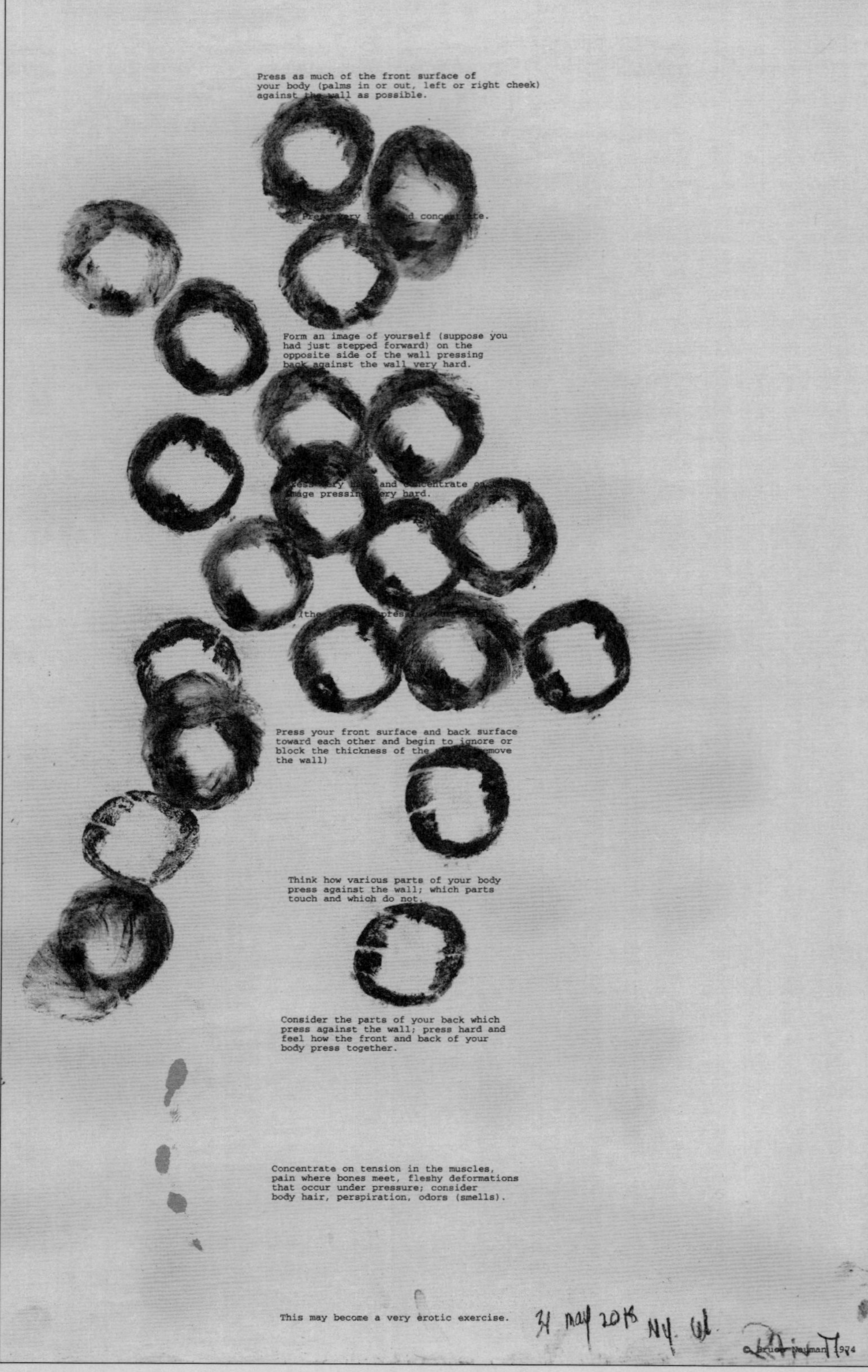
Body Pressure

Press as much of the front surface of
your body (palms in or out, left or right cheek)
against the wall as possible.

Press very hard and concentrate.

Form an image of yourself (suppose you
had just stepped forward) on the
opposite side of the wall pressing
back against the wall very hard.

Press very hard and concentrate on
image pressing very hard.

(the image of pressing very hard)

Press your front surface and back surface
toward each other and begin to ignore or
block the thickness of the wall (remove
the wall)

Think how various parts of your body
press against the wall; which parts
touch and which do not.

Consider the parts of your back which
press against the wall; press hard and
feel how the front and back of your
body press together.

Concentrate on tension in the muscles,
pain where bones meet, fleshy deformations
that occur under pressure; consider
body hair, perspiration, odors (smells).

This may become a very erotic exercise.

## MODERN ORNAMENT

Modern architects began to make the back the front, symbolizing the configurations of the shed to create a vocabulary for their architecture but denying in theory what they were doing in practice. They said one thing and did another. Less may have been more, but the I-section on Mies van der Rohe's fire-resistant columns, for instance, is as complexly ornamental as the applied pilaster on the Renaissance pier or the incised shaft in the Gothic pier. (In fact, less was more work.) Acknowledged or not, Modern ornament has seldom been symbolic of anything non-architectural since the Bauhaus vanquished Art Deco and the decorative arts. More specifically, its content is consistently spatial and technological. Like the Renaissance vocabulary of the Classical orders, Mies's structural ornament, although specifically contradictory to the structure it adorns, reinforces the architectural content of the building as a whole. If the Classical orders symbolized "rebirth of the Golden Age of Rome," modern I-beams represent "honest expression of modern technology as space"—or something like that. Note, however, it was "modern" technology of the Industrial Revolution that was symbolized by Mies, and this technology, not current electronic technology, is still the source for Modern architectural symbolism today.

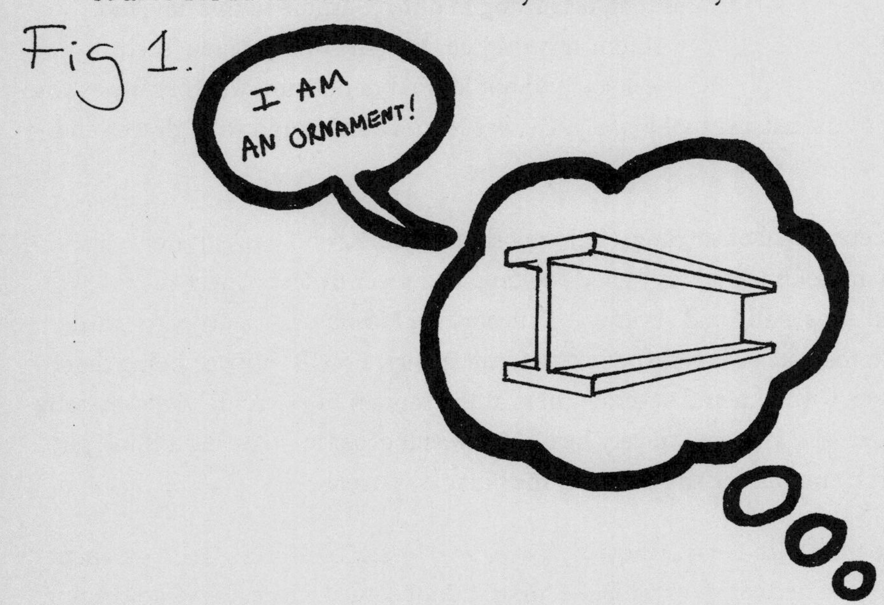



3. George Howe, "Some Experiences and Observations of an Elderly Architect," *Perspecta 2, The Yale Architectural Journal*, New Haven (1954), p. 4.

4. Donald Drew Egbert, "Lectures in Modern Architecture" (unpublished), Princeton University, c. 1945.

## For a while I sat with Paul while he jerked off beside me and gave a monologue of his petty crimes, the telling of which kept him very excited.

I got the impression nobody knew or cared who I was, possibly because they were not expecting me here and possibly because Bob hadn't told them. No one said science fiction writer, although I used my real nickname Chip, and I think at least once gave my last name.

George was the only person there who was probably older than I was. It was hard to tell, but the youngest and, by my lights, best-looking character was an extremely fat young man of perhaps forty, who was very active but seemed slightly slow. He was certainly over 300 pounds and with a working-class face and demeanor and one of the several people who, at least to me, seemed unremittingly masculine. From time to time, I managed to get a few stories. For a while I sat with Paul, ignoring his claw-like big toenail while he jerked off beside me and gave me a fifteen-minute monologue of his petty crimes that, according to him, continue to this day, the telling of which apparently kept him very excited. My part was to listen, seem interested, maintain physical contact, and not leave. I'm not sure whether it was true or whether it was just a sexual fantasy. He was lean, swarthy, and with glasses and said he was in his sixties.

There was a good deal of sucking. (I did my share.) Mark, who was fifty-four, again traditionally masculine and very good-looking, had recently lost a lover in his nineties, and apparently had severe ADD, according to Bob. He was very forward sexually with me and with everybody else in the group. I really enjoyed being there and having sex with him and several others at the same time. He did, however, hang around the longest, and next to very heavy Joe was the last to leave and I think put Bob out a bit by not taking the hint that the party was over.

I spent some time with Larry, who misplaced his shoes at one point. Then we spent some time on the bed together while he talked about some lectures he was planning to give in a couple weeks, again with sexual play all through. I wondered if I was going to have a similar shoe problem, but I found mine pretty easily in the confusion of clothes in the corner. Besides me, there was one other tall obviously black guy, not by my lights particularly good-looking, but he was, rather like the cliché, the tallest and best hung in the group. At one point I was talking to him while he was being serviced by someone else. His name was Philip and he explained that he had started coming to these parties when he was thirty-five, and he was now forty-three. Clearly he was having fun and lots of guys wanted to play with him. Among other things, he was shaped rather like a bowling pin and had a deep, irregular, fourteen-inch-plus scar up his belly. He wore large, black-rimmed glasses, and whenever he looked at me, he seemed dazzled. I don't think it was drugs. In fact, I got the impression that, other than Viagra, there were no drugs involved. (But I suspect I wasn't the only one there who'd had cataract operations.)

Now, as one after the other got dressed and said goodbye to Bob and Chuck, Joe seemed to be passed out and having some trouble breathing. In the other room, Bob mentioned that Joe probably needed a CPAP machine. Actually, I'd brought my own in my rollaway, though I'd decided not to use it, but Joe's weight seemed to militate for it as something necessary. Finally, we got him up and more or less into some clothes. I went to hug him goodbye, which he returned very good-heartedly. "You know," I said, "you could probably use a CPAP machine."

Still in the hug, he said, "I have one, but the mask is so uncomfortable, I never use it." Moments later, he pulled a wheelchair from behind the door and got into it. (I hadn't realized he had been using one when he came.) He let himself out to roll away down the hall.

At least two people had made it known that they had come twice. While I had fun and generally enjoyed the sucking and affection and some of the stories even more, I had not had an orgasm at all nor was I particularly looking for one.

My general take on the group? They seemed like nice guys trying to have fun. I have no idea whether I will seek out this kind of entertainment again or not.

The next day over breakfast in the hotel—Bob had a coupon that allowed us both to get the hotel buffet—he explained that he hadn't started to play till he was thirty-five. Ten years ago he'd run into an older gay guy who'd taken him to Houston, when he'd started the parties. Events like Charon Rising and the Celebration of Friends, which are well-known annual sex parties for gay men, had interested him, but he had also always liked older men.

*Can my perspective through the camera be as open as these words*

# DEMOLITION

ABRAHAM CRUZVILLEGAS ANNOTATED DEMOLICION, 1965, LOS SAICOS, WILD TEEN PUNK FROM PERÚ, 1999, ELECTRO HARMONIX

Tatatatatattayyayayayayayyaa
Let's tear down the train station
Demolish, demolish, demolish, demolish
Let's tear down the train station
Demolish, demolish the train station
Tatatatatattatayayyayayaya
We like to tear down the train station
Demolish, demolish, demolish, demolish
ye ye ye ye yeye ye
ye ye ye ye yeye ye
Demolish, demolish, demolish, demolish
ahhh
Tatatatatattayyayayayayayyaa

*DEMOLITION*, LOS SAICOS, 1965

# DEMOLICIÓN

Tatatatatattayyayayayayayyaa
Echemos abajo la estación del tren
demoler demoler demoler demoler
echemos abajo la estación del tren
demoler demoler la estación del tren
Tatatatatattatayayyayayaya
nos gusta volar la estación del tren
demoler demoler demoler demoler
ye ye ye ye yeye ye
ye ye ye ye yeye ye
Demoler demoler demoler demoler
ahhh
tatatatatatyayyayaya

*DEMOLICIÓN*, LOS SAICOS, 1965

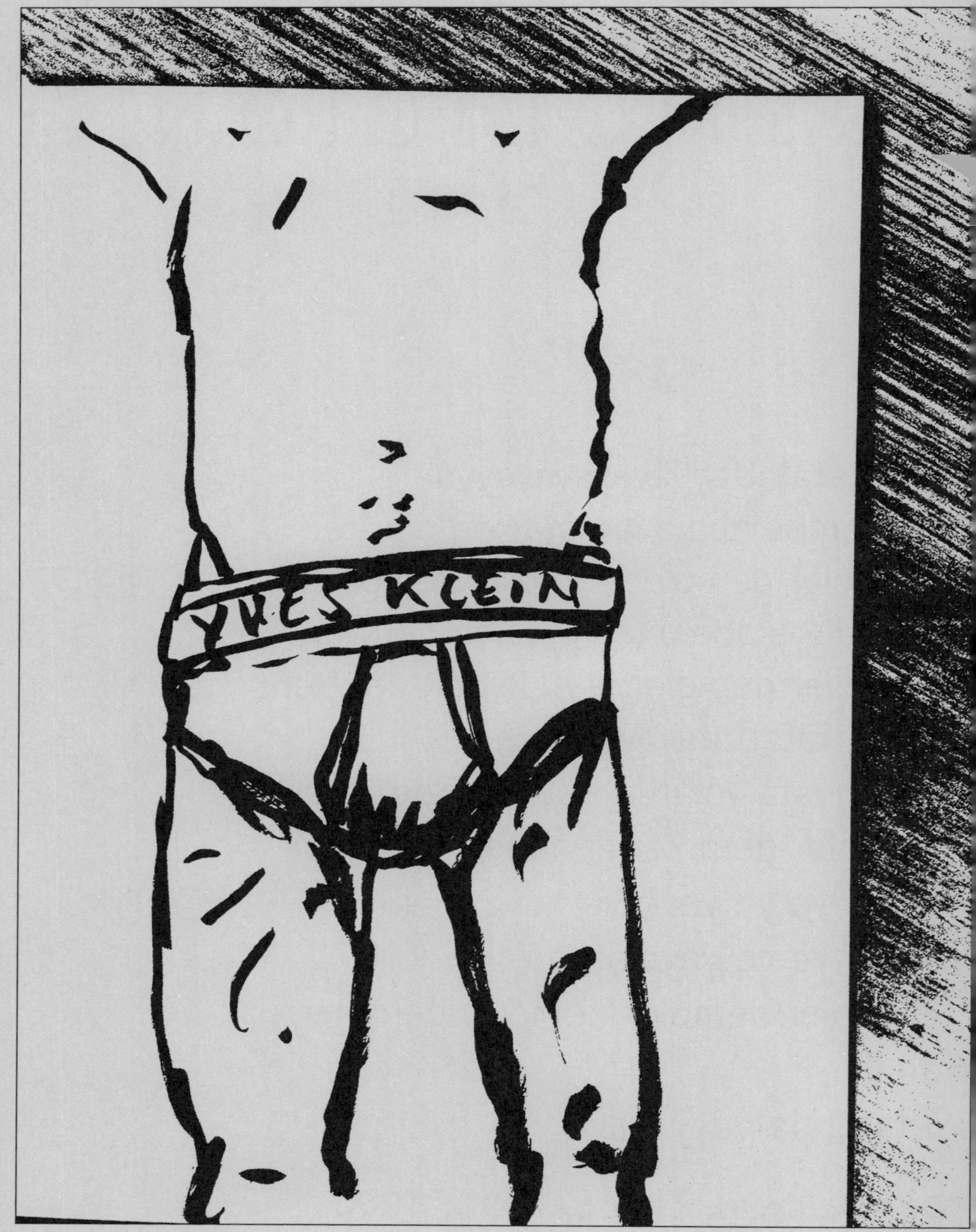

YVES KLEIN

Then, as if in excuse, and because I stood there without saying anything, 'I've known him a long time,' she added. 'I haven't dared bring him in before; I was afraid of tiring you, or perhaps vexing you.'

'Why in the world!' I cried. 'Bring in all the children you like, if it amuses you!' And I thought, with a little irritation at not having done so, that I might have perfectly well brought in Ashour.

And yet, as I thought this, I looked at my wife; how maternal and caressing she was! Her tenderness was so touching that the little fellow went off warm and comforted. I spoke of my walk and gently explained to Marceline why I preferred going out alone.

At that time, my nights were generally disturbed by my constantly waking with a start – either frozen with cold or bathed in sweat. That night was a very good one. I hardly woke up at all. The next morning, I was ready to go out by nine o'clock. It was fine; I felt rested, not weak, happy – or rather, amused. The air was calm and warm, but nevertheless, I took my shawl to serve as a pretext for making acquaintance with the boy who might turn up to carry it. I have said that the garden ran alongside our terrace, so that I reached it in a moment. It was with rapture I passed into its shade. The air was luminous. The cassias, whose flowers come very early, before their leaves, gave out a delicious scent – or was it from all around me that came the faint, strange perfume, which seemed to enter me by several senses at once and which so uplifted me? I was breathing more easily too, and so I walked more lightly; and yet at the first bench I sat down, but it was because I was excited – dazzled – rather than tired.

I looked. The shadows were transparent and mobile;

they did not fall upon the ground – seemed barely to rest on it. Light! Oh, light!

I listened. What did I hear? Nothing; everything; every sound amused me.

I remember a shrub some way off whose bark looked of such a curious texture that I felt obliged to go and feel it. My touch was a caress; it gave me rapture. I remember . . . Was that the morning that was at last to give me birth?

I had forgotten I was alone, and sat on, expecting nothing, waiting for no one, forgetting the time. Up till that day, so it seemed to me, I had felt so little and thought so much that now I was astonished to find my sensations had become as strong as my thoughts.

I say, 'it *seemed* to me', for from the depths of my past childhood, there now awoke in me the glimmerings of a thousand lost sensations. The fact that I was once more aware of my senses enabled me to give them a half fearful recognition. Yes; my reawakened senses now remembered a whole ancient history of their own – recomposed for themselves a vanished past. They were alive! Alive! They had never ceased to live; they discovered that even during those early studious years they had been living their own latent, cunning life.

I met no one that day, and I was glad of it; I took out of my pocket a little Homer, which I had not opened since Marseille, re-read three lines of the *Odyssey* and learned them by heart; then, finding in their rhythm enough to satisfy me, I dwelled on them awhile with leisurely delight, shut the book, and sat still, trembling, more alive than I had thought it possible to be, my mind benumbed with happiness . . .

the truth. Then there was a man who could tell his whole life story in a couple of hours. He would always finish at 5am with his mustache burning due to the speed of his words. An hour later a woman would wake up in her wedding bed and start doing yoga exercises. On the way to her office she would have coffee in a place that had just opened one month ago. "Are your beans fair-trade?" she would ask a waiter and hurry some sugar into her cup before receiving an answer. Two spoons usually, what a sweet tooth! A man across the bar sued her because he was convinced that the woman's character was based on his own life: same amount of sugar, same social concerns, same office. "I will never come back to that body I've left in jail, I am free now and I want you to be free too," he would say. "I am a rabbit and a hat," she would respond. But no one has even come close to a person who thought he was a book written without an author. To complement the existence of this thinker there was a woman who entertained a fantasy of being a writer. She would never write a single line, only stare at me gleefully as if I was jealous of her not writing yet still being a writer. What an insinuator.

I've never been introduced to the man of bad analogy, but I've been told that he was very good at bad analogies. The fellow would always speak with some kind of comparison, choosing the most abstract entity in the room and setting it alongside something more familiar. "Singing in the rain is like singing in the train," he would say. What the hell was that supposed to mean? Heaven only knows. A similarly debilitating character was ardently involved in totalization exercises. "What would happen if all the people who ever died returned back to life today?", "What would be the total hair length of all people living in New York?", "What would be the size of a gate through which all mankind could walk through in one step?" he would not stop asking. When digital visualization tools became available for these sort of nerds, their life reached the full swing. I should not forget to mention that a woman who sang every night in a choir of vocoders had a husband who was ready to pay all of his savings to have sex behind one of the O's of the HOLLYWOOD sign. "With anybody." Everybody waited for this to happen, but no one really wanted to crawl behind the O. "Maybe the W?" a French-speaking neighbor suggested, but the alternative was not discussed further. A tattoo on the neighbor's biceps was mesmerizing enough for me to ask: "Is

The dependency of childhood
Distorted images of one's parents
The omnipotentiality of adolescence
The "freedom" of uncommitment
The agility of youth
The sexual attractiveness and/or potency of youth
The fantasy of immortality
Authority over one's children
Various forms of temporal power
The independence of physical health
And, ultimately, the self and life itself.

### Renunciation and Rebirth

In regard to the last of the above, it may seem to many that the ultimate requirement—to give up one's self and one's life—represents a kind of cruelty on the part of God or fate, which makes our existence a sort of bad joke and which can never be completely accepted. This attitude is particularly true in present-day Western culture, in which the self is held sacred and death is considered an unspeakable insult. Yet the exact opposite is the reality. It is in the giving up of self that human beings can find the most ecstatic and lasting, solid, durable joy of life. And it is death that provides life with all its meaning. This "secret" is the central wisdom of religion.

The process of giving up the self (which is related to the phenomenon of love, as will be discussed in the next section of this book) is for most of us a gradual process which we get into by a series of fits and starts. One form of temporary giving up of the self deserves special mention because its practice is an absolute requirement for significant learning during adulthood, and therefore for significant growth of the human spirit. I am referring to a subtype of the discipline of balancing which I call "bracketing." Bracketing is essentially the act of balancing the need for stability and assertion of the self with the need for new knowledge and greater understanding by temporarily giving up one's self—putting one's self aside, so to speak—so as to make room for the incorporation of new material into the self. This discipline has been well described by the theologian Sam Keen in *To a Dancing God*:

> The second step requires that I go beyond the idiosyncratic and egocentric perception of immediate experience. Mature awareness is possible only when I have digested and compensated for the biases and prejudices that are the residue of my personal history. Awareness of what presents itself to me involves a double movement of attention: silencing the familiar and welcoming the strange. Each time I approach a strange object, person, or event, I have a tendency to let my present needs, past experience, or expectations for the future determine what I will see. If I am to appreciate the uniqueness of any datum, I must be sufficiently aware of my preconceived ideas and characteristic emotional distortions to bracket them long enough to welcome strangeness and novelty into my perceptual world. This discipline of bracketing, compensating, or silencing requires sophisticated self-knowledge and courageous honesty. Yet, without this discipline each present moment is only the repetition of something already seen or experienced. In order for genuine novelty to emerge, for the unique presence of things, persons, or events to take root in me, I must undergo a decentralization of the ego.*

The discipline of bracketing illustrates the most consequential fact of giving up and of discipline in general:

* New York: Harper & Row, 1970, p. 28.

LENNEBERG (9)

i.e. Verbal behaviour "activated" within situations presenting a certain kind of demand, of involvement."

– very often expressive disorders of language are less severe in emotional discourse than in propositional discourse. For instance, sudden, passionate exclamations may still occur at a time when the patient can no longer use language to explain something or to ask polite questions — (see 9d) See (9a) (preceding).

(etiology — the study of causes)       (9b)

CHAPTER (6)  If accept that man has innate mechanism for language then this theory cannot stand.
Critique.                                            Dar-winian thesis that since man
PAGE 228 Continuity theory language development, descended from more primitive forms
Non-specific intelligence. communication. The "need" for    modes of communication must also be so
         communication to man    descended, study will ∴ give the origins of
                                   language development in man.

229. Impossibility of comparative (intelligence testing ∴ lack of objective criteria)    see (9b) (9c) (9d)

Hockett & Ascher. Current Anthropology 5 135–168.

─────────────────────────────────────────────

CHAPTER (7). see (9e)        Reference relationship between an individual word and
                              some aspect or object of the physical environment
Page 273.   Meaning & reference. Meaning – semantic interpretation of verbal behaviour. "Because discourse is not encountered in anything but the essential form of sentences and sentences can be interpreted only through grammatical analysis, meaning cannot be divorced from grammatical structure" (Chomsky)

① colourless green ideas sleep furiously        SKINNER
② furiously sleep ideas green colourless         meaning?

273 → 275 problem of language complexity.

Wittgenstein      The linguistic development of utterances does not seem to begin by a composition
Philosophical 279  of individual, independently movable items but as a whole tonal pattern.
Investigations I
134          and see (9e)
281    Correct but over generalized usage in child developing language.

Page 294 -295. Differentiation c.f. earlier account of ontogeny, and (nervous — tissue linkage. Progressive differentiation of
progressive
syntactic, & semantic, phonetic } over generalized responses characteristic of ontogenetic development.
         other
See (10a)    301 Development of differentiation verbal   perceptual   support biological foundation language - because of way of development by differentiation special
                              transformational ability   acoustic
                                                         motor.

302.  If phrase structure and transformations are simply special application of general modes of organization, modes that are common to the organization of the behaviour of all higher animals, why is language species-specific? There is only one possible answer. In order to achieve such special adaptation, cognitive processes must be highly adapted biologically. The slightest alterations in the peculiarities of data-acceptance, data-storage and temporal integration apparently interferes with the proper reception and production of the peculiar patterns called sentences.

(304) Apparently pastness is first learned as a semantic phenomenon
305. Language acquisition in the absence of speech production (case history)
    — See (10a) — [congenital anarthria]

307 - 319. Parroting. e.f. Skinner echoic behaviour.

ie. application of structuration principle' to maintain the sense

Parroting is resorted to when the grammar of the original sentence is simply not understood." ie. when grammatical structure is complex, outside of experience.    ┃TABLES┃

────────────────────────────────

SUMMARY         (Neonate?)  (324)→(326).

    In the mechanism of language we find a natural extension of very general principles of organization of behaviour which are biologically adapted to a highly specific ethological function. With maturation the neonate begins to organize the perceptually available stimuli surrounding him and also to organize the movements of his muscles. Sensory data become grouped into as yet undifferentiated global classes of gross patterns, and these, subsequently become differentiated into more specific patterns, c.f. the development of and progressive discrimination discrimination of motor skills. (organize)
phrase structure - phrase markers. application of of differentiation principle to acoustic patterns of language

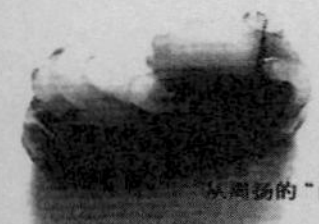

### "当代"批评家的道德问题

从周扬的"两面派"谈起

"文革"期间正式或非正式的出版物上，刊登有大量的文艺批判文章。今天看来，有点"学术含量"还值得一读的，姚文元著名的《评反革命两面派周扬》[1] 是少数几篇之一。所以说"著名"，是因为自1965

、欺骗"鲁迅，这一事实的揭发让会场上的许广平十分……站起来当面痛斥冯雪峰"是一个大骗子"。不过，到了19……等的"再批……为"文艺黑线头目"之后，许广平的关于"欺骗……年代在延安……便也部分投向周扬、夏衍他们的身上[15]。

反革命的文……

"当代"这样的关注点，和相应的论述方式的产生，原因其实复杂。从"大"的方面看，20世纪社会主义运动内部，在意识形态和权力分配问题上，始终存在区分真假、正伪、正统异端（修正主义）的激烈冲突。中国"当代"推动的又是一种"泛道德化"的政治实践。而对于许多革命作家、批评家来说，他们普遍持有对文学的道德承担的信仰。他们大多有掌握"客观真理"，并为捍卫这一"真理"奋斗的激情。不管是坚守的秉持，还是自我构建的幻觉，至少从表面，从姿态看，都在孜孜扮演着分辨真伪的道德主义者的角色。在涉及与辨明"真相"和"真理"的道德问题上，他们的言辞表情常常峻烈、庄严而凌厉。"潜意识"中也明白如何能激发读者（听众）的或同情或愤恨的情绪。

1957年批判丁玲的时候，涉及她30年代所谓自首变节的旧案。批判会上的发言有这样的话：

## 道德与权力的关系

度，和"两面派"相对立的真实、真诚等自然不……个体品格修养，还是从社会关系的维系层面上看……判者（江青，姚文元）采用的，总是怎样怎样……不诚实"的方法。而"文革"过后，当年"真理化身"的姚……

义正词严的……甚至可以说……延安之后已……首，然后滥……以作家的思……

文元，也同样获得"两面派""披上革命外衣"的评语[18]。指控者与受辱者位置的错动甚至互换，是当代史的奇观。当受辱者被推上"不老实""两面派"的审判台的时候，指控者自然获得了道德优势，一旦他们的权力地位失去，立于"道德制高点"上的就是另一些人。"两面派"的道德恶名，原由周扬等加诸丁玲、冯雪峰头上，不久就落到他们自身。而当初道义凛然的姚文元，也没有逃脱这样的命运。历史的吊诡，也许可以用"悲喜剧"来描述。

这样描述发生在当代文艺界的这些事情，并不是要把水搅浑，将历史视作一笔糊涂账，以为人和事没有正误、美丑、善恶之分，那被锁定在"历史链条"上的"零件"（参与者）的思想品格没有高低、贵贱之别，而在于让我们能廓清"当代"政治生活中权力与道德的关系的实质。这也就如有学者在分析历史某个时期权力与道德关系时指出的：在两者无法分辨的时代，"道德唯有在权力的强制之中并且在实体化之形式下始能存在，而权力也是作为道德权威体系之一始能显现其本身的社会意义"[19]。

文学批评家特里林在《诚与真》一书中，讨论了"真诚"的起源所……

人在自己生命处理上的无奈，在陈翔鹤60年代初写的短篇《陶……明写"挽歌"》《广陵散》中有所流露。就是说，在一个"言论的强迫统一"的社会里，"优秀的人注定只能沉默，大多数人则学会讲两种语言，一种在他们自己的四壁里的本来的语言，以及一种不是本来的，在公共领域里所说的语言"[24]。不追问社会情境、制度，不解析权力的性质和作方式，只严苛地纠缠个人道德，只能说是轻重不分。

从这里可以提出的问题有，为什么"道德"拥有"超凡权力"的规范性力量？为什么它具有"终极评价"的地位？谁有资格、权力做出……

"目的"和"手段"的关系。50年代斯大林事件……宣布脱离共产党，中国文艺界对他展开批判。巴金在他的文章里就触及了令自由知识分子苦恼的这个问题[25]。"目的"的崇高自然可以抵消在……

手段上的"不道德"。不过，从"当代"文艺史看，当年标榜的正义、崇高目的（捍卫"正确文艺路线"、还原"历史真相"等等），许多都未能经得起检验。退一步说，即使承认目的的崇高性，这样的忧虑也不能完全消弭："以太过无情手段促进的人性理想，有变成其相反物的危险，自由，变成以自由为名而行压迫，平等，变成以维护平等为名而久居不去的新寡头体制，公道，变成要打破一切不妥协，人类爱则变成怨恨所有反对以残暴手段达成人类爱之人。"[26]

也是在1957年，施蛰存在《才与德》的文章中说，"任人以德，现在恐怕不很妥当，因为我们在最近20年中，经过好几次大变革，可以说是一个乱离之世，有德之人，实在太少，'老子打过游击'，只能算是'功'，不能算是'德'。有功则酬以利禄，何必以位？"[27] 这看起来是"士"对"君主"谏言的现代版本，目的当在争取"知识分子"的"话语权"。不过，里面似乎也透露了对"当代""道德主义"趋向的警惕：这种"道德主义"是在承担推进"一体化"思想政治体制的功能，是在促使这样的现象产生——一边是绝对的纯洁正义，另一边则完全是欺骗和邪恶——端看谁掌握着权力而进行这种二元的道德分配。

# "真诚"上的迷思

与"伪装""两面派"相对立的，是真实、真诚的道德操守。"真诚"

> 苏珊·桑塔格在《乔治·卢卡奇的文学批评》这篇文章中，谈到卢
卡奇在匈牙利的处境，说他具有一种"能使自己在个人和政治两方面幸
存下来的巨大才能——这就是说，对众多不同的人意味着众多东西的那
种才能"，其中之一是那种被称为"内部放逐"的东西，这"明显地见于
他对所要撰述的主题的选择"。桑塔格说，卢卡奇最全神贯注的作家是
歌德、巴尔扎克、司各特和托尔斯泰，"由于他的年纪以及他所拥有的共
产主义文化准则出现前形成的一种感受力"，他能够"通过从现代（从
精神上）移民出去而保护自己。唯一得到他无保留的赞许的现代作家，
是那些基本上延续着 19 世纪小说传统的作家——曼、高尔斯华绥、高
尔基以及罗歇·马丁·杜伽尔"[31]。这种"在个人和政治"两方面保护
自己的表现，在当代中国批评家中也普遍存在，也表现为各种各样的形
态。不同的是，在 50—70 年代的中国，可以容许"内部"放逐、移民的
空间相较而言更加窄小，而限制、窄化这种可供"边缘性移民"空间的
办法，就是使用这种道德评价的手段。

> 人们不正是通过正视自己内在的矛盾分裂，通过激化或协调"自
我"与环境之间的龃龉，在"抵抗"中取得情感上和认知上的深化吗？
因此，特里林的《诚与真》在谈及歌德的《少年维特之烦恼》时说，

表的一致，言和行

，言行，表里的一

为不需论证的准

值得崇敬，也是需

> 将这种"整体性"的"一贯"绝对化，从个人说，可能是为了维护
在他人心目中的形象；从社会体制上，着眼的却是达到排斥"异端"，不
承认"选择"的合理性的目的。在这样的环境中，对"老实""真诚"的
绝对化强调，就有可能成为可疑的道德棍棒。而不少作家、批评家，也
转而对自己身上的分裂、矛盾，或者不愿承认，或者意识到了，也怀着
不安、羞愧的罪感加以掩盖。他们想努力维护一个让他心安的无裂痕的
"自我"。但是，"自我"如果拒绝（事实上也不大可能）这种变化和分
裂，就是强调对"外部"的，和内化于"内部"的权力的服从。从当代文
学批评实践看，倒是分裂、变易、不统一，有可能摆脱各种有形无形的
制约，承认在变化中选择的合理。这样，也就意味着发现、创造的活力，
意味着对抗的可能，包括抵抗内在的"顺从"。

# 并非多余的话

写到这里，还有两点意思需要补充，相信它们不是多余的话。

诗人牛汉有题为《为冯雪峰辩诬》的文章，说到 1957 年底冯雪峰
撰写《鲁迅全集》第 6 卷中《答徐懋庸并关于抗日统一战线问题》的注
的感叹？

> "真诚"一词昔日所有的尊荣如今已消失殆尽。我们今天
听到这个词时，会有一种恍若隔世的古怪感觉。如果我们说真
诚，我们可能会不太自在或含讥带讽。[35]

2011 年 3—5 月

*Notes x from the letters of Phil King (to me) 2016 – 2017 (on painting)*

Hello Stevie,

As I read your thoughts and write this the figure of Antoinin Artaud comes to mind very strongly… ~~initially because your description of a sense of disappearance in terms of emotion when you complete a painting (I totally get this and have the same thing when I finish. It's almost like a kind of loss of this act followed by a rediscovery in wholly new terms later, sometimes much later)~~ anyway Artaud wrote somewhere, I've been trying to find it. of how a completed poem would disappear for him, become unconscious. once fulfilled.    In looking unsuccessfully for where he says this, (in some poem I think,) I came across this:

> "For in the space of that minute the illumination of a lie can last, I manufacture a notion of escape; I rush off in any wrong direction my blood takes. I close the eyes of my intelligence and open my mouth to the speech of the unspoken; I give myself the illusion of a system whose vocabulary escapes me. But from this minute of error there remains the feeling that I have snatched something real from the unknown. I believe in spontaneous bewitchments. It is impossible that I shall not some day discover a truth somewhere on the routes my blood carries me."

… Jon Thompson, … said that:

"I have come to realize more and more that internationalism, that much vaunted shibboleth of the high modernist, is, at the very best, only skin deep. Just a geopolitical stones-throw across the other side of the English Channel, and you find yourself a stranger in an art world shaped by distinctly different attitudes and values. Of a sudden you are surrounded by artists who seem to talk about art in a fairly unfamiliar way. Furthermore, the take that you have on the art world you have left behind – the pool in which you once swam, almost oblivious of its culturally specific peculiarities – makes it seem like a very distant place indeed. It comes as quite a shock to discover that there is, after all, something called Englishness, just as there is Belgianess or Dutchness, although, like English artists speaking from the security of their own patch, most Belgian and Dutch artists fiercely deny it."

He felt that these: "almost subliminal traces of nationhood serve to colour the art of different countries in wonderfully subtle, complex, and in the case of certain artists, a thoroughly definitive way."

I think Brexit has come as an enormous shock in the UK for artists, especially for the many that have come here from abroad, and has opened a real problem of trust. Trust is a powerful emotion. A certain sense of the future has been X'd-out by many of our fellow subjects ( right there there is a culture shock . There is, I think, a real sense of betrayal and un-mooring. We aren't living in the internationally open country in which we thought that we were living. I was impressed that you were able to mount a show that bluntly addressed the issue and have the confidence to directly put your paintings in its context. Part of the traction of UK art came from it rapidly becoming nominally part of a continental European Bourgeois civilization with its pavement cafes and galleries and suddenly all that feels vulnerable. It's a lot to take on board – and the result I think is a kind of vacuum or emptiness that I can sense that you address in your paintings – always an element in the work, it now feels weaponised.

My sense of your work is that you constantly walk on tightropes – between abstract and figural, between exterior and interior drama and that to stress any one thing brings with it the risk of loosing sight of the other. This tightrope walk can only be achieved and keep achieving through the continued work of painting – its meaning is a kind of movement – a *wandering.*

Anyway thanks for such a great correspondence over the last year and sharing your paintings and thoughts so fully. It has really stretched my ability to respond (productively I hope) as great painting should.

Bonne chance!

_First shape evolution model **ever**._

Why is it that the so-called pebbles found on beaches are round, though they are originally formed from stones and shells which are elongated in shape? Is it because objects whose outer surfaces are far removed from their middle point _[Center of mass]_ are borne along more quickly by the movements to which they are subjected? The middle of such objects acts at the centre and the distance thence to the exterior becomes the radius, and _[(monotonicity)]_ a longer radius always describes a greater circle than a shorter radius when the force which moves them is equal. An object which traverses a greater space in the _[differential calculus?]_ same time travels more quickly, and objects which travel more quickly from an equal distance strike harder against other objects, and the more they strike _[Newton's Third Law?]_ the more they are themselves struck. It follows, therefore, that objects in which the distance from the middle to the exterior is greater always become broken, _[convergence to the sphere]_ and in this process they must necessarily become round. So in the case of pebbles, because the sea moves and they move with it, the result is that they are always in motion, and as they roll about, they come into collision with other objects; and it is their extremities which are necessarily most affected. _[shape evolution]_

_[idea of collective evolution]_

_2000 years old partial differential equation?_

GÁBOR DOMOKOS ANNOTATED QUESTION 15, MINOR WORKS, MECHANICAL PROBLEMS, ARISTOTLE, 1936, ED./TRANSLATED BY WALTER STANLEY HETT

$V = f(R)$

flea left him. 'There's nowhere to hide on a bald tw
lion,' he said and hopped                    it. H
bribed a part-time hairy ant-eater to sit on his head;
really looked like real hair, but the lion got hick-uj
and, each time, hairy ant-eater fell off. 'I'm off,' he sa
(which was obvious as he'd just fallen off). Lion w
heart-broken. 'Sad growls,' he said and then did what r
lion had ever done before, not even in the Ark, he la
himself down on the World and cried. 'Boo-hoo, bo
hairless-hoo.' The animals, having no television, gathere
around him to look and feel sad. 'He must have an ups
tummy,' said a monkey's stomach. 'I would say he's ha
bad news,' said a teenage coconut. 'Rubbish,' said a da
penguin and his cousin. 'Lions never get bad news. N
one can ever get near enough to tell them.' 'I think
know what it is,' said an owl from his bed. 'His grea
great grandfather was a baboon who tried to fly to the su
and he has just heard about it.' All the animals shook the
heads, and some fell off. It wasn't a very good day for th
Jungle or the animals. To make it worse a mole made
mole hill that turned into a mountain and hurt its bacl

Spirit of Spike Milligan, in
take life with a pinch of
absurdity — its the only way
to describe certain things th
happen...
(+ accept) expect the unexpected, follow
the change.

[70]

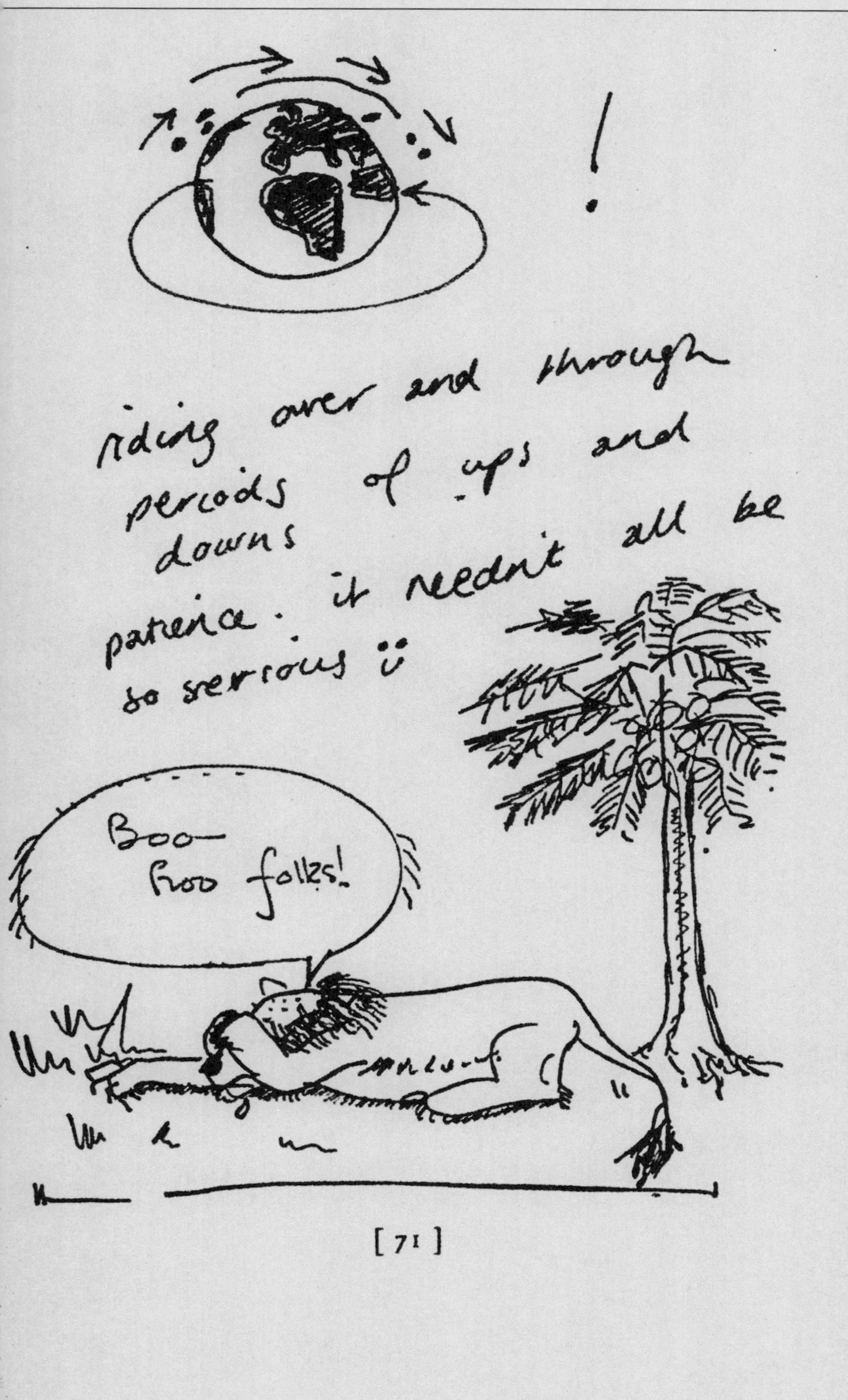

!
riding over and through
periods of ups and
downs
patience. it needn't all be
so serious ¨
Boo—
hoo folks!

their gazes into a sheaf, a skein.

It had been afternoon and raining when we entered the hall. The gray light had soon died out of the slit-windows under the eaves. Now whitish strips of light stretched like slanting phantasmal sails, long triangles and oblongs, from wall to floor, over the faces of the nine; dull scraps and shreds of light from the moon rising over the forest, outside. The fire had burned down long since and there was no light but those strips and slants of dimness creeping across the circle, sketching out a face, a hand, a moveless back. For a while I saw Faxe's profile rigid as pale stone in a diffuse dust of light. The diagonal of moonlight crept on and came to a black hump, the kemmerer, head bowed on his knees, hands clenched on the floor, body shaken by a regular tremor repeated by theslutter-pat-pat of the Zany's hands on stone in darkness across the circle. They were all connected, all of them, as if they were the suspension-points of a spiderweb. I felt, whether I wished or not, the connection, the communication that ran, wordless, inarticulate, through Faxe, and which Faxe was trying to pattern and control, for he was the center, the Weaver. The dim light fragmented and died away creeping up the eastern wall. The web of force, of tension, of silence, grew.

I tried to keep out of contact with the minds of the Foretellers. I was made very uneasy by that silent electric tension, by the sense of being drawn in, of becoming a point or figure in the pattern, in the web. But when I set up a barrier, it was worse: I felt cut off and cowered inside my own mind obsessed by hallucinations of sight and touch, a stew of wild images and notions, abrupt visions and sensations all sexually charged and grotesquely violent, a red-and-black seething of erotic rage. I was surrounded by great gaping pits with ragged lips, vaginas, wounds, hellmouths, I lost my balance, I was falling… If I could not shut out this chaos I would fall indeed, I would go mad, and there was no shutting it out. The empathic and paraverbal forces at work, immensely powerful and confused, rising out of the perversion and frustration of sex, out of an insanity that distorts time, and out of an appalling discipline of total concentration and apprehension of immediate reality, were far beyond my restraint or control. And yet they were controlled: the center was still Faxe. Hours and seconds passed, the moonlight shone on the wrong wall, there was no moonlight only darkness, and in the center of all darkness Faxe: the Weaver: a woman, a woman dressed in light. The light was silver, the silver was armor, an armored woman with a sword. The light burned sudden and intolerable,—the light along her limbs, the fire, and she screamed aloud in terror and pain, "Yes, yes, yes!"

The crooning laugh of the Zany began, "Ah-ah-ah-ah," and rose higher and higher into a wavering yell that went on and on, much longer than any voice could go on yelling, right across time. There was movement in the darkness, scuffling and shuffling, a redistribution of ancient centuries, an evasion of foreshadows. "Light, light," said an immense voice in vast syllables once or innumerable times. "Light. Log on the fire, there. Some light." It was the physician from Spreve. He had entered the circle. It was all broken. He was kneeling by the Zanies, the frailest ones, the fuse-points; both of them lay huddled up on the floor. The kemmerer lay with his head on Faxe's knees, breathing in gasps, still trembling; Faxe's hand, with absent gentleness, stroked his hair. The Pervert was off by himself in a corner, sullen and dejected. The session was over, time passed as usual, the web of power had fallen apart into indignity and weariness. Where was my answer, the riddle of the oracle, the ambiguous utterance of prophecy?

I knelt down beside Faxe. He looked at me with his clear eyes. For that instant I saw him as I had seen him in the dark, as a woman armed in light and burning in a fire, crying out, "Yes—"

Faxe's soft speaking-voice broke the vision. "Are you answered, Asker?"

"I am answered, Weaver."

Indeed I was answered. Five years from now Gethen would be a member of the Ekumen: yes. No riddles, no hedging. Even then I was aware of the quality of that answer, not so much a prophecy as an observation. I could not evade my own certainty that the answer was right. It had the imperative clarity of a hunch.

We have NAFAL ships and instantaneous transmission and mindspeech, but we haven't yet tamed hunch to run in harness; for that trick we must go to Gethen.

"I serve as the filament," Faxe said to me a day or two after the Foretelling. "The energy builds up and builds up in us, always sent back and back, redoubling the impulse every time, until it breaks through and the light is in me, around me, I am the light… The Old Man of Arbin Fastness once said that if the Weaver could be put in a vacuum at the moment of the Answer, he'd go on burning for years. That's what the Yomeshta believe of Meshe: that he saw past and future clear, not for a moment, but all during his life after the Question of Shorth. It's hard to believe. I doubt a man could endure it. But no matter…"

Nusuth, the ubiquitous and ambiguous negative of the Handdara.

We were strolling side by side, and Faxe looked at me. His face, one of the most beautiful human faces I ever saw, seemed hard and delicate as carved stone. "In the darkness," he said, "there were ten; not nine. There was a stranger."

"Yes, there was. I had no barrier against you. You are a Listener, Faxe, a natural empath; and probably a powerful natural telepath as well. That's why you're the Weaver, the one who can keep the tensions and responses of the group running in a self-augmenting pattern until the strain breaks the pattern itself and you reach through for your answer."

He listened with grave interest. "It is strange to see the mysteries of my discipline from outside, through your eyes. I've only seen them from within, as a disciple."

"If you permit—if you wish, Faxe, I should like to communicate with you in mindspeech." I was sure now that he was a natural Communicant; his consent and a little practice should serve to lower his unwitting barrier.

"Once you did that, I would hear what others think?"

"No, no. No more than you do already as an empath. Mindspeech is communication, voluntarily sent and received."

"Then why not speak aloud?"

"Well, one can lie, speaking."

"Not mindspeaking?"

"Not intentionally."

Faxe considered a while. "That's a discipline that must arouse the interest of kings, politicians, men of business.

"Men of business fought against the use of mindspeech when it first was found to be a teachable skill; they outlawed it for decades."

Faxe smiled. "And kings?"

"We have no more kings."

"Yes. I see that… Well, I thank you, Genry. But my business is unlearning, not learning. And I'd rather not yet learn an art that would change the world entirely."

"By your own foretelling this world will change, and within five years."

"And I'll change with it, Genry. But I have no wish to change it."

It was raining, the long, fine rain of Gethenian summer. We walked under the hemmen-trees on the slopes above the Fastness, where there were no paths. Light fell gray among dark branches, clear water dropped from the scarlet needles. The air was chill yet mild, and full of the sound of rain.

"Faxe, tell me this. You Handdarata have a gift that men on every world have craved. You have it. You can predict the future. And yet you live like the rest of us— it doesn't seem to matter—"

."How should it matter, Genry?"

"Well, look. For instance, this rivalry between Karhide and Orgoreyn, this quarrel about the Sinoth Valley. Karhide has lost face badly these last weeks, I gather. Now why didn't King Argaven consult his Foretellers, asking which course to take, or which member of the kyorremy to choose as prime minister, or something of that sort?"

"The questions are hard to ask."

"I don't see why. He might simply ask, Who'll serve me best as prime minister?—and leave it at that."

"He might. But he doesn't know whatserving him best may mean. It might mean the man chosen would surrender the valley to Orgoreyn, or go into exile, or assassinate the king; it might mean many things he wouldn't expect or accept."

"He'd have to make his question very precise."

"Yes. Then there'd be many questions, you see. Even the king must pay the price."

"You'd charge him high?"

"Very high," said Faxe tranquilly. "The Asker pays what he can afford, as you know. Kings have in fact come to the Foretellers; but not very often…"

"What if one of the Foretellers is himself a powerful man?"

"Indwellers of the Fastness have no ranks or status. I may be sent to Erhenrang to the kyorremy; well, if I go, I take back my status and my shadow, but my foretelling's at an end. If I had a question while I served in the kyorremy, I'd go to Orgny Fastness there, pay my price, and get my answer. But we in the Handdara don't want answers. It's hard to avoid them, but we try to."

"Faxe, I don't think I understand."

"Well, we come here to the Fastnesses mostly to learn what questions not to ask."

"But you're the Answerers!"

"You don't see yet, Genry, why we perfected and practice Foretelling?"

"No—"

"To exhibit the perfect uselessness of knowing the answer to the wrong question."

I pondered that a good while, as we walked side by side through the rain, under the dark branches of the Forest of Otherhord. Within the white hood Faxe's face was tired and quiet, its light quenched. Yet he still awed me a little. When he looked at me with his clear, kind, candid eyes, he looked at me out of a tradition thirteen thousand years old: a way of thought and way of life so old, so well established, so integral and coherent as to give a human being the unselfconsciousness, the authority, the completeness of a wild animal, a great strange creature who looks straight at you out of his eternal present…

"The unknown," said Faxe's soft voice in the forest, "the unforetold, the unproven, that is what life is based on. Ignorance is the ground of thought. Unproof is the ground of action. If it were proven that there is no God there would be no religion. No Handdara, no Yomesh, no hearthgods, nothing. But also if it were proven that there is a God, there would be no religion… Tell me, Genry, what is known? What is sure, predictable, inevitable—the one certain thing you know concerning your future, and mine?"

"That we shall die."

"Yes. There's really only one question that can be answered, Genry, and we already know the answer. … The only thing that makes life possible is permanent, intolerable uncertainty: not knowing what comes next."

6. One Way into Orgoreyn

Contents-Prev /Next

the cook, whowas always at the house very early, woke me up; I sleep sound, and he had to shake me and say in my ear, "Wake up, wake up, Lord Estraven, there's a runner come from the King's House!" At last I understood him, and confused by sleep and urgency got up in haste and went to the door of my room, where the messenger waited, and so I entered stark naked and stupid as a newborn child into my exile.

**Snow**

Walking through a field with my little brother Seth

I pointed to a place where kids had made angels in the snow.
For some reason, I told him that a troop of angels
had been shot and dissolved when they hit the ground.

He asked who had shot them and I said a farmer.

Then we were on the roof of the lake.
The ice looked like a photograph of water.

Why he asked. Why did he shoot them.

I didn't know where I was going with this.

They were on his property, I said.


When it's snowing, the outdoors seem like a room.

Today I traded hellos with my neighbor.
Our voices hung close in the new acoustics.
A room with the walls blasted to shreds and falling.

We returned to our shoveling, working side by side in silence.


But why were they on his property, he asked.

—David Berman

## Top 100 Living Artists
### 2011—2014

| RANK | ARTIST | VALUE SOLD (USD)* | LOTS SOLD* |
|---|---|---|---|
| 1 | Gerhard Richter (b.1932) | $839,444,861 | 893 |
| 2 | Jeff Koons (b.1955) | $286,954,285 | 436 |
| 3 | Zeng Fanzhi (b.1964) | $241,137,224 | 227 |
| 4 | Christopher Wool (b.1955) | $182,865,836 | 188 |
| 5 | Cui Ruzhuo (b.1944) | $177,257,855 | 202 |
| 6 | Fan Zeng (b.1938) | $163,932,683 | 1441 |
| 7 | Richard Prince (b.1949) | $109,426,554 | 249 |
| 8 | Damien Hirst (b.1965) | $107,212,136 | 1126 |
| 9 | Zhou Chunya (b.1955) | $106,175,069 | 377 |
| 10 | Peter Doig (b.1959) | $105,225,320 | 154 |
| 11 | Zhang Xiaogang (b.1958) | $104,677,133 | 197 |
| 12 | Yayoi Kusama (b.1929) | $101,297,426 | 1744 |
| 13 | Hu Jiaying (b.1957) | $94,231,232 | 406 |
| 14 | Wayne Thiebaud (b.1920) | $92,240,611 | 256 |
| 15 | Huang Yongyu (b.1924) | $31,310,369 | 955 |
| 16 | Pierre Soulages (b.1919) | $69,936,445 | 418 |
| 17 | Fernando Botero (b.1932) | $67,938,713 | 267 |
| 18 | Ju Ming (b.1938) | $67,641,667 | 384 |
| 19 | Luo Zhongli (b.1948) | $66,742,000 | 279 |
| 20 | Liu Wei (b.1965) | $66,333,212 | 166 |
| 21 | Ed Ruscha (b.1937) | $65,477,064 | 529 |
| 22 | Georg Baselitz (b.1938) | $62,510,703 | 365 |
| 23 | Takashi Murakami (b.1962) | $59,412,502 | 1776 |
| 24 | Wang Yidong (b.1955) | $56,980,415 | 135 |
| 25 | Cindy Sherman (b.1954) | $55,072,913 | 371 |
| 26 | Anselm Kiefer (b.1945) | $54,374,713 | 125 |
| 27 | Andreas Gursky (b.1955) | $54,102,579 | 135 |
| 28 | Jin Shangyi (b.1934) | $53,584,316 | 37 |
| 29 | Anish Kapoor (b.1954) | $53,356,356 | 162 |
| 30 | Mark Grotjahn (b.1968) | $52,258,670 | 71 |
| 31 | Robert Indiana (b.1928) | $52,049,519 | 614 |
| 32 | David Hockney (b.1937) | $51,739,303 | 1414 |
| 33 | Enrico Castellani (b.1930) | $50,088,400 | 187 |
| 34 | Chen Peiqiu (b.1922) | $49,338,477 | 892 |
| 35 | Rudolf Stingel (b.1956) | $48,901,936 | 90 |
| 36 | Yoshitomo Nara (b.1959) | $47,787,909 | 595 |
| 37 | Fang Lijun (b.1963) | $47,467,278 | 133 |
| 38 | Liu DaWei (b.1945) | $46,862,884 | 539 |
| 39 | Shi Guoliang (b.1956) | $46,040,508 | 537 |
| 40 | Yang Feiyun (b.1954) | $46,013,646 | 93 |
| 41 | Wang Mingming (b.1952) | $45,580,591 | 653 |
| 42 | Jia Youfu (b.1942) | $45,293,712 | 382 |
| 43 | Liu Ye (b.1964) | $45,167,818 | 163 |
| 44 | Frank Stella (b.1936) | $44,418,104 | 574 |
| 45 | Robert Ryman (b.1930) | $44,035,421 | 46 |
| 46 | Ai Xuan (b.1947) | $42,862,387 | 168 |
| 47 | Lee Ufan (b.1936) | $41,362,521 | 298 |
| 48 | Glenn Brown (b.1966) | $41,187,253 | 21 |
| 49 | Wade Guyton (b.1972) | $40,326,862 | 75 |
| 50 | Ellsworth Kelly (b.1923) | $36,030,912 | 388 |



*Handwritten annotations (right margin):*

Research —
cross reference
to taxes paid,
sales tax etc.

duty free ports?

Sales by country
where sold
where bought
where stored
capital flows
comparison to
original price
paid to artist —

Should artists get
share of profit?
Do they indirectly
profit?

how so?



**137**

| Rank | | Artist | Total Sales | Lots |
|---|---|---|---|---|
| 51 | - | Miquel Barceló (b.1957) | $35,802,977 | 120 |
| 52 | | John Currin (b.1962) | $34,152,580 | 42 |
| 53 | | Jasper Johns (b.1930) | $33,483,256 | 457 |
| 54 | - | Sayed Haider Raza (b.1922) | $33,353,407 | 265 |
| 55 | ▼ | Frank Auerbach (b.1931) | $32,880,513 | 101 |
| 56 | ▼ | Liu Xiaodong (b.1963) | $32,393,624 | 45 |
| 57 | - | Michelangelo Pistoletto (b.1933) | $31,859,547 | 342 |
| 58 | - | Yue Minjun (b.1962) | $31,791,261 | 149 |
| 59 | ▼ | Wang Zhwu (b.1936) | $30,964,525 | 376 |
| 60 | - | George Condo (b.1957) | $30,906,113 | 258 |
| 61 | - | Sean Scully (b.1945) | $28,425,887 | 216 |
| 62 | - | Günther Uecker (b.1930) | $28,145,127 | 419 |
| 63 | - | Liu Wenxi (b.1933) | $27,783,547 | 357 |
| 64 | ▼ | Fang Chuxiong (b.1950) | $27,673,560 | 874 |
| 65 | - | Xue Liang (b.1956) | $27,458,749 | 462 |
| 66 | ▼ | Urs Fischer (b.1973) | $27,201,805 | 44 |
| 67 | ▼ | Brice Marden (b.1938) | $26,926,358 | 100 |
| 68 | - | Fan Yang (b.1955) | $25,057,593 | 733 |
| 69 | | Antony Gormley (b.1950) | $24,519,263 | 109 |
| 70 | . | Albert Oehlen (b.1954) | $24,286,953 | 24 |
| 71 | - | Tian Liming (b.1955) | $22,921,996 | 377 |
| 72 | ▼ | Zhou Yansheng (b.1942) | $22,726,808 | 261 |
| 73 | . | Song Yugui (b.1940) | $22,584,071 | 166 |
| 74 | - | Thomas Schütte (b.1954) | $22,569,264 | 67 |
| 75 | - | David Hammons (b.1943) | $22,384,006 | 30 |
| 76 | - | Xu Lele (b.1955) | $22,235,100 | 442 |
| 77 | ▼ | Lin Yong (b.1942) | $21,810,955 | 688 |
| 78 | - | Maurizio Cattelan (b.1960) | $21,656,347 | 90 |
| 79 | | Wang Guangyi (b.1957) | $21,511,774 | 142 |
| 80 | | Bridget Riley (b.1931) | $21,306,013 | 745 |
| 81 | | Yang Zhiguang (b.1930) | $20,936,726 | 564 |
| 82 | . | Marc Quinn (b.1964) | $20,786,023 | 161 |
| 83 | | | $20,692,991 | 512 |
| 84 | ▼ | Mark Bradford (b.1961) | $20,601,069 | 15 |
| 85 | . | Mark Tansey (b.1949) | $19,808,583 | 20 |
| 86 | | Chen Danqing (b.1953) | $19,202,456 | 72 |
| 87 | | Guo Runwen (b.1955) | $18,924,620 | 75 |
| 88 | . | Banksy (b.1974) | $18,225,807 | 428 |
| 89 | | Richard Serra (b.1939) | $18,186,670 | 219 |
| 90 | - | Ren Zhong (b.1976) | $18,159,439 | 200 |
| 91 | . | Martial Raysse (b.1936) | $17,940,056 | 55 |
| 92 | - | Feng Yuan (b.1952) | $17,419,977 | 268 |
| 93 | ▼ | Julie Mehretu (b.1970) | $17,352,069 | 41 |
| 94 | - | Carlos Cruz-Diez (b.1923) | $17,176,492 | 166 |
| 95 | - | He Duoling (b.1948) | $17,097,742 | 79 |
| 96 | ▼ | Vija Celmins (b.1938) | $17,021,887 | 78 |
| 97 | . | Manolo Valdés (b.1942) | $16,995,172 | 125 |
| 98 | ▼ | Howard Terpning (b.1927) | $16,868,229 | 56 |
| 99 | . | Lang Jun (b.1963) | $16,671,646 | 115 |
| 100 | ▼ | Shen Peng (b.1931) | $16,362,411 | 874 |

*Measured from January 1, 2011 through October 31, 2014.
Arrows indicate a change in rank from the previous month.

**artnet** analytics

Data courtesy of artnet Analytics.

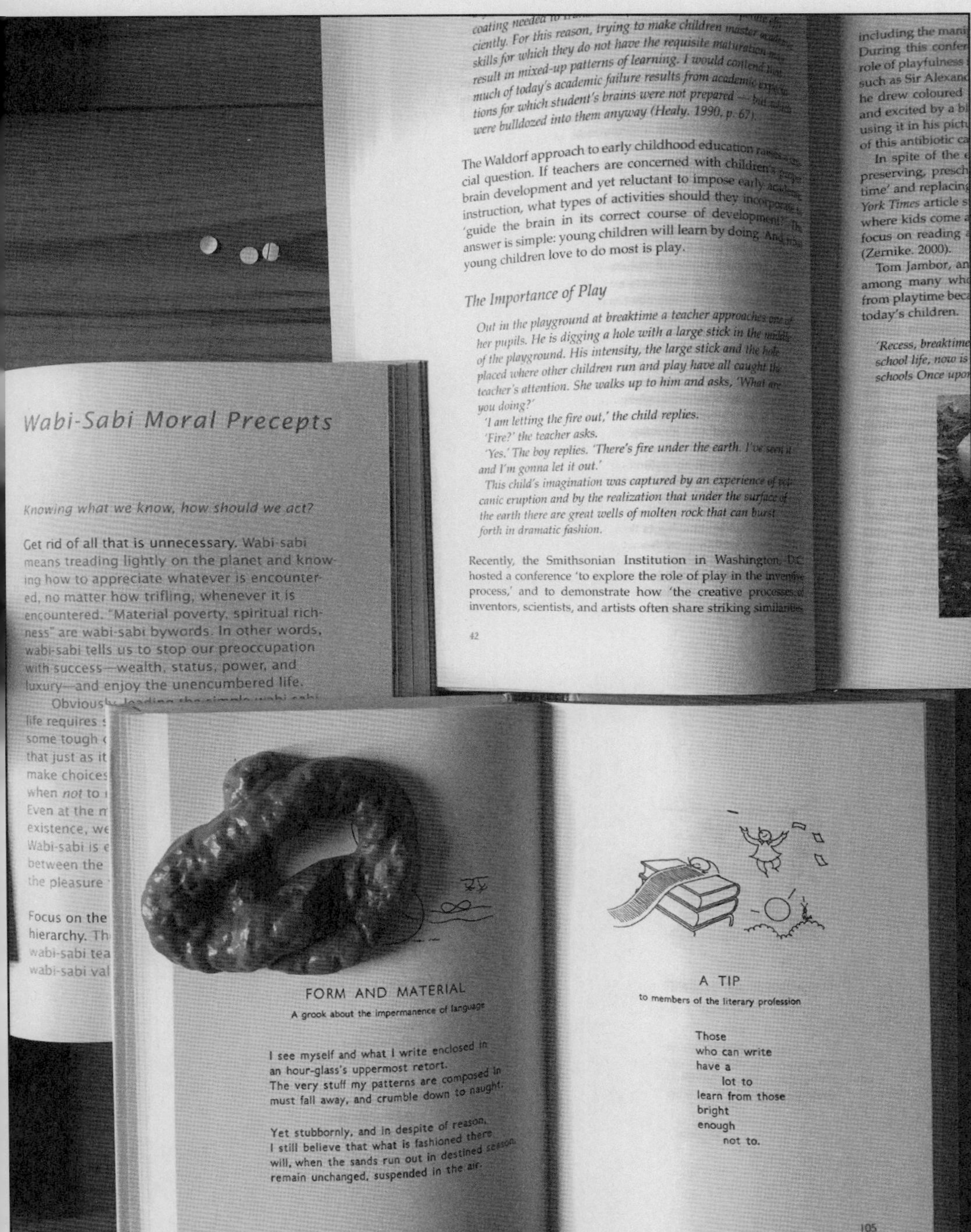

coating needed to tra...
ciently. For this reason, trying to make children master academic
skills for which they do not have the requisite maturation...
result in mixed-up patterns of learning. I would contend that
much of today's academic failure results from academic expectations for which student's brains were not prepared — but which
were bulldozed into them anyway (Healy, 1990, p. 67).

The Waldorf approach to early childhood education raises a crucial question. If teachers are concerned with children's proper
brain development and yet reluctant to impose early academic
instruction, what types of activities should they incorporate to
'guide the brain in its correct course of development?' The
answer is simple: young children will learn by doing. And what
young children love to do most is play.

The Importance of Play

Out in the playground at breaktime a teacher approaches one of
her pupils. He is digging a hole with a large stick in the middle
of the playground. His intensity, the large stick and the hole
placed where other children run and play have all caught the
teacher's attention. She walks up to him and asks, 'What are
you doing?'
'I am letting the fire out,' the child replies.
'Fire?' the teacher asks.
'Yes.' The boy replies. 'There's fire under the earth. I've seen it
and I'm gonna let it out.'
This child's imagination was captured by an experience of volcanic eruption and by the realization that under the surface of
the earth there are great wells of molten rock that can burst
forth in dramatic fashion.

Recently, the Smithsonian Institution in Washington, D.C.
hosted a conference 'to explore the role of play in the inventive
process,' and to demonstrate how 'the creative processes of
inventors, scientists, and artists often share striking similarities'

42

including the man...
During this confer...
role of playfulness...
such as Sir Alexan...
he drew coloured...
and excited by a bl...
using it in his pictu...
of this antibiotic ca...
In spite of the e...
preserving, presch...
time' and replacing...
York Times article s...
where kids come a...
focus on reading...
(Zernike, 2000).
Tom Jambor, an...
among many who...
from playtime beca...
today's children.

'Recess, breaktime...
school life, now is...
schools Once upon...

Wabi-Sabi Moral Precepts

Knowing what we know, how should we act?

Get rid of all that is unnecessary. Wabi-sabi
means treading lightly on the planet and knowing how to appreciate whatever is encountered, no matter how trifling, whenever it is
encountered. "Material poverty, spiritual richness" are wabi-sabi bywords. In other words,
wabi-sabi tells us to stop our preoccupation
with success—wealth, status, power, and
luxury—and enjoy the unencumbered life.
Obviously, leading the simple wabi-sabi
life requires
some tough
that just as it
make choices
when not to
Even at the m
existence, we
Wabi-sabi is e
between the
the pleasure

Focus on the
hierarchy. Th
wabi-sabi tea
wabi-sabi val

FORM AND MATERIAL
A grook about the impermanence of language

I see myself and what I write enclosed in
an hour-glass's uppermost retort.
The very stuff my patterns are composed in
must fall away, and crumble down to naught;

Yet stubbornly, and in despite of reason,
I still believe that what is fashioned there
will, when the sands run out in destined season,
remain unchanged, suspended in the air.

104

A TIP
to members of the literary profession

Those
who can write
have a
    lot to
learn from those
bright
enough
    not to.

105

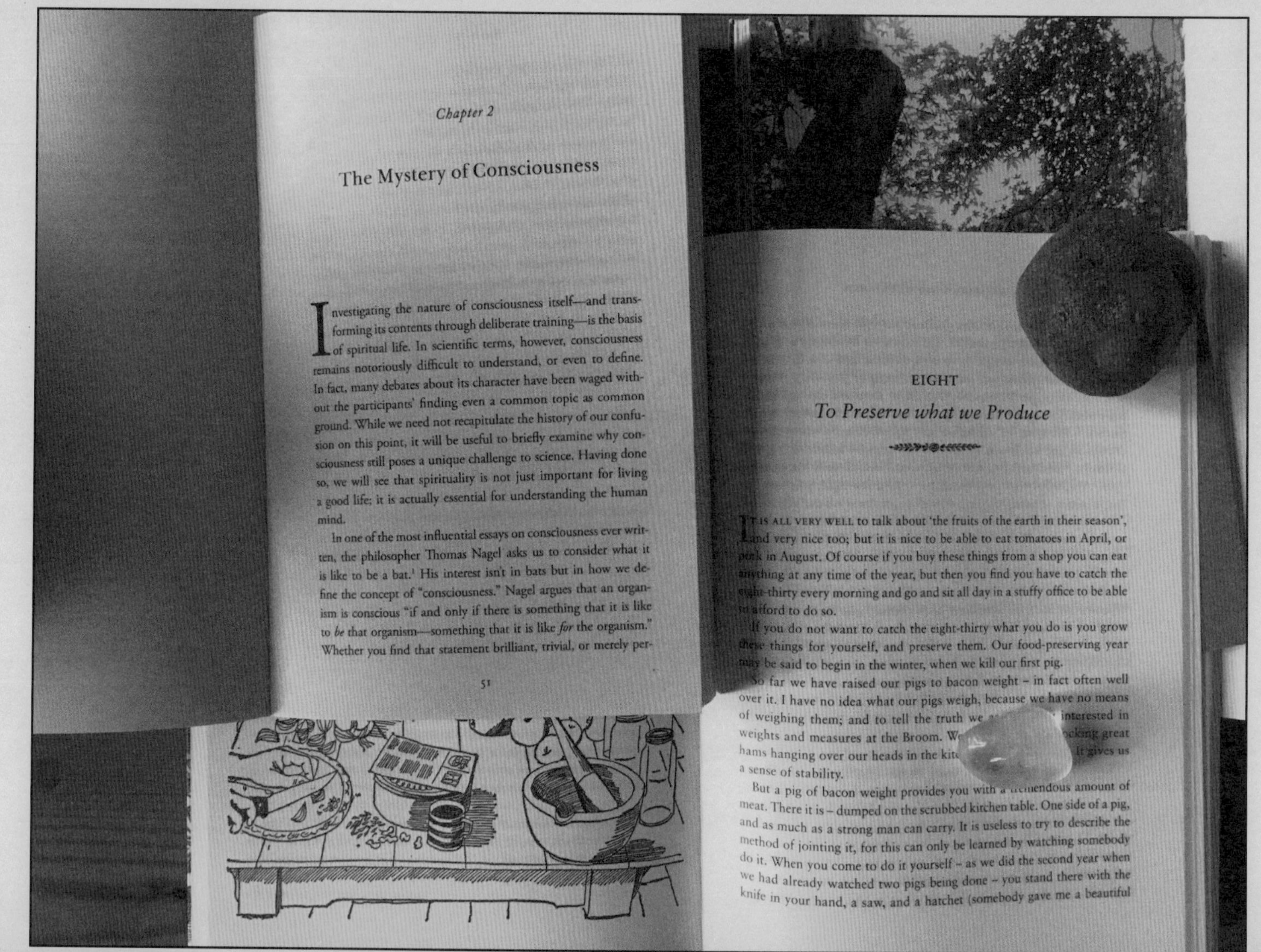



# The Mystery of Consciousness

Investigating the nature of consciousness itself—and transforming its contents through deliberate training—is the basis of spiritual life. In scientific terms, however, consciousness remains notoriously difficult to understand, or even to define. In fact, many debates about its character have been waged without the participants' finding even a common topic as common ground. While we need not recapitulate the history of our confusion on this point, it will be useful to briefly examine why consciousness still poses a unique challenge to science. Having done so, we will see that spirituality is not just important for living a good life; it is actually essential for understanding the human mind.

In one of the most influential essays on consciousness ever written, the philosopher Thomas Nagel asks us to consider what it is like to be a bat.[1] His interest isn't in bats but in how we define the concept of "consciousness." Nagel argues that an organism is conscious "if and only if there is something that it is like to *be* that organism—something that it is like *for the organism*." Whether you find that statement brilliant, trivial, or merely per-



---



## EIGHT

## *To Preserve what we Produce*

It is all very well to talk about 'the fruits of the earth in their season', and very nice too; but it is nice to be able to eat tomatoes in April, or pork in August. Of course if you buy these things from a shop you can eat anything at any time of the year, but then you find you have to catch the eight-thirty every morning and go and sit all day in a stuffy office to be able to afford to do so.

If you do not want to catch the eight-thirty what you do is you grow these things for yourself, and preserve them. Our food-preserving year may be said to begin in the winter, when we kill our first pig.

So far we have raised our pigs to bacon weight – in fact often well over it. I have no idea what our pigs weigh, because we have no means of weighing them; and to tell the truth we are not very interested in weights and measures at the Broom. We find the sight of these great hams hanging over our heads in the kitchen reassuring. It gives us a sense of stability.

But a pig of bacon weight provides you with a tremendous amount of meat. There it is – dumped on the scrubbed kitchen table. One side of a pig, and as much as a strong man can carry. It is useless to try to describe the method of jointing it, for this can only be learned by watching somebody do it. When you come to do it yourself – as we did the second year when we had already watched two pigs being done – you stand there with the knife in your hand, a saw, and a hatchet (somebody gave me a beautiful

## SOUND AND SEMBLANCE

*—"mu" twenty-sixth part—*

A sand-anointed wind spoke of
survival, wood scratched raw,
  scoured bough. And of low sky
    poked at by branches,    blown
rush,    thrown voice,    legbone
            flute…
  Wind we all filled up with caught
  in the tree we lay underneath…
Tree filled up with wind and more
            wind,

more than could be said of it said…
  So-called ascendancy of shadow,
  branch, would-be roost, now not
    only a tree, more than a tree…

It was the bending of boughs we'd
  read about, Ibn 'Arabi's reft
ipseity, soon-come condolence,
             thetic
  sough. We saved our breath, barely
            moved,

  said nothing, soon-come suzerainty
volubly afoot,    braided what we'd
read and what we heard and what
  stayed sayless,    giggly wind,
            wood,
riffling wuh…    A Moroccan
  reed-flute's desert wheeze took
  our breath,    floor we felt we
    stood on, caustic earth we rode
across… It was Egypt or Tennessee
            we
  were in. No one, eyes exed out,
  could say which. Fleet, millenarian
  we it now was whose arrival the wind
            an-

nounced

55





---

Handwritten annotations:

- wind / wind instrument
- Sunni Islam / Sufism / Sufi mystic, / poet, and / philosopher / "the great / master" and / also "genuine / saint" / overlord
- eyes exed out
- "containing a / thousand"
- reft – past tense of reave / & / rob (a person or / place) of / something by / force
- 'ipseity – noun. selfhood; / individual identity; / individuality.'
- theft / reft ipseity – to steal somebody / of Ibn 'Arabi's / personhood
- reft breath – stolen breath / stolen song
- thetic is the term applied to every collection of / dogmatical propositions. The Critique of Pure / Reason – KANT.

Night found us the far side of
Steal-Away Ridge, eyes crossed
out, X's what were left, nameless
what we saw we not-saw. We ducked
and ran, rained on by tree-sap,
dreaming,
chattered at by wind and leaf-stir,
more than we'd have dreamt or
thought. We lay on our backs looking
up at the limbs of the tree we lay
underneath, leaves our pneumatic
book,
*We lay on our backs'* unceased reprise.

North of us was all an emolument,
more than we'd have otherwise run.
We worked at crevices, cracks,
convinced we'd pry love loose,
wrote
our names out seven times in dove's
blood,
kings and queens, crowned ourselves
in sound. Duke was there,   Pres, Lady,
Count,   Pharoah came later. The
Soon-Come Congress we'd heard so much
about, soon come even sooner south…
So
there was a new mood suddenly, blue
but uptempo,
parsed, bitten into,   all of us got our
share… Pecks what had been kisses, beaks
what once were lips, other than we
were as we lay under tree limbs, red-beaked
birds
known as muni what we were, heads crowned
in
sound only in
sound

the studio. I built a table, put my goggles on, and cut stone month after month. I learned a lot about stone. And I didn't make one piece of sculpture that I wanted to show anybody. People would come to the studio and I would throw quilting over whatever I was working on. I took ·this piece into the backyard here, set it up, and started to cut the final piece of limestone. I began to move the limestone around the table and it became an activity. Every day I would go outdoors and move this piece of limestone from one corner of the table to the other, occasionally hitting it with a hammer, occasionally getting sort of angry at it, and literally bouncing it until it looked in the right position to be cut into this unnamed sculpture. After a couple of weeks I realized that that's what it's all about, and literally just placed it on the table, paying absolutely no attention to how I placed it. I think I went out for a drink and told people that I had finally solved my problem about how to make a limestone sculpture. I invited a lot of artists back and, with flashlights and candles, presented my piece of sculpture. Surprisingly enough, not only did it satisfy my needs at the moment, it satisfied theirs. I realized sculpture was about "Put in Place," volume or mass put in place. It's a matter of transportation; you move it from one place to the other, which was a rejection of the Duchampian ethic. I still find myself engaged in rejecting the idea that changing the context of a material constitutes an aesthetic gesture. I think that all materials normally change their context and it's not necessarily an aesthetic gesture. There is nothing that's not out of context.

**LG:** Can you explain further your interest in materials?

**LW:** Sure. I honestly cannot explain it in the terms that I would have explained it in the sixties because I don't remember them. For me, it seems to be now that art essentially is the relationship of human beings to objects and objects to objects in relation to human beings. The way that human beings understand their relationships to materials always relates back to a human being's use of it. If that's our activity as artists, then there is no other need for justification. It took a long time to get that straight. Art is not a metaphor, although it can function as metaphor in the culture sometimes. It also functions as illustration in the culture. But just because something functions as something within a culture does not mean that that's inherently what it is. Human beings function as soldiers and as rapists, but that

is not the definition of human being. Sometimes I used material as metaphor. The nice thing about using language is that you don't have to subjugate your own personality to make an objective piece of work. The work itself is objective in its relationship of one material to another, but you know what things stand for. A reasonable example is *RED AS WELL AS GREEN AS WELL AS BLUE*, a book I did in '72, where for the purpose of building the sculpture, I completely ignore the context of what red, green, and blue mean politically.* When the book

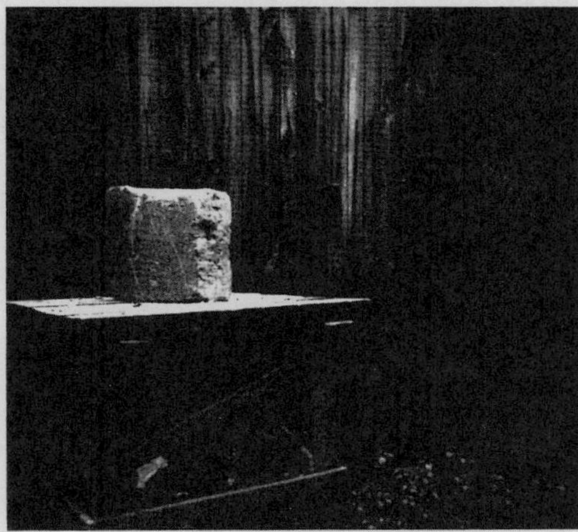

*Untitled*, 1960–62. Limestone and wood, dimensions unknown.

was finished, it had two different meanings; the work on the wall has two different meanings. We made a videotape with Kathryn Bigelow doing a commentary on it, called *RED AS WELL AS GREEN AS WELL AS BLUE*, where we discussed the fact that we know red means "left," blue is invariably a working-class color, and green is a fascist color.** We accepted that, so one can use that to talk about their feelings about politics at the time—and it was a very heavy time because of Vietnam. But the work itself was out of this immediate political context. When it was recently reshown in London in 1981, it was sold to a Belgian collector who bought it on the assumption that the work itself stood for the relationship of red to green to blue, not its political connotations, which are now becoming old-fashioned. They don't work any longer. We know it is historical because we know the thirties, the fifties. But that's about as close as it gets.

---

* Lawrence Weiner, *GREEN AS WELL AS BLUE AS WELL AS RED*, London: Jack Wendler, 1972.
** Lawrence Weiner, *GREEN AS WELL AS BLUE AS WELL AS RED*, produced by Moved Pictures, New York, 1975–76; see pp. 77–79 in the present volume.



SEAN EDWARDS ANNOTATED HAVING BEEN SAID: WRITINGS AND INTERVIEWS OF LAWRENCE WEINER 1968–2003, 2004, LAWRENCE WEINER, ED. BY GERTI FIETZEK & GREGOR STEMMRICH

**LG:** Are you conscious of how your attitudes toward your work have changed?

**LW:** As far as I can imagine, I'm conscious of it, but we all have this problem, we might be deluding ourselves that we're always aware of what we're doing.

**LG:** Looking back, do you see certain work as being more successful?

**LW:** Yes.

**LG:** How do you determine that?

**LW:** By its use to me as an artist today. When I rummage through papers, drawings, or an old notebook and start to work off of that, it is almost as a practice session, the way a musician would sit down and practice. There are still areas within that perception or insight that are useful today in relationship to materials, and as you grow older you learn more about the materials you use every day. I'd say the most successful works were the ones that allow themselves to be reused or reworked. Not because of their historical placement, but because of their content. I still believe that the content, not the context, is the reason for artists making art.

**LG:** "Put in Place" then has its relevance in both terms of the sculpture and the statement that was first published in 1978 [1977].

**LW:** Yes it does. In Geneva I wanted to make a piece that was complex, yet totally understandable to the public. What I did was make a sound tape involved with "Put in Place"* and devise a game in which I was able to take what I had learned from the limestone and place it within the context of a new work. I rather like to do that sometimes. It's a good way as well for checking out work that you are sentimentally attached to. You never know whether or not it's any good unless you try to reuse it.

**LG:** When you're working in the studio, do you always construct the pieces? Or is it sufficient to know that the pieces can be constructed?

**LW:** All of the work that's been presented publicly in language has the possibility of being built. It might sound a little simplistic, but it's really important that the artist can build a piece. A piece can be fabricated or it can just be presented in its language form. I wouldn't say I did anything regularly. When I find myself with materials I don't quite understand, I go out and schlepp a lot of it to the studio. I'm still basically a studio artist. I play with materials, I'll build a piece, I'll schlepp in stone, I'll make ice, I'll do the whole thing. I see that as research. For example, if you're not sure what the modular flexibility of a piece of plywood is, and you're working on an piece about a piece of plywood, you set up vises and a measuring device. You bend the plywood and build up your modules—I'm in the middle of doing that right now for a piece on glaciers.** But the central thing is basic research between the relation of human beings to objects.

**LG:** One thing that comes out in the early paintings as well is the importance of the receiver in determining whether or not the work may be constructed, its size, color, etc.

**LW:** I think that honestly and truly has been an obsession of mine since I was a teenager. When you deal with things as philosophical relationships to society, you begin to realize that the content is the most essential thing. It's not the context, but the content of what you're presenting. When one makes art, it

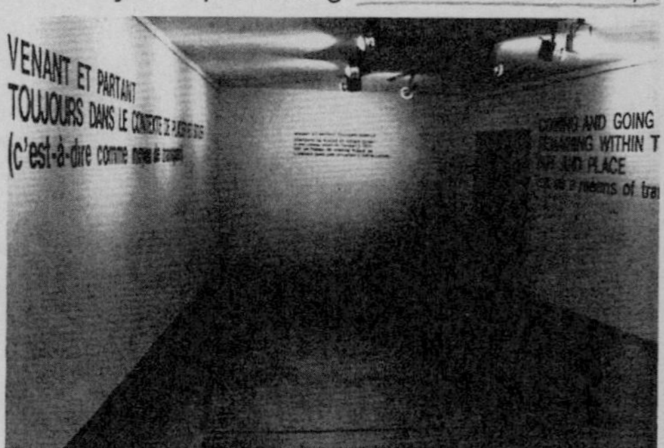


COMING AND GOING REMAINING WITHIN THE CONTEXT OF PUT AND PLACE (i.e. as a means of transport), Cat. #448 (1977). Installation, Centre d'art contemporain, Salle Patiño, Geneva, 21 September–20 October 1977.

is always for other people. It sounds very pretentious and very humanist, and I'm not a humanist, but you make art essentially to communicate your perceptions of the relationship of human beings to objects to other people. In other words, if I was stranded on a desert island, would I make art? If I didn't think that there was any chance that I'd be found, I would say I wouldn't make art. There'd be no need to make art. When I present something in public, I'm convinced that I know what it's about. If

---

* "COMING & GOING" (1977) on Weiner's audio cassette, *THE PERFORMANCE TAPES*, New York: Moved Pictures, [1984]. See also Weiner's book *COMING AND GOING / VENANT ET PARTANT*, Geneva: Centre d'art contemporain / Ecart Publications, 1977.

** A MASS OF SUFFICIENT QUANTITY MOVED A SUFFICIENT DISTANCE TO LEAVE HUMPS AND BOSSES IN THE WAKE OF PROGRESS (ROCHES MOUTONNÉES) and PRESSURE SUFFICIENT TO FORM AN ICE OF MASS ENOUGH TO CARRY UPON WITHIN AND BENEATH ITSELF SOME OF THAT WITHIN THE VECTOR OF MOTION, Cat. #489 and #490 (1982). Both works were first shown in 1983 at David Bellman Gallery, Toronto.

# Carbon

he reader, at this point, will have realized for some time now that this is not a chemical treatise: my presumption does not reach so far – '*ma voix est foible, et même un peu profane.*' Nor is it an autobiography, save in the partial and symbolic limits in which every piece of writing is autobiographical, indeed every human work; but it is in some fashion a history.

It is – or would have liked to be – a micro-history, the history of a trade and its defeats, victories, and miseries, such as everyone wants to tell when he feels close to concluding the arc of his career, and art ceases to be long. Having reached this point in life, what chemist, facing the Periodic Table, or the monumental indices of Beilstein or Landolt, does not perceive scattered among them the sad tatters, or trophies, of his own professional past? He only has to leaf through any treatise and memories rise up in bunches: there is among us he who has tied his destiny, indelibly, to bromine or to propylene, or the -NCO group, or glutamic acid; and every chemistry student, faced by almost any treatise, should be aware that on one of those pages, perhaps in a single line, formula, or word, his future is written in indecipherable characters, which, however, will become clear 'afterward': after success, error, or guilt, victory or defeat. Every no longer young chemist, turning again to the *verhängnisvoll* page in that same treatise, is struck by love or disgust, delights or despairs.

So it happens, therefore, that every element says something to someone (something different to each) like the mountain valleys or beaches visited in youth. One must perhaps make an exception for carbon, because it says everything to everyone, that is, it is not specific, in the same way that Adam is not specific as an ancestor – unless one discovers today (why

not?) the chemist-stylite who has dedicated his life to graphite or the diamond. And yet it is exactly to this carbon that I have an old debt, contracted during what for me were decisive days. To carbon, the element of life, my first literary dream was turned, insistently dreamed in an hour and a place when my life was not worth much: yes, I wanted to tell the story of an atom of carbon.

Is it right to speak of a 'particular' atom of carbon? For the chemist there exist some doubts, because until 1970 he did not have the techniques permitting him to see, or in any event isolate, a single atom; no doubts exist for the narrator, who therefore sets out to narrate.

Our character lies for hundreds of millions of years, bound to three atoms of oxygen and one of calcium, in the form of limestone: it already has a very long cosmic history behind it, but we shall ignore it. For it time does not exist, or exists only in the form of sluggish variations in temperature, daily or seasonal, if, for the good fortune of this tale, its position is not too far from the earth's surface. Its existence, whose monotony cannot be thought of without horror, is a pitiless alternation of hots and colds, that is, of oscillations (always of equal frequency) a trifle more restricted and a trifle more ample: an imprisonment, for this potentially living personage, worthy of the Catholic Hell. To it, until this moment, the present tense is suited, which is that of description, rather than the past tense, which is that of narration – it is congealed in an eternal present, barely scratched by the moderate quivers of thermal agitation.

But, precisely for the good fortune of the narrator, whose story could otherwise have come to an end, the limestone rock ledge of which the atom forms a part lies on the surface. It lies within reach of man and his pickax (all honor to the pickax and its modern equivalents; they are still the most important intermediaries in the millennial dialogue between the elements and man): at any moment – which I, the narrator, decide out of pure caprice to be the year 1840 – a blow of the pickax detached it and sent it on its way to the lime kiln, plunging it into the world of things that change. It was roasted until it separated from the calcium, which remained so to speak with its feet on the ground and went to meet a less brilliant destiny, which we shall not narrate. Still firmly clinging to two of its three former oxygen companions, it issued from the chimney

*(the pickax has its own story, wooden handle, steel head)*



and took the path of the air. Its story, which once was immobile, now turned tumultuous.

It was caught by the wind, flung down on the earth, lifted ten kilometers high. It was breathed in by a falcon, descending into its precipitous lungs, but did not penetrate its rich blood and was expelled. It dissolved three times in the water of the sea, once in the water of a cascading torrent, and again was expelled. It traveled with the wind for eight years: now high, now low, on the sea and among the clouds, over forests, deserts, and limitless expanses of ice; then it stumbled into capture and the organic adventure.

Carbon, in fact, is a singular element: it is the only element that can bind itself in long stable chains without a great expense of energy, and for life on earth (the only one we know so far) precisely long chains are required. Therefore carbon is the key element of living substance: but its promotion, its entry into the living world, is not easy and must follow an obligatory, intricate path, which has been clarified (and not yet definitively) only in recent years. If the elaboration of carbon were not a common daily occurrence, on the scale of billions of tons a week, wherever the green of a leaf appears, it would by full right deserve to be called a miracle.

The atom we are speaking of, accompanied by its two satellites which maintained it in a gaseous state, was therefore borne by the wind along a row of vines in the year 1848. It had the good fortune to brush against a leaf, penetrate it, and be nailed there by a ray of the sun. If my language here becomes imprecise and allusive, it is not only because of my ignorance: this decisive event, this instantaneous work *a tre* – of the (3) carbon dioxide, the light, and the vegetal greenery – has not yet been described in definitive terms, and perhaps it will not be for a long time to come, so different is it from that other 'organic' chemistry which is the cumbersome, slow, and ponderous work of man: and yet this refined, minute, and quick-witted chemistry was 'invented' two or three billion years ago by our silent sisters, the plants, which do not experiment and do not discuss, and whose temperature is identical to that of the environment in which they live. If to comprehend is the same as forming an image, we will never form an image of a happening* whose scale is a



millionth of a millimeter, whose rhythm is a millionth of a second, and whose protagonists are in their essence invisible. Every verbal description must be inadequate, and one will be as good as the next, so let us settle for the following description.

Our atom of carbon enters the leaf, colliding with other innumerable (but here useless) molecules of nitrogen and oxygen. It adheres to a large and complicated molecule that activates it, and simultaneously receives the decisive message from the sky, in the flashing form of a packet of solar light: in an instant, like an insect caught by a spider, it is separated from its oxygen, combined with hydrogen and (one thinks) phosphorus, and finally inserted in a chain, whether long or short does not matter, but it is the chain of life. All this happens swiftly, in silence, at the temperature and pressure of the atmosphere, and gratis: dear colleagues, when we learn to do likewise we will be *sicut Deus*, and we will have also solved the problem of hunger in the world.

But there is more and worse, to our shame and that of our art. Carbon dioxide, that is, the aerial form of the carbon of which we have up till now spoken: this gas which constitutes the raw material of life, the permanent store upon which all that grows draws, and the ultimate destiny of all flesh, is not one of the principal components of air but rather a ridiculous remnant, an 'impurity,' thirty times less abundant than argon, which nobody even notices. The air contains 0.03 percent; if Italy was air, the only Italians fit to build life would be, for example, the fifteen thousand inhabitants of Milazzo in the province of Messina. This, on the human scale, is ironic acrobatics, a juggler's trick, an incomprehensible display of omnipotence-arrogance, since from this ever renewed impurity of the air we come, we animals and we plants, and we the human species, with our four billion discordant opinions, our millenniums of history, our wars and shames, nobility and pride. In any event, our very presence on the planet becomes laughable in geometric terms: if all of humanity, about 250 million tons, were distributed in a layer of homogeneous thickness on all the emergent lands, the 'stature of man' would not be visible to the naked eye; the thickness one would obtain would be around sixteen thousandths of a millimeter.

Now our atom is inserted: it is part of a structure, in an architectural sense; it has become related and tied to five companions so identical

* English in original – TRANS.

with it that only the fiction of the story permits me to distinguish them. It is a beautiful ring-shaped structure, an almost regular hexagon, which however is subjected to complicated exchanges and balances with the water in which it is dissolved; because by now it is dissolved in water, indeed in the sap of the vine, and this, to remain dissolved, is both the obligation and the privilege of all substances that are destined (I was about to say 'wish') to change. And if then anyone really wanted to find out why a ring, and why a hexagon, and why soluble in water, well, he need not worry: these are among the not many questions to which our doctrine can reply with a persuasive discourse, accessible to everyone, but out of place here.

It has entered to form part of a molecule of glucose, just to speak plainly: a fate that is neither fish, flesh, nor fowl, which is intermediary, which prepares it for its first contact with the animal world but does not authorize it to take on a higher responsibility: that of becoming part of a proteic edifice. Hence it travels, at the slow pace of vegetal juices, from the leaf through the pedicel and by the shoot to the trunk, and from here descends to the almost ripe bunch of grapes. What then follows is the province of the winemakers: we are only interested in pinpointing the fact that it escaped (to our advantage, since we would not know how to put it in words) the alcoholic fermentation, and reached the wine without changing its nature.

It is the destiny of wine to be drunk, and it is the destiny of glucose to be oxidized. But it was not oxidized immediately: its drinker kept it in his liver for more than a week, well curled up and tranquil, as a reserve aliment for a sudden effort; an effort that he was forced to make the following Sunday, pursuing a bolting horse. Farewell to the hexagonal structure: in the space of a few instants the skein was unwound and became glucose again, and this was dragged by the bloodstream all the way to a minute muscle fiber in the thigh, and here brutally split into two molecules of lactic acid, the grim harbinger of fatigue: only later, some minutes after, the panting of the lungs was able to supply the oxygen necessary to quietly oxidize the latter. So a new molecule of carbon dioxide returned to the atmosphere, and a parcel of the energy that the sun had handed to the vine-shoot passed from the state of chemical energy to that of mechanical energy, and thereafter settled



slowly disintegrated, and the ex-drinker, ex-cedar, ex-wood worm has once again taken wing.

We will let it fly three times around the world, until 1960, and in justification of so long an interval in respect to the human measure we will point out that it is, however, much shorter than the average: which, we understand, is two hundred years. Every two hundred years, every atom of carbon that is not congealed in materials by now stable (such as, precisely, limestone, or coal, or diamond, or certain plastics) enters and reenters the cycle of life, through the narrow door of photosynthesis. Do other doors exist? Yes, some syntheses created by man; they are a title of nobility for man-the-maker, but until now their quantitative importance is negligible. They are doors still much narrower than that of the vegetal greenery; knowingly or not, man has not tried until now to compete with nature on this terrain, that is, he has not striven to draw from the carbon dioxide in the air the carbon that is necessary to nourish him, clothe him, warm him, and for the hundred other more sophisticated needs of modern life. He has not done it because he has not needed to: he has found, and is still finding (but for how many more decades?) gigantic reserves of carbon already organicized, or at least reduced. Besides the vegetable and animal worlds, these reserves are constituted by deposits of coal and petroleum: but these too are the inheritance of photosynthetic activity carried out in distant epochs, so that one can well affirm that photosynthesis is not only the sole path by which carbon becomes living matter, but also the sole path by which the sun's energy becomes chemically usable.

It is possible to demonstrate that this completely arbitrary story is nevertheless true. I could tell innumerable other stories, and they would all be true: all literally true, in the nature of the transitions, in their order and data. The number of atoms is so great that one could always be found whose story coincides with any capriciously invented story. I could recount an endless number of stories about carbon atoms that become colors or perfumes in flowers; of others which, from tiny algae to small crustaceans to fish, gradually return as carbon dioxide to the waters of the sea, in a perpetual, frightening round-dance of life and death, in which every devourer is immediately devoured; of others which instead attain a decorous semi-eternity in the yellowed pages of some archival

down in the slothful condition of heat, warming up imperceptibly the air moved by the running and the blood of the runner. 'Such is life,' although rarely is it described in this manner: an inserting itself, a drawing off to its advantage, a parasitizing of the downward course of energy, from its noble solar form to the degraded one of low-temperature heat. In this downward course, which leads to equilibrium and thus death, life draws a bend and nests in it.

Our atom is again carbon dioxide, for which we apologize: this too is an obligatory passage; one can imagine and invent others, but on earth that's the way it is. Once again the wind, which this time travels far; sails over the Apennines and the Adriatic, Greece, the Aegean, and Cyprus: we are over Lebanon, and the dance is repeated. The atom we are concerned with is now trapped in a structure that promises to last for a long time: it is the venerable trunk of a cedar, one of the last; it is passed again through the stages we have already described, and the glucose of which it is a part belongs, like the bead of a rosary, to a long chain of cellulose. This is no longer the hallucinatory and geological fixity of rock, this is no longer millions of years, but we can easily speak of centuries because the cedar is a tree of great longevity. It is our whim to abandon it for a year or five hundred years: let us say that after twenty years (we are in 1868) a wood worm has taken an interest in it. It has dug its tunnel between the trunk and the bark, with the obstinate and blind voracity of its race; as it drills it grows, and its tunnel grows with it. There it has swallowed and provided a setting for the subject of this story; then it has formed a pupa, and in the spring it has come out in the shape of an ugly gray moth which is now drying in the sun, confused and dazzled by the splendor of the day. Our atom is in one of the insect's thousand eyes, contributing to the summary and crude vision with which it orients itself in space. The insect is fecundated, lays its eggs, and dies: the small cadaver lies in the undergrowth of the woods, it is emptied of its fluids, but the chitin carapace resists for a long time, almost indestructible. The snow and sun return above it without injuring it: it is buried by the dead leaves and the loam, it has become a slough, a 'thing,' but the death of atoms, unlike ours, is never irrevocable. Here are at work the omnipresent, untiring, and invisible gravediggers of the undergrowth, the microorganisms of the humus. The carapace, with its eyes by now blind, has



document, or the canvas of a famous painter; or those to which fell the privilege of forming part of a grain of pollen and left their fossil imprint in the rocks for our curiosity; of others still that descended to become part of the mysterious shape-messengers of the human seed, and participated in the subtle process of division, duplication, and fusion from which each of us is born. Instead, I will tell just one more story, the most secret, and I will tell it with the humility and restraint of him who knows from the start that his theme is desperate, his means feeble, and the trade of clothing facts in words is bound by its very nature to fail.

It is again among us, in a glass of milk. It is inserted in a very complex, long chain, yet such that almost all of its links are acceptable to the human body. It is swallowed; and since every living structure harbors a savage distrust toward every contribution of any material of living origin, the chain is meticulously broken apart and the fragments, one by one, are accepted or rejected. One, the one that concerns us, crosses the intestinal threshold and enters the bloodstream: it migrates, knocks at the door of a nerve cell, enters, and supplants the carbon which was part of it. This cell belongs to a brain, and it is my brain, the brain of the *me* who is writing; and the cell in question, and within it the atom in question, is in charge of my writing, in a gigantic minuscule game which nobody has yet described. It is that which at this instant, issuing out of a labyrinthine tangle of yeses and nos, makes my hand run along a certain path on the paper, mark it with these volutes that are signs: a double snap, up and down, between two levels of energy, guides this hand of mine to impress on the paper this dot, here, this one.

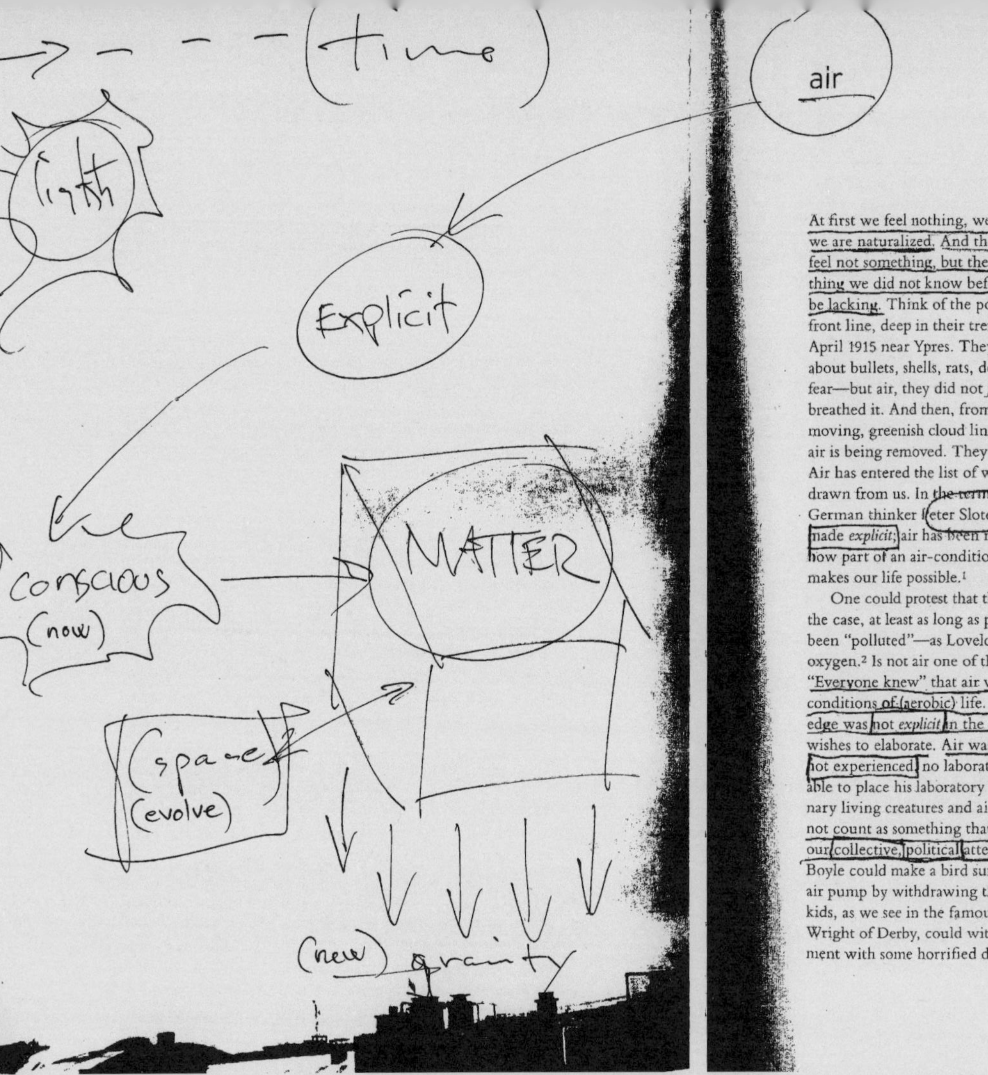


At first we feel nothing, we are insensitive, we are naturalized. And then suddenly we feel not something, but the absence of something we did not know before could possibly be lacking. Think of the poor soldiers on the front line, deep in their trenches, the 22nd of April 1915 near Ypres. They knew everything about bullets, shells, rats, death, mud, and fear—but air, they did not *feel* air, they just breathed it. And then, from this ugly, slow-moving, greenish cloud lingering over them, air is being removed. They begin to suffocate. Air has entered the list of what could be withdrawn from us. In the terms of the great German thinker Peter Sloterdijk, air has been made *explicit*; air has been reconfigured; it is now part of an air-conditioning *system* that makes our life possible.[1]

One could protest that this has always been the case, at least as long as planet Earth has been "polluted"—as Lovelock claimed—by oxygen.[2] Is not air one of the four elements? "Everyone knew" that air was one of the conditions of (aerobic) life. Yet this knowledge was not *explicit* in the sense Sloterdijk wishes to elaborate. Air was not felt; it was not experienced; no laboratory scientist was able to place his laboratory in between ordinary living creatures and air itself. Air did not count as something that had to come to our collective, political attention. To be sure, Boyle could make a bird suffocate inside his air pump by withdrawing the oxygen—and kids, as we see in the famous picture by Wright of Derby, could witness this experiment with some horrified delight, but they

themselves were not inside the glass dome: The bird's agony was lived only by proxy. Nineteenth-century hygienists had also brought the air to the attention of physicians, statisticians, educators, and city planners. But it was the air of miasmas that was in question, the infected mephitic air of lower classes, polluted cities, and dangerous industries. What happened in Ypres was different: air had become public; gas had become a branch of the military; a whole science of atmospheric manipulation had been declared.

Sloterdijk's argument is that if you want to understand what it is to feel something, it's not by rehearsing the tired old scenography of empiricism, the positivist protocols of sensation, the tiny repertoire of situations that philosophers like to use for their best examples: "Suppose I see a rock." "Let me touch a mug." "Have a child burn herself on a fire rod." "Look at this Manet." No, feeling is something much less direct than this face to face between a sentient being and some object to be felt. Feeling is more roundabout; it's the slow realization that something is missing. It resides, in a way, behind you, behind your back, or maybe even outside of you in an untouchable greenish cloud-—something you don't exactly understand and in charge of which are people you can only see through peripheral vision. As if you were resting in a hotel on a hot day and, after the air conditioning broke down, you overheard



OLAFUR ELIASSON ANNOTATED SENSORIUM – EMBODIED EXPERIENCE, TECHNOLOGY, AND CONTEMPORARY ART, 2006, BRUNO LATOUR, ED. BY CAROLINE A. JONES the hesitant conversation of the repair crew. Or suppose that you wake up in the Space Station, and realize that every single one of your innocent and inconsiderate gestures might break something essential to the breathing condition of the place you have "landed," so to speak. This is Sloterdijk's explicitness: You are on life support, it's fragile, it's technical, it's public, it's political, it could break down—it is breaking down—it's being fixed, you are not too confident of those who fix it. Our current condition merely relies on our more explicit understanding that this tentative technological system, this "life support," entails the whole planet—even its *atmosphere*.

The movement to make all this explicit has been hidden during the preceding century by other movements, those of revolution, modernization, emancipation. These describe our history as a move *out* of the sensorium, a great lesson in insensitivity and liberty. Less attachment. Finally, the great unmediated direct access to things. Nature a stable object at last. But although this process of desensitization, of indifferentiation certainly occurred, it's nothing for Sloterdijk but mere escapism. Modernisms, revolutions, avant-gardes (from the Right or from the Left) are but so many variations in escaping from an explicit awareness of what we are here calling the sensorium: how to avoid being caught up by the great inverse movement of folding in, of envelopment, of attachment, of things becoming explicit. At first air itself is being made part of our normal routine, our military-industrial complex (and "complex" itself is another word for being tucked in, embedded, implicated, attached). Since Ypres, of course, many more of those taken-for-granted life supports have been made explicit and have become part of the necessary management of the sensorium, part of industry, commerce, laboratory science, surveillance technologies, public debates. The whole ecology has become part of this explication/management routine. Now the gentle hum of the air conditioner is heard at all times, and at all scales—including that of the global warming of planet Earth itself—even though some people don't hear it, remain somehow still insensitive to it, don't feel the broken mechanism, don't see why some repair crews should be sent to fix it.

Sloterdijk is the philosopher who began to take seriously what Heidegger meant when he said we are "thrown in the world." Fine, but what does it mean to be "in" some place? It always means being inside some sphere, (some atmo-sphere), hence recasting philosophy as "spherology." And hence a whole

series of very practical, irreverent, funny questions. What is the envelope of this space? Through which door do you get in and out? What sort of air do you breathe in it? How do you become aware of the living conditions inside this glass house? What sort of technical crew is in attendance? To answer those questions, however, Sloterdijk does not share Heidegger's spite for science and technology; he does not take them as so many instances of mastery, control, domination, or emancipation. He takes the sciences very seriously, but sees them as just so many examples of a continuing exploration of the sensorium. He considers the sciences and their technical apparatus as an expansion of the sensorium, a set of elaborated and fascinating ways to make explicit the fragile envelopes inside which tiny bubbles of life sustain their existence. As if laboratories had been conceived as a huge, expanding Crystal Palace, as in some of the work by the artist Olafur Eliasson, with whom he shares an obsession for artificial atmospheres. Hence Sloterdijk's interest in obstetrics, botany, immunology, architecture, media studies, every discipline concerned with what it is to be "inside" something. On this account, Biosphere 1 (the Earth) becomes a back-formation of Biosphere 2, this strange (and failed) experiment on life support pursued in the Arizona desert inside a huge glass house.

For the first time in philosophy since the time of German *Naturphilosophie*, it might be possible to get a different feel for nature— a feel that would no longer alternate between the two present forms of escapism: "naturalization," on the one hand, this desensitized version of what it is to be thrown in the world; and, on the other, "symbolization," this strange idea that something "human" should be added to the sciences, as if those sciences were not precisely exploring what sort of life supports humans need to live in. "Once out

of nature," says the poet Yeats. Sloterdijk may explain this strange expression. It does not mean that we are going to flee out of "Space Ship Earth," but that we are finally out of this strange idea of a nature that could remain infinitely distant from the fragile life-support system that we are slowly making explicit. Art and nature have merged, folding into one another and forming a continuous sensorium. "Once back to nature?" But a nature, O so very different.

NOTES

1. Peter Sloterdijk, "Foreword to the Theory of Spheres," in M. Ohanian and J. C. Royoux, eds., *Cosmograms* (New York: Lucas and Sternberg, 2005), 223-41.

2. James Lovelock, *The Ages of Gaia. A Biography of our Living Earth* (New York: Bantam Books, 1988).

Dear Sir,

I write in order to ask your advice on a personal matter. There are people who make money, others nervous wrecks of themselves, others children. There are those who make us laugh. There are those who make love, those who make people pity them.

How long I've been trying to *make* something of my life! You alone can help me out of trouble. As soon as you have something to propose, please contact me.


Kind regards,

René M...

gerlach en koop ANNOTATED LORD PATCHOGUE & OTHER TEXTS, 1993, JACQUES RIGAUT, TRANSLATED BY TERRY HALE

Dear,

this letter is taken from *Lord Patchogue & Other texts* by Jacques
Rigaut, translated by Terry Hale. It was first published in a magazine
called *Littérature* in 1921. After Rigaut's death in 1929 the manuscript
was found amongst his papers. It is written on the back of stationery of
Brasserie Lutétia in Paris, but the handwriting is not his. It was suggested
that he could have dictated it, but we consider appropriation far more
likely. A ready-made. Brasserie Lutétia belongs to the famous hotel with
the same name and was probably just as luxurious and expensive then,
as it is now.

We remember reading the plea out loud to one another at the time
when we were just trying to built a practice as artists. At around the same
time we studied the work of Marcel Broodthaers and noticed how the
letter that marked Broodthaers' entry into the art world in 1964 resembled
Rigaut's: 'I, too, wondered whether I could not sell something and
succeed in life. For some time I had been no good at anything. I am forty
years old ...'. And it was silk screened on top of actual magazine ads.

Not long after, one of us read *Roland Barthes par Roland Barthes*, in
Dutch, possibly seduced by both books having an identically coloured
cover: the exact colour of egg yolk. In Barthes' autobiography, which
begins with a disclaimer 'It all must be considered as if spoken by a
character in a novel', he writes how at the age of 24 he was inclined to
copy the behaviour of a writer, affecting his gestures, posture and all
—as a way to be in the world—after seeing it displayed by Andre Gide,
sitting in the back of the same Brasserie Lutétia eating a pear and reading
a book.

Hotel stationery has fallen into disuse, even in the more expensive hotels,
just as handwritten letters have, but the stack of letter headed paper we
imagined sitting in some drawer in the Brasserie Lutétia has been on our
minds ever since, and so has the unknown René M. who might not even
have been someone Jacques Rigaut actually knew.

Best regards,

gerlach en koop

### The Little _Puppy_ That Could

The little puppy came bounding and tumbling over the fallow fields. Here he comes, bounding, tumbling. Like all the most adorable little puppies, this little puppy had large pleading brown eyes, wobbly half-cocked ears, and loose folds of flesh on the join of his neck. His coat was a subtle grey (like silver in shadow), with a triangle of white on his chest, like a shirtfront, and white tufts on each paw, like socks, like shoes, like little spats! He was a bit plump, this little puppy, it had to be said – but adorably so. Puppy fat, not doggy fat. He had been running and running for days and days. Where had the little puppy come from? Where was the little puppy heading, and so eagerly? His proud tail high, his front paws gaily out-thrust, his – whoops! Over he goes again. Then he's up, undismayed, bounding, tumbling, towards huge discoveries, towards wonderful transformations. Of course, the little puppy had no idea where he had come from or where he was heading. But he was going to get there.

Now, the puppy probably sniffed or sensed the village before he saw it – the fires, the crescents, the human place. In truth, his eyesight was not all that reliable, floppy, tousled, subject to passionate distortions of fear and desire. But he saw something new out there, shape and pattern, evidence, a great manifestation pressed or carved upon the random world through which he bounded. The little puppy tumbled to a halt, then wriggled himself upright. He knew at once that he had found the place that his heart sought – his destination. Down in the round valley 25

he could descry moving figures, and circles within circles, and, at their crux, a flaming parabola: a swan-neck, a scythe, a query of fire! The little puppy stood there, anxiously snapping his jaws. His head craned forward, urging the little puppy on, but his paws just jostled and danced. His tail started wagging, hesitantly at first, then with such reckless vigour that he almost pulled a muscle in his plump little rump. On he bounded, nearer, nearer, down through the dawn shadows, almost flying, his young blood aflame – until he saw a human group moving stolidly from a gateway in the low palisade. Now the little puppy really turned on the speed. He hurtled towards them, then leapt into the air and swivelled, skidlanding back-first at their feet – the four paws limply raised, the shivering tail, his soft belly exposed in reflexive surrender and trust.

And nothing happened ... The puppy awoke in a pool of bafflement and hurt. He hadn't been asleep or anything, but life was like that for the little puppy, it all being so much more fervent down there, so pressing, so sudden. The people just stood there in a stoical arc, six or seven of them; some faces wore fear, some disgust; none showed kindness. At last the puppy climbed sadly to his feet and looked up at them with beseeching eyes, his worked jaw forming a question. His question was your question. Why should they want to act this way towards a little puppy, his puzzled heart full of bruised love, a puppy made for cuddles and romps? And the people had no answer. They too (the puppy seemed to sense) were full of confusion, full of pain. Wishing to comfort them, and hoping there had been some sort of misunderstanding, the little puppy crept forward again, in trembling supplication. But now the people began to turn away. The men mumbled and sneered. One woman yelled; another woman spat – spat at the little puppy. Blinking, he watched 26

them go through the gate. It was strange. The little puppy didn't know much but he did know this: that the people were not unkind. No, they were not. They were not unkind.

And so, keeping his distance, foraging for food (grubs, roots, a special kind of flower, certain intoxicating though regrettable substances that his nose liked but his tongue loathed), and with many an exhausted sigh, the little puppy padded round the human place, until the day began to turn. As he searched for the tongue-tickling ants and the fairy toast of butterflies among the rocks and hollows, he kept glancing hopefully towards the ringed settlement – itself a termitary, full of erratic yet significant motion. His hunger appeased, propitiated, the puppy waited, there on the hillside, watching, sighing. Despite his wretchedness he nursed an intense presentiment of great things, of marvellous revelations – a feeling that may well have been delusive, since he always had it. Later in the day he encountered a damp and steaming hillock whose very interesting smells he investigated busily. Moments later he found himself lying on his side, being helplessly sick. The little puppy kept away from that hillock and all others with the same smell, a smell he came to think of as meaning danger. As night fell in folds over the disquieted landscape, he heard from across the valley the frazzled snarling of a beast, tireless and incarnadine, a sound that chimed in his head with the jeopardy of the special smell. All the little puppy could see or hear of the village now was the dreadful fire, the long flaming curve at the heart of the human place.

It was love, unquestionably love, and with classic symptoms. Each morning the little girl came with her basket, over the hills and far away, to gather flowers, and to swim in the varnished creek. Her wandering gait brought her there, punctually (the day 27

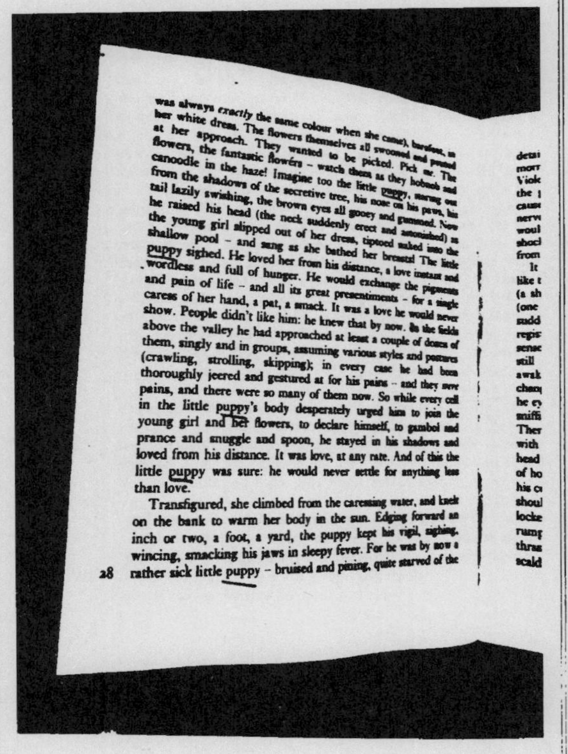

was always _exactly_ the same colour when she came), barefoot, in her white dress. The flowers themselves all swooned and pressed at her approach. They wanted to be picked. Pick me. The flowers, the fantastic flowers – watch them as they hobnob and canoodle in the haze! Imagine too the little puppy, nursing out from the shadows of the secretive tree, his nose on his paws, his tail lazily swishing, the brown eyes all gooey and gummed. Now he raised his head (the neck suddenly erect and astonished) as the young girl slipped out of her dress, tiptoed naked into the shallow pool – and sang as she bathed her breasts! The little puppy sighed. He loved her from his distance, a love instant and wordless and full of hunger. He would exchange the pigments and pain of life – and all its great presentiments – for a single caress of her hand, a pat, a smack. It was a love he would never show. People didn't like him: he knew that by now. In the fields above the valley he had approached at least a couple of dozen of them, singly and in groups, assuming various styles and postures (crawling, strolling, skipping); in every case he had been thoroughly jeered and gestured at for his pains – and they were pains, and there were so many of them now. So while every cell in the little puppy's body desperately urged him to join the young girl and her flowers, to declare himself, to gambol and prance and snuggle and spoon, he stayed in his shadows and loved from his distance. It was love, at any rate. And of this the little puppy was sure: he would never settle for anything less than love.

Transfigured, she climbed from the caressing water, and knelt on the bank to warm her body in the sun. Edging forward an inch or two, a foot, a yard, the puppy kept his vigil, sighing, wincing, smacking his jaws in sleepy fever. For he was by now a rather sick little puppy – bruised and pining, quite starved of the 28

detailed tenderness that every little puppy needs. And this
morning he lay there doubly traumatized by fear and relief.
Violent events had forced him actually to skip the assignation of
the previous day; and, in the little puppy's drowsy world of
cause and effect, he believed that if he failed to appear at the
nervous creek then, well, the loved one would fail to appear also,
would never reappear, would disappear for ever. Hence his
shock of relief, his seizure of consolation, when he peered out
from the secretive shadows and saw her there once more.

It happened the night before the night before. It happened
like this. The little puppy was soundly sleeping in his usual place
(a sheltered hollow by a leaning tree) and in his usual posture
(one of utter abandonment), when a flurry of sounds and smells
suddenly wrestled him to his feet. Frowning, the little puppy
registered curious stirrings in the texture of the earth, and
sensed faint splittings and crashings, drawing nearer. The scent,
still diluted by distance, keenly intrigued the puppy but also
awakened in him the glands of danger. He hesitated, there in the
changeable night. Too weak and confused to make a run for it,
he eyed the burrow where he had recently spent a pleasant hour,
sniffing and scratching and trying out a powerful new bark.
Then the sounds were upon him: louder, worse, hot and toxic
with limitless hunger. And still the little puppy hesitated, the
head bending slightly in its trance, the tail twitching in a reflex
of hope – of play. But now the gust of gas and blood swept over
his coat: the little puppy slithered whimpering to the burrow and
shouldered himself into the clinging damp. Or he tried. The
locked front paws searched for purchase, yet that plump little
rump of his was still exposed while the back legs skidded and
thrashed. And now he could actually feel the torch of breath, the
scalding saliva playing on his rear. Terror couldn't do it – but     29

horror could. Horror gouged him into the earth with an audible
pop; and he lay there coughing and weeping until the infamous
rage had vented, had wrecked itself on the ground above his
head . . . So shaken was the little puppy that he failed to emerge
for a good thirty-six hours, and then only a famished despair had
him backing towards the daylight. It wasn't easy getting into the
burrow, but it was easy getting out. For the little puppy, it
seemed, was getting littler all the time.

And so he sighed and gazed, and gazed and sighed. The
flowers had all lost their swoon and now arched and strained to
meet the young girl's touch. Oh, how they longed to be picked.
Light and naked she moved among them, leaning to free a stem
from the earth, then straightening to fix the petals in her costly
black hair. Loved by the little puppy (mutely, proudly – how
many lifetimes would he not joyously spend, unrequited, unre-
garded, in this half-love, this half-life?), the young girl sang, the
young girl swam, the young girl lay back on her dress, drying
herself and dreaming of growth, of change, of mysterious metamorphoses. Humming, murmuring, she sought another sun-
dazed shape in which to drowse, opened her eyes – and what
should she see? Why, a little puppy, a very tentative little puppy,
inching through the flowers, its tail anxiously shrivelled, the hot
nose brushing the grass. The puppy had had absolutely no
intention of approaching the girl in this way. But then, the
puppy just found that he'd gone ahead and done it – as little
puppies will. The girl sat up and, with no waste of attention,
stared at him strictly, a hand raised to her mouth. The little
puppy, sensing the gravity of his error, was about to slink
miserably away, to the ends of the earth, never to return – but
then she laughed and said,

30     'Hello. Who are you then? Come on. Come here. It's all right.

---

'Ooh, what a funny little creature you are. I'd take you home
with me. But they won't like you. Because of the dog. Keithette
won't like you. I don't think Tom will either. My name is
Andromeda. And I like you. Yes, I really do.'

All this of course was pure Greek to the little puppy but who
cared? Her voice, with its infant lilt and music, was just another
vast extra in his ambient bower of bliss. Not in his dreams, in
his wagging, whimpering dreams . . . While it might be pushing
it to say that little puppies have fantasies, it is certainly the case
that they have sentiments, powerful ones too – down there,
where everything rips and tears like hunger. Lying on his back
among the envious flowers, her hand on his tummy (lightly
steadied by a speculative paw), the tail in tune with the slow
heartbeat, the little puppy fairly choked and drowned in his little
sea of joy. Ah, the piercing peace. All covered in heaven – puppy
heaven! For many hours they rolled and cuddled and snuggled
and nuzzled, until the colour of the day began to change.

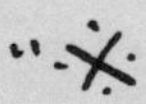

'Oh no,' said the girl.

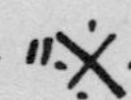

She ran away in vivid terror. Told to stay, the little puppy
followed her, as unobtrusively as possible, averting his glance
whenever she turned to shoo him back (as though he believed
that if he couldn't see her, then she couldn't see him). But now
Andromeda paused in her flight and stood her ground to give
warning.

'Stay. Be careful of the dog. Come tomorrow. Promise. Stay,
but please don't go away. Stay! Oh stay.'

Deeply puzzled, his tail uncertainly working, the little puppy
watched her run, down the valley towards the gaping crater,
where the fires were already boiling, black-veined, as they started
to consume the air of the dusk.

31

To Those Born Later

by

Bertolt Brecht


I

Truly I live in dark times!
Frank speech is naïve. A smooth forehead
Suggests insensitivity. The man who laughs
Has simply not yet heard
The terrible news.

What kind of times are these, when
To talk about trees is almost a crime
Because it implies silence about so many horrors?
When the man over there calmly crossing the street
Is already perhaps beyond the reach of his friends
Who are in need?

It's true that I still earn my daily bread
But, believe me, that's only an accident. Nothing
I do gives me the right to eat my fill.
By chance I've been spared. (If my luck breaks, I'm lost.)

They say to me: Eat and drink! Be glad you have it!
But how can I eat and drink if I snatch what I eat
From the starving
And my glass of water belongs to someone dying of thirst?
And yet I eat and drink.

I would also like to be wise.
In the old books it says what wisdom is:
To shun the strife of the world and to live out
Your brief time without fear
Also to get along without violence
To return good for evil
Not to fulfill your desires but to forget them
Is accounted wise.
All this I cannot do.
Truly, I live in dark times.

II

I came to the cities in a time of disorder
When hunger reigned.
I came among men in a time of revolt
And I rebelled with them.
So passed my time
Given me to on earth.
I ate my food between battles
I lay down to sleep among murderers
I practiced love carelessly
And I had little patience for nature's beauty.
So passed my time
Given to me on earth.

All roads led into the mire in my time.

My tongue betrayed me to the butchers.
There was little I could do. But those in power
Sat safer without me: that was my hope.
So passed my time
Given to me on earth.

Our forces were slight. Our goal
Lay far in the distance
Clearly visible, though I myself
Was unlikely to reach it.
So passed my time
Given to me on earth.

III

You who will emerge from the flood
In which we have gone under
Bring to mind

When you speak of our failings
Bring to mind also the dark times
That you have escaped.

Changing countries more often than our shoes,
We went through the class wars, despairing
When there was only injustice, no outrage.

And yet we realized: Hatred, even of meanness
Contorts the features.
Anger, even against injustice
Makes the voice hoarse. O,
We who wanted to prepare the ground for friendship
Could not ourselves be friendly

But you, when the time comes at last
When man is helper to man
Think of us with forbearance.


If I were to annotate this text as fully as I would wish, I would underline every line, and write next to it
'essential'. The poem would therefore become its own amplified commentary, which is perhaps how it
should be. Following this logic I will instead annotate it with the sister poem that followed it in the equall
necessary collection of Brecht's poems in English from which this comes. Brecht is almost peerless. Bu
was a true creative and political collaborator.

**Motto**

In the dark times
Will there also be singing?
Yes, there will be singing
About the dark times.


German; trans. John Willett

Onwards is the only direction of travel.

Gareth Evans, 2 July 2018

# The Big Toe

The big toe is the most *human* part of the human body, in the sense that no other element of this body is as differentiated from the corresponding element of the anthropoid ape (chimpanzee, gorilla, orangutan, or gibbon). This is due to the fact that the ape is tree dwelling, whereas man moves on the earth without clinging to branches, having himself become a tree, in other words raising himself straight up in the air like a tree, and all the more beautiful for the correctness of his erection. In addition, the function of the human foot consists in giving a firm foundation to the erection of which man is so proud (the big toe, ceasing to grasp branches, is applied to the ground on the same plane as the other toes).

But whatever the role played in the erection by his foot, man, who has a light head, in other words a head raised to the heavens and heavenly things, sees it as spit, on the pretext that he has this foot in the mud.

Although within the body blood flows in equal quantities from high to low and from low to high, there is a bias in favor of that which elevates itself, and human life is erroneously seen as an elevation. The division of the universe into subterranean hell and perfectly pure heaven is an indelible conception, mud and darkness being the *principles* of evil as light and celestial space are the *principles* of good: with their feet in mud but their heads more or less in light, men obstinately imagine a tide that will permanently elevate them, never to return, into pure space. Human life entails, in fact, the rage of seeing oneself as a back and

forth movement from refuse to the ideal, and from the ideal to refuse—a rage that is easily directed against an organ as *base* as the foot.

The human foot is commonly subjected to grotesque tortures that deform it and make it rickety. In an imbecilic way it is doomed to corns, calluses, and bunions, and if one takes into account turns of phrase that are only now disappearing, to the most nauseating filthiness: the peasant expression "her hands are as dirty as feet," while no longer true of the entire human collectivity, was so in the seventeenth century.

Man's secret horror of his foot is one of the explanations for the tendency to conceal its length and form as much as possible. Heels of greater or lesser height, depending on the sex, distract from the foot's low and flat character.

Besides, this uneasiness is often confused with a sexual uneasiness; this is especially striking among the Chinese, who, after having atrophied the feet of women, situate them at the most excessive point of deviance. The husband himself must not see the nude feet of his wife, and it is incorrect and immoral in general to look at the feet of women. Catholic confessors, adapting themselves to this aberration, ask their Chinese penitents "if they have not looked at women's feet."

The same aberration is found among the Turks (Volga Turks, Turks of Central Asia), who consider it immoral to show their nude feet and who even go to bed in stockings.

Nothing similar can be cited from classical antiquity (apart from the use of very high soles in tragedies). The most prudish Roman matrons constantly allowed their nude toes to be seen. On the other hand, modesty concerning the feet developed excessively in the modern era and only started to disappear in the nineteenth century. M. Salomon Reinach has studied this development in detail in the article entitled "Pieds pudiques" ["Modest Feet"],[1] insisting on the role of Spain, where women's feet have been the object of the most dreaded anxiety and thus were the cause of crimes. The simple fact of allowing the shod foot to be seen, jutting out from under a skirt, was regarded as indecent. Under no circumstances was it possible to touch the foot of a woman, this liberty being, with one exception, more grave than any other. Of course, the foot of the queen was the object of the most terrifying prohibition. Thus, according to Mme D'Aulnoy, the Count of Villamediana, in love with Queen Elizabeth, had the idea of starting a fire in order to have the pleasure of carrying her in his arms: "Almost the entire house, worth 100,000 écus, was burned, but he was consoled by the fact that, taking advantage of so favorable an occasion, he took the sovereign in his arms and carried her into a small staircase. He took some liberties there, and, *something very much noticed in this country, he even touched her foot.* A little page saw it, reported it to the king, and the latter had his revenge by killing the count with a pistol shot."

It is possible to see in these obsessions, as M. Reinach does, a progressive refinement of modesty that little by little has been able to reach the calf, the ankle, and the foot. This explanation, in part well founded, is however not sufficient if one wants to account for the hilarity commonly produced by simply imagining the *toes*. The play of fantasies and fears, of human necessities and aberrations, is in fact such that fingers have come to signify useful action and firm character, the toes stupor and base idiocy. The vicissitudes of organs, the profusion of stomachs, larynxes, and brains traversing innumerable animal species and individuals, carries the imagination along in an ebb and flow it does not willingly follow, due to a hatred of the still painfully perceptible frenzy of the bloody palpitations of the body. Man willingly imagines himself to be like the god Neptune, stilling his own waves, with majesty; nevertheless, the bellowing waves of the viscera, in more or less incessant inflation and upheaval, brusquely put an end to his dignity. Blind, but tranquil and strangely despising his obscure baseness, a given person, ready to call to mind the grandeurs of human history, as when his glance ascends a monument testifying to the grandeur of his nation, is stopped in mid-flight by an atrocious pain in his big toe because, though the most noble of animals, he nevertheless has corns on his feet; in other words, he has feet, and these feet independently lead an ignoble life.

Corns on the feet differ from headaches and toothaches by their baseness, and they are only laughable because of an ignominy explicable by the mud in which feet are found. Since by its physical attitude the human race distances itself *as much as it can* from terrestrial mud—whereas a spasmodic laugh carries joy to its summit each time its purest flight lands man's own arrogance spread-eagle in the mud—one can imagine that a toe, always more or less damaged and humiliating, is psychologically analogous to the brutal fall of a man—in other words, to death. The hideously cadaverous and at the same time loud and proud appearance of the big toe corresponds to this derision and gives a very shrill expression to the disorder of the human body, that product of the violent discord of the organs.

The form of the big toe is not, however, specifically monstrous: in this it is different from other parts of the body, the inside of a gaping mouth, for example. Only secondary (but common) deformations have been able to give its ignominy an exceptionally burlesque value. Now it is easy, most often, to account for burlesque values by means of extreme seductiveness. But we are led here to distinguish categorically two radically opposed kinds of seductiveness (whose habitual confusion entails the most absurd misunderstandings of language).

If a seductive element is to be attributed to the big toe, it is evidently not one to satisfy such exalted aspirations as, for example, the perfectly indelible taste



that, in most cases, leads one to prefer elegant and correct forms. On the contrary, if one chooses, for example, the case of the Count of Villamediana, one can affirm that the pleasure he derived from touching the queen's foot specifically derived from the ugliness and infection represented by the baseness of the foot, in practice by the most deformed feet. Thus, supposing that the queen's foot was perfectly pretty, it still derived its sacrilegious charm from deformed and muddy feet. Since a queen is *a priori* a more *ideal* and ethereal being than any other, it was human to the point of laceration to touch what in fact was not very different from the stinking foot of a thug. Here one submits to a seduction radically opposed to that caused by light and ideal beauty; the two orders of seduction are often confused because a person constantly moves from one to the other, and, given this back and forth movement, whether it finds its end in one direction or the other, seduction is all the more acute when the movement is more brutal.

As for the big toe, classic foot fetishism leading to the licking of toes categorically indicates that it is a phenomenon of base seduction, which accounts for the burlesque value that is always more or less attached to the pleasures condemned by pure and superficial men.

The meaning of this article lies in its insistence on a direct and explicit questioning of *seductiveness*, without taking into account poetic concoctions that are, ultimately, nothing but a diversion (most human beings are naturally feeble and can only abandon themselves to their instincts when in a poetic haze). A return to reality does not imply any new acceptances, but means that one is seduced in a base manner, without transpositions and to the point of screaming, opening his eyes wide: opening them wide, then, before a big toe.

**Note**

1. In *L'Anthropologie*, 1903, pp. 733-36; reprinted in *Cultes, mythes et religions*, 1905, vol 1, pp. 105-10.

result that he didn't have a girl. Sometimes he talked, not caring who might be listening, about the healing properties of masturbation (he cited Kant as an example), to be practiced from the earliest years to the most advanced age, which mostly tended to provoke laughter in the girls from the Town of Chattering Girls who happened to hear him, and which exceedingly bored and disgusted his acquaintances in Berlin, who were already overfamiliar with this theory and who thought that Vogel, in explaining it with such stubborn zeal, was really masturbating in front of them or using them as masturbation aids.

But bravery was another thing he held in high esteem, and when he saw that a boy, though at first he mistook him for seaweed, was drowning, he didn't hesitate a second before throwing himself into the sea, which wasn't exactly calm near the rocks just there, to rescue him. One further thing must be noted, which is that Vogel's blunder (mistaking a boy with brown skin and blond hair for a tangle of seaweed) tormented him that night, after it was all over. In bed, in the dark, Vogel relived the day's occurrences just as he always did, that is, with great satisfaction, until suddenly he saw the drowning boy again and himself watching, not sure whether it was a human being or seaweed. Sleep deserted him. How could he have mistaken a boy for seaweed? he asked himself. And then: in what sense can a boy resemble seaweed? And then: can a boy and seaweed have anything in common?

Before he formulated a fourth question, Vogel thought that possibly his doctor in Berlin was right and he was going mad, or perhaps not mad in the usual sense, but he was approaching the path of madness, so to speak, because a boy, he thought, has nothing in common with seaweed, and an observer from the rocks who mistakes a boy for seaweed is a person with a half-loosened screw, not a madman, exactly, with a screw altogether loose, but a man whose screw is loosening, and who, as a result, must tread more carefully in all matters regarding his mental health.

LOGIC MEETS INSTINCT MONTESSORI

## Programmed Reading

*If you have a pre-school or kindergarten age child who you feel is ready to learn to read but you don't know how to start, this series of programs may be your answer. The series of twenty-two books begins with a set of eight sound-symbol cards. Each 8 x 10" card has a picture and the sound (letter) it stands for.*

*When the child has learned all eight sounds without the help of the pictures, he is ready to begin the primer, which uses only the eight familiar sounds plus 'I', 'yes', and 'no'. Learning the sounds and getting into the primer may take a long time and plenty of help from you, depending on the age of the child and how much he can absorb in one sitting. Our children started short sessions before age four and it was several months before they reached the self-teaching level, about half-way through the primer. After that they were on their own, going through each book at their own rate and becoming fairly good readers by the time they started kindergarten.*

*The material in every book is presented in a highly entertaining way; drawings by Carol Andrews are funny and colorful so that learning to read never becomes a drag.*

*The main characters throughout the series are Sam, Ann, their little brother Walter, Nip the dog and Tab the cat. The beginning books are about their daily adventures and how they get into and out of trouble. In the more advanced books, when the mob is looking for adventure they visit the Roundabouts who live in a land where anything can happen. The last three books, also in the form of self-teaching programs, are stories from Greek mythology meaningfully written for seven and eight year olds.*

*Cynthia Buchanan has also written a three-part series, Programmed Geography (Macmillan) including The Earth in Space, Continents & Oceans, Latitudes and Climates. Our children were able to do this series successfully at eight years or so. Another excellent program by the Sullivan Associates is Programmed Astronomy (2 books).*

[Suggested and reviewed by Gretchen Guard.]

## Cuisenaire Rods

*The first rod is a small wooden cube with a 1 centimeter side. The second is twice as long with the same cross section. The third is three times as long as the first. Each length has its own color. With these rods, a child can learn arithmetical operations and mathematical relationships even though he recognizes no mathematical symbols. (Children are capable of grasping mathematical concepts before they have the mechanical ability to write. Therein lies one of the great advantages of Cuisenaire rods.) For example, if a child puts the first (white) and the second (red) rods end to end he can see that together they are equal in length to the third (green) rod. Once he realizes that a white and a red always equal a green, he has learned something quite general about addition and equality. If, later, the numeral '1' is associated with the first rod, '2' with the second rod and '3' with the third, he will be in a position to grasp at once that $1 + 2 = 3$. But the rods have no absolute numerical value so that if the value '1' were assigned to the third rod rather than the first, the truth $1/3 + 2/3 = 1$ would also be forthcoming as 'proved' by the general rule that the child discovered with the rods.*

*What is happening here is that algebra (the general case) is being learned before arithmetic (specific cases), as logically, it should be.*

*This is undoubtedly one of the best pieces of teaching equipment ever invented. But it is important that you don't show children the truths that the rods demonstrate. They must be allowed to discover these themselves or it won't work.* **Mathematics with Numbers in Color**, *books A, B, C, D, are a worthwhile purchase if you don't feel sure of how to use the rods. Also,* **For the Teaching of Elementary Mathematics** *will give an idea of what's going on when a child learns (as opposed to memorizing) math.*

[Suggested by Virginia Baker
Reviewed by Jane Burton]

**Catalog** free from:

Basic classroom kit for 25 kids (includes above books) **$57.50** postpaid

Cuisenaire Home Mathematics Kit **$12.50** postpaid
from Cuisenaire Co. of America, Inc.
9 Elm Avenue
Mt. Vernon, N. Y.

Home Math Kit available from
WHOLE EARTH CATALOG

# 112

## Programmed Reading
Cynthia D. Buchanan
Sullivan Associates.

Programmed reading. The pre-reading series. 3 bks. bk. 1, Programmed pre-reader. 1966. $1.60; 2nd ed. 1968. $0.92; bk. 2, Programmed reading, 1963. $2.40; bk. 3, Programmed primer, $1.32; readiness test, $2.80; teacher's alphabet cards, $3.60; student's alphabet cards, $1.84; sound-symbol cards, $1.92; teacher's guide to Pre-reader, stage 2, 1968, $2.72; teacher's guide to Reading readiness, stage 1, 1966. $2.00.

Programmed reading. 2 series. 1963. series 1. 2 vols. vol. 1, Programmed pre-reading, $1.48; vol. 2, Programmed primer, $1.24; reading readiness test, $2.40 per pkg. of 10; series 2, Programmed reading, bk. 1, $1.32; teacher's guide, $0.72.

Programmed reading. 21 bks. 3 ser. 1963-66. Teachers guide to ser. 1, $2.40; bks. 1-2, $1.60 ea; teacher's guides to bk. 1, $0.72; to bk. 2, o.p. bks. 3-7, $1.68 ea; teacher's guides to bks. 3-7. o.p. pupils response bks. for bks. 3-7, $0.32 ea; test bklet, $0.96; teacher's guide, $0.96; placement test, set, $8.00; guide to reading tests, $0.32. 7 filmstrips set, $30.00; teacher's guide to filmstrips, $0.96; Series 2, bks. 1-2, $1.56 ea; bks. 3-7, $1.68 ea; bks. 8-14 ea; teacher's guide to ser. 2. $2.40; pupil's response bks. $0.32 ea; Webster master's bks. 8-14, $16.00; sound symbol cards, $4.40; alphabet strips, $1.48; test bklet, $0.96; teacher's guide. $0.96; text films available; Series 3. bks. 8-21, $1.60 ea; pupil's response bks. 15-21, $0.32 ea; teacher's guide, $3.60; tests. $0.96; teacher's guide to tests,$0.96; bk. 16. 2nd ed. 1968. $1.60; programmed reading evaluation set, $130.00.

Programmed reading classroom starter set. 1967. $360.00.

from:
McGraw-Hill Book Co.
Princeton Road
Hightstown, N. J. 08520

Manchester Road
Manchester, MO 63062
8171 Redwood Highway
Novato, CA 94947

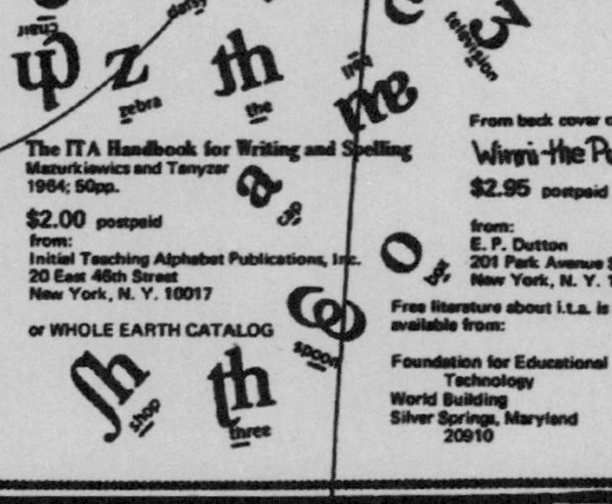


## Initial Teaching Alphabet

*As everyone knows, the English language is inconsistent. For instance, here are four different pronunciations of the letter "a":*

ape    apple    arm    all

*I.t.a. eliminates all such inconsistencies by spelling with a separate symbol for each "a" sound:*

*Eliminating contradictions in spelling and pronunciation makes learning to read and write a logical process, one whose mind can grasp logic—and this includes three and four year olds—can learn to read with i.t.a. There are none of the complicated rules of the normal alphabet. Capitals in i.t.a. are just the regular size i.t.a. symbol written or printed a little larger. Each sound has its own symbol; there are 44 altogether.*

*After learning to read in i.t.a., the switch can be made to conventional alphabet easily. The irregularities are most troublesome at this point, because the reader can read words at a time—not letter by letter—and can read for content.*

*i.t.a. is great for pre-school age children who want to read; at that age, kids get frustrated easily. The i.t.a. alphabet eliminates the frustration by its consistency. We taught our 4 year old the sound of i.t.a. letter. Then we showed him how words could be made by blending sounds together. It took a while before he was able to blend the sounds by himself. Once that happened, he was then able to read.*

*i.t.a. is also good for teaching English to foreigners (and foreign languages also have one symbol or one group of symbols for each sound) and for remedial reading instruction. It is also a good tool for writing: once all the sounds and symbols are learned, one can write anything he can say.*

[Reviewed by Lora Ferguson]

ther wos nœ wind tœ blœ him near
tœ the tree sœ ther hee stœd. hee cœd smell
the huny, hee cœd smell the huny, but
cœdn't kwiet reech the huny.

after a littl whiel hee cauld dœn tœ yœ
"cristofer robin!" hee sed in a loud
whisper.

"halœ!"

"ie think the bees suspect sumthig!"

"whot sort ov thig?"

"ie dœn't nœ. but sumthig tells me
that ther suspishius!"

"perhaps the
think that yœ'r
after ther huny?"

"it mæ bee that.
yœ never can tell
with bees."

ther wos anuther littl sielens, and then
he cauld dœn tœ yœ agæn.

"cristofer robin!"

"yes?"

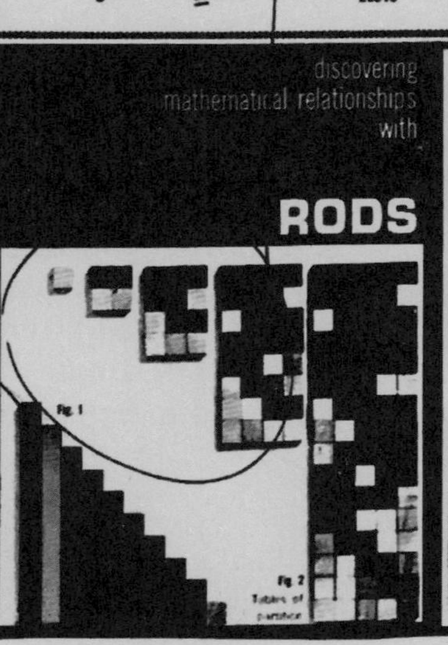


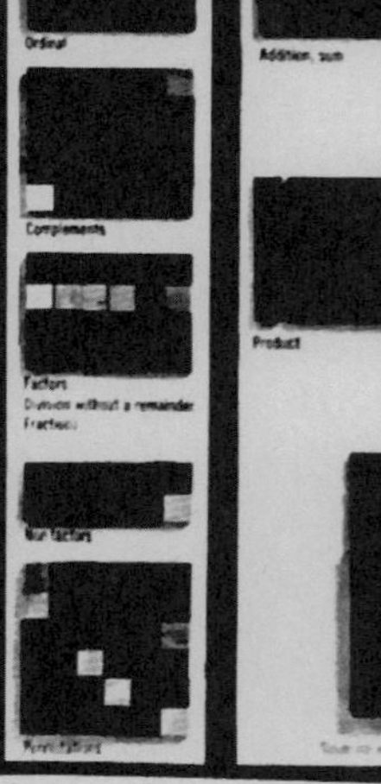

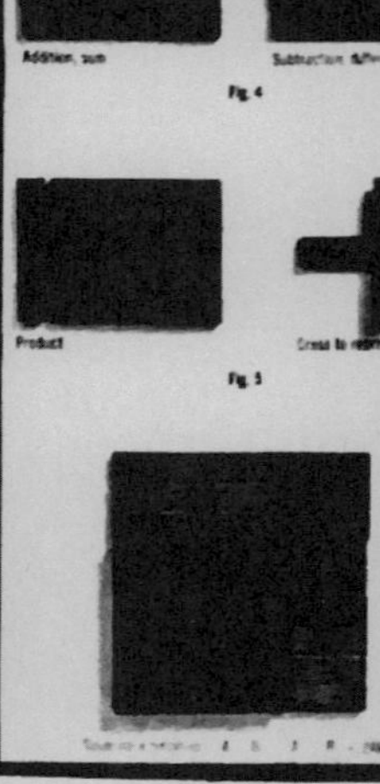

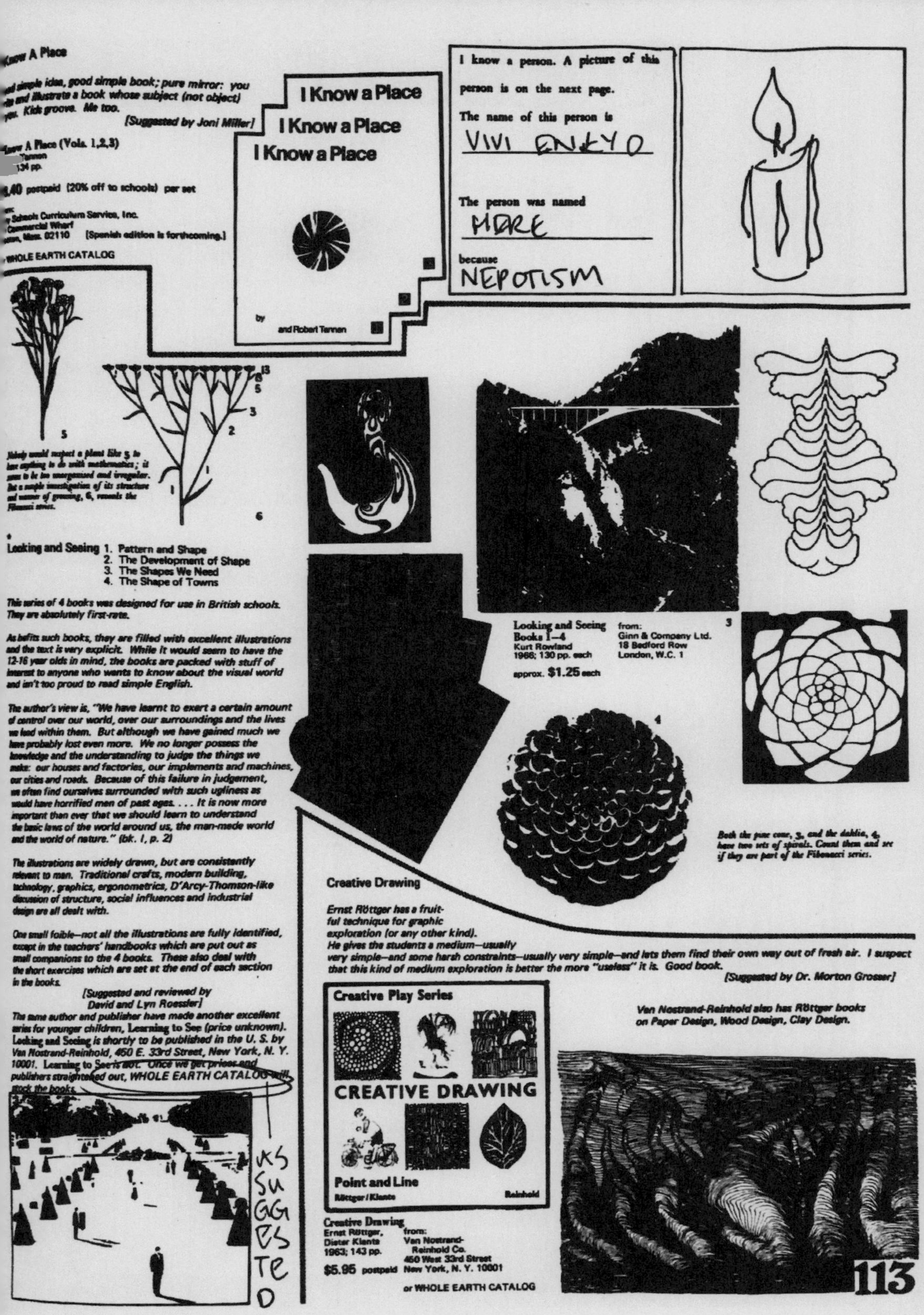

I Know A Place

...d simple idea, good simple book; pure mirror: you ... and illustrate a book whose subject (not object) ... you. Kick groove. Me too.

[Suggested by Joni Miller]

I Know A Place (Vols. 1,2,3)
... Tannen
134 pp.

8.40 postpaid (20% off to schools) per set

from:
... Schools Curriculum Service, Inc.
... Commercial Wharf
..., Mass. 02110   [Spanish edition is forthcoming.]

or WHOLE EARTH CATALOG





Looking and Seeing   1. Pattern and Shape
2. The Development of Shape
3. The Shapes We Need
4. The Shape of Towns

*This series of 4 books was designed for use in British schools. They are absolutely first-rate.*

*As befits such books, they are filled with excellent illustrations and the text is very explicit. While it would seem to have the 12-16 year olds in mind, the books are packed with stuff of interest to anyone who wants to know about the visual world and isn't too proud to read simple English.*

*The author's view is, "We have learnt to exert a certain amount of control over our world, over our surroundings and the lives we lead within them. But although we have gained much we have probably lost even more. We no longer possess the knowledge and the understanding to judge the things we make: our houses and factories, our implements and machines, our cities and roads. Because of this failure in judgement, we often find ourselves surrounded with such ugliness as would have horrified men of past ages. . . . It is now more important than ever that we should learn to understand the basic laws of the world around us, the man-made world and the world of nature." (bk. I, p. 2)*

*The illustrations are widely drawn, but are consistently relevant to man. Traditional crafts, modern building, technology, graphics, ergonometrics, D'Arcy-Thomson-like discussion of structure, social influences and industrial design are all dealt with.*

*One small foible—not all the illustrations are fully identified, except in the teachers' handbooks which are put out as small companions to the 4 books. These also deal with the short exercises which are set at the end of each section in the books.*

[Suggested and reviewed by David and Lyn Roessler]

*The same author and publisher have made another excellent series for younger children, Learning to See (price unknown). Looking and Seeing is shortly to be published in the U. S. by Van Nostrand-Reinhold, 450 E. 33rd Street, New York, N. Y. 10001. Learning to See is not. Once we get prices and publishers straightened out, WHOLE EARTH CATALOG will stock the books.*

Looking and Seeing
Books 1—4
Kurt Rowland
1968; 130 pp. each

approx. **$1.25** each

from:
Ginn & Company Ltd.
18 Bedford Row
London, W.C. 1

*Both the pine cone, 3, and the dahlia, 4, have two sets of spirals. Count them and see if they are part of the Fibonacci series.*

### Creative Drawing

*Ernst Röttger has a fruitful technique for graphic exploration (or any other kind).*
*He gives the students a medium—usually very simple—and some harsh constraints—usually very simple—and lets them find their own way out of fresh air. I suspect that this kind of medium exploration is better the more "useless" it is. Good book.*

[Suggested by Dr. Morton Grosser]

*Van Nostrand-Reinhold also has Röttger books on Paper Design, Wood Design, Clay Design.*



Creative Drawing
Ernst Röttger,
Dieter Klante
1963; 143 pp.

$5.95 postpaid

from:
Van Nostrand-
Reinhold Co.
450 West 33rd Street
New York, N. Y. 10001

or WHOLE EARTH CATALOG

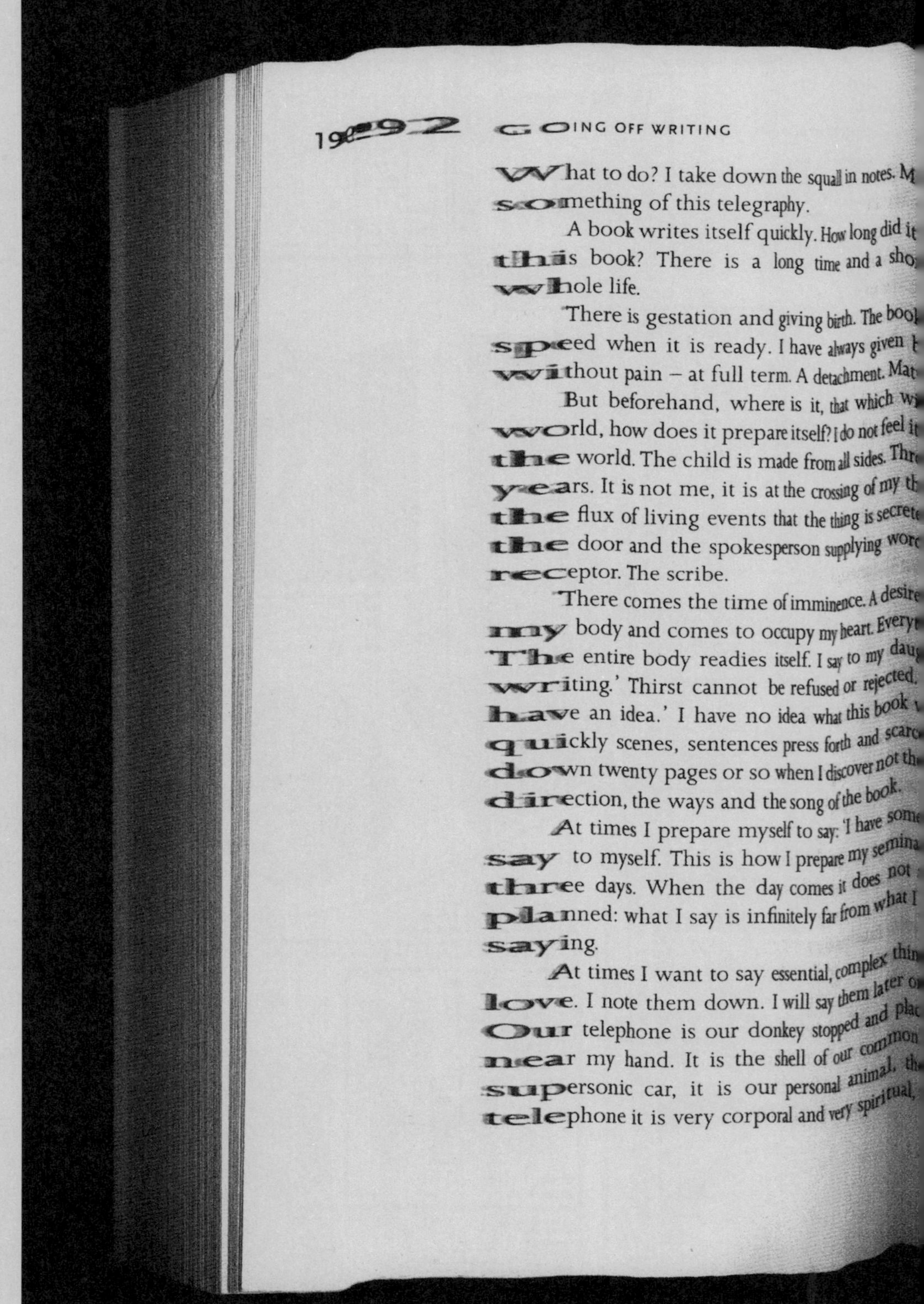



What to do? I take down the squall in notes. M[...] something of this telegraphy.

A book writes itself quickly. How long did it [...] this book? There is a long time and a sho[rt...] whole life.

There is gestation and giving birth. The boo[k...] speed when it is ready. I have always given [...] without pain – at full term. A detachment. Mat[...]

But beforehand, where is it, that which w[...] world, how does it prepare itself? I do not feel it [...] the world. The child is made from all sides. Thre[e...] years. It is not me, it is at the crossing of my th[...] the flux of living events that the thing is secrete[d...] the door and the spokesperson supplying word[s...] receptor. The scribe.

There comes the time of imminence. A desire [...] my body and comes to occupy my heart. Everyt[...] The entire body readies itself. I say to my daug[hter...] writing.' Thirst cannot be refused or rejected. [...] have an idea.' I have no idea what this book [...] quickly scenes, sentences press forth and scarc[e...] down twenty pages or so when I discover not th[...] direction, the ways and the song of the book.

At times I prepare myself to say: 'I have some[...] say to myself. This is how I prepare my semina[r...] three days. When the day comes it does not [...] planned: what I say is infinitely far from what I [...] saying.

At times I want to say essential, complex thin[gs...] love. I note them down. I will say them later o[...] Our telephone is our donkey stopped and plac[...] near my hand. It is the shell of our common [...] supersonic car, it is our personal animal, th[...] telephone it is very corporal and very spiritual, [...]

our exterior hut while being g our miracle mount and
good fortune. There is no more living

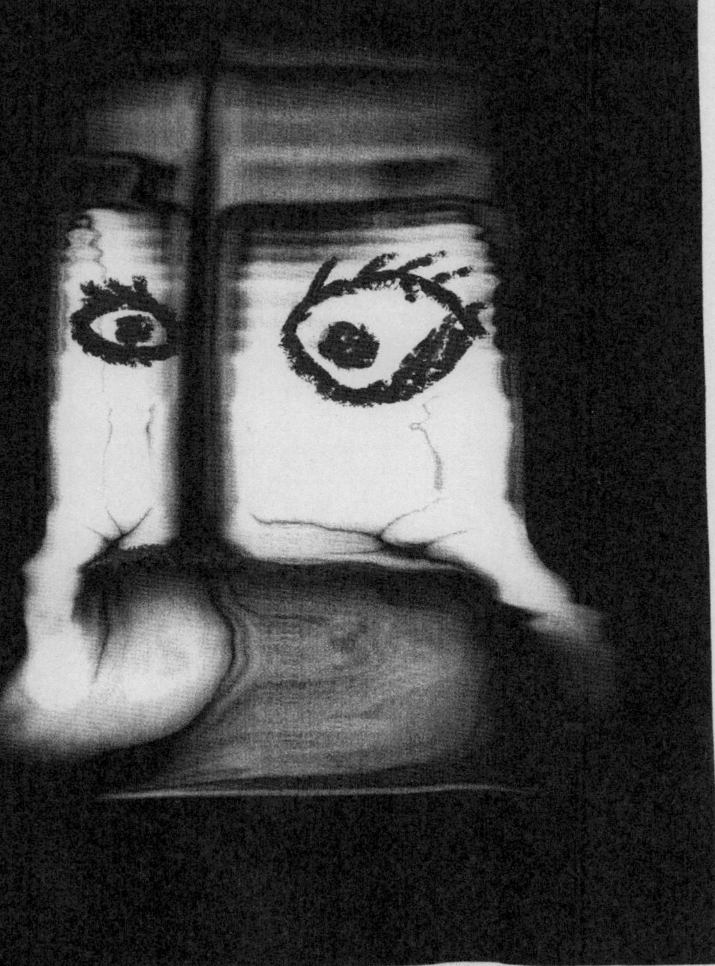

does not have a head and feet. It does not have a front
written from all over at once, you enter it through a

Wordless, we split up. We were on our turf; we could lose ourselves in the neighborhood backyards, everyone for himself. I paused and considered. Everyone had vanished except Mikey Fahey, who was just rounding the corner of a yellow brick house. Poor Mikey, I trailed him, and the driver of the Buick sensibly picked the two of us to follow. The man apparently had all day.

He chased Mikey and me around the yellow house and up a backyard path we knew by heart: under a low tree, up a bank, through a hedge, down some snowy steps, and across the grocery store's delivery driveway. We smashed through a gap in another hedge, entered a scruffy backyard, and ran around its back porch and tight between houses to Edgerton Avenue; we ran across Edgerton to an alley and up our own sliding woodpile to the Halls' front yard; he kept coming. We ran up Lloyd Street and wound through mazy backyards toward the steep hilltop at Willard and Lang.

He chased us silently, block after block. He chased us silently over picket fences, through thorny hedges, between houses, around garbage cans, and across streets. Every time I glanced back, choking for breath, I expected he would have quit. He must have been as breathless as we were. His jacket strained over his body. It was an immense discovery, pounding into my hot head with every sliding, joyous step, that this ordinary adult evidently

knew what I thought only children who trained at football knew: that you have to fling yourself at what you're doing, you have to point yourself, forget yourself, aim, dive.

Mikey and I had nowhere to go, in our own neighborhood or out of it, but away from this man who was chasing us. He impelled us forward; we compelled him to follow our route. The air was cold; every breath tore my throat. We kept running, block after block; we kept improvising, backyard after backyard, running a frantic course and choosing it simultaneously, failing always to find small places or hard places that might slow him down, and discovering always, exhilarated, dismayed, that only bare speed could save us—for he would never give us up, this man—and we were beginning to lose speed.

Ten blocks he chased us through the backyard labyrinths before he finally caught us by our jackets. He caught us and we all stopped.

We three stood staggering, half-blinded, coughing, in an obscure hilltop backyard, a man in his twenties, a boy, a girl. He had released our jackets, our pursuer, our captor, our hero: for he knew we weren't going anywhere. We all played by the rules. Mikey and I unzipped our jackets. I pulled off my sopping mittens. We looked back over our tracks multiplied in the backyard's new



IMPROVISATION, PASSION, CONVICTION, GLORY, VIOLENCE, STUPIDITY, snow. All morning we had been breaking that soft white surface. We didn't look at each other. I was cherishing my excitement. The man's lower pants legs were wet; his cuffs were full of snow, and there was a prow of snow beneath them on his shoes and socks. Some trees bordered the little flat backyard, some messy winter trees. There was no one around: a clearing in a grove, and we the only players.

It was a long time before he could speak. I had some difficulty at first recalling why we were even there. My lips felt swollen; I couldn't see out of the sides of my eyes; I kept coughing.

"You stupid kids," he began perfunctorily.

We listened perfunctorily, too, if we listened at all, for the chewing out was redundant, a mere formality, and beside the point. The point was that he had chased us passionately without giving up, and that he had caught us. I wanted the glory to last forever.

But how could it? We could have run through every backyard in North America until we got to Panama. And when he trapped us at the lip of the Panama Canal? What precisely could he have done to prolong the drama of the chase and cap its glory?

I brooded about this for the next few years. He could have fried Mikey Fahey and me in boiling oil, say, or dismembered us piecemeal, or staked us to anthills.



CHILDHOOD, EXHILERATION, EXHAUSTION

None of which I really wanted, and none of which any adult was likely to do, even in the spirit of fun. He could only chew us out there in the Panamanian jungle, after months or years of exalting pursuit. He could only begin, "You stupid kids," and continue in his ordinary Pittsburgh accent with his normal righteous anger and the usual common sense.

———

If in that snowy backyard the driver of the black Buick had cut off our heads, Mikey's and mine, I would have died happy, for nothing since has required so much of me as being chased all over Pittsburgh in the middle of winter—running terrified, exhausted—by this sainted, skinny, furious redheaded man who wished to have a word with us.

I don't know how he found his way back to his car.

———

In another story Dillard says: "There is another world, but its in this world."

Law is as you know I suppose,
Law is but let me explain it once more,
Law is The Law.

Yet law-abiding scholars write:
Law is neither wrong nor right,
Law is only crimes
Punished by places and by times,
Law is the clothes men wear
Anytime, anywhere,
Law is Good-morning and Good-night.

Others say, Law is our Fate;
Others say, Law is our State;
Others say, others say
Law is no more
Law has gone away.

And always the loud angry crowd
Very angry and very loud
Law is We,
And always the soft idiot softly Me.

If we, dear, know we know no more
Than they about the law,
If I no more than you
Know what we should and should not do
Except that all agree
Gladly or miserably
That the law is
And that all know this,
If therefore thinking it absurd
To identify Law with some other word,
Unlike so many men
I cannot say Law is again,
No more than they can we suppress
The universal wish to guess
Or slip out of our own position
Into an unconcerned condition.

90

Although I can at leas
Your vanity and mine
To stating timidly
A timid similarity,
We shall boast anywa
Like love I say.

Like love we don't know where or why
Like love we can't compel or fly
Like love we often weep
Like love we seldom keep.

September 1939

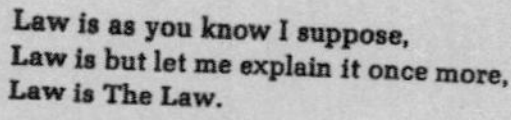

49

In Memory of Sigmund Freud

(d. September 1939)

When there are so many we shall have to mourn,
When grief has been made so public, and exposed
To the critique of a whole epoch
The frailty of our conscience and anguish,

Of whom shall we speak? For every day they die
Among us, those who were doing us some good,
And knew it was never enough but
Hoped to improve a little by living.

Such was this doctor: still at eighty he wished
To think of our life, from whose unruliness
So many plausible young futures
With threats or flattery ask obedience.

91

But his wish was denied him; he closed his eyes
Upon that last picture common to us all,
    Of problems like relatives standing
    Puzzled and jealous about our dying.

For about him at the very end were still
Those he had studied, the nervous and the nights,
    And shades that still waited to enter
    The bright circle of his recognition

Turned elsewhere with their disappointment as he
Was taken away from his old interest
    To go back to the earth in London,
    An important Jew who died in exile.

Only Hate was happy, hoping to augment
His practice now, and his shabby clientele
    Who think they can be cured by killing
    And covering the gardens with ashes.

They are still alive but in a world he changed
Simply by looking back with no false regrets;
    All that he did was to remember
    Like the old and be honest like children.

He wasn't clever at all: he merely told
The unhappy Present to recite the Past
    Like a poetry lesson till sooner
    Or later it faltered at the line where

Long ago the accusations had begun,
And suddenly knew by whom it had been judged,
    How rich life had been and how silly,
    And was life-forgiven and more humble,

Able to approach the Future as a friend
Without a wardrobe of excuses, without
    A set mask of rectitude or an
    Embarrassing over-familiar gesture.



No wonder the ancient cultures of conceit
In his technique of unsettlement foresaw
    The fall of princes, the collapse of
    Their lucrative patterns of frustration.

If he succeeded, why, the Generalised Life
Would become impossible, the monolith
    Of State be broken and prevented
    The co-operation of avengers.

Of course they called on God: but he went his way,
Down among the Lost People like Dante, down
    To the stinking fosse where the injured
    Lead the ugly life of the rejected.

And showed us what evil is: not as we thought
Deeds that must be punished, but our lack of faith,
    Our dishonest mood of denial,
    The concupiscence of the oppressor.

And if something of the autocratic pose,
The paternal strictness he distrusted, still
    Clung to his utterance and features,
    It was a protective imitation

For one who lived among enemies so long:
If often he was wrong and at times absurd,
    To us he is no more a person
    Now but a whole climate of opinion

Under whom we conduct our differing lives:
Like weather he can only hinder or help,
    The proud can still be proud but find it
    A little harder, and the tyrant tries

To make him do but doesn't care for him much.
He quietly surrounds all our habits of growth;
    He extends, till the tired in even
    The remotest most miserable duchy



Have felt the change in their bones and are cheered,
And the child unlucky in his little State,
    Some hearth where freedom is excluded,
    A hive whose honey is fear and worry,

Feels calmer now and somehow assured of escape,
While as they lie in the grass of our neglect,
    So many long-forgotten objects
    Revealed by his undiscouraged shining

Are returned to us and made precious again;
Games we had thought we must drop as we grew up,
    Little noises we dared not laugh at,
    Faces we made when no one was looking.

But he wishes us more than this: to be free
Is often to be lonely; he would unite
    The unequal moieties fractured
    By our own well-meaning sense of justice,

Would restore to the larger the wit and will
The smaller possesses but can only use
    For arid disputes, would give back to
    The son the mother's richness of feeling.

But he would have us remember most of all
To be enthusiastic over the night
    Not only for the sense of wonder
    It alone has to offer, but also

Because it needs our love: for with sad eyes
Its delectable creatures look up and beg
    Us dumbly to ask them to follow;
    They are exiles who long for the future

That lies in our power. They too would rejoice
If allowed to serve enlightenment like him,
    Even to bear our cry of "Judas,"
    As he did and all must bear who serve it.

One rational voice is dumb: over a grave
The household of Impulse mourns one dearly loved.
    Sad is Eros, builder of cities,
    And weeping anarchic Aphrodite.

                      *November 1939*

## 50

Lady, weeping at the crossroads
Would you meet your love
In the twilight with his greyhounds,
And the hawk on his glove?

Bribe the birds then on the branches,
Bribe them to be dumb,
Stare the hot sun out of heaven
That the night may come.

Starless are the nights of travel,
Bleak the winter wind;
Run with terror all before you
And regret behind.

Run until you hear the ocean's
Everlasting cry;
Deep though it may be and bitter
You must drink it dry.

Wear out patience in the lowest
Dungeons of the sea,
Searching through the stranded shipwrecks
For the golden key.

Push on to the world's end, pay the
Dread guard with a kiss;
Cross the rotten bridge that totters
Over the abyss.

EVEN LESS SO NOW
READERS READ
WORDS ON THE
PHONES

You are holding a hunk of old journalism. The prospect is not immediately appealing. Who, like Oliver Twist, will have either the nerve or the appetite to ask for more? Yet Oliver *did* want more; he knew what would land on his plate, if the beadle consented to his request, but he asked anyway. Even gruel has its uses, and so, more alarmingly, does a half-forgotten film review. There is surprising nourishment to be had from revisiting earlier judgments, if only for the pleasure of reversing them, wondering what curious conditions led one to cast them in the first place, or serving them up with relish to those who are constitutionally doomed to disagree. If this book has any concrete effect, it will be, I hope, in a small back room in a country town, where a reader will suddenly jump up and down in unprecedented fury, enraged by my appraisal of *Speed* or *The Bridges of Madison County*, and bang his head on the ceiling.

The book contains a selection of work from *The New Yorker*, at which I arrived in 1993. That I have now been with the magazine for almost a decade means that, if all goes well, I can soon expect to outgrow the status of stumbling novice; beyond that lie the ranks of the merely bewildered, and, forty years down the line, a cherished post as an acceptable part of the scenery. As a rule, writers should be treated like rubber plants—lightly pruned, occasionally watered, but basically left to do their own thing in a corner, away from direct sunlight. Even now, people ask wonderingly how my original appointment came about. All I can say is that, at some point, there must have been a clerical error of such embarrassing proportions that the magazine has spent the last nine years trying to cover it up. I myself wonder whether there is another and far more qualified Anthony Lane living quietly with his frustrations in a distant land, still waiting for the call from Tina Brown; in that case, I am a kindred spirit of William Boot, the malleable hero of Evelyn Waugh's *Scoop*, who, after a mixup with

NICE REFERENCE TO MYTHOLOGY OF
JOURNALISM

/ xiii

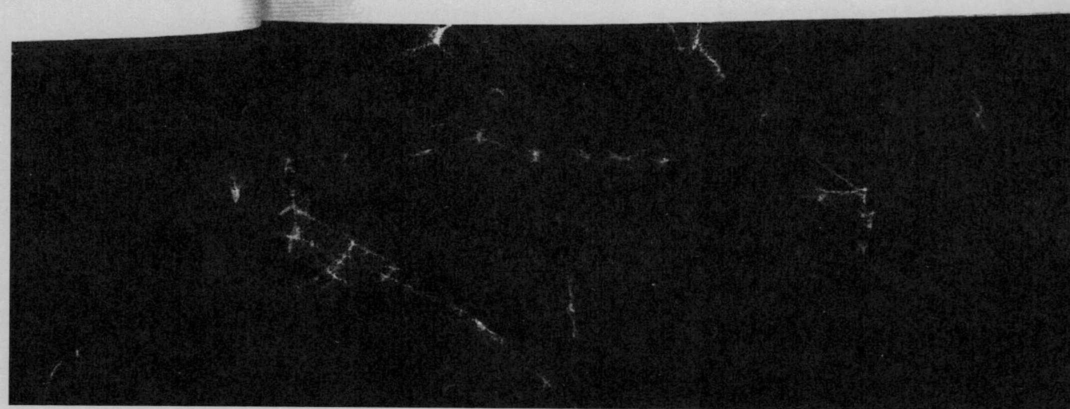

### Brechtian Theater Techniques (1973)

After hearing psychedelic music, I became a rock music fan and went to many concerts. In the early 1970s, the general trend was for pompous, self-involved rock theatrics. The beatnik notion of "poet-is-priest"[6] became "rock star-is-priest," and the rock concert audience was transformed into a hedonized mass, generating a group consciousness orchestrated by the rock singer. As at a church service or football game, the audience was enticed to sing along or raise lit matches in unison. Two concerts changed everything for me: one by Sun Ra at the Ann Arbor Blues and Jazz Festival,[7] the other by Iggy and the Stooges at a small biker bar in Wayne, Michigan.[8]

The two shows were quite different. Sun Ra's shows at this time were huge, showy, and spectacular. The stage was filled with tons of equipment and many musicians, his "Arkestra," as well as dancers and props. The aesthetic was a mix of African music, exotica, big band, science fiction, Greek chorus, and political rally. It was unlike anything I had ever seen or heard. The audience would be excited into a dancing frenzy by throbbing, African-style drumming, and then Sun Ra, or Mr. Mystery as he sometimes called himself, would start to fuck with your head, shifting at breakneck speed from schmaltzy big band arrangements, to strange neo-Egyptian poetry and long nonsense chants, to weird skits about "outer space employment agencies." You were constantly being asked to shift gears abruptly. At one point, you might be swept up bodily, only to be dropped on your ass by twenty minutes of harsh electronic white noise. It was the most intellectually and physically demanding show I have ever seen.[9] Afterward, I climbed a fence, got backstage, and met Sun Ra. He was very approachable. When I asked him how he felt his show differed from James Brown's equally elaborate but more pleasure-oriented performance,[10] Sun Ra replied, "James Brown gives the people what they want; I give them what they need."

During an intense winter snowstorm, I braved hitchhiking from Ann Arbor through a particularly redneck rural area outside Detroit to see the Stooges. When I arrived at the "club," I found it was a small biker bar. I was the first one there. Passing the time, I asked the bouncer, a huge, fat biker, whether he had ever seen the Stooges. "No," he said, "But if that prick throws up on stage, I'm going to kick his ass." When the Stooges arrived, Iggy was dressed in a ridiculous jazz-dancer's outfit, a kind of leotard with spangled skirt. His eyes were sloppily ringed with eyeliner, and a cigarette drooped from his lips. His whole demeanor said, "Fuck you." I could feel the current of hatred

spread through the bikers. Iggy was the total front man; the rest of the band barely moved. They stood stiff and erect like store window dummies, their faces blank. They were the perfect foil; all eyes were focused on Iggy, a master of body gesture. Every move was charged, and his moronic, contorted dancing seemed inspired, like an acrobat possessed by the spirit of an epileptic Jerry Lewis. The show started off simply enough with a few upbeat rock tunes that got the crowd going. Iggy incited the audience to respond to him, got them heated up—*they want Iggy.* Then, all of a sudden, he stopped, singling out a girl pushed up against the stage, one of the fans to whom a second earlier he had been gesturing and enticing. The room went silent.

"Get this bitch out of here. She tried to touch me! We won't play unless she is removed." The tension started to build. She moved out of sight. Then Iggy asked, "What do you want to hear?" The crowd yelled back an incomprehensible roar of song titles.

"Oh . . . 'Louie, Louie.'"[11]

So the band launched into "Louie, Louie." It is hard to explain now what "Louie, Louie" meant at that time, when rock music was trying to be important. It was the first song a hillbilly rocker would learn on his guitar to impress the girls at a school dance—a throwback to an embarrassing time when rock music was entertainment for fraternity boys, not an instrument of social change. It was a slap in the face to the audience. But they politely suffered through it, even goodnaturedly hoopin' and hollerin' a little bit.

Then Iggy asked again, "What do you want to hear?" The same roar came back.

"Oh . . . 'Louie, Louie.'"

And the band tore into "Louie, Louie" for a second time. "Louie, Louie" was played three times in a row. The audience was starting to get antsy. The band did another rocker and the audience regained its faith, only to have Iggy pull some other disruptive stunt.

He was an amazing performer. I have never seen better. He played the audience like a fish. The crowd was in the palm of his hand. They would suffer insult after insult, have their faces rubbed over and over again in their own complicity, and come running back for more. This doesn't sound like much after fifteen years of punk music, in which these stage antics are the norm. But Iggy invented this stuff.

After about five or six songs, a big biker shouted, "Hey, Poodle Boy," and hit Iggy with an egg. The next thing I saw was Iggy doing a belly flop into the audience; and then a riot broke out—

a real traditional biker bar fistfight. Chairs and tables overturned, the place was cleared within fifteen minutes. The lights were turned up, the band had run out the door, and I was left standing there babbling, "What happened?" It was the best piece of theater I have ever seen.[12]

Everything of major importance that I know about performing, I learned from these two concerts.

### Grassroots Aesthetics (1974–76)

In 1974, fellow University of Michigan art student Jim Shaw and I ran into two people we knew slightly at a party. Their names were Cary Loren and Niagara. Loren was a photographer and filmmaker studying at Eastern Michigan University at Ypsilanti, and Niagara had dropped out of the U of M art department. We were talking about the sad state of current music and the evils of country and arena rock. We decided right there and then to start a band, which we called Destroy All Monsters, after a Japanese monster movie.[13] It was a very democratic affair. No one knew how to play an instrument except Cary, who played guitar a bit. My solution to this problem was to go to garage sales and buy any old piece of electronic equipment with a speaker, and set it up to produce feedback. I amassed quite a pile of noisy, industrial suburban waste. We didn't get to play out very often. Our way of getting gigs was to crash parties, set up, and play. We were always thrown out. Our first gig was a comic book convention. We crashed it and asked the Trekkie band if we could use their PA system. We played one song: two lines from Black Sabbath's "Iron Man"[14] repeated over and over against a wall of feedback. We were thrown out.

### Group Dynamics (1978)

The year I graduated from Cal Arts, I moved to Hollywood. Hermann Nitsch came to town to do one of his elaborate Orgies Mysteries Theater rituals,[15] and a call was put out for volunteers to work on it. Based on photographs I had seen, I was interested in his work, and ended up playing in the noise orchestra. I was very impressed with Nitsch as a director. He was able to take a large group of people and, in a very short time, devise a system for them to work together: simple hand-cues, triggered various sounds or activities. The performance was very tightly choreographed. As a lapsed Catholic, I had great reservations about the symbology of Nitsch's work. I was worried that it might just

5. a: "Poster contest winners," *Westland Eagle*, April 23, 1969, p.10. b: A dance at St. Mary's gymnasium, Wayne, Michigan, circa 1970–71, Mike Kelley far right, half in frame. c: Mike Kelley with a hand-sewn doll, Westland, Michigan, 1970. d: Sun Ra and his Omniverse Jet Set Arkestra, New Year's Eve, 1980, at the Detroit Jazz Center. Photo: Leni Sinclair. Courtesy Book Beat Gallery, Oak Park, Michigan. e: Iggy and the Stooges at the Grande Ballroom, Detroit, 1968. Photo: Leni Sinclair. Courtesy Book Beat Gallery, Oak Park, Michigan. f: Some of the Destroy All Monsters circle annoying Andy Warhol during his book-signing tour for *The Philosophy of Andy Warhol*, Ann Arbor, Michigan, 1975. left, Andy Warhol, center, Niagara and David Keeps, far right, Jim Shaw. Photo: Cary Loren. g: Hermann Nitsch's Orgies Mysteries Theater, Venice, California, 1978. Mike Kelley second from left with face obscured.

From *Territorium Artis*, exhibition catalogue, edited by P. Hulten, Bonn 1992.

## Pablo Picasso

'So one day I took a bicycle seat and the handlebar and put one on top of the other, making them into the head of a bull. It was strong. But what I did later was to throw the bull's head away. I threw it away—into the rain gutter, or somewhere—but far away from me. Then a worker came along and picked it out of the gutter and decided that maybe he could make a bicycle seat and a handlebar out of this bull's head. And he would have done it [...] it would have been a magnificent thing. That's the art of transformation.

'Guess how I made that head of a bull? One day in a rubbish heap, I found an old bicycle seat, lying beside a rusted handlebar [...] and my mind instantly linked them together. The idea for this *tête de taureau* [bull head] came to me before I had even realised it. I just soldered them together! [...] it is incredible what a bronze solder can create between two totally dissimilar objects, just as at times it is not easy to determine all the elements that form part of a creation as a whole that begins with [...]. Certainly the danger lurks easily: if everything you see could be a head, if you don't immediately recognise the handlebar and the bicycle seat out of all the rest, the final result won't be interesting.

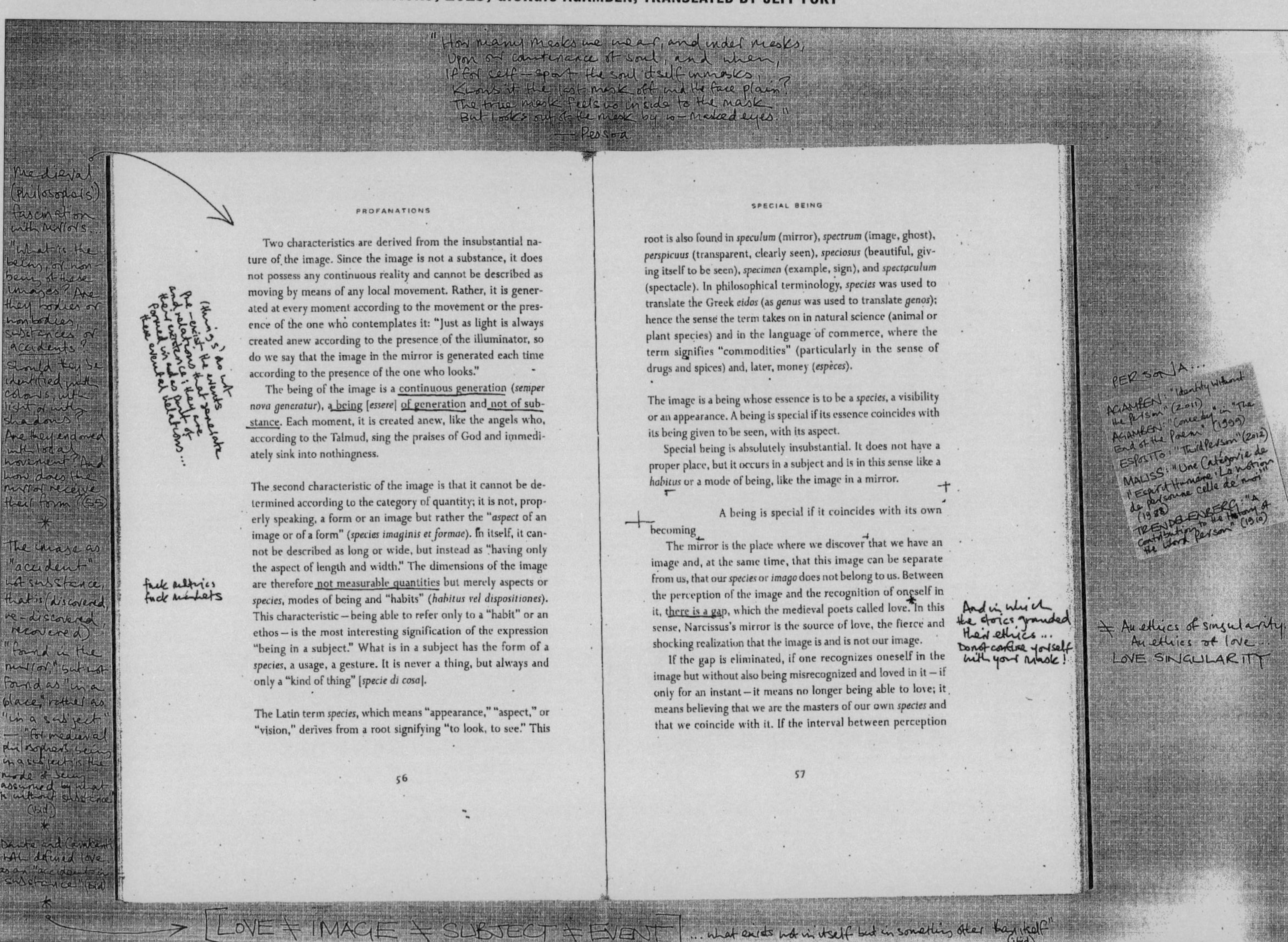



### PROFANATIONS

Two characteristics are derived from the insubstantial nature of the image. Since the image is not a substance, it does not possess any continuous reality and cannot be described as moving by means of any local movement. Rather, it is generated at every moment according to the movement or the presence of the one who contemplates it: "Just as light is always created anew according to the presence of the illuminator, so do we say that the image in the mirror is generated each time according to the presence of the one who looks."

The being of the image is a continuous generation (*semper nova generatur*), a being [*essere*] of generation and not of substance. Each moment, it is created anew, like the angels who, according to the Talmud, sing the praises of God and immediately sink into nothingness.

The second characteristic of the image is that it cannot be determined according to the category of quantity; it is not, properly speaking, a form or an image but rather the "*aspect* of an image or of a form" (*species imaginis et formae*). In itself, it cannot be described as long or wide, but instead as "having only the aspect of length and width." The dimensions of the image are therefore not measurable quantities but merely aspects or *species*, modes of being and "habits" (*habitus vel dispositiones*). This characteristic—being able to refer only to a "habit" or an ethos—is the most interesting signification of the expression "being in a subject." What is in a subject has the form of a *species*, a usage, a gesture. It is never a thing, but always and only a "kind of thing" [*specie di cosa*].

The Latin term *species*, which means "appearance," "aspect," or "vision," derives from a root signifying "to look, to see." This

56

### SPECIAL BEING

root is also found in *speculum* (mirror), *spectrum* (image, ghost), *perspicuus* (transparent, clearly seen), *speciosus* (beautiful, giving itself to be seen), *specimen* (example, sign), and *spectaculum* (spectacle). In philosophical terminology, *species* was used to translate the Greek *eidos* (as *genus* was used to translate *genos*); hence the sense the term takes on in natural science (animal or plant species) and in the language of commerce, where the term signifies "commodities" (particularly in the sense of drugs and spices) and, later, money (*espèces*).

The image is a being whose essence is to be a *species*, a visibility or an appearance. A being is special if its essence coincides with its being given to be seen, with its aspect.

Special being is absolutely insubstantial. It does not have a proper place, but it occurs in a subject and is in this sense like a *habitus* or a mode of being, like the image in a mirror.

A being is special if it coincides with its own becoming.

The mirror is the place where we discover that we have an image and, at the same time, that this image can be separate from us, that our *species* or *imago* does not belong to us. Between the perception of the image and the recognition of oneself in it, there is a gap, which the medieval poets called love. In this sense, Narcissus's mirror is the source of love, the fierce and shocking realization that the image is and is not our image.

If the gap is eliminated, if one recognizes oneself in the image but without also being misrecognized and loved in it—if only for an instant—it means no longer being able to love; it means believing that we are the masters of our own *species* and that we coincide with it. If the interval between perception

57

πρόσωπον(e)

PROFANATIONS

and recognition is indefinitely prolonged, the image becomes internalized as a fantasy and love falls into psychology.

In the Middle Ages, *species* was also called *intentio*, intention. The term names the internal tension (*intus tensio*) of each being, that which pushes it to become an image, to communicate itself. The *species* is nothing other than the tension, the love with which each being desires itself, desires to persevere in its own being. In the image, being and desire, existence and *conatus* coincide perfectly. To love another being means to desire its *species*, that is, to desire the desire with which it desires to persevere in its being. In this sense, special being is the being that is common or generic, and this is something like the image or the ..... of humanity.

The *species* does not subdivide the genus; it exposes it. The being that desires and is desired becomes *species*, makes itself visible, within the genus. And special being does not mean the individual, identified by this or that quality which belongs exclusively to it. On the contrary, it means a being insofar as it is whatever being [*essere qualunque*], a being such that it is — generically and indifferently — each one of its qualities, adhering to them without allowing any of them to identify it.

"Whatever being is desirable" is a tautology.

*Specious* first meant "beautiful" and only later came to mean "untrue, apparent." *Species* was first defined as that which makes visible and only later became the principle of classification and equivalence. "To be special [*far specie*]" can mean "to surprise and astonish" (in a negative sense) by not fitting into

58

SPECIAL·BEING

established rules, but the notion that individuals constitute a species and belong together in a homogeneous class tends to be reassuring.

Nothing is more instructive than this double meaning. The species is what presents and communicates itself to the gaze, what renders visible and, at the same time, what can — and must, at all costs — be fixed in a substance and in a specific difference in order to constitute an identity.

Originally, *persona* meant "mask," that is, something eminently "special." Nothing shows more clearly the meaning of the theological, psychological, and social processes with which the person is invested than the fact that the Christian theologians used this term to translate the Greek *hypostasis*, linking the mask to a substance (three persons in a single substance). The person is the containment of the *species*, anchoring it in a substance in order to identify it. Identity papers contain a photograph (or some other means of capturing the *species*).

Everywhere the special must be reduced to the personal and the personal to the substantial. The transformation of the *species* into a principle of identity and classification is the original sin of our culture, its most implacable apparatus [*dispositivo*]. Something is personalized — is referred to as an identity — at the cost of sacrificing its specialness. A being — a    , a gesture, an event — is special when, without resembling *any* other, it resembles *all* the others. Special being is delightful, because it offers itself eminently to common use, but it cannot be an object of personal property. But neither use nor enjoyment is possible with the personal; there can be only appropriation and jealousy.

59

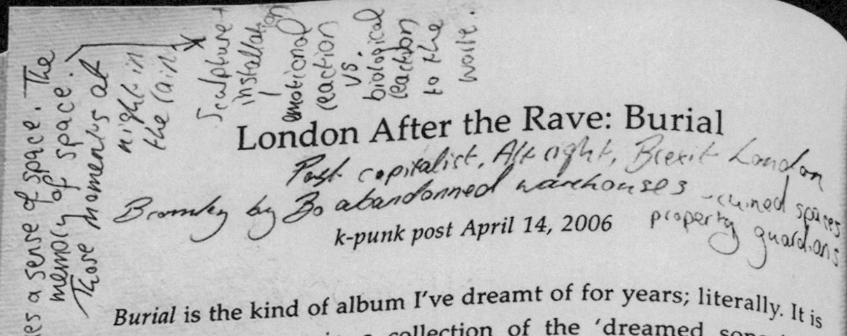



# London After the Rave: Burial

k-punk post April 14, 2006

*Burial* is the kind of album I've dreamt of for years; literally. It is oneiric dance music, a collection of the 'dreamed songs' Ian Penman imagined in his epochal piece on Tricky's *Maxinquaye*. *Maxinquaye* would be a reference point here, as would Pole – like both these artists, Burial conjures audio-spectres out of crackle, foregrounding rather than repressing sound's accidental materialities. Tricky and Pole's 'cracklology' was a further development of dub's materialist sorcery in which 'the seam of its recording was turned inside out for us to hear and exult in' (Penman). But rather than the hydroponic heat of Tricky's Bristol or the dank caverns of Pole's Berlin, Burial's sound evokes what the press release calls a 'near future South London underwater. You can never tell if the crackle is the burning static off pirate radio, or the tropical downpour of the submerged city out of the window.'

Near future, maybe . . . But listening to Burial as I walk through damp and drizzly South London streets in this abortive Spring, it strikes me that the LP is very London Now – which is to say, it suggests a city haunted not only by the past but by lost futures. It seems to have less to do with a near future than with the tantalising ache of a future just out of reach. *Burial* is haunted by what once was, what could have been, and – most keeningly – what could still happen. The album is like the faded ten year-old tag of a kid whose Rave dreams have been crushed by a series of dead end jobs.

*Burial* is an elegy for the hardcore continuum, a *Memories From the Haunted Ballroom* for the Rave generation. It is like walking into the abandoned spaces once carnivalised by Raves and finding them returned to depopulated dereliction. Muted air horns flare like the ghosts of Raves past. Broken glass cracks underfoot. MDMA flashbacks bring London to unlife in the way that hallucinogens brought demons crawling out of the subways in *Jacob's Ladder*'s New York. Audio hallucinations transform the city's rhythms into inorganic beings, more dejected than malign. You see faces in the clouds and hear voices in the crackle. What you momentarily thought was muffled bass turns out only to be the rumbling of tube trains.

Burial's mourning and melancholia sets it apart from dubstep's emotional autism and austerity. My problem with dubstep has been that in constituting dub as a positive entity, with no relation to the Song or to pop, it has too often missed the spectrality wrought by dub's subtraction-in-process. The emptying out has tended to produce not space but an oppressive claustrophobic flatness. If, by contrast, Burial's schizophonic hauntology has a 3D depth of field it is in part because of the way it grants a privileged role to voices under erasure, returning to dub's phono-decentrism. Snatches of plaintive vocal skitter through the tracks like fragments of abandoned love letters blowing through streets blighted by an unnamed catastrophe. The effect is as heartbreakingly poignant as the long tracking shot in Tarkovsky's *Stalker* (1979) that lingers over sublime objects-become trash.

Burial's London is a wounded city, populated by ecstasy casualties on day release from psychiatric units, disappointed lovers on night buses, parents who can't quite bring themselves to sell their Rave 12 inches at a carboot sale, all of them with haunted looks on their faces, but also haunting their interpassively nihilist kids with the thought that things weren't always like this. The sadness in the Dem 2 meets *Vini Reilly*-era Durutti Column 'You Hurt Me' and 'Gutted' is almost overwhelming. 'Southern Comfort' only deadens the pain. Ravers have become deadbeats, and Burial's beats are accordingly undead – like the tik-tok of an off-kilter metronome in an abandoned Silent Hill school, the klak-klak of graffiti-splashed ghost trains idling in

Paris 1972. Things had been going badly in the studio. Optimism, which had made transforming the closed-down hospital into a cutting edge complex of contemporary art workspaces such a collective joy, was fast evaporating. The government grant was spent. Nobody was coming to the private views, although the bus routes were clearly marked on all the invitations and a sense of futility hung in the air like bad aromatherapy. When the local junkies broke into Jean-Paul's studio they took the broken tape machine, a mug without a handle and two rolls of masking tape, but they left the paintings. The public's faith in the bourgeois attributes of line, form and harmonious colour combination remained stubborn. The roof leaked. There was a big meeting later that year. It was the second Friday in July, with the traffic outside gridlocked halfway to Belgium and the heat enough to make Marie-Joelle's wax casts of her naked body look like forensic shots of an acid-bath accident. Anything was better than this. 'Anything is better than this,' said Anton, when it was his turn to speak. 'I've got an idea,' said Dominique, when it was hers. Her plan was as brilliant as it was simple, and the artists adopted it immediately. It was true to the spirit of radicalism that had informed their project from the outset, and yet it promised considerable lifestyle benefits. It would be collective, but allow for individual freedom. Above all, it would represent the coming of the dream of the avant-garde – art and life merged seamlessly together. They sold the hospital to a property developer and bought the tiny abandoned fishing village of Inutile-sur-Mer. They made the long journey south in a convoy of borrowed vans, dormobiles, hand-painted 2CVs. Each of the artists had conceived a project that would contribute to the whole. Marie-Joelle installed an oven in her cottage and, using only flour, water, yeast and salt, constructed exact replicas of loaves of bread. Henri, as a tribute to Joseph Beuys, opened a shop that sold dead hares, and also rabbits, pheasant and a range of cured meat. Anton, inspired by Tinguely, set up a small workshop in which he worked on a variety of strange machinery, but principally the old Peugeots of the local farmers. Jean-Paul painted ironic watercolours of the surrounding countryside, which he sold to tourists.

The winters were mild and passed quickly, the summers were hot and lasted forever and the tensions of metropolitan life melted into the heat haze like so many bad dreams. The days, the weeks, the months, the years went by. The project took root and nourished. The artists became skilled in their new media, but the pile of press releases, hand-set an printed on home-made paper by Dominique and Jacques in the excitement of the community's formation lay yellowing and dust-covered, unsent. The world's ignorance of the artists' groundbreaking activities remained profound. In the local bar (motto- 'the act of drinking beer with friends is the highest form of art') the debate strayed ever further from the need to dematerialise the object and refine the aims of social sculpture, towards love affairs, problems with the harvest, roof maintenance, the poor run of form of the local football team. Marriages were celebrated with non-religious rites, personal vows or pagan rituals. Soon the first children were born. There were hard times too, of course, but the struggle had a meaning and what resources the villagers had were shared without bitterness. The artists ingenuity had not been dulled by their rural idyll, far from it. When things got difficult, Anton would sabotage harvesters or grain elevators on the surrounding farms and then turn up the next morning, toolbox in hand, asking whether by any chance they needed a mechanic. Angelique and Claude grew three acres of Morocco's finest on their small holding. There was a wine festival for the tourists with the artists dressed authentically as peasants. They sold there 2CVs and got bicycles. They claimed welfare at false addresses. They got by, in fact they thrived. One day a stranger came to the village, out of season for a tourist but dressed like a city dweller. The children laughed at him as he passed in his bright clothes, his impractical footwear. He wandered around for a whole afternoon, bought wine and cheese from the artists' little shops and picnicked down by the disused harbour. He took photographs and wrote in a spiral-bound notebook. Two weeks later he was back, looking for a room to rent. He was, he explained, a painter. He'd been working in Paris but had just received a grant and decided to spend a few months developing some ideas in isolation. Things hadn't been going too well. He felt his work lacked relevance. He needed to examine his practice, perhaps rebuild it entirely. A room was found that easily doubled as a studio if

# "GOOD WORK," HE SAID, AND

"Good work," he said, and
went out the door. What
work? We never saw him
before. There was no door.

45

MARK GEFFRIAUD ANNOTATED "GOOD WORK," HE SAID, AND, DATE UNKNOWN, RICHARD BRAUTIGAN

*LOVE,*

Mari thought quickly about whether she should be offended or relieved, couldn't decide, and said nothing. Jonna moved on, took pictures down and put them back up, her hammer blows inaugurating a new era.

"I know," she said, "rejection's not easy. But you reject words, whole pages, long impossible stories, and it feels good once it's done. It's no different rejecting pictures, a picture's right to hang on a wall. And most of these have hung here too long; you don't even see them any more. The best stuff you have, you don't see any more. And they kill each other because they're badly hung. Look, here's a thing of mine and here's your drawing, and they clash. We need distance, it's essential. And different periods need distance to set them apart – unless you're just cramming them together for the shock effect! You simply have to feel it... There should be an element of surprise when people's eyes move across a wall covered with pictures. We don't want to make it too easy for them. Let them catch their breath and look again because they can't help it. Make them think, make them mad, even... Now we'll give our colleagues here better light. Why did you leave so much space right here?"

"I don't know," Mari said. But she did know. Suddenly she knew very well that deep down she didn't like the painter colleagues who had done these undeniably very fine works. Mari began paying attention. As she watched Jonna rehang the pictures, it seemed to her that lots of things, including their life together, fell into perspective and into place, a summary expressed in distance or self-evident clustering. The room had changed completely.

When Jonna had taken her tape home with her, Mari marvelled all evening at how easy it is in the end to understand the simplest things.

London, commitments for the opportunity of getting some loot.

An immigrant drifting through a chain of events, highly, in a dream without limits.

Approaching the narroway, smoke billowed, abstract pleasure is at play.

The present mind cannot be attained. We're in one place-an obscure little corner.

An inebriated woman grabbing and kissing me in fluorescent jacket.

Unified intentionality, come to affirm the experience as something they'd happily do again.

Which makes its conclusion, dashing lines and depth rolling backwards. Back to Bristol

and Nottingham, contorting metaphysical hijinks, embedded in culture.

Untangling the narrative endoskeleton isn't easy, but it also poetry - not.

The dilemma is existential and moral. This film.


-   Amir George

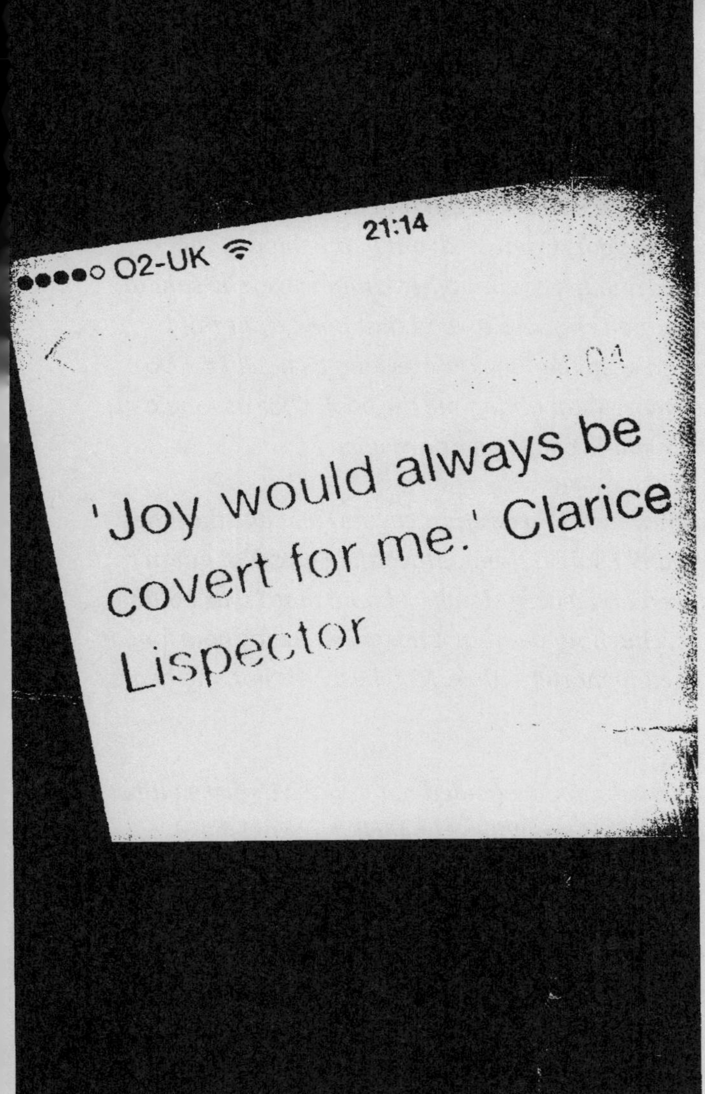



On Friday the 3rd February 2014 at 23:04pm I missed the train to Saxmundham. At the time I didn't know I was getting the train but looking back I recognise that I missed it nonetheless. I exhale now knowing that I can return to that missed connection and make amends through annotation.

Clarice (if I can myself familiar to her in this way) explores in her writing what's missing. The missing pieces of a version of our lived experience that are often unspeakable, unnameable or unknowable... and missing nonetheless.

This image represents a line, seven words, kept on a phone (my phone?) lifted from a story by Clarice. These words were somehow 'gifted' to me by two sisters, artists, who knew somehow that I felt this too.

At the time I missed the proverbial train, the sisters, the artists, wanted me to know that the this line tells me that thing we sometimes call joy is something else, and that the something else, is, itself, a kind of joy.

These sisters, the artists, pointed me to the story *Covert* Joy, which centres on a young girl living where Clarice grew up.  She loves books totally. There is a rich girl, a cruel bully, who lords it over her poorer fellow students. The narrator cannot afford to buy books, so the bully keeps telling her to come to her house and she will loan her a book which she never does. Eventually the bully's mother intervenes and give the girl a book.



ALEXIE GLASS–KANTOR ANNOTATED QUOTE: CLARICE LISPECTOR, DATE UNKNOWN, SOURCE UNKNOWN

This is the conclusion of the story:

*And the worst thing for that woman wasn't realizing what was going on. It must have been the horrified realization of the kind of daughter she had. She eyed us in silence: the power of perversity in the daughter she didn't know and the little blond girl standing at the door, exhausted, out in the wind of the streets of Recife. That was when, finally regaining her composure, she said to her daughter firmly and calmly: you're going to lend that book right this minute. And to me: "And you can keep that book for as long as you like." Do you understand? It was worth more than giving me the book: "for as long as I liked" is all that a person, big or small, could ever dare wish for.*

*How can I explain what happened next? I was stunned, and just like that the book was in my hand. I don't think I said a thing. I took the book. No, I didn't go skipping off as usual. I walked away very slowly. I know that I was holding the thick book with both hands, clutching it against my chest. As for how long it took to get home, that doesn't really matter either. My chest was hot, my heart thoughtful.*

*When I got home, I didn't start reading. I pretended not to have it, just so later on I could feel the shock of having it. Hours later I opened it, read a few wondrous lines, closed it again, wandered around the house, stalled even more by eating some bread and butter, pretended not to know where I'd put the book, found it, opened it for a few seconds. I kept inventing the most contrived obstacles for that covert thing that was joy.* **Joy would always be covert for me.** *I must have already sensed it. Oh how I took my time! I was living in the clouds …There was pride and shame inside me. I was a delicate queen.*

*Sometimes I'd sit in the hammock, swinging with the book open on my lap, not touching it, in the purest ecstasy.*

*I was no longer a girl with a book: I was a woman with her lover.*

This moment it is now Friday 13th July 2018 at 19:27pm and I am in Liverpool, UK, which is some distance from Saxmundham but farther still from home.

I write this annotation for Ryan as I sit by a window in riverside hotel feeling anonymous and indistinct. Later tonight in a bar I will hand him, the artist, this annotation.

Here is what I know: in these seven words I sense that before all is said and done I will miss many more trains, and still, somehow, joy would always be covert for me.

I'VE CHOSEN THIS POEM BY SIMON ARMITAGE. SOME OF
MY POETRY BUFF FRIENDS WOULD PROBABLY TURN THEIR NOSES
UP AT THIS BECAUSE THEY THINK HE'S TOO POP OR TRIVIAL
OR SOMETHING BUT I LIKE HIM.

## It Ain't What You Do It's What It Does to You

MOCKING KEROUAC CLICHÉS
AND OFF-THE-SHELF
ADVENTURE

I WENT TO MIAMI ONCE.
IT WAS FASCINATING UNTILL I
REALISED IT WASN'T

I have not bummed across America
with only a dollar to spare, one pair
of busted Levi's and a bowie knife.
I have lived with thieves in Manchester.

I LIVED WITH THIEVES ONCE. NOT IN
MANCHESTER MIND YOU. LUKAS MY
OLD FLAT MATE WOULD ROUTINELY
PILFER DAIRY PRODUCTS... NOT JUST
A BIT OF MILK FOR THE TEA OR
SOMETHING — WE'RE TALKING PINTS
EGGS, CHEESE.  I WOULDN'T HAVE
MINDED IT'S JUST THAT HE WAS
SO TIGHT HIMSELF — A WRETCHED
MAN WITH TEETH AS WHITE AS
PISSED ON SNOW + A RECEADING
HAIR LINE REPTILIAN EGG CRANIUM

IMMATERIAL CONSUMERISM!!
POST-BOHEMIANS ARE OSTENSIBLY
ANTI-CONSUMERIST IN A
WORLD WHERE CONSUMERISM IS THE
ONLY THING ON THE MENU. CONSUMER
GOODS MUST BE INCIDENTAL
[I 'FOUND THIS', RATHER THAN 'I
"I BOUGHT THIS"]
OR 'MERELY' PRACTICLE
[EXPENSIVE RUNNING SHOES]
OR EXPERIENTIAL RATHER
THAN MATERIAL. [TRAVELING
RATHER THAN HOLIDAYING, IMMERSIVE
THEATRE, UNUSUAL EXERCISE CLASSES]

I have not padded through the Taj Mahal,
barefoot, listening to the space between
each footfall picking up and putting down
its print against the marble floor. But I

skimmed flat stones across Black Moss on a day
so still I could hear each set of ripples
as they crossed. I felt each stones' inertia
spend itself against the water; then sink.

(ARE EGGS DAIRY PRODUCTS?)

I have not toyed with a parachute chord
while perched on the lip of a light-aircraft;
but I held the wobbly head of a boy
at the day centre, and stroked his fat hands.

15 SIBILANTS ARE USED IN
THIS STANZA. SEE THE 'S' SOUND
IN STYLE AND RHYMES THEY
SKIP LIKE THE RIPPLES

LIKE THE BYGONE BOHEMIANS
THEY/WE ARE AGAINST BOTH
STANDARDISED PRODUCTION AND
STANDARDISED CONSUMPTION BUT IN A
CRUEL TWIST ANTI-STANDARDISATION
IS THE STANDARD OF THE DAY.
UNIQUENESS IS PERSUED BY ALL
THE CONVENTION IS TO DECRY
CONVENTIONALITY. EVERYONE MUST
THINK OUTSIDE THE BOX.

And I guess that the tightness in the throat
and the tiny cascading sensation
somewhere inside us are both part of that
sense of something else. That feeling, I mean.

A DEFENCE OF
NON-INSTAGRAMABLE
ADVENTURES.

EVERYONE SIMPLY MUST
GO TO INDIA.

GOING 'TRAVELING' IS
JUST SCRUFFY TOURISM
PLUS S.T.D.s

IF YOU CAN'T 'DISCOVER' YOURSELF AT A
DESERTED TRAIN STATION IN THE MIDDLE OF THE NIGHT
IN SAXMUNDHAM THE PERHAPS THERE IS NOT MUCH
TO DISCOVER. PARACHUTING INTO THE TAJ MAHAL
WITH A BOWIE KNIFE ISN'T GOING TO HELP.
WHERE EVER YOU GO, THERE YOU ARE.

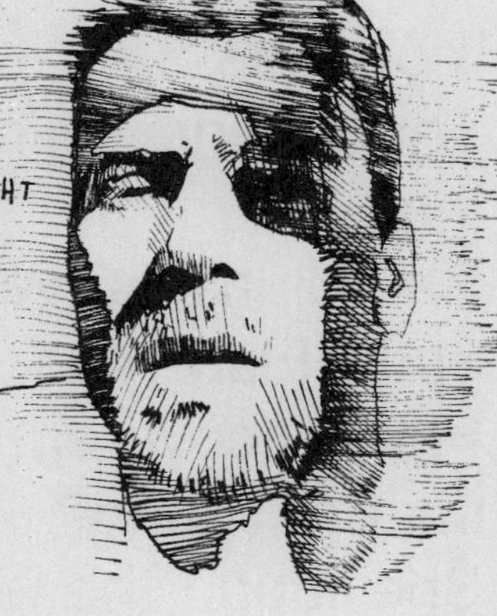

# D E P A R T M E N T S
## Sarah　　　　　　　　　　　　　　　　　Godfrey

The newly appointed director decided to end the feuding and knocked down the wall that divided sales and purchasing. Walls were painted a fresh coat of magnolia and the floor was laid with a new hardwearing c a r p e t . Marking a new era, a unique and eye catching bespoke aquarium was erected in its place. The ultra slim line design promised hours of relaxing viewing time. A single fish arrived. Restricted by the aquariums stylish specifications Fish could swim up, down, forwards and backwards, but not around. With one fish eye on marketing and one fish eye on purchasing, he spent a large proportion of his viewing time observing spreadsheets, office dynamics and internal p o l i t i c s . For one hour only, the cleaner would make an appearance. She would frantically dart between both fish eyes, disappearing in one, only to arrive in the next, moments later. The cleaner failed to make an appearance one morning, in either eye. She didn't arrive the next day, nor the one after that, until Fish had forgotten when he saw her last. Fully recovered, the cleaner returned to her morning shift after taking a week off sick. She found the aquarium empty. There lie, close by, a rigid Fish. One fish eye was touching the carpet, the other fish eye, wide open, was facing the ceiling above.

The Time Falling Bodies Take to Light
William Irwin Thompson

The revisioning of history is, therefore, also an act of prophecy—not prophecy in the sense of making predictions, for the universe is too free and open-ended for the manipulations of a religious egotism—but prophecy in the sense of seeing history in the light of myth. Technological Man has consciously excluded myth from his consciousness; this has brought him back under the sway of the collective *unconscious*. He feels a strong motivation to travel in space, to escape the confinement of mother earth, to rebuild his own version of nature and culture in the imagined total freedom of a space colony. In his utopian fantasy of technology, he creates a mirror-image of the utopian who hopes to find total freedom by escaping society and returning to nature. But in the jungle of Guyana with Reverend Jim Jones, or in the space colonies of NASA, "man" will painfully discover that wherever he goes, he brings his evil along with him.

In the classical era the person who saw history in the light of myth was the prophet, an Isaiah or Jeremiah; in the modern era the person who saw history in the light of myth was the artist, a Blake or a Yeats. But now in our postmodern era the artists have become a degenerate priesthood; they have become not spirits of liberation, but the interior decorators of Plato's cave. We cannot look to them for revolutionary deliverance. If history becomes the medium of our imprisonment, then history must become the medium of our liberation; (to rise, we must push against the ground to which we have fallen). For this radical task, the boundaries of both art and science must be redrawn. *Wissenschaft* must become *Wissenkunst*.

What I am talking about is the resacralization of culture and, in particular, the resacralization of scholarship. I am talking about a movement from ratio to Logos. Under the sway of ratio, a unit is

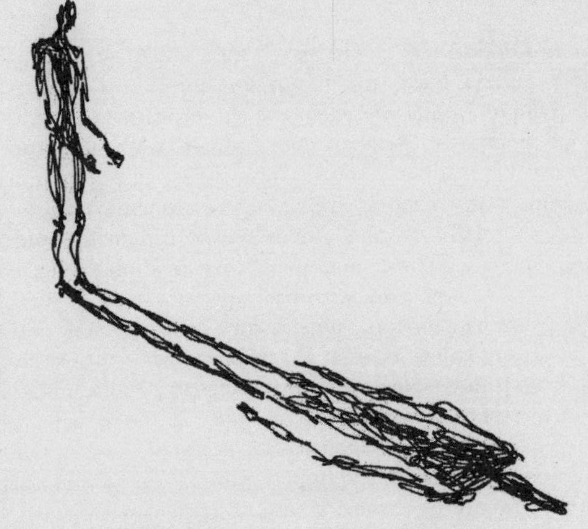



ANTONY GORMLEY ANNOTATED THE TIME FALLING BODIES TAKE TO LIGHT: MYTHOLOGY, SEXUALITY AND THE ORIGINS OF CULTURE, 1996, WILLIAM IRWIN THOMPSON

uniform and capable of measurement and mass production; in the light of Logos, each being is unique and yet capable of universal expression. In *Wissenschaft* you train a neutral observer to read a meter with objectivity; all observers everywhere should see the same event and describe it in the same way. In *Wissenkunst* the historian, like the musical composer, creates a unique narrative of time, and in this unique narrative the reader recognizes the universal truth of events. The art of *Wissenkunst* comes from research, for the historian is not free to make up characters and events any more than Aeschylus was free to invent Agamemnon and the Trojan War. In such a narrative, history loses the characteristic absolutism of science and religion; the reader is under no cultural compulsion to *believe in* what he reads, for what he reads is offered in the freedom of imaginative reception that characterizes artistic expression. As in the fictional histories of Jorgé Luis Borges or Stanislaw Lem, the boundaries between truth and fiction are intentionally blurred for the best of artistic and epistemological reasons.

A leader of a cult, whether the cult is religious, political, or scientific, says: "I have the Truth; follow me!" But the *Wissenkunstler* knows that no one can monopolize the Truth. The Truth cannot be expressed in an ideology, for the Truth is that power which overlights the conflict of opposed ideologies. And so the *Wissenkunstler* does not seek to turn his narrative into an apology for a new cult or the propaganda for an aspiring class of priests in a new theocracy. As a revolutionary act of prophecy in an age of political science, *Wissenkunst* is a unique and anarchic expression of freedom, and not a new and aspiring system of indoctrination. If *Wissenkunst* is itself turned into political apologetics, then the fabulous plumed serpent is turned into a monster, a basilisk.

To study myth one must go to a different kind of school from our universities, but the ancient schools are long since gone. Vibrating in another ether, the mystery schools are made out of music, not matter. To go there to study myth, one has to be drawn out of the body in sympathetic resonance with what it is. If one has never floated out of the body in meditation or sleep, then one should be disqualified from writing explanations of Egyptian religion with its Khat, Ba, Ka, Sahu, and Khu. We have built up a

materialistic civilization that is concerned almost exclusively with technology, power, and wealth, but the ancient Egyptians built up an entire civilization concerned, almost exclusively, with the psychic and the evolution of the human body as a vehicle for Illumination. The states of consciousness and the psychic experiences which are marginal for us were central for them. What we repress or ignore as a distraction from our proper attention on the physical, or as a possible seductive diversion from our central task of the conquest and domination of nature, or as a path to madness and schizophrenia, was to the ancient Egyptians the *donnée* of human consciousness that had to be dealt with if humanity was to understand its place in the cosmos. Cultures, like artists, focus on different subject matters and media of expression; some develop mastery over the subtle bodies, others choose to build rockets and walk in space suits on the moon. Each culture casts its own shadow, a shadow which is a perfect description of its own form and nature.

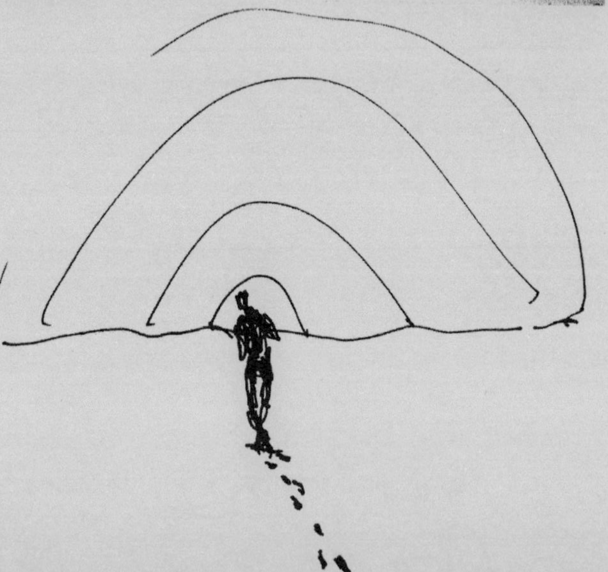

THE FIVE UNKNOWABLES

TEXT 1

You remove your shoes.

You stand on the grassy slope to read.

Is the viewer looking at you or the view?
Is the sun on your back?

Does the viewer catch you unawares?

Is there dew on the grass?

Shall we sip on it and sink into the moist ground?

Deeper and deeper, out of view.

TEXT 2

I walked over to her in the darkening courtyard. I am still handsome and upright. My accumulating years are not substantiated by my stature.

I've come to say goodbye to your parents. Where are they?

I'm sorry, they have left, they didn't say goodbye to me. They asked Zoe to say goodbye to me from them. Did Zoe say goodbye to you too?

Who is Zoe? I said.

~

As I removed my shoes I said, do you remember a show of conceptual art in

1971 at Bonython Gallery? It had ███ ███ and ████████ and many others. They were all young men.

And ███████████

That would be right I said.

I rolled my eyes. Nice guys, I said, but a waste of time.

Why? I said. Well it's a dead end, concept art. There's no-where to go. It's dead. It doesn't answer anything.

~

Art needs to answer The Five Unknowables.

The Unknowables? I said. Tell me more.

Only Sculpture answers all Five Unknowables simultaneously.

Maybe sculpture is all you know I said.

I disagreed. No, this is the only truth.

And I said what about poetry? and you laughed.

Let me explain I said.

I raised my voice and my arms. I swam in moving energy – protons and neutrons swimming around my gesticulating hands guiding me onwards.

The rush of force beneath my wings lifted me, the words flowing in the dark courtyard like shards of light pouring from my orifices. My audience was absorbed. I am alive again I shouted, I am here, I am in the company of young and old, I am heard.

It has to be behind you in front of you,

around you. You have to feel it. Feel it. I felt it.

Poetry by itself is simply not enough, I concluded.

I was dizzy.

~

Wasn't poetry one of the requirements I asked?

Sculpture, I began, is the only thing that can answer all Five Unknowables at once.

What are The Unknowables again? I asked.

I smirked. I'll tell you when you're not drunk (I'm not drunk, I thought).

You shrink away, making some excuse to me as you back away from my light into the crowded darkness.

TEXT 3

*I saw the sculpture you were describing – the one that answered all five calls.*

*It was a slinky mess, cast in shadows, cowering, hiding between the legs of all the people at the opening. It glared at me as I approached, and when I came from the other direction it turned quickly with a glint in its eye.*

*I felt its dewy ooze between my fingers as I stalked it on all fours, through the damp night's air, trying to see it clearly. As I closened it escaped my proximity again, darting in out of covered legs and swimming hands, circling smoke and aging cigarettes, shimmering mobile devices cradled in fists and pockets.*

*As I sat down close by it didn't welcome me, although it was aware of my interest. It didn't laugh. It's curling lip (an attempt at a smile?) wasn't warm, or even wry. It had dynamic thorns that grew longer the closer I sat.*

*Thorns, I learnt yesterday from a picture book, have a direct line to our nervous system.*

*1800 – N-E-R-V-O-U-S-S-Y-S-T-E-M*

*What are thorns? I ask the operator.*

*They help us know what hurt looks like before it happens, they tell me.*

TEXT 4

THE FIVE UNKNOWABLES

ONE Something about being caught unawares ~~IN THE GASLIGHT~~.

TWO Something about ~~FEMALE SCULPTORS~~ hanging ~~their~~ neurosis' on a flimsy copper frame.

THREE Something about how sculptors don't wear lipstick.

FOUR  Something about poetry being only part of the problem.

~~FIVE Something about how I will never call you again.~~

OR

THE PICTURE

 AGS 2018

AGATHA GOTHE–SNAPE ANNOTATED THE FIVE UNKNOWABLES, 2018 (TRANSCRIBED FROM MEMORY BY AGATHA GOTHE–SNAPE FOLLOWING DISCUSSION WITH AN UNDISCLOSED AUSTRALIAN SCULPTOR, BIENNALE OF AUSTRALIAN ART 2018, TARRAWARRA) my living through the birth and death of *Mahagonny* itself. More detailed theoretical information concerning the general method of approach to, and the background of the film, could be found in the original application." When I said—and this is also not in the letter —but when I said I have to spend all my time working at it, I'm doing that now in reading this letter for the first time. Because I don't even get Saturday or Friday night off. I wanted to go see a movie. I seldom go to a movie. I guess *Jaws* was the only important Hollywood film that I have seen recently, which I went to so that I could tell people fifty years from now the same way Seymour Stern is able to tell people how he went to the opening of a Buster Keaton film, *The General,* which is one of my very favorite films.

Good, good, good, et cetera, et cetera, et cetera, blah blah blah. The doctor himself is a little balmy, dating the letter January 3rd, 1976, and in a spasm of garbled syntax, seemingly makes CAPS responsible for my drunkenness of twenty years standing. There is no doubt that the CAPS grant precipitated a drinking and eating frenzy unparalleled in my recent history. A frenzy terminated only when I was strapped in bed with a twenty percent chance of living, a raving maniac suffering for two weeks of hallucinatory colors that rival those the Senate President delineates so skillfully in his *Memoirs of My Nervous Illness*, which I would like to add for the interviewers as one of the books *Heaven and Earth Magic* was based on. *Memoirs of My Nervous Illness*, edited by MacAlpine and Hunter, in Volume I of *Nervous and Mental Disease Monographs,* which was printed—that whole series being printed very lavishly to prove such things as shock therapy, telephones. [phone rings] Hello. Can you wait just a minute? Hold the telephone. Only when I was strapped in bed with a twenty percent chance of living, a raving maniac suffering for two weeks from hallucinatory colors that—the other book that we basically used in making film *Number 12* was Penfield and whatever his name is at the Montreal Neurological Institute called *Epilepsy and the Functional Anatomy of the Human Brain,* which outlines 1,800 brain operations of a most extraordinary nature, of which 1 300 of the patients died. But they

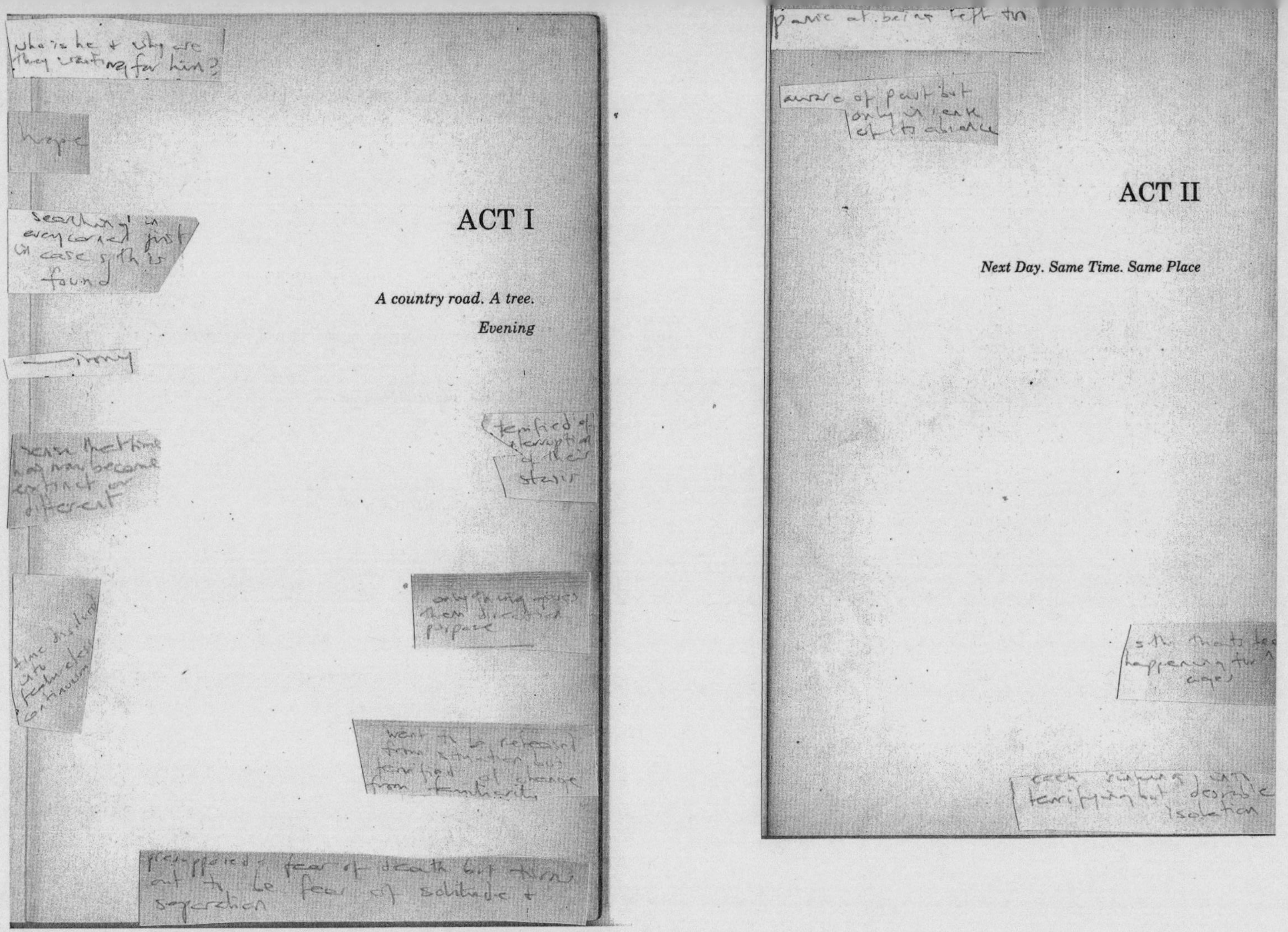

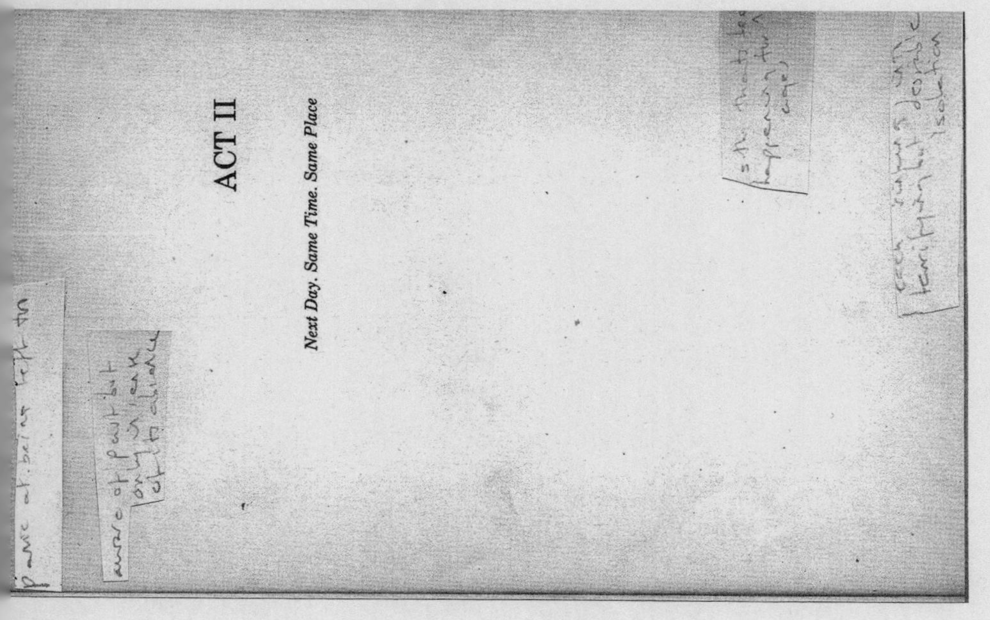


LAVINIA GREENLAW ANNOTATED WAITING FOR GODOT, 1953, SAMUEL BECKETT

**Waiting for Godot: Annotations 1980**

<u>Act I</u>

who is he & why are they waiting for him?

hope

searching in every corner just in case something is found

irony

sense that time has now become extinct or different

terrified of interruptions of their stasis

time dissolved into featureless continuum

only thing gives them direction purpose

want to be released from situation but terrified of change from familiarity

presupposed fear of death but turns out to be fear of solitude & separation

<u>Act II</u>

panic at being left too

aware of past but only in sense of its absence

something that's been happening for ages

each sinking into terrifying but desirable isolation

Bhanu Kapil, Ban en Banlieue, Nightboat Books, 2015.

I wanted to write a book that was like lying down.

That took some time to write, that kept forgetting something, that took a diversion: from which it never returned.

I wanted to write a book on a butcher's table in New Delhi: the shop-front open to the street, a bare light bulb swinging above the table and next to it a hook.

Swinging from that hook in the window, I wanted to write a book. Inverted, corrupted, exposed to view: a person writes a book in their free time, calling that time what they want to call it.

I wanted to write a book about England.

I wanted to write a book about lying on the floor of England. I wanted to return to England. I went to England. I was born in England. I lived in a house in England until I was thirty years old. My parents were English. I was English. After 1984, we all shared the same nationality, but by 2006 or 7, this was no longer true. Between September 2010 and late December 2012, I studied a piece of the earth, no longer or wider than a girl's body prone upon it. The asphalt. As dusk fell: violet/amber—and filled—with the reflected lights coming from the discs, the tiny mirrors, positioned in the ivy as she "slept."

On a balcony or street.

The asphalt's green stars, the shed parts of a ragged elm come Spring.

Ban is a portal, a vortex, a curl: a mixture of clockwise and anti-

42

clockwise movements in the sky above the street. I study the vapor as it rises, accumulates then starts to move. How a brisk wind organizes the soot or casings and bits of bark into whorls.

2017, Bhanu writes: -- we...
I don't know, decided?
To go back to.

Eng.
I am just going to call it Eng because I don't even know what a country is anymore. No, no, no.
Hate countries.
Basically hate the idea of a country. ⤷ (Get Away from He: Lalco')

That's how I feel now — got to go back to Eng., grudgingly — although I share none of the same family history, migrational history, history of exile as Bhanu. that I want to lie down.

After talking to A. about Partition (it's the anniversary), learning more about the violent details of the dividing up of / laid to make India, a history that we were never taught in school, and a history that forced his family to move (like Bhanu's, I have a dream, which I record the next day as follows:

I ask a boy:
Why do your hands smell like soil?
and he says: 43
I was burying part of myself
at the partition.

Hannah Gregory

Visiting.

↓
Emily, periods,
shame / prudery,
scene.

Bhanu., Bar en Banlieue.

"I wanted to write a book that was like lying
down.
. . . .

Like eyes in the time that follows talking.

103 Gorz's formulation of the fragment — * 'rough' — where
the edge of it is, like glass or fur or light, so that it
adheres to other fragments, not through historical or
phatic means; but through the force of attraction."
// resentment.

Adorno on fragment : "Fragment is the intrusion of
death into the work. While destroying (it), it removes the
stain of semblance."

— somatic residue. shows the psychological work is not
gut feeling / stomach stones.          complete.

⊛ In a note from a 'stray (she says 'rogue')
notebook included at the end of this book, BK
writes : "To write about England far from England.
To approach Englishness as the thing that decays,
and to watch it decay."

ing pockets and little pools and explore the best methods of fishing this type of water. If the brook is not more than four or five feet across in most places, and most of them won't be, then it is best to pick a section of stream a couple of hundred yards in length and begin fishing at the upper end working your way slowly back downstream. Keep in mind that the trout in a stream of this type will be lying next to the small boulders or in the little holding pools waiting to catch feed as it comes drifting by them. Also remember that in any stream, the bigger and stronger fish will predominate, taking the positions where the most amount of food will be washed or tumbled in to meet its needs. The term "reading the water" is the most important phrase in the whole concept of fly fishing or, in fact, any type of stream fishing. It simply means determining where the fish will be hiding at a particular time by studying the immediate environment surrounding the fish. This eliminates wasting a lot of time casting to areas where there are no fish. Since all underwater obstacles act as catchers for insects and other food, the fish will stay next to these obstacles both for cover and feeding purposes. The currents are the vehicles that carry the food to the fish, so the more converging currents, the greater amount of food being delivered to that section of the stream. This will be where your bigger trout will take position, so your first cast should present the fly so that it will drift into that feeding lane and appear to the trout in the most natural manner possible. Since we are dealing here with streams of smaller dimensions in the East that contain brook trout, we must determine what patterns work best a majority of time. Also keep in mind that these same methods and patterns apply equally well on the smaller Western streams where other types of fish predominate.

The effectiveness of certain patterns will vary with the different times of the season and the different types of insects in the water, water temperature also being an important factor. In the early spring when the water is very cold, the trout's metabolism is slowed and the fish will be lying dormant on or near the bottom of the pools or in the deeper water beneath the boulders. It is, therefore, necessary to get your fly down near the bottom as the fish will not be inclined to expend any amount of energy to go after or chase the fly to capture it. That is one criterion for determining the pattern to use and how to fish it. Another factor is the stream level and color of the water. If you have a combination of conditions such as high water after a spring run-off, discolored water and icewater, then the fish will not only be lying near the bottom but will also be handicapped from seeing any dull or neutral colors that do not catch their eye quick enough to allow them time to strike. Under these conditions, it is better to use brighter or more colorful patterns or flies such as the mini-muddler with a gold or silver body. Since brook trout prefer brighter colored flies than do brown trout, these patterns are consistently good producers and probably should be the first ones to try.

Another very effective way of fishing this type of stream is letting the fly drift down below you and hang in the currents as it works its way down into the hiding places alongside the rocks. The fly can then be retrieved very slowly to give it a more lifelike action. Keep in mind that when the water is very cold, a slow methodical retrieve or just letting the fly hang in the currents for a couple of minutes next to a boulder or under a little waterfall where the water swirls about is most effective.

If you are approaching this same section of stream later on in the season, say in June when the water is at normal level and the stream temperature has warmed, then it is appropriate to use slightly different methods and different patterns as well. The brook trout's diet during this time consists of insects of which the black fly larvae is one of the most important sources of feed. From mid-May until the end of June, small black nymphs will be consistently productive. A little trick I've found to be extremely helpful and one that almost always doubles my take of fish on any given outing is tying the black nymph with three or four winds of very fine gold ribbing over the body of the fly. This in effect combines the basic color of the fly on which the trout are feeding at the same time making the fly more visable to the fish. It also takes advantage of the fish's

POETICS OF RELATION, ÉDOUARD GLISSANT (1990)

## For Opacity

Several years back, if I made the statement, "We demand the right to opacity," or argued in favor of this, whoever I was speaking to would exclaim indignantly: "Now it's back to barbarism! How can you communicate with what you don't understand?" But in 1989, and before very diverse audiences, when the same demand was formulated, it aroused new interest. Who knows? Maybe, in the meanwhile, the topicality of the question of differences (the right to difference) had been exhausted.

The theory of difference is invaluable. It has allowed us to struggle against the reductive thought produced, in genetics for example, by the presumption of racial excellence or superiority. Albert Jacquard (*Éloge de la différence*, Éditions du Seuil, 1978) dismantled the mechanisms of this barbaric notion and demonstrated how ridiculous it was to claim a "scientific" basis for them. (I call the reversal and exasperation of self barbaric, and just as inconceivable as the cruel results of these mechanisms.) This theory has also made it possible to take in, perhaps, not their existence but at least the rightful entitlement to recognition of the minorities swarming throughout the world and the defense of their status. (I call "rightful" the escape far from any legitimacy anchored silently or resolutely in possession and conquest.)

But difference itself can still contrive to reduce things to the Transparent.

If we examine the process of "understanding" people and ideas from the perspective of Western thought, we discover that its basis is this requirement for transparency. In order to understand and thus accept you, I have to measure your solidity with the ideal scale providing me with grounds to make comparisons and, perhaps, judgments. I have to reduce.

Accepting differences does, of course, upset the hierarchy of this scale. I understand your difference, or in other words, without creating a hierarchy, I relate it to my norm. I admit you to existence, within my system. I create you afresh. —But perhaps we need to bring an end to the very notion of a scale. Displace all reduction.

Agree not merely to the right to difference but, carrying this further, agree also to the right to opacity that is not enclosure within an impenetrable autarchy but subsistence within an irreducible singularity. Opacities can coexist and converge, weaving fabrics. To understand these truly one must focus on the texture of the weave and not on the nature of its components. For the time being, perhaps, give up this old obsession with discovering what lies at the bottom of natures. There would be something great and noble about initiating such a movement, referring not to Humanity but to the exultant divergence of humanities. Thought of self and thought of other here become obsolete in their duality. Every Other is a citizen and no longer a barbarian. What is here is open, as much as this there. I would be incapable of projecting from one to the other. This-here is the weave, and it weaves no boundaries. The right to opacity would not establish autism; it would be the real foundation of Relation, in freedoms.

And now what they tell me is. "You calmly pack your poetics into these craters of opacity and claim to rise so serenely beyond the prodigiously elucidating work that the West has accomplished, but there you go talking nonstop about this West." —"And what would you rather I talk about at the beginning, if not this transparency whose aim was to reduce us? Because, if I don't begin there, you will see me consumed with the sullen jabber of childish refusal, convulsive and powerless. This is where I start. As for my identity, I'll take care of that myself." There has to be dialogue with the West, which, moreover is contradictory in itself (usually this is the argument raised when I talk about cultures of the One); the complementary discourse of whoever wants to give-on-and-with must be added to the West. And can you not see that we are implicated in its evolution?

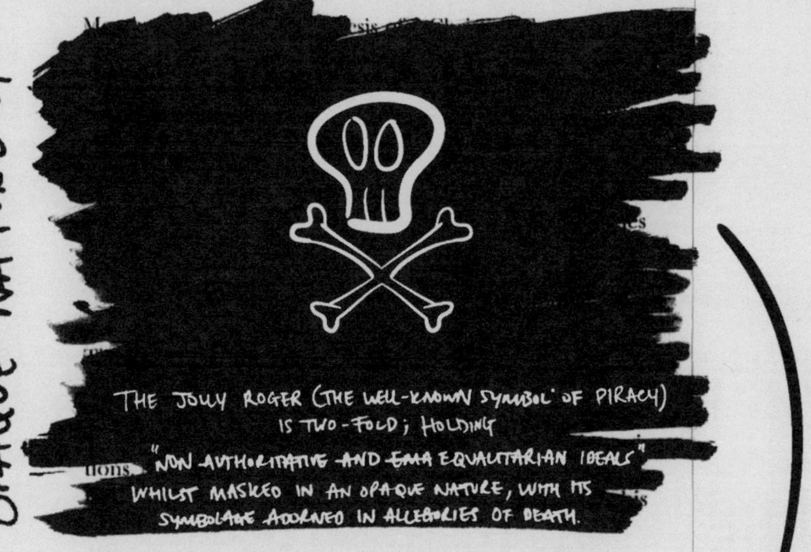


The opaque is not the obscure, though it is possible for it to be so and be accepted as such. It is that which cannot be reduced, which is the most perennial guarantee of participation and confluence. We are far from the opacities of Myth or Tragedy, whose obscurity was accompanied by exclusion and whose transparency aimed at "grasping." In this version of understanding the verb *to grasp* contains the movement of

hands that grab their surroundings and bring them back to themselves. A gesture of enclosure if not appropriation. Let our understanding prefer the gesture of giving-on-and-with that opens finally on totality.

( .... )

On the other hand, if an opacity is the basis for a Legitimacy, this would be the sign of its having entered into a political dimension. A formidable prospect, less dangerous perhaps than the erring ways to which so many certainties and so many clear, so-called lucid truths have led. The excesses of these political assurances would fortunately be contained by the sense not that everything is futile but that there are limits to absolute truth. How can one point out these limits without lapsing into skepticism or paralysis? How can one reconcile the hard line inherent in any politics and the questioning essential to any relation? Only by understanding that it is impossible to reduce anyone, no matter who, to a truth he would not have generated on his own. That is, within the opacity of his time and place. Plato's city is for Plato, Hegel's vision is for Hegel, the griot's town is for the griot. Nothing prohibits our seeing them in confluence, without confusing them in some magma or reducing them to each other. This same opacity is also the force that drives every community: the thing that would bring us together forever and make us permanently distinctive. Widespread consent to specific opacities is the most straightforward equivalent of nonbarbarism.

We clamor for the right to opacity for everyone.





GLISSANT'S OPACITY X MISUNDERSTANDING OF THE JOLLY ROGER

# NOTES ON SEEING

*Siri Hustvedt*

1. To look and not see: an old problem. It usually means a lack of understanding, an inability to divine the meaning of something in the world around us.

2. Cognitive scientists have repeatedly conducted the following experiment and, without fail, they come up with same results. An audience is asked to watch a film of two teams playing basketball. The observers are given a job to count the number of times the ball changes hands. I have done this, and one has to be very attentive to follow the motion of the ball. In the middle of the game, a man wearing a gorilla suit walks onto the court, turns to the camera, thumps his chest, and leaves. Half the people do not see the great ape. They do not believe that he was actually there until the film is replayed and, indeed, a gorilla strolls in and out of the game. Nearly everyone sees the gorilla if he is *not* given the assignment. This has been named *inattentional blindness.*

3. Writing at my desk now, I see the screen, but this sentence dominates my attention. In fact, my momentary awareness that there is much around the words distracts me: the blue screen of the computer beyond the white edge of the page; various icons above and below; the surface of my desk cluttered with small Post-it squares which, when I turn my head, I can read, "Habermas 254–55," "Meany et al., implications for adrenocortical responses to stress" scrawled on pink paper (residue of arcane research); a black stapler; and countless other objects that enter my awareness the moment I turn to them. What is crucial is that I don't turn to them. For hours every day, I have little, if any, consciousness of them. I live in a circumscribed phenomenal world. An internal narrator speaks words and dictates to my fingers, which type automatically. There is no need to think about the connection between head and hands. I am subsumed by the link. Were another object suddenly to materialize on my desk and then vanish, I might well have no knowledge of either its appearance or disappearance.

4. Once, in an unfamiliar hallway, I mistook myself for a stranger because I did not understand I was looking in a mirror. My own form took me by surprise because I was not oriented in space. Expectation is crucial to perception.

5. There are days when I think I see an old friend in the street, but it is a stranger. The recognition ignites like a match and then is instantly extinguished when I understand I am wrong. The recognition is felt, not thought. I can't trace what created the error, can't tell you why one person reminded me of another. Was the old friend a subliminal presence in my mind on that particular day or was the confusion purely external—a jut of the chin or slope of the shoulders or rhythm of a walk?

6. We do not become anesthetized to horrible photographs of death or suffering. We may choose to avoid them. When I see a gruesome image in the newspaper in the morning, I sometimes turn away, registering in seconds that looking too long will hurt me. People who gorge on horror films and violent thrillers do it not because they have learned to feel too little, but because they indulge in the limbic rush that floods their systems as they safely witness exploding bodies. It seems that these viewers are mostly men.

7. We feel colors before we can name them. Colors act on us pre-reflectively. A part of me feels red before I can name red. My cognitive faculties lag behind the color's impact. Standing in a room, I look first at the vase of red tulips because they are red and because they are alive.

8. My mother once told me about coming home to find our cat dead on the lawn. She saw the poor animal from many yards away, but she said she knew with absolute assurance that it was dead. An inert thing. An it.

9. Photographs of the beloved dead draw me in. I am fascinated. There is the good, dear face, one that changed over time. It is the picture that preserves the face, not my memory, which is befogged by the many faces he had over the years. Or is it the single face that grew old? Sometimes I cannot bear to look. The image has become a token of grief. And yet, there is nothing so banal as the pictures of strange families. After my father died, I found Christmas cards with photographs of unknown people among his papers—happy families—grinning into an invisible lens. I threw them away.

10. Galvanic skin response registers a change in the heat and electricity passed through the skin by nerves and sweat during emotional states. People in white coats attach electrodes to your hands and track what happens. When they show you a picture of your mother, your GSR goes up. Meaning in the body.

11. Is our visual world rich or poor? There are fights about this. People do not agree. Philosophers, scientists, and other academics ponder this richness and poverty question in papers and books and lectures. Human beings have very limited peripheral vision, but we can turn our heads and take in more of the world. When I'm writing, my vision is severely limited by my attention, but sometimes when I let my eyes roam in a space, I discover its density of light and color and feel surprised by what I find. When I focus, say, just on the shadows here on my desk, they become remarkable. My small round clock casts a double shadow from either side of its circular base, one darker than the other, a gray and a paler gray. There is a spot of brilliant light at the edge of the darker oval. As I look, this sight has become beautiful.

12. Why is a face beautiful?

13. If an image is flashed too quickly to be perceived consciously, we take it in unconsciously and respond to it without knowing what is happening. A picture of a scowling face I can't say I've seen affects me anyway. Scientists call this *masking.* Blindsight patients have cortical blindness. They lose visual consciousness but not visual unconsciousness. They see but don't know they are seeing. If you ask them to guess what you're holding (a pencil) they will guess far better than people who are truly blind. Words and consciousness are connected. How much do I see of the world that never registers in my awareness? When I walk in the street, I sometimes glimpse a scene for just an instant, but I cannot tell you what I have witnessed until a fraction of a second later, when the puzzling image falls into place: that furry thing was a stuffed animal, and a little boy was dangling it from his stroller. The lag again.

14. We are picture-making creatures. We scribble and draw and paint. When I draw what I see, I touch the thing I am looking at with my mind, but it is as if my hand is caressing its outline. People who stopped drawing as children continue to make pictures in their dreams or in the hallucinations that arrive just before they go to sleep. Where do those images come from? I dreamed that grass and brush and sticks were growing out of my arm, and I got to work busily trimming myself with a pair of scissors. I wasn't alarmed; it was a job handled in a matter-of-fact way. If I painted a self-portrait with bushy arms, I would be called a surrealist.

15. Some people who go blind see vivid images and colors. Some people who are losing their vision hallucinate while awake. An old man saw cows grazing in his living room, and a woman saw cartoon characters running up and down her doctor's arm. Charles Bonnet syndrome. Just before I fell asleep, I saw a little man speeding over pink and violet cliffs. Once I saw an explosion of melting colors—green, blues, reds, and then a great flash of light that devoured them all. Hypnagogic hallucinations. Freud said dreams protect sleep. At night the world is taken from us and we make up our own scenes and stories. If you wake up slowly, you will remember more of that human underground than if you wake up quickly.

16. Deprived of sight, we make visions. Seeing is also creating.

17. There are things in the world to see. Do I see what you see? We can talk about it and verify the facts. Through my window is the back of a house. One of its windows is completely covered by

a blue shade. But if I tell you I see a flying zebra you will say, Siri, you are hallucinating. You are dreaming while awake.

18. Sometimes artists can make a hallucination real. A painting of a flying zebra is a real thing in the world, a real thing to see.

19. Why do I not like the word *taste* when applied to art? Because it has lost its connection to the mouth and food and chewing. I don't like the way this picture tastes. It's bitter. If we thought about actual tastes, the word would still work. It would be a form of synesthesia, a crossing of our senses: seeing as tasting. But usually it is not used like that anymore, so I avoid it entirely when I talk about art.

20. Looking at a human being or even a picture of a human being is different from looking at an object. Newborn babies, only hours old, copy the expressions of adults. They pucker up, try to grin, look surprised, and stick out their tongues. The photographs of imitating infants are both funny and touching. They do not *know* they are doing it; this response is in them from the beginning. Later, people learn to suppress the imitation mechanism; it would not be good if we went on forever copying every facial expression we saw. Nevertheless, we human beings love to look at faces because we find ourselves there. When you smile at me, I feel a smile form on my own face before I am aware it is happening, and I smile because I am seeing me in your eyes and know that you like what you see.

21. I am looking at a small reproduction of Johannes Vermeer's *Study of a Young Woman*, which hangs in a room at the Metropolitan Museum here in New York. It is a girl's head and face. I say *girl* because she is very young. From her face I would guess she is no more than ten years old. When I look up the picture in one of my books on Vermeer, I see that there it is called *Portrait of a Young Girl*, a far better title. We should not turn girls into women too soon. She is smiling, but not a wide smile. Her lips are sealed. My impression is that she is looking at me, but I cannot quite catch her eye. What is certain is that she is answering someone else's gaze. Someone has made her smile. She is not a beautiful child; it is her looking that is beautiful, her connection to the invisible person. There is shyness in her expression, reserve, maybe a hint of hesitancy. I think she is looking at an adult, probably the artist, because she has not let herself go. She looks over her shoulder at him. I have great affection for this girl. That is the magic of the painting; it is not that I have affection for a representation of a child's head that was painted some time between 1665 and 1667. No, I feel I have actually fallen for her, the way I fall for a child who looks up at me on the street and smiles, perhaps a homely child, who with a single look calls forth a burst of maternal feeling and sympathy. But my emotion is made of something more; I remember my own girlhood and my shyness with grown-ups I didn't know well. I was not a bold child, and in her face I see myself at the same age.

22. In some of Gerhard Richter's painted-over photographs, he painted over his wife's face and parts of her body. He covered the bodies of his children, too, in snapshots of them as babies and growing children. In these gestures, I felt he was keeping them for himself, keeping the private hidden. Other times, he framed them with swaths of color, turning them into featured subjects. I love those pictures.

23. Mothers have a need to look at their children. We cannot help it.

24. Lovers have a need to look at each other. They cannot help it.

25. Sometimes I like to look at my husband's face in photographs because he becomes a stranger in the pictures, an object fixed in time. Over many years, I have come to know him through my other senses, too—the feel of his skin, the changing smell of his body in winter and spring and fall and summer, the sound of his voice, his breathing, and sometimes his snoring at night. When I look at him in a photograph, my other senses are quiet. I simply see him, and because I find him beautiful, his unmoving face excites me.

26. Looking at pornography is exciting but loses its interest after orgasm.

27. Reading the end of James Joyce's *Ulysses* when Molly Bloom is remembering is erotic because she gives permission, gives up and gives way, and this is always exciting and interesting because it is personal, not impersonal. Isn't it strange that looking at little abstract symbols on a white page can make a person feel such things? I see her in his arms. I am in his arms. I remember your arms.

28. When I read stories, I see them. I make pictures and often they remain in my mind after I have finished a novel, along with some phrases or sentences. I ground the characters in places, real and imagined. But I always remember the feeling of a book best, unless I have forgotten it altogether.

29. I do not usually *see* philosophy—with some exceptions: Plato, Pascal, Kierkegaard, and Nietzsche, because they are also storytellers.



30. Some people cannot make visual imagery. They do not see pictures in their minds. They do not turn words into images. I didn't know such a thing was possible until a short time ago. They see abstractly. They remember the symbols on the page.

31. "I see" can also mean "I understand."

32. There is a small part of the brain called the fusiform gyrus that is crucial for recognizing faces. If you lose this ability, your deficit is called prosopagnosia. It happens that a person with brain damage looks at herself in the mirror and believes she is seeing, not herself, but a double. It seems that what has vanished is not reason but that special feeling we get when we look at our reflections, that warm sense of ownership. When that disappears, the image of one's self becomes alien.

33. I look and sometimes I see.

2010

else I might be tempted to say. When, for example, Pascal makes the famous remark that the heart has its reasons as well as the head, when Goethe says that no matter how hard we try there will always be an irreducible element of anthropomorphism in everything we do and think, these remarks strike people as profound for this reason, because wherever we apply them they open new vistas, and these vistas are not reducible, not embraceable, not describable, not collectable; you have no formula which will by deduction lead you to all of them. This is the fundamental notion of depth in the romantics, and it is to this, in a large degree, that most of their talk about the finite standing for the infinite, the material standing for the immaterial, the dead standing for the living, space standing for time, words standing for something which is in itself wordless, relates. 'Can the sacred be seized?' asked Friedrich Schlegel, and he replied, 'No, it can never be seized because the mere imposition of form deforms it.' This is what runs through their entire theory of life and of art.

This leads to two quite interesting and obsessive phenomena which are then very present both in nineteenth- and in twentieth-century thought and feeling. One is nostalgia, and the other is paranoia of a certain kind. The nostalgia is due to the fact that, since the infinite cannot be exhausted, and since we are seeking to embrace it, nothing that we do will ever satisfy us. When Novalis was asked where he thought he was tending, what his art was about, he said 'I am always going home, always to my father's house.' This was in one sense a religious remark, but he also meant that all these attempts at the exotic, the strange, the foreign, the odd, all these attempts to emerge from the empirical framework of daily life, the writing of fantastic stories with transformations and transmogrifications of a most peculiar kind, attempts at writing down stories which are symbolic or allegorical or contain all kinds of mystical and veiled references, esoteric imagery of a most peculiar kind which has preoccupied critics for years, are all attempts to go back, to go home to what is pulling and drawing him, the famous infinite *Sehnsucht* of the romantics, the search for the blue flower, as Novalis called it. The search for the blue flower is an attempt either to absorb the infinite into myself, to make myself at one with it, or to dissolve myself into it. This is a which frustrates our dearest wishes. Sometimes it is conceived as a kind of indifferent or even hostile nature, sometimes as the cunning of history, which optimists think bears us towards ever more glorious goals, but which pessimists such as Schopenhauer think is simply a huge fathomless ocean of undirected will upon which we bob like a little boat with no direction, no possibility of really understanding the element in which we are, or directing our course upon it; and this is a huge, powerful, ultimately hostile force, to resist which or even to come to terms with which is never of the slightest use.

This paranoia takes all kinds of other, sometimes much cruder, forms. It takes the form, for example, of looking for all kinds of conspiracies in history. People begin to think that perhaps history is formed by forces over which we have no control. Someone is at the back of it all: perhaps the Jesuits, perhaps the Jews, perhaps the Freemasons. This attitude was much stimulated by attempts to explain the course of the French Revolution. We the enlightened, we the virtuous, we the wise, we the good and the kind seek to do this or that, but somehow all our efforts end in nothing, and therefore there must be some fearful hostile force lying in wait for us which trips us up when we are on the brink, as we think, of great success. This view takes, as I say, crude forms, such as the conspiracy theory of history, by which you always look for concealed enemies, sometimes for larger and larger conceptions such as economic forces, the forces of production or class war (as in Marx), or the much vaguer and more metaphysical notion of the cunning of reason or of history (as in Hegel), which understands its goal much better than we do and plays tricks upon us. Hegel says, 'The spirit cheats us, the spirit intrigues, the spirit lies, the spirit triumphs.' He almost conceives of it as a kind of huge, ironical, Aristophanic force which mocks the poor human beings who are trying to construct their little homes upon the slopes of what they regard as a green and flowery mountain, but which turns out to be the vast volcano of human history, which is about to erupt once again, ultimately perhaps for human good, ultimately in order to realise itself towards an ideal, but in the short run destroying a large number of innocent persons and causing a great deal of suffering and damage.

*"What sad irony in human history!"*

*(James quotes Saurès.)*

The George Padmore Research Library
Gamal Abdul Nasser Avenue
Accra
Ghana
February 2013

## Prologue

The Black Jacobins
by
C.L.R. James

*Toussaint Louverture and the San Domingo Revolution, 1938*

Christopher Columbus landed first in the New World at the island of San Salvador, and after praising God enquired urgently for gold. The natives, Red Indians, were peaceable and friendly and directed him to Haiti, a large island (nearly as large as Ireland), rich, they said, in the yellow metal. He sailed to Haiti. One of his ships being wrecked, the Haitian Indians helped him so willingly that very little was lost and of the articles which they brought on shore not one was stolen.

The Spaniards, the most advanced Europeans of their day, annexed the island, called it Hispaniola, and took the backward natives under their protection. They introduced Christianity, forced labour in mines, murder, rape, bloodhounds, strange diseases, and artificial famine (by the destruction of cultivation to starve the rebellious). These and other requirements of the higher civilization reduced the native population from an estimated half-a-million, perhaps a million, to 60,000 in fifteen years.

Las Casas, a Dominican priest with a conscience, travelled to Spain to plead for the abolition of native slavery. But without coercion of the natives how could the colony exist? All the natives received as wages was Christianity and they could be good Christians without working in the mines.

The Spanish Government compromised. It abolished the *repartimientos*, or forced labour, in law while its agents in the colony maintained it in fact. Las Casas, haunted at the prospect of seeing before his eyes the total destruction of a population within one generation, hit on the expedient of importing the more robust Negroes from a populous Africa; in 1517, Charles V authorized the export of 15,000 slaves to San Domingo, and thus priest and King launched on the world the American slave-trade and slavery.

*In a single page, James narrates the origins of global capitalism within the "discovery" of the Americas, resource extraction and forced labour, resulting in the 'moral' decision to begin the Atlantic slave trade.*

_life + inert matter — how we comprehend things through our bodies — as a "mixing" in the world + a border to it._

## Oh, Tomato Puree!

_A way of understanding our relationship with other <u>stuff</u>_

_mundane + vibrant_

Oh, Tomato Puree! When at last you occur to me it is as something <u>pro-fuse, fresh, and erupting.</u> Alas, when I open the door and reach for you, the chill light comes on and <u>shows you crumpled, cold, and, despite being well within your sell-by-date, in dire need of coaxing.</u>

_vision of the crumpled substance in the packaging as both geographical + graphic — a thick image — crumpled viscosity_

_Skins_

_self + substance convoluted bodies_

_material imagination ignite thoughts the hand_

_Sexy!_

Oh, Tomato Puree—let me lay you out and <u>pummel</u> those rigid furrows and creases! Reconnecting your fractured substance, so you might push aside the residue of previous abundance and come forth again, in all your <u>kitsch</u> and concentrated <u>splendour.</u>

_the previous fullness of being "emptied out"_

_Gaston Bachelard's definition of the infinitely malleable "ideal paste" (of which clay, dough + mashed potato can all fit within)_

_(not as kitsch as Heinz?)_

_rich + dumb_

_an ambition of giving depth + furnishing full bodied sensation puree as the flat essence + image of its former whole (tomato)_

_"a perfect synthesis of stiffness + softness, a marvellous equilibrium of yielding + resisting forces" (GB – 'An essay on the imaginations of matter)_

### VII. L'insubordination des faits matériels

La vie humaine, distincte de l'existence juridique et telle qu'elle a lieu en fait sur un globe isolé dans l'espace céleste, du jour à la nuit, d'une contrée à l'autre, la vie humaine ne peut en aucun cas être limitée aux systèmes fermés qui lui sont assignés dans des conceptions raisonnables. L'immense travail d'abandon, d'écoulement et d'orage qui la constitue pourrait être exprimé en disant qu'elle ne commence qu'avec le déficit de ces systèmes : du moins ce qu'elle admet d'ordre et de réserve n'a-t-il de sens qu'à partir du moment où les forces ordonnées et réservées se libèrent et se perdent pour des fins qui ne peuvent être assujetties à rien dont il soit possible de rendre des comptes. C'est seulement par une telle insubordination, même misérable, que l'espèce humaine cesse d'être isolée dans la splendeur sans condition des choses matérielles.

En fait, de la façon la plus universelle, isolément ou en groupe, les hommes se trouvent constamment engagés dans des processus de dépense. La variation des formes n'entraîne aucune altération des caractères fondamentaux de ces processus dont le principe est la perte. Une certaine excitation, dont la somme est maintenue au cours des alternatives à un étiage sensiblement constant, anime les collectivités et les personnes. Sous leur forme accentuée, les *états d'excitation* qui sont assimilables à des états toxiques, peuvent être définis comme des impulsions illogiques et irrésistibles au rejet des biens matériels ou moraux qu'il aurait été possible d'utiliser rationnellement (conformément au principe de la balance des comptes). Aux pertes ainsi réalisées se trouve liée – aussi bien dans le cas de la « fille *perdue* » que dans celui de la dépense militaire – la création de valeurs improductives, dont la plus absurde et en même temps celle qui rend le plus avide est la *gloire*. Complétée par la *déchéance*, celle-ci sous des formes tantôt sinistres et tantôt éclatantes, n'a pas cessé de dominer l'existence sociale et il reste impossible de rien entreprendre sans elle alors qu'elle est conditionnée par la pratique aveugle de la perte personnelle ou sociale.

C'est ainsi que le déchet immense de l'activité entraîne les intentions humaines – y compris celles qui sont associées aux opérations économiques – dans le jeu qualificatif de la matière universelle : la matière, en effet, ne peut être définie que par la *différence non logique* qui représente par rapport à l'*économie* de l'univers ce que le *crime* représente par rapport à la loi. La gloire qui résume ou symbolise (sans l'épuiser) l'objet de la dépense libre, alors qu'elle ne peut jamais exclure le crime, ne peut pas être distinguée de la qualification – du moins si l'on tient compte de la seule qualification qui ait une valeur comparable à celle de la matière, de la *qualification insubordonnée*, qui n'est la condition de rien d'autre.

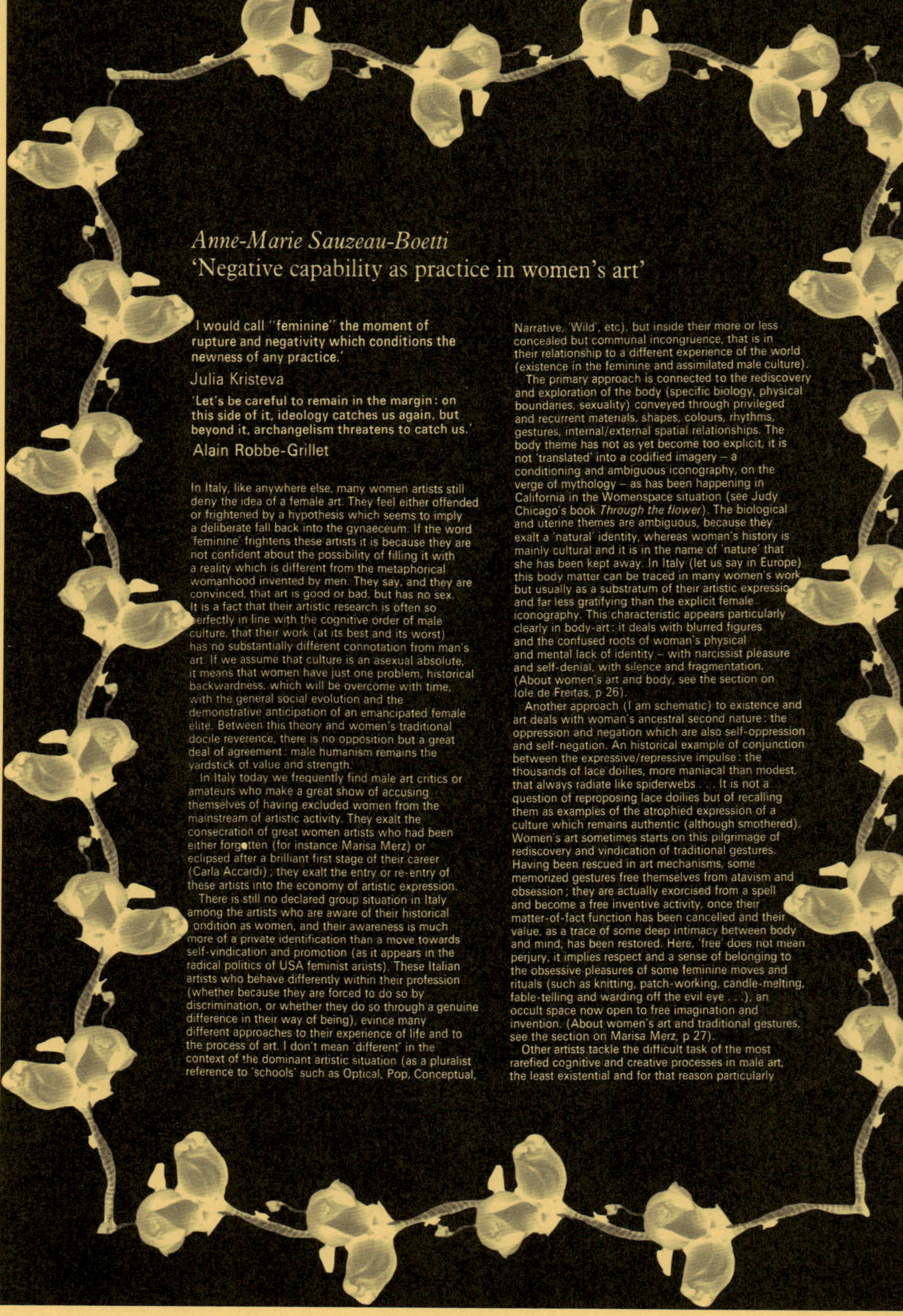

## Anne-Marie Sauzeau-Boetti
### 'Negative capability as practice in women's art'

I would call ''feminine'' the moment of rupture and negativity which conditions the newness of any practice.'

Julia Kristeva

'Let's be careful to remain in the margin: on this side of it, ideology catches us again, but beyond it, archangelism threatens to catch us.'

Alain Robbe-Grillet

In Italy, like anywhere else, many women artists still deny the idea of a female art. They feel either offended or frightened by a hypothesis which seems to imply a deliberate fall back into the gynaeceum. If the word 'feminine' frightens these artists it is because they are not confident about the possibility of filling it with a reality which is different from the metaphorical womanhood invented by men. They say, and they are convinced, that art is good or bad, but has no sex. It is a fact that their artistic research is often so perfectly in line with the cognitive order of male culture, that their work (at its best and its worst) has no substantially different connotation from man's art. If we assume that culture is an asexual absolute, it means that women have just one problem, historical backwardness, which will be overcome with time, with the general social evolution and the demonstrative anticipation of an emancipated female elite. Between this theory and women's traditional docile reverence, there is no opposition but a great deal of agreement: male humanism remains the yardstick of value and strength.

In Italy today we frequently find male art critics or amateurs who make a great show of accusing themselves of having excluded women from the mainstream of artistic activity. They exalt the consecration of great women artists who had been either forgotten (for instance Marisa Merz) or eclipsed after a brilliant first stage of their career (Carla Accardi); they exalt the entry or re-entry of these artists into the economy of artistic expression.

There is still no declared group situation in Italy among the artists who are aware of their historical condition as women, and their awareness is much more of a private identification than a move towards self-vindication and promotion (as it appears in the radical politics of USA feminist artists). These Italian artists who behave differently within their profession (whether because they are forced to do so by discrimination, or whether they do so through a genuine difference in their way of being), evince many different approaches to their experience of life and to the process of art. I don't mean 'different' in the context of the dominant artistic situation (as a pluralist reference to 'schools' such as Optical, Pop, Conceptual, Narrative, 'Wild', etc), but inside their more or less concealed but communal incongruence, that is in their relationship to a different experience of the world (existence in the feminine and assimilated male culture).

The primary approach is connected to the rediscovery and exploration of the body (specific biology, physical boundaries, sexuality) conveyed through privileged and recurrent materials, shapes, colours, rhythms, gestures, internal/external spatial relationships. The body theme has not as yet become too explicit, it is not 'translated' into a codified imagery – a conditioning and ambiguous iconography, on the verge of mythology – as has been happening in California in the Womenspace situation (see Judy Chicago's book *Through the flower*). The biological and uterine themes are ambiguous, because they exalt a 'natural' identity, whereas woman's history is mainly cultural and it is in the name of 'nature' that she has been kept away. In Italy (let us say in Europe) this body matter can be traced in many women's work but usually as a substratum of their artistic expression and far less gratifying than the explicit female iconography. This characteristic appears particularly clearly in body-art: it deals with blurred figures and the confused roots of woman's physical and mental lack of identity – with narcissist pleasure and self-denial, with silence and fragmentation. (About women's art and body, see the section on Iole de Freitas, p 26).

Another approach (I am schematic) to existence and art deals with woman's ancestral second nature: the oppression and negation which are also self-oppression and self-negation. An historical example of conjunction between the expressive/repressive impulse: the thousands of lace doilies, more maniacal than modest, that always radiate like spiderwebs . . . It is not a question of reproposing lace doilies but of recalling them as examples of the atrophied expression of a culture which remains authentic (although smothered). Women's art sometimes starts on this pilgrimage of rediscovery and vindication of traditional gestures. Having been rescued in art mechanisms, some memorized gestures free themselves from atavism and obsession; they are actually exorcised from a spell and become a free inventive activity, once their matter-of-fact function has been cancelled and their value, as a trace of some deep intimacy between body and mind, has been restored. Here, 'free' does not mean perjury, it implies respect and a sense of belonging to the obsessive pleasures of some feminine moves and rituals (such as knitting, patch-working, candle-melting, fable-telling and warding off the evil eye . . .), an occult space now open to free imagination and invention. (About women's art and traditional gestures, see the section on Marisa Merz, p 27).

Other artists tackle the difficult task of the most rarefied cognitive and creative processes in male art, the least existential and for that reason particularly

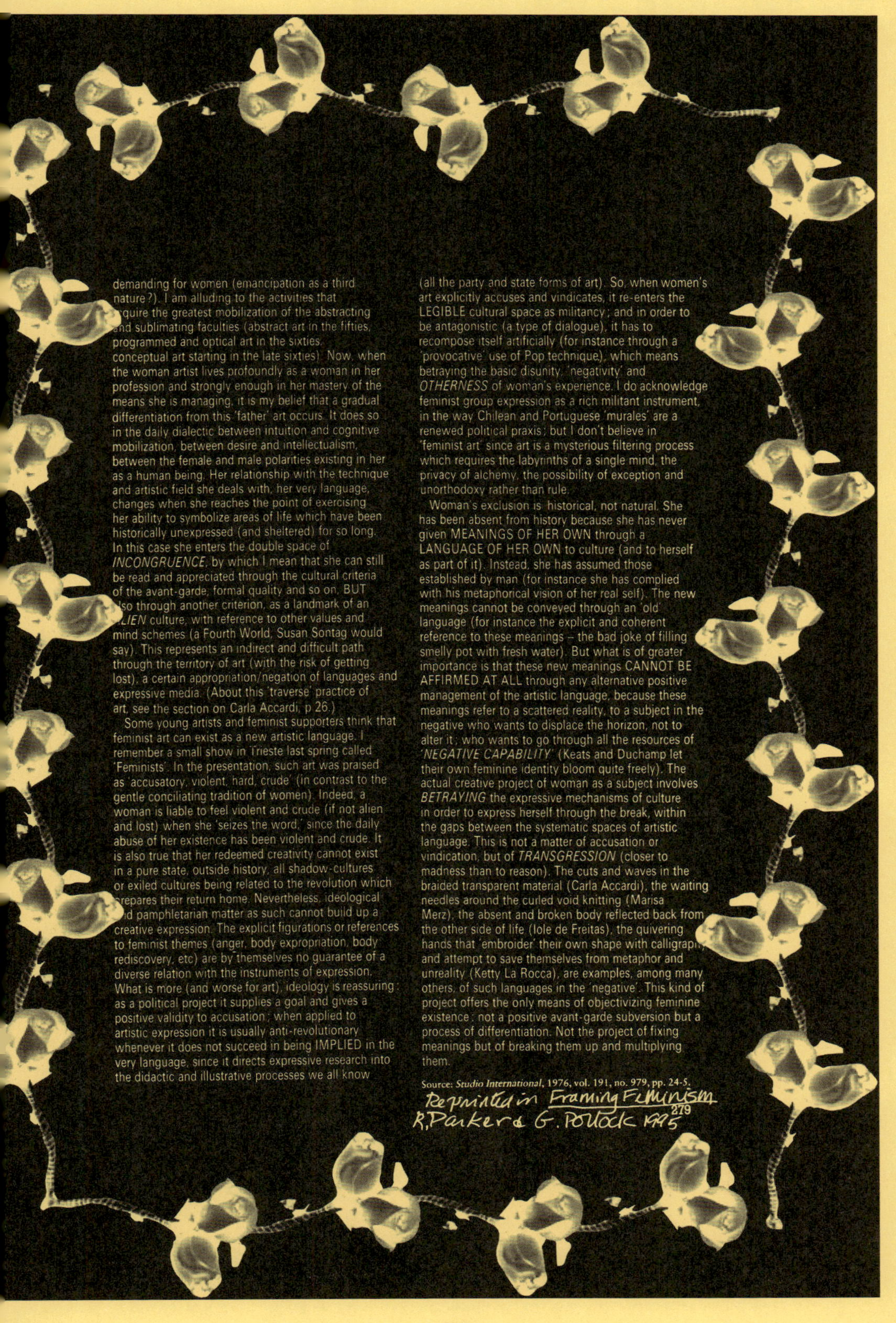

demanding for women (emancipation as a third nature?). I am alluding to the activities that require the greatest mobilization of the abstracting and sublimating faculties (abstract art in the fifties, programmed and optical art in the sixties, conceptual art starting in the late sixties). Now, when the woman artist lives profoundly as a woman in her profession and strongly enough in her mastery of the means she is managing, it is my belief that a gradual differentiation from this 'father' art occurs. It does so in the daily dialectic between intuition and cognitive mobilization, between desire and intellectualism, between the female and male polarities existing in her as a human being. Her relationship with the technique and artistic field she deals with, her very language, changes when she reaches the point of exercising her ability to symbolize areas of life which have been historically unexpressed (and sheltered) for so long. In this case she enters the double space of *INCONGRUENCE*, by which I mean that she can still be read and appreciated through the cultural criteria of the avant-garde, formal quality and so on, BUT also through another criterion, as a landmark of an *ALIEN* culture, with reference to other values and mind schemes (a Fourth World, Susan Sontag would say). This represents an indirect and difficult path through the territory of art (with the risk of getting lost), a certain appropriation/negation of languages and expressive media. (About this 'traverse' practice of art, see the section on Carla Accardi, p 26.)

Some young artists and feminist supporters think that feminist art can exist as a new artistic language. I remember a small show in Trieste last spring called 'Feminists'. In the presentation, such art was praised as 'accusatory, violent, hard, crude' (in contrast to the gentle conciliating tradition of women). Indeed, a woman is liable to feel violent and crude (if not alien and lost) when she 'seizes the word,' since the daily abuse of her existence has been violent and crude. It is also true that her redeemed creativity cannot exist in a pure state, outside history, all shadow-cultures or exiled cultures being related to the revolution which prepares their return home. Nevertheless, ideological and pamphletarian matter as such cannot build up a creative expression. The explicit figurations or references to feminist themes (anger, body expropriation, body rediscovery, etc) are by themselves no guarantee of a diverse relation with the instruments of expression. What is more (and worse for art), ideology is reassuring: as a political project it supplies a goal and gives a positive validity to accusation; when applied to artistic expression it is usually anti-revolutionary whenever it does not succeed in being IMPLIED in the very language, since it directs expressive research into the didactic and illustrative processes we all know

(all the party and state forms of art). So, when women's art explicitly accuses and vindicates, it re-enters the LEGIBLE cultural space as militancy; and in order to be antagonistic (a type of dialogue), it has to recompose itself artificially (for instance through a 'provocative' use of Pop technique), which means betraying the basic disunity, 'negativity' and *OTHERNESS* of woman's experience. I do acknowledge feminist group expression as a rich militant instrument, in the way Chilean and Portuguese 'murales' are a renewed political praxis; but I don't believe in 'feminist art' since art is a mysterious filtering process which requires the labyrinths of a single mind, the privacy of alchemy, the possibility of exception and unorthodoxy rather than rule.

Woman's exclusion is historical, not natural. She has been absent from history because she has never given MEANINGS OF HER OWN through a LANGUAGE OF HER OWN to culture (and to herself as part of it). Instead, she has assumed those established by man (for instance she has complied with his metaphorical vision of her real self). The new meanings cannot be conveyed through an 'old' language (for instance the explicit and coherent reference to these meanings – the bad joke of filling smelly pot with fresh water). But what is of greater importance is that these new meanings CANNOT BE AFFIRMED AT ALL through any alternative positive management of the artistic language, because these meanings refer to a scattered reality, to a subject in the negative who wants to displace the horizon, not to alter it; who wants to go through all the resources of *'NEGATIVE CAPABILITY'* (Keats and Duchamp let their own feminine identity bloom quite freely). The actual creative project of woman as a subject involves *BETRAYING* the expressive mechanisms of culture in order to express herself through the break, within the gaps between the systematic spaces of artistic language. This is not a matter of accusation or vindication, but of *TRANSGRESSION* (closer to madness than to reason). The cuts and waves in the braided transparent material (Carla Accardi), the waiting needles around the curled void knitting (Marisa Merz), the absent and broken body reflected back from the other side of life (Iole de Freitas), the quivering hands that 'embroider' their own shape with calligraphy and attempt to save themselves from metaphor and unreality (Ketty La Rocca), are examples, among many others, of such languages in the 'negative'. This kind of project offers the only means of objectivizing feminine existence: not a positive avant-garde subversion but a process of differentiation. Not the project of fixing meanings but of breaking them up and multiplying them.

Source: *Studio International*, 1976, vol. 191, no. 979, pp. 24-5.

Reprinted in Framing Feminism
R. Parker & G. Pollock 1995
279

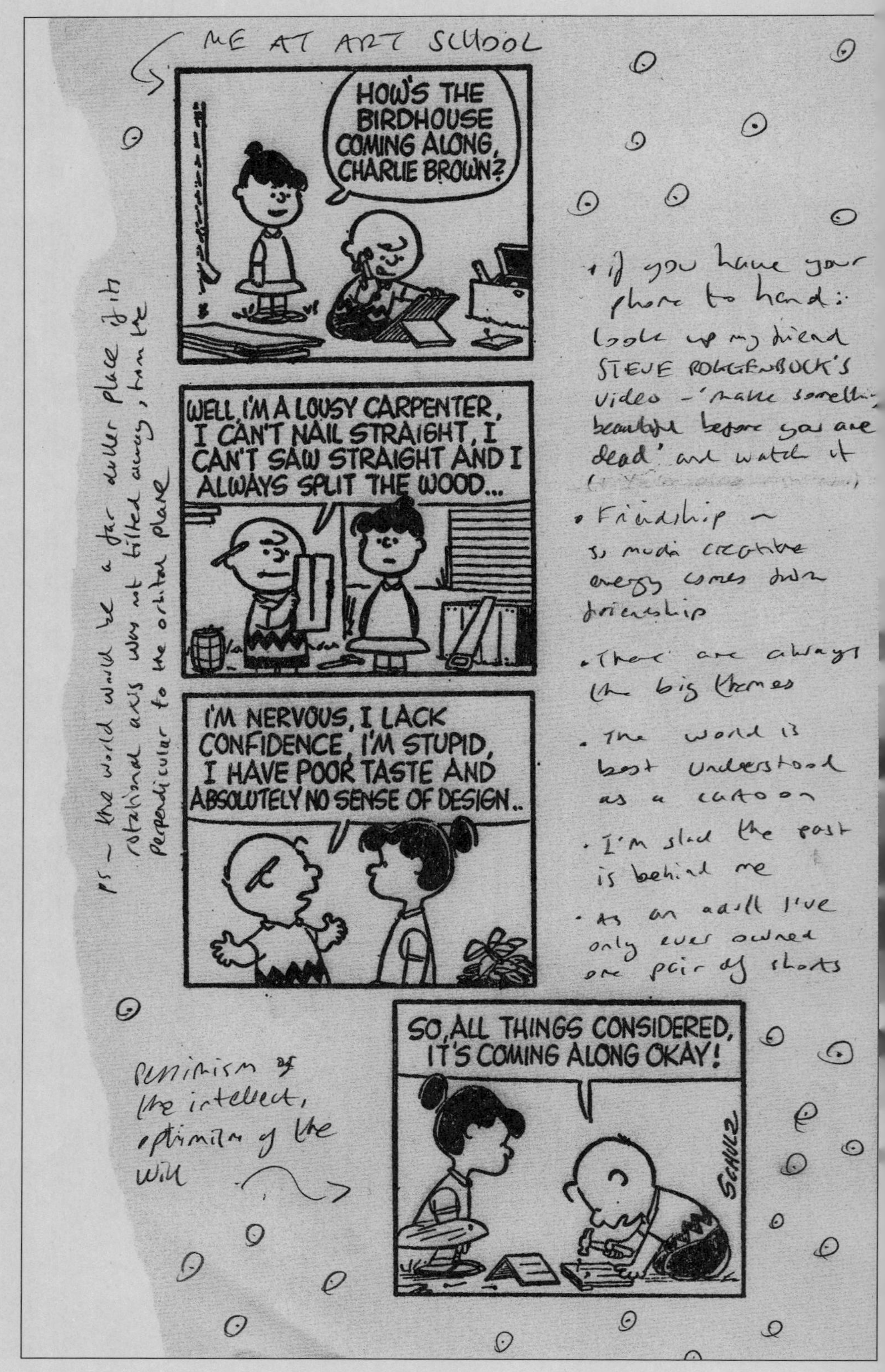

HOW'S THE BIRDHOUSE COMING ALONG, CHARLIE BROWN?
WELL, I'M A LOUSY CARPENTER, I CAN'T NAIL STRAIGHT, I CAN'T SAW STRAIGHT AND I ALWAYS SPLIT THE WOOD...
I'M NERVOUS, I LACK CONFIDENCE, I'M STUPID, I HAVE POOR TASTE AND ABSOLUTELY NO SENSE OF DESIGN..
SO, ALL THINGS CONSIDERED, IT'S COMING ALONG OKAY!
SCHULZ



PS — the world would be a far duller place if its rotational axis was not tilted away, from the perpendicular to the orbital plane

pessimism of the intellect, optimism of the will

• if you have your phone to hand: look up my friend STEVE ROGGENBUCK'S video — 'make something beautiful before you are dead' and watch it

• Friendship — so much creative energy comes down friendship

• There are always the big themes

• The world is best understood as a cartoon

• I'm glad the past is behind me

• As an adult I've only ever owned one pair of shorts

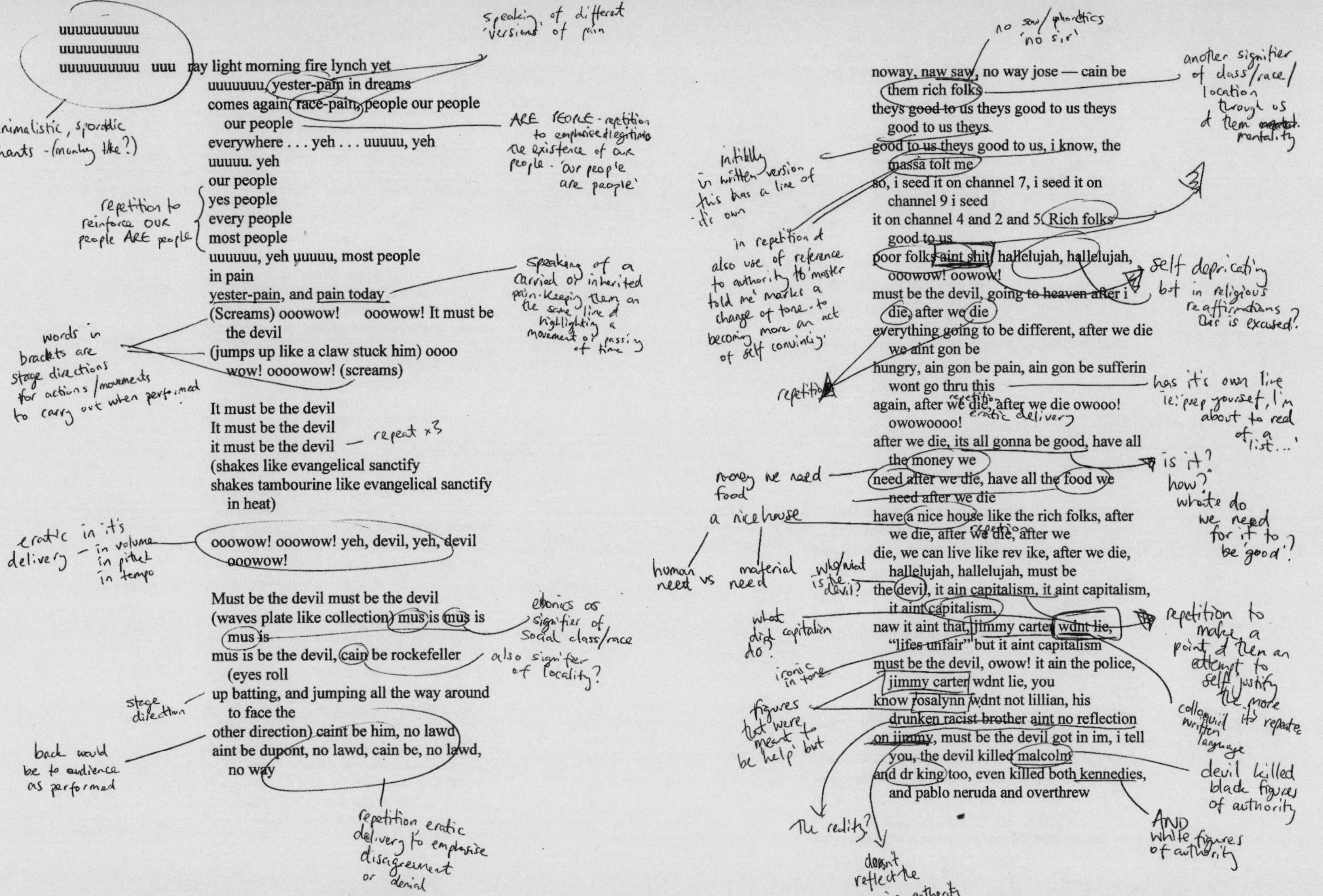

uuuuuuuuuu
uuuuuuuuuu
uuuuuuuuuu  uuu  ray light morning fire lynch yet
uuuuuuu. yester-pain in dreams
comes again, race-pain, people our people
our people
everywhere . . . yeh . . . uuuuu, yeh
uuuuu. yeh
our people
yes people
every people
most people
uuuuuu, yeh uuuuu, most people
in pain
yester-pain, and pain today
(Screams) ooowow!    ooowow! It must be
the devil
(jumps up like a claw stuck him) oooo
wow! oooowow! (screams)

It must be the devil
It must be the devil
it must be the devil
(shakes like evangelical sanctify
shakes tambourine like evangelical sanctify
in heat)

ooowow! ooowow! yeh, devil, yeh, devil
ooowow!

Must be the devil must be the devil
(waves plate like collection) mus is mus is
mus is
mus is be the devil, cain be rockefeller
(eyes roll
up batting, and jumping all the way around
to face the
other direction) caint be him, no lawd
aint be dupont, no lawd, cain be, no lawd,
no way

noway, naw saw, no way jose — cain be
them rich folks
theys good to us theys good to us theys
good to us theys
good to us theys good to us, i know, the
massa tolt me
so, i seed it on channel 7, i seed it on
channel 9 i seed
it on channel 4 and 2 and 5. Rich folks
good to us
poor folks aint shit, hallelujah, hallelujah,
ooowow! ooowow!
must be the devil, going to heaven after i
die, after we die
everything going to be different, after we die
we aint gon be
hungry, ain gon be pain, ain gon be sufferin
wont go thru this
again, after we die, after we die owooo!
owowoooo!
after we die, its all gonna be good, have all
the money we
need after we die, have all the food we
need after we die
have a nice house like the rich folks, after
we die, after we die, after we
die, we can live like rev ike, after we die,
hallelujah, hallelujah, must be
the devil, it ain capitalism, it aint capitalism,
it aint capitalism,
naw it aint that, jimmy carter wdnt lie,
"lifes unfair" but it aint capitalism
must be the devil, owow! it ain the police,
jimmy carter wdnt lie, you
know rosalynn wdnt not lillian, his
drunken racist brother aint no reflection
on jimmy, must be the devil got in im, i tell
you, the devil killed malcolm
and dr king too, even killed both kennedies,
and pablo neruda and overthrew



**ASHLEY HOLMES ANNOTATED DOPE, 1978, AMIRI BARAKA**

allende's govt. killed lumumba, and is
  negotiating with step and fetchit,
sleep n eat and birmingham, over there in
  "Rhodesia", goin' under the name
ian smith, must be the devil, caint be vortser,
  caint be apartheid, caint
be imperialism, jimmy carter wdnt lie, didnt
  you hear him say in his state
of the union message, i swear on rosalynn's
  face-lifted catatonia, i wdnt lie
nixon lied, haldeman lied, dean lied, hoover
  lied hoover sucked dicks too
but jimmy dont, jimmy wdnt jimmy aint lying,
  must be the devil, put yr
money on the plate, must be the devil, in
  heaven we'all all be straight
cain be rockefeller, he gave amos pootbootie a
  scholarship to Behavior
Modification Univ, and Genevieve Almoswhite
  works for his foundation
Must be niggers! Cain be Mellon, he gave
  Winky Suckass, a fellowship in
his bank put him in charge of closing out
  mortgages in the lowlife
Pittsburgh Hill nigger section, caint be him.
  (Goes on babbling, and wailing, jerking
  in pathocrazy grin stupor)
Yessuh, yessuh, yessuh, yessuh, yessuh, yes-
  suh, yessuh, yessuh, yessuh, yessuh,
put yr money in the plate, dont be late, dont
  have to wait, you gonna be in
heaven after you die, you gon get all you need
  once you gone, yessuh, i heard
it on the jeffersons, i heard it on the rookies,
  I swallowed it
whole on roots, wasn't it nice slavery was so
  cool and
all you had to do was wear derbies and vests
  and train chickens and buy your
way free if you had a mind to, must be the

devil, wasnt no white folks,
lazy niggers chained theyselves and threw
  they own black asses in the bottom
of the boats, [(well now that you mention it King
  Assblackuwasi helped throw yr ass in
the bottom of the boat, yo mamma, wife, and
  you never seed em no more)] must
a been the devil, gimme your money put your
  money on this plate, heaven be here soon,
just got to die, just got to stop living, close yr
  eyes stop
breathin and bammm-O heaven be here, you
  have all a what you need, Bam-O
all a sudden, heaven be here, you have all you
  need, that assembly line
you work on will dissolve in thin air owowoo!
  owowoo! Just gotta die
just gotta die, this ol world aint nuthin, must be
  the devil got you
thinkin so, it cain be rockefeller, it cain be mor-
  gan, it caint be capitalism
it caint be national oppression owow! No Way!
  Now go back to work and cool
it, go back to work and lay back, just a little
  while longer till you pass
its all gonna be alright once you gone. gimme
  that last bitta silver you got
stashed there sister, gimme that dust now brother man, itll be ok on the
other side, yo soul be clean be washed pure
  white, yes, yes, yes, owow.
now go back to work, go to sleep, yes, go to
  sleep, go back to work, yes
owow. owow. uuuuuuuuuuu, uuuuuuuuuuu,
  uuuuuuuuuuu, yes, uuuuuuu, yes.
uuuuuuuuuu.

a men.

---

*Handwritten marginal annotations:*

- killed the body/organisation higher than individual figure of power
- ZIMBABWE
- highlight wider social/racial historic problems.
- More figures of power
- reference to church collection
- written colloquidism
- speaking of romanticised future views
- requests of who? white American?
- exclamation mark to emphasise enthusi
- stage direction
- repetition 'yes sir'
- reference to church collection charity.
- Reference cultural show
- ref. to cultural film
- justification of
- What would you need to wear now?
- written in italics to emphasise how it should be read
- 'Theyselves' rather than 'themselves'
- self blaming
- name of a made up black 'African sounding' figure of authority
- instruction is demanding, adds aggressive tone
- almost at the goal
- Use of 'just' before instruction of how to attain happiness/peace
- indicates immediacy/instant impact
- written in present tense
- exclamation to emphasise how it should be read/delivered
- Theresa may?
- exclamation mark
- Switch in tone to signify return to previous state
- speaking of feelings of suicide?
- steal your chain (equivalent)
- indicating that when you have nothing, 'dust' being valuable
- Suggesting that once you're dead things will be better!
- no worries
- Change in tone to suggest movement of time/tense
- repetition as re assurance
- indicates a prayer?
- finishes as it starts? chants sporadic-(like) (monkey-like)
- Sound of intrigue
- OR PAI

# 24/7

## Late Capitalism and the Ends of Sleep

### Jonathan Crary

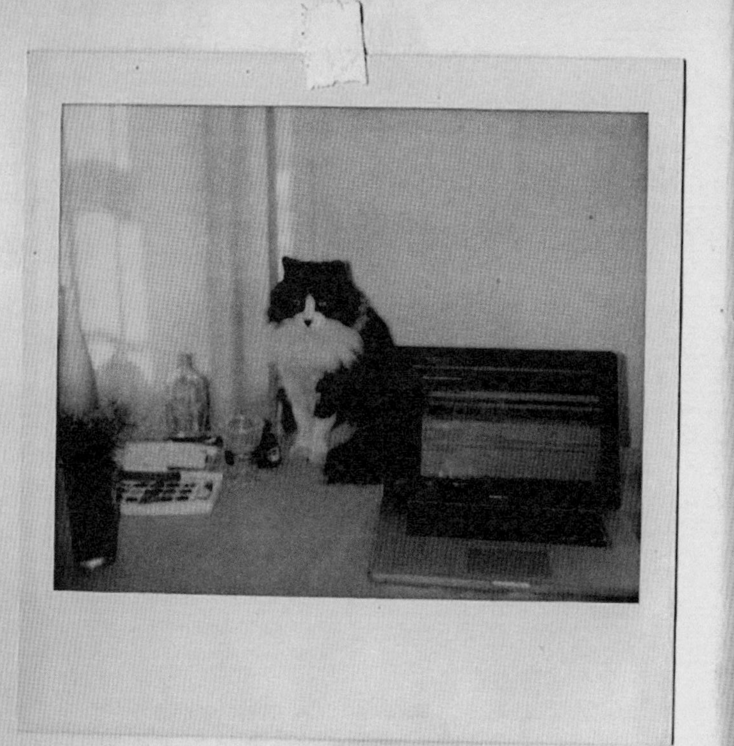

VERSO

London • New York

*we could consider the opposite or antonym to be ECOLOGY where even 'autonomous art' is but a connected ecosystem operating within the whole world of west.*

## Autonomy

*(A term to be retired)*



Autonomy is a tricky term to handle because in the field of art it has come to denote almost the opposite of what it set out to name. Literally, *auto / nomos* means to determine one's own laws. When art slowly but surely pried open a new social space for itself in nineteenth-century European society, on the basis of aesthetic principles laid out by Kant, Hegel, Diderot and others, it was in the name of giving itself its own laws. Its 'conquest of space,' as Pierre Bourdieu calls it, was about wresting art from the overarching control and hindrance of religious and political authorities, carving out a separate sphere for itself where it could develop in keeping with its own internal logic. This space of autonomous art determined the art of modernity. Of course, the autonomy was only ever relative – but it was effective, and jealously guarded. In fact it still is. Incursions from other fields were repulsed vigorously. Indeed, they still are. This autonomous sphere was seen as a place where art was free from the overcodes of the general economy (its own, utterly unregulated market notwithstanding) and the utilitarian rationality of market society – and as such, something be cherished and protected. This realm of autonomy was never supposed to be a comfort zone, but the place where art could develop audacious, scandalous, seditious works and ideas - which it set about doing.

However, autonomous art came at a cost – one that for many has become too much to bear. The price to pay for autonomy are the invisible parentheses that bracket art off from being taken seriously as a proposition having consequences beyond the aesthetic realm. Art judged by art's standards can be easily written off as, well... *just art*. Of contemplative value to people who like that sort of thing, but without teeth. Of course autonomous art has regularly claimed to bite the hand that feeds it, but never very hard. To gain use value, to find a usership, requires that art quit the autonomous sphere of purposeless purpose and disinterested spectatorship. For many practitioners today, autonomous art has become less a place of self-determined experimentation than a prison house – a sphere where one must conform to the law of permanent ontological exception, which has left the autonomous artworld rife with cynicism. *and a public cynical of it!*

*＊2 key terms of Kantian software or it's bite was captured by the market.*



*Compare to a contained 'each ecology' vs. 'galactic ecology' complicity with colonialism. → Economy is fundamentally ＊good house, keeping*

*＊Economy is galactic ecology*

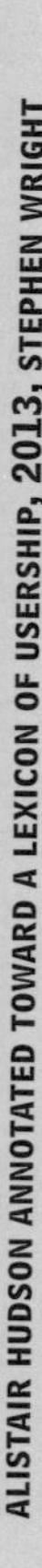

*Modernity hand in hand with industrialisation; middle dwelling, art world of west. free market, scientific environmentalism: classes emerging all*

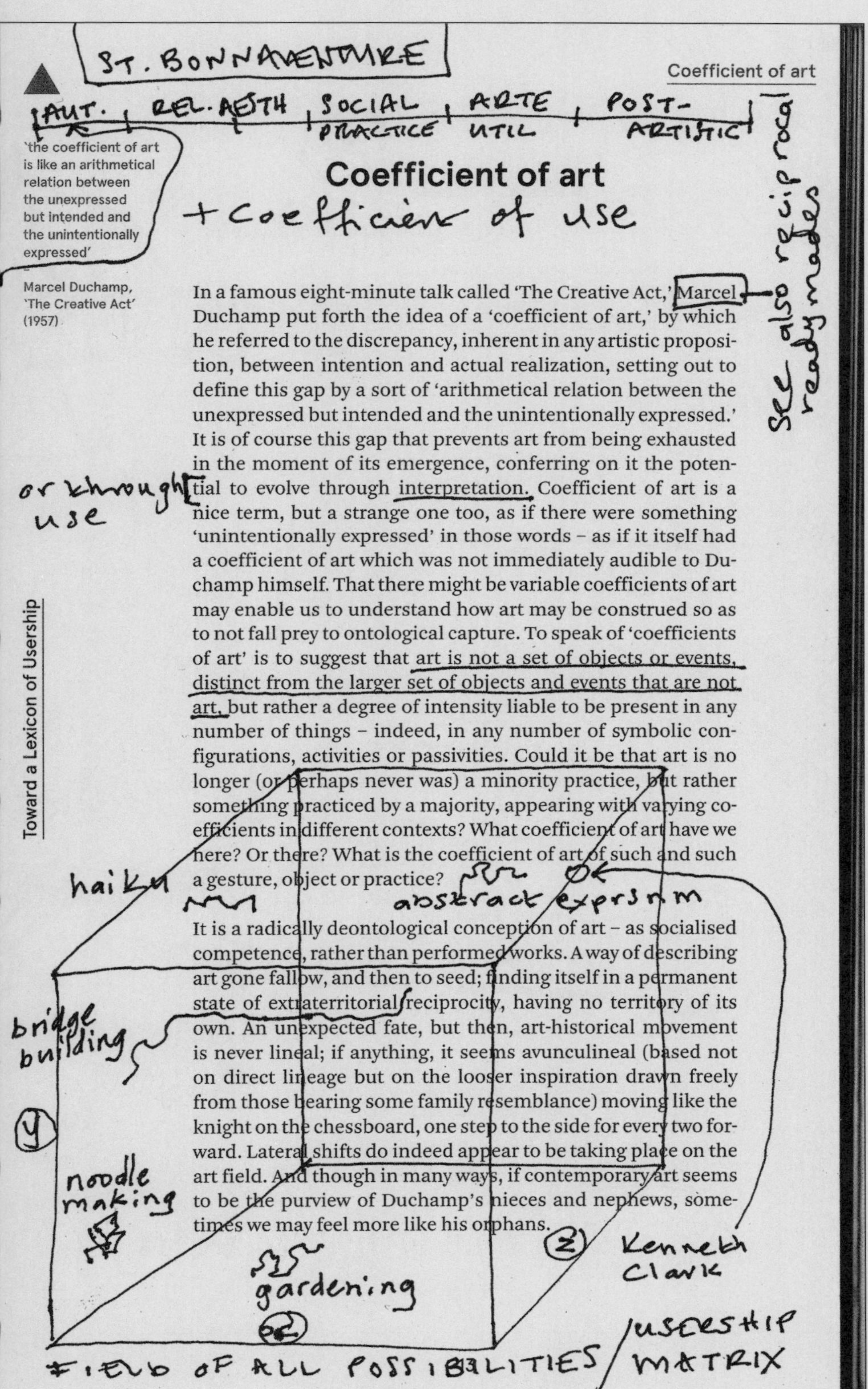

'the coefficient of art is like an arithmetical relation between the unexpressed but intended and the unintentionally expressed'

Marcel Duchamp, 'The Creative Act' (1957)

Toward a Lexicon of Usership

# Coefficient of art

In a famous eight-minute talk called 'The Creative Act,' Marcel Duchamp put forth the idea of a 'coefficient of art,' by which he referred to the discrepancy, inherent in any artistic proposition, between intention and actual realization, setting out to define this gap by a sort of 'arithmetical relation between the unexpressed but intended and the unintentionally expressed.' It is of course this gap that prevents art from being exhausted in the moment of its emergence, conferring on it the potential to evolve through interpretation. Coefficient of art is a nice term, but a strange one too, as if there were something 'unintentionally expressed' in those words – as if it itself had a coefficient of art which was not immediately audible to Duchamp himself. That there might be variable coefficients of art may enable us to understand how art may be construed so as to not fall prey to ontological capture. To speak of 'coefficients of art' is to suggest that art is not a set of objects or events, distinct from the larger set of objects and events that are not art, but rather a degree of intensity liable to be present in any number of things – indeed, in any number of symbolic configurations, activities or passivities. Could it be that art is no longer (or perhaps never was) a minority practice, but rather something practiced by a majority, appearing with varying coefficients in different contexts? What coefficient of art have we here? Or there? What is the coefficient of art of such and such a gesture, object or practice?

It is a radically deontological conception of art – as socialised competence, rather than performed works. A way of describing art gone fallow, and then to seed; finding itself in a permanent state of extraterritorial reciprocity, having no territory of its own. An unexpected fate, but then, art-historical movement is never lineal; if anything, it seems avunculineal (based not on direct lineage but on the looser inspiration drawn freely from those bearing some family resemblance) moving like the knight on the chessboard, one step to the side for every two forward. Lateral shifts do indeed appear to be taking place on the art field. And though in many ways, if contemporary art seems to be the purview of Duchamp's nieces and nephews, sometimes we may feel more like his orphans.

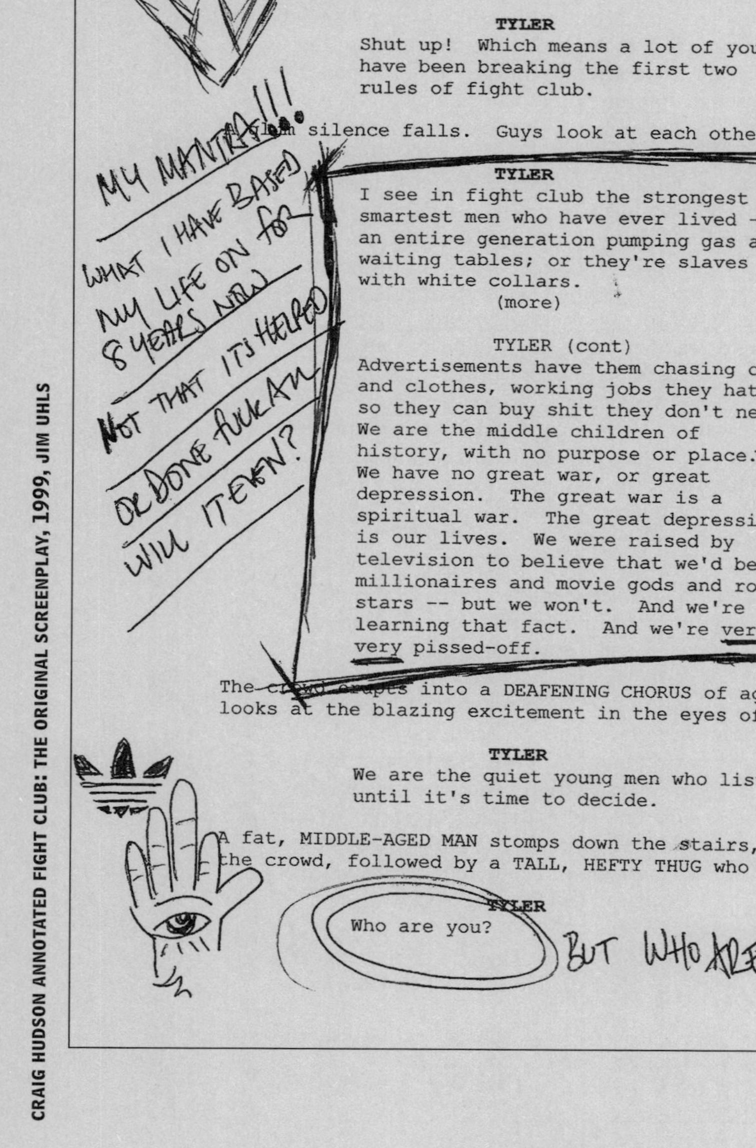

                TYLER
          Good for you.

INT. LOU'S TAVERN - BASEMENT - NIGHT

LOUD.  An enormous CROWD of guys, including Jack and Bob,
stands around Tyler, who's in the center of the circle,
holding up his hands to quiet them...

                TYLER
          I look around... I look around and
          see a lot of new faces.

An enthusiastic RUMBLE from the crowd.

                TYLER
          Shut up!  Which means a lot of you
          have been breaking the first two
          rules of fight club.

Then silence falls.  Guys look at each other.

                TYLER
          I see in fight club the strongest and
          smartest men who have ever lived --
          an entire generation pumping gas and
          waiting tables; or they're slaves
          with white collars.
                    (more)

                TYLER (cont)
          Advertisements have them chasing cars
          and clothes, working jobs they hate
          so they can buy shit they don't need.
          We are the middle children of
          history, with no purpose or place.
          We have no great war, or great
          depression.  The great war is a
          spiritual war.  The great depression
          is our lives.  We were raised by
          television to believe that we'd be
          millionaires and movie gods and rock
          stars -- but we won't.  And we're
          learning that fact.  And we're very,
          very pissed-off.

The crowd erupts into a DEAFENING CHORUS of agreement!  Jack
looks at the blazing excitement in the eyes of the crowd.

                TYLER
          We are the quiet young men who listen
          until it's time to decide.

A fat, MIDDLE-AGED MAN stomps down the stairs, pushing into
the crowd, followed by a TALL, HEFTY THUG who holds a GUM.

                TYLER
          Who are you?

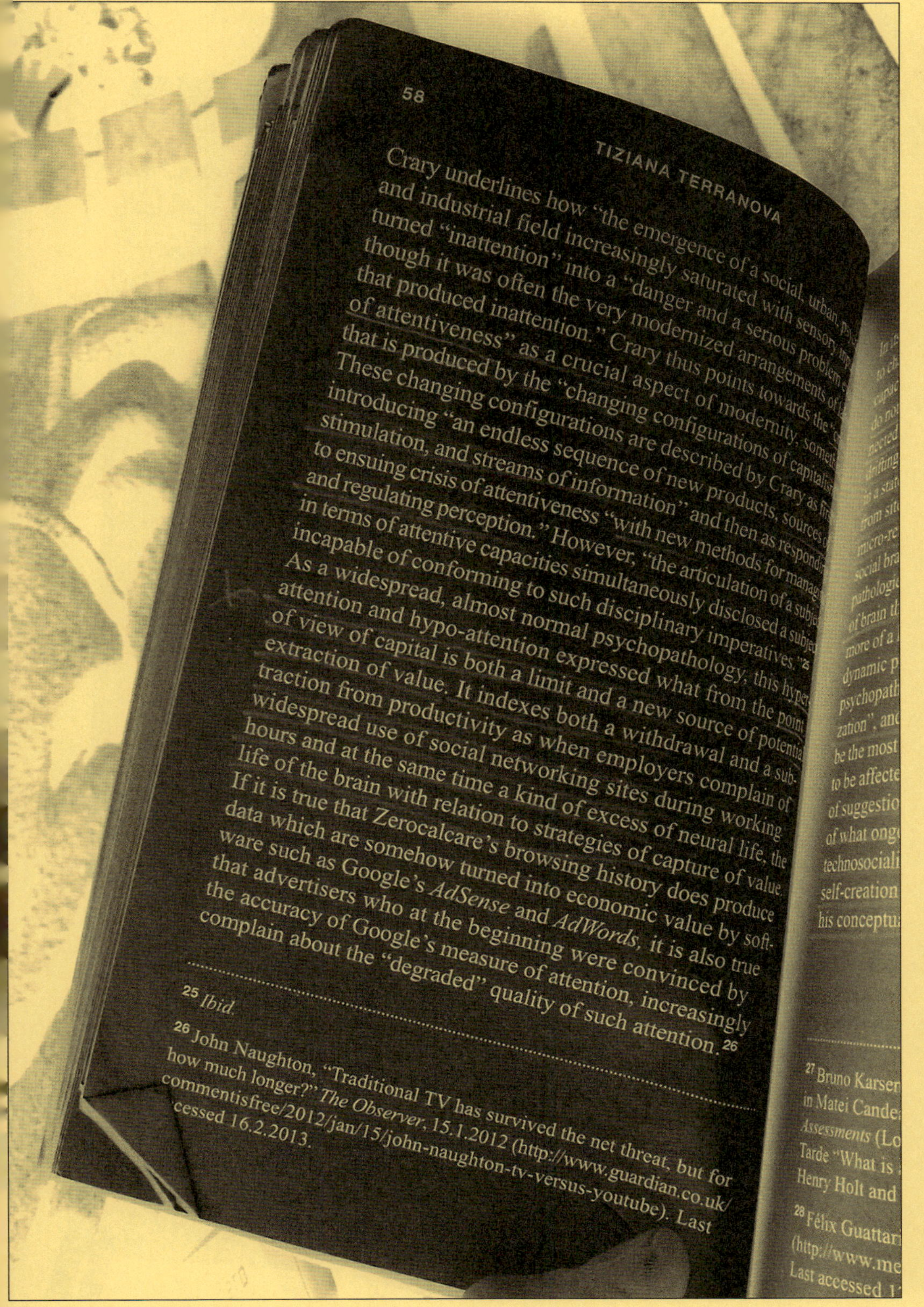



TIZIANA TERRANOVA

Crary underlines how "the emergence of a social, urban, psychic and industrial field increasingly saturated with sensory input turned "inattention" into a "danger and a serious problem," even though it was often the very modernized arrangements of [...] that produced inattention." Crary thus points towards the [...] of attentiveness" as a crucial aspect of modernity, something that is produced by the "changing configurations of capitalism."

These changing configurations are described by Crary as first introducing "an endless sequence of new products, sources of stimulation, and streams of information" and then as responding to ensuing crisis of attentiveness "with new methods for managing and regulating perception." However, "the articulation of a subject in terms of attentive capacities simultaneously disclosed a subject incapable of conforming to such disciplinary imperatives."[25]

As a widespread, almost normal psychopathology, this hyper-attention and hypo-attention expressed what from the point of view of capital is both a limit and a new source of potential extraction of value. It indexes both a withdrawal and a sub-traction from productivity as when employers complain of widespread use of social networking sites during working hours and at the same time a kind of excess of neural life, the life of the brain with relation to strategies of capture of value. If it is true that Zerocalcare's browsing history does produce data which are somehow turned into economic value by software such as Google's *AdSense* and *AdWords*, it is also true that advertisers who at the beginning were convinced by the accuracy of Google's measure of attention, increasingly complain about the "degraded" quality of such attention.[26]

25 *Ibid.*

26 John Naughton, "Traditional TV has survived the net threat, but for how much longer?" *The Observer*, 15.1.2012 (http://www.guardian.co.uk/commentisfree/2012/jan/15/john-naughton-tv-versus-youtube). Last accessed 16.2.2013.

Such pathologization of attention is an ordinary occurrence in the life of cognitive capitalism, expressing not so much a clear boundary between the normal and the pathological as a modulation of a general pathologization of neural life which crucially implicates our symbiotic relation with digital screens. Citing neuroscientific research on neuroplasticity, Carr has argued that multi-tasking and "always on" connectivity produce an excess of stimulation of the regions of the brain associated with short-term memory, while downplaying and atrophying long-term memory. The notion of the neuroplasticity of the brain is thus drawn on to emphasize the production by means of computers and communication networks, of a subject incapable of long-term memory and as a consequence of focused concentration and rational argumentation.

As attention is identified in new economy discourse as the new scarce resource in an economy of information, a new "crisis of attentiveness" is produced. It has been the merit of Jonathan Crary's work on early capitalism, to show how such crisis is far from being a new phenomenon.[23] It was in the late nineteenth century and early twentieth century that a crisis of attention was first denounced—triggered by a new commercial, urban culture of sensory stimulation. Looking back at the first expansion of industrial capitalism into the structures of perception in the nineteenth century, Crary shows how "at the moment when the dynamic logic of capital began to dramatically undermine any stable or enduring structure of perception, this logic simultaneously attempted to impose a disciplinary regime of attentiveness."[24] In the late nineteenth century, it was the new field of scientific psychology that identified attention as a fundamental problem.

[23] Jonathan Crary, *Suspensions of Perception. Attention, Spectacle and Modern Culture* (Cambridge, MA: MIT Press, 1999), 13.

[24] *Ibid.*

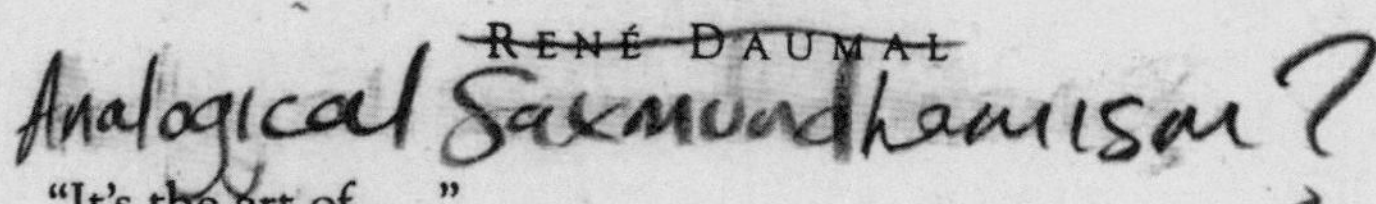




"It's the art of . . ."

"What is an art?"

"The value of danger:

     temerity—suicide.

     Short of that, no satisfaction."

"What is danger?"

"What is prudence?"

"What is a mountain?"

Keep your eyes fixed on the way to the top, but don't forget to look at your feet. The last step depends on the first. Don't think you have arrived jut because you see the peak. Watch your feet, be certain of your next step, but don't let this distract you from the *highest* goal. The first step depends on the last.

When you take off on your own, leave some trace of your passage that will guide your return: one rock set on top of another, some grass pierced by a stick. But if you come to a place you cannot cross or that is dangerous, remember that the trace you have left might lead the people following you into trouble. So go back the way you came and destroy any traces you have left. This is addressed to anyone who wants to leave traces of his passage in this world. And even without wanting to, we always leave traces. Answer to your fellow men for the traces you leave behind.

Never stop on a crumbling slope. Even if you believe your feet are firmly planted, while you take a breath and looking at the sky the earth is gradually piling up under your feet, the gravel is slipping imperceptibly, and suddenly you are launched like a ship. The mountain always lies in wait for the chance to trip you up.

If, after climbing up and down three times through gullies that end in sheer drops (visible only at the last moment), your legs begin to tremble from knee to heel and your teeth start to chatter, first

106

reach a little platform where you can stop safely; then, remember all the curse words you know and hurl them at the mountain, and spit on the mountain; finally, insult it in every way possible, swallow some water, have a bite to eat, and start climbing again, calmly, slowly, as if you had your whole lifetime to undo this bad move. In the evening, before going to sleep, when it all comes back to you, you will see then that it was just a performance. It wasn't the mountain you were talking to, it wasn't the mountain you conquered. The mountain is only rock or ice, with no ears or heart. But this performance may have saved your life.

Besides, in difficult moments you'll often surprise yourself talking to the mountain, sometimes flattering it, sometimes insulting it, sometimes promising, sometimes threatening. And you'll imagine that the mountain answers, as if you had said the right words by speaking gently, by humbling yourself. Don't despise yourself for this, don't feel ashamed of behaving like those men our social scientists call primitives and animists. Just keep in mind when you recall these moments later that your dialogue with nature was only the outward image of a dialogue with yourself.

Shoes are not like feet—we are not born with them. Therefore we can choose them. Let yourself be guided in this choice first by experienced people, then by your own experience. Very quickly you will be so used to your shoes that every nail will seem like a finger, capable of testing the rock and gripping it firmly; they will become a sensitive and reliable tool, like a part of yourself. And yet you were not born with them; and yet, when they wear out, you will throw them away and remain what you are.

Your life somewhat depends on your footwear. Care for them properly, but a quarter of an hour per day will be plenty, for your life depends on several other things as well.

A climber far more experienced than I told me, "When your feet

*ROBERT MUSIL*

shows, and even the avant-garde of the avant-garde; the family magazines have bobbed their hair; politicians like to sound off on the cultural arts, and newspapers make literary history. So what has been lost?

Something imponderable. An omen. An illusion. As when a magnet releases iron filings and they fall in confusion again. As when a ball of string comes undone. As when a tension slackens. As when an orchestra begins to play out of tune. No details could be adduced that would not also have been possible before, but all the relationships had shifted a little. Ideas whose currency had once been lean grew fat. Persons who would before never have been taken seriously became famous. Harshness mellowed, separations fused, intransigents made concessions to popularity, tastes already formed relapsed into uncertainties. Sharp boundaries everywhere became blurred, and some new, indefinable ability to form alliances brought new people and new ideas to the top. Not that these people and ideas were bad, not at all; it was only that a little too much of the bad was mixed with the good, of error with truth, of accommodation with meaning. There even seemed to be a privileged proportion of this mixture that got furthest on in the world; just the right pinch of makeshift to bring out the genius in genius and make talent look like a white hope, as a pinch of chicory, according to some people, brings out the right coffee flavor in coffee. Suddenly all the prominent and important positions in the intellectual world were filled by such people, and all decisions went their way. There is nothing one can hold responsible for this, nor can one say how it all came about. There are no persons or ideas or specific phenomena that one can fight against. There is no lack of talent or goodwill or even of strong personalities. There is just something missing in everything, though you can't put your finger on it, as if there had been a change in the blood or in the air; a mysterious disease has eaten away the previous period's seeds of genius, but everything sparkles with novelty, and finally one has no way of knowing whether the world has really grown worse, or oneself merely older. At this point a new era has definitively arrived.

So the times had changed, like a day that begins radiantly blue and then by degrees clouds over, without having the kindness to wait for Ulrich. He evened the score by holding the cause of these mysterious changes that made up the disease eating away genius to be simple, common stupidity. By no means in an insulting sense. For if stupidity, seen from within, did not so much resemble talent as possess the ability to be mistaken for it, and if it did not outwardly resemble progress, genius, hope, and improvement, the chances are that no one would want to be stupid, and so there would be no stupidity. Or fighting it would at least be easy. Unfortunately, stupidity has something uncommonly endearing and natural about it. If one finds that a reproduction, for instance, seems more of an artistic feat than a hand-painted original, well, there is a certain truth in that, and it is easier to prove than that van Gogh was a great artist. It is also easy and profitable to be a more powerful playwright than Shakespeare or a less uneven storyteller than Goethe, and a solid commonplace always contains more humanity than a new discovery. There is, in short, no great idea that stupidity could not put to its own uses; it can move in all directions, and put on all the guises of truth. The truth, by comparison, has only one appearance and only one path, and is always at a disadvantage.

I suppose you could annotate
but works can't be added
to those of Robert Musil.

Date??
Art World 2018?

I shall speak about women's writing: about *what it will do*. Woman must write her self: must write about women and bring women to writing, from which they have been driven away as violently as from their bodies – for the same reasons, by the same law, with the same fatal goal. Woman must put herself into the text – as into the world and into history – by her own movement.

The future must no longer be determined by the past. I do not deny that the effects of the past are still with us. But I refuse to strengthen them by repeating them, to confer upon them an irremovability the equivalent of destiny, to confuse the biological and the cultural. Anticipation is imperative.

Since these reflections are taking shape in an area just on the point of being discovered, they necessarily bear the mark of our time – a time during which the new breaks away from the old, and, more precisely, the (feminine) new from the old (*la nouvelle de l'ancien*). Thus, as there are no grounds for establishing a discourse, but rather an arid millennial ground to break, what I say has at least two sides and two aims: to break up, to destroy; and to foresee the unforeseeable, to project.

I write this as a woman, toward women. When I say "woman," I'm speaking of woman in her inevitable struggle against conventional man; and of a universal woman subject who must bring women to their senses and to their meaning in history. But first it must be said that in spite of the enormity of the repression that has kept them in the "dark" – that dark which people have been trying to make them accept as their attribute – there is, at this time, no general woman, no one typical woman. What they have in *common* I will say. But what strikes me is the infinite richness of their individual constitutions: you can't talk about a female sexuality, uniform, homogeneous, classifiable into codes – any more than you can talk about one unconscious resembling another. Women's imaginary is inexhaustible, like music, painting, writing: their stream of phantasms is incredible.

I have been amazed more than once by a description a woman gave me of a world all her own which she had been secretly haunting since early childhood. A world of searching, the elaboration of a knowledge, on the basis of a systematic experimentation with the bodily functions, a passionate and precise interrogation of her erotogeneity. This practice, extraordinarily rich and inventive, in particular as concerns masturbation, is prolonged or accompanied by a production of forms, a veritable aesthetic activity, each stage of rapture inscribing a resonant vision, a composition, something beautiful. Beauty will no longer be forbidden.

Nearly the entire history of writing is confounded with the history of reason, of which it is at once the effect, the support, and one of the privi-

I wished that that woman would write and proclaim this unique empire so that other women, other unacknowledged sovereigns, might exclaim: I, too, overflow; my desires have invented new desires, my body knows unheard-of songs. Time and again I, too, have felt so full of luminous torrents that I could burst – burst with forms much more beautiful than those which are put up in frames and sold for a stinking fortune. And I, too, said nothing, showed nothing; I didn't open my mouth, I didn't repaint my half of the world. I was ashamed. I was afraid, and I swallowed my shame and my fear. I said to myself: You are mad! What's the meaning of these waves, these floods, these outbursts? Where is the ebullient, infinite woman who, immersed as she was in her naiveté, kept in the dark about herself, led into self-disdain by the great arm of parental-conjugal phallocentrism, hasn't been ashamed of her strength? Who, surprised and horrified by the fantastic tumult of her drives (for she was made to believe that a well-adjusted normal woman has a . . . divine composure), hasn't accused herself of being a monster? Who, feeling a funny desire stirring inside her (to sing, to write, to dare to speak, in short, to bring out something new), hasn't thought she was sick? Well, her shameful sickness is that she resists death, that she makes trouble.

And why don't you write? Write! Writing is for you, you are for you; your body is yours, take it. I know why you haven't written. (And why I didn't write before the age of twenty-seven.) Because writing is at once too high, too great for you, it's reserved for the great-that is, for "great men"; and it's "silly." Besides, you've written a little, but in secret. And it wasn't good, because it was in secret, and because you punished yourself for writing, because you didn't go all the way; or because you wrote, irresistibly, as when we would masturbate in secret, not to go further, but to attenuate the tension a bit, just enough to take the edge off. And then as soon as we come, we go and make ourselves feel guilty – so as to be forgiven; or to forget, to bury it until the next time.

Write, let no one hold you back, let nothing stop you: not man; not the imbecilic capitalist machinery, in which publishing houses are the crafty, obsequious relayers of imperatives handed down by an economy that works against us and off our backs; and not *yourself*. Smug-faced readers, managing editors, and big bosses don't like the true texts of women – female-sexed texts. That kind scares them.

I write woman: woman must write woman. And man, man. So only an oblique consideration will be found here of man; it's up to him to say where his masculinity and femininity are at: this will concern us once men have opened their eyes and seen themselves clearly.[1]

1 Men still have everything to say about their sexuality, and everything to write. For

Now women return from afar, from always: from "without," from the heath where witches are kept alive; from below, from beyond "culture"; from their childhood which men have been trying desperately to make them forget, condemning it to "eternal rest." The little girls and their "ill-mannered" bodies immured, well-preserved, intact unto themselves, in the mirror. Frigidified. But are they ever seething underneath! What an effort it takes – there's no end to it – for the sex cops to bar their threatening return. Such a display of forces on both sides that the struggle has for centuries been immobilized in the trembling equilibrium of a deadlock.

Here they are, returning, arriving over and again, because the unconscious is impregnable. They have wandered around in circles, confined to the narrow room in which they've been given a deadly brainwashing. You can incarcerate them, slow them down, get away with the old Apartheid routine, but for a time only. As soon as they begin to speak, at the same time as they're taught their name, they can be taught that their territory is black: because you are Africa, you are black. Your continent is dark. Dark is dangerous. You can't see anything in the dark, you're afraid. Don't move, you might fall. Most of all, don't go into the forest. And so we have internalized this horror of the dark.

Men have committed the greatest crime against women. Insidiously, violently, they have led them to hate women, to be their own enemies, to mobilize their immense strength against themselves, to be the executants of their virile needs. They have made for women an antinarcissism! A narcissism which loves itself only to be loved for what women haven't got! They have constructed the infamous logic of antilove.

We the precocious, we the repressed of culture, our lovely mouths gagged with pollen, our wind knocked out of us, we the labyrinths, the ladders, the trampled spaces, the bevies-we are black and we are beautiful.

what they have said so far, for the most part, stems from the opposition activity/passivity, from the power relation between a fantasized obligatory virility meant to invade, to colonize, and the consequential phantasm of woman as a "dark continent" to penetrate and to "pacify." (We know what "pacify" means in terms of scotomizing the other and misrecognizing the self.) Conquering her, they've made haste to depart from her borders, to get out of sight, out of body. The way man has of getting out of himself and into her whom he takes not for the other but for his own, deprives him, he knows, of his own bodily territory. One can understand how man, confusing himself with his penis and rushing in for the attack, might feel resentment and fear of being "taken" by the woman, of being lost in her, absorbed, or alone.

( . . . )

We're stormy, and that which is ours breaks loose from us without our fearing any debilitation. Our glances, our smiles, are spent; laughs exude from all our mouths; our blood flows and we extend ourselves without ever reaching an end; we never hold back our thoughts, our signs, our writing; and we're not afraid of lacking.

reason, of which it is at once the effect, the support, and one of the privileged alibis. It has been one with the phallocentric tradition. It is indeed that same self-admiring, self-stimulating, self-congratulatory phallocentrism.

With some exceptions, for there have been failures – and if it weren't for them, I wouldn't be writing (I-woman, escapee) – in that enormous machine that has been operating and turning out its "truth" for centuries.

history, first at two levels that cannot be separated.

a) Individually. By writing her self, woman will return to the body which has been more than confiscated from her, which has been turned into the uncanny stranger on display – the ailing or dead figure, which so often turns out to be the nasty companion, the cause and location of inhibitions. Censor the body and you censor breath and speech at the same time.

Write your self. Your body must be heard. Only then will the immense resources of the unconscious spring forth. Our naphtha will spread, throughout the world, without dollars – black or gold – nonassessed values that will change the rules of the old game.

To write. An act which will not only "realize" the decensored relation of woman to her sexuality, to her womanly being, giving her access to her native strength; it will give her back her goods, her pleasures, her organs, her immense bodily territories which have been kept under seal; it will tear her away from the superegoized structure in which she has always occupied the place reserved for the guilty (guilty of everything, guilty at every turn: for having desires, for not having any; for being frigid, for being "too hot"; for not being both at once; for being too motherly and not enough; for having children and for not having any; for nursing and for not nursing ...) – tear her away by means of this research, this job of analysis and illumination, this emancipation of the marvelous text of her self that she must urgently learn to speak. A woman without a body, dumb, blind, can't possibly be a good fighter. She is reduced to being the servant of the militant male, his shadow. We must kill the false woman who is preventing the live one from breathing. Inscribe the breath of the whole woman.

b) An act that will also be marked by woman's seizing the occasion to speak, hence her shattering entry into history, which has always been based on her suppression. To write and thus to forge for herself the antilogos weapon. To become at will the taker and initiator, for her own right, in every symbolic system, in every political process.

It is time for women to start scoring their feats in written and oral language.

Every woman has known the torment of getting up to speak. Her heart racing, at times entirely lost for words, ground and language slipping away – that's how daring a feat, how great a transgression it is for a woman to speak – even just open her mouth – in public. A double distress, for even if she transgresses, her words fall almost always upon the deaf

8

male ear, which hears in language only that which speaks in the masculine.

It is by writing, from and toward women, and by taking up the challenge of speech which has been governed by the phallus, that women will confirm women in a place other than that which is reserved in and by the symbolic, that is, in a place other than silence. Women should break out of the snare of silence. They shouldn't be conned into accepting a domain which is the margin or the harem.

Listen to a woman speak at a public gathering (if she hasn't painfully lost her wind). She doesn't "speak," she throws her trembling body forward; she lets go of herself, she flies; all of her passes into her voice, and it's with her body that she vitally supports the "logic" of her speech. Her flesh speaks true. She lays herself bare. In fact, she physically materializes what she's thinking; she signifies it with her body. In a certain way she inscribes what she's saying, because she doesn't deny her drives the intractable and impassioned part they have in speaking. Her speech, even when "theoretical" or political, is never simple or linear or "objectified," generalized: she draws her story into history.

There is not that scission, that division made by the common man between the logic of oral speech and the logic of the text, bound as he is by his antiquated relation – servile, calculating – to mastery. From which proceeds the meager lip service which engages only the tiniest part of the body, plus the mask.

In women's speech, as in their writing, that element which never stops resonating, which, once we've been permeated by it, profoundly and imperceptibly touched by it, retains the power of moving us – that element is the song: first music from the first voice of love which is alive in every woman. Why this privileged relationship with the voice? Because no woman stockpiles as many defenses for countering the drives as does a man. You don't build walls around yourself, you don't forego pleasure as "wisely" as he. Even if phallic mystification has generally contaminated good relationships, a woman is never far from "mother" (I mean outside her role functions: the "mother" as nonname and as source of goods). There is always within her at least a little of that good mother's milk. She writes in white ink.

*Woman for women.*—There always remains in woman that force which produces/is produced by the other – in particular, the other woman. In her, matrix, cradler; herself giver as her mother and child; she is her own sister-daughter. You might object, "What about she who is the

9

hysterical offspring of a bad mother?" Everything will be changed once woman gives woman to the other woman. There is hidden and always ready in woman the source; the locus for the other. The mother, too, is a metaphor. It is necessary and sufficient that the best of herself be given to woman by another woman for her to be able to love herself and return in love the body that was "born" to her. Touch me, caress me, you the living no-name, give me my self as myself. The relation to the "mother," in terms of intense pleasure and violence, is curtailed no more than the relation to childhood (the child that she was, that she is, that she makes, remakes, undoes, there at the point where, the same, she others herself). Text: my body – shot through with streams of song; I don't mean the overbearing, clutchy "mother" but, rather, what touches you, the equivoice that affects you, fills your breast with an urge to come to language and launches your force; the rhythm that laughs you; the intimate recipient who makes all metaphors possible and desirable; body (body? bodies?), no more describable than god, the soul, or the Other; that part of you that leaves a space between yourself and urges you to inscribe in language your woman's style. In women there is always more or less of the mother who makes everything all right, who nourishes, and who stands up against separation; a force that will not be cut off but will knock the wind out of the codes. We will rethink womankind beginning with every form and every period of her body. The Americans remind us, "We are all Lesbians"; that is, don't denigrate woman, don't make of her what men have made of you.

Because the "economy" of her drives is prodigious, she cannot fail, in seizing the occasion to speak, to transform directly and indirectly *all* systems of exchange based on masculine thrift. Her libido will produce far more radical effects of political and social change than some might like to think.

Because she arrives, vibrant, over and again, we are at the beginning of a new history, or rather of a process of becoming in which several histories intersect with one another. As subject for history, woman always occurs simultaneously in several places. Woman un-thinks[4] the unifying, regulating history that homogenizes and channels forces, herding contradictions into a single battlefield. In woman, personal history blends together with the history of all women, as well as national and world history. As a militant, she is an integral part of all liberations. She must be farsighted, not limited to a blow-by-blow interaction. She foresees that her liberation will do more than modify power relations or toss the ball over to the other camp; she will bring about a mutation in human

4 "*De-pense,*" a neologism formed on the verb *penser*, hence "unthinks," but also "spends" (from *depenser*) (translator's note).

10

[...] thought, in all praxis: ners is not simply a class struggle, which she carries forward into a much vaster movement. Not that in order to be a woman-in-struggle(s) you have to leave the class struggle or repudiate it; but you have to split it open, spread it out, push it forward, fill it with the fundamental struggle so as to prevent the class struggle, or any other struggle for the liberation of a class or people, from operating as a form of repression, pretext for postponing the inevitable, the staggering alteration in power relations and in the production of individualities.

The new history is coming; it's not a dream, though it does extend beyond men's imagination, and for good reason. It's going to deprive them of their conceptual orthopedics, beginning with the destruction of their enticement machine.

It is impossible to *define* a feminine practice of writing, and this is an impossibility that will remain, for this practice can never be theorized, enclosed, coded – which doesn't mean that it doesn't exist. But it will always surpass the discourse that regulates the phallocentric system; it does and will take place in areas other than those subordinated to philosophico-theoretical domination. It will be conceived of only by subjects who are breakers of automatisms, by peripheral figures that no authority can ever subjugate.

Here we encounter the inevitable man-with-rock, standing erect in his old Freudian realm, in the way that, to take the figure back to the point where linguistics is conceptualizing it "anew," Lacan preserves it in the sanctuary of the phallos (Φ) "sheltered" from *castration's lack*! Their "symbolic" exists, it holds power – we, the sowers of disorder, know it only too well. But we are in no way obliged to deposit our lives in their banks of lack, to consider the constitution of the subject in terms of a drama manglingly restaged, to reinstate again and again the religion of the father. Because we don't want that. We don't fawn around the supreme hole. We have no womanly reason to pledge allegiance to the negative. The feminine (as the poets suspected) affirms: ". . . And yes," says Molly, carrying *Ulysses* off beyond any book and toward the new writing; "I said yes, I will Yes."

*The Dark Continent is neither dark nor unexplorable.*—It is still unexplored only because we've been made to believe that it was too dark to be explorable. And because they want to make us believe that what interests us is the white continent, with its monuments to Lack. And we believed. They riveted us between two horrifying myths: between the Medusa and the abyss. That would be enough to set half the world laughing, except that it's still going on. For the phallologocentric sublation[5] is with us, and it's militant, regenerating the old patterns, anchored in the dogma of castration. They haven't changed a thing: they've theorized their desire for reality! Let the priests tremble, we're going to show them our sexts!

Too bad for them if they fall apart upon discovering that women aren't men, or that the mother doesn't have one. But isn't this fear convenient for them? Wouldn't the worst be, isn't the worst, in truth, that women aren't castrated, that they have only to stop listening to the Sirens (for the Sirens were men) for history to change its meaning? You only have to look at the Medusa straight on to see her. And she's not deadly. She's beautiful and she's laughing.

Men say that there are two unrepresentable things: death and the feminine sex. That's because they need femininity to be associated with death; it's the jitters that gives them a hard-on! for themselves! They need to be afraid of us. Look at the trembling Perseuses moving backward toward us, clad in apotropes. What lovely backs! Not another minute to lose. Let's get out of here.

Let's hurry: the continent is not impenetrably dark. I've been there often. I was overjoyed one day to run into Jean Genêt. It was in *Pompes*

*funèbres.*[6] He had come there led by his Jean. There are some men (all too few) who aren't afraid of femininity.

Almost everything is yet to be written by women about femininity: about their sexuality, that is, its infinite and mobile complexity, about their eroticization, sudden turn-ons of a certain miniscule-immense area of their bodies; not about destiny, but about the adventure of such and such a drive, about trips, crossings, trudges, abrupt and gradual awakenings, discoveries of a zone at one time timorous and soon to be forthright. A woman's body, with its thousand and one thresholds of ardor – once, by smashing yokes and censors, she lets it articulate the profusion of meanings that run through it in every direction – will make the old single-grooved mother tongue reverberate with more than one language.

We've been turned away from our bodies, shamefully taught to ignore them, to strike them with that stupid sexual modesty; we've been made victims of the old fool's game: each one will love the other sex. I'll give you your body and you'll give me mine. But who are the men who give women the body that women blindly yield to them? Why so few texts? Because so few women have as yet won back their body. Women must write through their bodies, they must invent the impregnable language that will wreck partitions, classes, and rhetorics, regulations and codes, they must submerge, cut through, get beyond the ultimate reserve-discourse, including the one that laughs at the very idea of pronouncing the word "silence," the one that, aiming for the impossible, stops short before the word "impossible" and writes it as "the end."

Such is the strength of women that, sweeping away syntax, breaking that famous thread (just a tiny little thread, they say) which acts for men as a surrogate umbilical cord, assuring them – otherwise they couldn't come – that the old lady is always right behind them, watching them make phallus, women will go right up to the impossible.

When the "repressed" of their culture and their society returns, it's an explosive, *utterly* destructive, staggering return, with a force never yet unleashed and equal to the most forbidding of suppressions. For when the Phallic period comes to an end, women will have been either annihilated or borne up to the highest and most violent incandescence. Muffled throughout their history, they have lived in dreams, in bodies (though muted), in silences, in aphonic revolts.

6 Jean Genêt, *Pompes funèbres* (Paris, 1948), p. 185.

14

And with such force in their fragility; a fragility, a vulnerability, equal to their incomparable intensity. Fortunately, they haven't sublimated; they've saved their skin, their energy. They haven't worked at liquidating the impasse of lives without futures. They have furiously inhabited these sumptuous bodies: admirable hysterics who made Freud succumb to many voluptuous moments impossible to confess, bombarding his Mosaic statue with their carnal and passionate body words, haunting him with their inaudible and thundering denunciations, dazzling, more than naked underneath the seven veils of modesty. Those who, with a single word of the body, have inscribed the vertiginous immensity of a history which is sprung like an arrow from the whole history of men and from biblico-capitalist society, are the women, the suppliants of yesterday, who come as forebears of the new women, after whom no intersubjective relation will ever be the same. You, Dora, you the indomitable, the poetic body, you are the true "mistress" of the Signifier. Before long your efficacity will be seen at work when your speech is no longer suppressed, its point turned in against your breast, but written out over against the other.

*In body.*—More so than men who are coaxed toward social success, toward sublimation, women are body. More body, hence more writing. For a long time it has been in body that women have responded to persecution, to the familial-conjugal enterprise of domestication, to the repeated attempts at castrating them. Those who have turned their tongues 10,000 times seven times before not speaking are either dead from it or more familiar with their tongues and their mouths than anyone else. Now, I-woman am going to blow up the Law: an explosion henceforth possible and ineluctable; let it be done, right now, in language.

Let us not be trapped by an analysis still encumbered with the old automatisms. It's not to be feared that language conceals an invincible adversary, because it's the language of men and their grammar. We mustn't leave them a single place that's any more theirs alone than we are.

If woman has always functioned within the discourse of man, a signifier that has always referred back to the opposite signifier which annihilates its specific energy and diminishes or stifles its very different sounds, it is time for her to dislocate this "within," to explode it, turn it around, and seize it; to make it hers, containing it, taking it in her own mouth, biting that tongue with her very own teeth to invent for herself a language to get inside of. And you'll see with what ease she will spring forth from that "within" – the "within" where once she so drowsily crouched – to overflow at the lips she will cover the foam.

15

Let's hurry: the continent is not impenetrably dark. I've been there often. I was overjoyed one day to run into Jean Genêt. It was in *Pompes*

5 Standard English term for the Hegelian *Aufhebung*, the French *la relève*.

13

Nor is the point to appropriate their instruments, their concepts, their places, or to begrudge them their position of mastery. Just because there's a risk of identification doesn't mean that we'll succumb. Let's leave it to the worriers, to masculine anxiety and its obsession with how to dominate the way things work – knowing "how it works" in order to "make it work." For us the point is not to take possession in order to internalize or manipulate, but rather to dash through and to "fly."[7]

Flying is woman's gesture – flying in language and making it fly. We have all learned the art of flying and its numerous techniques; for centuries we've been able to possess anything only by flying; we've lived in flight, stealing away, finding, when desired, narrow passageways, hidden cross-overs. It's no accident that *voler* has a double meaning, that it plays on each of them and thus throws off the agents of sense. It's no accident: women take after birds and robbers just as robbers take after women and birds. They (*illes*)[8] go by, fly the coop, take pleasure in jumbling the order of space, in disorienting it, in changing around the furniture, dislocating things and values, breaking them all up, emptying structures, and turning propriety upside down.

What woman hasn't flown/stolen? Who hasn't felt, dreamt, performed the gesture that jams sociality? Who hasn't crumbled, held up to ridicule, the bar of separation? Who hasn't inscribed with her body the differential, punctured the system of couples and opposition? Who, by some act of transgression, hasn't overthrown successiveness, connection, the wall of circumfusion?

A feminine text cannot fail to be more than subversive. It is volcanic; as it is written it brings about an upheaval of the old property crust, carrier of masculine investments; there's no other way. There's no room for her if she's not a he. If she's a her-she, it's in order to smash everything, to shatter the framework of institutions, to blow up the law, to break up the "truth" with laughter.

For once she blazes her trail in the symbolic, she cannot fail to make of it the chaosmos of the "personal" – in her pronouns, her nouns, and her clique of referents. And for good reason. There will have been the long history of gynocide. This is known by the colonized peoples of yester-day, the workers, the nations, the species off whose backs the history of men has made its gold; those who have known the ignominy of persecution derive from it an obstinate future desire for grandeur; those who are

7 Also, "to steal." Both meanings of the verb *voler* are played on, as the text itself explains in the following paragraph (translator's note).

8 *Illes* is a fusion of the masculine pronoun *ils*, which refers back to birds and robbers, with the feminine pronoun *elles*, which refers to women (translator's note).

16

14

locked up know better than their jailers the taste of free air. Thanks to their history, women today know (how to do and want) what men will be able to conceive of only much later. I say woman overturns the "personal," for if, by means of laws, lies, blackmail, and marriage, her right to herself has been extorted at the same time as her name, she has been able, through the very movement of mortal alienation, to see more closely the inanity of "propriety," the reductive stinginess of the masculine-conjugal subjective economy, which she doubly resists. On the one hand she has constituted herself necessarily as that "person" capable of losing a part of herself without losing her integrity. But secretly, silently, deep down inside, she grows and multiplies, for, on the other hand, she knows far more about living and about the relation between the economy of the drives and the management of the ego than any man. Unlike man, who holds so dearly to his title and his titles, his pouches of value, his cap, crown, and everything connected with his head, woman couldn't care less about the fear of decapitation (or castration), adventuring, without the masculine temerity, into anonymity, which she can merge with without annihilating herself: because she's a giver.

I shall have a great deal to say about the whole deceptive problematic of the gift. Woman is obviously not that woman Nietzsche dreamed of who gives only in order to.[9] Who could ever think of the gift as a gift-that-takes? Who else but man, precisely the one who would like to take everything?

If there is a "propriety of woman," it is paradoxically her capacity to depropriate unselfishly: body without end, without appendage, without principal "parts." If she is a whole, it's a whole composed of parts that are wholes, not simple partial objects but a moving, limitlessly changing ensemble, a cosmos tirelessly traversed by Eros, an immense astral space not organized around any one sun that's any more of a star than the others.

This doesn't mean that she's an undifferentiated magma, but that she doesn't lord it over her body or her desire. Though masculine sexuality gravitates around the penis, engendering that centralized body (in political anatomy) under the dictatorship of its parts, woman does not bring about the same regionalization which serves the couple head/genitals and which is inscribed only within boundaries. Her libido is cosmic,

9 Reread Derrida's text, "Le Style de la femme," in *Nietzsche aujourd'hui* (Paris: Union Generale d'Editions, Coll. 10/18), where the philosopher can be seen operating an *Aufhebung* of all philosophy in its systematic reducing of woman to the place of seduction: she appears as the one who is taken for; the bait in person, all veils unfurled, the one who doesn't give but who gives only to (take).

17

just as her unconscious is worldwide. Her writing can only keep going, without ever inscribing or discerning contours, daring to make these vertiginous crossings of the other(s) ephemeral and passionate sojourns in him, her, them, whom she inhabits long enough to look at from the point closest to their unconscious from the moment they awaken, to love them at the point closest to their drives; and then further, impregnated through and through with these brief, identificatory embraces, she goes and passes into infinity. She alone dares and wishes to know from within, where she, the outcast, has never ceased to hear the resonance of fore-language. She lets the other language speak – the language of 1,000 tongues which knows neither enclosure nor death. To life she refuses nothing. Her language does not contain, it carries; it does not hold back, it makes possible. When id is ambiguously uttered – the wonder of being several – she doesn't defend herself against these unknown women whom she's surprised at becoming, but derives pleasure from this gift of alterability. I am spacious, singing flesh, on which is grafted no one knows which I, more or less human, but alive because of transformation.

Write! and your self-seeking text will know itself better than flesh and blood, rising, insurrectionary dough kneading itself, with sonorous, perfumed ingredients, a lively combination of flying colors, leaves, and rivers plunging into the sea we feed. "Ah, there's her sea," he will say as he holds out to me a basin full of water from the little phallic mother from whom he's inseparable. But look, our seas are what we make of them, full of fish or not, opaque or transparent, red or black, high or smooth, narrow or bankless; and we are ourselves sea, sand, coral, seaweed, beaches, tides, swimmers, children, waves .... More or less wavily sea, earth, sky – what matter would rebuff us? We know how to speak them all.

Heterogeneous, yes. For her joyous benefit she is erogenous; she is the erotogeneity of the heterogeneous: airborne swimmer, in flight, she does not cling to herself; she is dispersible, prodigious, stunning, desirous and capable of others, of the other woman that she will be, of the other woman she isn't, of him, of you.

Woman be unafraid of any other place, of any same, or any other. My eyes, my tongue, my ears, my nose, my skin, my mouth, my body-for-(the)-other – not that I long for it in order to fill up a hole, to provide against some defect of mine, or because, as fate would have it, I'm spurred on by feminine "jealousy"; not because I've been dragged into the whole chain of substitutions that brings that which is substituted back to its ultimate object. That sort of thing you would expect to come straight out of "Tom Thumb," out of the *Penisneid* whispered to us by old grandmother ogresses, servants to their father-sons. If they believe,

18

I feel I should be trying to complete my life, whatever "completing a life" means. Some of my patients in their nineties or hundreds say *nunc dimittis*—"I have had a full life, and now I am ready to go." For some of them, this means going to heaven—it is always heaven rather than hell, though Samuel Johnson and James Boswell both quaked at the thought of going to hell and got furious with David Hume, who entertained no such beliefs. I have no belief in (or desire for) any postmortem existence, other than in the memories of friends and the hope that some of my books may still "speak" to people after my death.

W. H. Auden often told me he thought he would live to eighty and then "bugger off" (he lived only to sixty-seven). Though it is forty years since his death, I often dream of him, and of my parents and of former patients—all long gone but loved and important in my life.

At eighty, the specter of dementia or stroke

8

looms. A third of one's contemporaries are dead, and many more, with profound mental or physical damage, are trapped in a tragic and minimal existence. At eighty, the marks of decay are all too visible. One's reactions are a little slower, names more frequently elude one, and one's energies must be husbanded, but even so, one may often feel full of energy and life and not at all "old." Perhaps, with luck, I will make it, more or less intact, for another few years and be granted the liberty to continue to love and work, the two most important things, Freud insisted, in life.

When my time comes, I hope I can die in harness, as Francis Crick did. When he was told that his colon cancer had returned, at first he said nothing; he simply looked into the distance for a minute and then resumed his previous train of thought. When pressed about his diagnosis a few weeks later, he said, "Whatever has a beginning must have an end-

9

ing." When he died, at eighty-eight, he was still fully engaged in his most creative work.

My father, who lived to ninety-four, often said that the eighties had been one of the most enjoyable decades of his life. He felt, as I begin to feel, not a shrinking but an enlargement of mental life and perspective. One has had a long experience of life, not only one's own life, but others' too. One has seen triumphs and tragedies, booms and busts, revolutions and wars, great achievements and deep ambiguities. One has seen grand theories rise, only to be toppled by stubborn facts. One is more conscious of transience and, perhaps, of beauty. At eighty, one can take a long view and have a vivid, lived sense of history not possible at an earlier age. I can imagine, feel in my bones, what a century is like, which I could not do when I was forty or sixty. I do not think of old age as an ever grimmer time that one must somehow endure and make the best of, but



as a time of leisure and freedom, freed from the factitious urgencies of earlier days, free to explore whatever I wish, and to bind the thoughts and feelings of a lifetime together.

I am looking forward to being eighty.

### *I will write a poem about nothing*
#### William of Aquitaine
#### 1071-1127

I will write a poem about nothing
not about myself or other people,
nor about love or youth,
   nor about anything else;
composed, in fact, as I slept
   on horseback.

I don't know how I was born,
I'm neither happy nor sad,
neither stranger nor intimate,
   nor can act otherwise,
entranced thus, by night,
   on a high hill.

I don't know if I'm awake
or asleep unless told.
My heart is near broken
   with real grief,
yet I don't give a hoot
   by Saint Martial.

Sick and afraid to die,
I know only what I hear.
I'll find my kind of doctor
   though I know none such:
a good doctor, should he cure me
   – but if not, a quack.

I have a mistress, I don't know who,
whom I've never seen, I swear.
She's neither a pleasure nor a pain
   nor of interest to me.
And I've never had Normans or French
   at my house.

I've never seen her and adore her.
She's never done me right nor even wrong.
When I don't see her, that's fine
   I couldn't care less:
I know someone nobler, lovelier,
   who means much more.

So I've made a poem about I don't know what,
and I'll send it on to him
who will send it on to another
   and on to Anjou,
so that he, from his own pocket,
   may send the key to me.

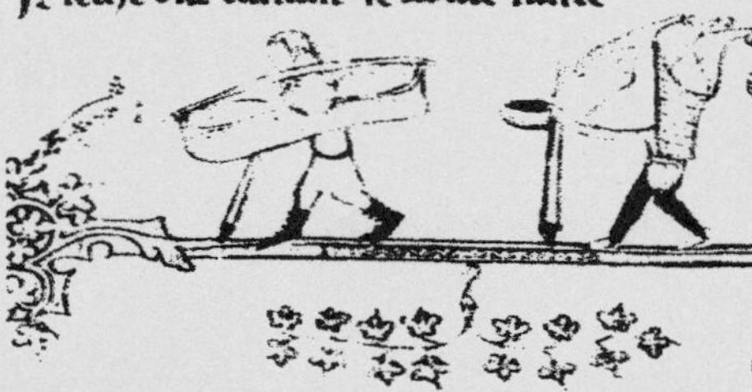



*— pure transmission*

*(everything he says he contradicts in this way he creates a wheel which moves things forward....)*

*life*
*me*
*you*

*already home*

*Give me back what I had to lose in order to have it restored, eternally*



ALLISON KATZ ANNOTATED I WILL WRITE A POEM ABOUT NOTHING, C. 12TH CENTURY, WILLIAM OF AQUITAINE figure, as if it corresponds to some truth or even our truth. Another black trainer describes the self-questioning entailed by living with this figure: "The other point as well about being a black trainer is that I've got to rapport build. Do I do that by being a member of the black and white minstrel show or do I do that by trying to earn respect with my knowledge? Do I do it by being friendly or do I do it by being cold, aloof and detached? And what does all this mean to the people now? From my point of view, it probably has nothing to do with the set of people that are in that room because actually the stereotype they've got in their heads is well and truly fixed" (cited in Ahmed et al. 2006: 59). Building rapport becomes a requirement because of a stereotype, as that which is fixed, no matter whom you encounter. The demand to build rapport takes the form of a perpetual self-questioning—the emotional labor of asking yourself what to do when there is an idea of you that persists, no matter what you do. Indeed, the consequences of racism are in part managed as a question of self-presentation, of trying not to fulfill a stereotype:

> Don't give white people nasty looks straight in their eyes; don't show them aggressive body positions. I mean, for example I am going to go and buy a pair of glasses because I know the glasses soften my face and I keep my hair short because I'm going bald, so I need something to soften my face. But actually what I am doing, I am countering a stereotype, I'm countering the black male sexual stereotype and yes, I spend all my time, I counter that stereotype, I couch my language behaviour and tone in as English a tone as I can. I am very careful, just very careful. (Cited in Ahmed et al. 2006: 60)

Being careful is about softening the form of your appearance so you do not appear "aggressive" because you are already assumed to be aggressive before you appear.[17] The demand not to be aggressive might be lived as a form of body politics or as a speech politics: you have to be careful what you say, how you appear, to maximize the distance between you and their idea of you ("the black male sexual stereotype"). The *encounter* with racism is experienced as the intimate labor of *countering* their idea of you. We might note here the specificity of the experience of being a black man, and thus of the gendered nature of racial stereotypes. The quote recalls the

writings of Frantz Fanon ([1952] 1986) and his powerful phenomenological description of the fright of being "the cause" of white fear as a black man (see Ahmed 2004: 62–63). A stereotype is a repetition (see Bhabha 2004: 153). The repetition of a stereotype allows it to accumulate negative affective value. A stereotype *is* a sticky sign.[18] The experience of being a black male subject in the institutions of whiteness is that of being on perpetual guard: of having to defend yourself against those who perceive you as someone to be defended against.

The experience of racism can involve self-censorship: because racism exists, people of color have to conceal its existence. The concealment of racism is understandable—it can be a way of coping with all that whiteness —but it still has far-reaching consequences. Those who do speak about racism are heard as all the more insistent. When people of color talk about racism, we are heard as the angry people they have already assumed us to be.

Feminists of color know very well the trouble it can cause just to bring racism up. If we talk about how racism affects us, then we are getting in the way of reconciliation, as if our talk is what prevents us all from "just" getting along. As Audre Lorde describes: "When women of Color speak out of the anger that laces so many of our contacts with white women, we are often told that we are 'creating a mood of helplessness,' 'preventing white women from getting past guilt,' or 'standing in the way of trusting communication and action'" (1984: 131). To preserve the possibility of getting on and moving on, we are asked to put racism behind us.

Another example: I publish an article on whiteness in the journal *Feminist Theory*, which also included a paper by Suneri Thobani (2007). I had previously written about Thobani's important critiques of the war against terrorism and the politics of how she was dismissed as an angry black woman (Ahmed 2004: 168–69). In this special issue, Thobani's article offers a critique of Phyllis Chesler, Zillah Eisenstein, and Judith Butler for how their writings are complicit with imperialism (albeit in very different ways). The journal publishes a response from Chesler alongside Thobani's article. The response draws on racist vocabularies with quite extraordinary ease. "It will be a good pedagogic tool," I say to a black feminist colleague at a conference. It will show students how racism works in academic practices. I don't convince myself or my colleague. We both know very well we have no need for any such tools. We have too many already.

What does Chesler say? She describes Thobani's article as "ideological, not scholarly" (2007: 228) and as trying "to pass for an academic or even intellectual work" (228). She describes the article as an "angry and self-righteous declaration of war" (228). She suggests "'white' folk have sorrows too" and then suggests that Thobani "is perfectly free to criticise, even to demonize the West, *in* the West because she is living in a democracy where academic freedom and free speech are (still) taken seriously" (230).[19]

The familiarity of these kinds of statements is exhausting. When I read them, I kept thinking of Audre Lorde and how I wished she were here to help us describe the moment. Description gets hard at this point. The woman of color isn't a real scholar; she is motivated by ideology. The woman of color is angry. She occupies the moral high ground. The woman of color declares war by pointing to the complicity of white feminists in imperialism. The woman of color is racist (and we hurt, too). The woman of color should be grateful, as she lives in our democracy. We have given her the right and the freedom to speak. The woman of color is the origin of terror, and she fails to recognize violence other than the violence of white against black. The exercising of this figure does more than make her work: *it is a defense against hearing her work.*

The stakes are indeed very high: to talk about racism is to occupy a space saturated with tension. History is saturation. It is because of how racism saturates everyday and institutional spaces that people of color often make strategic decisions *not* to use the language of racism. If you already pose a problem, or appear "out of place" in the institutions of whiteness, there can be good reasons not to exercise what is heard as a threatening or aggressive vocabulary. We learn also that hearing a language as a threat is a way of not hearing: if the organization has ears, it can block them, to stop the word "racism" from getting through.

If racism tends to recede from social consciousness, then it appears as if the ones who "bring it up" are bringing it into existence. A recession is possible if we make a concession. To recede is to go back or withdraw. To concede is to give way, yield. People of color are asked to concede to the

recession of racism: we are asked to "give way" by letting it "go back." Not only that: more than that. We are asked to embody a commitment to diversity. We are asked to smile in their brochures. The smile of diversity is a form of political recession.

### Diversity and Repair

One of my aims in this book has been to write about experiences of being included. Inclusion could be read as a technology of governance: not only as a way of bringing those who have been recognized as strangers into the nation, but also of making strangers into subjects, those who in being included are also willing to consent to the terms of inclusion. A national project can also be understood as a project of inclusion—a way others as would-be citizens are asked to submit to and agree with the task of reproducing that nation.[20]

Others have written of the current moment as a time in which the liberal promises of happiness and freedom have been extended to those who were previously excluded. For example, Jasbir Puar elegantly describes how a new class of (affluent, white, male) queer subjects are being "folded into life" (2007: xii, 24, 35, 36). The fold into life is an invitation to live; more than that, it is an invitation to live well, to flourish. The good ethnic as well as the good homosexual might be the ones who choose life, where life means being willing to become worthy of receiving state benevolence. To be included can thus be a way of sustaining and reproducing a politics of exclusion, where a life sentence for some is a death sentence for others.

I think this analysis provides an astute reading of both the politics of the state and those forms of politics premised on being willing to be the recipients of benevolence. If we start from our own experiences as persons of color in the institutions of whiteness, we might also think about how those benevolent acts of giving are *not what they seem*: being included can be a lesson in "being not" as much as "being in." The "folding into life" of minorities can also be understood as a national fantasy: it can be a "fantasy fold." We come up against the limits of this fantasy when we encounter the brick wall; we come up against the limits when we refuse to be grateful for what we receive. As Gail Lewis has convincingly shown,

# A SEDIMENTATION OF THE MIND: EARTH PROJECTS (1968)

*[handwritten annotation at top:] such a geo-logic oozes the confluence of the ancient and geo-mythical with technological, in resonant vectors, contingent + conspiratorial discoursing to ever shift our [—] earth ...*

The earth's surface and the figments of the mind have a way of disintegrating into discrete regions of art. Various agents, both fictional and real, somehow trade places with each other—one cannot avoid muddy thinking when it comes to earth projects, or what I will call "abstract geology." One's mind and the earth are in a constant state of erosion, mental rivers wear away abstract banks, brain waves undermine cliffs of thought, ideas decompose into stones of unknowing, and conceptual crystallizations break apart into deposits of gritty reason. Vast moving faculties occur in this geological miasma, and they move in the most physical way. This movement seems motionless, yet it crushes the landscape of logic under glacial reveries. This slow flowage makes one conscious of the turbidity of thinking. Slump, debris slides, avalanches all take place within the cracking limits of the brain. The entire body is pulled into the cerebral sediment, where particles and fragments make themselves known as solid consciousness. A bleached and fractured world surrounds the artist. To organize this mess of corrosion into patterns, grids, and subdivisions is an esthetic process that has scarcely been touched.

*[handwritten annotation at left:] in any non-muddy episteme there always a containment of work: avoiding the recursion of explaining its means of description (such as 'the sun will rise tomorrow' as in a smuggled inductive reasoning) and that any 'excess' of description will always be erased or put on hold as a 'copy-out' or 'undecidable'...*

The manifestations of technology are at times less "extensions" of man

Artforum, September 1968

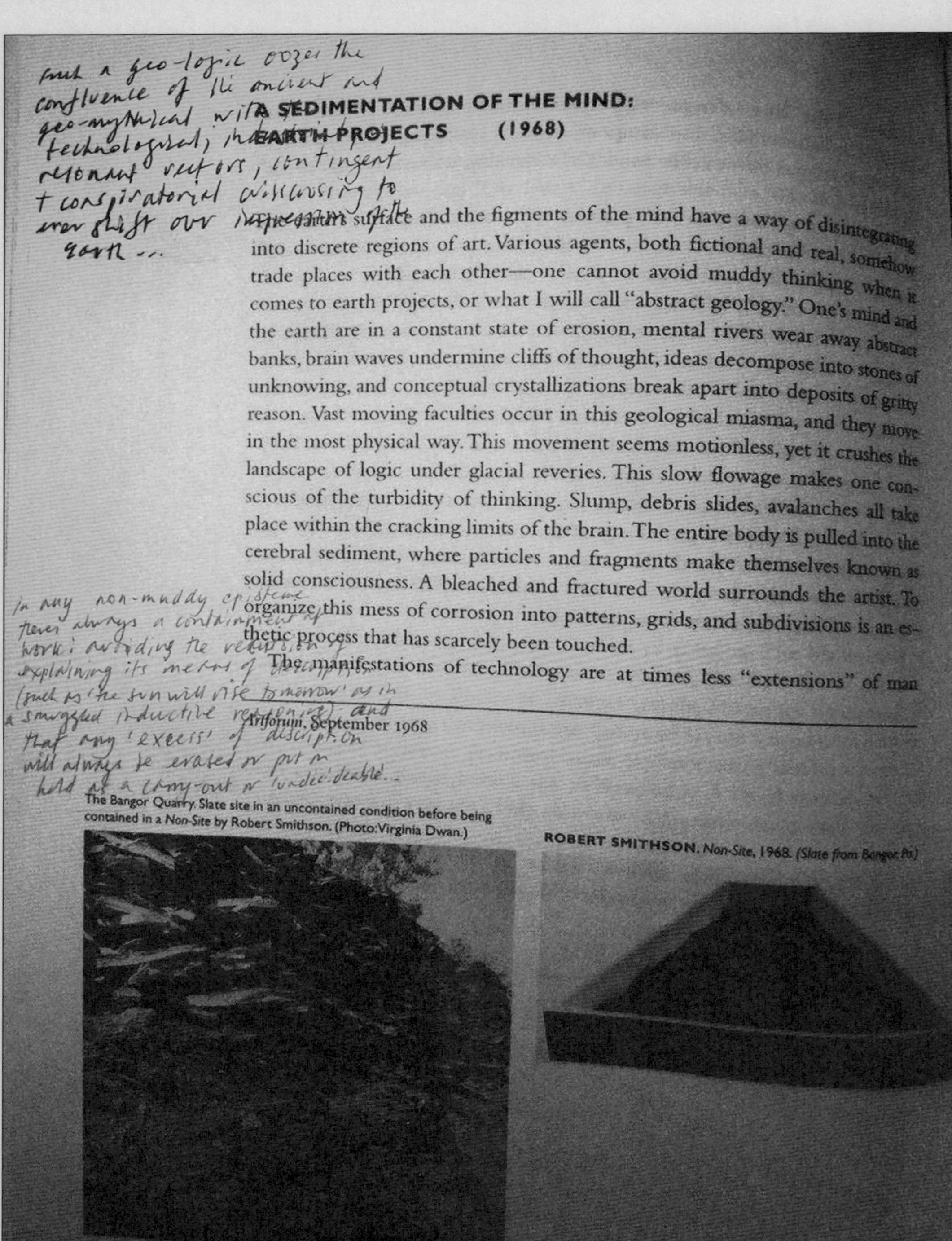

The Bangor Quarry. Slate site in an uncontained condition before being contained in a *Non-Site* by Robert Smithson. (Photo: Virginia Dwan.)

**ROBERT SMITHSON.** *Non-Site*, 1968. *(Slate from Bangor, Pa.)*

(Marshall McLuhan's anthropomorphism), than they are aggregates of elements. Even the most advanced tools and machines are made of the raw matter of the earth. Today's highly refined technological tools are not much different in this respect from those of the caveman. Most of the better artists prefer processes that have not been idealized, or differentiated into "objective" meanings. Common shovels, awkward looking excavating devices, what Michael Heizer calls "dumb tools," picks, pitchforks, the machine used by suburban contractors, grim tractors that have the clumsiness of armored dinosaurs, and plows that simply push dirt around. Machines like Benjamin Holt's steam tractor (invented in 1885)—"It crawls over mud like a caterpillar." Digging engines and other crawlers that can travel over rough terrain and steep grades. Drills and explosives that can produce shafts and earthquakes. Geometrical trenches could be dug with the help of the "ripper"—steel toothed rakes mounted on tractors. With such equipment construction takes on the look of destruction; perhaps that's why certain architects hate bulldozers and steam shovels. They seem to turn the terrain into unfinished cities of organized wreckage. A sense of chaotic planning engulfs site after site. Subdivisions are made—but to what purpose? Building takes on a singular wildness as loaders scoop and drag soil all over the place. Excavations form shapeless mounds of debris, miniature landslides of dust, mud, sand and gravel. Dump trucks spill soil into an infinity of heaps. The dipper of the giant mining power shovel is 25 feet high and digs 140 cu. yds. (250 tons) in one bite. These processes of heavy construction have a devastating kind of primordial grandeur, and are in many

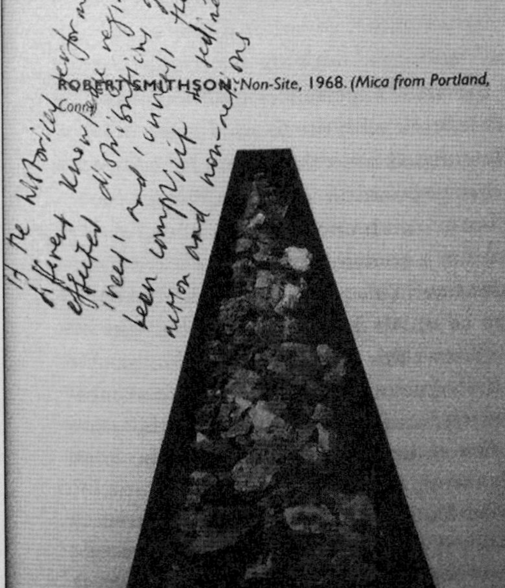

ROBERT SMITHSON: *Non-Site*, 1968. *(Mica from Portland, Conn.)*

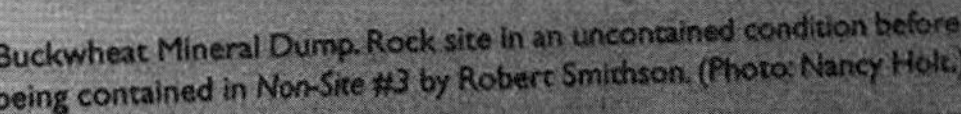

Buckwheat Mineral Dump. Rock site in an uncontained condition before being contained in *Non-Site #3* by Robert Smithson. (Photo: Nancy Holt.)

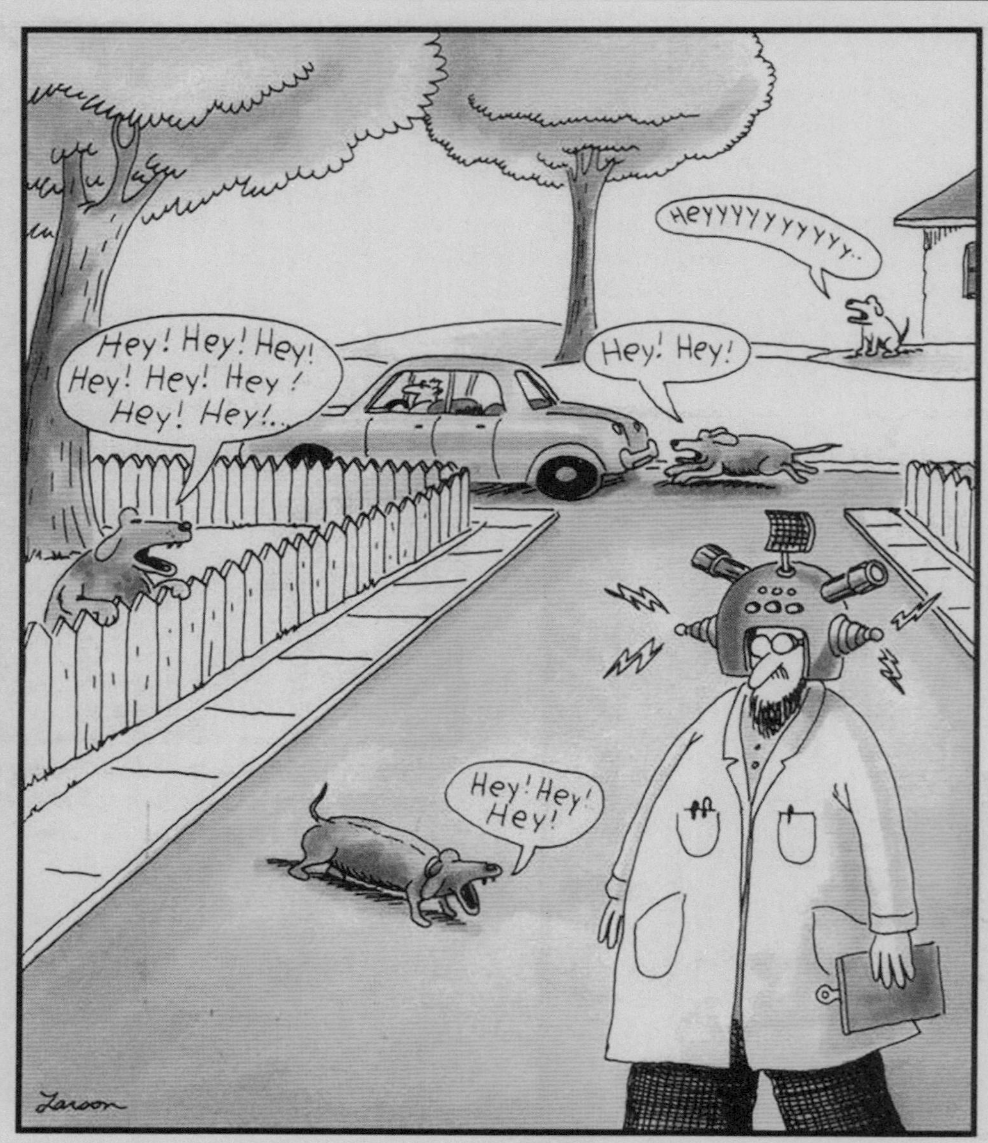


Donning his new canine decoder, Professor Schwartzman becomes the first human being on Earth to hear what barking dogs are actually saying.

with the dream, a criterion which gives us a concept of 'truth' as distinct from 'truthfulness' here.)

There is a game of 'guessing thoughts'. A variant of it would be this: I tell A something in a language that B does not understand. B is supposed to guess the meaning of what I say.—Another variant: I write down a sentence which the other person cannot see. He has to guess the words or their sense.—Yet another: I am putting a jig-saw puzzle together; the other person cannot see me but from time to time guesses my thoughts and utters them. He says, for instance, "Now where is this bit?"—*"Now* I know how it fits!"—"I have no idea what goes in here,"—"The sky is always the hardest part" and so on——but *I* need not be talking to myself either out loud or silently at the time.

All this would be guessing at thoughts; and the fact that it does not actually happen does not make thought any more hidden than the unperceived physical proceedings.

"What is *internal* is hidden from us."—The future is hidden from us. But does the astronomer think like this when he calculates an eclipse of the sun?

If I see someone writhing in pain with evident cause I do not think: all the same, his feelings are hidden from me.

We also say of some people that they are transparent to us. It is, however, important as regards this observation that one human being can be a complete enigma to another. We learn this when we come into a strange country with entirely strange traditions; and, what is more, even given a mastery of the country's language. We do not *understand* the people. (And not because of not knowing what they are saying to themselves.) We cannot find our feet with them.

"I cannot know what is going on in him" is above all a *picture.* It is the convincing expression of a conviction. It does not give the reasons for the conviction. *They* are riot readily accessible.

If a lion could talk, we could not understand him.

It is possible to imagine a guessing of intentions like the guessing of thoughts, but also a guessing of what someone is actually *going to do.*

To say "He alone can know what he intends" is nonsense: to say "He alone can know what he will do", wrong. For the prediction contained in my expression of intention (for example "When it strikes

MATTHEW DE KERSAINT GIRAUDEAU ANNOTATED PHILOSOPHICAL INVESTIGATIONS, 1953, LUDWIG WITTGENSTEIN

'One day a dachshund followed Wittgenstein and bit him in the left ankle. Without grimacing Ludwig responded by saying "If only it knew how to continue!" When I asked him whether it hurt he got angry and yelled at me "You of all people should not ask such a stupid question – see what philosophy has done to you!" Wittgenstein then demonstratively threw some mud at a traffic sign and added "Think about this!" Later he mellowed down and offered me some soup. He never spoke of dogs again.'

written by workers like Pottier, stealing time in the late night hours their schedules allowed them, was not a means of revindication—neither the form nor the thematic content of the poetry were what mattered. "It is not through its descriptive content nor its revindications that worker poetry becomes a *social* oeuvre, but rather through its pure act of existing."[17] The poetry illustrates neither the misery of the worker's conditions nor the heroism of his struggle—what it says, rather, is aesthetic capacity, the transgression of the division that assigns to some manual work and to others the activity of thinking. It is the proof that one participates in another life. When Marx says that the greatest accomplishment of the Paris Commune was "its own working existence" he is saying much the same thing. More important than any laws the Communards were able to enact was simply the way in which their daily workings inverted entrenched hierarchies and divisions—first and foremost among these the division between manual and artistic or intellectual labor. The world is divided between those who can and those who cannot afford the luxury of playing with words or images. When that division is overcome, as it was under the Commune, or as it is conveyed in the phrase "communal luxury," what matters more than any images conveyed, laws passed, or institutions founded are the capacities set in motion. You do not have to start at the beginning—you can start anywhere.

It was Courbet who started things off by issuing on April 6 an open "Call to Artists" to come to a political meeting the following week. There, in the Sorbonne's Medical School Amphitheater—the faculty of the medical school having all fled to Versailles—Eugène Pottier read aloud the Manifesto for an Artists' Federation developed by a preparatory committee and written by Pottier. Courbet's contribution to the manifesto seems to have been the essentially corporatist insistence that artists be allowed to administer the arts themselves—that they assume control of the museums and art collections. Artists must be entrusted to manage their own interests. The first basis for the Federation's existence was "the free expression of art, released

---

17   Jacques Rancière, "Ronds de fumé (Les poètes ouvriers dans la France de Louis-Philippe)," *Revue des sciences humaines*, 41:190 (April–June 1983), p. 46. His emphasis.

from all government supervision and all privilege."[18] The Federation envisaged liberty for the arts as the autonomy of art and artists vis-à-vis state power: it instituted total freedom from state subsidy, which had been used throughout the Second Empire as a means of promoting a particular artist or a particular theater over another. Any subsidy was understood by the Commune as a form of enslavement, a means of restricting that "freedom of the individual" the bourgeoisie claimed to promote but instead undermined. Abolition of the subsidy—essentially a kind of state bribery of artists—brought an end to the idea of an "official" style, or of the state's approval of academic or "safe" painters. In the place of state subsidies, the Federation looked to cooperation among the artists themselves as a way forward, rather like a trade union whereby each artist's dignity was protected by all the others: "Equality between members of the Federation that all artists adhering to the communal Republic constitute ... the independence and dignity of each artist is placed under the safeguard of all." Association meant a reconfiguration of alliances: artists were linked to each other and to their self-management in complete independence from the state. And all would share equally among themselves the ordinary tasks and requisitions commissioned by the Commune. Traces of Fourier can be detected in the educational mission the federation undertook for itself. To "regenerate the future through education," members of the committee would found and oversee the teaching of drawing in the schools, "favoring instruction according to attractive and logical methods." The federation also established a tribune, *L'Officiel des Arts*, open to everyone, where anyone who desired could discuss aesthetic questions, or issues concerning the relation between the artist and the public: "The Committee invites any citizen to communicate any proposition, project, thesis or opinion whose aim is artistic progress, the moral or intellectual emancipation of artists, or the material amelioration of their condition."

Liberty for the arts was thus in part a demand for artists' control over museum administrations, curators, and the organization of the

---

18   Manifesto of the Artists' Federation of Paris, April 15, 1871, in *Journal Officiel*, tome 2, pp. 273–4.

fishing gear and are in danger of having their wages reduced in the quarry or of losing their jobs altogether. I am a poet. I am the man who could never carry rocks, let alone have a share in a boat—that was what I meant when I said I was outside everything. I'm the village good-for-nothing whom everyone jeers at because I stay up at night and write books about men who were just as useless as I am myself. But for that very reason there is no thief so powerful that he can steal anything from me. Some say I'm allowed to work at the fish yards because I'm in tow with Pétur Pálsson the manager, but that's not true; I have never done anything for the manager except to compose twelve elegies for him, which is the least one can do for anyone. But even though both king and bishop allowed me and no one else to work in their fish yards, and promised to pay me in gold and diamonds, I'd never dream of touching a single fin, except only because fish are the same color as the sunshine, and because the smell of fish matches the breeze off the sea."

The meeting had already begun to interrupt him occasionally, but the poet Ólafur Kárason had now started and did not want to stop.

"Yes," he said, "I can hear what you say. I have never thought of anything except being a poet and a scholar, and so I don't care what others call me—fool, good-for-nothing, layabout, every bad name imaginable. But whatever I'm called, it doesn't alter the fact that whoever is a poet and a scholar loves the world more than all others do, even though he has never owned a share in a boat, yes, and not even managed to be classed as a quarryman. The fact is that it is much more difficult to be a poet and write poetry about the world than it is to be a man and live out in the world. You hump rocks for next to no pay and have lost your livelihood to thieves, but the poet is the emotion of the world, and it is in the poet that all men suffer. 'From the hoof of this damned world, O Lord, remove the small nails,' says the old hymn. The poet is the quick in this hoof, and there is no stroke of luck, neither higher wages nor better catches, which can cure the poet of suffering—nothing but a better world. On the day the world becomes good, the poet will cease to suffer, and not before; but at the same time he will also cease to be a poet."

He fell silent, looked around, and realized that the cobweb was gone from his face. And what he saw before him was wide, blue eyes, hot with the expectation of great, great things. Was it they which had called forth all this eloquence? He was not finished even yet.

"To be a poet is to be a visitor on a distant shore until one dies. In the land where I belong, but which I shall never reach, individuals have no cares, and that is because industry runs by itself without anyone trying to steal from others. My land is a land of plenty; it is the world that Nature has given to mankind, where society is not a thieves' society, where the children aren't sickly but healthy and contented, and young men and women can fulfill their aspirations because it is natural to do so. In my world it is possible to fulfill all aspirations, and therefore all aspirations are in themselves good, quite unlike here, where people's aspirations are called wicked because it isn't possible to fulfill them. In my land one can be content with looking at the clouds being mirrored in the sea, or lying on the grass listening to the brook purling through the dell. And when the great storms rage, people stoke their home fires generously, happy to own a sturdy house. And we hear a Voice which doesn't express any pain, and makes no demands, but which never sounds sweeter than when the poet is silenced at last; and in my land, all men can hear it. But here on this shore . . ."

The men were getting restless and were searching their pockets for tobacco; it caused them almost physical pain to hear someone baring his soul like this. But Jórunn, the daughter of Hjörtur of Veghús, stood up in a trance, walked over to him, gave him her long, strong hand and said:

"It is the Dream of Happiness."

The girl's father bellowed with laughter.

Everyone had started mewing at one another again. The poet felt that no one had understood him except this girl, who had certainly been the cause of his speech, and yet he doubted whether she had understood him correctly; her unexpected handshake burned in the palm of his hand. Her hand was larger than his and undoubtedly stronger. But what worried him most was to have aroused Faroese-

**There are these two young fish** swimming along and they happen to meet an older fish swimming the other way, who nods at them and says, »Morning, boys. How's the water?« And the two young fish swim on for a bit, and then eventually one of them looks over at the other and goes, »What the hell is water?«

This is a standard requirement of US commencement speeches, the deployment of didactic little parable-ish stories.

The story thing turns out to be one of the better, less bullshitty conventions of the genre …

~ 39 ~

center of all creation. This kind of freedom has much to recommend it.

But of course there are all different kinds of freedom, and the kind that is most precious you will not hear much talked about in the great outside world of winning and achieving and displaying.

The really important kind of freedom involves attention, and awareness, and discipline, and effort, and being able truly to care about other people and to sacrifice for them, over and over, in myriad petty little unsexy ways, every day.

That is real freedom.

That is being taught how to think.

The alternative is unconsciousness, the default setting, the »rat race« – the constant, gnawing sense of having had and lost some infinite thing.

I know that this stuff probably doesn't sound fun and breezy or grandly inspirational the way a commencement speech's central stuff



should sound. What it is, so far as I can see, is the truth, with a whole lot of rhetorical bullshit pared away. Obviously, you can think of it whatever you wish. But please don't dismiss it as some finger-wagging Dr. Laura sermon. None of this is about morality, or religion, or dogma, or big fancy questions of life after death.

The capital-T Truth is about life *before* death. It is about making it to thirty, or maybe even fifty, without wanting to shoot yourself in the head. It is about the real value of a real education, which has nothing to do with grades or degrees and everything to do with simple awareness – awareness of what is so real and essential, so hidden in plain sight all around us, that we have to keep reminding ourselves over and over:

»This is water.«

»This is water.«

»These Eskimos might be much more than they seem.«

Gauls." I believe it is necessary to become a child again in order to grasp certain psychic realities. This is where Jung was an innovator: He wanted to go back to the childhood of the world, but he made a remarkable mistake: He went back only to the childhood of Europe.

In the remotest depth of the European unconscious an inordinately black hollow has been made in which the most immoral impulses, the most shameful desires lie dormant. And as every man climbs up toward whiteness and light, the European has tried to repudiate this uncivilized self, which has attempted to defend itself. When European civilization came into contact with the black world, with those savage peoples, everyone agreed: Those Negroes were the principle of evil.

Jung consistently identifies the foreign with the obscure, with the tendency to evil: He is perfectly right. This mechanism of projection—or, if one prefers, transference—has been described by classic psychoanalysis. In the degree to which I find in myself something unheard-of, something reprehensible, only one solution remains for me: to get rid of it, to ascribe its origin to someone else. In this way I eliminate a short circuit that threatens to destroy my equilibrium. One must be careful with waking dreams in the early sessions, because it is not good if the obscenity emerges too soon. The patient must come to understand the workings of sublimation before he makes any contact with the unconscious. If a Negro comes up in the first session, he must be removed at once; to that end, suggest a stairway or a rope to the patient, or propose that he let himself be carried off in a helicopter. Infallibly, the Negro will stay in his hole. In Europe the Negro has one function: that of symbolizing the lower emotions, the baser inclinations, the dark side of the soul. In the collective unconscious of *homo occidentalis*, the Negro—or, if one prefers, the color black—symbolizes evil, sin, wretchedness, death, war, famine. All birds of prey are black. In Martinique, whose collective unconscious makes it a European country, when a "blue" Negro—a coal-black one—comes to visit, one reacts at once: "What bad luck is he bringing?"

<u>The collective unconscious is not dependent on cerebral heredity; it is the result of what I shall call the unreflected imposition of a culture.</u> Hence there is no reason to be surprised when an Antillean exposed to waking-dream therapy relives the same fantasies as a European. It is because the Antillean partakes of the same collective unconscious as the European.

If what has been said thus far is grasped, this conclusion may be stated: It is normal for the Antillean to be anti-Negro. Through the collective unconscious the Antillean has taken over all the archetypes belonging to the European. The *anima* of the Antillean Negro is almost always a white woman. In the same way, the *animus* of the Antilleans is always a white man. That is because in the works of Anatole France, Balzac, Bazin, or any of the rest of "our" novelists, there is never a word about an ethereal yet ever present black woman or about a dark Apollo with sparkling eyes. . . . But I too am guilty, here I am talking of Apollo! There is no help for it: I am a white man. For unconsciously I distrust what is black in me, that is, the whole of my being.

I am a Negro—but of course I do not know it, simply because I am one. When I am at home my mother sings me French love songs in which there is never a word about Negroes. When I disobey, when I make too much noise, I am told to "stop acting like a nigger."

Somewhat later I read white books and little by little I take into myself the prejudices, the myths, the folklore

## ✳ CÓMO PONER LOS PUNTOS SUSPENSIVOS

En «Cómo reconocer una película porno» se ha dicho que para distinguir una película pornográfica de una película que simplemente representa vicisitudes eróticas, es suficiente establecer si, para ir de un sitio a otro en coche, los personajes emplean más tiempo del que desearía el espectador y la historia requeriría. Parecido criterio científico puede servir para distinguir al escritor profesional del escritor dominguero (que puede incluso volverse famoso). Se trata del uso de los puntos suspensivos en medio de la frase.

Los escritores usan los puntos suspensivos sólo al final de la frase para indicar que el discurso podría continuar («y sobre este argumento habría mucho que decir, pero ...»), y en medio de la frase o entre frases cuando se quiere indicar la fragmentariedad del texto («Aquel ramal del lago Como... toma casi de repente curso y figura de río»). Los no escritores usan los puntos suspensivos para hacerse perdonar una figura retórica que juzgan demasiado atrevida: «Estaba enfurecido como... un toro».

El escritor es alguien que ha decidido conducir el lenguaje más allá de sus límites, y por ello asume la responsabilidad de una metáfora incluso osada: «Cada vez que la miraba, salía un sol por su frente, de tantos rayos ceñido cuantos cabellos contiene». Estamos todos de acuerdo en que, en este romance, Góngora exagera, como buen barroco, pero por lo menos no ha tirado la piedra y escondido la mano. En cambio el no-escritor escribiría: «salía... un sol por su frente», como para decir «naturalmente, estoy bromeando».

El escritor escribe para los escritores, el no-escritor escribe para el vecino de rellano o para el director de la oficina de co-

220

rreos local, y teme (a menudo equivocadamente) que no comprendan o que, de todas formas, no perdonen su osadía. Usa los puntos suspensivos como contraseña: quiere hacer la revolución, pero con la autorización de la guardia civil.

Lo desdichados que son los puntos suspensivos, nos lo dice esta modesta serie de variaciones que cuentan qué le habría sucedido a la literatura si los escritores hubieran sido tímidos.

«A mitad del camino de... nuestra vida.»

«Nuestras vidas son... los ríos.»

«Si yo fuera... fuego, ardería el mundo.»

«Polvo serán, mas polvo... enamorado.»

«La vida es una... historia contada por un... idiota.»

«El hombre es un... dios cuando sueña.»

«No existe gran amor más que a la sombra de un gran... sueño.»

«Os mostraré el miedo en un puñado de... polvo.»

Y de ahí en adelante, desde «Una rosa es... una rosa, una... rosa» hasta «A las cinco en punto... de la tarde.»

Y paciencia por el papelón que aquellos Grandes habrían hecho. Pero nótese que la introducción de los puntos suspensivos, expresando temor por la osadía del hablar figurado, puede usarse también para inducir la sospecha de que es figura retórica una expresión que parece llanamente literal. Pongamos un ejemplo. El *Manifiesto* de los comunistas de 1848 empieza, como es sabido, con «Un fantasma recorre Europa» y admitiréis que es un gran buen incipit. Paciencia si Marx y Engels hubieran escrito «Un... fantasma recorre Europa», simplemente habrían puesto en duda que el comunismo fuera algo tan terrible e inasible, a lo mejor la revolución rusa se habría anticipado cincuenta años, quizá con el beneplácito del zar, y habría participado incluso Mazzini.

¿Pero, y si hubieran escrito «Un fantasma... recorre Europa»? ¿Entonces no la recorre? ¿Está? ¿Y dónde está? ¿O es que los fantasmas, al ser fantasmas, aparecen y desaparecen de golpe, en un abrir y cerrar de ojos y no pierden tiempo circulando? Pero no acaba aquí la cosa. ¿Y si hubieran escrito «Un fantasma... recorre Europa»? ¿Habrían querido decir que estaban exagerando, que el fantasma, aún gracias con que recorriera Tréveris, y los demás todavía podían estar tranquilos? ¿O habrían aludido al hecho de que el fantasma del comunismo ya estaba

221

obsesionando también a las Américas y, ojalá lo viéramos, a Australia?

«Ser o... no ser, este es el problema.»

«Ser o no ser, este es el... problema.»

«Ser o no... ser, este es el problema...»

Ved lo que habría debido trabajar la crítica shakespeariana sobre las intenciones recónditas del Bardo. ¿Y qué decir de nuestra constitución?

«Italia es una república fundada sobre el ... trabajo (¡anda!)»

«Italia es, digamos. una... república fundada sobre el trabajo.»

«Italia es una república... fundada (???) sobre el trabajo.»

«...Italia (si existiera) sería una república fundada sobre el trabajo.»

Italia es una república fundada sobre los puntos suspensivos.

(1991)

founded over ...

sobre over
sobre above ...

suspension ...

waiting...

a supporting role in his long-ago former wife's history. I imagine her living quietly during those mid-'60s years in remote San Diego, although doubtless ambivalent about whatever it meant to be a "young wife" during the *Peyton Place* era.

* * *

Before leaving Brandeis, Acker had been one of a handful of classics majors. Years later she'd boast that her undergrad papers were read by the renowned structural linguist Roman Jakobson, although this seems unlikely, since he taught at Harvard. Even if, as she'd elaborate, her Brandeis tutor had studied with Jakobson, it's hard to imagine the tutor sharing an undergrad student's papers with him. But to lie is to try. Like most fabulations, the story contains a kernel of truth, or at least of desire. There's no doubt that Acker wanted to study at Harvard with Roman Jakobson—or rather at Radcliffe, its sister school, because Harvard wouldn't enroll female undergraduate students until 1975.

Brandeis, known at the time as "Jew U," wasn't her first choice of school. By her mid-teens Acker was fiercely precocious, an outstanding student at the Lenox School, a staid and somewhat mediocre Upper East Side private girl's institution that has since merged with Birch Wathen. But until she met the future film scholar P. Adams Sitney, her knowledge of culture didn't extend much beyond the Lenox curriculum. Acker met Sitney at a summer study intensive at Trinity College in the summer of 1963, when she was sixteen, between her sophomore and junior years of high school. Sitney was eighteen. Two and a half years Acker's senior, he was about to begin his first (and, as it turned out, his last) semester at Yale, studying classics. A dazzling polymath, Sitney's poetic passions that summer included Charles Olson, Ezra Pound, Virgil, and Sextus Propertius. Acker had just discovered the Victorian poet Gerard Manley Hopkins. She was

## At the Dam



SINCE THE AFTERNOON in 1967 when I first saw Hoover Dam, its image has never been entirely absent from my inner eye. I will be talking to someone in Los Angeles, say, or New York, and suddenly the dam will materialize, its pristine concave face gleaming white against the harsh rusts and taupes and mauves of that rock canyon hundreds or thousands of miles from where I am. I will be driving down Sunset Boulevard, or about to enter a freeway, and abruptly those power transmission towers will appear before me, canted vertiginously over the tailrace. Sometimes I am confronted by the intakes and sometimes by the shadow of the heavy cable that spans the canyon and sometimes by the ominous outlets to unused spillways, black in the lunar clarity of the desert light. Quite often I hear the turbines. Frequently I wonder what is happening at the dam this instant, at this precise intersection of time and space, how much water is being released to fill downstream orders and what lights are flashing and which generators are in full use and which just spinning free.

I used to wonder what it was about the dam that made me think of it at times and in places where I once thought of the Mindanao Trench, or of the stars wheeling in their courses, or of the words *As it was in the beginning, is now and ever shall be, world without end, amen.* Dams, after all, are commonplace: we have all

198

seen one. This particular dam had existed as an idea in the world's mind for almost forty years before I saw it. Hoover Dam, showpiece of the Boulder Canyon project, the several million tons of concrete that made the Southwest plausible, the *fait accompli* that was to convey, in the innocent time of its construction, the notion that mankind's brightest promise lay in American engineering.

Of course the dam derives some of its emotional effect from precisely that aspect, that sense of being a monument to a faith since misplaced. "They died to make the desert bloom," reads a plaque dedicated to the 96 men who died building this first of the great high dams, and in context the worn phrase touches, suggests all of that trust in harnessing resources, in the meliorative power of the dynamo, so central to the early Thirties. Boulder City, built in 1931 as the construction town for the dam, retains the ambience of a model city, a new town, a toy triangular grid of green lawns and trim bungalows, all fanning out from the Reclamation building. The bronze sculptures at the dam itself evoke muscular citizens of a tomorrow that never came, sheaves of wheat clutched heavenward, thunderbolts defied. Winged Victories guard the flagpole. The flag whips in the canyon wind. An empty Pepsi-Cola can clatters across the terrazzo. The place is perfectly frozen in time.

But history does not explain it all, does not entirely suggest what makes that dam so affecting. Nor, even, does energy, the massive involvement with power and pressure and the transparent sexual overtones to that involvement. Once when I revisited the dam I walked through it with a man from the Bureau of Reclamation. For a while we trailed behind a guided

199

tour, and then we went out into parts of the dam where visitors do not generally go. Once in a while he would explain something, usually in that recondite language having to do with "peaking power," with "outages" and "dewatering," but on the whole we spent the afternoon in a world so alien, so complete and so beautiful unto itself that it was scarcely necessary to speak at all. We saw almost no one. Cranes moved above us as if under their own volition. Generators roared. Transformers hummed. The gratings on which we stood vibrated. We watched a hundred-ton steel shaft plunging down to that place where the water was. And finally we got down to that place where the water was, where the water sucked out of Lake Mead roared through thirty-foot penstocks and then into thirteen-foot penstocks and finally into the turbines themselves. "Touch it," the Reclamation said, and I did, and for a long time I just stood there with my hands on the turbine. It was a peculiar moment, but so explicit as to suggest nothing beyond itself.

There was something beyond all that, something beyond energy, beyond history, something I could not fix in my mind. When I came up from the dam that day the wind was blowing harder, through the canyon and all across the Mojave. Later, toward Henderson and Las Vegas, there would be dust blowing, blowing past the Country-Western Casino FRI & SAT NITES and blowing past the Shrine of Our Lady of Safe Journey STOP & PRAY, but out at the dam there was no dust, only the rock and the dam and a little greasewood and a few garbage cans, their tops chained, banging against a fence. I walked across the marble star map that traces a sidereal revolution of the equinox and fixes forever, the Reclamation man had told me, for all time and for all people who can read the stars, the date the dam was dedicated. The star map was, he had said, for when we were all gone and the dam was left. I had not thought much of it when he said it, but I thought of it then, with the wind whining and the sun dropping behind a mesa with the finality of a sunset in space. Of course that was the image I had seen always, seen it without quite realizing what I saw, a dynamo finally free of man, splendid at last in its absolute isolation, transmitting power and releasing water to a world where no one is.

Woman, Art, Class



bert, Rilke, Joseph Conrad; Thomas Wolfe's *Story of a Novel*, Valéry's *Course in Poetics*. What do they explain of the silences?

"Constant toil is the law of art, as it is of life," says (and demonstrated) Balzac:

> To pass from conception to execution, to produce, to bring the idea to birth, to raise the child laboriously from infancy, to put it nightly to sleep surfeited, to kiss it in the mornings with the hungry heart of a mother, to clean it, to clothe it fifty times over in new garments which it tears and casts away, and yet not revolt against the trials of this agitated life—this unwearying maternal love, this habit of creation—this is execution and its toils.

"Without duties, almost without external communication," Rilke specifies, "unconfined solitude which takes every day like a life, a spaciousness which puts no limit to vision and in the midst of which infinities surround."

Unconfined solitude as Joseph Conrad experienced it:

> For twenty months I wrestled with the Lord for my creation . . . mind and will and conscience engaged to the full, hour after hour, day after day . . . a lonely struggle in a great isolation from the world. I suppose I slept and ate the food put before me and talked connectedly on suitable occasions, but I was never aware of the even flow of daily life, made easy and noiseless for me by a silent, watchful, tireless affection. — a woman, no doubt

So there is a homely underpinning for it all, the even flow of daily life made easy and noiseless.

"The terrible law of the artist"—says Henry James—"the law of fructification, of fertilization. The old, old lesson of the art of meditation. To woo combinations and inspirations into being by a depth and continuity of attention and meditation."

"That load, that weight, that gnawing conscience," writes Thomas Mann—

> That sea which to drink up, that frightful task . . . The will, the discipline and self-control to shape a sentence or follow out a hard train of thought. From the first rhythmical urge of the inward

creative force towards the material, towards casting in shape and form, from that to the thought, the image, the word, the line, what a struggle, what Gethsemane.

Does it become very clear what Melville's Pierre so bitterly remarked on, and what literary history bears out—why most of the great works of humanity have come from lives (able to be) wholly surrendered and dedicated? How else sustain the constant toil, the frightful task, the terrible law, the continuity? Full self: this means full time as and when needed for the work. (That time for which Emily Dickinson withdrew from the world.) But what if there is not that fullness of time, let alone totality of self? What if the writers, as in some of these silences, must work regularly at something besides their own work—as do nearly all in the arts in the United States today.

I know the theory (kin to "starving in the garret makes great art") that it is this very circumstance which feeds creativity. I know, too, that for the beginning young, for some who have such need, the job can be valuable access to life they would not otherwise know. A few (I think of the doctors, the incomparables: Chekhov and William Carlos Williams) for special reasons sometimes manage both. But the actuality testifies: substantial creative work demands time, and with rare exceptions only full-time workers have achieved it. Where the claims of creation cannot be primary, the results are atrophy; unfinished work; minor effort and accomplishment; silences. (Desperation which accounts for the mountains of applications to the foundations for grants—undivided time—in the strange bread-line system we have worked out for our artists.)

Twenty years went by on the writing of *Ship of Fools*, while Katherine Anne Porter, who needed only two, was "trying to get to that table, to that typewriter, away from my jobs of teaching and trooping this country and of keeping house." "Your subconscious needed that time to grow the layers of pearl," she was told. Perhaps, perhaps, but I doubt it. Subterranean forces can make you wait, but they are very finicky about the kind of waiting it has to be. Before they will feed the creator back, they must be fed, passionately fed, what needs to be worked on. "We hold up our desire as one places a magnet over a composite dust from which the particle of iron will suddenly jump up," says Paul Valéry. A receptive waiting, that means, not demands which prevent "an undistracted center of being." And when the response comes, availability to work must be immediate. If not used at once, all may vanish as a dream; worse, future creation be endangered —for only the removal and development of the material frees the forces for further work. / /

There is a life in which all this is documented: Franz Kafka's. For every one entry from his diaries here, there are fifty others that testify as unbearably to the driven stratagems for time, the work lost (to us), the damage to the creative powers (and the body) of having to deny, interrupt, postpone, put aside, let work die.

"I cannot devote myself completely to my writing," Kafka explains (in 1911). "I could not live by literature if only, to begin with, because of the slow maturing of my work and its special character." So he worked as an official in a state insurance agency, and wrote when he could.

> These two can never be reconciled. . . . If I have written something one evening, I am afire the next day in the office and can bring nothing to completion. Outwardly I fulfill my office duties satisfactorily, not my inner duties however, and every unfulfilled inner duty becomes a misfortune that never leaves. What strength it will necessarily drain me of.

1911

> No matter how little the time or how badly I write, I feel approaching the imminent possibility of great moments which could make me capable of anything. But my being does not have sufficient strength to hold this to the next writing time. During the day the visible world helps me; during the night it cuts me to pieces unhindered. . . . In the evening and in the morning, my consciousness of the creative abilities in me then I can encompass. I feel shaken to the core of my being. Calling forth such powers which are then not permitted to function.

. . . which are then not permitted to function . . .



1911

> I finish nothing, because I have no time, and it presses so within me.

1912

> When I begin to write after such a long interval, I draw the words as if out of the empty air. If I capture one, then I have just this one alone, and all the toil must begin anew.

1914

> Yesterday for the first time in months, an indisputable ability to do good work. And yet wrote only the first page. Again I realize that everything written down bit by bit rather than all at once in the course of the larger part is inferior, and that the circumstances of my life condemn me to this inferiority.

1915

> My constant attempt by sleeping before dinner to make it possible to continue working [writing] late into the night, senseless. Then at one o'clock can no longer fall asleep at all, the next day at work insupportable, and so I destroy myself.

1917

> Distractedness, weak memory, stupidity. Days passed in futility, powers wasted away in waiting. . . . Always this one principal anguish—if I had gone away in 1911 in full possession of all my powers. Not eaten by the strain of keeping down living forces.

Eaten into tuberculosis. By the time he won through to himself and time for writing, his body could live no more. He was forty-one.

I think of Rilke who said, "If I have any responsibility, I mean and desire it to be responsibility for the deepest and innermost essence of the loved reality [writing] to which I am inseparably bound"; and who also said, "Anything alive that makes demands, arouses in me an infinite capacity to give it its due, the consequences of which completely use me up." These were true with Kafka, too, yet how different their lives. When Rilke wrote that about responsibility, he is explaining why he will not take a job to support his wife and baby, nor live with them (years later will not come to his daughter's wedding nor permit a two-hour honeymoon visit lest it break his solitude where he awaits poetry). The

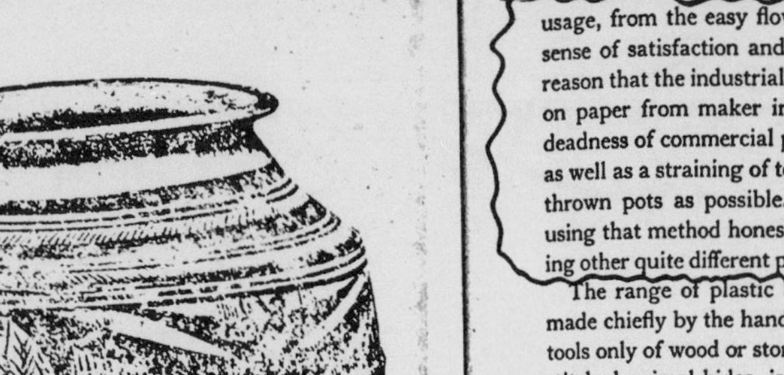

12. Primitive Persian Jar, circa 3000 B.C., wheel-thrown, pigmented but unglazed. The manner in which the painted pattern picks up and vitalises the subtle variations of the large form should be noted.

# TOWARDS A STANDARD

usage, from the easy flowing application of which follows the sense of satisfaction and adequacy of technique. It is for this reason that the industrial practice of rigidly separating designer on paper from maker in clay is responsible for much of the deadness of commercial pottery, for it is a waste of opportunity as well as a straining of technique to make moulded pots as like thrown pots as possible. The beauty of each method lies in using that method honestly, for what it is worth, not in imitating other quite different processes.[1]

The range of plastic beauty achieved in primitive pottery, made chiefly by the hands of women without a wheel and with tools only of wood or stone, basketry, textiles, leaves of trees or stitched animal hides, is immense. The whole world seems to have contributed to it during thousands of prehistoric years: Minoan, archaic Greek, African, North and South American, pots of the Black Earth Region and neolithic China, pigmented but unglazed, often so fine that one might be tempted to surrender all claim for the supremacy of eleventh and twelfth century China, were it not for the fact that the general cultural and technical achievements of the Sung Chinese were so much greater. For this reason I shall deal in this book for the most part with wheel-thrown forms, which reached their greatest perfection round about that period.

A pot thrown on a good wheel with responsive clay, but not too soapy in texture, is impressed and expressed, urged and

[1] Every designer either on paper or of model parts should have first-hand experience not only of the processes of manufacture, but also of the limitations no less than the potentialities of his materials. What is obviously needed is a new type of designer who knows both approaches to ~~pottery~~ and can therefore keep industry in touch with fresh artistic expression in the studio. Without such an alliance in the near future between artist-craftsman and factory, it is difficult to conceive how ~~ware~~ could be made ~~in Staffordshire~~ which would be even respectable in the scale of beauty the world has known. The ~~tendency to employ sculptors and painters of reputation~~ to make designs for the industry is useful up to a point, but it gives no guarantee that these artists know and feel their medium, nor that the factories and their reduplicating processes will do justice to the designs. The link is not close enough.

*Handwritten annotation:* Production Products

*Handwritten annotation (bottom right):* Without understanding how a material works, what it can do and what processes are available to you and how they work, then it's impossible to design a a product that's # both economic in its use of materials and efficient in the way its produced

*Handwritten annotation (bottom left):* * beautiful and works well, and is

## TOWARDS A STANDARD

character of the potter, his stock and his tradition live afresh in his work; objective in so far as his selection is drawn from the background of universal human experience.

Subordinate to form but intimately connected with it is the problem of decoration, and the question arises whether the increased orchestration adds to the total effect or not. Decoration will be treated more fully later on, here it is enough to say that, although some of the very finest pots are quite plain, it is nevertheless of the greatest significance. Many a good piece has been spoiled by a weak or tasteless design, printed or applied in one way or another: not only must the pattern be good in itself and freely executed, but it must combine with and improve the form and harmonize with the natural variations of both colour and texture of body and glaze.

The upshot of the argument is that a pot in order to be good should be a genuine expression of life. It implies sincerity on the part of the potter and truth in the conception and execution of the work. By this reasoning we are thrown back upon the oldest of questions, but there is no escaping fundamental issues in discussing problems of art at a period of break-up and change. Art is an epitome of life experience and in searching for a standard in pottery elastic enough to cover both past and present we are compelled to look far afield and to examine the principles upon which the best pots of East and West have been based. In a broad way the difference between the old potters and the new is between unconsciousness within a single culture and individual consciousness of all cultures. And to this one can only add that until a life synthesis is reached by humanity the individual potter can only hope to deepen and widen his consciousness in anticipation and contribution towards that end

The method by which a pot is formed determines its general character, whether hand modelled or built up out of coils or slices, or freely thrown on the wheel, or thrown in a mould, or cast entirely in a mould—each process conditions the interpretation of the original idea, and each has a limited range of right

20

11. English Mediaeval Pitcher, 14th century. Wheel thrown, combed, and with a pinched foot. The lead ore (galena) glaze has probably been dusted over a coating of damp slip. The severe dignity of form allies such monastic pitchers with Gothic architecture. Inset, part of an English mediaeval tile (see pages 11 and 32).

All processes have a place and honesty to a material's properties → But respect their idiosyncrasies of a processe is the supreme.

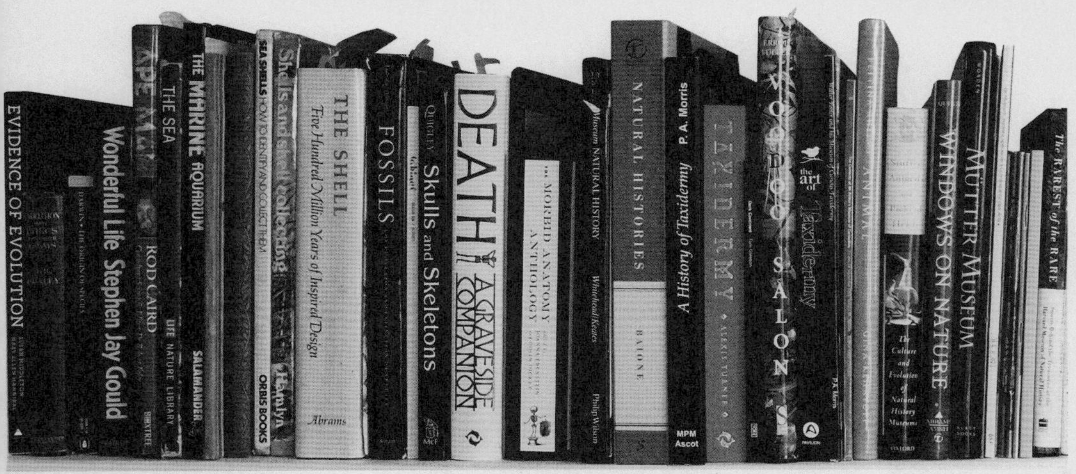

EVOLUTION –

THE SEA – SHELLS – FOSSILS – BONES – NATURAL HISTORY – TAXIDERMY – THE MUSEUM –

COLLECTING – CABINETS OF WONDER – SPECIAL CASES – IMAGINARY ANIMALS – MONSTERS

– GHOSTS

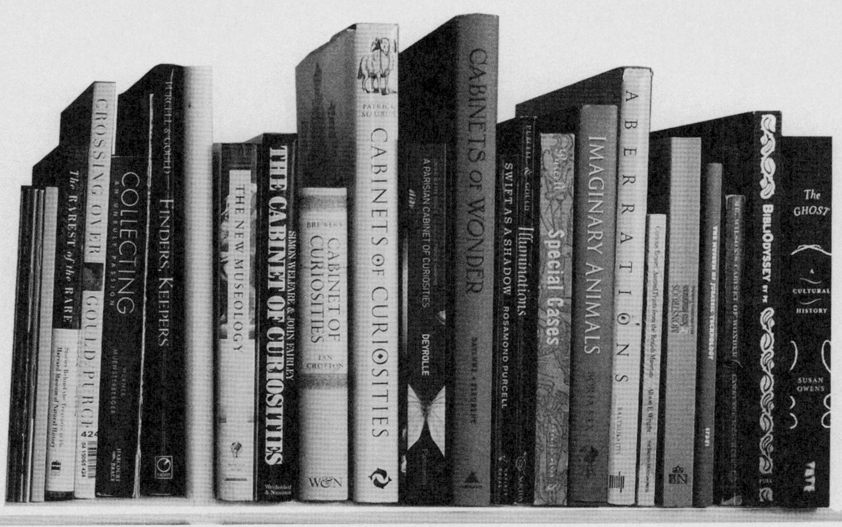



ABIGAIL LANE ANNOTATED BOOK SHELF EXCERPT 1 AND BOOK SHELF EXCERPT 2

GROWTH – BODIES – ANATOMY – SURGERY – DEATH – CRIME – WAR – DISASTER – NATURAL DISASTER – WEATHER – SPACE – ASTRONOMY – THE ENGINEER – THE ORIGIN OF EVERYDAY THINGS – HOME

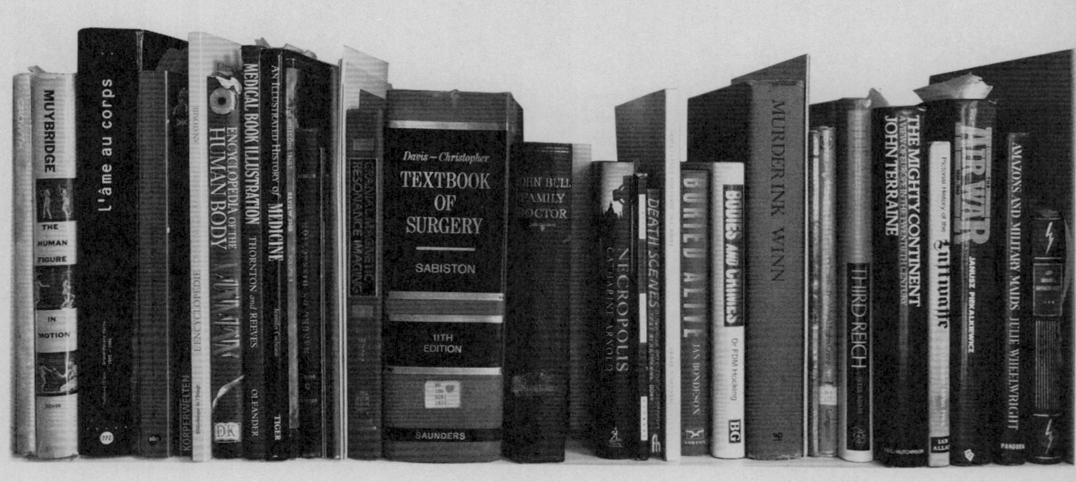

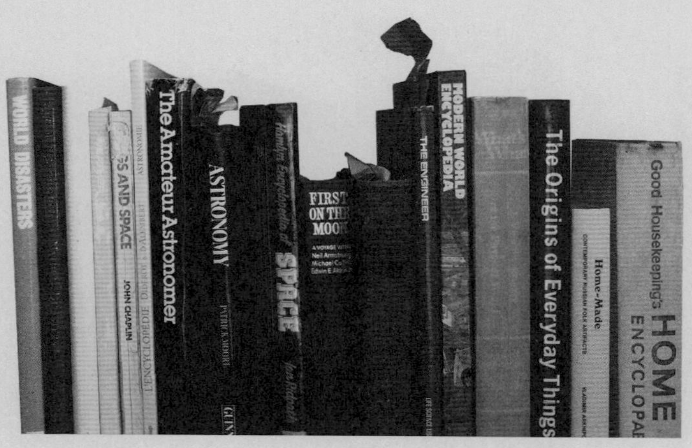

A work of art needs to feel complete and whole and I try to achieve this full feeling each time I make an object or image. But like the words that I find, read and treasure, art is most interesting to me as an evolving dialogue between multiple things

LETTER II

JUDGING from what you tell me and from what I hear, I feel that you show great promise. You do not tear from place to place and unsettle yourself with one move after another. Restlessness of that sort is symptomatic of a sick mind. Nothing, to my way of thinking, is a better proof of a well ordered mind than a man's ability to stop just where he is and pass some time in his own company. Be careful, however, that there is no element of discursiveness and desultoriness about this reading you refer to, this reading of many different authors and books of every description. You should be extending your stay among writers whose genius is unquestionable, deriving constant nourishment from them if you wish to gain anything from your reading that will find a lasting place in your mind. To be everywhere is to be nowhere. People who spend their whole life travelling abroad end up having plenty of places where they can find hospitality but no real friendships. The same must needs be the case with people who never set about acquiring an intimate acquaintanceship with any one great writer, but skip from one to another, paying flying visits to them all. Food that is vomited up as soon as it is eaten is not assimilated into the body and does not do one any good; nothing hinders a cure so much as frequent changes of treatment; a wound will not heal over if it is being made the subject of experiments with different ointments; a plant which is frequently moved never grows strong. Nothing is so useful that it can be of any service in the mere passing. A multitude of books only gets in one's way. So if you are unable to read all the books in your possession, you have enough when you have all the books you are able to read. And if you say, „But I feel like opening different books at different times", my answer will be this: tasting one dish after another is the sign of a fussy stomach, and where the foods are dissimilar and diverse in range they lead to contamination of the system, not nutrition. So always read well-tried authors, and if at any moment you find yourself wanting a change from a particular author, go back to ones you have read before. Each day, too, acquire something which will help you to face poverty, or death, and other ills as well. After running over a lot of different thoughts, pick out one to be digested thoroughly that day. This is what I do myself; out of the many bits I have been reading I, lay hold of one. My thought for today is something which I found in Epicurus (yes, I actually make a practice of going over to the enemy's camp – by way of reconnaissance, not as a deserter!). "A cheerful poverty," he says, "is an honorable state." But if it is cheerful it is not poverty at all. It is not the man who has too little who is poor, but the one who hankers after more. What difference does it make how much there is laid away in a man's safe or in his barns, how many head of stock he grazes or how much capital he puts out at interest, if he is always after what is another's and only counts what he has yet to get, never what he has already. You ask what is the proper limit to a person's wealth? First, having what is essential, and second, having what is enough.

LETTER VII

YOU ask me to say what you should consider it particularly important to avoid. My answer is this: a mass crowd. It is something to which you cannot entrust yourself yet without risk. I at any rate am ready to confess my own frailty in this respect. I never come back home with quite the same moral character I went out with; something or other becomes unsettled where I had achieved internal peace, someone or other of the things I had put to flight reappears on the scene. We who are recovering from a prolonged spiritual sickness are in the same condition as invalids who have been affected to such an extent by prolonged indisposition that they cannot once be taken out of doors without ill effects. Associating with people in large numbers is actually harmful: there is not one of them that will not make some vice or other attractive to us, or leave us carrying the imprint of it or bedaubed all unawares with it. And inevitably enough, the larger the size of the crowd we mingle with, the greater the danger. But nothing is as ruinous to the character as sitting away one's time at a show – for it is then, through the medium of entertainment, that vices creep into one with more than usual ease. What do you take me to mean? That I go home more selfish, more self-seeking and more self-indulgent? Yes, and what is more, a person crueler and less humane through having been in contact with human beings. I happened to go to one of these shows at the time of the lunch-hour interlude, expecting there to be some light and witty entertainment then, some respite for the purpose of affording people's eyes a rest from human blood. Far from it. All the earlier contests were charity in comparison. The nonsense is dispensed with now: what we have now is murder pure and simple. The combatants have nothing to protect them; their whole bodies are exposed to the blows; every thrust they launch gets home. A great many spectators prefer this to the ordinary matches and even to the special, popular demand ones. And quite naturally. There are no helmets and no shields repelling the weapons. What is the point of armor? Or of skill? All that sort of thing just makes the death slower in coming. In the morning men are thrown to the lions and the bears: but it is the spectators they are thrown to in the lunch hour. The spectators insist that each on killing his man shall be thrown against another to be killed in his turn; and the eventual victor is reserved by them for some other form of butchery; the only exit for the contestants is death. Fire and steel keep the slaughter going. And all this happens while the arena is virtually empty. "But he was a highway robber, he killed a man." And what of it? Granted that as a murderer he deserved this punishment, what have you done, you wretched fellow, to deserve to watch it? "Kill him! Flog him! Burn him! Why does he run at the other man's weapon in such a cowardly way? Why isn't he less half-hearted about killing? Why isn't he a bit more enthusiastic about dying? Whip him forward to get his wounds! Make them each offer the other a bare breast and trade blow for blow on them." And when there is an interval in the show: "Let's have some throats cut in the meantime, so that there's something happening!" Come now, I say, surely you people realize – if you realize nothing else – that bad examples have a way of recoiling on those who set them? Give thanks to the immortal gods that the men to whom you are giving a lesson in cruelty are not in a position to profit from it. When a mind is impressionable and has none too firm a hold on what is right, it must be rescued from the crowd: it is so easy for it to go over to the majority. A Socrates, a Cato or a Laelius might have been shaken in his principles by a multitude of people different from himself: such is the measure of the inability of any of us, even as we perfect our personality's adjustment, to withstand the onset of vices when they come with such a mighty following. A single example of extravagance or greed does a lot of harm – an intimate who leads a pampered life gradually makes one soft and flabby; a wealthy neighbor provokes cravings in one; a companion with a malicious nature tends to rub off some of his rust even on someone of an innocent and open-hearted nature – what then do you imagine the effect on a person's character is when the assault comes from the world at large? You must inevitably either hate or imitate the world. But the right thing is to shun both courses: you should neither become like the bad because they are many, nor be an enemy of the many because they are unlike you. Retire into yourself as much as you can. Associate with people who are likely to improve you. Welcome those whom you are capable of improving. The process is a mutual one: men learn as they teach. And there is no reason why any pride in advertising your talents abroad should lure you forward into the public eye, inducing you to give readings of your works or deliver lectures. I should be glad to see you doing that if what you had to offer them was suitable for the crowd I have been talking about: but the fact is, not one of them is really capable of understanding you. You might perhaps come across one here and there, but even they would need to be trained and developed by you to a point where they could grasp your teaching. "For whose benefit, then, did I learn it all?" If it was for your own benefit that you learnt it you have no call to fear that your trouble may have been wasted. Just to make sure that I have not been learning solely for my own benefit today, let me share with you three fine quotations I have come across, each concerned with something like the same idea – one of them is by way of payment of the usual debt so far as this letter is concerned, and the other two you are to regard as an advance on account. "To me," says Democritus, "a single man is a crowd, and a crowd is a single man." Equally good is the answer given by the person, whoever it was (his identity is uncertain), who when asked what was the object of all the trouble he took over a piece of craftsmanship when it would never reach more than a very few people, replied: "A few is enough for me; so is one; and so is none." The third is a nice expression used by Epicurus in a letter to one of his colleagues. "I am writing this," he says, "not for the eyes of the many, but for yours alone: for each of us is audience enough for the other." Lay these up in your heart, my dear Lucilius, that you may scorn the pleasure that comes from the majority's approval. The many speak highly of you, but have you really any grounds for satisfaction with yourself if you are the kind of person the many understand? Your merits should not be outward facing.

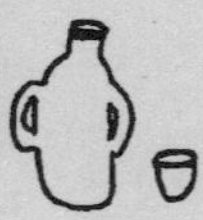

**4.**

In the firmament that we observe at night, the stars shine brightly, surrounded by a thick darkness. Since the number of galaxies and luminous bodies in the universe is almost infinite, the darkness that we see in the sky is something that, according to scientists, demands an explanation. It is precisely the explanation that contemporary astrophysics gives for this darkness that I would now like to discuss. In an expanding universe, the most remote galaxies move away from us at a speed so great that their light is never able to reach us. What we perceive as the darkness of the heavens is this light that, though traveling toward us, cannot reach us, since the galaxies from which the light originates move away from us at a velocity greater than the speed of light.

To perceive, in the darkness of the present, this light that strives to reach us but cannot—this is what it means to be contemporary. As such, contemporaries are rare. And for this reason, to be contemporary is, first and foremost, a question of courage, because it means being able not only to firmly fix your gaze on the darkness of the epoch, but also to perceive in this darkness a light that, while directed toward us, infinitely distances itself from us. In other words, it is like being on time for an appointment that one cannot but miss.

at dawn has immediately perceived this archaic *facies* of the present, this contiguousness with the ruin that the atemporal images of September 11th have made evident to all.

Historians of literature and of art know that there is a secret affinity between the archaic and the modern, not so much because the archaic forms seem to exercise a particular charm on the present, but rather because the key to the modern is hidden in the immemorial and the prehistoric. Thus, the ancient world in its decline turns to the primordial so as to rediscover itself. The avant-garde, which has lost itself over time, also pursues the primitive and the archaic. It is in this sense that one can say that the entry point to the present necessarily takes the form of an archeology; an archeology that does not, however, regress to a historical past, but returns to that part within the present that we are absolutely incapable of living. What remains unlived therefore is incessantly sucked back toward the origin, without ever being able to reach it. The present is nothing other than this unlived element in everything that is lived. That which impedes access to the present is precisely the mass of what for some reason (its traumatic character, its excessive nearness) we have not managed to live. The attention to this "unlived" is the life of the contemporary. And to be contempo-

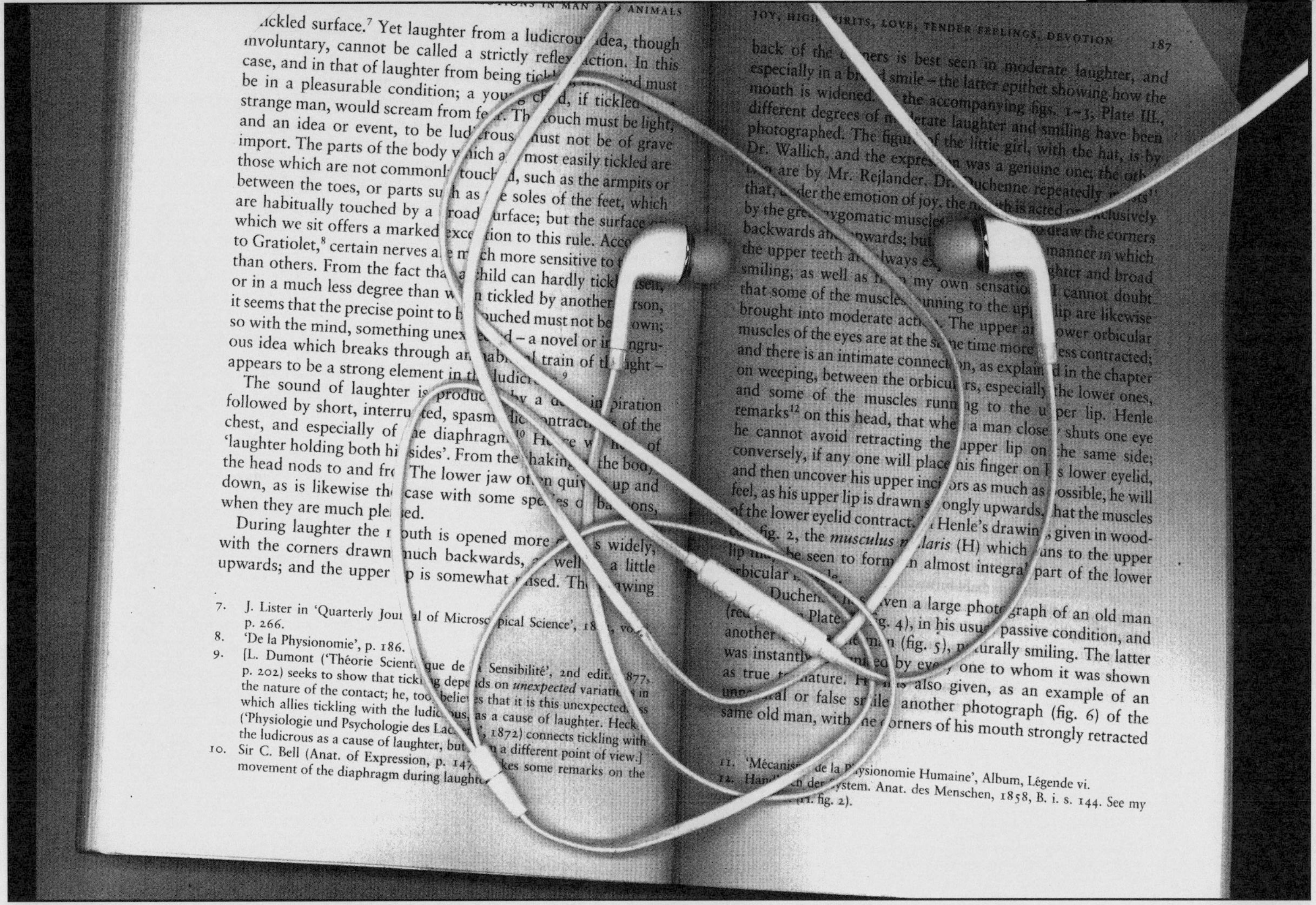

...ickled surface.[7] Yet laughter from a ludicrous idea, though involuntary, cannot be called a strictly reflex action. In this case, and in that of laughter from being tickled, the mind must be in a pleasurable condition; a young child, if tickled by a strange man, would scream from fear. The touch must be light, and an idea or event, to be ludicrous, must not be of grave import. The parts of the body which are most easily tickled are those which are not commonly touched, such as the armpits or between the toes, or parts such as the soles of the feet, which are habitually touched by a broad surface; but the surface on which we sit offers a marked exception to this rule. According to Gratiolet,[8] certain nerves are much more sensitive to touch than others. From the fact that a child can hardly tickle itself, or in a much less degree than when tickled by another person, it seems that the precise point to be touched must not be known; so with the mind, something unexpected – a novel or incongruous idea which breaks through an habitual train of thought – appears to be a strong element in the ludicrous.[9]

The sound of laughter is produced by a deep inspiration followed by short, interrupted, spasmodic contractions of the chest, and especially of the diaphragm.[10] Hence we hear of 'laughter holding both his sides'. From the shaking of the body, the head nods to and fro. The lower jaw often quivers up and down, as is likewise the case with some species of baboons, when they are much pleased.

During laughter the mouth is opened more or less widely, with the corners drawn much backwards, as well as a little upwards; and the upper lip is somewhat raised. The drawing

7.  J. Lister in 'Quarterly Journal of Microscopical Science', 18.., vo.. p. 266.
8.  'De la Physionomie', p. 186.
9.  [L. Dumont ('Théorie Scientifique de la Sensibilité', 2nd edit. 1877, p. 202) seeks to show that tickling depends on *unexpected* variations in the nature of the contact; he, too, believes that it is this unexpectedness which allies tickling with the ludicrous, as a cause of laughter. Heckel ('Physiologie und Psychologie des Lachens', 1872) connects tickling with the ludicrous as a cause of laughter, but from a different point of view.]
10.  Sir C. Bell (Anat. of Expression, p. 147) makes some remarks on the movement of the diaphragm during laughter.

back of the corners is best seen in moderate laughter, and especially in a broad smile – the latter epithet showing how the mouth is widened. In the accompanying figs. 1–3, Plate III., different degrees of moderate laughter and smiling have been photographed. The figure of the little girl, with the hat, is by Dr. Wallich, and the expression was a genuine one; the others are by Mr. Rejlander. Dr. Duchenne repeatedly insists[11] that, under the emotion of joy, the mouth is acted on exclusively by the great zygomatic muscles to draw the corners backwards and upwards; but from the manner in which the upper teeth are always exposed during laughter and broad smiling, as well as from my own sensations, I cannot doubt that some of the muscles running to the upper lip are likewise brought into moderate action. The upper and lower orbicular muscles of the eyes are at the same time more or less contracted; and there is an intimate connection, as explained in the chapter on weeping, between the orbiculars, especially the lower ones, and some of the muscles running to the upper lip. Henle remarks[12] on this head, that when a man closely shuts one eye he cannot avoid retracting the upper lip on the same side; conversely, if any one will place his finger on his lower eyelid, and then uncover his upper incisors as much as possible, he will feel, as his upper lip is drawn strongly upwards, that the muscles of the lower eyelid contract. In Henle's drawings, given in wood-cut, fig. 2, the *musculus malaris* (H) which runs to the upper lip may be seen to form an almost integral part of the lower orbicular muscle.

Duchenne has given a large photograph of an old man (reduced, Plate III. fig. 4), in his usual passive condition, and another of the same man (fig. 5), naturally smiling. The latter was instantly recognized by every one to whom it was shown as true to nature. He has also given, as an example of an unnatural or false smile another photograph (fig. 6) of the same old man, with the corners of his mouth strongly retracted

11.  'Mécanisme de la Physionomie Humaine', Album, Légende vi.
12.  Handbuch der ... System. Anat. des Menschen, 1858, B. i. s. 144. See my ... (11. fig. 2).

by the galvanisation of the great zygomatic muscles. That the expression is not natural is clear, for I showed this photograph to twenty-four persons, of whom three could not in the least tell what was meant, whilst the others, though they perceived that the expression was of the nature of a smile, answered in such words as 'a wicked joke', 'trying to laugh', 'grinning laughter', 'half-amazed laughter', &c. Dr. Duchenne attributes the falseness of the expression altogether to the orbicular muscles of the lower eyelids not being sufficiently contracted; for he justly lays great stress on their contraction in the expression of joy. No doubt there is much truth in this view, but not, as it appears to me, the whole truth. The contraction of the lower orbiculars is always accompanied, as we have seen, by the drawing up of the upper lip. Had the upper lip, in fig. 6, been thus acted on to a slight extent, its curvature would have been less rigid, the naso-labial furrow would have been slightly different, and the whole expression would, as I believe, have been more natural, independently of the more conspicuous effect from the stronger contraction of the lower eyelids. The corrugator muscle, moreover, in fig. 6, is too much contracted, causing a frown; and this muscle never acts under the influence of joy except during strongly pronounced or violent laughter.

By the drawing backwards and upwards of the corners of the mouth, through the contraction of the great zygomatic muscles, and by the raising of the upper lip, the cheeks are drawn upwards. Wrinkles are thus formed under the eyes, and, with old people, at their outer ends; and these are highly characteristic of laughter or smiling. As a gentle smile increases into a strong one, or into a laugh, every one may feel and see, if he will attend to his own sensations and look at himself in a mirror, that as the upper lip is drawn up and the lower orbiculars contract, the wrinkles in the lower eyelids and those beneath the eyes are much strengthened or increased. At the same time, as I have repeatedly observed, the eyebrows are slightly lowered, which shows that the upper as well as the lower orbiculars contract at least to some degree, though this passes unperceived, as far as our sensations are concerned. If



the original photograph of the old man, with his countenance in its usual placid state (fig. 4), be compared with that (fig. ), in which he is naturally smiling, it may be seen that the eyebrows in the latter are a little lowered. I presume that this is owing to the upper orbiculars being impelled, through the force of long-associated habit, to act to a certain extent in concert with the lower orbiculars, which themselves contract in connection with the drawing up of the upper lip.

The tendency in the zygomatic muscles to contract under pleasurable emotions is shown by a curious fact, communicated to me by Dr. Browne, with respect to patients suffering from *general paralysis of the insane.*[13]

In this malady there is almost invaria to wealth, rank, grandeur – insane jo profusion, while its very earliest ph at the corners of the mouth and a This is a well-recognised fact. Co inferior palpebral and great zyg the earlier stages of general p pleased and benevolent expres muscles become involved, b the prevailing expression

As in laughing and br are much raised, the nos on the bridge become other oblique longi teeth are commonl formed, which ru of the mouth; and

A bright and amused state o mouth and up eyes of micro

13.  See, also of Men

barbaric sounds" were a stimulus to "disorder and licence" (as Plutarch puts it).[36] Female sound was judged to arise in craziness and to generate craziness.

We detect a certain circularity in the reasoning here. If women's public utterance is perpetually enclosed within cultural institutions like the ritual lament, if women are regularly reassigned to the expression of nonrational sounds like the *ololyga* and raw emotion in general, then the so-called "natural" tendency of the female to shrieking, wailing, weeping, emotional display and oral disorder cannot help but become a self-fulfilling prophecy. But circularity is not the most ingenious thing about this reasoning. We should look a little more closely at the ideology that underlies male abhorrence of female sound. And it becomes important at this point to distinguish sound from language.

For the formal definition of human nature preferred by patriarchal culture is one based on articulation of sound. As Aristotle says, any animal can make noises to register pleasure or pain. But what differentiates man from beast, and civilization from the wilderness, is the use of rationally articulated speech: *logos*.[37] From such a prescription for humanity follow severe rules for what constitutes human *logos*. When the wife of Alexander Graham Bell, a woman who had been deafened in childhood and knew how to lipread but not how to talk very well, asked him to teach her sign language, Alexander replied, "The use of sign language is pernicious. For the only way by which language can be thoroughly mastered is by using it for the communication of thought without translation into any other language."[38] Alexander Graham Bell's wife, whom he had married the day after he patented the telephone, never did learn sign language. Or any other language.

What is it that is pernicious about sign language? To a husband like Alexander Graham Bell, as to a patriarchal social order like that of classical Greece, there is something disturbing or abnormal about the use of signs to transcribe upon the outside of the body a meaning from inside the body which does not pass through the control point of *logos*, a meaning which is not subject to the mechanism of dissociation that the Greeks called *sophrosyne* or self-control. Sigmund Freud applied the name "hysteria" to this process of transcription when it occurred in female patients whose tics and neuralgias and convul-



sions and paralyses and eating disorders and spells of blindness could be read, in his theory, as a direct translation into somatic terms of psychic events within the woman's body.[39] Freud conceived his own therapeutic task as the rechannelling of these hysteric signs into rational discourse.[40] Herodotos tells us of a priestess of Athene in Pedasa who did not use speech to prophesy but would grow a beard whenever she saw misfortune coming upon her community.[41] Herodotos does not register any surprise at the "somatic compliance" (as Freud would call it) of this woman's prophetic body nor call her condition pathological. But Herodotos was a practical person, less concerned to discover pathologies in his historical subjects than to congratulate them for putting "otherness" to cultural use. And the anecdote does give us a strong image of how ancient culture went about constructing the "otherness" of the female. Woman is that creature who puts the inside on the outside. By projections and leakages of all kinds—somatic, vocal, emotional, sexual—females expose or expend what should be kept in. Females blurt out a direct translation of what should be formulated indirectly. There is a story told about the wife of Pythagoras, that she once uncovered her arm while out of doors and someone commented, "Nice arm," to which she responded, "Not public property!" Plutarch's comment on this story is: "The arm of a virtuous woman should not be public property, nor her speech neither, and she should as modestly guard against exposing her voice to outsiders as she would guard against stripping off her clothes. For in her voice as she is blabbering away can be read her emotions, her character and her physical condition."[42] In spite of herself, Plutarch's woman has a voice that acts like a sign language, exposing her inside facts. Ancient physiologists from Aristotle through the early Roman empire tell us that a man can know from the sound of a woman's voice private data like whether or not she is menstruating, whether or not she has had sexual experience.[43] Although these are useful things to know, they may be bad to hear or make men uncomfortable. What is pernicious about sign language is that it permits a direct continuity between inside and outside. Such continuity is abhorrent to the male nature. The masculine virtue of *sophrosyne* or self-control aims to obstruct this continuity, to dissociate the outside surface of a man from what is going on inside him. Man breaks continuity by interposing *logos*—whose most important censor is the rational articulation sound.

Every sound we make is a bit of autobiography. It has a totally private interior yet its trajectory is public. A piece of inside projected to the outside. The censorship of such projections is a task of patriarchal culture that (as we have seen) divides humanity into two species: those who can censor themselves and those who cannot.

In order to explore some of the implications of this division let us consider how Plutarch depicts the two species in his essay "On Talkativeness."

To exemplify the female species in its use of sound Plutarch tells the story of a politician's wife who is tested by her husband. The politician makes up a crazy story and tells it to his wife as a secret early one morning. "Now keep your mouth closed about this," he warns her. The wife immediately relates the secret to her maidservant. "Now keep your mouth closed about this," she tells the maidservant, who immediately relates it to the whole town and before midmorning the politician himself receives his own story back again. Plutarch concludes this anecdote by saying, "The husband had taken precautions and protective measures in order to test his wife, as one might test a cracked or leaky vessel by filling it not with oil or wine but with water."[44] Plutarch pairs this anecdote with a story about masculine speech acts. It is a description of a friend of Solon's named Anacharsis:

> Anacharsis who had dined with Solon and was resting after dinner, was seen pressing his left hand on his sexual parts and his right hand on his mouth: for he believed that the tongue requires a more powerful restraint. And he was right. It would not be easy to count as many men lost through incontinence in amorous pleasures as cities and empires ruined through revelation of a secret.[45]

In assessing the implications of the gendering of sound for a society like that of the ancient Greeks, we have to take seriously the connexion Plutarch makes between verbal and sexual continence, between mouth and genitals. Because that connexion turns out to be a very different matter for men than for women. The masculine virtue of self-censorship with which Anacharsis responds to impulses from inside himself is shown to be simply unavailable to the female nature.





Plutarch reminds us a little later in the essay that perfect *sophrosyne* is an attribute of the god Apollo whose epithet Loxias means that he is a god of few words and concise expression, not one who runs off at the mouth.[46] Now when a woman runs off at the mouth there is far more at stake than waste of words: the image of the leaky water jar with which Plutarch concludes his first anecdote is one of the commonest figures in ancient literature for the representation of female sexuality.

The forms and contexts of this representation (the leaky jar of female sexuality) have been studied at length by other scholars including me,[47] so let us pass directly to the heart, or rather the mouth, of the matter. It is an axiom of ancient Greek and Roman medical theory and anatomical discussion that a woman has two mouths.[48] The orifice through which vocal activity takes place and the orifice through which sexual activity takes place are both denoted by the word *stoma* in Greek (*os* in Latin) with the addition of adverbs *ano* or *kato* to differentiate upper mouth from lower mouth. Both the vocal and the genital mouth are connected to the body by a neck (*auchen* in Greek, *cervix* in Latin). Both mouths provide access to a hollow cavity which is guarded by lips that are best kept closed. The ancient medical writers apply not only homologous terms but also parallel medications to upper and lower mouths in certain cases of uterine malfunction. They note with interest, as do many poets and scholiasts, symptoms of physiological responsion between upper and lower mouth, for example that an excess or blockage of blood in the uterus will evidence itself as strangulation or loss of voice,[49] that too much vocal exercise results in loss of menses,[50] that defloration causes a woman's neck to enlarge and her voice to deepen.[51]

"With a high pure voice because she has not yet been acted upon by the bull," is how Aiskhylos describes his Iphigeneia (*Agamemnon*).[52] The changed voice and enlarged throat of the sexually initiated female are an upward projection of irrevocable changes at the lower mouth. Once a woman's sexual life begins, the lips of the uterus are never completely closed again—except on one occasion, as the medical writers explain: in his treatise on gynecology Soranos describes the sensations that a woman experiences during fruitful sexual intercourse. At the moment of conception, the Hellenistic doctor Soranos alleges, the woman has a shivering sensation and the shook her head. The answer was obvious. He wanted her dependent. That was the reason for her continued isolation from her own kind. She was to be dependent on an Oankali—dependent and trusting. To hell with that!

"Tell me what you want of me," she demanded abruptly, "and what you want of my people."

His tentacles swung to examine her. "I've told you a great deal."

"Tell me the price, Jdahya. What do you want? What will your people take from us in return for having saved us?"

All his tentacles seemed to hang limp, giving him an almost comical droop. Lilith found no humor in it. "You'll live," he said. "Your people will live. You'll have your world again. We already have much of what we want of you. Your cancer in particular."

"What?"

"The ooloi are intensely interested in it. It suggests abilities we have never been able to trade for successfully before."

"Abilities? From cancer?"

"Yes. The ooloi see great potential in it. So the trade has already been useful."

"You're welcome to it. But before when I asked, you said you trade . . . yourselves."

"Yes. We trade the essence of ourselves. Our genetic material for yours."

Lilith frowned, then shook her head. "How? I mean, you couldn't be talking about interbreeding."

"Of course not." His tentacles smoothed. "We do what you would call genetic engineering. We know you had begun to do it yourselves a little, but it's foreign to you. We do it naturally. We *must* do it. It renews us, enables us to survive as an evolving species instead of specializing ourselves into extinction or stagnation."

"We all do it naturally to some degree," she said warily. "Sexual reproduction—"

"The ooloi do it for us. They have special organs for it. They can do it for you too—make sure of a good, viable gene mix.

It is part of our reproduction, but it's much more deliberate than what any mated pair of humans have managed so far.

"We're not hierarchical, you see. We never were. But we are powerfully acquisitive. We acquire new life—seek it, investigate it, manipulate it, sort it, use it. We carry the drive to do this in a minuscule cell within a cell—a tiny organelle within every cell of our bodies. Do you understand me?"

"I understand your words. Your meaning, though . . . it's as alien to me as you are."

"That's the way we perceived your hierarchical drives at first." He paused. "One of the meanings of Oankali is gene trader. Another is that organelle—the essence of ourselves, the origin of ourselves. Because of that organelle, the ooloi can perceive DNA and manipulate it precisely."

"And they do this . . . inside their bodies?"

"Yes."

"And now they're doing something with cancer cells inside their bodies?"

"Experimenting, yes."

"That sounds . . . a long way from safe."

"They're like children now, talking and talking about possibilities."

"What possibilities?"

"Regeneration of lost limbs. Controlled malleability. Future Oankali may be much less frightening to potential trade partners if they're able to reshape themselves and look more like the partners before the trade. Even increased longevity, though compared to what you're used to, we're very long-lived now."

"All that from cancer."

"Perhaps. We listen to the ooloi when they stop talking so much. That's when we find out what our next generations will be like."

"You leave all that to them? They decide?"

"They show us the tested possibilities. We all decide."

He tried to lead her into his family's woods, but she held back. "There's something I need to understand now," she said. "You call it a trade. You've taken something you value from and films, with "we" or "us" as the subject, as if there is any other. SL gave me those gifts—the movies and books and so on—because he knew, too, that I was like everyone else, except him: I identified with other people. His gifts were road maps to our love, the valley of the unconditional. 



As we became friends, the strangest thing happened: most of our acquaintances abused adverbs in their rush to condemn—violently, passionately—our becoming a we. We were something dark and unforeseen: two colored gentlemen who moved through the largely white social world we inhabited in New York (the world where art and fashion and journalism converged) who did not exploit each other or our obvious physical traits—their coloredness and maleness—for political sympathy or social gain. People looked at us and thought we were really evil. That we had pointy heads and forked tongues. That we wore furs and had no animal rights. That we knew the twelve steps but skipped intimacy. That we betrayed every confidence and judged without impunity. That we lauded women and then denigrated them. That we mentored young boys only to corrupt them. That we borrowed money with no thought of returning it. That we were indolent and crackled with ambition. That we were gluttons who drank from a bottomless well of envy. That we were gay and couldn't admit we were straight. That we were faithless Jesus freaks who had forsaken Him for tight pussy, credit cards we abused, and loose shoes. That we had lockjaw once but still managed to feed off our enemies. That we sold children down the river and watched them suffocate in an ocean of adult bitterness. That we were racists, especially against our own kind. That we were matricidal, especially toward our own mothers.

magical ambiguities. They are evil words, and we utter them in a loud voice only when we are not in control of ourselves. In a confused way they reflect our intimacy: the explosions of our vitality light them up and the depressions of our spirit darken them. They constitute a sacred language like those of children, poetry and sects. Each letter and syllable has a double life, at once luminous and obscure, that reveals and hides us. They are words that say nothing and say everything. Adolescents, when they want to appear like men, speak them in a hoarse voice. Women also repeat them, sometimes to demonstrate their freedom of spirit, sometimes to prove the truth of their feelings. But these words are definitive and categorical, despite their ambiguities and the ease with which their meanings change. They are the bad words, the only living language in a world of anemic vocables. They are poetry within the reach of everyone.

Each country has its own. In ours, with their brief, aggressive, electric syllables, resembling the flash given off by a knife when it strikes a hard opaque body, we condense all our appetites, all our hatreds and enthusiasms, all the longings that rage unexpressed in the depths of our being. The word is our sign and seal. By means of it we recognize each other among strangers, and we use it every time the real conditions of our being rise to our lips. To know it, to use it, to throw it in the air like a toy or to make it quiver like a sharp weapon, is a way of affirming that we are Mexican.

All of our anxious tensions express themselves in a phrase we use when anger, joy or enthusiasm cause us to exalt our condition as Mexicans: "*¡Viva México, hijos de la chingada!*" This phrase is a true battle cry, charged with a peculiar electricity; it is a challenge and an affirmation, a shot fired against an imaginary enemy, and an explosion in the air. Once again, with a certain pathetic and plastic fatality, we are presented with the image of a skyrocket that climbs into the sky, bursts in a shower of sparks and then falls in darkness. Or with the image of that howl that ends all our songs and possesses the same ambiguous resonance: an angry joy, a destructive affirmation ripping open the breast and consuming itself.

When we shout this cry on the fifteenth of September, the anniversary of our independence, we affirm ourselves in front of, against and in spite of the "others." Who are the "others"? They are the *hijos de la chingada:* strangers, bad Mexicans, our enemies, our rivals. In any case, the "others," that is, all those who are not as we are. And these "others" are not defined except as the sons of a mother as vague and indeterminate as themselves.

Who is the *Chingada?* Above all, she is the Mother. Not a Mother of flesh and blood but a mythical figure. The *Chingada* is one of the Mexican representations of Maternity, like *La Llorona* or the "long-suffering Mexican mother" we celebrate on the tenth of May.[1] The *Chingada* is the mother who has suffered — metaphorically or actually — the corrosive and defaming action implicit in the verb that gives her her name. It would be worth while to examine that verb.

Darío Rubio, in his *Anarquía del lenguaje en la América Española*, examines the origins of *chingar* and enumerates the meanings given it by almost all Spanish-American people. It probably comes from the Aztecs: *chingaste* (lees, residue, sediment) is *xinachtli* (garden seed) or *xinaxtli* (fermented maguey juice). The word and its derivatives are used in most of America

---

[1] The "Weeping Woman," who wanders through the streets late at night, weeping and crying out. This belief, still current in some parts of Mexico, derives from pre-Conquest times, when "La Llorona" was the earth-goddess Cihuacóatl. The 10th of May is Mother's Day. — *Tr.*

was a plain example of what a tree could be when given a chance. And the chance seemed mostly to be one of place: The acorn had rooted in rich soil, in an open space, in a latitude and longitude that favored acorns.

Yet between the pine and the beech there is a tension that has beauty too. The adaptation of the beech has the grace of submission to circumstances, and their conquest also, as its leaves glitter in the windy sunshine above a certain height and lend their delicate variety to the pine's harsh needles.

Every place is right for whatever is in it. Acceptance is more understandable to me now than to the child I was. But if I were a tree, I would prefer to be the Avonlea oak.

2 8   J U L Y

Yesterday my body began to feel right. The sick fatigue isn't there any more. I feel steady. This time I wasn't at all sure that my body would heal to vigor. Now I can begin to stockpile strength as I am stockpiling work. The protection of the regular routine—the studio hours, the silent days, the naps, the evening reading of Henry James and George Eliot and E. M. Forster, the delicious and balanced meals, the lack of responsibility—has cradled me, and I am recovering from last winter.

KEPT COMPANY

3 1   J U L Y

A group of resident poets read their work last night in the living room of West House. They read in sequence, a man's voice, a woman's voice, each a poem, sometimes quietly repeated until it had settled into us all.

The pain of poets seems to me unmitigated. They are denied the physical activity of studio work, which in it-

42

self makes a supportive context for thought and feeling. In my twenties, when I was writing poetry steadily, I heard words at a high pitch. On the deep, full notes of three-dimensional form, demanding for its realization the physical commitment of my whole body, I floated into spaciousness. Using all my faculties, I could plumb deeper, without sinking forever.

Poetry was drawn out of my life, pulled out into lines. Sculpture is not. The works stand as I stand; they keep me company. I realize this clearly here because I miss them. I brought only table sculptures with me. In making my work, I make what comforts me and is home for me.

I expanded into love with the discipline of sculpture. Although my intellectual reason for abandoning writing for sculpture in 1948 was that I found myself uninterested in the sequence of events in time, I think now that it was this love that tipped the balance. Artists have no choice but to express their lives. They have only, and that not always, a choice of process. This process does not change the essential content of their work in art, which *can* only be their life. But in my own case the fact that I have to use my whole body in making my work seems to disperse my intensity in a way that suits me.

6   A U G U S T

In skirting the role of the artist, I now begin to think that I have made too wide a curve, that I have deprived myself of a certain strength. Indeed, I am not sure that I can grow as an artist until I can bring myself to accept that I am one. This was not true, I think, before last winter. I was underground until the two retrospective exhibits of my work. Part of my intense discomfort this past year has been that I was pried out of my place there. I was attached

43

to my secret burrow, which now begins to feel a little stale.

And also egotistic, confined, even imprisoning. I begin to see that by clinging to this position I was limiting what I had to handle in the world to what I could rationalize. As long as I stayed within my own definition of myself, I could control what I admitted into that definition. By insisting that I was "just me," I held myself aloof. Let others claim to be artists, I said to myself, holding my life separate and unique, beyond all definition but my own.

The course of events in my life has blasted this fortification, as it had blasted another in Japan. The fact of financial insecurity since my divorce in 1971, and the momentum of my own work and my efforts to be responsible for it, have thrown me into the open.

The open being: I am an artist. Even to write it makes me feel deeply uneasy. I am, I feel, not good enough to be an artist. And this leads me to wonder whether my distaste for the inflated social definition of the artist is not an inverse reflection of secret pride. Have I haughtily rejected the inflation on the outside while entertaining it on the inside? In my passion for learning how to make true for others what I felt to be true for myself (and I cannot remember, except very, very early on, ever not having had this passion), I think I may have fallen into idolatry of those who were able to communicate this way. Artists. So to think myself an artist was self-idolatry.

In a clear wind of the company of artists this summer, I am gently disarmed. We are artists because we are ourselves.

9 AUGUST

Aleksis Rannit is right: "Patience is the sister of mystery and tirelessness the best of roads." In this family, humility

44

is the daughter of truth. As I work to understand my life, its scale seems to diminish, as a tree I gaze up into flattens when I walk up a mountain and look down on it. Humility is really more natural than pride, which seems to me always to involve a lie.

I remember when this lie began for me. I was in my mother's bedroom, standing in front of a gold-bordered pier glass. It was early afternoon. The light was sunny. It was warm. I had on a white batiste undergarment, all one piece with a drop-seat. The neck and arms were edged with narrow lace, and the same lace was on the ruffles gathered by elastic around my legs. I was being dressed for a party. My dress lay on the bed behind me, a translucent white cloud. My mother and my nurse were paying a new kind of attention to me, the same flavor of attention now paid to me at the openings of my exhibits. They were arranging my thin whitish blonde hair into a "roach" curl, which was to run from the back of my head along its crown to the center of my forehead. They brushed my hair up, used a little water to hold it, and brushed again. The curl was totally artificial and had to be forced into being. Admonished to stand still, puzzled by their excited determination (very unlike the usual matter-of-fact tenor of the household), I addressed my image in the mirror.

I had never, to my recollection, seen myself before. I looked all right to myself in general; my feeling for my body seemed pretty well matched by what I saw. In fact, I was interested and would have been glad to have been left alone to look. But the chirps about the curl went on and on, and I began to feel uncomfortable. Something was being added to me. They wanted me to be more, and the "more" was the curl. I began to want the curl too, and I remember the first sick feeling of anxiety as they worked to get it to stick there. My healthy self felt whole without it, and recognized quite clearly that I was being made a

45

ernism. In this book I investigate art practices, including my own, that are working in and with networked culture, but are not simply using and testing the new technologies of connection. Rather they are works that reflect in some ways on the new condition created by the network; effects felt either of time, space, social relations or the social imaginary. In fact these «uncertain» practices often employ low-tech strategies with little use for spectacle or high-end computing power, rather, through strategies of playful intervention and humorous situations they test the cultural logic of everyday life to peel back hidden layers of significance.

I also use the term «mediated public space» rather than simply «network culture» to point to the contemporary moment (that is crucial to understanding the work discussed). In so doing I am drawing attention to the way that people of all ages are carrying media of all sorts everywhere and using media in public space. I consider this an aspect of network culture now so taken for granted that the complexity and significance of its effects can be overlooked. That is, what I am calling «mediated public space» involves a reconfiguring not just of public/private and social behaviour and relations, but also subjectivity more broadly. In Chapter 2, I parallel John McGrath's perceptive analysis of surveillance media and «surveillance space» in _Loving big brother_ (2004)[11] and argue that the ubiquity and new uses of mobile media are creating a performative space of encounter in public. With the multiplication of media – besides the surveillance effect – there are other unexpected and possibly more positive effects which are changing the relationship between people and media, and which are producing a more active subject than the more passive subject of previous technologies. Following McGrath's argument for a more productive understanding of surveillance through the notion of performativity and what he calls «surveillance space,» I apply his insights to «mediated public space.» I see this performative space, created by mobile media, as a key condition for an unsitely aesthetics.

In order to go beyond the limits of traditional approaches to both public art and new media art I foreground the _situatedness_ of the making and reception of the work. I do this through the figure of site – playing on its situatedness. I use the idea of _site_ as a «fulcrum,» as Ehrlich and LaBelle (2003: 11) put it, to think through ideas of current media art practice that exist across sites of mediated public spaces. This contemporary art figure

## Media Art in Network Culture and Mediated Public Space

«Network culture» is a term used by Kazys Varnelis to describe the current moment of internet connections and mobile media. (Varnelis)[10] Network culture, for Varnelis and the contributors to his book, is the contemporary condition we find ourselves in, «the simultaneous superimposition of real and virtual space, the new participatory media.» In fact they go further to describe the network as the «dominant cultural logic» of our era and analogous to previous logics and periodisations like modernism and postmod-

and concept has much to offer us in order to understand a group of media art practices that in most cases have been understood through media art theories of distributed aesthetics, or other media theories of communication. That is, while site has been the subject of extensive and important scholarly work in art history, (Miwon Kwon 2004 and James Meyer 2000)[12] and sound studies (see Ken Ehrlich & Brandon LaBelle 2003) it has not been a significant figure for (new) media art theory.[13] In this book, then, I want to rework the figure of site to investigate and present media art in public places and, in turn, to suggest that media art in public s/places also opens new questions for scholarship about site and of course implicitly about place and our sense of place. What could *place* mean in a networked world?[14] In returning to the figure of site, my aim is to look again at the significance and potentialities of site, not to relocate media art back again into paradigms of site-specificity but, on the contrary, to understand site as it relates to and enframes contemporary media art practice as it plays out in network culture. And in looking at media art practices in public space we will also look again at a particularly important form of public space as a site of art – the internet.

In this sense «site» is operating much like a thaumatrope, a nineteenth century toy that flips between two images.[15] For now let us imagine site here as a sort of hinge and a way to open up and connect two seemingly incompatible histories and discourses – those of contemporary art and media art. In these discourses site has a distinct meaning. By making the term work *as if* a Duchampian door, I am attempting to conjure both meanings simultaneously and at once. If you swing the door in the direction of the internet and media art, its meaning is linked to the common term «website.» If you swing the door in the direction of contemporary art, site is situated within a rich and complex history of site-specificity, dating from the 1960s and described and analysed by Kwon in *One place after another*.

In investigating media art practices that exist at the intersection of media art and contemporary art,[16] I use the term «media art» in a similar spirit to that outlined by Darren Tofts in *Interzone*:

First, I have resisted using the term «digital art» because it is too reductive, foregrounding the computer as the decisive factor in the art-making process ... Secondly, I have also resisted using the term «new media art» because it is the one term most closely aligned



with the concept of interaction and therefore even more reductive than digital art. (Tofts 2005b: 8)

The term media art invokes contemporary art practices that engage with a range of different media, of which the computer is the predominant mode. (Tofts 2005b: 12)

Tofts assumes media art practices to be naturally part of the landscape of contemporary art practices, and in a way of course they are. Yet, I suggest there is also a discord within contemporary art institutions, which have on the whole been slow to accept the computer as another tool or medium for art practice. This has created a separate and specific history of the electronic arts; Tofts' book is testament to that history in the Australian context. (Tofts 2005b) Instead this book takes this historical separation of media art and contemporary art as a starting point and invitation to discuss work that is now ranged across this gap: work that for this very reason I am calling uncertain.

By foregrounding uncertain media art practices, I am responding to what has happened to some of the practices once defined as new media art. New media, especially during the 1990s, existed in a separate art world where the digital and new media was heralded as either the new avant-garde, or such a totally new phenomenon that it could only herald the end of art (again). Both sides share some responsibility for this estrangement of new media and contemporary art. On the one hand there was the disdain for new media art and rejection of it by art galleries and museums unwilling to engage with technology, and anchored in a phenomenological discourse of «presence» – specifically the presence of materiality. On the other hand this attitude was up against the hubristic attitude of the new media advocates – artists, technologists and media enthusiasts – unwilling to understand art discourse's historical concerns and terms. Ironically the position of media art was (and still is to a certain extent) just as uncertain in the field of media studies itself, as it was in the field of contemporary art. As Daniel Palmer remarks:

In contemporary media and cultural studies' obsession with «popular» and «ordinary» culture, artistic practices are increasingly rare as objects of study. Dismissed as the self-expression of a niche market for residual high-culture, their analysis is left to the specialised discipline of art history. (Palmer 2004: 169)

21. How do you know?    20. Do you love anybody?

16. Are you convinced by your own self-criticism?

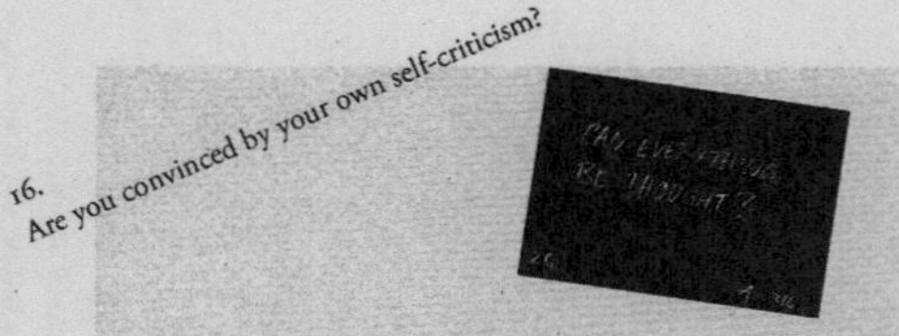


*Task Slips for Small-Talk Condition in Study 1*

*Set I*

→ or were you just wandering around daydreaming?

1. When was the last time you walked for more than an hour? Describe where you went and what you saw.
2. What was the best gift you ever received and why?
3. If you had to move from ~~California~~ where would you go, and what would you miss the most about ~~California~~?
4. How did you celebrate last ~~Halloween~~?
5. Do you read a newspaper often and which do you prefer? Why?
6. What is a good number of people to have in a ~~student~~ household and why?
7. If you could invent a new flavor of ice cream, what would it be?
8. What is the best restaurant you've been to ~~in the last month~~ that your partner hasn't been to? Tell your partner about it.
9. Describe the (last) pet you owned.
10. What is your favorite holiday? Why?
11. Tell your partner the funniest thing that ever happened to you when you were with a small child.
12. What gifts did you receive on your last birthday?

*Set II*

13. Describe the last time you went to the zoo.
14. Tell the names and ages of your family members, include grandparents, aunts and uncles, and where they were born (to the extent you know this information).
15. One of you say a word, the next say a word that starts with the last letter of the word just said. Do this until you have said 50 words. Any words will do—you aren't making a sentence.
16. Do you like to get up early or stay up late? Is there anything funny that has resulted from this?
17. Where are you from? Name all of the places you've lived.
18. What is your favorite class at ~~UCSC~~ so far? Why?
19. What did you do this summer?
20. What gifts did you receive last ~~Christmas/Hanukkah/etc.~~?
21. Who is your favorite actor of your own gender? Describe a favorite scene in which this person has acted.
22. What was your impression of ~~UCSC~~ the first time you ever came here?
23. What is the best ~~movie~~ you've seen in the last month that your partner hasn't seen? Tell your partner about it.
24. What is your favorite ~~holiday~~? Why?

*Set III*

25. Where did you go to ~~high~~ school? What was your ~~high~~ school like?

26. What is the best book you've read ~~in the last three months~~ that your partner hasn't read? Tell your partner about it.
27. What foreign country would you most like to visit? What attracts you to this place?
28. Do you prefer digital watches and clocks or the kind with hands? Why?
29. Describe your ~~mother~~'s best friend.
30. What are the advantages and disadvantages of artificial ~~Christmas~~ trees?
31. How often do you get your hair cut? Where do you go? Have you ever had a really bad haircut experience?
32. Did you have a class pet when you were in elementary school? Do you remember the pet's name?
33. Do you think left-handed people are more creative than right-handed people?
34. What is the last concert you saw? How many of that band's albums do you own? Had you seen them before? Where?
35. Do you subscribe to any magazines? Which ones? What have you subscribed to in the past?
36. Were you ever in a school play? What was your role? What was the plot of the play? Did anything funny ever happen when you were on stage?

1.
NOTES Are you sure you are really interested in the preservation of the human race once you and all the people you know are no longer alive?

2.
State briefly why.





6.
Would you like to have perfect memory?

15. When did you stop believing you could become wiser—or do you still believe it? Give your age.

13. Why not, if you think they are right?

12. If you had the power to put into effect things you consider right, would you do so against the wishes of the majority? (Yes or no)

17.
What in your opinion do others dislike about you, and what do you dislike about yourself? If not the same thing, which do you find it easier to excuse?

Would you rather have belonged to a different nation (or civilization)? If so, which?

18.
Do you find the thought that you might never have been born (if it ever occurs to you) disturbing?

and manufacturing choices in the Kalashnikov line—signs that the communist world's arms-manufacturing skills were higher than its critics in the West could appreciate—enabled the Type 56 rifles handed out for jungle duty in Vietnam to resist rust and corrosion, even in the monsoon season, and even with limited cleaning. The weapons *looked* primitive. Looks were deceiving. The rifle had been made to be a peasant's gun, and it worked exceptionally well in many conditions in which peasants fight.

The M-16 was the manifestation of a different set of design ideas. Its parts were made to be a snug fit, almost in the manner of a manually operated bolt-action rifle. The tight fit helped make the M-16 more accurate than the Kalashnikov, all the way out to the theoretically impressive five hundred yards. It also seemed to make it undependable. Dust, dirt, sand, rust, carbon buildup—all these things could slow or obstruct the movement of an M-16's bolt. Further, in the quest to keep down the weapon's weight, the main moving parts of its operating system had been made light. This added to the problems with reliability. The M-16 was easy to carry, aim, and shoot. But the small mass of its bolt gave its operation little excess potential energy; coupled with the tight fit, this was a design recipe for stoppages in harsh environments, especially if the weapons were pitted or corroding. If this were not enough, certain manufacturing standards at Colt's through 1967 were also behind those in the Soviet Union and China. Colt's, the sole-source provider of the M-16, neither chromed the rifles' chambers or bores nor applied an adequate protective finish to the weapons—a pair of oversights that made the rifle prone to corrosion in Vietnam.

By spring 1967, the problems had become so widely known that Congress took an interest. On May 3, 1967, Representative L. Mendel Rivers, Democrat of South Carolina and chairman of the House Armed Services Committee, appointed Representative Richard H. Ichord, Democrat of Missouri, as head of a special subcommittee to examine "the development, production, distribution and sale of M-16 rifles."[57] Ichord steered wide of the question of which weapon was better—the M-14 or the M-16—for Vietnam or elsewhere. He left such questions to soldiers.[58] If the military wanted the M-16, so be it. He wanted to know why the M-16 was malfunctioning at an unacceptably high rate.

The appointment of the subcommittee coincided with a fresh round of malfunctions of M-16s issued to the Marines, including those issued

Bridget Jones' Diary - Helen Fielding

**Tuesday 11 April**

8st 11, alcohol units 0, cigarettes 0, Instants 9 (this must stop).

All seems normal with Magda and Jeremy so maybe it was just a business meeting. Maybe the Zen and Flow notion is correct, for there is no doubt that by relaxing and going with the vibes I have done the right thing. Am invited to a glittering literati launch of *Kafka's Motorbike* next week at the Ivy. Determined, instead of fearing the scary party, panicking all the way through and going home pissed and depressed, am going to improve social skills, confidence and Make Parties Work for Me – as guided by article have just read in magazine.

Apparently, Tina Brown of the *New Yorker* is brilliant at dealing with parties, gliding prettily from group to group, saying, 'Martin Amis! Nelson Mandela! Richard Gere!' in a tone which at once suggests, 'My God, I have never been more enchanted to see anyone in my entire life! Have you met the most dazzling person at the party apart from you? Talk! Talk! Must network! Byeee!' Wish to be like Tina Brown, though not, obviously, quite so hardworking.

The article is full of useful tips. One should never, apparently, talk to anyone at a party for more than two minutes. When time is up, you simply say, 'I think we're expected to circulate. Nice to meet you,' and go off. If you get lost for words after asking someone what they do to which they reply 'Undertaker' or 'I work for the Child Support Agency', you must simply ask, 'Do you enjoy that?' When introducing people add a thoughtful detail or two about each person so that their interlocutor has a conversational kicking-off point. E.g., 'This is John – he's from New Zealand and enjoys windsurfing.' Or, 'Gina is a keen skydiver and lives on a barge.'

pp 96-97

this sterling advice is a brilliant tool to employ whilst ☆ networking at openings, art fairs etc. if you hate that shit, or at least find it hard...

My most oft used one was:
"...meet Lucy Clout, she's my best friend, Olive's godmother, an artist i represent and we met over an excruciating buffet at Cove Park."
Lucy used to hate it, i think.

N.B. I did learn stuff
at art school, but
mainly from David Batchelor
and mainly verbal, so
Bridget + Jilly ...
        Polo - Jilly Cooper



## CHARACTERS

| | |
|---|---|
| **BART ALDERTON** | An American airplane billionaire. Polo patron of the Alderton Flyers. |
| **GRACE ALDERTON** | His second wife. |
| **LUKE ALDERTON** | Bart's son by his first wife. A professional polo player. |
| **RED ALDERTON** | Bart's and Grace's son. An unprofessional polo player. |
| **BIBI ALDERTON** | Bart's and Grace's daughter – a poor little rich girl. |
| **THE HONOURABLE BASIL BADDINGHAM** | English polo player, jack of all trades. |
| **PHILIP BAGLEY** | A vet. |
| **DREW BENEDICT** | English polo player and a dashing Captain in the Welsh Guards. |
| **SUKEY BENEDICT** | His wife. An English heiress and jolly good sort. |
| **JAMES BENSON** | A smooth private doctor. |
| **MRS BODKIN** | Rupert Campbell-Black's housekeeper. |
| **MARGIE BRIDGWATER** | An American lawyer. |
| **JAIME CALAVESSI** | An Argentine polo player. |
| **RUPERT CAMPBELL-BLACK** | Show-jumping ace, later MP for Chalford and Bisley and Minister for Sport. |
| **TABITHA CAMPBELL-BLACK** | His daughter. |
| **BRIGADIER CANFORD** | Chairman of the Pony Club and later of the British Polo Association. |
| **DOMMIE AND SEB CARLISLE** | English polo players – known as the Heavenly Twins. |
| **WINSTON CHALMERS** | A shit-hot American lawyer. |
| **LUCY CHALMERS** | His ravishing much younger wife. |
| **DORIS CHOW** | A Chinese hooker. |

11

Jilly's cast of characters
inspired me. She laid
out the players at
the beginning. Such
a practical + helpful
approach and
introduction.

The tidbits are also
a bit funny.

<u>open</u>

<u>generous</u>

<u>funny</u>

(or at least willing to
have a laugh with
the craft)

good rules for
curators i
thought.

MAY 30, 2018

I REMEMBER ONE TIME HAVING LUNCH WITH
DAVID WOJNAROWICZ, AND I HAD THESE SMALL
WORK PRINTS OF CLOUDS WITH ME.... I FELT
GUILTY AND TORN. I FELT DETACHED — MY WORK
WAS SO SUBTLE AND ABSTRACT, SO APOLITICAL
ON THE SURFACE. I REMEMBER SHOWING THOSE
PICTURES TO DAVID AND TALKING THINGS OVER
WITH HIM AND HE SAID — I'M PARAPHRASING —
"DON'T EVER GIVE UP BEAUTY. WE'RE FIGHTING
SO THAT WE CAN HAVE THINGS LIKE THIS,
SO THAT WE CAN HAVE BEAUTY AGAIN."

YOU KNOW, WE WERE ALL JUST TOO BUSY FOR
BEAUTY. WE WERE TOO ANGRY FOR BEAUTY.
WE WERE TOO HEARTBROKEN FOR BEAUTY. I
FELT LIKE AN ASSHOLE WITH THESE PICTURES
OF CLOUDS, BUT DAVID WAS RIGHT. YOU GO
THROUGH ALL OF THE FIGHTING NOT BECAUSE
YOU WANT TO FIGHT, BUT BECAUSE YOU WANT TO
GET SOMEWHERE AS A PEOPLE. YOU WANT TO
HELP CREATE A WORLD WHERE YOU CAN SIT
AROUND AND THINK ABOUT CLOUDS. THAT
SHOULD BE OUR RIGHT AS HUMAN BEINGS.

— ZOE LEONARD



RUI MATEUS AMARAL ANNOTATED 945 MADISON AVENUE, SURVEY, 2018, DOUGLAS CRIMP & ZOE LEONARD

# What Children Say



Children never stop talking about what they are doing or trying to do: exploring milieus, by means of dynamic trajectories,[1] and drawing up maps of them. The maps of these trajectories are essential to psychic activity. Little Hans wants to leave his family's apartment to spend the night at the little girl's downstairs and return in the morning—the apartment building as milieu. Or again: he wants to leave the building and go to the restaurant to meet with the little rich girl, passing by the horses at the warehouse—the street as milieu. Even Freud deems the intervention of a map to be necessary.[2]

As usual, however, Freud refers everything back to the father-mother: oddly enough, he sees the demand to explore the building as a desire to sleep with the mother. It is as if parents had primary places or functions that exist independently of milieus. But a milieu is made up of qualities, substances, powers, and events: the street, for example, with its materials (paving stones), its noises (the cries of merchants), its animals (harnessed horses) or its dramas (a horse slips, a horse falls down, a horse is beaten . . .). The trajectory merges not only with the subjectivity of those who travel through a milieu, but also with the subjectivity of the milieu itself, insofar as it is reflected in those who travel through it. The map expresses the identity of the journey and what one journeys through. It merges with its object, when the object itself is movement. Nothing is more instructive than the paths of autistic children, such as those whose maps Deligny has revealed and superimposed, with their customary lines, wandering lines, loops, corrections, and turnings back—all their singularities.[3]

Thus the Australian Aborigines link nomadic itineraries to dream voyages, which together compose "an interstitching of routes," " in an immense cut-out [*découpe*] of space and time that must be read like a map." At the limit, the imaginary is a virtual image that is interfused with the real object, and vice versa, thereby constituting a crystal of the unconscious. It is not enough for the real object or the real landscape to evoke similar or related images; it must disengage *its own* virtual image at the same time that the latter, as an imaginary landscape, makes its entry into the real, following a circuit where each of the two terms pursues the other, is interchanged with the other. "Vision" is the product of this doubling or splitting in two [*doublement ou dédoublement*], this coalescence. It is in such crystals of the unconscious that the trajectories of the libido are made visible.

A cartographic conception is very distinct from the archaeological conception of psychoanalysis. The latter establishes a profound link between the unconscious and memory: it is a memorial, commemorative, or monumental conception that pertains to persons or objects, the milieus being nothing more than terrains capable of conserving, identifying, or authenticating them. From such a point of view, the superposition of layers is necessarily traversed by a shaft that goes from top to bottom, and it is always a question of penetration. Maps, on the contrary, are superimposed in such a way that each map finds itself modified in the following map, rather than finding its origin in the preceding one; from one map to the next, it is not a matter of searching for an origin, but of evaluating *displacements*. Every map is a redistribution of impasses and breakthroughs, of thresholds and enclosures, which necessarily go from bottom to top. There is not only a reversal of directions, but also a difference in nature: the unconscious no longer deals with persons and objects, but with trajectories and becomings; it is no longer an unconscious of commemoration but one of mobilization, an unconscious whose objects take flight rather than remaining buried in the ground.

Maps should not be understood only in extension, in relation to a space constituted by trajectories. There are also maps of intensity, of density, that are concerned with what fills space, what subtends the trajectory. Little Hans defines a horse by making out a list of its affects, both active and passive: having a big widdler, hauling heavy loads, having blinkers, biting, falling down, being whipped, making a row with its feet. It is this distribution of affects (with the widdler playing the role of a transformer or converter) that constitutes a map of intensity. It is always an affective constellation. Here again, it would be abusive to see this as a simple derivation from the father-mother, as does Freud—as if the "vision" of the street, so frequent at the time (a horse falls down, is whipped, struggles) were incapable of affecting the libido directly, and had to recall a lovemaking scene between the parents . . . Identifying the horse with the father borders on the grotesque and entails a misunderstanding of all the unconscious's relations with animal forces. And just as the map of movements or intensities was not a derivation from or an extension of the father-mother, the map of forces or intensities is not a derivation from the body, an extension of a prior image, or a supplement or afterword. On the contrary, it is the map of intensity that distributes the affects, and it is their links and valences that constitute the image of the body in each case—an image that can always be modified or transformed depending on the affective constellations that determine it.

A list or constellation of affects, an intensive map, is a becoming: Little Hans does not form an unconscious representation of the father with the horse, but is drawn into a becoming-horse to which his parents are opposed.

Becoming is what subtends the trajectory, just as intensive forces subtend motor forces. Hans's becoming-horse refers to a trajectory, from the apartment house to the warehouse. The passage alongside the warehouse, or even the visit to the henhouse, may be customary trajectories, but they are not innocent promenades. We see clearly why the real and the imaginary were led to exceed themselves, or even to interchange with each other: a becoming is not imaginary, any more than a voyage is real. It is becoming that turns the most negligible of trajectories, or even a fixed immobility, into a voyage; and it is the trajectory that turns the imaginary into a becoming. Each of the two types of maps, those of trajectories and those of affects, refers to the other.

What concerns the libido, what the libido invests, presents itself with an indefinite article, or rather is presented by the indefinite article: *an* animal as the qualification of a becoming or the specification of a trajectory (*a* horse, *a* chicken); a body or an organ as the power to affect and to be affected (*a* stomach, *some* eyes . . .); and even the characters that obstruct a pathway and inhibit affects, or on the contrary that further them (*a* father, *some* people . . .). Children express themselves in this manner—a father, a body, a horse. These indefinites often seem to result from a lack of determination due to the defenses of consciousness. For psychoanalysis, it is always a question of *my* father, *me*, *my* body. It has a mania for the possessive and the personal, and interpretation consists in recovering persons and possessions. "A child is being beaten" must signify "I am being beaten by my father," even if this transformation remains abstract; and "a horse falls down and kicks about with its legs" means that my father makes love with my mother. Yet the indefinite lacks nothing; above all, it does not lack determination. It is the determination of a becoming, its characteristic power, the power of an impersonal that is not a generality but a singularity at its highest point. For example, I do not play *the* horse, any more than I imitate *this or that* horse, but I become *a* horse, by reaching a zone of proximity where I can no longer be distinguished from what I am becoming.

Art also attains this celestial state that no longer retains anything of the personal or rational. In its own way, art says what children say.

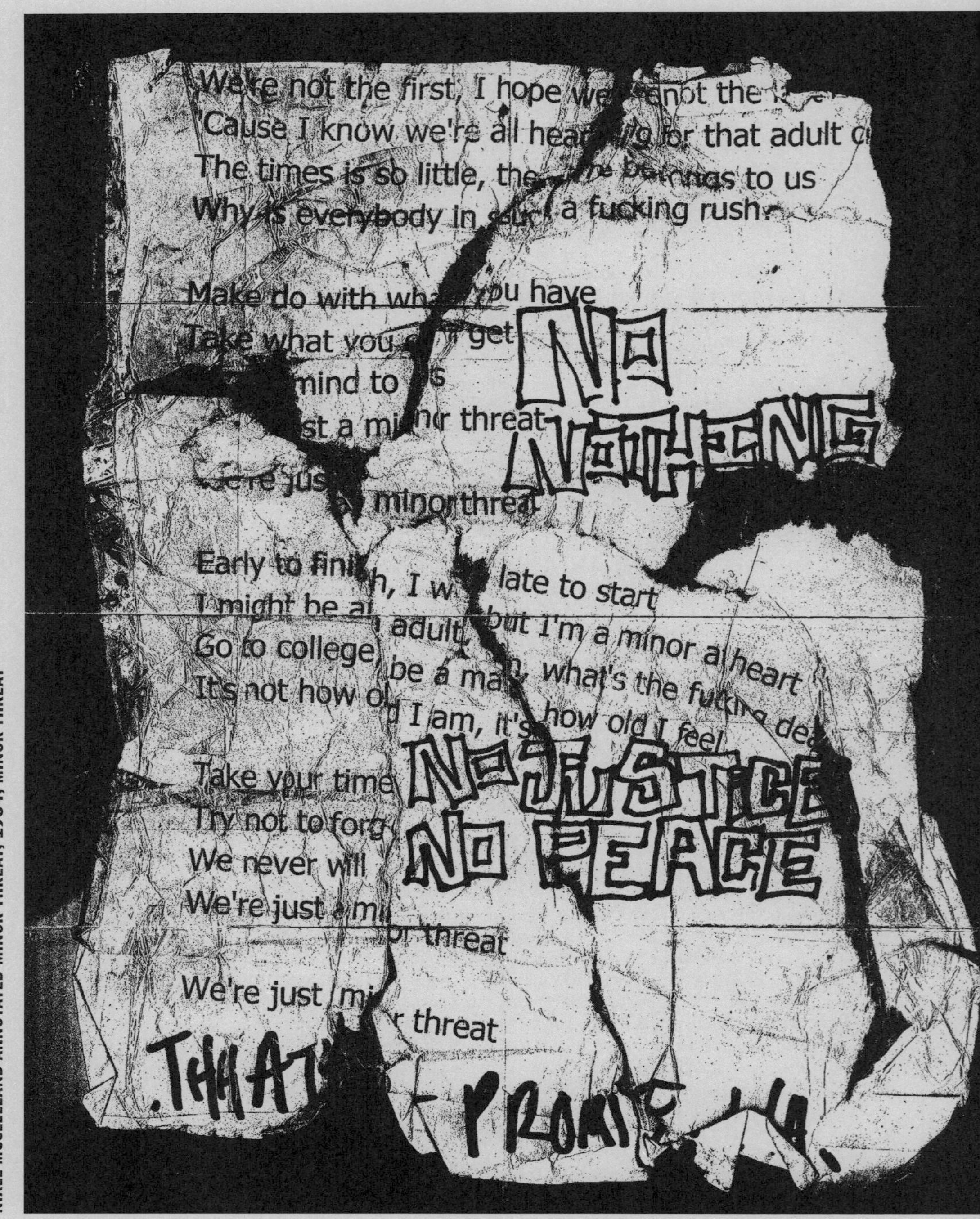
We're not the first, I hope we're not the last
'Cause I know we're all heading for that adult crash
The times is so little, the time belongs to us
Why is everybody in such a fucking rush

Make do with what you have
Take what you can get
mind to this
st a minor threat
We're just a minor threat

Early to finish, I was late to start
I might be an adult, but I'm a minor at heart
Go to college, be a man, what's the fucking deal
It's not how old I am, it's how old I feel

Take your time
Try not to forg
We never will
We're just a mi
or threat

We're just mi
r threat

NO NOTHING
NO JUSTICE NO PEACE
THAT
PROMISE '14

FREE
BOOKS

Let's also remark here that this new art criticism was mostly by women, and by a few brave boys, and that it managed to include gender and sexual preferences with other interests behind certain productions and receptions of art. Before, I guess, these issues were omitted by mistakes in the printing process, no doubt! And it is precisely because a certain number of artists were always thought to be better off unmentioned, because after all, in the service of the division of labor, artists are supposed to do something very specific – maybe to produce a work that could complement an embassy décor. Thank God we still have some "defending fathers" to unravel the truth for us. Just look at your TV, and check out the political ads – all we need to know is there. The state practices control, not only through the repressive methods of the state apparatus – such as the army, the police, the jails (by the way, we in the U.S. have one of the largest incarcerated populations of the industrialized world) – but through the ideological state apparatuses – such as the churches, the family, the media, and – in the most recent incarnation – through the NEA debate. The NEA debate is not actually a debate, but a rhetorical posturing about freedom of information, and the first amendment of so-called free speech – which was never free, you had to pay for it. It was about white, male, straight speech – or classical values. The Constitution was not written by single black mothers, or factory workers on a three-day work schedule somewhere in Chicago. No, it was written by free white men with properties and titles – what I call, "the other."

So if you ever get invited, or get invited again, to pretend that there is a debate about freedom, just remember a few things if you are a cultural producer. First, don't act "artistic." Screw the division of labor really good, and don't talk about how important it is for your "creative self" to smear shit all over your body as a metaphor. No, instead tell the audience – the American family – that perhaps we should be addressing ourselves to the more than $500 million with which the government is subsidizing the savings and loan orgies of the 1980s (for every dollar spent on social programs, we now spend six dollars for the savings and loan bailout. So this is no longer the welfare state but the savings and loan bailout state). Screw up the division of labor and recite – at the drop of a hat – numbers and statistics about the increase in infant mortality, the new cases of tuberculosis, the defunding of supplemental food programs for pregnant women, infants and children, the Women, Infants, and Children (WIC) programs, by the supposedly pro-family, pro-environment, pro-education administration.

Yes, really screw up the division of labor and your role – the divisions and rules of how you should look, and how you should act; or the things you should know if you're an artist. Don't give them what they are expecting from you. Reframe the terms of the argument. Make connections. Establish priorities. By taking over issues of housing, health care, queer rights, women's rights, the environment, the government coverups (and many more unfamiliar acts), we artists, critics, and art historians do in fact rearrange the divisions of cultural labor, and perhaps in this way, we might be able to put forward our own agenda. Maybe in this way, our voice of opposition will be a more complex voice – less easy to dissect and categorize. A voice, not only of more diverse contestation, but also of infiltration that upsets the expected narrative. Ultimately this will be a voice that truly attempts liberation through meaning and renaming, and reordering according to our own needs.

Originally delivered as a talk at Sites of Criticism: A Symposium. The Drawing Center, New York, March 10, 1992. Published in Acme Journal 1, no 2, (1992): 44–49. Reprinted by permission of Andrea Rosen.

133

---

*Handwritten annotations:*

Ian White forwarded me this pdf as part of a queer weekend of events for the periodical 'Little Joe' Saturday 13 April 2013.

'BAME individuals make up 3% of the UK black people / 12% of the population but make up 39% of the population but ⅓ of the prison population.' David Lammy

Félix González-Torres 'Practices: The Problem of Divisions of Cultural Labor.' 1992.

see Jesse Helms/Robert Mapplethorpe debates in 1989 when NEA pulled the exhibition for the work's sexual content. Height of HIV/Aids epidemic and resultant deaths.

see Broodthaers

FGT's point here is about how language itself avoids or suppresses other voices, bodies, lives.

'As a criminal, you have scarcely more rights, and arguably less respect, than a black man living in Alabama at the height of Jim Crow. We have not ended racial caste in America; we have merely redesigned it' The New Jim Crow, Michelle Alexander

see online spaces and paying for them with your personal data.

UK's hidden subsidies, direct grants, and tax breaks to big business amounted to £93bn per year – with £14bn in direct subsidies. The UK arms industry is subsidised by £750m – 1bn per year. Arts is subsidised by £500m. UK's art industries exported £46bn. Conversely Arms Industry only £2bn. Artnotes, Art Monthly April 2018.

against a backdrop of precarity and lack of social-mobility its hard to see whether this is still possible, but I like these provocations to act.

one example: language around 'trans' bodies has moved a great deal since this article was written.

see recent report on the state of prisons in Liverpool – 'worst ever seen' February 2018, Independent.

a think about the failings in mental healthcare in the UK. See Jenny Diski's review of Barbara Taylor's book 'The Last Asylum' in the LRB.

and whether I had somewhere here a place to live and what I had to do in order not to have to walk any more.

And now on top of everything this illness that has always affected me so peculiarly. I am certain it is underestimated. Just as one exaggerates the significance of other illnesses. This illness does not have any specific characteristics, it adopts the characteristics of the person it attacks. With a sleepwalking sureness it plucks from each person his deepest danger, one that seemed past, and places it before him again, quite close, in the next hour. Men who once during their school years tried the helpless vice whose deceived lover was the poor, hard hands of boys find themselves at it again, or an illness they overcame as children starts up in them again; or an abandoned habit recurs, a certain hesitant turning of the head that they had had years before. And together with whatever recurs a whole tangle of wild memories arises that clings to it as wet seaweed clings to a sunken thing. Lives one would never have known about rise to the surface and mingle with what really was and repress past things one thought one knew: for in what rises up there is a new, rested energy, but what was always there is tired from being too often remembered.

I am lying in my bed, up five flights of stairs, and my day, which nothing interrupts, is like a dial without a hand. Like a thing long lost, that one morning is lying in its place, preserved and good, newer almost than when it was lost, just as if it had been in someone's care— thus here and there on my bedspread lost things from childhood are lying, and are like new. All the lost fears are here again.

The fear that a small wool thread sticking out from the hem of a blanket is hard, hard and sharp as a steel needle; the fear that this small button on my nightshirt is bigger than my head, big and heavy;

46

CHRIS McCORMACK ANNOTATED THE NOTEBOOKS OF MALTE LAURIDS BRIGGE, 1915, RAINER MARIA RILKE

*Handwritten annotations:*

published 1915

Hypochondria; too well attuned to bodily sensation and mistake normal feelings for morbid ones — famous cases include Andy Warhol and Glenn Gould. The problem seems to be a reluctance to engage with the real world.

the energy of repressed thoughts.

the present continuous used here 'lying' gives a sense of inaction, powerlessness.

Freud, and his thinking of stairs sex, and the climax of reaching the top.

obsessive qualities, feverish surge of scale and dread.

# Formless



*Bound / unbound*

A dictionary begins when it no longer gives the meaning of words, but their tasks. Thus *formless* is not only an adjective having a given meaning, but a term that serves to bring things down in the world, generally requiring that each thing have its form. What it designates has no rights in any sense and gets itself squashed everywhere, like a spider or an earthworm. In fact, for academic men to be happy, the universe would have to take shape. All of philosophy has no other goal: it is a matter of giving a frock coat to what is, a mathematical frock coat. On the other hand, affirming that the universe resembles nothing and is only *formless* amounts to saying that the universe is something like a spider or spit.

*silent speech
mouth closed (if)
// object speech?*

31

*Reynardine*

One evening as I rambled
among the leaves so green,
*I overheard a young woman*
*converse with Reynardine.*

Her hair was black, her eyes
were blue, her lips as red as wine,
And he smiled to gaze upon her,
did that sly, bold Reynardine.

She said, "Kind sir, be civil,
my company forsake,
For in my own opinion
I fear you are some rake."

*"Oh no," he said, "no rake am I,*
*brought up in Venus' train,*
But I'm seeking for concealment
all along the lonesome plain."

"Your beauty so enticed me,
I could not pass it by
So it's with my gun I'll guard you
all on the mountain side."

"And if by chance you should look
for me, perhaps you'll not me find,
For I'll be in my castle,
inquire for Reynardine."

*Sun and dark she followed him, his teeth*
*did brightly shine,*
And he led her over the mountains, did
that sly bold Reynardine.

This is a transcription of the lyrics of 'Reynardine' as sung by Sandy Denny on Fairport Convention's album *Liege and Lief* (1969). There had been several previous recordings of the song but Fairport's seemed to appear from a parallel dimension. Repeated waves of cymbals break over sustained guitar and fiddle drones and an ethereal vocal slowly unfolds the enigmatic story of a werefox. The recording reflected the uncanny simplicity of the lyrics

The dark psychedelic landscape of the song draws knowingly on multiple traditions to create something dreamlike and unique.

The song had not always been so closely entwined with the supernatural. It can be found in nineteenth century broadsides, often travelling under another name, 'The Mountains High', and it was even being sung in Kentucky in the early 1800s. But there was no mention of a fox until 1909 when an Irish composer, Herbert Hughes, notes that "In the locality where I obtained this fragment, Reynardine is known as the name of a faery which changes into the shape of a fox."

Hughes unlocks the potential of the name Reynardine. It always had an echo of the medieval Reynard stories: the fox as anthropomorphic hero, regularly outwitting his enemies and escaping to his hideaway, the chateau Maupertuis. Now, he is a shape shifter too, moving between forms and worlds.

In the 1950s and '60s, the English folksinger and folklorist, A. L. Lloyd (Bert more commonly) introduced Reynardine to the new young audiences that were beginning to congregate in folk clubs across the country. His first recording of the song in 1956 laid the groundwork. Lloyd was seen at the time as a preserver of the folk tradition though never as dogmatic as his comrade, Ewan McColl.

He was one of the founders of Topic Records, a vital platform for the distribution of folk and field recordings. That's important as one of writers who contributed liner notes to Topic albums was Angela Carter who at that time ran a folk club with her husband Paul in Bristol (they also sang together as a duo and Angela played concertina).

Paul Carter was Bert Lloyd's colleague at Topic Records and Bert also performed at the Carter's club, The Bear, where Angela heard him tell the story of Mr Fox. Speaking of Reynardine on the liner notes to *The Foggy Dew* in 1956, Lloyd asked:

"Is he that dreadful Mr Fox in the English folk-tale, the elegant gentleman whose bedroom was full of skeletons and buckets of blood?" Angela Carter clearly thought so: she recounts 'Mr Fox' in her collection of classic fairy tales and it underpins her own infamous story, 'The Bloody Chamber'.

Bert Lloyd's subtle rewrite of the song is a pivotal moment in English folk, arguably in the wider British and Irish folk movement. With the simple addition of a few descriptive words across the lyrics he transforms the character of Reynardine into a dangerously seductive figure while his last verse evocation of 'sun and dark… over the mountains' places the action in a metaphysical landscape.

The song's popularity spread rapidly with versions by most of Britain's folk royalty including Bert Jansch, Anne Briggs, Martin Carthy, June Tabor, Maddy Prior. Shirley Collins and Davey Graham.

It was Fairport's version though that realised the full potential of the song to re-enchant the English landscape at a time when many musicians, possibly in a psychotropic haze, were launching themselves into the heavens from the shires   - 'Over the hills a swallow is resting, Set the controls for the heart of the sun'.

There were dissenters. It is regularly pointed out that Bert Lloyd's changes to the song have no real provenance. One folklorist claimed Lloyd had collected the song from a Tom Cook of Eastbridge though he never said so himself. In the liner notes for his LP of *English Drinking Songs* (1961) Lloyd did claim to have collected some material from this Tom Cook but academics claim no such person existed. There were a family of singers named Cook in Eastbridge, recorded several times by Lloyd, but none were called Tom: it was a convenient myth and, as a practiced mythologizer, Bert Lloyd would have known it was more convincing if rooted in a near truth. This is essentially the folk process in full flow — drawing on tradition, stressing authenticity and manufacturing, with occasional slight of hand, something newly relevant.

Stranded, at twilight,  on the platform at Saxmundham I can almost see the shifting form of a fox, flitting across the tracks. And Tom Cook, from neighbouring Eastbridge, is waiting for me on the approach.

Wherever the spirit ceases to be a principle it also ceases to be an end. Hence the close connection between collective "thought" under all its forms and the loss of the sense of and respect for souls. The soul is the human being considered as having a value in itself. To love the soul of a woman is not to think of her as serving one's own pleasure, etc. Love no longer knows how to contemplate, it wants to possess. (disappearance of Platonic love *).

It is a fault to wish to be understood before we have made ourselves clear to ourselves. It is to seek pleasures in friendship, and pleasures which are not deserved. It is something which corrupts even more than love. You would sell your soul for friendship.

Learn to thrust friendship aside, or rather the dream of friendship. To desire friendship is a great fault. Friendship should be a gratuitous joy like those afforded by art or life. We must refuse it so that we may be worthy to receive it; it is of the order of grace ("Depart from me, O Lord..."). It is one of those things which are added unto us. *Every* dream of friendship deserves to be shattered. It is not by chance that you have never been loved.... To wish to escape from solitude is cowardice. Friendship is not to be sought, not to be dreamed, not to be desired; it is to be exercised (it is a virtue). We must have done with all this impure and turbid border of sentiment. *Schluss!*

Or rather (for we must not prune too severely within our-

* Here "Platonic" love has nothing to do with what today goes by the same name. It does not proceed from the imagination but from the soul. It is purely spiritual contemplation. Cf., later, in the chapter on *Beauty* (*Editor's note*).

116



selves), everything in friendship which does not pass into real exchanges should pass into considered thoughts. It serves no useful purpose to do without the inspiring virtue of friendship. What should be severely forbidden is to dream of its sentimental joys. That is corruption. Moreover, it is as stupid as to dream about music or painting. Friendship cannot be separated from reality any more than the beautiful. It is a miracle, like the beautiful. And the miracle consists simply in the fact that it *exists*. At the age of twenty-five, it is high time to have done with adolescence once and for all....

Do not allow yourself to be imprisoned by any affection. Keep your solitude. The day, if it ever comes, when you are given true affection there will be no opposition between interior solitude and friendship, quite the reverse. It is even by this infallible sign that you will recognize it. Other affections have to be severely disciplined.

The same words (e.g., a man says to his wife, "I love you") can be commonplace or extraordinary according to the manner in which they are spoken. And this manner depends on the depth of the region in a man's being from which they proceed without the will being able to do anything. And by a marvelous agreement they reach the same region in him who hears them. Thus the hearer can discern, if he has any power of discernment, what is the value of the words.

Benefaction is permissible precisely because it constitutes a humiliation still greater than pain, a still more intimate

117

everse a Greek tra-
ounce, in a context
Christian mutation
friend? Let us note
ppears not to have
of its inauguration
or?) with Diogenes
self, but rather cites
pter on Aristotle in
*Philosophers*.

of Aristotle's testa-
tiful sayings" of the
uestion "What is a
dies." Further on,
*written* by Aristotle,
rinus' *Memorabilia*
ite of their surface
mble chains of aph-
An ethico-political
ain egalitarianism,
stice, and a certain
man person, with
, there is no (true)
d him for having
for the fact is also
e individual but to
the *Nichomachean*
friendship due to
e *Eudemian Ethics*
highest friendship
dship from which
en if they are not
t types of friend-
ing in an entirely
eaning of friend-
niversal meaning.
It is reserved for
eration (*bouleusis*)
God. There is no



friendship, at least in this first sense, with or between animals, with or between gods. But one is not allowed to talk *only* of friendship in the first sense without being caught in several paradoxes. For there is also friendship founded on utility (and this is the case for concord as a political friendship: cf. *Eud.* 1242 a b) or on pleasure, an unstable friendship found particularly among young people.

These three friendships imply equality, but a certain friendship can also imply superiority. The friendship of a divine being for a man, of a governor for the governed, of a father for his son, of a husband for his wife, is another kind of friendship, says Aristotle, and they also differ among each other, implying no absolute reciprocity. It is during the passage devoted to this inequality that Aristotle evokes friendship for the dead—the friendship that knows without being known (1239 a b).

What does the series of Aristotelian sayings reported by Diogenes Laertius signify? For example:

People reproached him for having given alms to a scoundrel: he answered [. . .] 'I did not give to the individual but to the man.' People asked him how one ought to conduct oneself with one's friends: 'As we would like to see them conduct themselves towards us.' He defined justice as a virtue of the soul which makes us give to each according to his own merit. He affirmed that study is the greatest asset in reaching old age. Favorinus says, finally, (*Memoirs*, book II) that he loved to exclaim: 'O my friends, there is no (true) friend.' And one can in fact find this sentence in the seventh book of the *Ethics*. (Aristotle 1925, 1.462–5)

The little word "true" ("there is no [true] friend") obviously bears almost the whole enigma, the other part coming back to the grammatical instability of the sentence, which can always have the O of the apostrophe understood as a sort of dative (the one for whom there are friends, many friends, for that one there are no friends).[5]

Very schematically, we could say that the interpretation can appeal to two great logics. The first can make true friend-

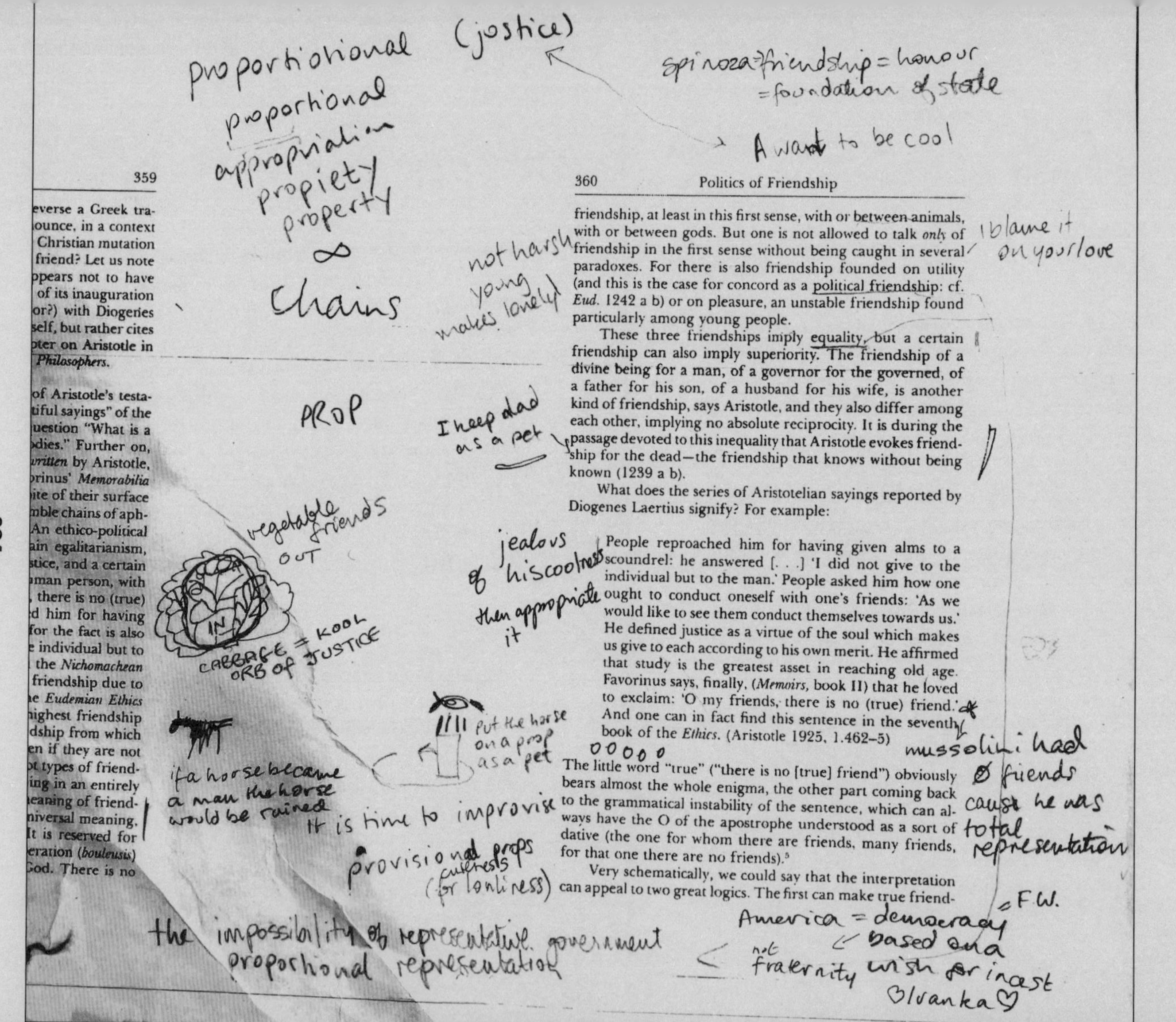

# Art

*Art is the expression of the self.* — Art is really the expression of the self. The more complicated and restricted the method, the less the opportunity for the expression of one's original sense of freedom.

↳ THE FIRST MOMENT IT IS FELT?

*Art and choiceless awareness.* — Artists in all fields must learn to observe choicelessly, to digest their observations, and to express them in their work.

↳ TO STAY IN A PERMENANT STATE OF OPENESS?

*Art begins with feelings.* — Art must originate with an experience or feeling of the artist.

*Art and emotion.* — Art is communication of feelings.

*Forget your mind and become one with the work.* — If [one] has any idea at all of displaying his art well, he ceases to be a good artist, for his mind "stops" with every movement he goes through. In all things, it is important to forget your "mind" and become one with the work at hand.

IF THE WORK IS PURE DISPLAY IT MIGHT NOT NEED IT WELL!

*Art requires creativity and freedom.* — Art lives where absolute freedom is, because where it is not, there can be no creativity — art has no ego rigidity.

↳ TO BE FREE FROM ONE'S OWN EGO.

134

*Art is not decorative.* — Art is never decoration, embellishment; instead it is work of enlightenment. Art, in other words, is a technique for acquiring liberty.

*The aim of art.* — The aim of art is to project an inner vision into the world without.

↳ STUDY THE WORLD TO CHECK IT DOESNT ALREADY HAVE IT.

*The artistic requisite.* — Requirement to be an artist: purity of heart.

*Art is transcendent.* — Art is an expression of life and transcends both time and space.

*Art is the music of the soul made visible.* — Behind every motion is the music of his soul made visible. Otherwise empty motion is like an empty word; no meaning. Postures without proper channeling of your emotions behind them are dead movements.

EMOTIONAL CONTENT!

*Art demands whole-hearted action.* — Art demands only immediated, honest and whole-hearted action. Through art our own souls are what we must employ to give a new form and a new meaning to Nature or the world.

135

285

*Art opens all human capacities.* — The aim of art is not the one-sided promotion of spirit, soul, and the senses, but the OPENING of all human capacities — thought, feeling, and will — to the life rhythm of the world of nature: so will the voiceless voice be heard and the self be brought into harmony with it.

*Immediacy in art.* — Would that we could at once paint with the eyes! In the long way from the eye through the arm to the pencil, how much is lost!

*If we cling to any artistic technique it can limit our artistic expression.* — Art is the expression of the self; the more complicated and restrictive a method is, the lesser the opportunity for expression of one's original sense of freedom. The techniques, although they play an important role in the earlier stage, should not be too complex, restrictive, or mechanical. If we cling to them, we will become bound by their limitations.

*Seamless art is perfect art.* — The perfection of art is to conceal art.

*Pseudo-art is the result of insincerity.* — Much pseudo-art comes from insincerity or the attempt to create a work of art which does not grow from an actual experience or feeling.





*The four postulates of effective art.* — Adequate form [in art] requires:

· Individuality rather than imitative repetitiousness

· Brevity rather than bulkiness

· Clarity rather than obscurity

· Simplicity of expression rather than complexity of form.

*Art requires soulful commitment.* — There are simply not enough soulful characters who are committed, dedicated, and at the same time professional.

*True art cannot be handed out.* — I insist and maintain that art — true art that is — cannot be handed out. Furthermore, art is never decoration or embellishment. Instead it is a constant process of *maturing* (in the sense of NOT having arrived!).

*Art is a means of acquiring personal liberty.* — Art, after all, is a means of acquiring "personal" liberty. Your way is not my way nor mine yours.

*The way of the artist.* — With all the training thrown to nowhere, with a mind (if there is such a verbal substance) perfectly unaware of its own working, with the "self" vanishing nowhere, art attains its perfection.

*[handwritten top margin: picture is of a cycle: appropriation ⇄ excretion / food → energy → output.]*

*[handwritten left margin: CONDITION of APPROPRIATION is homogeneity. → good homogeneity of the world.]*

have the opportunity to become aware of it. And (even though I am capable to a large extent of doing it now) I put off until later difficult and interminable explications, analogous to those of any other elaborated theory. At this point then I will set forth the propositions that, among other things, allow one to introduce the values established by the Marquis de Sade, obviously not in the domain of gratuitous impertinence, but rather directly in the very market in which, each day, the credit that individuals and even communities can give to their own lives is, in a way, registered.

*[handwritten: # remember an involved in appropriation — but issue perhaps balance between approp + excretion — more to what end?]*

### Appropriation and Excretion

1. The division of social facts into religious facts (prohibitions, obligations, and the realization of sacred action) on the one hand and profane facts (civil, political, juridical, industrial, and commercial organization) on the other, even though it is not easily applied to primitive societies and lends itself in general to a certain number of confusions, can nevertheless serve as the basis for the determination of two polarized human impulses: EXCRETION and APPROPRIATION. In other words, during a period in which the religious organization of a given country *is developing*, this organization represents the freest opening for excremental collective impulses (orgiastic impulses) established in opposition to political, juridical, and economic institutions.

2. Sexual activity, whether perverted or not; the behavior of one sex before the other; defecation; urination; death and the cult of cadavers (above all, insofar as it involves the stinking decomposition of bodies); the different taboos; ritual cannibalism; the sacrifice of animal-gods; omophagia; the laughter of exclusion; sobbing (which in general has death as its object); religious ecstasy; the identical attitude toward shit, gods, and cadavers; the terror that so often accompanies involuntary defecation; the custom of making women both brilliant and lubricious with makeup, gems, and gleaming jewels; gambling; heedless expenditure and certain fanciful uses of money, etc. together present a common character in that the object of the activity (excrement, shameful parts, cadavers, etc.) is found each time treated as a foreign body (*daz ganz Anderes*); in other words, it can just as well be expelled following a brutal rupture as reabsorbed through the desire to put one's body and mind entirely in a more or less violent state of expulsion (or projection). The notion of the (heterogeneous) *foreign body* permits one to note the elementary *subjective* identity between types of excrement (sperm, mentrual blood, urine, fecal matter) and everything that can be seen as sacred, divine, or marvelous: a half-decomposed cadaver fleeing through the night in a luminous shroud can be seen as characteristic of this unity.[1]

3. The process of simple appropriation is normally presented within the pro-

*[handwritten bottom margin: sort of homogeneity between possessor + object ('s the condition of appropriation (Bataille) — therefor app. fundamentally conservative.]*



NATHANIEL MELLORS ANNOTATED THE USE VALUE OF D. A. F. DE SADE (AN OPEN LETTER TO MY CURRENT COMRADES), 1930, GEORGES BATAILLE, VISIONS OF EXCESS – SELECTED WRITINGS, 1927 – 1939, 1985, GEORGES BATAILLE, ED. BY WLAD GODZICH & JOCHEN SCHULTE-SASS

## Contents

*Johannes Climacus
or: A life of doubt:
Søren Kierkegaard*



*the 1,2,3: ruptures chronologies
and opens up
duration to
propositional
immediacy*

*and Jo Melvin*


Translation copyright © 2001 T.H. Croxhall
Introduction copyright © 2001 Jane Chamberlain



First published in 2001 by
Serpent's Tail,
4 Blackstock Mews,
London N4 2BT




## Modern philosophy begins with doubt

*plays with mediacy: it throws the reader
into a space of uncertainty, an
in-between space; performative, authorial
dilemma of projected identifications.
We sit on his shoulder between the
character and space created*

What immediately struck him about these three theses was that they seemed by no means homogeneous. While the first two must in the strict sense, because of their universality, be regarded as philosophical – for they stated something universal about the philosophy of all times and all places, or about the philosophizer of all times and places – the third seemed to be a historical report that must first undergo a transformation before it could claim in a strict sense to be of a philosophical nature. Historically, of course, it could be interesting to know that modern philosophy begins with doubt, in the same way as it could be interesting to know whether it begins in Germany or in France, and with whom. If on the other hand a transformation did take place, then it probably could be subsumed under one of the foregoing theses.

In order to check whether this might be possible, he decided to explore the thesis in more detail.



*author, editor, translator and mediator: Kiekegaard's pseudonymous authorial project*

**Philosophy begins with doubt**

Johannes first juxtaposed this thesis with thesis number two, that in order to philosophize one must have doubted. He easily saw that they did not say the same thing, for while the first defined doubt as the beginning of philosophy, the second defined doubt as something which preceded the beginning. He had fixed his attention on these three theses because, among other things, they might shed light on the connection between the statement *de omnibus dubitandum est* and philosophy, and thereby make his prospects of being brought to philosophize more or less brighter. Naturally therefore thesis number one pleased him, for it seemed to be the quickest way. It did not speak of doubt as something preceding philosophy; it taught that in doubt one was at the beginning of philosophy.

49

Johannes Climacus is also the pseudonymous author of Kierkegaard's 'Philosophical Fragments' and 'Concluding unscientific postscript to philosophical fragments'

the conclusion is 5 X the length of the text preceding.

Try unpacking the three statements, unfix their order to make your order – frustrating, tantalising experience of an authorial dilemma.

**In order to philosophize one must have doubted**

It was, as the reader will remember, really the statement *de omnibus dubitandum est* that Johannes wanted to make the object of his deliberations. But first he wanted to encourage himself by exploring this statement's relation to philosophy. What he had discovered, after exhaustive labour, gave him little joy; for he was reduced to the paltry assertion that this statement lay outside philosophy and was a preparation. Yet even so, his efforts would not be without reward if by such preparation he made himself worthy of beginning philosophy later on.

In a certain sense there was nothing now to stop him from going on to that statement, for from it he surely must learn what he had to do, so that thereupon he might carry it out. Yet he thought it worth investigating what it could mean that philosophy should demand such preparation. And thesis number two gave him this opportunity.

That philosophy should demand such preparation seemed to him entirely in order – indeed it greatly appealed to him; his disposition, which was as humble as it was bold, wholly approved of it.

67

d'œuvres qui combinent deux sortes d'idées ou descriptions contradictoires voire mutuellement exclusives :

> «Je préfère les choses hybrides aux choses pures… équivoques plutôt que précises… j'adhère à l'idée de continuité et je suis le champion du dualisme… je préfère conserver deux éléments et leur ajouter quelque chose plutôt que de choisir entre l'un ou l'autre : je préfère le noir et blanc, et parfois le gris, au noir ou blanc.»[20]

Il dit encore :

> «Notre projet pour le *Franklin Delano Roosevelt Memorial* relevait de l'architecture et du paysagisme ; notre fondation pour la *Philadephia Fairmount Park Commission,* de l'architecture et de la sculpture ; notre plan pour *Copley Plaza,* de l'architecture et du design urbain… alors que le *National Football Hall of Fame* est un immeuble qui sert de panneau d'affichage.»[21]

Le but de l'art et de l'architecture n'est pas de résoudre les conflits sociaux ou idéologiques dans une belle œuvre, ni de construire un contre-contenu idéologique en sus ; l'œuvre d'art, au contraire, attire l'attention sur les failles des différentes représentations idéologiques (révélant ainsi les différentes contradictions des lectures idéologiques)[22]. Elle utilise pour cela une forme hybride, une forme qui participe à la fois du code populaire des médias de masse et du code «noble» de l'art et de l'architecture, du code populaire du divertissement et d'une analyse politique et théorique de la forme, enfin de ceux de l'information et de l'esthétique formelle.

---

Notes

20. Cf. note 13.

21. Robert Venturi cité dans Robert Maxwell «The Venturi Effect» in *Venturi and Rauch : The Public Buildings,* New York, 1978.

22. Cf. note 18.

観阿弥

ことである。（十体とは物真似の種類を指すが）年々去来の花とは、幼少の時の風姿、初心のころの態、壮年期のやり方、年寄ってからの風体というような、その時期時期に、自然と身にそなわっていた風体を、みないま現在の芸に、一ぺんにするから持つことである。ある時には子供・若者の能かと見え、ある時は壮年期の役者かと思われ、または随分年劫積んだようにも見えて、同じ本人だとも思われないように能をやるわけだ。これが、幼少の時から老後までの芸をみな一度に持つという理屈である。そこで、これを年々去来する花と言ったのである。

ただし、この芸境に達した役者は、昔も今も知らない。死んだ親父の若盛りの能で年劫を積んだ風体がことに得意であったと聞いている。四十からこっちは、実際に見なれていたことなので疑いない。自然居士の物まねで、高座の上の所作を、その時見た人が、十七、八の身体に見えたと評判したものだ。これは確かに見た人も言い、私自身も見たことだから、年々去来の花に当る達者な役者だと思ったことだ。このように、若い時分には、まだ先きの年齢の風体がうまくやれ、また、年をとってからは、過去の若い時の風体を身体に残している役者は、一人も見たことも聞いたこともなかった。（それは亡父ただ一人だ。）そこで、初心の時からこのかたの芸能の様々を身に残しておいて、それを必要に応じて取り出して演ずることができるのである。若い時には年寄の風体を見せ、年寄ってからは、年盛りの風体を身に残すということは、これまた珍らしいということになるではないか。

そうしてみると、芸能のくらいが上ると、過去の風体をすっかり捨てて忘れてしまうのは、ただもう花の種を失うことだ。その時々に咲いている花だけで、種が無いということになると、

---

手折った花の枝のようなものだ。種があれば、年々またその時節には、かならず咲きをおう。そこで、くれぐれも初心を忘れてはならぬ。世間でよくする批評に、若い役者を、早くもとを上っている、年劫を積んでいるなど賞め、年寄った役者を、若やいているなど言うことがある。これは珍らしさを賞でる原理ではないだろうか。十体の中を色々変えて工夫すれば百種にもなるわけだし、その上に年々去来の品々を、現在の身にそっくりそなえているということになれば、どれほどの花と言ったらよいか、それは大変なものだ。

一つ能をやる時に、万事に抜け目なく心を配ることが大切である。たとえば、はげしく動くような風体を演じようという時には、（相反する心のはたらき）柔かな心を忘れてはならぬ。これは、どんなにはげしく動いても、荒くならないようにという手段だ。はげしい時に柔かな心を持つということは、珍らしいという原理である。また、幽玄の物まねに強くということを忘れてはいけない。これは、舞・はたらき・物まね等、申楽全般において、すべてのことに一つに固まって停滞しないという理屈である。また、身体を使う場合にも、この心づかいが必要だ。上半身を強く動かす時には、足踏（下半身の動き）を加減するがよい。足を強く踏む時には、上半身をしずかに保つがよい。これは文章では説明しにくい。面と向って口で直接教えることである。（これまた心に余裕のある状態である。平凡人にはまねきかねる心のはたらきである。）

一つ秘することによる花の効果を知ることが大切だ。秘すれば花になる。秘せねば花とはならぬというわけだ。これをわきまえることが、花の大事である。そもそも世の中の一切のこと、諸道芸において、その専門の家々において秘事というものがあるが、その秘事は、秘密にす

# What Difference Does It Make?

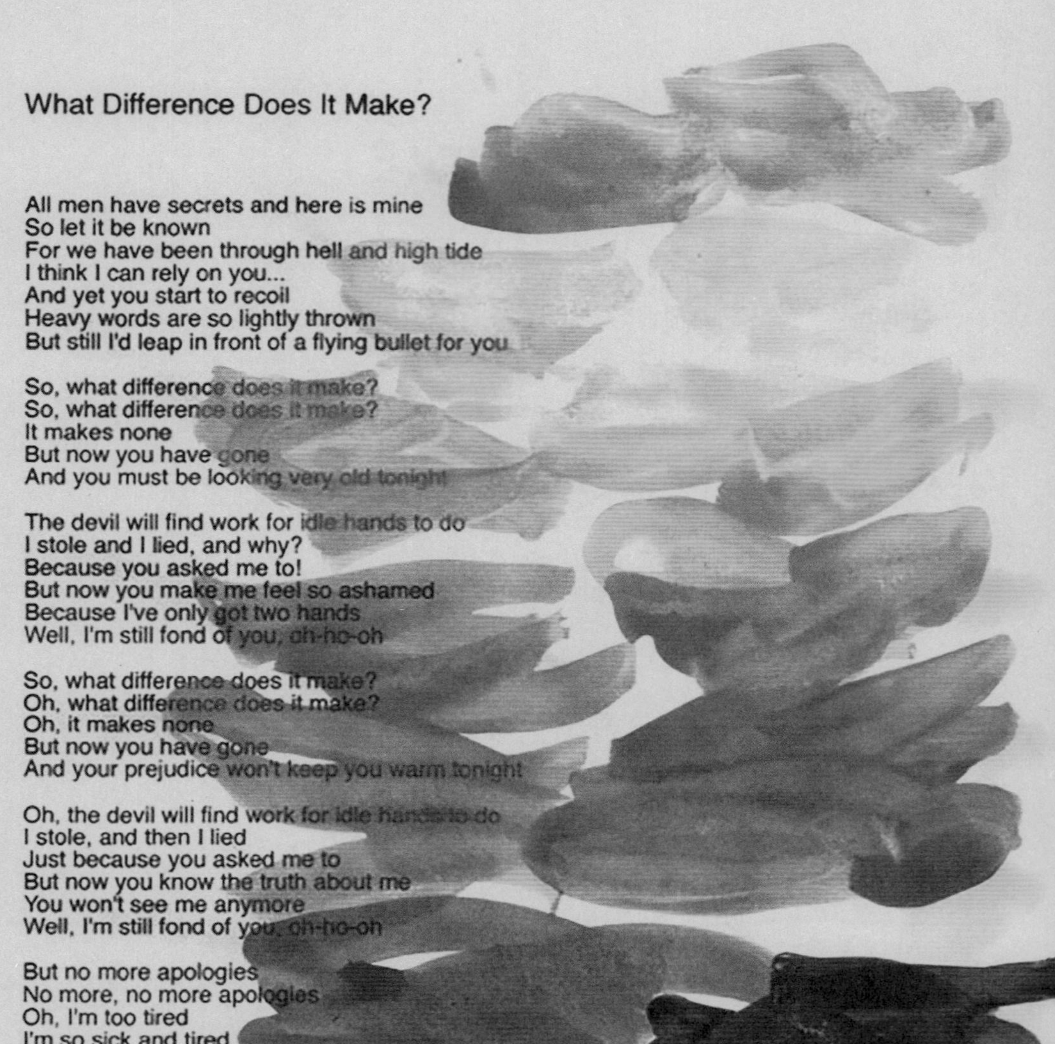

All men have secrets and here is mine
So let it be known
For we have been through hell and high tide
I think I can rely on you...
And yet you start to recoil
Heavy words are so lightly thrown
But still I'd leap in front of a flying bullet for you

So, what difference does it make?
So, what difference does it make?
It makes none
But now you have gone
And you must be looking very old tonight

The devil will find work for idle hands to do
I stole and I lied, and why?
Because you asked me to!
But now you make me feel so ashamed
Because I've only got two hands
Well, I'm still fond of you, oh-ho-oh

So, what difference does it make?
Oh, what difference does it make?
Oh, it makes none
But now you have gone
And your prejudice won't keep you warm tonight

Oh, the devil will find work for idle hands to do
I stole, and then I lied
Just because you asked me to
But now you know the truth about me
You won't see me anymore
Well, I'm still fond of you, oh-ho-oh

But no more apologies
No more, no more apologies
Oh, I'm too tired
I'm so sick and tired
And I'm feeling very sick and ill today
But I'm still fond of you, oh-ho-oh

Oh, my sacred one...
Oh...

Steven Morrissey / Johnny Marr

JONATHAN MONK ANNOTATED WHAT DIFFERENCE DOES IT MAKE?, 1984, STEVEN MORRISSEY & JOHNNY MARR tionary organization, which will pose to the people as problems their position in the historical process, the national reality, and manipulation itself. In the words of Francisco Weffert:

> All the policies of the Left are based on the masses and depend on the consciousness of the latter. If that consciousness is confused, the Left will lose its roots and certain downfall will be imminent, although (as in the Brazilian case) the Left may be deluded into thinking it can achieve the revolution by means of a quick return to power.[25]

In a situation of manipulation, the Left is almost always tempted by a "quick return to power," forgets the necessity of joining with the oppressed to forge an organization, and strays into an impossible "dialogue" with the dominant elites. It ends by being manipulated by these elites, and not infrequently itself falls into an elitist game, which it calls "realism."

Manipulation, like the conquest whose objectives it serves, attempts to anesthetize the people so they will not think. For if the people join to their presence in the historical process critical thinking about that process, the threat of their emergence materializes in revolution. Whether one calls this correct thinking "revolutionary consciousness" or "class consciousness," it is an indispensable precondition of revolution. The dominant elites are so well aware of this fact that they instinctively use all means, including physical violence, to keep the people from thinking. They have a shrewd intuition of the ability of dialogue to develop a capacity for criticism. While some revolutionary leaders consider dialogue with the people a "bourgeois and reactionary" activity, the bourgeoisie regard dialogue between the oppressed and the revolutionary leaders as a very real danger to be avoided.

One of the methods of manipulation is to inoculate individuals with the bourgeois appetite for personal success. This manipulation is sometimes carried out directly by the elites and sometimes indi-

25. Francisco Weffert, "Política de massas," *Política e Revolução social no Brasil* (Rio de Janeiro, 1967), p. 187.



rectly, through populist leaders. As Weffert points out, these leaders serve as intermediaries between the oligarchical elites and the people. The emergence of populism as a style of political action thus coincides causally with the emergence of the oppressed. The populist leader who rises from this process is an ambiguous being, an "amphibian" who lives in two elements. Shuttling back and forth between the people and the dominant oligarchies, he bears the marks of both groups.

Since the populist leader simply manipulates, instead of fighting for authentic popular organization, this type of leader serves the revolution little if at all. Only by abandoning his ambiguous character and dual action and by opting decisively for the people (thus ceasing to be populist) does he renounce manipulation and dedicate himself to the revolutionary task of organization. At this point he ceases to be an intermediary between the people and the elites, and becomes a contradiction of the latter; thereupon the elites immediately join forces to curb him. Observe the dramatic and finally unequivocal terms in which Getulio Vargas[26] spoke to the workers at a May 1 celebration during his last period as head of state:

> I want to tell you that the gigantic work of renewal which my Administration is beginning to carry out cannot be completed successfully without the support and the daily, steadfast cooperation of the workers.[27]

Vargas then spoke of his first ninety days in office, which he called "an estimate of the difficulties and obstacles which, here and there, are being raised in opposition to the actions of the government." He spoke directly to the people about how deeply he felt "the helplessness, poverty, the high cost of living, low salaries . . . the hope-

26. Getulio Vargas led the revolution which overthrew Brazilian President Washington Luis in 1930. He remained in power as a dictator until 1945. In 1950 he returned to power as elected president. In August 1954, when the opposition was about to overthrow him, he committed suicide.—Translator's note.

27. Speech given in Vasco da Gama Stadium on May 1, 1950, *O Governo Trabalhista no Brasil* (Rio), pp. 322–324.

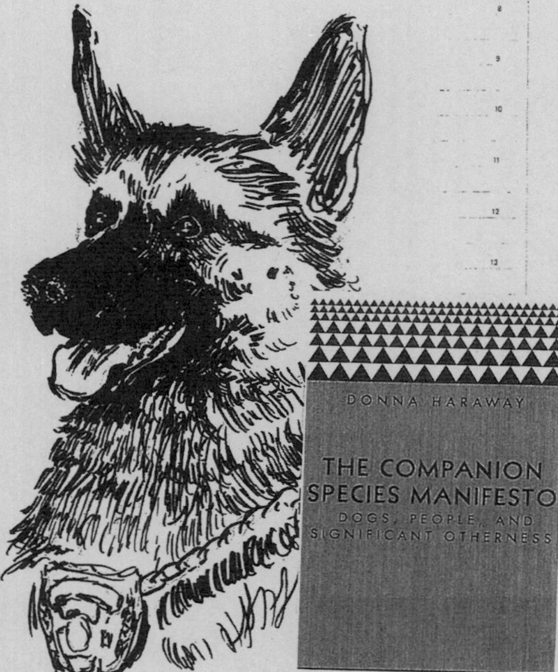


## Love Stories

Commonly in the US, dogs are attributed the capacity for "unconditional love." According t· this belief, people, burdened with misrecognition, contradiction, and complexity in their relations wi· other humans, find solace in unconditional love fr· their dogs. In turn, people love their dogs as child· In my opinion, both of these beliefs are not only b· on mistakes, if not lies, but also they are in themse· abusive—to dogs and to humans. A cursory glance shows that dogs and humans have always had a vas· range of ways of relating. But even among the pet-keeping folk of contemporary consumer cultures, o· maybe especially among these people, belief in "unconditional love" is pernicious. If the idea that man makes himself by realizing his intentions in his tools, such as domestic animals (dogs) and compute· (cyborgs), is evidence of a neurosis that I call huma· technophiliac narcissism, then the superficially opposed idea that dogs restore human beings' souls their unconditional love might be the neurosis of caninophiliac narcissism. Because I find the love of and between historically situated dogs and humans precious, dissenting from the discourse of uncondi-tional love matters.

J.R. Ackerley's quirky masterpiece, *My Dog Tulip* (first privately printed in England in 1956), about a relationship between the writer and his "Alsatian" bitch in the 1940s and 1950s, gives me a way to think through my dissent. History flickers in the reader's peripheral vision from the start of this

34 great love story. After two world wars, in one of those niggling examples of denial and substitution that allow us to go about our lives, a German Shepherd Dog in England was called an Alsatian. Tulip (Queenie, in real life) was the great love of Ackerley's life. An important novelist, famous homosexual, and splendid writer, Ackerley honored that love from the start by recog-nizing his impossible task—to wit, first, somehow to learn what *this* dog needed and desired and, second, to move heaven and earth to make sure she got it.

In Tulip, rescued from her first home, Ackerley hardly had his ideal love object. He also suspected he was not her idea of the loved one. The saga that followed was not about unconditional love, but about seeking to inhabit an inter-subjective world that is about meeting the other in all the fleshly detail of a mortal relationship. Barbara Smuts, the behavioral bioanthropologist who writes courageously about intersubjectivity and friendship with and among animals, would approve. No behavioral biologist, but attuned to the sexology of his culture, Ackerley comi-cally and movingly sets out to find an adequate sexual partner for Tulip in her periodic heats.

The Dutch environmental feminist Barbara Noske, who also called our attention to the scandal of the meat-producing "animal-industrial complex," suggested thinking about animals as "other worlds" in a science fictional sense. In his unswerving dedication to his dog's significant otherness, Ackerley would have understood. Tulip mattered, and that changed them both. He also mattered to her, in ways that could only be read with the tripping proper to any semiotic prac-

35 tice, linguistic or not. The misrecognitions were as important as the fleeting moments of getting things right. Ackerley's story was full of the fleshly, meaning-making details of worldly, face-to-face love. Receiving unconditional love from another is a rarely excusable neurotic fantasy; striving to fulfill the messy condi-tions of being in love is quite another matter. The permanent search for knowledge of the intimate other, and the inevitable comic and tragic mistakes in that quest, commands my respect, whether the other is

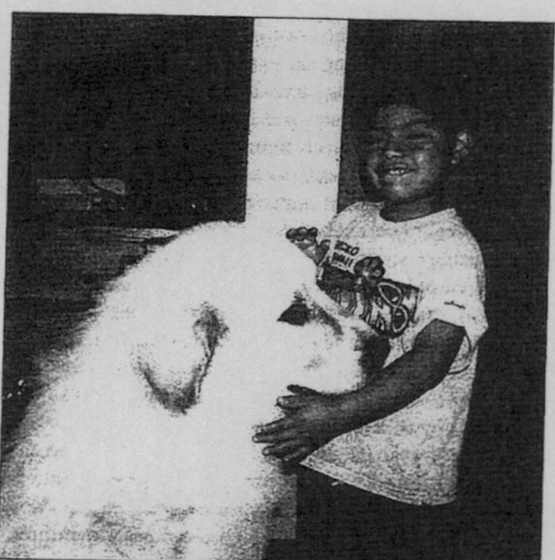

*Figure 2. Marco Harding and Willem DeKooning Caudill, a pet Great Pyrenees of Linda Weisser's breeding. Photo by the author.*

animal or human, or indeed, inanimate. Ackerley's relationship with Tulip earned the name of love.

I have benefited from the mentoring of several life-long dog people. These people use the word love sparingly because they loathe how dogs get taken for cuddly, furry, child-like dependents. For example, Linda Weisser has been a breeder for more than thirty years of Great Pyrenees livestock guardian dogs, a health activist in the breed, and a teacher on all aspects of these dogs' care, behavior, history, and well being. Her sense of responsibility to the dogs and to the people who have them is stunning. Weisser emphasizes love of a *kind* of dog, of a breed, and talks about what needs to be done if people care about these dogs as a whole, and not just about one's own dogs. Without wincing, she recommends killing an aggressive rescue dog or any dog who has bitten a child; doing so could mean saving the reputation of the breed and the lives of other dogs, not to mention children. The "whole dog" for her is both a kind and an individual. This love leads her and others with very modest middle-class means to scientific and medical self-education, public action, mentoring, and major commitments of time and resources.

Weisser also talks about the special "dog of her heart"—a bitch who lived with her many years ago and who still stirs her. She writes in acid lyricism about a current dog who arrived at her house at eighteen months of age and snarled for three days, but who now accepts cookies from her nine-year-old granddaughter, allows the child to take away both food and toys, and tolerantly rules the household's younger bitches.



## 37

I love this bitch beyond words. She is smart and proud and alpha, and if a snarl here and there is the price I pay for her in my life, so be it (Great Pyrenees Discussion List, 9/29/02).

Weisser plainly treasures these feelings and these relationships. She is quick to insist that at root her love is about

the deep pleasure, even joy, of sharing life with a different being, one whose thoughts, feelings, reactions, and probably survival needs are different from ours. And somehow in order for all the species in this 'band' to thrive, we have to learn to understand and respect those things (Great Pyrenees Discussion List, 11/14/01).

To regard a dog as a furry child, even metaphorically, demeans dogs and children—and sets up children to be bitten and dogs to be killed. In 2001 Weisser had eleven dogs and five cats in residence. All of her adult life, she has owned, bred, and showed dogs; and she raised three human children and carried on a full civic, political life as a subtle left feminist. Sharing human language with her children, friends, and comrades is irreplaceable.

While my dogs can love me (I think), I have never had an interesting political conversation with any of them. On the other hand, while my children can talk, they lack the true 'animal' sense that that allows me to touch, however briefly, the 'being' of another species so different from my own with all



the awe-inspiring reality that brings me (Great Pyrenees Discussion List, 11/14/01).

Loving dogs the way Weisser means is not incompatible with a pet relationship; indeed, pet relationships can and do frequently nurture this sort of love. Being a pet seems to me to be a demanding job for a dog, requiring self-control and canine emotional and cognitive skills matching those of good working dogs. Very many pets and pet people deserve respect. Further, play between humans and pets, as well as simply spending time peaceably hanging out together, brings joy to all the participants. Surely that is one important meaning of companion species. Nonetheless, the status of pet puts a dog at special risk in societies like the one I live in—the risk of abandonment when human affection wanes, when people's convenience takes precedence, or when the dog fails to deliver on the fantasy of unconditional love.

Many of the serious dog people I have met doing my research emphasize the importance to dogs of jobs that leave them less vulnerable to human consumerist whims. Weisser knows many livestock people whose guardian dogs are respected for the work they do. Some are loved and some are not, but their value does not depend on an economy of affection. In particular, the dogs' value—and life— does not depend on the humans' perception that the dogs love them. Rather, the dog has to do his or her job, and, as Weisser says, the rest is gravy.

Donald McCaig, the astute Border Collie writer and sheepdog trialer, concurs. His novels, *Nop's*



## 39

*Hope* and *Nop's Trial*, are a superb introduction to potent relationships between working sheepdogs and their people. McCaig notes that working sheepdogs, as a category, fall "somewhere between 'livestock' and 'co-worker'" (Canine Genetics Discussion List, 11/30/00). A consequence of that status is that the dog's judgment may sometimes be better than the human's on the job. Respect and trust, not love, are the critical demands of a good working relationship between these dogs and humans. The dog's life depends more on skill—and on a rural economy that does not collapse—and less on a problematic fantasy.

In his zeal to foreground the need to breed, train, and work to sustain the precious herding abilities of the breed he best knows and most cares about, I think McCaig sometimes devalues and mis-describes both pet and sport performance relationships in dogland. I also suspect that his dealings with his dogs might properly be called love if that word were not so corrupted by our culture's infantilization of dogs and the refusal to honor difference. Dog naturecultures need his insistence on the functional dog preserved only by deliberate work-related practices, including breeding and economically viable jobs. We need Weisser's and McCaig's knowledge of the job of a kind of dog, the whole dog, the specificity of dogs. Otherwise, love kills, unconditionally, both kinds and individuals.

dent on the way *his mother* experienced his *expression of needs and sensations* during his first days and weeks of life, then we must assume that it is here that the *beginning of a later tragedy* might be set. If a mother cannot take pleasure in her child as he is but must have him behave in a particular way, then the first value selection takes place for the child. Now "good" is differentiated from "bad," "nice" from "nasty," and "right" from "wrong." Against this background will follow all his further valuations of himself.

Such an infant must learn that there are things about him for which the mother has "no use." She will expect her child to control his bodily functions as early as possible. On the conscious level his parents apparently want him to do so in order not to offend against society, but unconsciously they are protecting their own repression dating from the time when they were themselves small children afraid of "offending."

Marie Hesse, the mother of the poet and novelist Hermann Hesse, described in her diaries how her own will was broken at the age of four. When her son was four years old, she suffered greatly under his defiant behavior and battled against it with varying degrees of success. At the age of fifteen, Hermann Hesse was sent to an institution for the care of epileptics and defectives in Stetten, "to put an end to his defiance once and for all." In an affecting and angry letter from Stetten, Hesse wrote to his parents: "If I were a bigot, and not a human being, I could perhaps hope for your understanding." All the same, his release from the home was made conditional upon his "improvement," and so the boy "improved."



In a later poem dedicated to his parents, denial and idealization are restored: he reproaches *himself* that it had been "his character" that had made life so difficult for his parents. Many people suffer all their lives from this oppressive feeling of guilt, the sense of not having lived up to their parents' expectations. This feeling is stronger than any intellectual insight they might have, that it is not a child's task or duty to satisfy his parent's needs. No argument can overcome these guilt feelings, for they have their beginnings in life's earliest period, and from that they derive their intensity and obduracy. They can be resolved only slowly, with the help of a revealing therapy.

Probably the greatest of wounds—not to have been loved just as one truly was—cannot heal without the work of mourning. It can be either more or less successfully resisted and covered up (as in grandiosity and depression), or constantly torn open again in the compulsion to repeat. We encounter this latter possibility in obsessive behavior and in perversion, where the mother's (or father's) scornful reactions to the child's behavior have stayed with him as repressed memory, stored up in his body. (The same happens with mistreatments and molestations that have been endured.) The mother often reacted with surprise and horror, aversion and disgust, shock and indignation, or fear and panic to the child's most natural impulses—his autoerotic behavior, investigation and discovery of his own body, urination and defecation, or his curiosity or rage in response to betrayal and injustice. Later, all these experiences remain closely linked with the mother's horrified eyes. They drive the former child to obsessions and perversions in which the

"We the people, in order to form a more perfect union."
Two hundred and twenty one years ago, in a hall that still stands across the street, a group of men gathered and, with these simple words, launched America's improbable experiment in democracy. Farmers and scholars; statesmen and patriots who had travelled across an ocean to escape tyranny and persecution finally made real their declaration of independence at a Philadelphia convention that lasted through the spring of 1787.

[handwritten: white men! — no blacks, woman, native Americans]

The document they produced was eventually signed but ultimately unfinished. It was stained by this nation's original sin of slavery, a question that divided the colonies and brought the convention to a stalemate until the founders chose to allow the slave trade to continue for at least twenty more years, and to leave any final resolution to future generations.

[handwritten: original sin! perpetuated in different guises!]

Of course, the answer to the slavery question was already embedded within our Constitution – a Constitution that had at its very core the ideal of equal citizenship under the law; a Constitution that promised its people liberty, and justice, and a union that could be and should be perfected over time. And yet words on a parchment would not be enough to deliver slaves from bondage, or provide men and women of every colour and creed their full rights and obligations as citizens of the United States. What would be needed were Americans in successive generations who were willing to do their part – through protests and struggle, on the streets and in the courts, through a civil war and civil disobedience and always at great risk - to narrow that gap between the promise of our ideals and the reality of their time.

[handwritten: — the myth of the American Dream!!]

I am the son of a black man from Kenya and a white woman from Kansas. I was raised with the help of a white grandfather who survived a Depression to serve in Patton's Army during World War II and a white grandmother who worked on a bomber assembly line at Fort Leavenworth while he was overseas. I've gone to some of the best schools in America and lived in one of the world's poorest nations. I am married to a black American who carries within her the blood of slaves and slave owners – an inheritance we pass on to our two precious daughters. I have brothers, sisters, nieces, nephews, uncles and cousins, of every race and every hue, scattered across three continents, and for as long as I live, I will never forget that in no other country on Earth is my story even possible.

[handwritten: Another American myth! Not true]

It's a story that hasn't made me the most conventional candidate. But it is a story that has seared into my genetic makeup the idea that this nation is more than the sum of its parts – that out of many, we are truly one.

As William Faulkner once wrote, "The past isn't dead and buried. In fact, it isn't even past." We do not need to recite here the history of racial injustice in this country. But we do need to remind ourselves that so many of the disparities that exist in the African-American community today can be directly traced to inequalities passed on from an earlier generation that suffered under the brutal legacy of slavery and Jim Crow.
Segregated schools were, and are, inferior schools; we still haven't fixed them, fifty years after Brown v. Board of Education, and the inferior education they provided, then and now, helps explain the pervasive achievement gap between today's black and white students.
Legalized discrimination - where blacks were prevented, often through violence, from owning property, or loans were not granted to African-American business owners, or black homeowners could not access FHA mortgages, or blacks were excluded from unions, or the police force, or fire departments – meant that black families could not amass any meaningful wealth to bequeath to future generations. That history helps explain the wealth and income gap between black and white, and the concentrated pockets of poverty that persists in so many of today's urban and rural communities.

[handwritten: Much of this NOT taught in schools]

But I have asserted a firm conviction – a conviction rooted in my faith in God and my faith in the American people – that working together we can move beyond some of our old racial wounds, and that in fact we have no choice if we are to continue on the path of a more perfect union.
For the African-American community, that path means embracing the burdens of our past without becoming victims of our past. It means continuing to insist on a full measure of justice in every aspect of American life. But it also means binding our particular grievances – for better health care, and better schools, and better jobs - to the larger aspirations of all Americans -- the white woman struggling to break the glass ceiling, the white man who's been laid off, the immigrant trying to feed

[handwritten: 's a collective effort]

[handwritten: A collective effort]



CLIVE MYRIE ANNOTATED SPEECH ON RACE, PHILADELPHIA, MARCH 2008, BARACK OBAMA his family. And it means taking full responsibility for own lives – by demanding more from our fathers, and spending more time with our children, and reading to them, and teaching them that while they may face challenges and discrimination in their own lives, they must never succumb to despair or cynicism; they must always believe that they can write their own destiny.

I would not be running for President if I didn't believe with all my heart that this is what the vast majority of Americans want for this country. This union may never be perfect, but generation after generation has shown that it can always be perfected. And today, whenever I find myself feeling doubtful or cynical about this possibility, what gives me the most hope is the next generation – the young people whose attitudes and beliefs and openness to change have already made history in this election.

Amen!

The conversation on race America is too ashamed to have, & so never has!

とが多かった。この解釈によれば、このように具体的な共有特性がなければ、二つの状況を結びつける基礎となるものが何もないことになる。転移には同一の具体的な要素が必要であるという見方は教育実践に対して強い影響を与え続けており、生徒が学校で学んだものは、教授されたときの課題と類似した課題でしか役に立たないという主張を生んでいる。複雑な現代世界の職業生活では、常に新たな仕事の要求に応えてゆく必要がある。もし同一の具体的要素が転移に必要であるのならば、公教育は実生活においてはあまり役に立たないことになる。しかし、同一の（あるいは特に類似した）要素を共有していなくても、二つのベースは同型だろう。このとき、二つの構造間で同一なのは、対象や属性ではなく、全体的な対応関係のシステム——つまり関係のパターンなのである。

したがって、同一要素がない場合にも、ベースからターゲットへの転移が有効な可能性がある。後の章で、新たな問題に直面したときでも転移は有効なのか、有効だとしたらそれはどんな場合かを調べる。無論、転移が同一要素を必要としない場合にも、同一要素があるのは悪いことではない。実際に、同一要素による転移は、私たちがこれまで論じてきた類似性の制約、つまり知覚的・意味的に類似した要素の対応づけと密接な関係がある。さらに、対象と一次の関係だけが意味的に類似しているのではなく、高次の関係もまた意味的に類似していることがあり得る。関係の関係の類似性である高次の類似性には、知覚的なレベルでの同一要素は必要ない。アナロジーを最も創造的に利用できるか否かは、高次の類似性を発見できるかどうか、そして同型な関係のシステムを対応づけることができるかどうかによって決まる。これらの制約によって、非常に異なった知識の領域からもってきた似ていない要素同士を対応づけることができるようになる。対応づけられる要素間には無視しなければならない多くの違いがあるので、この種のアナロジーの利用は難しい。それでもなお、音の動きと水の動きの平行性を認識したときのように、この種のアナロジーは創造的な飛躍の可能性をもたらすのである。

## 目的と因果

なぜ人はアナロジーを用いるのだろうか。音／水の例はアナロジーの説明的な利用の例である。このとき、ベースはターゲットについての新たな仮説を説明したり発展させたりするために用いられる。幾何の証明を行う・休暇の計画を立てるといった目的を達成するために何をしなければならないかが問題であるとき、アナロジーを利用して問題解決やプランニングを行うことができる。政治・法律・日常生活でよく見られるように、ある行為を行うよう他者を説得する議論を形成するのにもアナロジーはよく使われる。シェークスピアが恋人を夏の日と比較したように、文学的なアナロジーや比喩によって感情的な反応を引き起こすことができる。この後の章で、これらすべてのアナロジーについて、さらに詳しく考えることにする。

現実生活におけるアナロジーでは、アナロジーを利用する人の目的や状況が重要な役割を果たしている。ベースとターゲットについて非常に細かいことまですべて考えようとすれば、どちらにもならなくなることが多いだろう。それでも、同型性という理想的な基準を満たさないが、不

fantasy of a purely passive medium. Earlier prototypes of the perfect medium had been equally idealized: the peculiarities of real wax had always altered the impress of the seal to a greater or lesser extent, as can be clearly seen in the variability of ancient coins cast from the same mold[44]; when Flemish painters first began painting on white linen canvases (as opposed to wooden or copper panels) in the fourteenth and fifteenth centuries, they took special precautions to use fabric with a high thread count, to smooth over the surface by cutting off knots and filling in the space between threads with gesso, and sometimes followed the weave of the cloth in their painting.[45] The history of the blank slate embraces everything from wax tablets to parchment made from animal skins to paper made from materials ranging from papyrus to wood chips to rags to the flickering plastic screens of computers.[46]

Yet all these material peculiarities and resistances melt away in the dreams of the perfect medium. The wax loses its color and consistency; the canvas loses its warp and weft; the paper loses its texture and grain; the photographic plate loses its chemical odor. All that remains is purest softness, blankness, receptivity. But in this parade of abstract nouns for passivity taken to the limit is nonetheless preserved a material history that has bodied out the dreams of the perfect medium over almost three millennia. We no longer dream of seals imprinted in soft wax or magic lantern ghouls projected on white screens. Very few scientists nowadays would liken themselves to photographic plates. We are no longer haunted by nightmares about the subtle effluvia emitted by the imagination producing monsters or celestial apparitions. Neither the passive imagination in solitary reverie nor the active imagination deforming perception awakens epistemological fears any more. Projections of the imagination have, since Freud, become the tools of the psychologist, read in Rorschach blots and analyzed in a battery of standardized projective tests.[47]

Have we finally overcome our dreams of a perfect medium and our nightmares of the projective imagination? The power of the imagination has been steadily diluted since the Renaissance: demoted from physical force to optical image to mere psychological superposition. Nonetheless, it has remained projective: a thing thrown out, an emission of a hyperactive mind that refuses to be contained by the boundaries of reason and the body. Its counterweight was the yielding passive medium to be formed – or more often, deformed; the inchoate matter that was to be shaped into the perfect copy. Fidelity, both sexual and epistemological, depended on passivity.

It is in fears about violations of fidelity of both kinds that we must seek the explanation of the dreams of a perfect medium – and also the explanation of the strange conjunction of such dreams in both sexual reproduction and scientific representation. Historians of media – print, photography, telegraphy, film, the web – have repeatedly and rightly complained that the materiality of these very diverse ways of dispersing texts and images has been ignored. But they have not explained *why* materiality is so persistently overlooked, why soft flesh, linen canvases, clouds, and chemical-coated photographic plates are all »regarded as passive vehicles for the transmission of forms.«[48] This question is particularly urgent when the agent in question – here, the projective

44 Olga Krzyszkowska, *Aegean Seals: An Introduction*, London 2005.

45 Diane Wolfthal, *The Beginnings of Netherlandish Canvas Painting: 1400-1530*, Cambridge 1989, pp. 23-29.

46 On the history of ancient writing surfaces, see Jocelyn Penny Small, *Wax Tablets of the Mind: Cognitive Studies of Memory and Literacy in Classical Antiquity*, London 1997, pp. 141-159; of paper, Wilhelm Sandemann, *Papier. Eine spannende Kulturgeschichte*, Berlin 1992; and of its importance in the writing process, Claire Bustaret, »The Material Surface of the Modern Literary Manuscript«, in: *A History of Writing: From Hieroglyph to Multimedia*, ed. Anne-Marie Christin, Paris 2002, pp. 333-339.

47 On psychological tests that apply projection, see Lawrence Edwin Abt and Leopold Bellak (eds.), *Projective Psychology. Clinical Approaches to the Total Personality*, New York 1952; on the history of the Rorschach blot, see Peter Galison, »Image of Self«, in: Lorraine Daston (ed.), *Things that Talk. Object Lessons from Art and Science*, New York 2004, pp. 257-296.

48 See for example N. Katherine Hayles, *My Mother Was a Computer: Digital Subjects and Literary Texts*, Chicago 2005, p. 206.

4' 33"

FOR ANY INSTUMENT OR COMBINATION OF INSTRUMENTS

*John Cage*

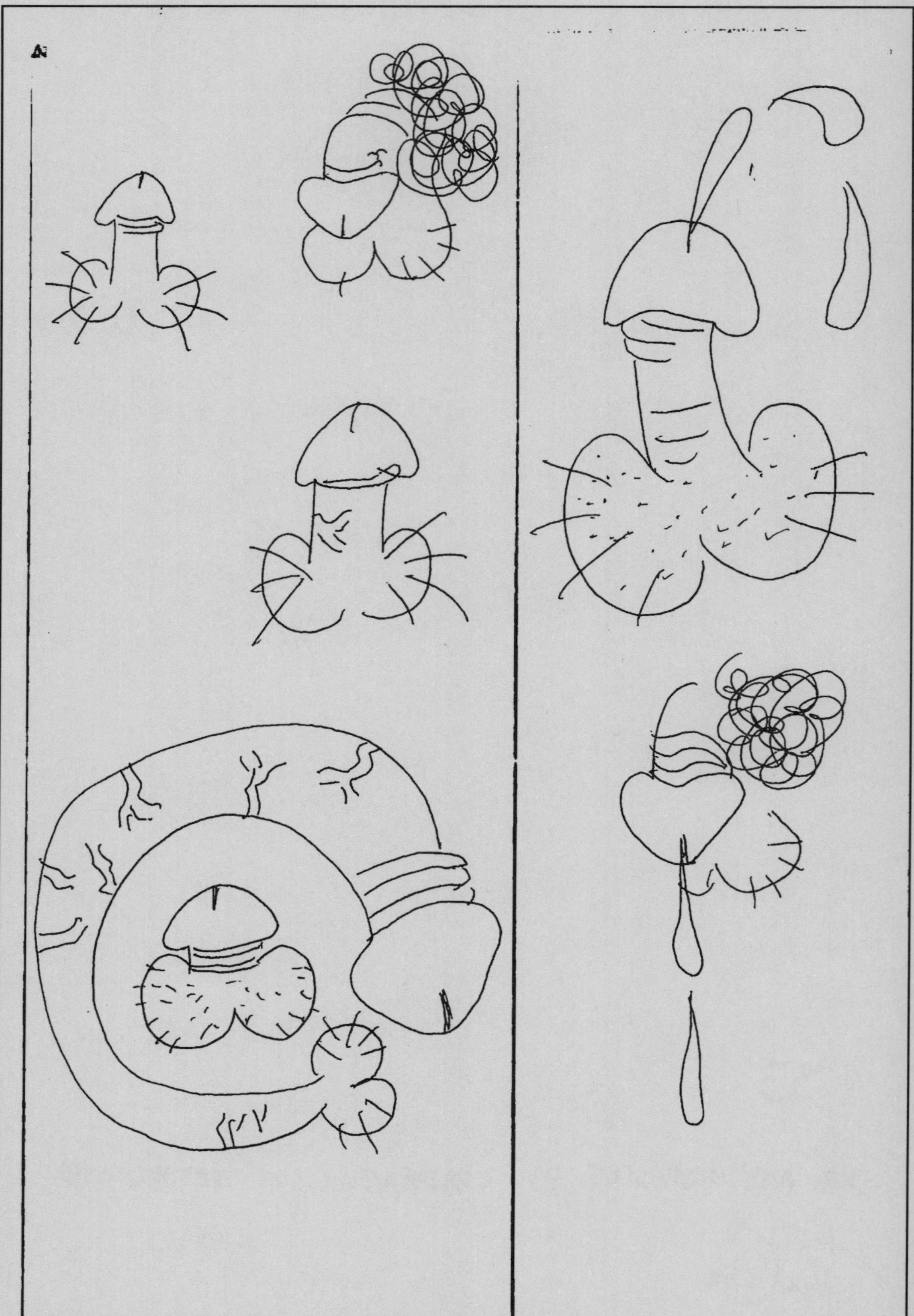

# FRANK O'HARA

## from **PERSONISM: A MANIFESTO**

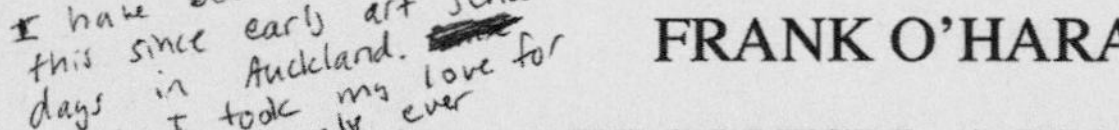

*[Handwritten annotation:] I have been reading this since early art school days in Auckland. Once I took my love for it into my only ever short film called: "Henry, a Flaneur, inspired by Frank O'Hara" It was made in 1999 and it was Henry walking around a street at night time. I Filmed it and the video camera needed an extension cord to be mobile. Flâneur.*

Everything is in the poems, but at the risk of sounding like the poor wealthy man's Allen Ginsberg I will write to you because I just heard that one of my fellow poets thinks that a poem of mine that can't be got at one reading is because I was confused too. Now, come on. I don't believe in god, so I don't have to make elaborately sounded structures. I hate Vachel Lindsay, always have, I don't even like rhythm, assonance, all that stuff. You just go on your nerve. If someone's chasing you down the street with a knife you just run, you don't turn around and shout, "Give it up! I was a track star for Mineola Prep."

That's for the writing poems part. As for their reception, suppose you're in love and someone's mistreating (mal aimé) you, you don't say, "Hey, you can't hurt me this way, I care!" you just let all the different bodies fall where they may, and they always do 'flay after a few months. But that's not why you fell in love in the first place, just to hang onto life, so you have to take your chances and try to avoid being logical. Pain always produces logic, which is very bad for you.

I'm not saying that I don't have practically the most lofty ideas of anyone writing today, but what difference does that make? they're just ideas. The only good thing about it is that when I get lofty enough I've stopped thinking and that's when refreshment arrives. *[handwritten:] This changed everything for me*

But how can you really care if anybody gets it, or gets what it means, or if it improves them. Improves them for what? for death? Why hurry them along? Too many poets act like a middle-aged mother trying to get her kids to eat too much cooked meat, and potatoes with drippings (tears). I don't give a damn whether eat or not. Forced feeding leads to excessive thinness (effete). Nobody should experience anything they don't need to, if they don't need poetry bully for them, I like the movies too. And all, only Whitman and Crane and Williams, of the American are better than the movies. As for measure and other technical apparatus, that's just common sense: if you're going to buy a of pants you want them to be tight enough so everyone will want to go to bed with you. *[handwritten:] makes all the sense in the world* There's nothing metaphysical about it. Unless of course, you flatter yourself into thinking that what You're experiencing is "yearning."

Abstraction in poetry, which Allen recently commented on in It is, is intriguing. I think it appears mostly in the minute particulars where decision is necessary. Abstraction (in poetry, not in painting) involves personal removal by the poet. For instance, the decision involved in the choice between "the nostalgia of the infinite" and "the nostalgia for the infinite" defines an attitude toward degree of abstraction. The nostalgia of the infinite representing the greater degree of abstraction, removal, and negative capability (as in Keats and Mallarmé). Personism, a movement which I *[handwritten:] Bold move –* recently founded and which nobody yet knows about, interests me a great deal, being so totally *[handwritten:] I love it…* opposed to this kind of abstract removal that it is verging on a true abstraction for the first time, really, in the history of poetry. Personism is to Wallace Stevens what la poésie pure was to Béranger. Personism has nothing to do with philosophy, it's all art. It does not have to do with personality or intimacy, far from it! But to give you a vague idea, one of its minimal aspects is to address itself to one person (other than the poet himself), thus evoking overtones of love without destroying love's life-giving vulgarity, and sustaining the poet's feelings towards the poem while preventing love from distracting him into feeling about the person. That's part of personism. It was founded by me after lunch with LeRoi Jones on August 27, 1959, a day in which I was in love with someone (not Roi, by the way, a blond). I went back to work and wrote a poem for this person. While I was writing it I was realizing that if I wanted to I could use the telephone instead of writing the poem, and so Personism was born. It's a very exciting movement which will undoubtedly have lots of adherents. It puts the poem squarely between the poet and the person, Lucky Pierre style, and the poem is correspondingly gratified. The poem is at last between two persons instead of two pages.

*[handwritten:] That's it.*





**303**

[9/3/59]

[Frank O'Hara. "Personism: A Manifesto," *Yugen* #7, 1961.]

Eileen Myles

"Once I was introduced at a reading by someone whom I thought of as a Language poet, and when they described me as "New York School" I experienced it as a critique — like I was retro. But, yes, those were the writers (O'Hara, Ashbery, Koch, Guest) who woke me up, who gave me a sense of what an adventure being a poet could be... Ultimately, though, "New York School" just means I learned to be a poet in New York. As an aesthetic it means putting yourself in the middle of a place and being excited and stunned by it, and trying to make sense of it in your work." (Richard, 25)

# On the Road Again
## Bob Dylan

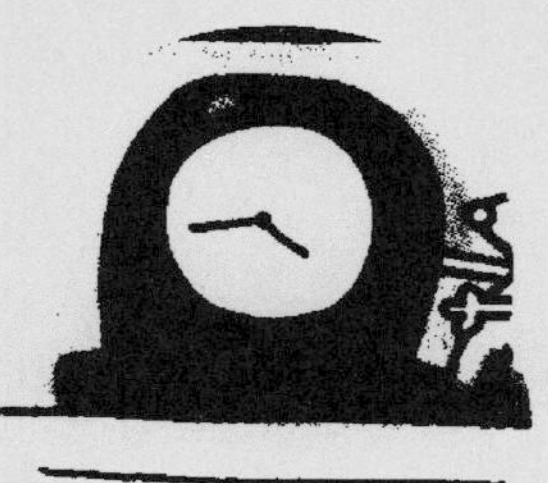

Well, I woke up in the morning
There's frogs inside my socks
Your mama, she's a-hidin'
Inside the icebox
Your daddy walks in wearin'
A Napoleon Bonaparte mask
Then you ask why I don't live here
Honey, do you have to ask?

Well, I go to pet your monkey
I get a face full of claws
I ask who's in the fireplace
And you tell me Santa Claus
The milkman comes in
He's wearing a derby hat
Then you ask why I don't live here
Honey, how come you have to ask me that?

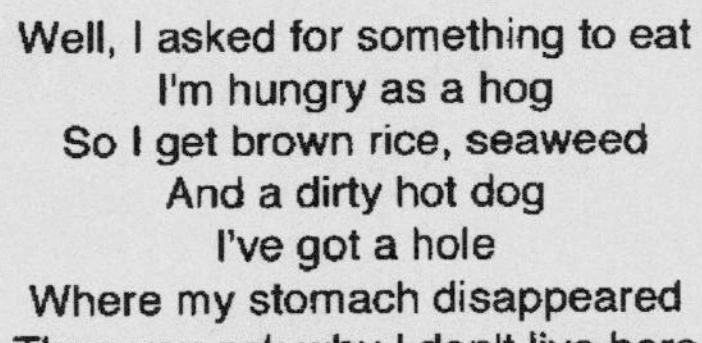

Well, I asked for something to eat
I'm hungry as a hog
So I get brown rice, seaweed
And a dirty hot dog
I've got a hole
Where my stomach disappeared
Then you ask why I don't live here
Honey, I gotta think you're really weird

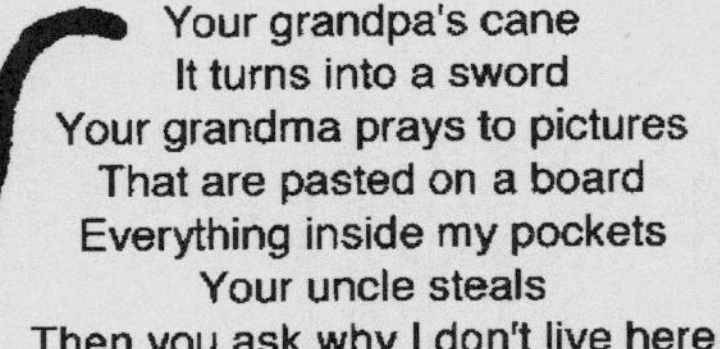

Your grandpa's cane
It turns into a sword
Your grandma prays to pictures
That are pasted on a board
Everything inside my pockets
Your uncle steals
Then you ask why I don't live here
Honey, I can't believe that you're for real

Well, there's fist fights in the kitchen
They're enough to make me cry
The mailman comes in
Even he's gotta take a side
Even the butler
He's got something to prove
Then you ask why I don't live here
Honey, how come you don't move

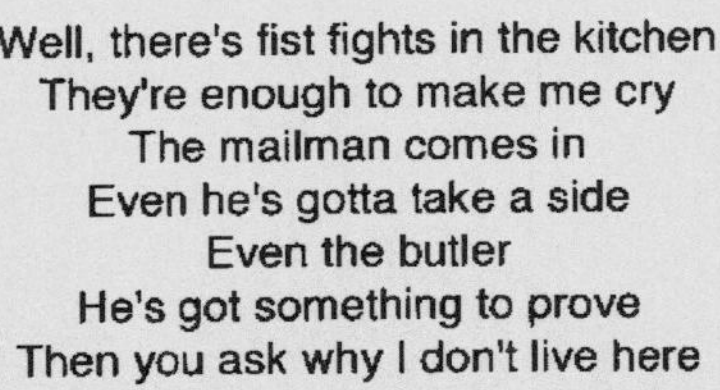

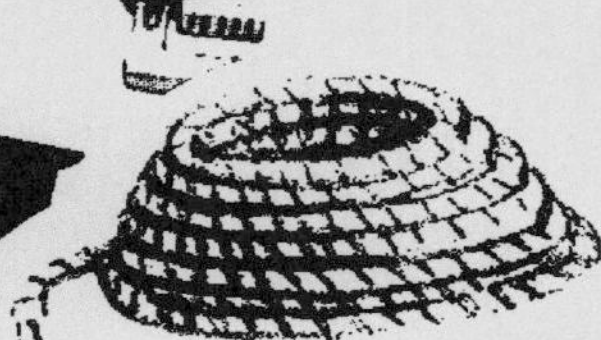

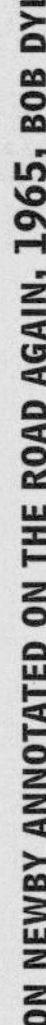

*[handwritten: THROUGH TALKING ABOUT FORM WE EMPHASISE THE ENDLESS]*

*[handwritten: STRUCTURE NOT DISSIMILAR TO THE O.U.L.I.P.O]*

nudo, e una quiete altissima, empieranno lo spazio immenso. Così questo arcano mirabile e spaventoso dell'esistenza universale, innanzi di essere dichiarato nè inteso, si dileguerà e perderassi" (a naked silence and a most profound quiet will fill the immensity of space. So this marvelous and frightening mystery of universal existence, before being declared or understood, will fade away and be lost). Here we see that what is terrifying and inconceivable is not the infinite void, but existence.

This talk is refusing to be led in the direction I set myself. I began by speaking of exactitude, not of the infinite and the cosmos. I wanted to tell you of my fondness for geometrical forms, for symmetries, for numerical series, for all that is combinatory, for numerical proportions; I wanted to explain the things I had written in terms of my fidelity to the idea of limits, of measure . . . . . But perhaps it is precisely this idea of forms that evokes the idea of the endless: the sequence of whole numbers, Euclid's straight lines . . . . . Rather than speak to you of what I have written, perhaps it would be more interesting to tell you about the problems that I have *not* yet resolved, that I don't know how to resolve, and what these will cause me to write: Sometimes I try to concentrate on the story I would like to write, and I realize that what interests me is something else entirely or, rather, not anything precise but everything that does not fit in with what I ought to write—the relationship between a given argument and all its possible variants and alternatives, everything that can happen in time and space. This is a devouring and destructive obsession, which is enough to render writing impossible. In order to combat it, I try to limit the field of what I have to say, divide it into still more limited fields, then subdivide these again, and so on and on. Then another kind of vertigo seizes me, that of the detail of the detail



*[handwritten: MAGNIFICATION (POWERS OF TEN — EAMES)]*

of the detail, and I am drawn into the infinitesimal, the infinitely small, just as I was previously lost in the infinitely vast.

"Le bon Dieu est dans le détail." This statement of Flaubert's I would explain in the light of the philosophy of Giordano Bruno, that great visionary cosmologist, who sees the universe as infinite and composed of innumerable worlds but who cannot call it "totally infinite" because each of these worlds is finite. God, on the other hand, *is* totally infinite: "tutto lui è in tutto il mondo, ed in ciascuna sua parte infinitamente e totalmente" (the whole of him is in the whole world, and in each of his parts infinitely and totally).

Among the Italian books in the last few years which I have most often read, reread, and thought about is Paolo Zellini's *Breve storia dell' infinito* (Short History of the Infinite, 1980). It opens with Borges' famous invective against the infinite from "Avatares de la tortuga" (Avatars of the Tortoise)—it is the one concept that corrupts and confuses all others—and then goes on to review all arguments on the subject, with the result that it dissolves and reverses the extension of the infinite into the density of the infinitesimal.

I think that this bond between the formal choices of literary composition and the need for a cosmological model (or else for a general mythological framework) is present even in those authors who do not explicitly declare it. This taste for geometrical composition, of which we could trace a history in world literature starting with Mallarmé, is based on the contrast of order and disorder fundamental to contemporary science. The universe disintegrates into a cloud of heat, it falls inevitably into a vortex of entropy, but within this irreversible process there may be areas of order, portions of the existent that tend toward a form, privileged points in which we seem to discern a design or perspective. A work of literature is one of these minimal portions in which

*[handwritten: THE EXISTENT CRYSTALLIZES INTO A FORM, ACQUIRES A MEANING - NOT FIXED, NOT DEFINATIVE, NOT HARDENED INTO A MINERAL IMMOBILITY, BUT ALIVE AS AN ORGANISM.]*

foreigner knew how to express himself fluently in his language, but it was not this fluency that amazed him.

"Here is a thicker pore: perhaps it was a larvum's nest; not a woodworm, because, once born, it would have begun to dig, but a caterpillar that gnawed the leaves and was the cause of the tree's being chosen for chopping down . [. This edge was scored by the wood carver with his gouge so that it would adhere to the next square, more protruding. . . ."

The quantity of things that could be read in a little piece of smooth and empty wood overwhelmed Kublai; Polo was already talking about ebony forests, about rafts laden with logs that come down the rivers, of docks, of women at the windows . . .*

From the moment I wrote that page it became clear to me that my search for exactitude was branching out in two directions: on the one side, the reduction of secondary events to abstract patterns according to which one can carry out operations and demonstrate theorems; and on the other, the effort made by words to present the tangible aspect of things as precisely as possible.

The fact is, my writing has always found itself facing two divergent paths that correspond to two different types of knowledge. One path goes into the mental space of bodiless rationality, where one may trace lines that converge, projections, abstract forms, vectors of force. The other path goes through a space crammed with objects and attempts to create a verbal equivalent of that space by filling the page with words, involving a most careful, painstaking effort to adapt what is written to what is not written, to the sum of what is sayable and not sayable. These are two different drives toward exactitude that will never attain com-

*Invisible Cities, translated by William Weaver (New York: Harcourt Brace Jovanovich, 1974), pp. 131–132.



plete fulfillment, one because "natural" languages always say something more than formalized languages can—natural languages always involve a certain amount of noise that impinges upon the essentiality of the information—and the other because, in representing the density and continuity of the world around us, language is revealed as defective and fragmentary, always saying something less with respect to the sum of what can be experienced.

I continually switch back and forth between these two paths, and when I feel I have fully explored the possibilities of one, I rush across to the other, and vice versa. Thus in the last few years I have alternated my exercises in the structure of the story with other exercises in description, today a very neglected art. Like a schoolboy whose homework is to "Describe a giraffe" or "Describe the starry sky," I applied myself to filling a notebook with such exercises and made a book out of the material. This is Mr. Palomar, which was recently published in English translation (1985). It is a kind of diary dealing with minimal problems of knowledge, ways of establishing relationships with the world, and gratifications and frustrations in the use of both silence and words.

In my quests of this sort I have always borne in mind the practice of poets. I think of William Carlos Williams, who describes the leaves of the cyclamen so minutely that we can visualize the flower poised above the leaves he has drawn for us, thereby giving the poem the delicacy of the plant. I think of Marianne Moore who, in depicting her scaly anteater and her nautilus and all the other animals in her bestiary, blends information from zoology books with symbolic and allegorical meanings that make each of her poems a moral fable. And I think also of Eugenio Montale, who may be said to sum up the achievement of both in his poem, "L'anguilla." This is a poem consisting of a

The following is an excerpt from the transcript of the Apollo 12 flight crew communications — November 18, 1969 – Day 4 of the mission. Communicators in the text are identified as follows: (CDR) Commander Charles Conrad, Jr. (CMP) Command Module Pilot Richard F. Gordon, Jr. and (LMP) Lunar Module Pilot Alan L. Bean.

| | | |
|---|---|---|
| 03 11 33 48 | LMP | Look at that Moon bugger! I'll tell you, I may be colorblind, but that looks gray as hell to me. |
| 03 11 33 58 | CDR | What are you doing? Oh, you're rolling. |
| 03 11 33 59 | CMP | I'm rolling, for attitude, Pete, for attitude. I'm working. |
| 03 11 34 02 | CDR | Save that gas, babe! Save it! |
| 03 11 34 04 | CMP | I'm saving it. |
| 03 11 34 05 | CDR | Good Godfrey! That's a God-forsaken place; but it's beautiful, isn't it? |
| 03 11 34 10 | CMP | That old turtleback dome hanging there — look at it. |
| 03 11 34 14 | CDR | Look — look how black the sky is … |
| 03 11 34 15 | LMP | That's gray and something else. |
| 03 11 34 17 | CDR | Chalky white — those craters have been there for … |
| 03 11 34 20 | LMP | A few days. |
| 03 11 34 21 | CDR | Yes. |
| 03 11 34 26 | CMP | Man, this is good to be here is all I can say. |
| 03 11 34 29 | CDR | Has quite a horizon to it, doesn't it? |
| 03 11 34 31 | LMP | Yes. |
| 03 11 34 32 | CDR | It is smaller — and it's got a nice arch to it. |

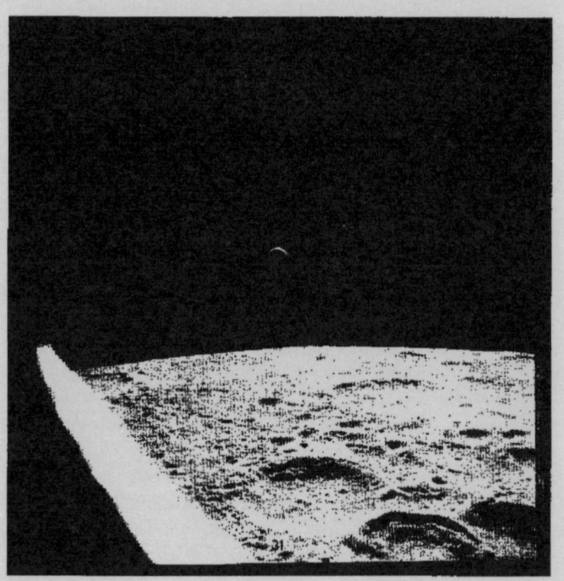

Helen,

These words are very special to me. They give me strength on my weak days. I hope they do the same for you. Enjoy them sweetie.

We are women we are strong
lots + lots of love + solidarity
Peace love and forward to a world socialist revolution.

bell hooks' WOUNDS OF PASSION: A WRITING LIFE given to me by a very important pal from university who helped me to affirm my politics and find my feminist voice She was older than me and said I reminded her of the characters in Alan Warner's THE SOPRANOS. I haven't seen her in a while but I think about her a LOT and look over this book so often ♡

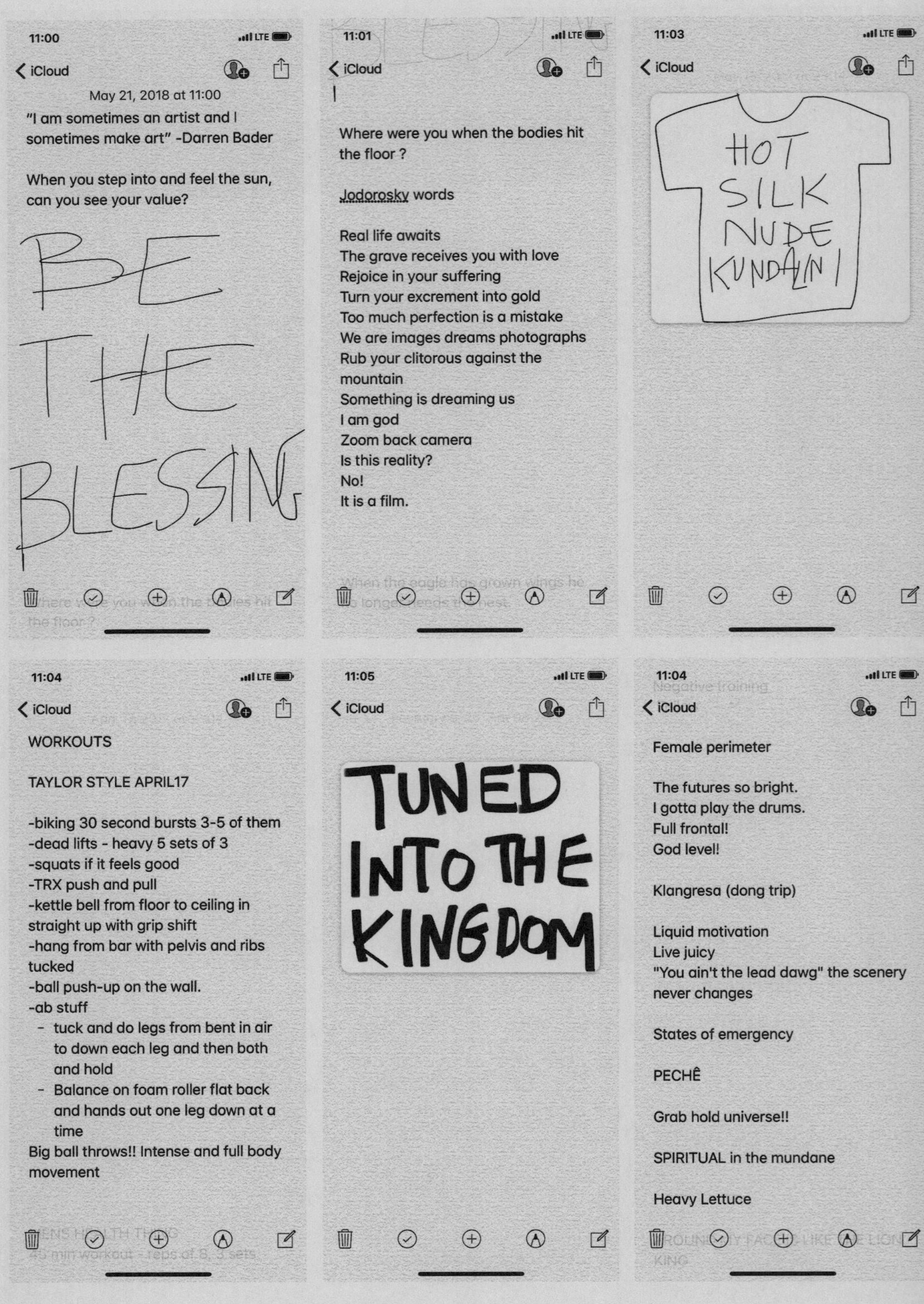
11:00
iCloud
May 21, 2018 at 11:00
"I am sometimes an artist and I sometimes make art" -Darren Bader

When you step into and feel the sun, can you see your value?

BE THE BLESSING

11:01
iCloud
Where were you when the bodies hit the floor ?

Jodorosky words

Real life awaits
The grave receives you with love
Rejoice in your suffering
Turn your excrement into gold
Too much perfection is a mistake
We are images dreams photographs
Rub your clitorous against the mountain
Something is dreaming us
I am god
Zoom back camera
Is this reality?
No!
It is a film.

11:03
iCloud

HOT SILK NUDE KUNDALINI

11:04
iCloud
WORKOUTS

TAYLOR STYLE APRIL17

-biking 30 second bursts 3-5 of them
-dead lifts - heavy 5 sets of 3
-squats if it feels good
-TRX push and pull
-kettle bell from floor to ceiling in straight up with grip shift
-hang from bar with pelvis and ribs tucked
-ball push-up on the wall.
-ab stuff
 - tuck and do legs from bent in air to down each leg and then both and hold
 - Balance on foam roller flat back and hands out one leg down at a time
Big ball throws!! Intense and full body movement

11:05
iCloud

TUNED INTO THE KINGDOM

11:04
iCloud
Female perimeter

The futures so bright.
I gotta play the drums.
Full frontal!
God level!

Klangresa (dong trip)

Liquid motivation
Live juicy
"You ain't the lead dawg" the scenery never changes

States of emergency

PECHÊ

Grab hold universe!!

SPIRITUAL in the mundane

Heavy Lettuce

7

the mexican

        hummmmmmmmming bird

  hummmmmmmmmmmmmmmming

'mhmumimtmzmimlmompmomcmhmtmlmim' !!!

8

rain
sings   -   i too have
             the
          heartflower

read
downwards



HANA NOORALI ANNOTATED 12 DANCEPOEMS FROM THE COSMIC TYPEWRITER BY DSH, 1969, DOM SYLVESTER HOUÉDARD, CONTRIBUTION BY DAVID MEDALLA

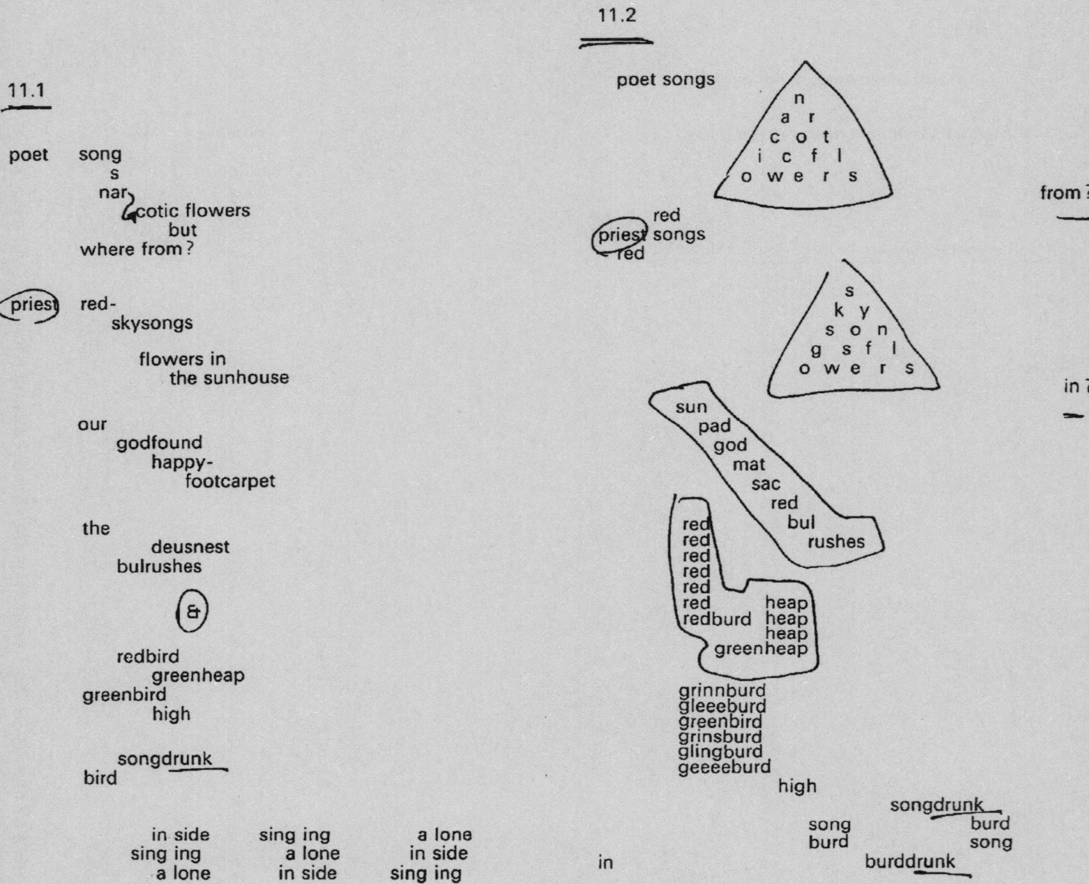



```
11.1                                            poet songs          n
                                                                   a r
poet    song                                                      c o t
           s                                                     i c f l
        nar cotic flowers                                         o w e r s
              but
      where from?                                         red
                                                 priest songs
                                                    red
priest  red-
        skysongs                                                    s
                                                                   k y
           flowers in                                             s o n
              the sunhouse                                       g  s f l
                                                                 o w e r s
our
     godfound                                         sun
        happy-                                         pad
           footcarpet                                   god
                                                         mat
the                                                       sac
        deusnest                                           red
     bulrushes                                    red       bul
                                                  red     rushes
          &                                       red
                                                  red
                                                  red
      redbird                                     red      heap
         greenheap                                redburd  heap
greenbird                                                  heap
      high                                            greenheap

      songdrunk                                  grinnburd
bird                                             gleeeburd
                                                 greenbird
                                                 grinsburd
                                                 glingburd
                                                 geeeeburd
                                                              high
   in side    sing ing    a lone                    song        songdrunk
   sing ing   a lone      in side                   burd              burd
    a lone    in side     sing ing        in              burddrunk   song

                                    a lone    in side   sing ing
                                    in side   sing ing  a lone
                                    sing ing  a lone    in side
```

from?

in?

to . .

→

a genius with bad
behaviours

ART = An activity by means of which one man, having experienced a feeling, intentionally transmits it to others. Tolstoy

If a boy out for a walk sees a bull coming towards him and is terrified, and if on reaching home he tells the story of how the bull coming towards him lowered its head and looked fierce, and of how he hurried away, stumbled, recovered his balance climbed over a stile, and was happy to escape—and if he tells the story so that his parents are infected by his emotion and feel what he has gone through—he has achieved a work of art. So also if he did not see any bull, but only imagined how he would feel if he met one, and then recalling that feeling, imagined and told the tale so that his parents shared the feelings he had experienced, that too would be a work of art.

Or again: if a man passing through a crowded room treads on a lady's toe and causes her to shriek with pain so that her feeling is communicated to others—that is *not* a work of art, because her transmission of feeling is spontaneous and instinctive at the very moment she herself experiences it. But if the man passes her again *without* stepping on her toe, and it occurs to her to pretend that he has, and in order to cause others to share the sense of discomfort she had experienced she recalls it, and by voice and gesture expresses it, pretending that he has hurt her again, that might be a work of art. It would depend on how she used her voice and her

# MILAN KILLS ME

We come from the middle classes or from a more or less settled proletariat families who want respectability. As Pere Gimferrer says: in the old days, ARTISTS came from the upper classes or the aristocracy, and by choosing ART they chose — at least for a certain period that might be a lifetime or four or five years — social censure, the destruction of learned values, mockery and constant criticism. Now, on the other hand, especially in ITALY, ARTISTS come from the lower middle classes or from the ranks of the proletariat and what they want, at the end of the day, is a light veneer of respectability. That is, ARTISTS today seek recognition, though not the recognition of their peers but of what are often called "political authorities," the usurpers of power, (the young ARTISTS don't care!), and thereby the recognition of the public, or sales, which makes GALLERISTS happy but makes ARTISTS even happier, because these are ARTISTS who, as children at home, saw how hard it is to work eight hours a day, or nine or ten, which was how long their parents worked, and this was when there was work, because the only thing worse than working ten hours a day is not being able to work at all and having to drag oneself around looking for a job (paid, of course)

So young ARTISTS have been burned, as they say, and they devote themselves body and soul to selling. Some rely more on their bodies, others on their souls, but in the end it's all about selling.

(...) Where does the new ITALIAN ART come from? The answer is very simple. It comes from fear. It comes from the terrible (and in a certain way fairly understandable) fear of working in an office. It comes from the desire for respectability, which is simply a cover for fear. To those who don't know any better, we might seem like extras from a New York gangster movie, always talking about respect. Frankly, at first glance we're a pitiful group of ARTISTS in our thirties and forties, along with the occasional fifty-year-old, waiting for Godot,

. I hope no one takes what I just said the wrong way. I was kidding. I didn't mean what I wrote, or what I said. At this stage in my life I don't want to make any more unnecessary enemies. I'm here because I want to teach you to be men. Not true. Just kidding. Actually, it makes me insanely envious to look at you. Not just you but all young ITALIAN ARTISTS. You have a future, I promise you. Sorry. Kidding again.

It's a promising scene, especially if viewed from a bridge. The river is wide and mighty and its surface is broken by the heads of at least twenty-five ARTISTS under fifty, under forty, under thirty. How many will drown? I'd say all of them.

The treasure left to us by our parents, or by those we thought were our putative parents, is pitiful. In fact, we're like children trapped in the mansion of a pedophile. Some of you will say that it's better to be at the mercy of a pedophile than a killer. You're right. But our pedophiles are also killers.

Today the exercising and enjoyment of cultural mores of whatever form, tend to generate in age groups rather than those demarked by nationality or wealth.

Such grouping in appetite for, production and appreciation of various cultural mores will, inevitably, be succeeded by further demarkation.

This continuous rhythm of changing cultures should be enabled, rather than merely be mirrored by a 'cultural centre'.

A valid cultural centre must create conditions of communal and private delight, productivity and appreciation previously unimaginable.

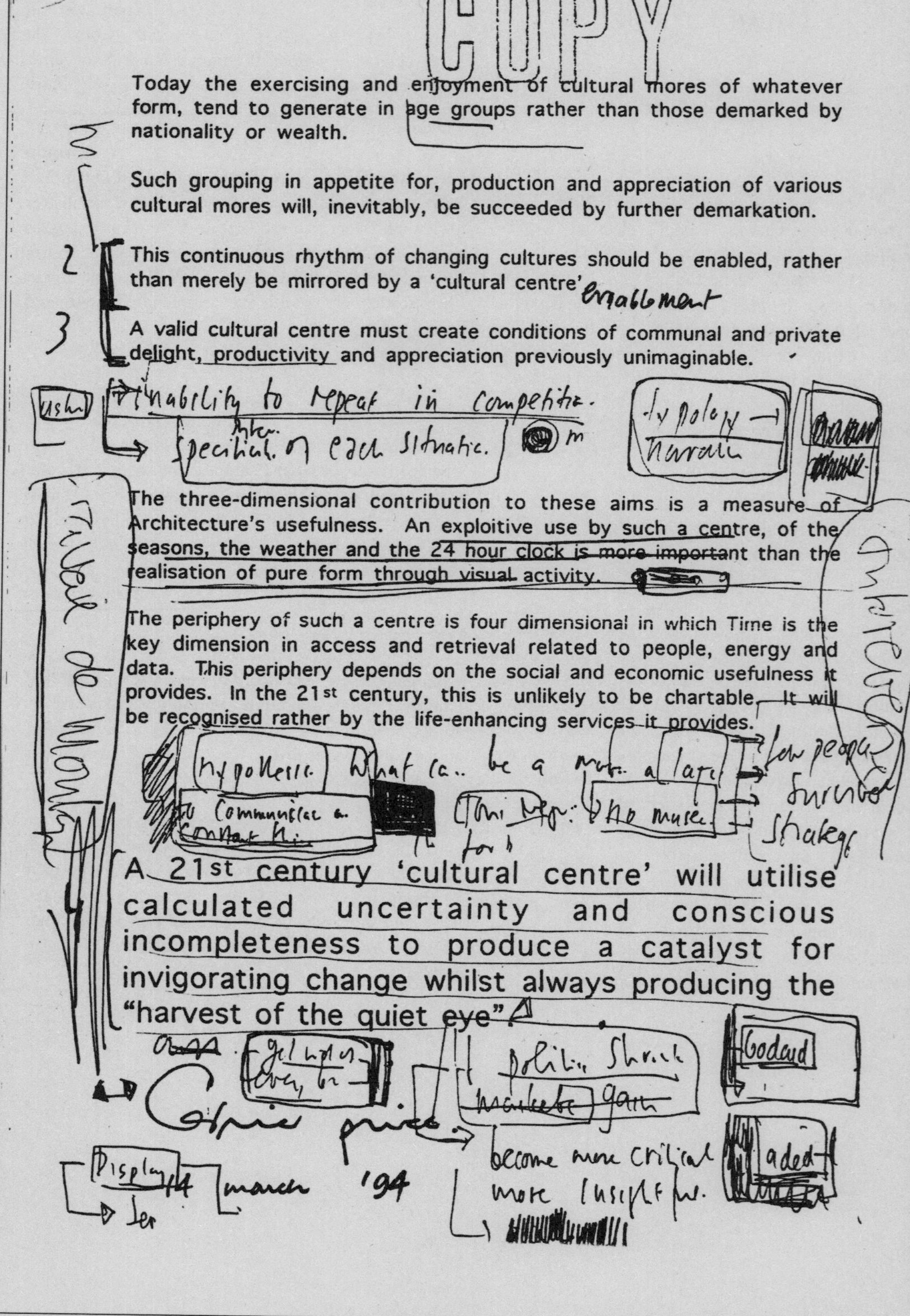


The three-dimensional contribution to these aims is a measure of Architecture's usefulness. An exploitive use by such a centre, of the seasons, the weather and the 24 hour clock is more important than the realisation of pure form through visual activity.

The periphery of such a centre is four dimensional in which Time is the key dimension in access and retrieval related to people, energy and data. This periphery depends on the social and economic usefulness it provides. In the 21st century, this is unlikely to be chartable. It will be recognised rather by the life-enhancing services it provides.

A 21st century 'cultural centre' will utilise calculated uncertainty and conscious incompleteness to produce a catalyst for invigorating change whilst always producing the "harvest of the quiet eye".

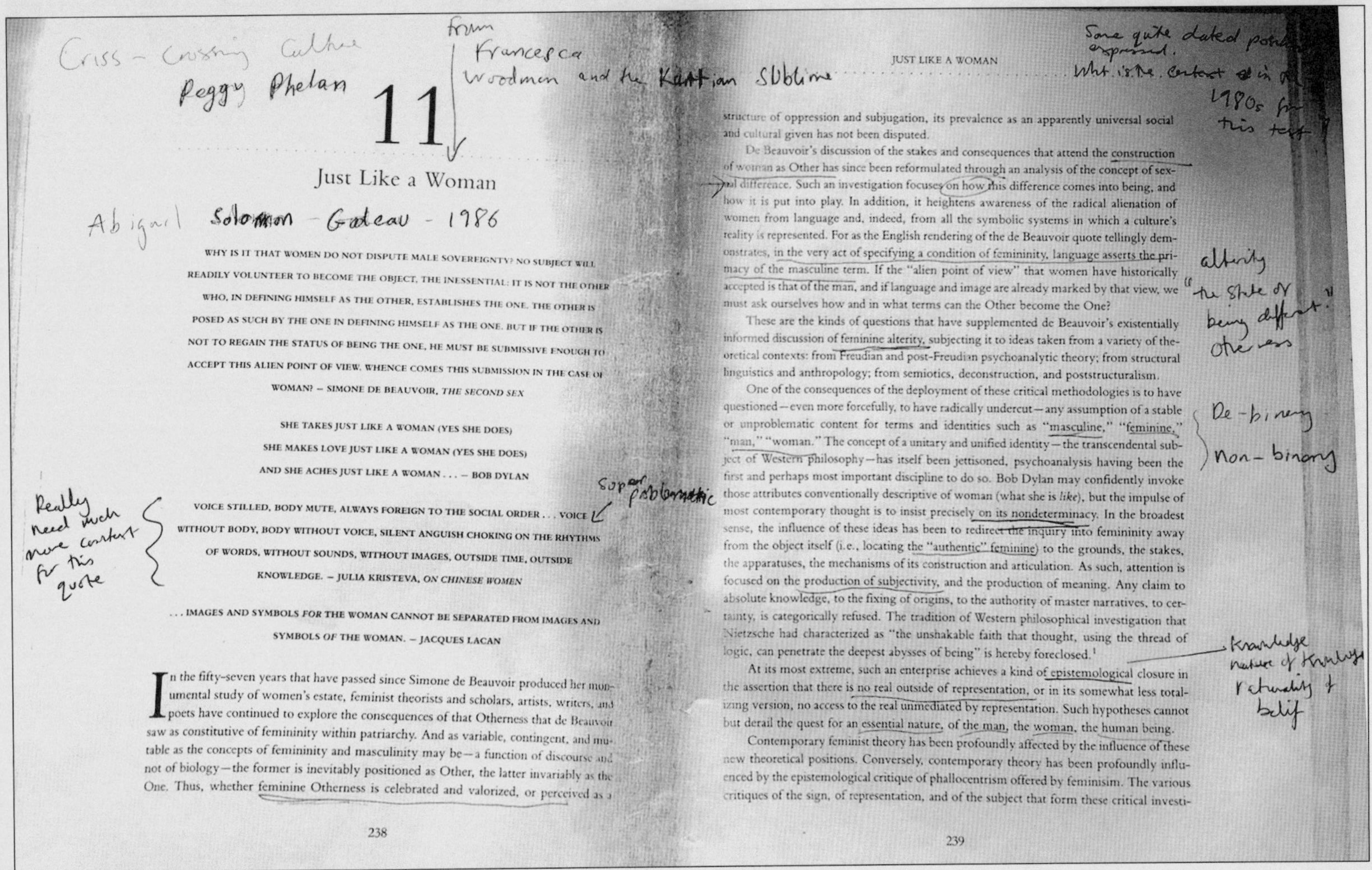

# 11

## Just Like a Woman

WHY IS IT THAT WOMEN DO NOT DISPUTE MALE SOVEREIGNTY? NO SUBJECT WILL
READILY VOLUNTEER TO BECOME THE OBJECT, THE INESSENTIAL: IT IS NOT THE OTHER
WHO, IN DEFINING HIMSELF AS THE OTHER, ESTABLISHES THE ONE. THE OTHER IS
POSED AS SUCH BY THE ONE IN DEFINING HIMSELF AS THE ONE. BUT IF THE OTHER IS
NOT TO REGAIN THE STATUS OF BEING THE ONE, HE MUST BE SUBMISSIVE ENOUGH TO
ACCEPT THIS ALIEN POINT OF VIEW. WHENCE COMES THIS SUBMISSION IN THE CASE OF
WOMAN? – SIMONE DE BEAUVOIR, *THE SECOND SEX*

SHE TAKES JUST LIKE A WOMAN (YES SHE DOES)
SHE MAKES LOVE JUST LIKE A WOMAN (YES SHE DOES)
AND SHE ACHES JUST LIKE A WOMAN . . . – BOB DYLAN

VOICE STILLED, BODY MUTE, ALWAYS FOREIGN TO THE SOCIAL ORDER . . . VOICE
WITHOUT BODY, BODY WITHOUT VOICE, SILENT ANGUISH CHOKING ON THE RHYTHMS
OF WORDS, WITHOUT SOUNDS, WITHOUT IMAGES, OUTSIDE TIME, OUTSIDE
KNOWLEDGE. – JULIA KRISTEVA, *ON CHINESE WOMEN*

. . . IMAGES AND SYMBOLS *FOR* THE WOMAN CANNOT BE SEPARATED FROM IMAGES AND
SYMBOLS OF THE WOMAN. – JACQUES LACAN

In the fifty-seven years that have passed since Simone de Beauvoir produced her monumental study of women's estate, feminist theorists and scholars, artists, writers, and poets have continued to explore the consequences of that Otherness that de Beauvoir saw as constitutive of femininity within patriarchy. And as variable, contingent, and mutable as the concepts of femininity and masculinity may be—a function of discourse and not of biology—the former is inevitably positioned as Other, the latter invariably as the One. Thus, whether feminine Otherness is celebrated and valorized, or perceived as a

238



structure of oppression and subjugation, its prevalence as an apparently universal social and cultural given has not been disputed.

De Beauvoir's discussion of the stakes and consequences that attend the construction of woman as Other has since been reformulated through an analysis of the concept of sexual difference. Such an investigation focuses on how this difference comes into being, and how it is put into play. In addition, it heightens awareness of the radical alienation of women from language and, indeed, from all the symbolic systems in which a culture's reality is represented. For as the English rendering of the de Beauvoir quote tellingly demonstrates, in the very act of specifying a condition of femininity, language asserts the primacy of the masculine term. If the "alien point of view" that women have historically accepted is that of the man, and if language and image are already marked by that view, we must ask ourselves how and in what terms can the Other become the One?

These are the kinds of questions that have supplemented de Beauvoir's existentially informed discussion of feminine alterity, subjecting it to ideas taken from a variety of theoretical contexts: from Freudian and post-Freudian psychoanalytic theory; from structural linguistics and anthropology; from semiotics, deconstruction, and poststructuralism.

One of the consequences of the deployment of these critical methodologies is to have questioned—even more forcefully, to have radically undercut—any assumption of a stable or unproblematic content for terms and identities such as "masculine," "feminine," "man," "woman." The concept of a unitary and unified identity—the transcendental subject of Western philosophy—has itself been jettisoned, psychoanalysis having been the first and perhaps most important discipline to do so. Bob Dylan may confidently invoke those attributes conventionally descriptive of woman (what she is *like*), but the impulse of most contemporary thought is to insist precisely on its nondeterminacy. In the broadest sense, the influence of these ideas has been to redirect the inquiry into femininity away from the object itself (i.e., locating the "authentic" feminine) to the grounds, the stakes, the apparatuses, the mechanisms of its construction and articulation. As such, attention is focused on the production of subjectivity, and the production of meaning. Any claim to absolute knowledge, to the fixing of origins, to the authority of master narratives, to certainty, is categorically refused. The tradition of Western philosophical investigation that Nietzsche had characterized as "the unshakable faith that thought, using the thread of logic, can penetrate the deepest abysses of being" is hereby foreclosed.[1]

At its most extreme, such an enterprise achieves a kind of epistemological closure in the assertion that there is no real outside of representation, or in its somewhat less totalizing version, no access to the real unmediated by representation. Such hypotheses cannot but derail the quest for an essential nature, of the man, the woman, the human being.

Contemporary feminist theory has been profoundly affected by the influence of these new theoretical positions. Conversely, contemporary theory has been profoundly influenced by the epistemological critique of phallocentrism offered by feminisim. The various critiques of the sign, of representation, and of the subject that form these critical investi-

239

have become weak under the preponderance of the strong, but by the strong who have emasculated them.

For the oppressors, however, it is always the oppressed (whom they obviously never call "the oppressed" but—depending on whether they are fellow countrymen or not—"those people" or "the blind and envious masses" or "savages" or "natives" or "subversives") who are disaffected, who are "violent," "barbaric," "wicked," or "ferocious" when they react to the violence of the oppressors.

Yet it is—paradoxical though it may seem—precisely in the response of the oppressed to the violence of their oppressors that a gesture of love may be found. Consciously or unconsciously, the act of rebellion by the oppressed (an act which is always, or nearly always, as violent as the initial violence of the oppressors) can initiate love. Whereas the violence of the oppressors prevents the oppressed from being fully human, the response of the latter to this violence is grounded in the desire to pursue the right to be human. As the oppressors dehumanize others and violate their rights, they themselves also become dehumanized. As the oppressed, fighting to be human, take away the oppressors' power to dominate and suppress, they restore to the oppressors the humanity they had lost in the exercise of oppression.

It is only the oppressed who, by freeing themselves, can free their oppressors. The latter, as an oppressive class, can free neither others nor themselves. It is therefore essential that the oppressed wage the struggle to resolve the contradiction in which they are caught; and the contradiction will be resolved by the appearance of the new man: neither oppressor nor oppressed, but man in the process of liberation. If the goal of the oppressed is to become fully human, they will not achieve their goal by merely reversing the terms of the contradiction, by simply changing poles.

This may seem simplistic; it is not. Resolution of the oppressor-oppressed contradiction indeed implies the disappearance of the oppressors as a dominant class. However, the restraints imposed by the former oppressed on their oppressors, so that the latter cannot reassume their former position, do not constitute *oppression*. An act as oppressed must be among the developers of this pedagogy. No pedagogy which is truly liberating can remain distant from the oppressed by treating them as unfortunates and by presenting for their emulation models from among the oppressors. The oppressed must be their own example in the struggle for their redemption.

The pedagogy of the oppressed, animated by authentic, humanist (not humanitarian) generosity, presents itself as a pedagogy of humankind. Pedagogy which begins with the egoistic interests of the oppressors (an egoism cloaked in the false generosity of paternalism) and makes of the oppressed the objects of its humanitarianism, itself maintains and embodies oppression. It is an instrument of dehumanization. This is why, as we affirmed earlier, the pedagogy of the oppressed cannot be developed or practiced by the oppressors. It would be a contradiction in terms if the oppressors not only defended but actually implemented a liberating education.

But if the implementation of a liberating education requires political power and the oppressed have none, how then is it possible to carry out the pedagogy of the oppressed prior to the revolution? This is a question of the greatest importance, the reply to which is at least tentatively outlined in Chapter 4. One aspect of the reply is to be found in the distinction between *systematic education*, which can only be changed by political power, and *educational projects*, which should be carried out *with* the oppressed in the process of organizing them.

The pedagogy of the oppressed, as a humanist and libertarian pedagogy, has two distinct stages. In the first, the oppressed unveil the world of oppression and through the praxis commit themselves to its transformation. In the second stage, in which the reality of oppression has already been transformed, this pedagogy ceases to belong to the oppressed and becomes a pedagogy of all people in the process of permanent liberation. In both stages, it is always through action in depth that the culture of domination is culturally confronted.[10] In the first stage this confrontation occurs through the

---

10. This appears to be the fundamental aspect of Mao's Cultural Revolution.

IMA–ABASI OKON ANNOTATED OTHER PLANES, DIFFERENT PHASES, MY GEOMETRY, TIMES, MOVEMENTS: BECOMINGS ONGOING, OTHER PLANES OF THERE, 2014, RENÉE GREEN

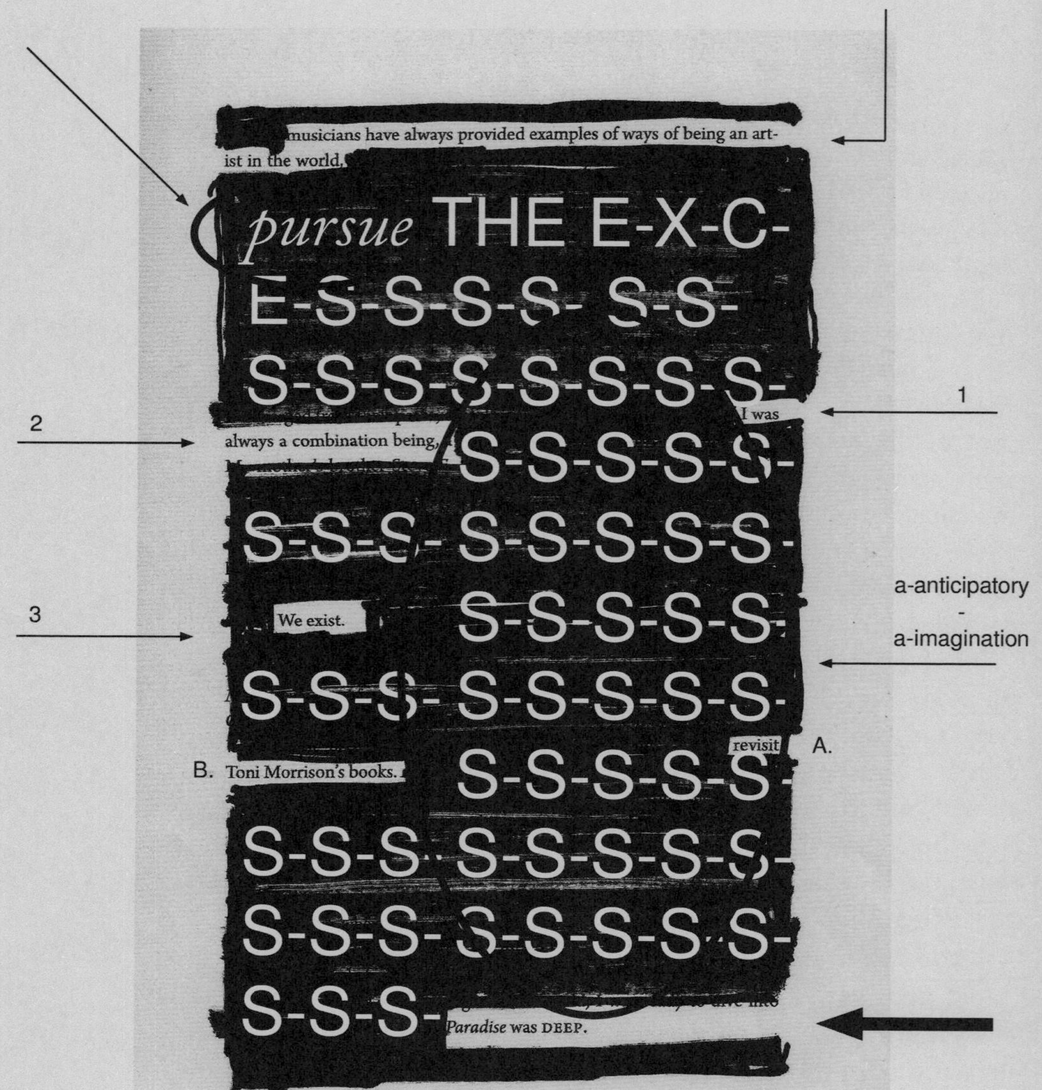
musicians have always provided examples of ways of being an artist in the world,
pursue THE E-X-C-E-S-S-S-S-S-S-S-S-S-S-S-S-S-S-S-S-S-S-S-S-S-S-S-S-S-S-S-S-S-S-S-S-S-S-S-S-S-S-S-S-S-S-S-S-S-S-S-S-S-S-S-S-S-S-S-S-S-S-S-S-S-S-S-S-S-S-S-S-S-S-S-S-
I was
always a combination being,
We exist.
B. Toni Morrison's books.
revisit A.
Paradise was DEEP.
Other Planes, Different Phases   15
1
2
3
a-anticipatory
-
a-imagination

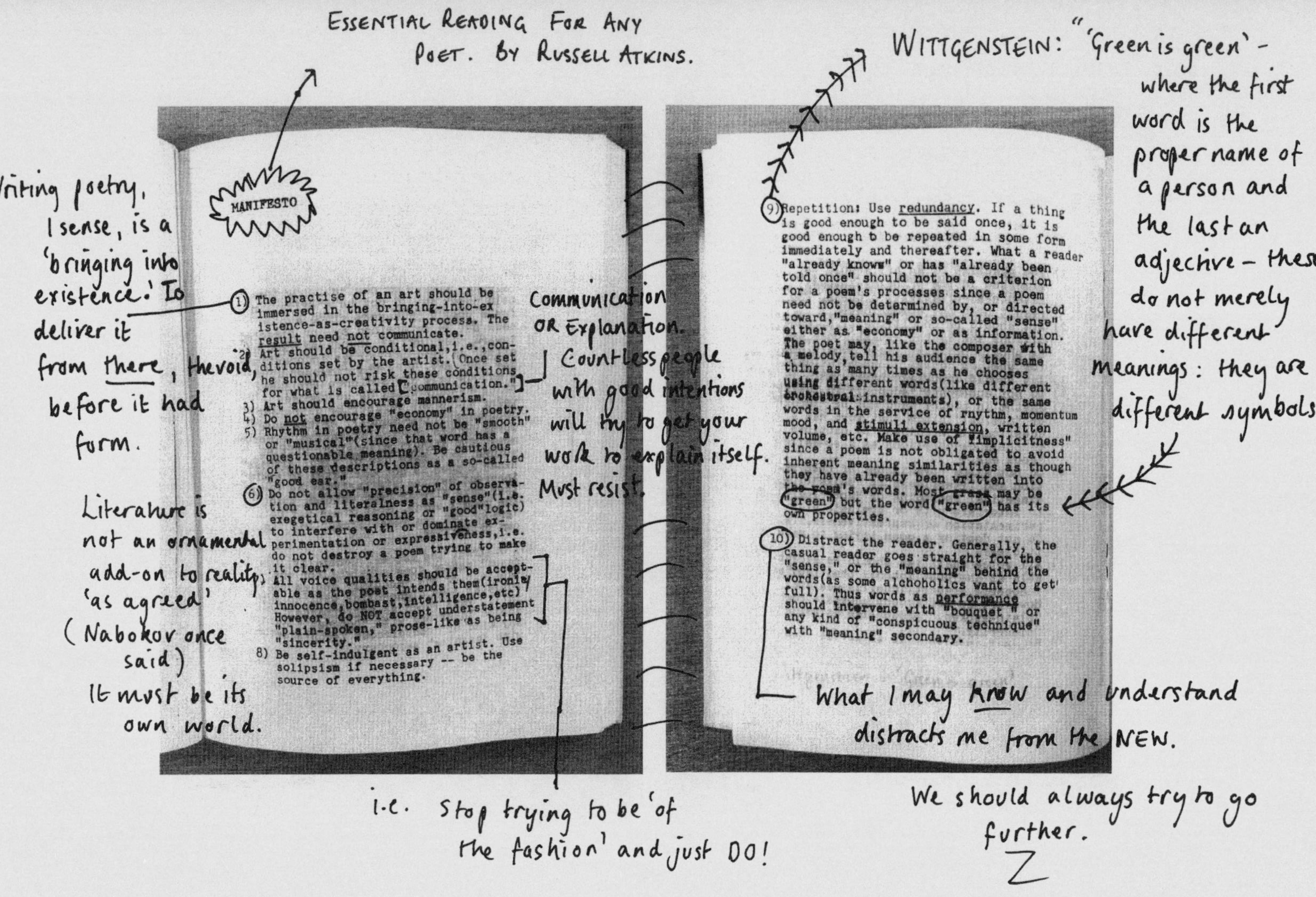


ESSENTIAL READING FOR ANY
POET. BY RUSSELL ATKINS.

WITTGENSTEIN: "Green is green" -
where the first
word is the
proper name of
a person and
the last an
adjective - these
do not merely
have different
meanings: they are
different symbols.

Writing poetry,
I sense, is a
'bringing into
existence.' To
deliver it
from there, the void,
before it had
form.

Literature is
not an ornamental
add-on to reality,
'as agreed'
(Nabokov once
said)
It must be its
own world.

Communication
or Explanation.
Countless people
with good intentions
will try to get your
work to explain itself.
Must resist.

What I may know and understand
distracts me from the NEW.

i.e. stop trying to be 'of
the fashion' and just DO!

We should always try to go
further.
Z

MANIFESTO

1) The practise of an art should be
immersed in the bringing-into-ex
istence-as-creativity process. The
result need not communicate.
2) Art should be conditional, i.e., conditions set by the artist. (Once set
he should not risk these conditions
for what is called "communication.")
3) Art should encourage mannerism.
4) Do not encourage "economy" in poetry.
5) Rhythm in poetry need not be "smooth"
or "musical"(since that word has a
questionable meaning). Be cautious
of these descriptions as a so-called
"good ear."
6) Do not allow "precision" of observation and literalness as "sense"(i.e.
exegetical reasoning or "good"logic)
to interfere with or dominate experimentation or expressiveness, i.e.
do not destroy a poem trying to make
it clear.
7) All voice qualities should be acceptable as the poet intends them(irony,
innocence, bombast, intelligence, etc)
However, do NOT accept understatement
"plain-spoken," prose-like as being
"sincerity."
8) Be self-indulgent as an artist. Use
solipsism if necessary -- be the
source of everything.

9) Repetition: Use redundancy. If a thing
is good enough to be said once, it is
good enough to be repeated in some form
immediately and thereafter. What a reader
"already knows" or has "already been
told once" should not be a criterion
for a poem's processes since a poem
need not be determined by, or directed
toward, "meaning" or so-called "sense"
either as "economy" or as information.
The poet may, like the composer with
a melody, tell his audience the same
thing as many times as he chooses
using different words(like different
orchestral instruments), or the same
words in the service of rhythm, momentum
mood, and stimuli extension, written
volume, etc. Make use of "implicitness"
since a poem is not obligated to avoid
inherent meaning similarities as though
they have already been written into
the poem's words. Most grass may be
"green" but the word "green" has its
own properties.

10) Distract the reader. Generally, the
casual reader goes straight for the
"sense," or the "meaning" behind the
words(as some alchoholics want to get
full). Thus words as performance
should intervene with "bouquet " or
any kind of "conspicuous technique"
with "meaning" secondary.

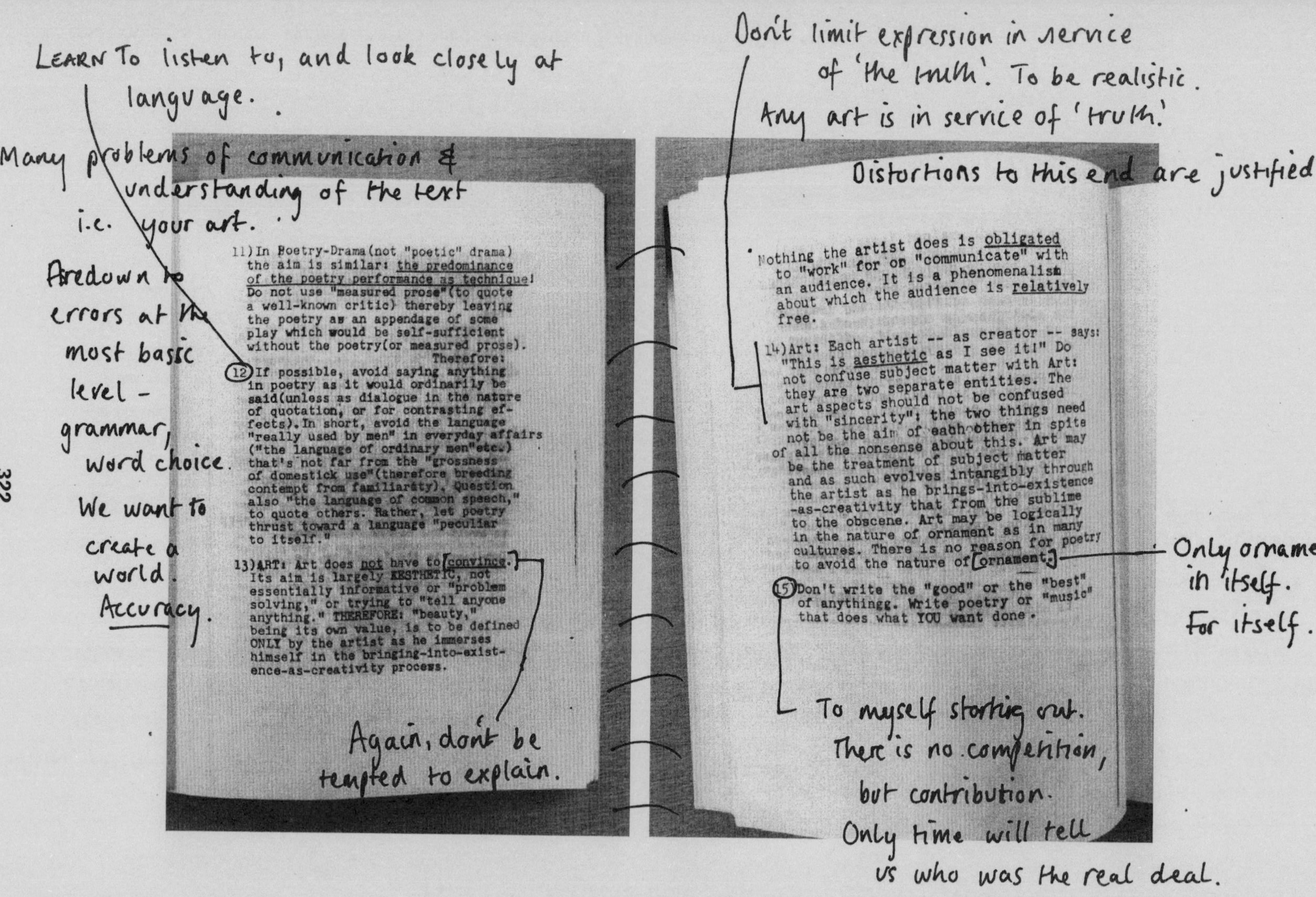


11) In Poetry-Drama (not "poetic" drama)
the aim is similar: the predominance
of the poetry performance as technique!
Do not use "measured prose"(to quote
a well-known critic) thereby leaving
the poetry as an appendage of some
play which would be self-sufficient
without the poetry(or measured prose).
                          Therefore:
12) If possible, avoid saying anything
in poetry as it would ordinarily be
said(unless as dialogue in the nature
of quotation, or for contrasting effects).In short, avoid the language
"really used by men" in everyday affairs
("the language of ordinary men"etc.)
that's not far from the "grossness
of domestick use"(therefore breeding
contempt from familiarity). Question
also "the language of common speech,"
to quote others. Rather, let poetry
thrust toward a language "peculiar
to itself."

13) ART: Art does not have to convince.
Its aim is largely AESTHETIC, not
essentially informative or "problem
solving," or trying to "tell anyone
anything." THEREFORE: "beauty,"
being its own value, is to be defined
ONLY by the artist as he immerses
himself in the bringing-into-exist-
ence-as-creativity process.

Nothing the artist does is obligated
to "work" for or "communicate" with
an audience. It is a phenomenalism
about which the audience is relatively
free.

14) Art: Each artist -- as creator -- says:
"This is aesthetic as I see it!" Do
not confuse subject matter with Art:
they are two separate entities. The
art aspects should not be confused
with "sincerity"; the two things need
not be the aim of each other in spite
of all the nonsense about this. Art may
be the treatment of subject matter
and as such evolves intangibly through
the artist as he brings-into-existence
-as-creativity that from the sublime
to the obscene. Art may be logically
in the nature of ornament as in many
cultures. There is no reason for poetry
to avoid the nature of ornament.

15) Don't write the "good" or the "best"
of anythingg. Write poetry or "music"
that does what YOU want done.

# LES MOTS ET LES IMAGES

Un objet ne tient pas tellement à son nom qu'on ne puisse lui en trouver un autre qui lui convienne mieux

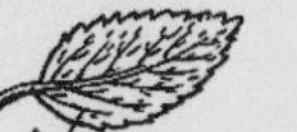


AN OBJECT DOES NOT HOLD ITS NAME THAT WE CANNOT FIND ANOTHER WHICH BETTER SUITS IT...( IDENTITY CAN BE FLUID )

Il y a des objets qui se passent de nom :



THERE ARE OBJECTS THAT GO BY WITHOUT A NAME ... ( IDENTITY CAN BE PROXIMATE )

Un mot ne sert parfois qu'à se désigner soi-même :



A WORD SOMETIMES ONLY SERVES TO DESIGNATE ITSELF : ( AS IMAGE )

Un objet rencontre son image, un objet rencontre son nom. Il arrive que l'image et le nom de cet objet se rencontrent ·



AN OBJECT MEETS ITS IMAGE. AN OBJECT MEETS ITS NAME. IT HAPPENS THE IMAGE AND THE NAME OF THE OBJECT MEET. ( SYMBOLIC SYMBIOSIS )

Parfois le nom d'un objet tient lieu d'une image

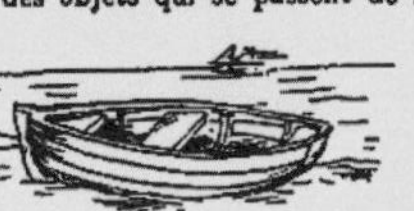


SOMETIMES THE NAME OF AN OBJECT TAKES THE PLACE OF AN IMAGE ... ( AS SUBSTITUTE )

Un mot peut prendre la place d'un objet dans la réalité :

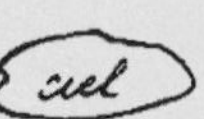


A WORD CAN TAKE THE PLACE OF AN OBJECT IN REALITY ...

Une image peut prendre la place d'un mot dans une proposition ·



A PICTURE CAN TAKE THE PLACE OF A WORD AS A PROPOSITION ... ( NATURALLY )

Un objet fait supposer qu'il y en a d'autres derrière lui :

AN OBJECT SUGGESTS THAT THERE ARE OTHERS BEHIND IT... ( A HIDDEN NARRATIVE )

Tout tend à faire penser qu'il y a peu de relation entre un objet et ce qui le représente



EVERYTHING TENDS TO SUGGEST THAT THERE IS LITTLE RELATIONSHIP BETWEEN AN OBJECT AND WHAT REPRESENTS IT...( OBJECT / IMAGE )

Les mots qui servent à désigner deux objets différents ne montrent pas ce qui peut séparer ces objets l'un de l'autre

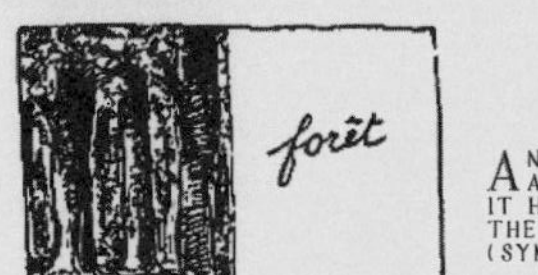


WORDS THAT SERVE TO DESIGNATE TWO DIFFERENT OBJECTS DO NOT SHOW WHAT CAN SEPARATE THESE OBJECTS FROM EACH OTHER.

Dans un tableau, les mots sont de la même substance que les images



IN A PAINTING, THE WORDS ARE THE SAME SUBSTANCE AS IMAGES ( LIQUID )

On voit autrement les images et les mots dans un tableau ·



WE SEE DIFFERENTLY IMAGES AND WORDS IN PAINTINGS ... ( THE SENSATION OF PERCEPTION )

Une forme quelconque peut remplacer l'image d'un objet



SOME FORMS CAN REPLACE THE IMAGE OF AN OBJECT ( AS A MEANS OF DECEPTION )

Un objet ne fait jamais le même office que son nom ou que son image



AN OBJECT NEVER DOES THE SAME THING AS ITS NAME OR ITS IMAGE ( DISLOCATED )

Or, les contours visibles des objets, dans la réalité, se touchent comme s'ils formaient une mosaïque :

THE VISIBLE CONTOURS OF OBJECTS IN REALITY TOUCH EACH OTHER AS IF THEY WERE A MOSAIC ( PLAIN FLAT / PLANE )

Les figures vagues ont une signification aussi nécessaire aussi parfaite que les précises ·

THE VAGUE FIGURES HAVE A NECESSARY MEANING AS PERFECT AS THE PRECISE... ( GUNKY OBJECTS )

Parfois, les noms écrits dans un tableau désignent des choses précises, et les images des choses vagues ·

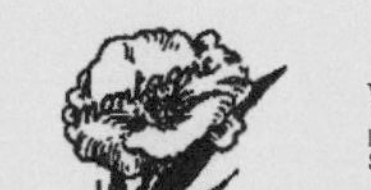


SOMETIMES THE NAMES WRITTEN IN A PAINTING REFER TO PRECISE THINGS, AND IMAGES OF VAGUE THINGS ... ( ALLUDE )

Ou bien le contraire :



OR THE OPPOSITE ... FOG ( ALL SOLIDS MELT INTO AIR )

René MAGRITTE.

SET IN MOCK MODERNICA / DAVID OSBALDESTON ( ADAPTED )

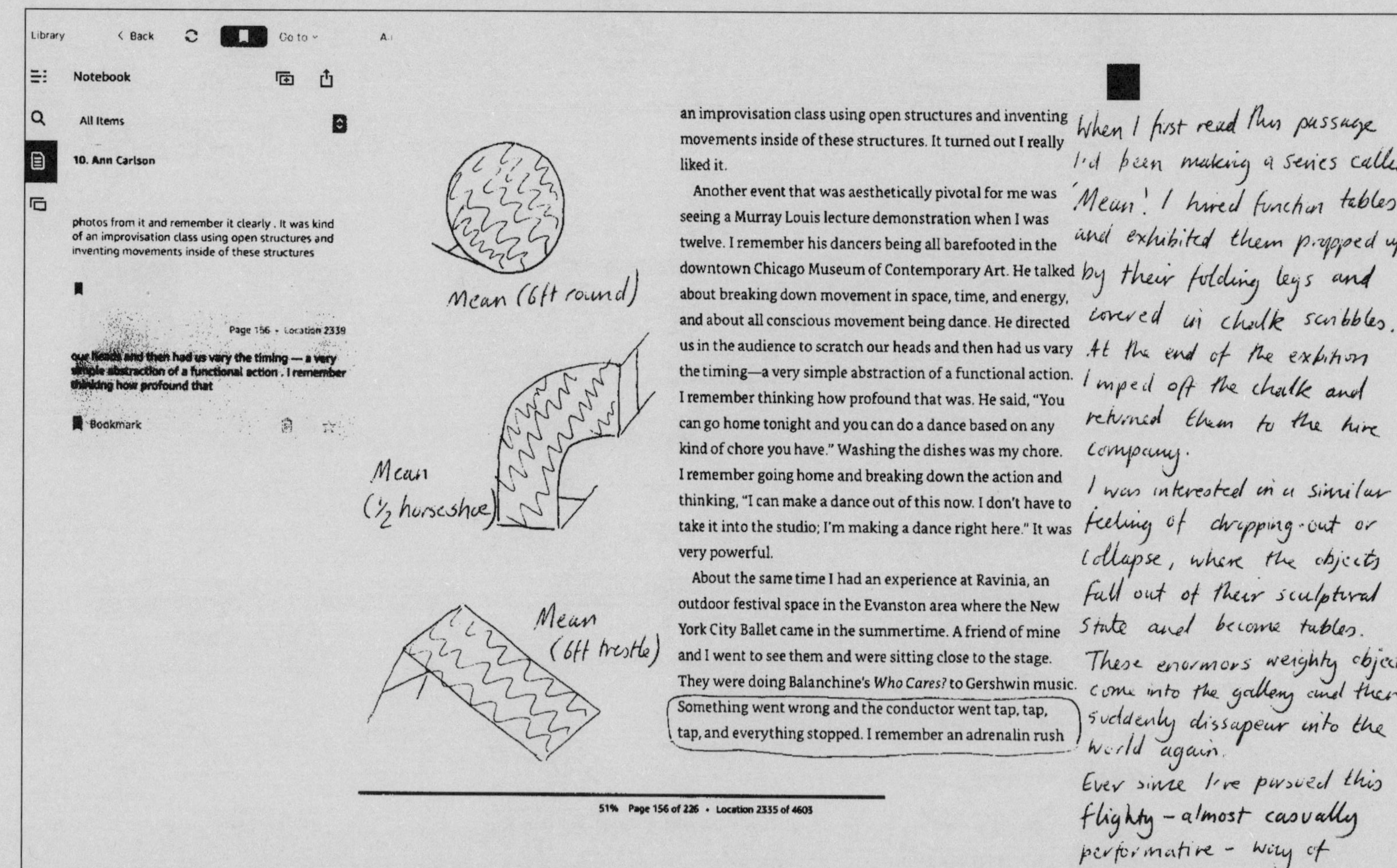



an improvisation class using open structures and inventing movements inside of these structures. It turned out I really liked it.

Another event that was aesthetically pivotal for me was seeing a Murray Louis lecture demonstration when I was twelve. I remember his dancers being all barefooted in the downtown Chicago Museum of Contemporary Art. He talked about breaking down movement in space, time, and energy, and about all conscious movement being dance. He directed us in the audience to scratch our heads and then had us vary the timing—a very simple abstraction of a functional action. I remember thinking how profound that was. He said, "You can go home tonight and you can do a dance based on any kind of chore you have." Washing the dishes was my chore. I remember going home and breaking down the action and thinking, "I can make a dance out of this now. I don't have to take it into the studio; I'm making a dance right here." It was very powerful.

About the same time I had an experience at Ravinia, an outdoor festival space in the Evanston area where the New York City Ballet came in the summertime. A friend of mine and I went to see them and were sitting close to the stage. They were doing Balanchine's *Who Cares?* to Gershwin music. Something went wrong and the conductor went tap, tap, tap, and everything stopped. I remember an adrenalin rush



When I first read this passage I'd been making a series called 'Mean'. I hired function tables and exhibited them propped up by their folding legs and covered in chalk scribbles. At the end of the exhbition I mped oft the chalk and returned them to the hire company.

I was interested in a similar feeling of dropping-out or collapse, where the objects fall out of their sculptural state and become tables. These enormous weighty objects come into the gallery and then suddenly dissapeur into the world again.

Ever since I've pursued this flighty – almost casually performative – way of making.

photos from it and remember it clearly . It was kind of an improvisation class using open structures and inventing movements inside of these structures

Page 156 · Location 2339

our heads and then had us vary the timing — a very simple abstraction of a functional action . I remember thinking how profound that

Bookmark

through my body. When the dancers stopped, they dropped out of the imaginary world and suddenly their feet looked like duck's feet and their tutus flipped forward as they stood there. I had a strong visceral reaction to it: I suddenly saw ballet as a form. I realized I had been making a decision to study this form thinking the standards of ballet were the only way.

I felt an excitement at seeing that immediate break from the dancers' *doing* something to their *being* the *people* doing that something. It excited me visually, kinesthetically, and aesthetically. They stood there and stared at the conductor for a minute, then ran upstage, got into place, and started again. At the time, I didn't include that moment of their dropping out as part of my concept of dance. It looked so separate. That separation is what eventually really interested me and still does.

The other odd layer to this event was that my friend, who had been looking at her program, missed it all. It happened very fast. I had to wonder, "Did it happen at all?" I trust my memory that it did. But the person I was with didn't see it, so there's that wonderful bit of doubt, did I make it up? That story became the opening in my work *Grass/Bird/Rodeo* about authenticity of memory and what is real.

I studied modern dance more and more in high school and then went to undergraduate school in Utah. My parents encouraged me to go far away to college. They thought I should

# Preface to the First Edition

There are professions more harmful than industrial design, but only a very few of them. And possibly only one profession is phonier. Advertising design, in persuading people to buy things they don't need, with money they don't have, in order to impress others who don't care, is probably the phoniest field in existence today. Industrial design, by concocting the tawdry idiocies hawked by advertisers, comes a close second. Never before in history have grown men sat down and seriously designed electric hairbrushes, rhinestone-covered shoe horns, and mink carpeting for bathrooms, and then drawn up elaborate plans to make and sell these gadgets to millions of people. Before (in the "good old days"), if a person liked killing people, he had to become a general, purchase a coal mine, or else study nuclear physics. Today, industrial design has put murder on a mass-production basis. By designing criminally unsafe automobiles that kill or maim nearly one million people around the world each year, by creating whole new species of permanent garbage to clutter up the landscape, and by choosing materials and processes that pollute the air we breath, designers have become a dangerous breed. And the skills needed in these activities are carefully taught to young people.

In this age of mass production when everything must be planned and designed, design has become the most powerful tool with which man shapes his tools and environments (and, by extension, society and himself). This demands high social and moral responsibility from the designer. It also demands greater understanding of the people by those who practice demoutonnent les nuages, et la vue d'un seul coquelicot hissant au bout de son cordage et faisant cingler au vent sa flamme rouge, au-dessus de sa bouée graisseuse et noire, me faisait battre le cœur, comme au voyageur qui aperçoit sur une terre basse une première barque échouée que répare un calfat, et s'écrie, avant de l'avoir encore vue : « La Mer ! »

Puis je revenais devant les aubépines comme devant ces chefs-d'œuvre dont on croit qu'on saura mieux les voir quand on a cessé un moment de les regarder, mais j'avais beau me faire un écran de mes mains pour n'avoir qu'elles sous les yeux, le sentiment qu'elles éveillaient en moi restait obscur et vague, cherchant en vain à se dégager, à venir adhérer à leurs fleurs. Elles ne m'aidaient pas à l'éclaircir, et je ne pouvais demander à d'autres fleurs de le satisfaire. Alors me donnant cette joie que nous éprouvons quand nous voyons de notre peintre préféré une œuvre qui diffère de celles que nous connaissions, ou bien si l'on nous mène devant un tableau dont nous n'avions vu jusque-là qu'une esquisse au crayon, si un morceau entendu seulement au piano nous apparaît ensuite revêtu des couleurs de l'orchestre, mon grand-père m'appelant et me désignant la haie de Tansonville, me dit : « Toi qui aimes les aubépines, regarde un peu cette épine rose ; est-elle jolie ! » En effet c'était une épine, mais rose, plus belle encore que les blanches. Elle aussi avait une parure de fête – de ces seules vraies fêtes que sont les fêtes religieuses, puisqu'un caprice contingent ne les applique pas comme les fêtes mondaines à un jour quelconque qui ne leur est pas spécialement destiné, qui n'a rien d'essentiellement férié – mais une parure plus riche encore, car les fleurs attachées sur la branche, les unes au-dessus des autres, de manière à ne laisser aucune place qui ne fût décorée, comme des pompons qui enguirlandent une houlette rococo, étaient « en couleur », par conséquent d'une qualité supérieure selon l'esthétique de Combray, si l'on en jugeait par l'échelle des prix dans le « magasin » de la Place, ou chez Camus où étaient plus chers ceux des biscuits qui étaient roses. Moi-même j'appréciais plus le fromage à la crème rose, celui où l'on m'avait permis d'écraser des fraises. Et justement ces fleurs avaient choisi une de ces teintes de chose mangeable, ou de tendre embellissement à une toilette pour une grande fête, qui, parce qu'elles leur présentent la raison de leur supériorité, sont celles qui semblent belles avec le plus d'évidence aux yeux des enfants, et à cause de cela, gardent toujours pour eux quelque chose de plus vif et de plus naturel que les autres teintes, même lorsqu'ils ont compris qu'elles ne promettaient rien à leur gourmandise et n'avaient pas été choisies par la couturière. Et certes, je l'avais tout de suite senti, comme devant les épines blanches mais avec plus d'émerveillement, que ce n'était pas facticement, par un artifice de fabrication humaine, qu'était traduite l'intention de festivité dans les fleurs, mais que c'était la nature qui, spontanément, l'avait exprimée avec la naïveté d'une commerçante de village travaillant pour un reposoir, en surchargeant

"What are you gawking at?"

I didn't feel like talking, it was stuffy, the tea. I replied:

"That line there, in the corner, behind the island, and that sort of a triangle . . . Next to the straits."

"What?"

"Nothing."

"What about it?"

"Well . . ."

After a long while I asked:

"What does it remind you of?"

"That smudge and the line?" he took it up eagerly, and I knew why so eagerly, I knew this would distract him from Drozdowski. "That? I'll tell you, just a minute. A rake."

"Maybe a rake."

Lena joined in the conversation because we were playing at guessing, a parlor game, easy and in keeping with her shyness.

"What do you mean a rake?! It's a little arrow."

Fuks protested: "Nonsense, it's not an arrow!"

A couple of minutes filled with something else, Ludwik asked Leon, "Would you like to play chess, father?" I had a broken fingernail that was bothering me, a newspaper fell to the floor, dogs barked outside the window (two little dogs, young, amusing, off their leashes at night, there was also a cat), Leon said, "One game," Fuks said:

"Maybe it is an arrow."

"Maybe an arrow, maybe not an arrow," I remarked, I picked up the newspaper, Ludwik rose, a bus rolled down the road, Roly-Poly asked "did you make that phone call?"



*Witold Gombrowicz*



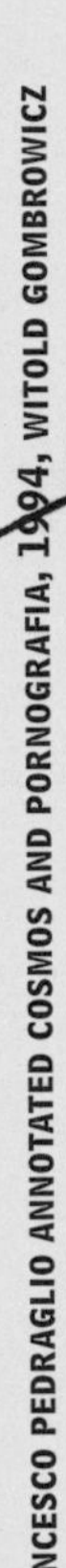

## chapter 2

I don't know how to tell this . . . this story . . . because I'm telling it *ex post.* The arrow, for instance . . . The arrow, for instance . . . The arrow, at that time, at supper, was no more important than Leon's chess, or the newspaper, or tea, everything—equally important, everything—was contributing to a given moment, a kind of consonance, the buzzing of a swarm. But today, *ex post,* I know it was the arrow that was the most important, so in telling this I move it to the forefront, from a myriad of undifferentiated facts I extract the configuration of the future. But how can one describe something except *ex post?* Can nothing be ever truly expressed, rendered in its anonymous becoming, can no one ever render the babbling of the nascent moment, how is it that, born out of chaos, we can never encounter it again, no sooner do we look than order . . . and form . . . are born under our very eyes? No matter. Never mind. Katasia made me with breakfast every morning and, with my eyes just opened from sleep, I would catch above me the impropriety of her mouth, that slippery slipaway lip superimposed on her peasant woman's

This Book discusses the idea of Cultural Capital which means NON Financial assets such as education, which promotes social mobility beyond economic means, and how this is likely to ~~determine~~ determine what constitutes TASTE specifically talking about those with LOW overall capital who are unable to access "high" culture because they dont have the means to access it.

I would also recommend reading "why working class kids get working class jobs" by Paul Willis. Both talk of the acceptance of dominant forms of taste as a form of symbolic violence AND that the "working class aesthetic is a Dominated aestetic obligated to defign itself interms of the Rulling class.

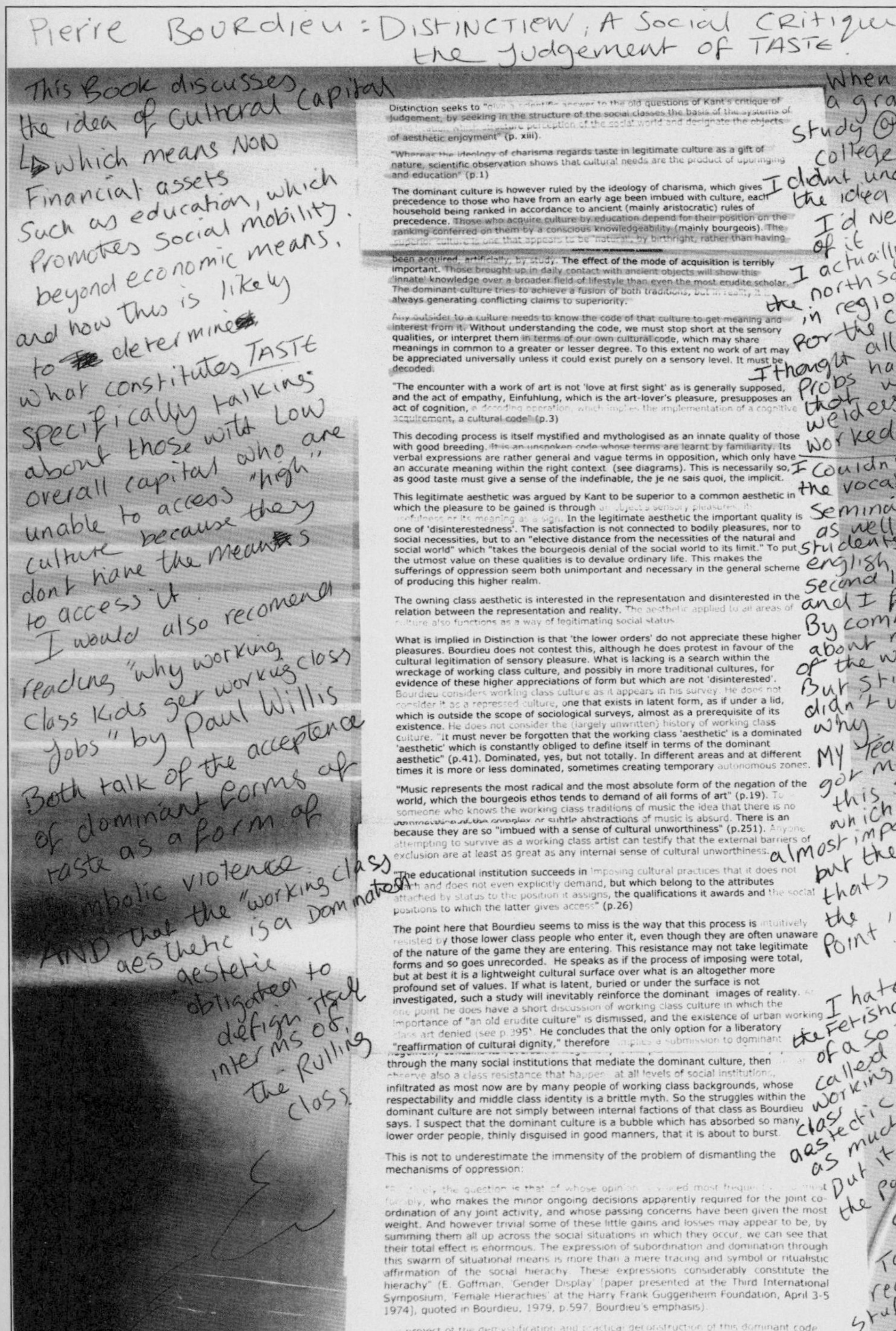

Distinction seeks to "give a scientific answer to the old questions of Kant's critique of judgement, by seeking in the structure of the social classes the basis of the systems of classification which structure perception of the social world and designate the objects of aesthetic enjoyment" (p. xiii).

"Whereas the ideology of charisma regards taste in legitimate culture as a gift of nature, scientific observation shows that cultural needs are the product of upbringing and education" (p.1)

The dominant culture is however ruled by the ideology of charisma, which gives precedence to those who have from an early age been imbued with culture, each household being ranked in accordance to ancient (mainly aristocratic) rules of precedence. Those who acquire culture by education depend for their position on the ranking conferred on them by a conscious knowledgeability (mainly bourgeois). The superior culture is one that appears to be "natural", by birthright, rather than having been acquired, artificially, by study. The effect of the mode of acquisition is terribly important. Those brought up in daily contact with ancient objects will show this 'innate' knowledge over a broader field of lifestyle than even the most erudite scholar. The dominant culture tries to achieve a fusion of both traditions, but in reality it is always generating conflicting claims to superiority.

Any outsider to a culture needs to know the code of that culture to get meaning and interest from it. Without understanding the code, we must stop short at the sensory qualities, or interpret them in terms of our own cultural code, which may share meanings in common to a greater or lesser degree. To this extent no work of art may be appreciated universally unless it could exist purely on a sensory level. It must be decoded.

"The encounter with a work of art is not 'love at first sight' as is generally supposed, and the act of empathy, Einfuhlung, which is the art-lover's pleasure, presupposes an act of cognition, a decoding operation, which implies the implementation of a cognitive acquirement, a cultural code" (p.3)

This decoding process is itself mystified and mythologised as an innate quality of those with good breeding. It is an unspoken code whose terms are learnt by familiarity. Its verbal expressions are rather general and vague terms in opposition, which only have an accurate meaning within the right context (see diagrams). This is necessarily so, as good taste must give a sense of the indefinable, the je ne sais quoi, the implicit.

This legitimate aesthetic was argued by Kant to be superior to a common aesthetic in which the pleasure to be gained is through an object's sensory pleasures, its usefulness or its meaning as a sign. In the legitimate aesthetic the important quality is one of 'disinterestedness'. The satisfaction is not connected to bodily pleasures, nor to social necessities, but to an "elective distance from the necessities of the natural and social world" which "takes the bourgeois denial of the social world to its limit." To put the utmost value on these qualities is to devalue ordinary life. This makes the sufferings of oppression seem both unimportant and necessary in the general scheme of producing this higher realm.

The owning class aesthetic is interested in the representation and disinterested in the relation between the representation and reality. The aesthetic applied to all areas of culture also functions as a way of legitimating social status.

What is implied in Distinction is that 'the lower orders' do not appreciate these higher pleasures. Bourdieu does not contest this, although he does protest in favour of the cultural legitimation of sensory pleasure. What is lacking is a search within the wreckage of working class culture, and possibly in more traditional cultures, for evidence of these higher appreciations of form but which are not 'disinterested'. Bourdieu considers working class culture as it appears in his survey. He does not consider it as a repressed culture, one that exists in latent form, as if under a lid, which is outside the scope of sociological surveys, almost as a prerequisite of its existence. He does not consider the (largely unwritten) history of working class culture. "It must never be forgotten that the working class 'aesthetic' is a dominated 'aesthetic' which is constantly obliged to define itself in terms of the dominant aesthetic" (p.41). Dominated, yes, but not totally. In different areas and at different times it is more or less dominated, sometimes creating temporary autonomous zones.

"Music represents the most radical and the most absolute form of the negation of the world, which the bourgeois ethos tends to demand of all forms of art" (p.19). To someone who knows the working class traditions of music the idea that there is no appreciation of the complex or subtle abstractions of music is absurd. There is an because they are so "imbued with a sense of cultural unworthiness" (p.251). Anyone attempting to survive as a working class artist can testify that the external barriers of exclusion are at least as great as any internal sense of cultural unworthiness.

"The educational institution succeeds in imposing cultural practices that it does not teach and does not even explicitly demand, but which belong to the attributes attached by status to the position it assigns, the qualifications it awards and the social positions to which the latter gives access" (p.26)

The point here that Bourdieu seems to miss is the way that this process is intuitively resisted by those lower class people who enter it, even though they are often unaware of the nature of the game they are entering. This resistance may not take legitimate forms and so goes unrecorded. He speaks as if the process of imposing were total, but at best it is a lightweight cultural surface over what is an altogether more profound set of values. If what is latent, buried or under the surface is not investigated, such a study will inevitably reinforce the dominant images of reality. At one point he does have a short discussion of working class culture in which the importance of "an old erudite culture" is dismissed, and the existence of urban working class art denied (see p. 395). He concludes that the only option for a liberatory "reaffirmation of cultural dignity," therefore implies a submission to dominant hegemony, through the many social institutions that mediate the dominant culture, then observe also a class resistance that happens at all levels of social institutions, infiltrated as most now are by many people of working class backgrounds, whose respectability and middle class identity is a brittle myth. So the struggles within the dominant culture are not simply between internal factions of that class as Bourdieu says. I suspect that the dominant culture is a bubble which has absorbed so many lower order people, thinly disguised in good manners, that it is about to burst.

This is not to underestimate the immensity of the problem of dismantling the mechanisms of oppression:

"Ultimately, the question is that of whose opinion is voiced most frequently and most forcibly, who makes the minor ongoing decisions apparently required for the joint co-ordination of any joint activity, and whose passing concerns have been given the most weight. And however trivial some of these little gains and losses may appear to be, by summing them all up across the social situations in which they occur, we can see that their total effect is enormous. The expression of subordination and domination through this swarm of situational means is more than a mere tracing and symbol or ritualistic affirmation of the social hierachy. These expressions considerably constitute the hierachy" (E. Goffman, 'Gender Display' [paper presented at the Third International Symposium, 'Female Hierachies' at the Harry Frank Guggenheim Foundation, April 3-5 1974], quoted in Bourdieu, 1979, p.597, Bourdieu's emphasis).

The project of the demystification and practical deconstruction of this dominant code of manners is our main historic task and one that is well within human capabilities. But first we must dare to face it fairly and squarely.

When i got a grant to study @ goldsmiths college for free, I didnt understand the idea of 'class', I'd never heard of it I actually mistook the north south devide in regional accents for the class divide. I thought all northerns had parents probs were welders or worked in Texico. I couldn't understand the vocabulary in Seminars half as well as some students where english was there second language and I felt hurt By comments about my tastes of the way i dressed. But still, didn't understand why My teachers got me reading this sort of stuff which was almost impossible but then, thats the point!

I hate the fetisharion of a so-called working class aastectic just as much, But it was the painfully gruelling Task of reading this stuff that helped me understand why

Thank god for free education....



HANNAH PERRY ANNOTATED DISTINCTION: A SOCIAL CRITIQUE OF THE JUDGEMENT OF TASTE, 1979, PIERRE BOURDIEU

# Listening

## The Exercise

Sit either on the floor or in a chair.
If on the floor, use a cushion to raise the sitz bones.
If sitting in a chair, feet are flat on the floor.
The legs should be crossed either in full lotus position,[48] or tucked in close to the body with the knees relaxed downward to the floor.
Posture is relaxed upper body, chin tucked in slightly, balanced on the 'sitz' bones and knees.
Palms rest on the thighs, or palms folded close to the belly.
Eyes are relaxed with the lids half or fully closed.

At the sound of a bell or gong listen inclusively for the interplay of sounds in the whole space/time continuum. Include the sounds of your own thoughts. Can you imagine that you are the center of the whole?

Use this mantra[49] to aid your listening:
*With each breath I return to the whole of the space/time continuum.*

If a sound takes your attention to a focus, then follow the sound all the way to the end as you return to the whole of the space/time continuum.

At the sound of the bell prepare to review your experience and describe it in your journal.

## Commentary

The sitting position described for the exercise is common to many meditation practices. However the two forms of attention—focal and global—are directed in Deep Listening practice to sound/silence. An objective is to feel the sharp contrast between the two forms of attention—the clear detail of a sound or sequence of sounds using focal attention and the expansion to multiple sources sounding simultaneously in multi-dimensions with global attention.

It is important to review your listening experience and to compare your prior and after feelings, sensations, intuitions and thoughts and write them in your journal. As experiences accumulate in your journal, patterns of listening may become discernable and progress will become apparent.

# Ways of Listening

## Forms of Attention

Focal attention, like a lens, produces clear detail limited to the object of attention. Global attention is diffuse and continually expanding to take in the whole of the space/time continuum of sound. Sensitivity is to the flow of sounds and details are not necessarily clear. For example, the crowd noise at a baseball game changes when the focal crack of a bat against a ball is heard. If there is a home run, then the voices of the crowd unify from a fuzzy global rumble into a loud focused roar.

The practice of Deep Listening encourages the balancing of these two forms of attention so that one can flexibly employ both forms and recognize the difference between these two forms of listening.

There are many ways of listening to be discovered and explored. Listening is used in innumerable ways. Here are some of the ways:

"Detection, isolation, and interpretation of subtle variations in a sonic environment…listening in search, listening in readiness, and background listening…highly attuned to direction, timbre, and texture… Confessional—configuration of listening and speaking".[50]

Lou Gottlieb's secret for listening to non-stop rappers: "Just listen to the melody of their talk, not to the content, as you would listen to a babbling brook".[51]

## Sending and Receiving

If you are speaking, singing, performing with an instrument or otherwise sounding, then you are sending. Are you receiving what you send and also receiving the whole of the space/time continuum of sound?

Use this mantra:
*With each breath I send sound and receive sound.*

## Sound/Silence

There is no sound without silence before and after. Sound/silence is a symbiotic relationship. Sound and silence are relative to one another. Time relationships may be instantaneous to very long. Listening to sounds means listening to silences, and vice versa.

There is no absolute silence unless there is zero vibration. Silence means that we can hear no sounds. Silence is the space between sounds.

## Palms of Hands

Rub the palms of the hands together vigorously to make them very warm and to energize the nerve endings.

Hold the palms a little apart and parallel in front of you and sense the energy field* between them as if you were holding a sphere or ball. Your hands maybe close together or further apart to perceive the effect.

Massage this ball of energy and gradually bring the palms of your hands to a folded position just under your navel. (Men place left hand under right hand, women right hand under left hand).[52]

Receive the warmth from your palms into this lower body center (dan t'ien)[53]

If you don't feel the subtle tingling sensations, your energy may be blocked by stiff shoulders or other tensions elsewhere in the body. Breathe deeply to release the tension and continue to sense the palms of your hands.

## Soles of Feet

The soles of the feet are your connection to earth (even through the floor). The sole is sensitive with many nerve endings and connections to the inner organs.[54]

As you stand, allow energy to flow to the soles of the feet.

Soften the knees and grip the earth.

Follow the sensations that return from the soles of the feet throughout the body. As you grip the earth with the soles of your feet, there is a reaction force—a return of energy from the earth. This reaction force can give you a feeling of strength.

By bringing attention to the soles of the feet,[55] energy can be raised in the body. The reaction force of gripping the earth with the feet in natural stance can help to promote circulation in the body.

## Whole Body

As you listen, notice the impact and effects of sound throughout the body.

Notice when you feel sound in your body.

If you are in conversation, receive with your whole body what is being said.

## Multi-dimensional Listening

Sounds are both temporal and spatial. As we converse with a partner, there is space between us created by the sound of our voices and the proximity of our bodies. The sound of the conversation can radiate out of the intended intimate space and be heard by others not necessarily included in the conversation. The intimate dimension is overlapping with a more public dimension that we may or may not be aware of. We can hear the dimensions of the space consciously and unconsciously. Simultaneously we may be taking in other dimensions—a dog barking outside, other conversations in the same room, passing traffic and so forth. Our global attention is engaging with numerous overlapping dimensions created by sounds. At the same time we may be imagining what to say next. We then feel the dimension of imagination or memory.

We are giving attention to more than one flow of sound, in parallel or simultaneously, as well as discerning the direction and context. For example, attending to a conversation, music and external sounds that are cues for something to happen, like a siren or telephone, without breaking any flow. Readiness to listen is always present while already engaged in listening.

Dimensions of sound/silence are the space created by the sound/silence, the instant of the sound/silence, the duration, the quality, the relationship between the listener and the sound/silence, the volume and location (actual and perceived).

The depth of listening is related to the expansion of consciousness brought about by inclusive listening. Inclusive listening is impartial, open and receiving and employs global attention. Deep Listening has limitless dimensions.

Attention narrows for exclusive listening. Exclusive listening gathers detail and employs focal attention. Focal attention is necessarily limited and specific. The depth of exclusive listening is clarity.

# FREE CULTURE

**THE NATURE AND FUTURE OF CREATIVITY**

## LAWRENCE LESSIG

PENGUIN BOOKS


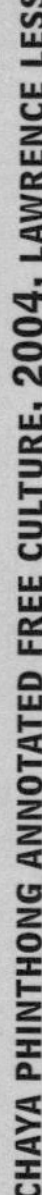

PENGUIN BOOKS
Published by the Penguin Group
Penguin Group (USA) Inc., 375 Hudson Street, New York, New York 10014, U.S.A.
Penguin Group (Canada), 90 Eglinton Avenue East, Suite 700, Toronto,
Ontario, Canada M4P 2Y3 (a division of Pearson Penguin Canada Inc.)
Penguin Books Ltd, 80 Strand, London WC2R 0RL, England
Penguin Ireland, 25 St Stephen's Green, Dublin 2, Ireland (a division of Penguin Books Ltd)
Penguin Group (Australia), 250 Camberwell Road, Camberwell, Victoria 3124, Australia
(a division of Pearson Australia Group Pty Ltd)
Penguin Books India Pvt Ltd, 11 Community Centre, Panchsheel Park,
New Delhi - 110 017, India
Penguin Group (NZ), 67 Apollo Drive, Rosedale, North Shore 0632, New Zealand
(a division of Pearson New Zealand Ltd)
Penguin Books (South Africa) (Pty) Ltd, 24 Sturdee Avenue,
Rosebank, Johannesburg 2196, South Africa

Penguin Books Ltd, Registered Offices: 8o Strand, London WC2R 0RL, England

First published in the United States of America by The Penguin Press,
a member of Penguin Group (USA) Inc. 2004
Published in Penguin Books 2005

7  9  10  8

Copyright © Lawrence Lessig, 2004
All rights reserved

Excerpt from an editorial titled 'The Coming of Copyright Perpetuity," *The New York Times*,
January 16, 2003. Copyright © 2003 by The New York Times Co.
Reprinted with permission.
Cartoon by Paul Conrad on page 159. Copyright Tribune Media Services, Inc.
All rights reserved. Reprinted with permission.
Diagram on page 164 courtesy of the office of FCC Commissioner, Michael J. Copps.

THE LIBRARY OF CONGRESS HAS CATALOGED THE HARDCOVER EDITION AS FOLLOWS:
Lessig, Lawrence.
Free culture : how big media uses technology and the law to lock down culture and control creativity /
Lawrence Lessig.
p. cm.
Includes index.
ISBN 1-59420-006-8 (hc.)
ISBN 978-0-14-303465-0 (pbk.)
1. Intellectual property—United States.   2. Mass media—United States.   3. Technological
innovations—United States.   4. Art—United States.   I. Title.
KF2979.L47  2004
343.7309'9—dc22      2003063276

Printed in the United States of America
Designed by Marysarah Quinn

SOME HERO-TOOLS OF PATRIARCHAL HISTORY _ WHAT GETS SAVED VS. WHAT IS DEEMED NOT VALUABLE THESE STORIES ARE TOLD:

UNCHANGING FOREVER NSURPRISE

NOT SURPRISE

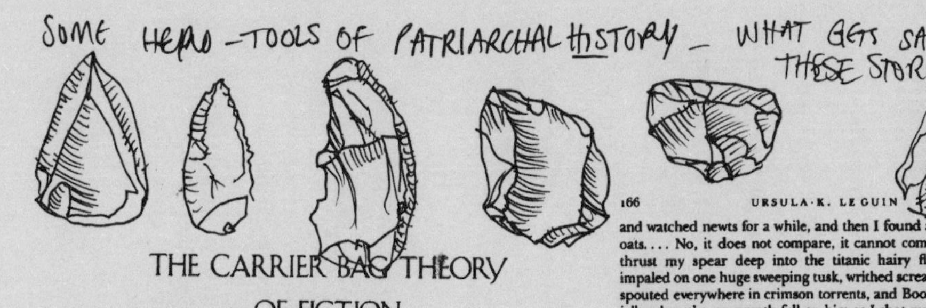

## THE CARRIER BAG THEORY
## OF FICTION

RACHEL PIMM ON     (1986)
URSULA K. LE GUIN  OCT 21, 1929 –
JAN 22, 2018

336

In the temperate and tropical regions where it appears that hominids evolved into human beings, the principal food of the species was vegetable. Sixty-five to eighty percent of what human beings ate in those regions in Paleolithic, Neolithic, and prehistoric times was gathered; only in the extreme Arctic was meat the staple food. The mammoth hunters spectacularly occupy the cave wall and the mind, but what we actually did to stay alive and fat was gather seeds, roots, sprouts, shoots, leaves, nuts, berries, fruits, and grains, adding bugs and mollusks and netting or snaring birds, fish, rats, rabbits, and other tuskless small fry to up the protein. And we didn't even work hard at it—much less hard than peasants slaving in somebody else's field after agriculture was invented, much less hard than paid workers since civilization was invented. The average prehistoric person could make a nice living in about a fifteen-hour work week.

Fifteen hours a week for subsistence leaves a lot of time for other things. So much time that maybe the restless ones who didn't have a baby around to enliven their life, or skill in making or cooking or singing, or very interesting thoughts to think, decided to slope off and hunt mammoths. The skillful hunters then would come staggering back with a load of meat, a lot of ivory, and a story. It wasn't the meat that made the difference. It was the story.

It is hard to tell a really gripping tale of how I wrested a wild-oat seed from its husk, and then another, and then another, and then another, and then another, and then I scratched my gnat bites, and Ool said something funny, and we went to the creek and got a drink

165

166     URSULA·K·LE GUIN

and watched newts for a while, and then I found another patch of oats. . . . No, it does not compare, it cannot compete with how I thrust my spear deep into the titanic hairy flank while Oob, impaled on one huge sweeping tusk, writhed screaming, and blood spouted everywhere in crimson torrents, and Boob was crushed to jelly when the mammoth fell on him as I shot my unerring arrow straight through eye to brain.

That story not only has Action, it has a Hero. Heroes are powerful. Before you know it, the men and women in the wild-oat patch and their kids and the skills of the makers and the thoughts of the thoughtful and the songs of the singers are all part of it, have all been pressed into service in the tale of the Hero. But it isn't their story. It's his.

When she was planning the book that ended up as *Three Guineas*, Virginia Woolf wrote a heading in her notebook, "Glossary"; she had thought of reinventing English according to a new plan, in order to tell a different story. One of the entries in this glossary is *heroism*, defined as "botulism." And *hero*, in Woolf's dictionary, is "bottle." The hero as bottle, a stringent reevaluation. I now propose the bottle as hero.

Not just the bottle of gin or wine, but bottle in its older sense of container in general, a thing that holds something else.

If you haven't got something to put it in, food will escape you—even something as uncombative and unresourceful as an oat. You put as many as you can into your stomach while they are handy, that being the primary container; but what about tomorrow morning when you wake up and it's cold and raining and wouldn't it be good to have just a few handfuls of oats to chew on and give little Oom to make her shut up, but how do you get more than one stomachful and one handful home? So you get up and go to the damned soggy oat patch in the rain, and wouldn't it be a good thing if you had something to put Baby Oo Oo in so that you could pick the oats with both hands? A leaf a gourd a shell a net a bag a sling a sack a bottle a pot a box a container. A holder. A recipient.

The first cultural device was probably a recipient. . . . Many theorizers feel that the earliest cultural inventions must have been a container to hold gathered products and some kind of sling or net carrier.

So says Elizabeth Fisher in *Women's Creation* (McGraw-Hill, 1975). But no, this cannot be. Where is that wonderful, big, long, hard

THE CARRIER BAG THEORY OF FICTION     167

thing, a bone, I believe, that the Ape Man first bashed somebody with in the movie and then, grunting with ecstasy at having achieved the first proper murder, flung up into the sky, and whirling there it became a space ship thrusting its way into the cosmos to fertilize it and produce at the end of the movie a lovely fetus, a boy of course, drifting around the Milky Way without (oddly enough) any womb, any matrix at all? I don't know. I don't even care. I'm not telling that story. We've heard it, we've all heard all about all the sticks and spears and swords, the things to bash and poke and hit with, the long, hard things, but we have not heard about the thing to put things in, the container for the thing contained. That is a new story. That is news.

And yet old. Before—once you think about it, surely long before—the weapon, a late, luxurious, superfluous tool; long before the useful knife and ax; right along with the indispensable whacker, grinder, and digger—for what's the use of digging up a lot of potatoes if you have nothing to lug the ones you can't eat home in—with or before the tool that forces energy outward, we made the tool that brings energy home. It makes sense to me. I am an adherent of what Fisher calls the Carrier Bag Theory of human evolution.

This theory not only explains large areas of theoretical obscurity and avoids large areas of theoretical nonsense (inhabited largely by tigers, foxes, and other highly territorial mammals); it also grounds me, personally, in human culture in a way I never felt grounded before. So long as culture was explained as originating from and elaborating upon the use of long, hard objects for sticking, bashing, and killing, I never thought that I had, or wanted, any particular share in it. ("What Freud mistook for her lack of civilization is woman's lack of *loyalty* to civilization," Lillian Smith observed.) The society, the civilization they were talking about, these theoreticians, was evidently theirs; they owned it, they liked it; they were human, fully human, bashing, sticking, thrusting, killing. Wanting to be human too, I sought for evidence that I was; but if that's what it took, to make a weapon and kill with it, then evidently I was either extremely defective as a human being, or not human at all.

That's right, they said. What you are is a woman. Possibly not human at all, certainly defective. Now be quiet while we go on telling the Story of the Ascent of Man the Hero.

Go on, say I, wandering off towards the wild oats, with Oo Oo in the sling and little Oom carrying the basket. You just go on telling how the mammoth fell on Boob and how Cain fell on Abel and how

BAGS: BODY(IES), WOMEN, WOMXN, HUMANS, STOMACHP, GUTS, HANDS, VAGINAS, MOUTHS, EAR CANALS, ELBOW DITCHES, HEDGEROWS, DITCHES, CRACKS, ANUSES, BODY BAGS, GLOVES, SOCKS, CLOTHES, PILL CAPSULES, VOLCANOS, FOLDS, FAULTS, SHELLS, EXOSKELETONS, CELL WALLS, the bomb fell on Nagasaki and how the burning jelly fell on the villagers and how the missiles will fall on the Evil Empire, and all the other steps in the Ascent of Man.

If it is a human thing to do to put something you want, because it's useful, edible, or beautiful, into a bag, or a basket, or a bit of rolled bark or leaf, or a net woven of your own hair, or what have you, and then take it home with you, home being another, larger kind of pouch or bag, a container for people, and then later on you take it out and eat it or share it or store it up for winter in a solider container or put it in the medicine bundle or the shrine or the museum, the holy place, the area that contains what is sacred, and then next day you probably do much the same again—if to do that is human, if that's what it takes, then I am a human being after all. Fully, freely, gladly, for the first time.

Not, let it be said at once, an unaggressive or uncombative human being. I am an aging, angry woman laying mightily about me with my handbag, fighting hoodlums off. However I don't, nor does anybody else, consider myself heroic for doing so. It's just one of those damned things you have to do in order to be able to go on gathering wild oats and telling stories.

It is the story that makes the difference. It is the story that hid my humanity from me, the story the mammoth hunters told about bashing, thrusting, raping, killing, about the Hero. The wonderful, poisonous story of Botulism. The killer story.

It sometimes seems that that story is approaching its end. Lest there be no more telling of stories at all, some of us out here in the wild oats, amid the alien corn, think we'd better start telling another one, which maybe people can go on with when the old one's finished. Maybe. The trouble is, we've all let ourselves become part of the killer story, and so we may get finished along with it. Hence it is with a certain feeling of urgency that I seek the nature, subject, words of the other story, the untold one, the life story.

It's unfamiliar, it doesn't come easily, thoughtlessly to the lips as the killer story does; but still, "untold" was an exaggeration. People have been telling the life story for ages, in all sorts of words and ways. Myths of creation and transformation, trickster stories, folktales, jokes, novels . . .

The novel is a fundamentally unheroic kind of story. Of course the Hero has frequently taken it over, that being his imperial nature and uncontrollable impulse, to take everything over and run it while making stern decrees and laws to control his uncontrollable impulse



to kill it. So the Hero has decreed through his mouthpieces the Lawgivers, first, that the proper shape of the narrative is that of the arrow or spear, starting here and going straight there and THOK! hitting its mark (which drops dead); second, that the central concern of narrative, including the novel, is conflict; and third, that the story isn't any good if he isn't in it.

I differ with all of this. I would go so far as to say that the natural, proper, fitting shape of the novel might be that of a sack, a bag. A book holds words. Words hold things. They bear meanings. A novel is a medicine bundle, holding things in a particular, powerful relation to one another and to us.

One relationship among elements in the novel may well be that of conflict, but the reduction of narrative to conflict is absurd. (I have read a how-to-write manual that said, "A story should be seen as a battle," and went on about strategies, attacks, victory, etc.) Conflict, competition, stress, struggle, etc., within the narrative conceived as carrier bag / belly / box / house / medicine bundle, may be seen as necessary elements of a whole which itself cannot be characterized either as conflict or as harmony, since its purpose is neither resolution nor stasis but continuing process.

Finally, it's clear that the Hero does not look well in this bag. He needs a stage or a pedestal or a pinnacle. You put him in a bag and he looks like a rabbit, like a potato.

That is why I like novels: instead of heroes they have people in them.

So, when I came to write science-fiction novels, I came lugging this great heavy sack of stuff, my carrier bag full of wimps and klutzes, and tiny grains of things smaller than a mustard seed, and intricately woven nets which when laboriously unknotted are seen to contain one blue pebble, an imperturbably functioning chronometer telling the time on another world, and a mouse's skull; full of beginnings without ends, of initiations, of losses, of transformations and translations, and far more tricks than conflicts, far fewer triumphs than snares and delusions; full of space ships that get stuck, missions that fail, and people who don't understand. I said it was hard to make a gripping tale of how we wrested the wild oats from their husks, I didn't say it was impossible. Who ever said writing a novel was easy?

If science fiction is the mythology of modern technology, then its myth is tragic. "Technology," or "modern science" (using the words as they are usually used, in an unexamined shorthand standing for



the "hard" sciences and high technology founded upon continuous economic growth), is a heroic undertaking, Herculean, Promethean, conceived as triumph, hence ultimately as tragedy. The fiction embodying this myth will be, and has been, triumphant (Man conquers earth, space, aliens, death, the future, etc.) and tragic (apocalypse, holocaust, then or now).

If, however, one avoids the linear, progressive, Time's-(killing)-arrow mode of the Techno-Heroic, and redefines technology and science as primarily cultural carrier bag rather than weapon of domination, one pleasant side effect is that science fiction can be seen as a far less rigid, narrow field, not necessarily Promethean or apocalyptic at all, and in fact less a mythological genre than a realistic one.

It is a strange realism, but it is a strange reality.

Science fiction properly conceived, like all serious fiction, however funny, is a way of trying to describe what is in fact going on, what people actually do and feel, how people relate to everything else in this vast sack, this belly of the universe, this womb of things to be and tomb of things that were, this unending story. In it, as in all fiction, there is room enough to keep even Man where he belongs, in his place in the scheme of things; there is time enough to gather plenty of wild oats and sow them too, and sing to little Oom, and listen to Ool's joke, and watch newts, and still the story isn't over. Still there are seeds to be gathered, and room in the bag of stars.

LIKE GETTING WET — THIS IS A LIE

THIS ISN'T A RECORD COVER IT IS THE WRITING

This is a RECORD COVER. This writing is the DESIGN upon the

FROM AN XTC RECORD COVER. I'M SORT OF

record cover. The DESIGN is to help SELL the record. We hope

INDIFFERENT ABOUT XTC, MAKING PLANS FOR

to draw your attention to it and encourage you to pick it up.

NIGEL IS A FUN SONG, BUT I REALLY LIKE THIS

When you have done that maybe you'll be persuaded to listen to

ALBUM COVER. I USED TO READ IT OVER AND OVER

the music — in this case XTC's Go 2 album. Then we want you

AGAIN WHEN I WAS WORKING IN AN OFFICE

to BUY it. The idea being that the more of you that buy this

FOR AN ART SHIPPING COMPANY CALLED MOMART

record the more money Virgin Records, the manager Ian Reid and

AND I FELT LIKE I WAS WIPING DAMIEN HIRST'S ARSE

XTC themselves will make. To the aforementioned this is known

FOR HIM AND I VERY QUICKLY WORKED OUT THAT

as PLEASURE. A good cover DESIGN is one that attracts more

THE ARSE END OF ARTS ADMINISTRATION WAS

buyers and gives more pleasure. This writing is trying to pull

A VALUABLE EDUCATION IF YOU WANT TO BE

you in much like an eye-catching picture. It is designed to get

AN EXPERT IN THE **MULTIPLE, PREDICTABLE AND**

you to READ IT. This is called luring the VICTIM, and you are

**BANAL HIERARCHIES OF** THE ARTS INDUSTRY.

the VICTIM. But if you have a free mind you should STOP READING

SHIPPING HAD PRIMARILY WORKING CLASS *[ASSUMPTION BASED ON EXPERIENCE]*

NOW! because all we are attempting to do is to get you to read

EMPLOYEES, MOST OF WHOM WERE ASPIRING TO

1. Yet this is a DOUBLE BIND because if you indeed stop you'll

BECOME GALLERY REGISTRARS — A PRIZE I THINK

be doing what we tell you, and if you read on you'll be doing what

A FEW RESENTED WHEN THEY WON THE TITLE

we've wanted all along. And the more you read on the more you're

AND I USED TO SIT THERE AND THINK "ITS PAYING

falling for this simple device of telling you exactly how a good

THE RENT EMILY ITS PAYING THE RENT."¹ DO

commercial design works. They're TRICKS and this is the worst

NOT ACTUALLY POKE YOUR BOSS (OR INFACT

TRICK of all since it's describing the TRICK whilst trying to

NEVER PUT MY FOOT IN THE SAME RIVER TWICE I DON'T

HOW BAD AND HOW GOOD DOES IT NEED GET? NOT SURE

UNMENTIONABLE SNOB GALLERINA AT SADIE
COLES) IN THE EYE - SOMEONE IS SHITTING
ON HER FROM A GREAT HEIGHT TOO - HAVE
A BIT OF COMPASSION FOR THE TERMINALLY
RUDE - COMPASSION I HAVE NOW LOST -
YEAH ANYWAY - I NEARLY GOT THE SACK
FROM MOMART A FEW TIMES FOR NOT
DOING WHAT I WAS TOLD AND BEING ON
GOOGLE TOO MUCH. I FOUND THAT GOOGLE
WAS EXCELLENT - INSTEAD OF WORKING OUT
HOW TO GET A MOTH INFESTATION OUT OF
A TIBETAN TENT IMPORTED FOR AN INSTALLATION
BY A FAMOUS XXXX ARTIST (HAD TO ORDER A RENTOKIL
BUBBLE) I COULD LEARN A LOT ONLINE. I USED
TO OBSESSIVELY google THE DEFINITIONS OF
'CAPITALISM' + 'COMMUNISM' AND RESEARCH
'TEXT ART' BECAUSE I WANTED TO GET SMART
AND THIS CAME UP WHEN I SEARCHED 'TEXT ART'
AND I USED TO READ IT OVER AND OVER AGAIN
ALONG WITH DEAD DOLL PARTS BY ACKER AND
IT WAS AN INTRODUCTION TO BEING COMPLICIT
IN OWN PARODY AS A WAY OF MAKING, AND
I STILL QUESTION THE PRODUCTIVITY OF THIS
STANCE AND I NO LONGER WORK IN ART
SHIPPING.

SO SENATOR SO JANITOR

TRICK you, and if you've read this far then you're TRICKED but you wouldn't have known this unless you'd read this far. At least we're telling you directly instead of seducing you with a beautiful or haunting visual that may never tell you. We're letting you know that you ought to buy this record because in essence it's a PRODUCT and PRODUCTS are to be consumed and you are a consumer and this is a good PRODUCT. We could have written the band's name in special lettering so that it stood out and you'd see it before you'd read any of this writing and possibly have bought it anyway. What we are really suggesting is that you are FOOLISH to buy or not buy an album merely as a consequence of the design on its cover. This is a con because if you agree then you'll probably like this writing – which is the cover design – and hence the album inside. But we've just warned you against that. The con is a con. A good cover design could be considered as one that gets you to buy the record, but that never actually happens to YOU because YOU know it's just a design for the cover. And this is the RECORD COVER.

DOM COM = DOMESTIC COMEDY. YOBBY. HALF GIRL HALF DOG. HALF RENT.

I REALLY DON'T LIKE MORRISEY, ALTHOUGH I LOVE THE SMITHS JUST LIKE EVERYBODY ELSE DOES X IE THAT WAS A CANIS MONETISETTE I'D PROBABLY FORGIVE HER ANYTHING FOR THAT ONE LINE. I RUN MY NAILS DOWN EVERY TIME. I RUN MY NAILS DOWN SOMEONE ELSE'S BACK, I HOPE YOU FEEL IT

RATHER BE A 50 GAL WORK GRL

"MAKE CHRISTMAS CARDS FOR THE MOST TALL ILL"

— THIS my way and corrodes my soul

~~it or not, and women—suicides—who wake up in the night screaming.~~

'You hold meetings, then, like the AA?'

'No, of course not. You get a phone number, an answering service you can call. Nobody knows anybody else's name; just the number in case it gets so bad you can't handle it alone. We're isolates, Arnold. Meetings would destroy the whole point of it.'

'What about the person who comes to sit with you? Suppose yo fall in love with them?'

'They go away,' he said. 'You never see them twice. The answering service dispatches them, and they're careful not to hav any repeats.'

~~How did the post horn come in? That went back to their founding.~~ In the early '60s a Yoyodyne executive living near LA and located someplace in the corporate root-system above supervisor but below vice-president, found himself, at age 39, automated out of a job. Having been since age 7 rigidly instructe in an eschatology that pointed nowhere but to a presidency and death, trained to do absolutely nothing but sign his name to specialized memoranda he could not begin to understand and to take blame for the running-amok of specialized programmes tha failed for specialized reasons he had to have explained to him, th executive's first thoughts were naturally of suicide. But previous training got the better of him: he could not make the decision without first hearing the ideas of a committee. He placed an ad i the personal column of the LA *Times*, asking whether anyone who'd been in the same fix had ever found any good reasons for committing suicide. His shrewd assumption being that no suicid would reply, leaving him automatically with only valid inputs. The assumption was false. After a week of anxiously watching mailbox through little Japanese binoculars his wife had given hi for a going-away present (she'd left him the day after he was p slipped) and getting nothing but sucker-list stuff through the regular deliveries that came each noon, he was jolted out of a boozy, black and white dream of jumping off The Stack into ru hour traffic, by an insistent banging at the door. It was late on a Sunday afternoon. He opened his door and found an aged bum with a knitted watch cap on his head and a hook for a hand, wl presented him with a bundle of letters and loped away without

78

word. Most of the letters were from suicides who had failed, either through clumsiness or last-minute cowardice. None of them, however, could offer any compelling reasons for staying alive. Still the executive dithered: spent another week with pieces of paper on which he would list, in columns headed 'pro' and 'con', reasons for and against taking his Brody. He found it impossible, in the absence of some trigger, to come to any clear decision. Finally one day he noticed a front page story in the *Times*, complete with AP wirephoto, about a Buddhist monk in Viet Nam who had set himself on fire to protest government policies. 'Groovy!' cried the executive. He went to the garage, siphoned all the gasoline from his Buick's tank, put on his green Zachary All suit with the vest, stuffed all his letters from unsuccessful suicides into a coat pocket, went in the kitchen, sat on the floor, proceeded to douse himself good with the gasoline. He was about to make the farewell flick of the wheel on his faithful Zippo, which had seen him through the Normandy hedgerows, the Ardennes, Germany, and postwar America, when he heard a key in the front door, and voices. It was his wife and some man, whom he soon recognized as the very efficiency expert at Yoyodyne who had caused him to be replaced by an IBM 7094. Intrigued by the irony of it, he sat in the kitchen and listened, leaving his necktie dipped in the gasoline as a sort of wick. From what he could gather, the efficiency expert wished to have sexual intercourse with the wife on the Moroccan rug in the living-room. The wife was not unwilling. The executive heard lewd laughter, zippers, the thump of shoes, heavy breathing, moans. He took his tie out of the gasoline and started to snigger. He closed the top on his Zippo. 'I hear laughing,' his wife said presently. 'I smell gasoline,' said the efficiency expert. Hand in hand, naked, the two proceeded to the kitchen. 'I was about to do the Buddhist monk thing,' explained the executive. 'Nearly three weeks it takes him,' marvelled the efficiency expert, 'to decide. You know how long it would've taken the IBM 7094? Twelve microseconds. No wonder you were replaced.' The executive threw back his head and laughed for a solid ten minutes, along towards the middle of which his wife and her friend, alarmed, retired, got dressed and went out looking for the police. The executive undressed, showered and hung his suit out on the line to dry. ~~There he noticed a curious thing. The stamps on some of the~~

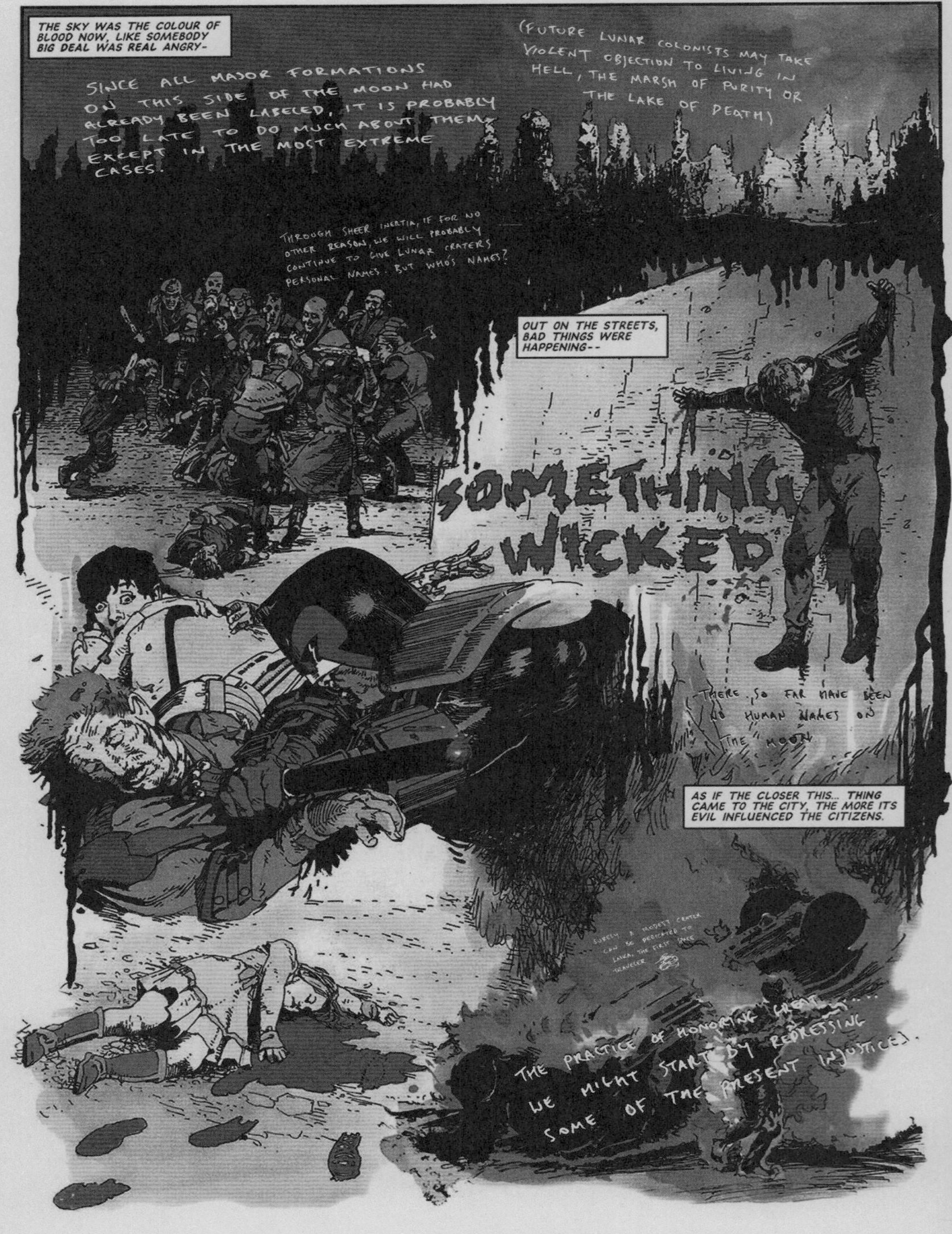
THE SKY WAS THE COLOUR OF BLOOD NOW, LIKE SOMEBODY BIG DEAL WAS REAL ANGRY--
SINCE ALL MAJOR FORMATIONS ON THIS SIDE OF THE MOON HAD ALREADY BEEN LABELED, IT IS PROBABLY TOO LATE TO DO MUCH ABOUT THEM, EXCEPT IN THE MOST EXTREME CASES.
(FUTURE LUNAR COLONISTS MAY TAKE VIOLENT OBJECTION TO LIVING IN HELL, THE MARSH OF PURITY OR THE LAKE OF DEATH)
THROUGH SHEER INERTIA, IF FOR NO OTHER REASON, WE WILL PROBABLY CONTINUE TO GIVE LUNAR CRATERS PERSONAL NAMES. BUT WHO'S NAMES?
OUT ON THE STREETS, BAD THINGS WERE HAPPENING--
SOMETHING WICKED
THERE, SO FAR HAVE BEEN NO HUMAN NAMES ON THE MOON.
AS IF THE CLOSER THIS... THING CAME TO THE CITY, THE MORE ITS EVIL INFLUENCED THE CITIZENS.
SURELY A MODEST CRATER CAN BE DEDICATED TO LANAI, THE FIRST LUNAR TRAVELER
(THE PRACTICE OF HONORING GREAT... WE MIGHT START BY REDRESSING SOME OF THE PRESENT INJUSTICE)

MY FAVOURITE PUBLIC-HOUSE, THE MOON UNDER WATER, IS ONLY TWO MINUTES FROM A BUS STOP, BUT IT IS ON A SIDE-STREET, AND DRUNKS AND ROWDIES NEVER SEEM TO FIND THEIR WAY THERE, EVEN ON SATURDAY NIGHTS.

ITS CLIENTELE, THOUGH FAIRLY LARGE, CONSISTS MOSTLY OF 'REGULARS' WHO OCCUPY THE SAME CHAIR EVERY EVENING AND GO THERE FOR CONVERSATION AS MUCH AS THE BEER.

IF YOU ARE ASKED WHY YOU FAVOUR A PARTICULAR PUBLIC-HOUSE, IT WOULD SEEM NATURAL TO PUT THE BEER FIRST, BUT THE THING THAT MOST APPEALS TO ME ABOUT THE MOON UNDER WATER IS WHAT PEOPLE CALL 'ATMOSPHERE'.

TO BEGIN WITH, ITS WHOLE ARCHITECTURE AND FITTINGS ARE UNCOMPROMISINGLY VICTORIAN. IT HAS NO GLASS-TOPPED TABLES OR OTHER MODERN MISERIES, AND, ON THE OTHER HAND, NO SHAM ROOF-BEAMS, INGLE-NOOKS OR PLASTIC PANELS MASQUERADING AS OAK.

THE GRAINED WOODWORK, THE ORNAMENTAL MIRRORS BEHIND THE BAR, THE CAST-IRON FIREPLACES, THE FLORID CEILING STAINED DARK YELLOW BY TOBACCO-SMOKE, THE STUFFED BULL'S HEAD OVER THE MANTELPIECE EVERYTHING HAS THE SOLID, COMFORTABLE UGLINESS OF THE NINETEENTH CENTURY.

IN WINTER THERE IS GENERALLY A GOOD FIRE BURNING IN AT LEAST TWO OF THE BARS, AND THE VICTORIAN LAYOUT OF THE PLACE GIVES ONE PLENTY OF ELBOW-ROOM. THERE ARE A PUBLIC BAR, A SALOON BAR, A LADIES BAR, A BOTTLE-AND-JUG FOR THOSE WHO ARE TOO BASHFUL TO BUY THEIR SUPPER BEER PUBLICLY, AND, UPSTAIRS, DINING ROOM.

IN WINTER THERE IS GENERALLY A GOOD FIRE BURNING IN AT LEAST TWO OF THE BARS, AND THE VICTORIAN LAYOUT OF THE PLACE GIVES ONE PLENTY OF ELBOW-ROOM. THERE ARE A PUBLIC BAR, A SALOON BAR, A LADIES BAR, A BOTTLE-AND-JUG FOR THOSE WHO ARE TOO BASHFUL TO BUY THEIR SUPPER BEER PUBLICLY, AND, UPSTAIRS, DINING ROOM.

THE BARMAIDS KNOW MOST OF THEIR CUSTOMERS BY NAME, AND TAKE A PERSONAL INTEREST IN EVERYONE. THEY ARE MIDDLE-AGED WOMEN — TWO OF THEM HAVE THEIR HAIR DYED IN QUITE SURPRISING ... IRRESPECTIVE OF AGE OR SEX. ('DEAR' NOT MAID CALLING YOU ... RAFFISH ...

UNLIKE MOST PUBS, THE MOON UNDER WATER, SELLS TOBACCO AS WELL AS CIGARETTES, AND IT ALSO SELLS ASPIRINS AND STAMPS, AND IS OBLIGING ABOUT LETTING YOU USE THE TELEPHONE. YOU CANNOT GET DINNER AT THE MOON UNDER WATER, BUT THERE IS ALWAYS THE SNACK COUNTER WHERE YOU CAN GET LIVER-SAUSAGE SANDWICHES, MUSSELS (A SPECIALITY OF THE HOUSE), CHEESE, PICKLES AND THOSE LARGE BISCUITS WITH CARAWAY SEEDS IN THEM WHICH ONLY SEEM TO EXIST IN PUBLIC-HOUSES. UPSTAIRS, SIX DAYS A WEEK, YOU CAN GET A GOOD, SOLID LUNCH — FOR EXAMPLE, A CUT OFF THE JOINT, TWO VEGETABLES AND BOILED JAM ROLL — FOR ABOUT THREE SHILLINGS. THE SPECIAL PLEASURE OF THIS LUNCH IS THAT YOU CAN HAVE DRAUGHT STOUT WITH IT. I DOUBT WHETHER AS MANY AS 10 PERCENT OF LONDON PUBS SERVE DRAUGHT STOUT, BUT THE MOON UNDER WATER IS ONE OF THEM.

IT IS A SOFT, CREAMY SORT OF STOUT, AND IT GOES BETTER IN A PEWTER POT. THEY ARE PARTICULAR ABOUT THEIR DRINKING VESSELS AT THE MOON UNDER WATER, AND NEVER, FOR EXAMPLE, MAKE THE MISTAKE OF SERVING A PINT OF BEER IN A HANDLELESS GLASS. APART FROM GLASS AND PEWTER MUGS, THEY HAVE SOME OF THOSE PLEASANT STRAWBERRY PINK CHINA ONES WHICH ARE NOW SELDOM SEEN IN LONDON. CHINA MUGS WENT OUT ABOUT 30 YEARS AGO, BECAUSE MOST PEOPLE LIKE THEIR DRINK TO BE TRANSPARENT, BUT IN MY OPINION BEER TASTES BETTER OUT OF CHINA.

THE GREAT SURPRISE OF THE MOON UNDER WATER IS ITS GARDEN. YOU GO THROUGH A NARROW PASSAGE LEADING OUT OF THE SALOON, AND FIND YOURSELF IN A FAIRLY LARGE GARDEN WITH PLANE TREES, UNDER WHICH THERE ARE LITTLE GREEN TABLES WITH IRON CHAIRS AROUND THEM.

BECAUSE IT ALLOWS WHOLE FAMILIES TO GO OUT THERE INSTEAD OF HIM HAVING TO STAY AT HOME AND WIFE THE BABY WHILE DAD GOES OUT ALONE. AND THOUGH STRICTLY SPEAKING THEY ARE ONLY ALLOWED IN THE GARDEN, THE CHILDREN TEND TO SEEP INTO THE PUB EVEN TO FETCH DRINKS FOR THEIR PARENTS. THIS, I BELIEVE, IS AGAINST THE LAW, BUT IT IS A LAW THAT DESERVES TO BE BROKEN, FOR IT IS THE PURITANICAL NONSENSE OF EXCLUDING CHILDREN — AND THEREFORE (TO SOME EXTENT) WOMEN — FROM PUBS THAT HAS TURNED THESE PLACES INTO

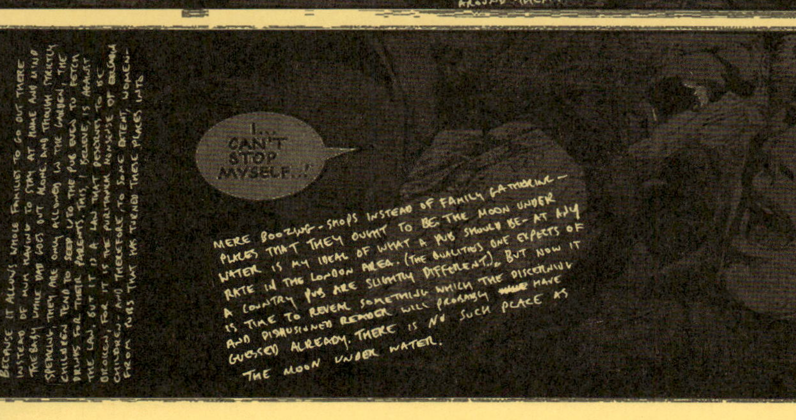


MERE BOOZING-SHOPS INSTEAD OF FAMILY GATHERING-PLACES THAT THEY OUGHT TO BE. THE MOON UNDER WATER IS MY IDEAL OF WHAT A PUB SHOULD BE — AT ANY RATE IN THE LONDON AREA. (THE QUALITIES ONE EXPECTS OF A COUNTRY PUB ARE SLIGHTLY DIFFERENT.) BUT NOW IT IS TIME TO REVEAL SOMETHING WHICH THE DISCERNING AND DISILLUSIONED READER WILL PROBABLY HAVE GUESSED ALREADY. THERE IS NO SUCH PLACE AS THE MOON UNDER WATER.

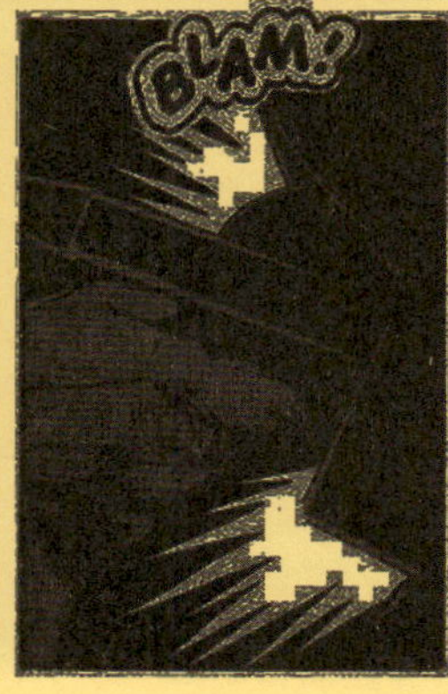


LIV PRESTON ANNOTATED THE MEN ON THE MOON, REPORT ON PLANET THREE, 1973, ARTHUR C. CLARKE // THE MOON UNDER WATER, REVIEW OF THE PUB AND THE PEOPLE BY MASS-OBSERVATION (THE LISTENER), 1943, GEORGE ORWELL

intolerable for being "too polished". So the purview of electronic music, its stereotypical conceits of coldness, detachment, mechanisation – the attributes of robot-mindedness and laboratory clinicism in old-fashioned hard sci-fi – were displaced by a determination to transmute machine sequencing and electronic sounds into organic, changeable, "soft" substances. Speaking in 1989 to Manchester's 808 State, the first UK post-acid-house act to make a long-term pop career for itself, I found the same attitude. "Some of the best records are shoestring", said Graham Massey. Then, later in the interview, key words defined the difference between the emerging techno generation and most of its predecessors from the 1970s and early 1980s – Gary Numan, OMD, Jean Michel-Jarre, Tomita and Vangelis. Key words and phrases such as "alchemy", "getting your hands in the mud", "accident".

## night drive thru babylon

But techno's machine-age coldness has a basis in mass production, mass consumption and the human – machine interface of Henry Ford's assembly line, an urban workforce marshalled and entrained by heavy industry and then left stranded by its relocation in Asia. The central inspiration for European techno came from the black housing projects of Detroit. In the late 1980s, Kirk DeGiorgio, a London-born techno musician who has recorded under the names of Future/Past, As One and Esoterik, travelled to Detroit as a record buyer. Anxious to meet his idols – Derrick May, Juan Atkins, Carl Craig – he experienced a shock of realisation. "I remember driving in from Chicago", he says, "and seeing the hi-tech headquarters for Ford and then I was in the most extreme poverty I've ever seen in my life, five minutes later. There's just no hope at all. It's just complete despair. Young girls on the street. You can really understand the melancholy feel of a lot of those early Detroit records, the coldness people associate with them. You can imagine Derrick May sitting up in his flat and looking out on Detroit. You can really see a city shaping a music."

Having grown up with the latter-day effects of Fordism, the Detroit techno musicians read futurologist Alvin Toffler's *The Third Wave* and found that Toffler's soundbite predictions for change – "blip culture", "the intelligent environment", "the infosphere", "de-massification of the media de-massifies our minds", "the techno rebels", "appropriate technologies" – accorded with some, though not all, of their own intuitions. First came the George Clinton-inspired electro-funk of Cybertron, a duo of Juan Atkins and a Vietnam vet named Rick Davies who called himself 3070. I am a number, not a name. Their music was explicit in its cold precision and roboticism. Track titles – "Clear", "Techno City", "Cosmic Cars" – dwelled on familiar Futurist themes of transcendence through movement and immersion in the smart city, the wired megalopolis. After Cybertron came another Atkins recording pseudonym – Model 500 – as well as Derrick May's Rhythim Is Rhythim and Mayday, Kevin Saunderson's Reese & Santonio, Carl Craig, Kenny Larkin, Stacey Pullen, Mark Kinchin and Underground Resistance. This was the canon, and tracks such as Derrick May's "Strings of Life", Carl Craig's "Crackdown" or Model 500's "Info World" and "Ocean To Ocean" established an intricate, subtle aesthetic that was difficult to match.

The repercussions of this music rippled out to European musicians, labels and DJs, particularly in Britain, Belgium, Germany, Holland, Scandinavia and Italy – A Guy Called Gerald, Orbital, The Black Dog, Moody Boyz, Future Sound of London, Dr Motte, Jam & Spoon, Carl Cox, Bandulu, Autechre, Redcell, Speedy J, Aqua Regia, Dave Angel, The Irresistible Force, C.J. Bolland, Frank De Wulf, Source, Stefan Robbers, Sun Electric, Thomas Fehlmann, Global Communication, Higher Intelligence Agency, Sweet Exorcist, Seefeel, Bedouin Ascent, Mouse On Mars, Sketch, Oval, and then the next generation of UK jungle producers, whose innovations in rhythm programming and edit experimentation swept

die proletarischen Parteien in den bestimmenden imperialistischen Ländern Deutschland, Japan und Italien in "einem langwierigen legalen Kampf"' - wie es Mao beiläufig empfahl - die Arbeitermassen hätten mobilisieren können.
Nach dem 2. Weltkrieg, dessen Ausgang die entscheidende Rolle der Sowjetunion und Volkschinas begründete, muß die Perspektive der Verwandlung imperialistischer Kriege in sozialrevolutionäre Bürgerkriege neu bestimmt werden. Lenin ging bei seiner Analyse imperialistischer Kriege von bewaffneten Auseinandersetzungen unter den kapitalistischen Großmächten aus. Diese Art des imperialistischen Krieges ist überholt. Eine neue Erscheinungsform bewaffneter imperialistischer Unterdrückung ist in den Vordergrund getreten:
der Einsatz der Militärmaschinen der kapitalistischen Großmächte gegen nationale und soziale Befreiungsbewegungen - heute zunächst in den unterentwickelt gehaltenen Ländern. Unter diesen Bedingungen ist die von den Black Panthers und dem amerikanischen SDS ausgegebene Losung: "bring the war home" die folgerichtige Weiterentwicklung der leninschen These von der Verwandlung imperialistischer Kriege in emanzipatorische Bürgerkriege.
Wenn Mao sagt, daß der Bürgerkrieg in den Metropolen erst begonnen werden sollte, wenn die Mehrheit des Proletariats zum bewaffneten Kampf entschlossen sei, dann sicher nicht als Ausdruck eines metaphysischen Demokratismus, sondern weil er es offensichtlich nicht für möglich hielt, daß sich der Bürgerkrieg in urbanisierten Zonen unter anderen Bedingungen entwickeln und mit einem Sieg des Proletariats enden könnte. Seine These steht und fällt also mit der Antwort auf die Frage, ob sich eine mit Waffen kämpfende Bewegung unter den Bedingungen der entwickelten Metropole bilden, erhalten und erweitern kann, bevor die proletarischen Massen für den bewaffneten Kampf mobilisiert sind. Diese Frage bedarf einer sorgfältigen Untersuchung. Mao hat sich insoweit auf die Einschätzungen der KP's in den Metropolen verlassen. Diese Einschätzung aber war falsch.

(2)  E. Mandel: Die Lehre vom Mai 1968 in "Revolution in Frankreich 1968" EVA S 123
(3)  Mandel aaO S 126 Fußnote 8
(4)  Vgl. "Neue Zeit" 30. Jahrg. 2. Bd. 1912, daselbst A. Pannekoek: Massenaktion und Revolution
(5)  Letztere hat erst im Feuer der Novemberrevolution die Dimensionen des konterrevolutionären Terrors erahnt. Vgl. "Was will der Spartacusbund?" Ges. Schriften II (EVA) S 164
(6)  Lenin: Was tun?; Werke Bd. 5 S 536 f
(7)  Lenin: Was tun?; Werke Bd. 5 S 386/394ff und S 479
(8)  Lenin: Werke Bd. 5 S 386
(9)  Lenin: Was tun?;Werke Bd. 5 S 393
(10) Rosa Luxemburg: Rede auf dem Londoner Parteitag der SDAPR; Ausgew. Reden und Schriften I S 287

The universe is infinite creativity. But what is spontaneity? Is it a kind of energy? If it is energy it is *unconservable*, if the meaning of spontaneity should be kept consistent. We must, therefore, differentiate between two varieties of energy, conservable and unconservable energy. There is an energy which is conservable in the form of "cultural" conserves, which can be saved up, which can be spent at will in selected parts and used at different points in time; it is like a robot at the disposal of its owner. There is another form of energy which emerges and which is spent in a moment, which must emerge to be spent and which must be spent to make place for emergence, like the life of some animals which are born and die in the love-act.

It is a truism to say that the universe cannot exist without physical and mental energy which can be preserved. But it is more important to realize that without the other kind of energy, the unconservable one—or spontaneity—the creativity of the universe could not start and could not run, it would come to a standstill.

There is apparently little spontaneity in the universe, or, at least, if there is any abundance of it only a small particle is available to man, hardly enough to keep him surviving. In the past he has done everything to discourage its development. He could not rely upon the instability and insecurity of the moment, with an organism which was not ready to deal with it adequately; he encouraged the development of devices as intelligence, memory, social and cultural conserves, which would give him the needed support with the result that he gradually became the slave of his own crutches. If there is a neurological localization of the spontaneity-creativity process it is the least developed function of man's nervous system. The difficulty is that one cannot store spontaneity, one either is spontaneous at a given moment or one is not. If spontaneity is such an important factor for man's world why is it so little developed? The answer is: man *fears* spontaneity, just like his ancestor in the jungle feared fire; he feared fire until he learned how to make it. Man will fear spontaneity until he will learn how to train it.

impact remained unexplored, the film spectator was turned into a *voyeur*. By contrast, when we speak of site-seeing we imply that, because of film's spatio-corporeal mobilization, the spectator is rather a *voyageur*, a passenger who traverses a haptic, emotive terrain. Through this shift, my aim is to reclaim *emotion* and to argue, from the position of a film *voyageuse*, for the haptic as a feminist strategy of reading space.

The premise of site-seeing contests another aspect of the theory of the gaze as well: its favoring of a perspectival, optical geometry as a model for film. Confined to an optical position, this theory has tended to conceive of film space as a direct heir of Renaissance perspective and, understanding this in a narrow and reductive way, has reduced spectatorship to the fixed, unified geometry of a transcendental, disembodied gaze.[3] We now recognize that an optical model of this kind is unfit to account for the type of displacements that are represented, conveyed, and negotiated in the moving image. It not only has excluded a spectatorial articulation of the notion of public but has failed to engage in the sentient voyage and embodied psychogeography housed in the movie "house." In order to explore this realm and to expose the shortcomings of the optical-geometric model of film and its ocularcentrism, we do not, however, need to subscribe simply to an oppositional dichotomy. That is, we need not insist on positions that are skeptical or denigratory of visuality; nor need we treat visuality solely as a site of regulatory power over our bodies. There is another path to follow in tracing a composite genealogy for a filmic architectonics.[4] It involves an engagement with environmental history and its inhabited, lived space.

To build a theoretical map of an architectonics as mobile as that of motion pictures, one must use a traveling lens and make room for the sensory spatiality of film, for our apprehension of space, including filmic space, occurs through an engagement with touch and movement. Our site-seeing tour follows this intimate path of mobilized visual space, "erring" from architectural and artistic sites to moving pictures. Haptically driven, the atlas finds a design for filmic space within the delicate cartography of *emotion*, that sentient place that exists between the map, the wall, and the screen.

## PANORAMAS OF MODERNITY

> *Mobility lies at the heart of the historian's method. . . . Knowledge depends upon travel, upon a refusal to respect boundaries, upon a restless drive toward the margins.*
> Stephen Greenblatt

In keeping with the kinetic origins of the cinema, known in its early days as the "kinema," a passage to site-seeing involves, first of all, locating a geography of movement for cinema within the haptic map designed by the modern age. In this respect, my efforts converge with recent work in cinema studies that focuses on early

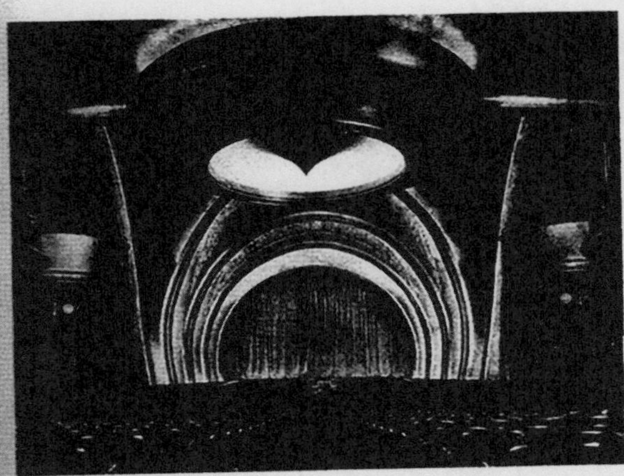

1.2. Interior of the Titania Palace Cinema, Berlin, 1928. Schöffler, Schlönbach and Jacobi, architects.

cinema and gives attention to film space.[5] Looking at the emergence of cinema in terms of a cultural space enables us to articulate the link between cinema and the culture of modernity.[6] Film came to place itself within the perceptual field that has been described by art historian Jonathan Crary as the "techniques of the observer."[7] It emerged out of this shifting observational arena and was affected, in particular, by the panoramic spectacle of display (especially anatomical display). A product of this representational architectonics, the motion picture developed from what cultural historian Wolfgang Schivelbusch has called "panoramic vision," and especially from the architectural configurations of modern life and their circulation.[8]

On the eve of cinema's invention, a network of architectural forms produced a new spatiovisuality. Such venues as arcades, railways, department stores, the pavilions of exhibition halls, glass houses, and winter gardens incarnated the new geography of modernity.[9] They were all sites of transit. Mobility—a form of cinematics—was the essence of these new architectures. By changing the relation between spatial perception and bodily motion, the new architectures of transit and travel culture prepared the ground for the invention of the moving image, the very epitome of modernity.

Film shared much in common with this geography of travel culture, especially with regard to its constant reinvention of space. I have argued elsewhere that spectatorship is to be conceived as an embodied and kinetic affair, and that the anatomy of movement that early film engendered is particularly linked to notions of flânerie, urban "streetwalking," and modern bodily architectures.[10] As wandering was incorporated into the cinema, early film viewing became an imaginary form of flânerie, an activity that was—both historically and phantasmatically—fully open to women. By way of the cinema, new horizons opened up for female explorations. A relative of the railway passenger and the urban stroller, the female spectator—a flâneuse—traveled along sites.

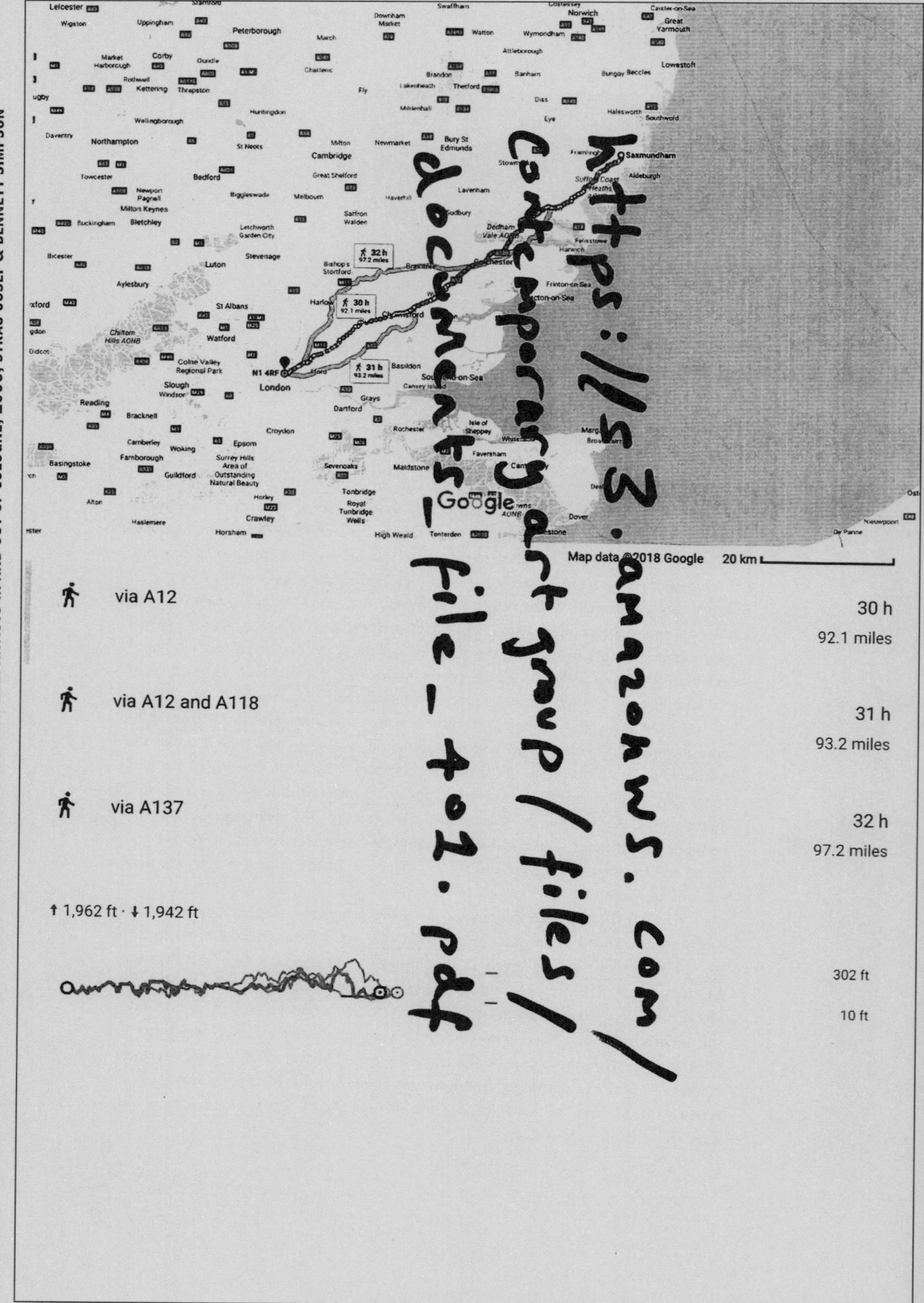


via A12

30 h
92.1 miles

via A12 and A118

31 h
93.2 miles

via A137

32 h
97.2 miles

↑ 1,962 ft · ↓ 1,942 ft

302 ft

10 ft

351

**I.**

**The public** men's room, architecturally speaking, is rarely a room with a view—or rarely, at least, a room that affords a view outside itself. Like the closet, to which it is near allied (both as "water closet" and as site of bodily relations discursively tabooed) the men's room tends to lack windows. And on those occasions when windows do figure as part of its structural design, the glass, more often translucent than transparent, generally precludes any visual commerce between the areas without and within. Substituting mirrors for windows, satisfying the eye's desire for depth of field by returning its look to itself, the men's room, through a segmentation of space that can justly be called self-reflexive, gestures, despite the accessibility of that space to a subset of the "public," towards an idea of interiority, towards a principle of containment, implicit in the architectural imperative that shapes the subject—forming and informing him as the subject of ideology—in its own monumentalizing image, modeling the subject as container of space through the articulation of structural, because structuring, identities.

Closed in on itself as if to exemplify the very notion of constructed space, but always, of course, designed to permit exchanges between inside and outside analogous to those that would seem most successfully arrested by its circumscription of the visual, this locus of functional attention to culturally abjected bodily functions always necessarily functions in excess of a logic of mere functionality. The men's room, that is, though clearly conceived as a technological response to the hygienic concerns associated with bodily necessities, constitutes a social technology in itself to necessitate a certain relation between the male subject and his body. The design of the men's room, simply put, has palpable designs on men: it aspires, that is, to design them. As a site of representation, as a space intended to "serve" the subject it collaborates to call into being, the men's room gives the male subject his body in its relation to symbolic space—effectively locating him within his body as he is located within space itself—by allowing him, before the only public, the male one, whose witness can matter, to enact, as if in a theater, the law of its mandatory closeting. I refer, with this, not only to the law of (heterosexual) masculinity as we know it—the law that reads the male body, in its potential to be seized, overwhelmed, by erotic stimuli not provoked by the "proper" object (a woman) or centered in the "proper" place (the genitals), as requiring consignment to a psychic space analogous to a closet—but also to the law whereby the straight male body becomes a closet itself: a spatial enclosure for an autonomous subject able to imagine inhabiting his body only by conceiving his body simultaneously as container and thing contained; as *being* and *needing* a closet; as bestowing upon him the social protection, the cultural shelter, it uniquely affords within our patriarchal sex-gender system, but only so long as he performatively shelters the structural flaw that opens his body, by way of its multiple openings (ocular, oral, anal, genital), to the various psychic vicissitudes able to generate illicit desires. As a prime arena for that performance, for that enactment of the body's compliance with the cultural regulation of desire, the men's room marks a critical stage both for and in the solicitation of masculine subjectivity.

**II.**

But just as soliciting the subject can define the social project of the men's room, so it also names the threat against which the solicited subject must be sheltered. However much the men's room may prompt the performers within it to heed its own subjectifying call—the call it slyly assimilates to the irresistible call of nature itself—it allows for the possibility of error, for what the penal code calls soliciting for the purpose of committing unnatural acts. And the habitual structuring of the men's room to ensure the possibility of this error makes clear that whatever shelter it provides requires the presence of the threat its very design apparently solicits.

The men's room, set apart as it is to provide a culturally designated "privacy" in which to respond to the body's demands, houses two highly differentiated spaces that reestablish within it the consequential distinction between public and private zones, mapping each of those attributes onto specified zones of the male subject's body. Thus, the genitals, though figured as the "private parts," acquire, through the openness of the urinal, a relatively "public" status here, while the anus and its functional necessity bear weightier burdens of social embarrassment.[1] In the men's room the norms of male bodily display reverse the values that the laws of *pudeur* assign to the privatized portions of male anatomy in the world outside: you don't show your ass in the men's room, and you don't conceal your dick. The partition that distinguishes the privacy of the stalls from the exposure of the urinals and sinks, therefore, defines the men's room, like the U.S. Congress, as strategically bicameral, allowing each part of its legislative body to hold the other in check. As *camera lucida* and *camera obscura* at once, the men's room might simply come out and proclaim as its motto "I am a camera" were it not that it operates more saliently as a factory for turning into cameras themselves all those who enter to confront, as if *in camera*, the unblinking eye of the law that keeps watch, through every patron's eye—including, signally, their own—to see that what is publicly displayed is never directly observed.

**III.**

The law of the men's room decrees that men's dicks be available for public contemplation at the urinal precisely to allow a correlative mandate: that such contemplation must never take place. The performative bravado, "naturalized" only

[1] These sentences condense an argument I have made at greater length in "Tearooms and Sympathy; Or, The Epistemology of the Water Closet," in my *Homographesis: Essays in Gay Literary and Cultural Theory* (New York and London: Routledge, 1994), pp. 148-170. Since I will focus in this essay primarily on the significations informing the logic of the urinal, I cite here, by way of contextualization, a passage from "Tearooms and Sympathy" that may help to trace the lineaments of my argument concerning the space of the stall:

"I want to suggest that the men's room . . . is the site of a particular heterosexual anxiety about the potential inscriptions of homosexual desire and about the possibility of knowing or recognizing whatever might constitute 'homosexual difference.'

"This can be intuited more readily when the restroom is considered not, as it is by Lacan, in terms of 'urinary segregation'—a context that establishes the phallus from the outset as the token of anatomical difference—but as the site of a loosening of sphincter control, evoking, therefore, an older eroticism, undifferentiated by gender, because anterior to the genital tyranny that raises the phallus to its privileged position. Precisely because the phallus marks the putative stability of the divide between "Ladies" and "Gentlemen," because it articulates the concept of sexual difference in terms of 'visible perception,' the 'urinary' function in the institutional men's room customarily takes place within view of others—as if to indicate its status as an act of definitional display; but the private enclosure of the toilet stall signals the potential anxiety at issue in the West when the men's room becomes the locus not of urinary but of intestinal relief. For the satisfaction that such relief affords abuts dangerously on homophobically abjectified desires, and because that satisfaction marks an opening onto difference that would challenge the phallic supremacy and coherence of the signifier on the men's room door, it must be isolated and kept in view at once lest its erotic potential come out" (pp. 160-161).

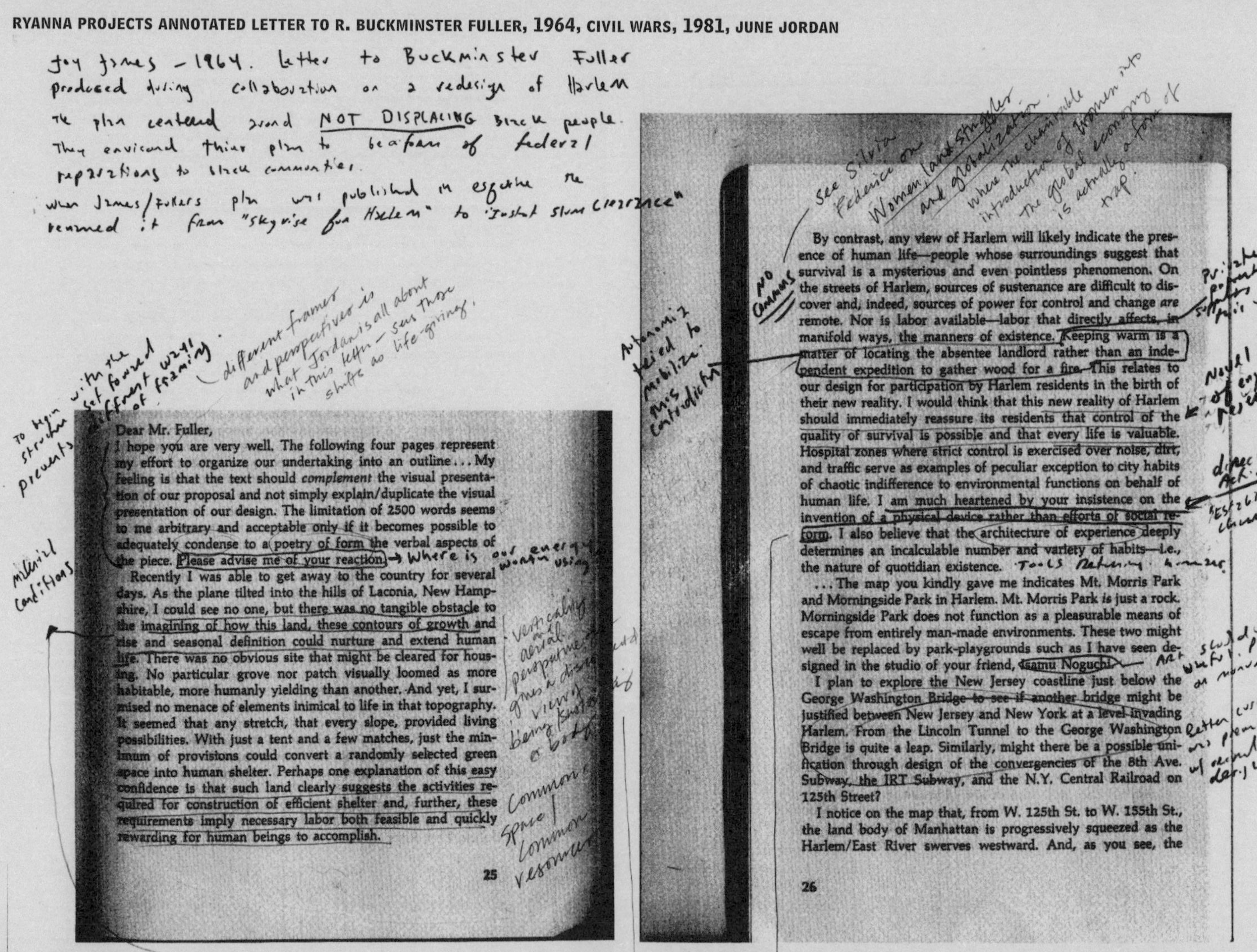

Dear Mr. Fuller,

I hope you are very well. The following four pages represent my effort to organize our undertaking into an outline... My feeling is that the text should *complement* the visual presentation of our proposal and not simply explain/duplicate the visual presentation of our design. The limitation of 2500 words seems to me arbitrary and acceptable only if it becomes possible to adequately condense to a poetry of form the verbal aspects of the piece. Please advise me of your reaction.

Recently I was able to get away to the country for several days. As the plane tilted into the hills of Laconia, New Hampshire, I could see no one, but there was no tangible obstacle to the imagining of how this land, these contours of growth and rise and seasonal definition could nurture and extend human life. There was no obvious site that might be cleared for housing. No particular grove nor patch visually loomed as more habitable, more humanly yielding than another. And yet, I surmised no menace of elements inimical to life in that topography. It seemed that any stretch, that every slope, provided living possibilities. With just a tent and a few matches, just the minimum of provisions could convert a randomly selected green space into human shelter. Perhaps one explanation of this easy confidence is that such land clearly suggests the activities required for construction of efficient shelter and, further, these requirements imply necessary labor both feasible and quickly rewarding for human beings to accomplish.

25

By contrast, any view of Harlem will likely indicate the presence of human life—people whose surroundings suggest that survival is a mysterious and even pointless phenomenon. On the streets of Harlem, sources of sustenance are difficult to discover and, indeed, sources of power for control and change are remote. Nor is labor available—labor that directly affects, in manifold ways, the manners of existence. Keeping warm is a matter of locating the absentee landlord rather than an independent expedition to gather wood for a fire. This relates to our design for participation by Harlem residents in the birth of their new reality. I would think that this new reality of Harlem should immediately reassure its residents that control of the quality of survival is possible and that every life is valuable. Hospital zones where strict control is exercised over noise, dirt, and traffic serve as examples of peculiar exception to city habits of chaotic indifference to environmental functions on behalf of human life. I am much heartened by your insistence on the invention of a physical device rather than efforts of social reform. I also believe that the architecture of experience deeply determines an incalculable number and variety of habits—i.e., the nature of quotidian existence.

... The map you kindly gave me indicates Mt. Morris Park and Morningside Park in Harlem. Mt. Morris Park *is* just a rock. Morningside Park does not function as a pleasurable means of escape from entirely man-made environments. These two might well be replaced by park-playgrounds such as I have seen designed in the studio of your friend, Isamu Noguchi.

I plan to explore the New Jersey coastline just below the George Washington Bridge to see if another bridge might be justified between New Jersey and New York at a level invading Harlem. From the Lincoln Tunnel to the George Washington Bridge is quite a leap. Similarly, might there be a possible unification through design of the convergencies of the 8th Ave. Subway, the IRT Subway, and the N.Y. Central Railroad on 125th Street?

I notice on the map that, from W. 125th St. to W. 155th St., the land body of Manhattan is progressively squeezed as the Harlem/East River swerves westward. And, as you see, the

26

352

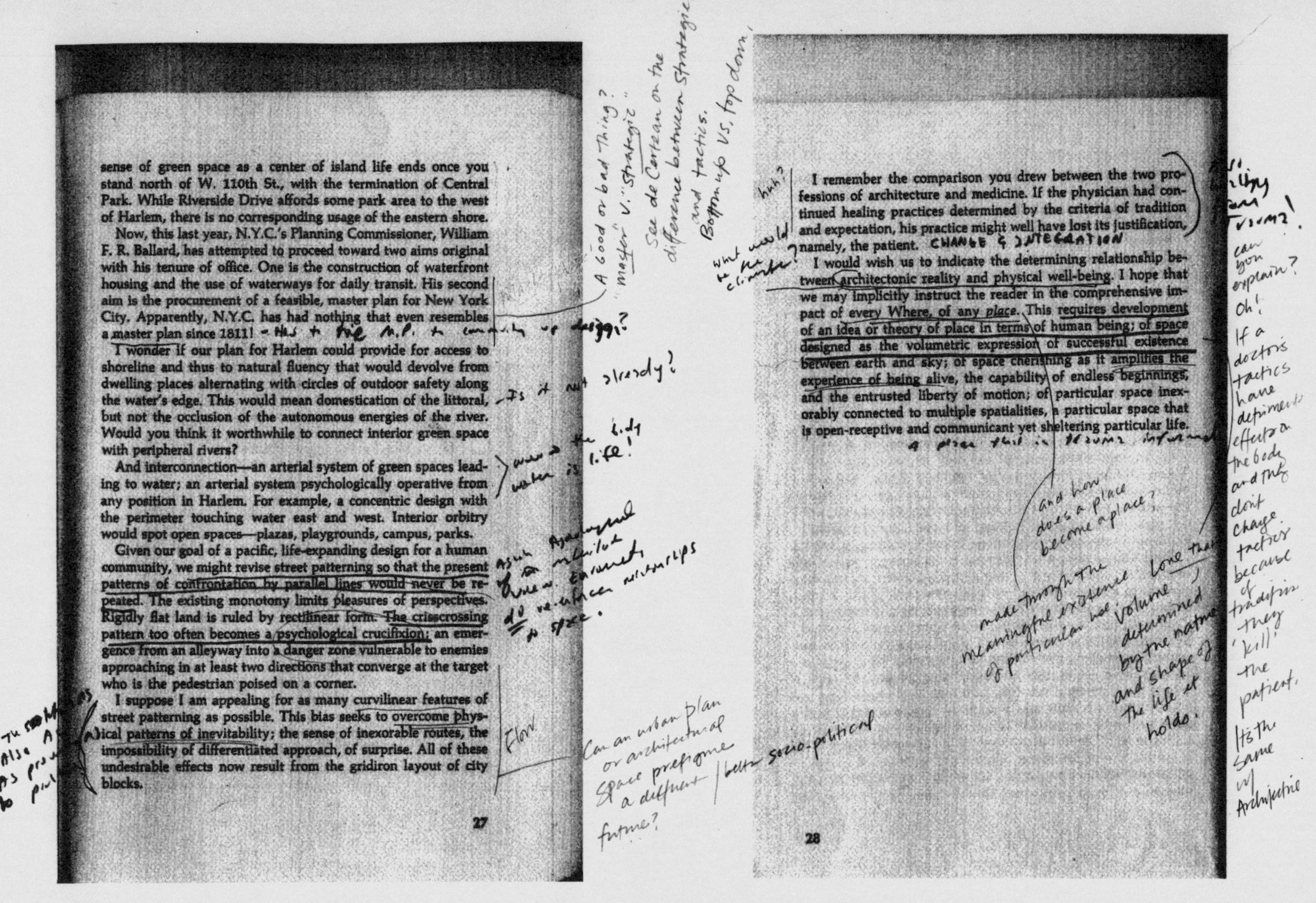



sense of green space as a center of island life ends once you stand north of W. 110th St., with the termination of Central Park. While Riverside Drive affords some park area to the west of Harlem, there is no corresponding usage of the eastern shore.

Now, this last year, N.Y.C.'s Planning Commissioner, William F. R. Ballard, has attempted to proceed toward two aims original with his tenure of office. One is the construction of waterfront housing and the use of waterways for daily transit. His second aim is the procurement of a feasible, master plan for New York City. Apparently, N.Y.C. has had nothing that even resembles a master plan since 1811!

I wonder if our plan for Harlem could provide for access to shoreline and thus to natural fluency that would devolve from dwelling places alternating with circles of outdoor safety along the water's edge. This would mean domestication of the littoral, but not the occlusion of the autonomous energies of the river. Would you think it worthwhile to connect interior green space with peripheral rivers?

And interconnection—an arterial system of green spaces leading to water; an arterial system psychologically operative from any position in Harlem. For example, a concentric design with the perimeter touching water east and west. Interior orbitry would spot open spaces—plazas, playgrounds, campus, parks.

Given our goal of a pacific, life-expanding design for a human community, we might revise street patterning so that the present patterns of confrontation by parallel lines would never be repeated. The existing monotony limits pleasures of perspectives. Rigidly flat land is ruled by rectilinear form. The crisscrossing pattern too often becomes a psychological crucifixion; an emergence from an alleyway into a danger zone vulnerable to enemies approaching in at least two directions that converge at the target who is the pedestrian poised on a corner.

I suppose I am appealing for as many curvilinear features of street patterning as possible. This bias seeks to overcome physical patterns of inevitability; the sense of inexorable routes, the impossibility of differentiated approach, of surprise. All of these undesirable effects now result from the gridiron layout of city blocks.

27

I remember the comparison you drew between the two professions of architecture and medicine. If the physician had continued healing practices determined by the criteria of tradition and expectation, his practice might well have lost its justification, namely, the patient.

I would wish us to indicate the determining relationship between architectonic reality and physical well-being. I hope that we may implicitly instruct the reader in the comprehensive impact of every Where, of any place. This requires development of an idea or theory of place in terms of human being; of space designed as the volumetric expression of successful existence between earth and sky; of space cherishing as it amplifies the experience of being alive, the capability of endless beginnings, and the entrusted liberty of motion; of particular space inexorably connected to multiple spatialities, a particular space that is open-receptive and communicant yet sheltering particular life.

28

ME

# MELT

REVISED, FINALLY (APRIL, 1961 – APRIL, 1973), FOR GORDON MUMM.

# Robert Ashley

## Outside of Time

### Ideas about Music

## Außerhalb der Zeit

### Gedanken über Musik

MusikTexte

history beyond their grandparents and don't know anything about their place history, because the family was always moving.) It was apparent that Americans in a new and raw country had to create a new kind of mythology. By the end of the nineteen-seventies it seemed that every composer I knew was writing an opera or wanted to.

And of course the form of opera we got from Europe didn't fit the new stories. So there were many works in musical theater that were in fact operas of a new sort but that weren't called "opera." For the first five "operas" I composed for the ONCE Group I tried to find a new term—"electronic music theater" or something of the sort. But when I realized that I was simply creating a new term that no one would understand, I had to go back to the word "opera." Finally, in 1967, I called the composition THAT MORNING THING an opera. And only then I began to understand what an "opera" could be. It was as though a huge burden had been lifted.

These new kinds of stories or ideas set to music—mine and pieces by Pauline Oliveros, David Behrman, Robert Wilson and many others—had to have a new form. To generalize, I would say that these new pieces were not stories as such, but were more likely to be an assembly or collage of "characters" that seemed to belong together and that being brought together gave the characters some meaning.

Critics often have gone after me because my operas had no "plot." What can I say? Plots abounded in television serials, movies, detective stories. But those media mostly had the shortcoming of not attaching memorable emotion to a character in the way that music can. This was amply demonstrated in popular music. We know more emotionally about Eleanor Rigby or Maybellene ("Why can't you be true?") or the man who says "Goodnight, Irene" or Madame Butterfly or Tosca than we do about characters in other media, even the famous ones like Citizen Kane. We live with Citizen Kane while the projector is running. Then we walk away and the emotion becomes blurred. We don't walk away from Eleanor Rigby or the many others. They stay with us for decades or probably forever.

The opera ATALANTA (ACTS OF GOD) (actually three operas with interchangeable scenes and characters) is simply a huge group of characters grouped around three central characters, Max Ernst, Willard Reynolds and Bud Powell. The plot ("such as it is," to quote my friend, the critic John Rockwell), suggested by Lawrence Brickman, who was the stage designer for the touring performances, is flimsy to the point of being facetious: the characters are entertaining "The Odalisque" in her private room in the harem (where nobody but entertainers are allowed). There are a number of subplots, barely explained, to show who the entertainers are and where they come from, but the stories are simply the stories the characters tell to entertain "The Odalisque."

<table>
<tr><td>134</td><td style="text-align:right">Contemporary Opera</td></tr>
</table>

This interpreting and filling in is the spectator's version of the cinematic imagination at work. It creates an almost continuous impetus toward convergence with the objects and bodies on the screen. In this and its withholding can be found the attraction and many of the "photogenic" qualities of film images. Films exceed normal observation and yet throw up huge barriers to it. They give us the privileged viewpoints of the close-up, the enclosing frame, the photographic "look" of things—their lighted textures, their extended focal lengths, their monochrome range in black and white—indeed, everything that heightens or defamiliarizes everyday perception—yet at the same time they confine us to limited frames, give us limited time to inspect them, and in other ways deprive us of our will. This becomes a gap on a larger scale, of a different order. It can create a compulsion to see, even to see something terrible.

The receptive, dreamlike state of film viewing adds a sense of inevitability to one's perceptions of how people behave on the screen, a sensation that seems to increase with the repeated viewing of a film. The mythic status of film stars derives partly from this accumulated exposure and redundancy. The effect may be better understood if one observes what happens when a filmmaker sees his or her own film. At various points along the way the filmmaker has actively controlled the images of the people in the film, but this disappears once the images have become fixed. Viewing the film can then become almost insupportable, for there is a renewed sense of responsibility for images that have by now assumed a life of their own, often in what seems an arbitrary fashion. A process that was thought to be completed returns with an intimation of its original indeterminacy, leaving the filmmaker powerless, with the sense of being stranded in the present.

## The Body of the Filmmaker

Film viewing involves the conjunction of two acts of looking and two bodies, at the very least. The spectator views the objects on the screen—objects that have already been seen and selected with the camera. It thus goes without saying that whatever is seen has already been mediated by the filmmaker's vision, but this is more than a process of thought: it is as much a physical act. The presence of the filmmaker's body becomes a "residue" in the work of the kind alluded to by Gell. The human beings in the film create another residue that is not so different from the filmmaker's own, for both are imprinted in the film's images as equivalent facts. This is perhaps most evident when the filmmaker is holding the camera, for the camera then records the filmmaker's movements and



those of the film's subjects in parallel. The image is affected as much by the body behind the camera as those before it.

Like other artists, filmmakers see many transient events that they would like to show to others. In effect, they want these events to repeat themselves for others to see. It seems an unattainable dream, and yet with a camera it is almost possible. The mimetic longings of the filmmaker are satisfied by the camera with an immediacy quite unprecedented in previous times in the production of poems, novels, and paintings.

Exactly why one should wish to show others what one has seen is another matter. Is it an affirmation of the thing itself, or of one's own vision, or a desire to command the consciousness of others? Or is it perhaps to transcend oneself, to overflow one's self-containment? Sometimes the descriptions of the filmmaking process sound rather like the last. For all the avant-gardists' descriptions of the camera's mechanical autonomy, they sound suspiciously like the experiencing body of the filmmaker. This begins historically with still photography and is not merely an expression of male *jouissance*. Julia Margaret Cameron, who began making photographs in 1863, wrote: "I longed to arrest all beauty that came before me, and at length the longing has been satisfied."[40] In Vertov's celebrations of the mobile camera, the camera is not so much anthropomorphized as that Vertov himself becomes a flying object. Basil Wright is mesmerized by the flight of kingfishers, the movements of a fisherman's arms, the legs of children in a dance. While filming, Rouch experiences *ciné-transe*. "Filmmaking for me is to write with one's eyes, one's ears, with one's body; it's to enter into something. . . . I am a ciné-Rouch in ciné-trance in the act of ciné-filming. . . . It's the joy of filming, the 'ciné-plaisir.' "[41] Rouch notes the synchrony of himself with his subject, the "harmony . . . which is in perfect balance with the movements of the subjects."[42] The ecstasy of the filming-body is captured in John Marshall's description: "You have this feeling, 'I'm on; I'm on.' You know, 'I'm getting it. It's happening; it's happening.' "[43] Here it is definitely Marshall who is "on," not the camera. The sensation, for Robert Gardner, is "as close to cinematic orgasm as I'll get."[44]

We must conclude that for many filmmakers there is an ecstatic, even erotic pleasure in filming others. This resembles the creative process in other arts but differs from it in its relation to its materials, which are almost always "found" objects, even if prepared to be discovered by the film. Perhaps a maker of collages or life-masks feels something equivalent, even though not responding so directly to the living human body and its fleeting expressions. The filmmaker "makes" nothing in an obvious sense but conducts an activity in conjunction with the living world. The pleasure of filming erodes the boundaries between filmmaker and subject, between the bodies filmmakers see and the images they make. Filming is fundamentally acquisitive in "incorporating" the bodies of others. The filmmaker's consciousness must also expand to accommodate these other bodies, but it cannot hold them all; they must be given to others—or at least returned to the world. In achieving this, the bodies of the subject, the filmmaker, and the viewer become interconnected and in some ways undifferentiated.

To speak of the dissolution of boundaries in this way is really to speak of the often fragile identity of the filmmaker at the moment of filming and, later, when viewing a film. Sometimes indifferent, sometimes obsessed, filmmakers experience a wide range of feelings toward their subjects. Occasionally another person's physical presence overpowers the filmmaker's consciousness. This results partly from the synchrony that Hoffman and Rouch both note, and from an internal mimicry of the other person's gestures, postures, voice, and emotional states. It can produce a sensation of power and expectancy, a willing of others to be precisely what they are, and to do precisely what they are doing, as they appear in the viewfinder. This becomes a spiritual synchrony, perhaps best expressed in Marshall's words: It's happening. I'm on.

## The Body of the Film

The human body has often been pictured as a machine. Early in the twentieth century it began to be described as a factory consuming and processing raw materials.[45] Well before this, however, the dissection of bodies by Leonardo and Vesalius had established the mechanical principles governing the joints and the circulation of blood. In the sixteenth century, human vision was often equated with the *camera obscura*, the principle of which had been known since antiquity. As well, the camera obscura was taken to reflect the physical structure of the human eye and, at a more abstract level, the relation of the eye to the mind. Soon after its invention, the camera became a mechanical extension of the body, to be enlisted in surveillance, initially for police "mug shots" and later in prisons, banks, shopping malls, and offices.[46] The interplay of body and machine subsequently became a recurrent theme in discussions of films and what they do. As in the idea of photogénie, photographic images were held to transcend normal vision. For Louis Delluc, the camera took on the characteristics of a body, but a body liberated from previous physical, cultural, and psychological constraints. For Fernand Léger and the Futurists the film camera produced a new "machine aesthetic." Jean Epstein called it "a standardized metal brain, manufactured and sold in thousands of copies, which transforms the external world into art."[47] In Vertov's rapturous imagining, the camera was the "kino-eye," capable of a vision freed for-



ever from "human immobility." Such conceptions of the camera as an autonomous body are partly signs of rebellion against academic art, but they are also a paradoxical way of acknowledging the camera's connection with the bodies it touches, including that of the filmmaker. Vertov went on to imagine the camera as a body fused with his own. "I am in constant motion. I draw near, then away, from objects. I crawl under, I climb onto them. I move apace with the muzzle of a galloping horse. I plunge full speed into a crowd."[48] Nineteenth-century novelists had already produced a mobile eye, sometimes anonymous, sometimes associated with an identifiable narrator. The focus on the senses, often dissociated from one another and yet creating a heightened sensory awareness, continued apace in the modern novel. Joyce conceived of *Ulysses* (1922) as an "encyclopaedia of the body," with fifteen of its eighteen chapters corresponding to separate bodily organs.[49] In novels and in many films (especially in the silent era), there is a shifting hypertrophy of one sense or another, brought about by their separation. As in *The Act of Seeing with one's own eyes*, lack of sound is capable of producing an almost unbearable acuity of vision. Equally, a dark or severely limited screen makes sounds more evocative, an effect explored as soon as the sound film was invented by Hitchcock, Lang, and, later, Bresson.

Unlike Joyce's procedure in *Ulysses*, it is unusual for filmmakers to relate their films so closely to the human body and its organs, perhaps because a film is already so closely identified with the eye and ear. (A very few fiction films, such as *The Last Laugh* [1924], *Lady in the Lake* [1946], and *Sunset Boulevard* [1950], do, however, turn the camera into a living or dead character.) Yet filmmakers have inherited from classical thought certain notions about the body of the work as well as the "corpus" of works of an artist. Aristotle compared the plots of tragedies to living organisms compounded of specific parts. Similarly, filmmakers often conceive of a film as an organic whole with a beginning, middle, and end, corresponding roughly to exposition, conflict, and resolution. These, in turn, can be seen in a more corporeal light, corresponding first to cognition and sensory-perception, then the muscle of action, and finally the emotional or organic processes of release. Filmmakers are known to refer to the skeleton and flesh of a film, its intellectual framework versus its "heart" or "guts," and so on. Films are also seen to have a life of their own in the public domain, a time span not unlike the stages of life of an organism. And although far in spirit from the mechanical-body notions of the avant-gardists, the psychoanalytical film criticism of the 1970s linked film to many of the attributes of the (mostly male) body—its desires, its "gaze," its self-reflection.

Films are thus seen in several different contexts as symbolic bodies—but to whose body do they correspond? Is it the body of the subject? Is it

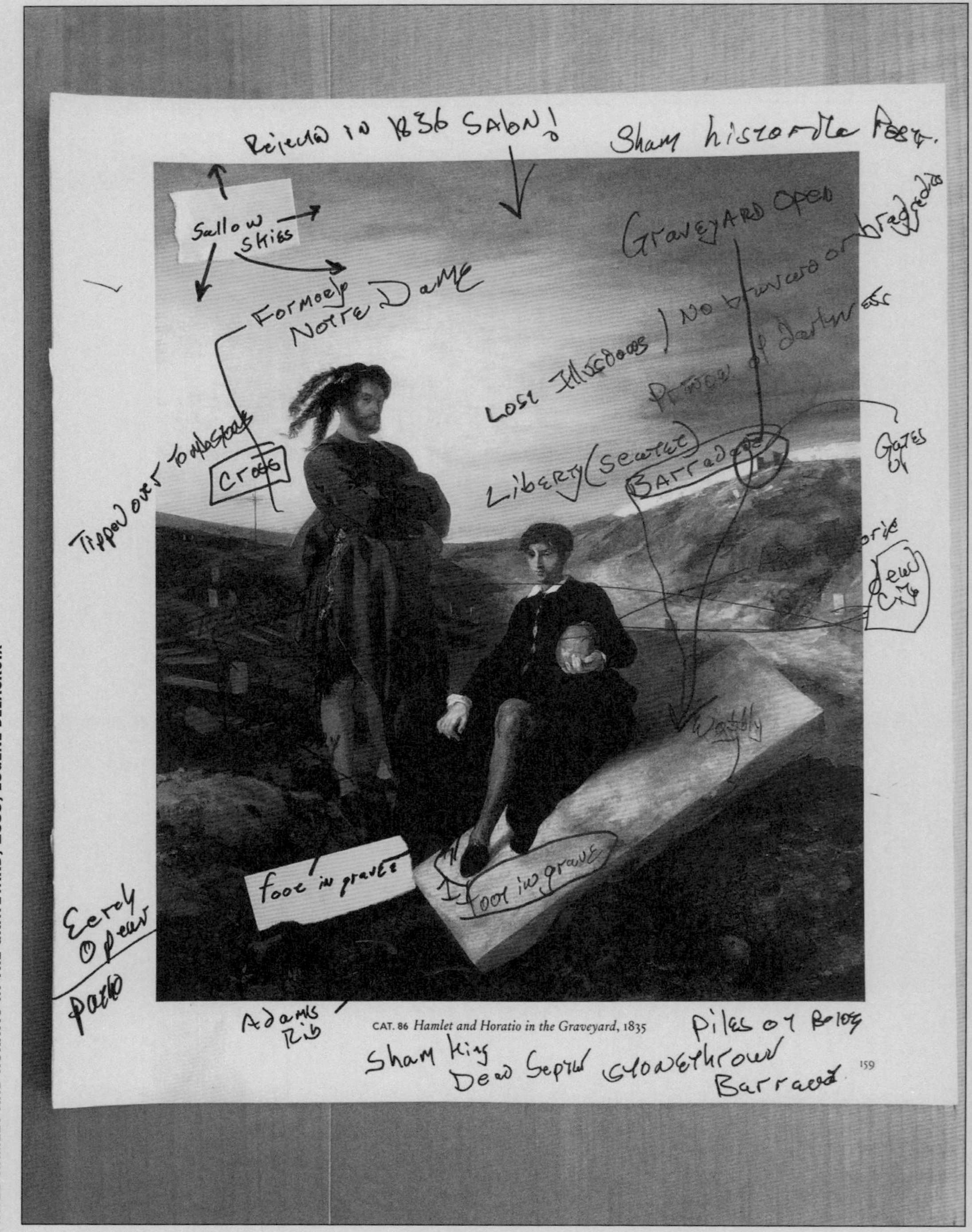


CAT. 86 *Hamlet and Horatio in the Graveyard, 1835*

# A Cartography of the Ecstatic and Meditative States

The experimental and experiential features of a perception-hallucination continuum are considered.

Roland Fischer

In this age so concerned with travel in outer as well as inner space, it is strange that, while we have detailed charts of the moon, we have no cartography of the varieties of human experience. In order to draft a map of inner space, I am ready to be your travel guide and take you on two voyages: one along the perception-hallucination continuum of increasing ergotropic (*1*) arousal, which includes creative, psychotic, and ecstatic experiences; and another along the perception-meditation continuum of increasing trophotropic (*1*) arousal, which encompasses the hypoaroused states of Zazen and Yoga samadhi.

Along the perception-hallucination continuum of increasing arousal of the sympathetic nervous system (ergotropic arousal), man—the self-referential system—perceptually-behaviorally (cortically) interprets the change (drug-induced or "natural") in his subcortical activity as creative, psychotic, and ecstatic experiences (*2*). These states are marked by a gradual turning inward toward a mental dimension at the expense of the physical. The normal state of daily routine, our point of departure, is followed by an aroused, creative state, which can be characterized by an increase in both data content (a description of space) and rate of data processing ["flood of inner sensation" (*3*), or most intense time] (*4*). However, in the next aroused state on the continuum, the acute schizophrenic [or rather, "hyperphrenic" (*5*)] state, a further increase in data content may not be matched by a corresponding increase in the rate of data processing. While the creative state is conducive to the evolution of novel relations and new meaning, the psychotic "jammed computer" state interferes with the individual's creative interpretation of the activity of his central nervous system (CNS). At the peak of ecstatic rapture, the outside (physical) world "retreats to the fringe of consciousness" (*6*), and the individual reflects himself in his own "program." One can conceptualize the normal, creative, "hyperphrenic," and ecstatic states along the perception-hallucination continuum as the ledges of a homeostatic step function (*7*). While the creative person may travel freely between "normal" and creative states, the chronic schizophrenic patient is stranded in the "jammed computer" state. And the talented mystic, of course, does not need to go through every intermediate step to attain ecstasy.

The mutually exclusive relationship between the ergotropic and trophotropic systems (*8*) justifies a separate perception-meditation continuum of increasing trophotropic arousal (hypoarousal) that is continuous with, and to the right of, the perception-hallucination continuum (Fig. 1). The course of our second trip, therefore, will take us in the opposite direction, along the tranquil perception-meditation continuum, where man may symbolically interpret his gradually increasing trophotropic arousal as Zazen and, ultimately, samadhi.

That the two continua in Fig. 1 represent two mutually exclusive states of arousal has been well documented by Hess (*1*) and Gellhorn (*8*, *9*). The mutual exclusiveness of the ergotropic and trophotropic systems can also be illustrated by characteristic changes in the frequency of the small, involuntary, micronystagmoid movements of the eye. These rapid scanning movements (with a mean frequency of one per second and an amplitude of 5 to 10 minutes of arc) are regarded as a prerequisite for the fixation of an object in physical space-time (*10*). The frequency of saccadic movements is increased five- to eightfold in response to the ergotropic arousal induced by moderate doses of mescaline, psilocybin, or LSD (D-lysergic acid diethylamide) (*10*). This increase is also present without drugs in acute schizophrenics (*11*) [that is, patients in a state of ergotropic arousal, the "alarm reaction" (*12*) stage of Selye's general adaptation syndrome (*13*)].

On the other hand, 0.9 gram of alcohol per kilogram of body weight, and even sleepiness and fatigue, decreases saccadic frequency (*14*); more precisely, 0.01 milligram of Valium (diazepam) per kilogram of body weight reduces the saccadic frequency by 9 degrees per second (*15*). Such a progressive decrease seems to be a characteristic feature of trophotropic arousal along the perception-meditation continuum. That the alpha rhythm appearing on the electroencephalogram (EEG) appears to be phase-locked to the onset of saccades (*16*) may also be of significance, since states of progressively greater trophotropic arousal along the perception-meditation continuum are characterized by EEG waves of progressively lower frequencies (measured in hertz) (*17*) (see Fig. 1, right). Moreover, since a complete arrest of saccadic frequency, [for example, by optical immobilization of the retinal image (*18*)] results in periodic fading, disintegration, and fragmented reconstruction of the image, we may postulate that reduced saccadic frequency may be linked with the Yogi's comment that, at the peak of a meditative experience, he can still see "objects," but they have no predicative properties (*19*).

## What Are Hallucinations and How Can They Be Measured?

The hallucinatory or waking-dream states along the perception-hallucination continuum can best be described as experiences of intense sensations that cannot be verified through voluntary motor activity. Note that such a definition does not differentiate between dreams and hallucinations: for example, see the "Three Wise Men" (Fig. 2). Two of the three wise men dream with eyes closed, while the third, with eyes open, hallucinates the angel who carries all three away from the "real" world into a mental dimension.

We can describe verifiable perceptions, therefore, by assigning to them low sensory-to-motor (S/M) ratios (*20*), while nonverifiable hallucinations and dreams can be characterized by increasing S/M ratios as one moves along the perception-hallucination or perception-meditation continuum toward ecstasy or samadhi, the two most hallucinatory states (*21*) (Fig. 1, left and right, respectively). Moderate doses of the hallucinogenic drugs LSD, psilocybin, and mescaline (*22*) can get one "moving" along the perception-hallucination continuum, whereas minor tranquilizers and some muscle relaxants may initiate travel along the perception-meditation continuum.

If high S/M ratios do, indeed, reflect hallucinatory experiences, as my definition of hallucinations would imply, it would be important to quantify S/M ratio as a measure of hallucinatory intensity. In fact, a quantitative meaning has been given to the S/M ratio by measuring the components of a psychomotor performance, specifically, handwriting area and handwriting pressure (*20*), in volunteers during a psilocybin-induced waking-dream state.

The techniques for measuring handwriting area (S) (in square centimeters), as well as for obtaining handwriting pressure (M) (in $10^4$ dynes averaged over time), with an indicator that operates on a pressure-voltage-to-frequency basis, have been described elsewhere (*20*). Using these two parameters prior to ($T_1$) and at the peak ($T_2$) of a psilocybin-induced experience [160 to 250 micrograms of psilocybin per kilogram of body weight], we found in a sample of 47 college-age volunteers a 31 percent ($T_2 - T_1$) increase in mean S/M ratio.

I should note that the standard deviation on handwriting area at $T_1$ is

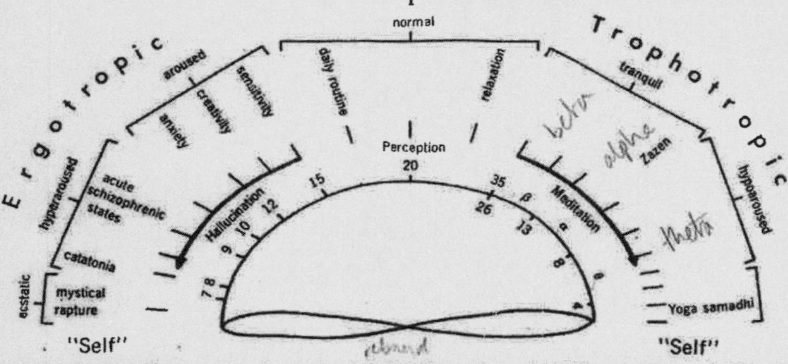


Fig. 1. Varieties of conscious states mapped on a perception-hallucination continuum of increasing ergotropic arousal (left) and a perception-meditation continuum of increasing trophotropic arousal (right). These levels of hyper- and hypoarousal are interpreted by man as normal, creative, psychotic, and ecstatic states (left) and Zazen and samadhi (right). The loop connecting ecstasy and samadhi represents the rebound from ecstasy to samadhi, which is observed in response to intense ergotropic excitation. The numbers 35 to 7 on the perception-hallucination continuum are Goldstein's coefficient of variation (*46*), specifying the decrease in variability of the EEG amplitude with increasing ergotropic arousal. The numbers 26 to 4 on the perception-meditation continuum, on the other hand, refer to those beta, alpha, and theta EEG waves (measured in hertz) that predominate during, but are not specific to, these states (*17*).

significantly related to the S/M at $T_1$ ($r = 0.4888$, $P < .01$, $N = 47$) and that the standard deviation is a simple and useful indicator of the ensuing drug-induced increase in S/M ratio ($r = 0.372$, $P < .01$, $N = 47$). Moreover, subjects with a large standard deviation on handwriting area at $T_1$ (that is, "variable" subjects), tend to be "perceivers," whereas volunteers with a small standard deviation at $T_1$ ("stable" subjects) tend to be "judgers," in terms of the Myers-Briggs Type Indicator. This self-reporting, Jungian-type personality indicator yields simple, continuous scores on four dichotomous scales: extroversion-introversion, sensation-intuition, thinking-feeling, and judging-perceiving (23). The perceivers also overestimate or contract time more than judgers do at the peak of a psilocybin-induced experience (4); this implies that perceivers move faster and farther along the perception-hallucination continuum than do judgers, who apparently require a larger dose for a comparable experience.

### Space and Increasing Hyper- and Hypoarousal

We call man's symbolic interpretation of his CNS activity "perception-behavior" and regard creative, "hyperphrenic," and ecstatic states, as well as Zazen and samadhi, as perceptual-behavioral interpretations of ergotropic and trophotropic arousal, respectively. We may now consider some of the perceptual-behavioral changes, or transformations, that gradually develop as the level of arousal increases and decreases along each continuum. One of the most conspicuous transformations is that of "constancies" (24), which in the normal state of daily routine form a learned structure of primary ordering of space and time "out there." Although the newborn infant's only reality, in the beginning, is his CNS activity, he soon learns, by bumping into things, to erect a corresponding model "out there." Ultimately, his forgetting that his CNS activity had been the only reality will be taken by society as proof of his maturity, and he will be ready to conduct his life "out there" in (container) space and (chronological) time (4). This gradually learned and projected model, then, is the re-presentation of a world ordered and stabilized by self-programmed invariances. The adult interprets his CNS activity within this structure of similarity criteria, or "constancies," and thus experience can be said to consist of two processes: the programmed (subcortical) CNS activity; and the symbolic or perceptual-behavioral (cortical) interpretation, or metaprograms, of the CNS activity.

I have studied the transformation of certain constancies along the perception-hallucination continuum and find, for example, that the ability to readapt to optically induced spatial distortions, or to maintain the constancy of the visual world, gradually diminishes as a subject turns inward under the influence of psilocybin (25). Another finding revealed that the preferred level of (the constancy of) brightness increases under the influence of hallucinogenic drugs (26), but only in "variable" subjects (20, 27)—that is, those subjects whose large standard deviations on a variety of perceptual and behavioral tasks indicate a large and varied interpretive repertoire. However, in "stable" subjects, who are characterized by small standard deviations and, thus, by smaller and more predictable interpretive repertoires, the level of preferred brightness decreases when they are under the influence of hallucinogenic drugs. In addition, nearby visual space was found to gradually close in as subjects moved along the perception-hallucination continuum under the influence of moderate doses of psilocybin. This contraction of nearby visual space was observed with two different techniques: monitoring the apparent fronto-parallel plane (28), and handwriting measurements (29).

The transformation of constancies under ergotropic arousal—specifically, as manifested in the psilocybin-induced contraction of nearby visual space—can also be observed in acute schizophrenics under "natural" ergotropic arousal (that is, without hallucinogenic

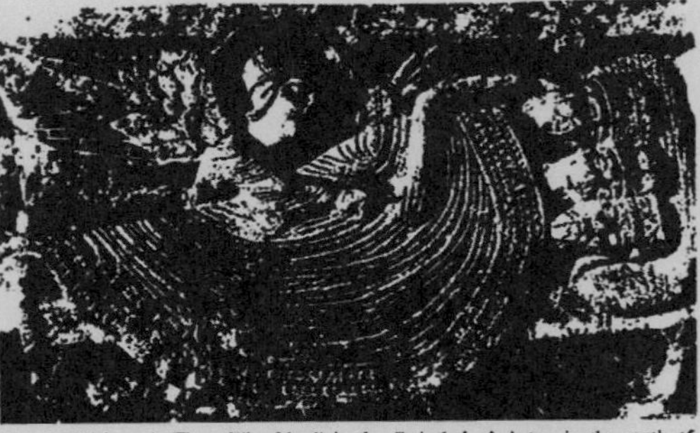

Fig. 2. Gislebertus' "Three Wise Men," in the Cathedral of Autun in the south of France, dramatizes the intense sensations and concomitant loss of voluntary motor activity which are the common features of both hallucinations (see the wise man with eyes open) and dreams (see the two dreaming wise men).

drugs). The transformation of constancies during acute psychotic episodes apparently gives rise to a "vertical displacement of the visual angle," which is implicit in a contraction of visual space and which results in an elevation of the horizon (30). Rennert (30), who for years has studied the angle tions of the projected type like adults, but only of the introjected type. They hear voices inside their head or other parts of the body, feel that they originate inside themselves and do not feel persecuted by them" (34).

The constancy of corporeal awareness also undergoes transformations as one moves along the perception-hallucination continuum. For instance, phantom sensations [that is, readaptation phenomena compensating for and correcting distortions of corporeal awareness in physical space-time (35)] gradually diminish and disappear as one moves into the mental dimension under the influence of hallucinogenic drugs (36). Depersonalization phenomena, on the other hand, manifest themselves as changes in body image, and usually accompany the dissolution of ego boundaries during creative, psychotic, ecstatic, or meditative states—whether "natural" or drug-induced—as well as while falling asleep. All of this is to say that the constancy of the "I" is interfered with as one moves along the perception-hallucination continuum from the "I" of the physical world to the "Self" of the mental dimension. Analogously, the perception-meditation continuum (Fig. 1, right) also involves quinine, and so on) to taste a JND in sweetness or bitterness. On the other hand, under the influence of tranquilizers of the phenothiazine type, the Weber fraction becomes larger; more molecules are needed to taste a JND (32). Since the Weber fraction is constant at levels of arousal associated with daily routine (within the customary middle range of taste sensitivity) (33), I interpret the above as examples of arousal-induced transformations of constancies. Because the number of molecules necessary to elicit the sensation of a JND gradually decreases during a voyage from the physical to the mental dimension along the perception-hallucination continuum, it might be extrapolated that no sapid molecules at all are needed for the experience of taste during ecstasy, the most hyperaroused hallucinatory state.

It should be emphasized that the projection of our CNS activity as location in the physical dimension of space and time "out there" was learned at, and is hence bound to, the lower levels of arousal characteristic of our daily survival routines. That this projection is gradually learned can be supported by Bender's observation that schizophrenic children "do not experience hallucinations of the projected type like adults, but only of the introjected type. They hear voices inside their head or other parts of the body, feel that they originate inside themselves and do not feel persecuted by them" (34).

The constancy of corporeal awareness also undergoes transformations as one moves along the perception-hallucination continuum. For instance, phantom sensations [that is, readaptation phenomena compensating for and correcting distortions of corporeal awareness in physical space-time (35)] gradually diminish and disappear as one moves into the mental dimension under the influence of hallucinogenic drugs (36). Depersonalization phenomena, on the other hand, manifest themselves as changes in body image, and usually accompany the dissolution of ego boundaries during creative, psychotic, ecstatic, or meditative states—whether "natural" or drug-induced—as well as while falling asleep. All of this is to say that the constancy of the "I" is interfered with as one moves along the perception-hallucination continuum from the "I" of the physical world to the "Self" of the mental dimension. Analogously, the perception-meditation continuum (Fig. 1, right) also involves a departure from the "I" to the "Self." These two continua can thus be called "I-Self" continua. As will become clear later, the "Self" of ecstasy and the "Self" of samadhi are one and the same 'Self.'

The further we progress on the perception-hallucination continuum from the normal through the creative, psychotic, and, ultimately, to the ecstatic state (Fig. 1), the more complete is the transformation, or "unlearning," of the constancies of the physical dimension. Input, or outside information in general, is gradually reduced along this continuum. Thus, Saint Teresa of Avila tells us in her autobiography that, at the peak of a mystical experience, ". . . the soul neither hears nor sees nor feels. While it lasts, none of the senses perceives or knows what is taking place" (6). Space, then, which was gradually established in ever-widening circles during childhood, gradually contracts with increasing arousal and ultimately disappears.

### Time and Increasing Hyper- and Hypoarousal

A gradual contraction and ultimate disappearance is also the fate of chronological time in the physical dimension (of the "I" state) as one progresses along the perception-hallucination or the perception-meditation continuum. In particular, we find that LSD (37) and psilocybin (4) cause an overestimation of time, the magnitude of which is related to a subject's variability on a perceptual or behavioral test before ingesting the given drug. The greater a subject's variability before ingesting a drug—for example, the retest-variance on his quinine taste-threshold or the standard deviation on his handwriting area—the greater will be his contraction or overestimation of time at drug peak [that is, 150 minutes after the oral administration of 160 to 200 micrograms of psilocybin per kilogram of body weight, when 63 minutes of chron-

Act 4:
The introduction
is published as an
248  <u>Afterword</u>  in 2011

to Morocco, are just as native to the region as those who converted to Islam. Are they all to be stifled and suppressed under the outmoded conformity of Islam dressed up in the new garb of Arab nationalism? Some, like the Kurds and Israelis, resist. Others, like the Copts, must at present lie low. But few, if any, consent simply to disappear.

Behind the dramatic Israeli-Arab confrontation the fate of many other people and the future of the region itself hang in the balance. The Kurds have a better chance to achieve their independence as long as Israel constitutes a major preoccupation for the Iraqi rulers; the Maronites in Lebanon cannot be absorbed or eliminated by the Moslem majority as long as Israel is there. Some of them surely know that, even if a deep-rooted anti-Semitism has prevented many groups struggling for their own survival to fully appreciate the significance for their own sake of Israel's existence. The grave mistake of Syrian and Lebanese Christians might well have been to support Arabism for the immediate advantage it gave them over other minorities (Greeks, Armenians, Copts, and Jews) who had no claim to "Arabism," while forgetting that their own survival hinged on a pluralistic Levantine framework rather than on a monolithic Arab or Moslem one.

We have all clung to old hostilities from our pasts—ethnic, theological, and national—and made no attempt to reinterpret them in terms that would be mutually inclusive rather than exclusive. Reviving the notion of the Levant as a geographic entity, comprising many genuinely native peoples and cultures, may help us to create a consensus between Israel and other people in the region that stems from the acceptance of diversity not as an inevitable evil, but as a necessary good. Our own fears about assimilation and Levantinization have prevented us from stressing to best advantage the importance of a strong, independent Israel in the Levant, which can have a dynamic impact. The very fact that we are intensely particularistic as regards our own history, language, and culture provides an assurance that what may be termed our "expansionism" and "imperialism" cannot be indefinite, but will be limited in time, as was the case with Byzantium and Islam. A Jewish Israel promises the best guarantee for the freedom of other people in the region who are just as particularistic and are no more prepared to be absorbed by us than we are to be absorbed by them. Even those now in the grips

... there are other dramas, like the one recounting the dramaturgy of publishing

Act 2:

A collection under the same title, published in Hebrew translation, does not include the introduction. Nor it includes the translator's name, thus suggesting that the essays were written in Hebrew.



ERAN SCHAERF ANNOTATED AFTERWORD FROM EAST THE SUN, 1978, JACQUELINE SHOHET KAHANOFF, MONGRELS OR MARVELS: THE LEVANTINE WRITINGS OF JACQUELINE SHOHET KAHANOFF, 2011, ED. BY DEBORAH A. STARR & SASSON SOMEKH of revolutionary Pan-Arabism may yet discover that a pluralistic Levantine solution is a reasonable alternative to the anarchy created in the name of an all-embracing, if largely illusory, Arab unity.

The concept of a reconstructed Levant may help us to redefine ourselves in relation to others. While Zionism has little meaning for the people in the area among whom we live, an independent Israel which defends its right to be itself may have far greater impact. But Western concepts, unfortunately, often prevent us from finding a language that expresses our perception of ourselves, and we may need to circumvent them in order to communicate directly in terms of our own historical sensitivities.

The concept of the nation-state appears modern or advanced in regard to the Levant's hodgepodge of communities, but in global terms nation-states may be already obsolete. Yet, psychologically, human beings still feel the need to belong to smaller, cozier communities, and still care about their personal pasts. Strikingly, while Europe unites, the Bretons, Basques, Welsh, Flemish, Irish, and Scots assert their own cultural autonomy against the all-inclusive nation-state. Furthermore, newer groups crystallize, as a result of immigration following the breakup of the European empires—Africans, Pakistanis, West Indians, Indochinese, Algerians, etc. They constitute new social and cultural enclaves in Europe—much as Jews almost exclusively once did—with no territorial claims in their new surroundings. They are not, and do not want to be, totally integrated or absorbed in the nation-state; they maintain ties with their countries of origin. They constitute *ummot*—folk—much on the old Levantine pattern. In other words, the Western nation-state itself is being Levantinized. Various types of communities, incorporated in a wider, rather loosely organized entity, might provide a solution in the many cases where different people have to share the same geographic space. Human groupings thus comprise concentric, intersecting, and overlapping circles, and ethnic, spiritual, or cultural identities do not and can not correspond to neatly fixed territorial units.

Significantly, Israel has as yet no fixed or recognized boundaries, so that, while some may debate whether we should exist at all, Israelis argue about the fate of Hebron, Shekhem, and Jericho. But what to us

BY KEEPING ITS INNER CRISIS INNER (CHASTE IN THE SENSE OF FOCUS, KEEPING ITSELF UNTOUCHED BY WHAT DOESN'T TOUCH IT, WHAT IS UNRELATED TO THE TASK) WHILE SOMETHING NOW IS IN THE PROCESS OF GESTATION, WHAT'S GOING TO HAPPEN

Aussi garde-toi et sois là.

KEEP YOUR EYES OPEN AND BE THERE. (SOMETHING WILL HAPPEN, DON'T MISS IT)

La poésie, sacre ; qui essaie, en de chastes crises isolément, pendant l'autre gestation en train.

POETRY, SACRED JUST INSOFAR AS AN ATTEMPT (BUT AN ATTEMPT AT WHAT?

Publie.

PUBLISH! PUT THINGS OUT IN PUBLIC (NO MATTER IF THERE IS NO PUBLIC)

Le Livre, où vit l'esprit satisfait, en cas de malentendu, un obligé par quelque pureté d'ébat à secouer le gros du moment. Impersonnifié, le volume, autant qu'on s'en sépare comme auteur, ne réclame approche de lecteur. Tel, sache, entre les accessoires humains, il a lieu tout seul : fait, étant. Le sens enseveli se meut et dispose, en chœur, des feuillets.

NOT SPECIFIC TO ANY INDIVIDUAL ESP. THE AUTHOR

BURIED BUT NOT DEAD - ACTIVE: THE SENSE OF THE BOOK

THICKNESS? DENSITY?

IT'S NOT CLICK BAIT

THE ONLY HUMAN-MADE THING THAT IS THOROUGHLY MADE, THAT THEREFORE FULLY EXISTS

Loin, la superbe de mettre en interdit, même quant aux fastes, l'instant : on constate qu'un hasard y dénie les matériaux de confrontation à quelques rêves ; ou aide une attitude spéciale.

HOPES THAT BY SOME CHANCE IT LACKS THE MATERIAL (THE MATERIALITY?) TO CONFRONT (IMMATERIAL) IDEAS

Toi, Ami, qu'il ne faut frustrer d'années à cause que parallèles au sourd labeur général, le cas est étrange : je te demande, sans jugement, par manque de considérants soudains,

DON'T BE FRUSTRATED JUST BECAUSE YOU FIND YOURSELF IN THE THICK OF A COLLECTIVE LABOR THAT REMAINS UNHEARD

YOU CAN TAKE WHAT I SAY AS FOLLY — BUT A CERTAIN WISDOM
TEMPERS IT — NAMELY TO HAZARD (DESPITE CONDITIONS NOT
BEING PROPITIOUS FOR IT) CERTAIN CONCLUSIONS OF AN ART
TAKEN TO THE EXTREME

que tu traites mon indication comme une folie je ne le défends, rare. Cependant la tempère déjà cette sagesse, ou discernement, s'il ne vaut pas mieux — que de risquer sur un état à tout le moins incomplet environnant, certaines conclusions d'art extrêmes qui peuvent éclater, diamantairement, dans ce temps à jamais, en l'intégrité du Livre — les jouer, mais et par un triomphal renversement, avec l'injonction tacite que rien, palpitant en le flanc inscient de l'heure, aux pages montré, clair, évident, ne la trouve prête ; encore que n'en soit peut-être une autre où ce doive illuminer.

WHICH CAN EXPLODE FROM NOW TO WHENEVER —
TO PLAY THEM (TO GAMBLE, TO BET ON THEM)
WITH THE PROVISO THAT NOTHING — EVER,
IN THOSE "SEEDS OF TIME," ~~HOWEVER~~ HOWEVER
CLEAR AND EVIDENT ON THE PAGE, WILL FIND
ITS MOMENT OF READINESS. (THE PRESENT NEVER
ARRIVES.) AND YET THERE ALWAY REMAINS
ANOTHER TIME FOR IT TO ILLUMINATE
(IN ADVANCE).

(tel qu'il fut présenté au public du Café au Go-Go, N.Y., 8 février 1965) :
Moi, m'adressant au public : « mon nom est Filliou, donc le titre de mon poème est :

LE FILLIOU IDÉAL

C'est un poème-action et je vais le présenter :

> ne rien décider
> ne rien choisir
> ne rien vouloir
> ne rien posséder
> conscient de soi
> pleinement éveillé
> TRANQUILLEMENT ASSIS
> SANS RIEN FAIRE ».

(Puis je me suis assis en tailleur sur la scène, immobile et silencieux.)



102

STEPHEN SHEEHAN ANNOTATED JUMPERS: THE FATAL GRANDEUR OF THE GOLDEN GATE BRIDGE, THE NEW YORKER, OCTOBER 13 2003, TAD FRIEND

that everything in my life that I'd thought was unfixable was totally fixable—except for having just jumped." *[handwritten: realised in the final moments everything could be changed…]*

# Kevin Hines was eighteen when he took a municipal bus to the bridge one

day in September, 2000. After treating himself to a last meal of Starbursts and Skittles, he paced back and forth and sobbed on the bridge walkway for half an hour. No one asked him what was wrong. A beautiful German tourist approached, handed him her camera, and asked him to take her picture, which he did. "I was like, 'Fuck this, nobody cares,'" he told me. *[handwritten: Why should we though??]* "So I jumped." But after he crossed the chord, he recalls, "My first thought was What the hell did I just do? I don't want to die." *[handwritten: exactly — "He" doesn't want to die]*

Paul Alarab never told his colleagues about his first experience on the bridge. He didn't even tell his wife, whom he married in 1990 and divorced in 1995. The only hint of his fascination was his business card, which he resisted changing despite his boss's complaint that it looked unprofessional. The card featured a photo of Alarab on the shore of the Bay; behind him lurked the Golden Gate. *[handwritten: — Derren Brown shit go on here.]*

On that March morning, facing the camera, Alarab read an ambiguous handwritten addendum to his statement: "I would sacrifice myself as a symbol of children that will die. If you are antiwar, e-mail me at alarabpaul@hotmail.com." After forty minutes, CNN had not arrived and it seemed that Alarab had done all he could. It was 11:33 A.M. He bent to put his statement on the bridge, then placed his cell phone on it. He then unwound his wrist from the securing rope and stepped off the chord. The officers on the walkway craned their necks in a horrified line, watching him fall. *[handwritten: Madness. Again cos nobody cared, but he cared. Yet he stepped off the bridge.]*

At a 1977 rally on the Golden Gate supporting the building of an anti-suicide barrier above the railing, a minister, speaking to six hundred of his followers, tried to explain the bridge's power. Matchless in its Art Deco splendor, the Golden Gate is also unrivalled as a symbol: it is a threshold that presides over the end of the continent and a gangway to the void beyond. Just being there, the minister said, his words growing increasingly

*[left-margin handwritten: I think we need to not give a fuck about what people that — not give a fuck about our existence.]*

*[left-margin handwritten: I would say that's the problem today. We expect people to care about our problems and our existence because social media makes us feel about us that, we don't.]*

*[right-margin handwritten: I wonder if it is the rush of adrenaline that makes people alive for those final seconds that makes them want to live, for many it's too late! splash.]*

incoherent, left him in a rather suicidal mood. The Golden Gate, he said, is "a symbol of human ingenuity, technological genius, but social failure."

Eighteen months later, that minister, the Reverend Jim Jones, who had decamped with his People's Temple to Jonestown, Guyana, ordered his adherents to kill themselves by drinking grape Kool-Aid mixed with potassium cyanide. Nine hundred and twelve of them did.

Every two weeks, on average, someone jumps off the Golden Gate Bridge. It is the world's leading suicide location. In the eighties, workers at a local lumberyard formed "the Golden Gate Leapers Association"—a sports pool in which bets were placed on which day of the week someone would jump. At least twelve hundred people have been seen jumping or have been found in the water since the bridge opened, in 1937, including Roy Raymond, the founder of Victoria's Secret, in 1993, and Duane Garrett, a Democratic fund-raiser and a friend of Al Gore's, in 1995. The actual toll is probably considerably higher, swelled by legions of the stealthy, who sneak onto the bridge after the walkway closes at sundown and are carried to sea with the neap tide. Many jumpers wrap suicide notes in plastic and tuck them into their pockets. "Survival of the fittest. Adios—unfit," one seventy-year-old man said in his valedictory; another wrote, "Absolutely no reason except I have a toothache."

There is a fatal grandeur to the place. Like Paul Alarab, who lived and worked in the East Bay, several people have crossed the Bay Bridge to jump from the Golden Gate; there is no record of anyone traversing the Golden Gate to leap from its unlovely sister bridge. Dr. Richard Seiden, a professor emeritus at the University of California at Berkeley's School of Public Health and the leading researcher on suicide at the bridge, has written that studies reveal "a commonly held attitude that romanticizes suicide from the Golden Gate Bridge in such terms as aesthetically pleasing and beautiful, while regarding a Bay Bridge suicide as tacky."

Unlike the Bay Bridge—or most bridges, for that matter—the Golden Gate has a footpath adjacent to a low exterior railing. "Jumping from the bridge is seen as sure, quick, clean, and available—which is the most potent factor,"

**New York Times** DEC. 18, 2000

***WRITERS ON WRITING; Directions: Write, Read, Rewrite. Repeat Steps 2 and 3 as Needed.***

## By SUSAN SONTAG

Reading novels seems to me such a normal activity, while writing them is such an odd thing to do. . . . At least so I think until I remind myself how firmly the two are related. (No armored generalities here. Just a few remarks.)

First, because to write is to practice, with particular intensity and attentiveness, the art of reading. You write in order to read what you've written and see if it's O.K. and, since of course it never is, to rewrite it -- once, twice, as many times as it takes to get it to be something you can bear to reread. You are your own first, maybe severest, reader. "To write is to sit in judgment on oneself," Ibsen inscribed on the flyleaf of one of his books. Hard to imagine writing without rereading.

But is what you've written straight off never all right? Yes, sometimes even better than all right. And that only suggests, to this novelist at any rate, that with a closer look, or voicing aloud -- that is, another reading -- it might be better still. I'm not saying that the writer has to fret and sweat to produce something good.

"What is written without effort is in general read without pleasure," said Dr. Johnson, and the maxim seems as remote from contemporary taste as its author. Surely, much that is written without effort gives a great deal of pleasure.

No, the question is not the judgment of readers -- who may well prefer a writer's more spontaneous, less elaborated work -- but a sentiment of writers, those professionals of dissatisfaction. You think, "If I can get it to this point the first go around, without too much struggle, couldn't it be better still?"

And though the rewriting -- and the rereading -- sound like effort, they are actually the most pleasurable parts of writing. Sometimes the only pleasurable parts. Setting out to write, if you have the idea of "literature" in your head, is formidable, intimidating. A plunge in an icy lake. Then comes the warm part: when you already have something to work with, upgrade, edit.

Let's say it's a mess. But you have a chance to fix it. You try to be clearer. Or deeper. Or more eloquent. Or more eccentric. You try to be true to a world. You want the book to be more spacious, more authoritative. You want to winch yourself up from yourself. You want to winch the book out of your balky mind. As the statue is entombed in the block of marble, the novel is inside your head. You try to liberate it. You try to get this wretched stuff on the page closer to what you think your book should be -- what you know, in your spasms of elation, it can be. You read the sentences over and over. Is this the book I'm writing? Is this all?

Or let's say it's going well; for it does go well, sometimes. (If it didn't, some of the time, you'd go crazy.) There you are, and even if you are the slowest of scribes and the worst of touch typists, a trail of words is getting laid down, and you want to keep going; and then you reread it. Perhaps you don't dare to be satisfied, but at the same time you like what you've written. You find yourself taking pleasure -- a reader's pleasure -- in what's there on the page.

Writing is finally a series of permissions you give yourself to be expressive in certain ways. To invent. To leap. To fly. To fall. To find your own characteristic way of narrating and insisting; that is, to find your own inner freedom. To be strict without being too self-excoriating. Not stopping too often to reread. Allowing yourself, when you dare to think it's going well (or not too badly), simply to keep rowing along. No waiting for inspiration's shove.

Blind writers can never reread what they dictate. Perhaps this matters less for poets, who often do most of their writing in their head before setting anything down on paper. (Poets live by the ear much more than prose writers do.) And not being able to see doesn't mean that one doesn't make revisions. Don't we imagine that Milton's daughters, at the end of each day of the dictation of "Paradise Lost," read it all back to their father aloud and then took down his corrections?

But prose writers, who work in a lumberyard of words, can't hold it all in their heads. They need to see what they've written. Even those writers who seem most forthcoming, prolific, must feel this. (Thus Sartre announced, when he went blind, that his writing days were over.) Think of portly, venerable Henry James pacing up and down in a room in Lamb House composing "The Golden Bowl" aloud to a secretary. Leaving aside the difficulty of imagining how James's late prose could have been dictated at all, much less to the racket made by a Remington typewriter circa 1900, don't we assume that James reread what had been typed and was lavish with his corrections?

When I became, again, a cancer patient two years ago and had to break off work on the nearly finished "In America," a kind friend in Los Angeles, knowing my despair and fear that now I'd never finish it, offered to take a leave from his job and come to New York and stay with me as long as needed, to take down my dictation of the rest of the novel. True, the first eight chapters were done (that is, rewritten and reread many times), and I'd

from "Speak, Memory"
VLADIIMIR NABOKOV 1967

Chapter 6

The mysteries of mimicry had a special attraction for me. Its phenomena showed an artistic perfection usually associated with [man] wrought things. Consider the imitation of oozing poison by bubblelike macules on a wing (complete with pseudo-refraction) or by glossy yellow knobs on a chrysalis ('Don't eat me - I have already been squashed, sampled and rejected). Consider the tricks of an acrobatic caterpillar (of the Lobster Moth) which in infancy looks like a birds's dung, but after molting develops scrabbly hymenopteroid appendages and baroque characteristics, allowing the extraordinary [fellow] to play two parts at once (like the actor in ~~~~~~ shows who *becomes* a pair of intertwisted wrestlers): that of a writhing larva and that of a big ant seemingly harrowing it. When a certain moth resembles a certain wasp in shape and colour, it also walks and moves its antennae in a waspish, unmothlike manner. When a butterfly has to look like a leaf, not only are all the details of the leaf beautifully rendered but markings mimicking grub-bored holes are generously thrown in. 'Natural selection', in the Darwinian sense, could not explain the miraculous coincidence of imitative behaviour, nor could one appeal to the theory of 'the struggle for life' when a protective device was carried to a point of mimetic subtlety exuberance, and <u>luxury far in excess of a predator's power of appreciation</u>. I discovered in nature the <u>nonutilitarian delights</u> that I sought in art. Both were a form of magic, both were a game of intricate enchantment and deception.



ANJ SMITH ANNOTATED SPEAK, MEMORY: AN AUTOBIOGRAPHY REVISITED, 2000, VLADIMIR NABOKOV

from "Speak, Memory" 1964
Vladimir Nabokov

I confess I do not believe in time. I like to fold my magic carpet, after use, in such a way as to superimpose one part of the pattern upon the other. Let visitors trip. And the highest enjoyment of timelessness - in a landscape selected at random - is when I stand among rare butterflies and their food plants. This is ecstasy, and behind the ecstasy is something else, which is hard to explain. It is like a momentary vacuum into which rushes all that I love. A sense of oneness with sun and stone. A thrill of gratitude to whom it may concern - to the lucky contrapuntal genius of human fate or to ghosts humoring a lucky mortal.

Chapter 6

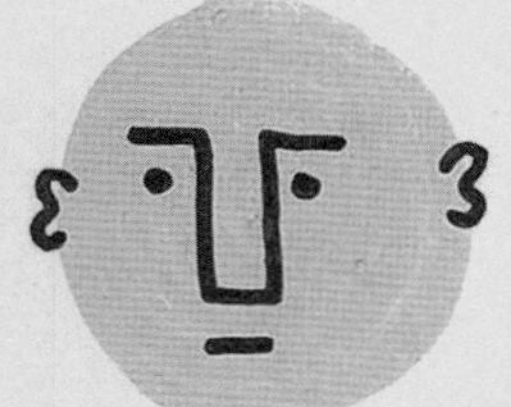
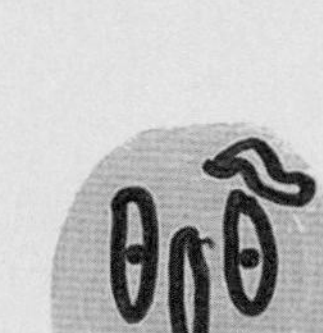
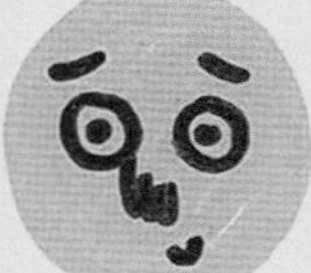
THERE IS STILL ART THERE IS STILL HOPE

## Responsive Movements

In front of the motor cortex are the **premotor** cortex and **supplementary** cortex. These areas **select** movements that the motor cortex will execute.

Premotor cortex selects movements in response to *external* triggers.

Supplementary cortex selects movements in response to *internal* triggers.

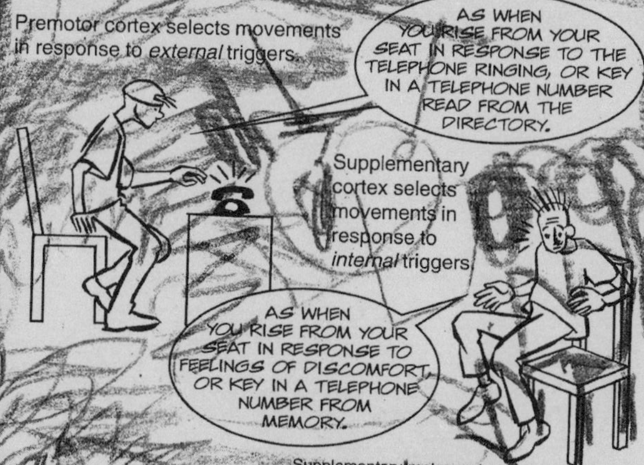

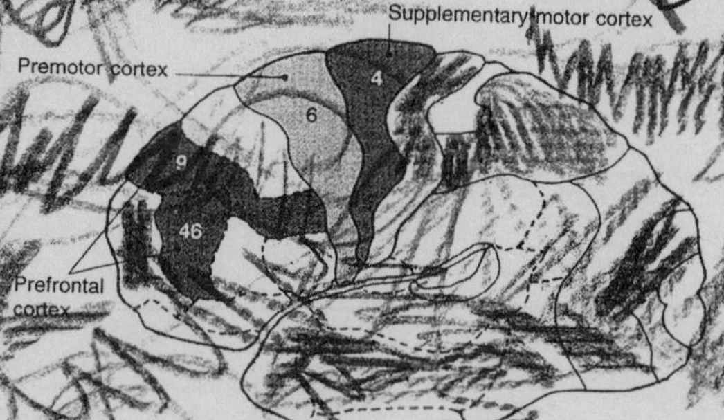

Forward of premotor and supplementary cortex lies the **prefrontal** cortex. This area has many incoming and outgoing connections. The upper and lower visual pathways from the parietal and temporal lobes terminate here.

140

374

## Free Will and the Frontal Lobes

When **Penfield** stimulated the motor cortex of conscious surgical patients, they assured him that they experienced their consequent movements as involuntary, not willed.

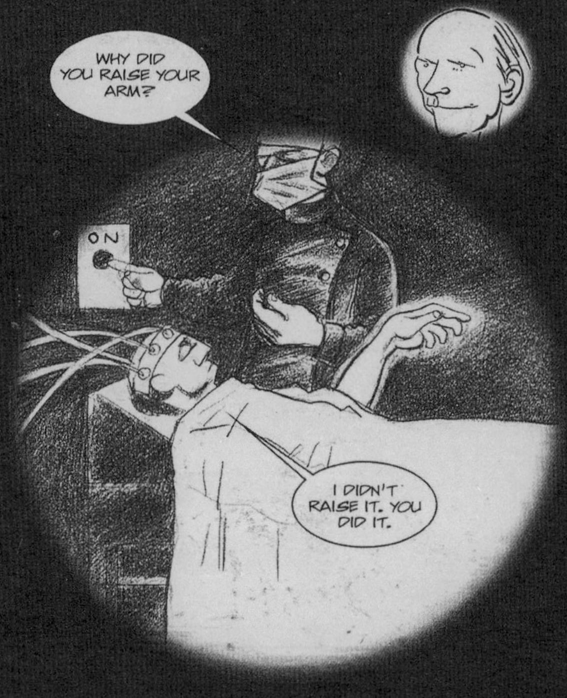

The **motor cortices** are at the back of the frontal lobes (FLs). Their role is to initiate execution of cortically generated movements, as opposed to movements generated sub-cortically or spinally (as we saw in the section on movement). But Penfield's patients bear eloquent witness that they are not **the seat of the will**.

139

Well Great Crikes!'

He got up and brushed his hair with a flat hand back along his skull and looked out of the window for a long interval, his eyes popping and dancing and his face like an empty bag with no blood in it.

Then he walked around to put back the circulation and took a little spear from a place he had on the shelf.

'Put your hand out,' he said.

I put it out idly enough and he held the spear at it. He kept putting it near me and nearer and when he had the bright point of it about half a foot away, I felt a prick and gave a short cry. There was a little bead of my red blood in the middle of my palm.

'Thank you very much,' I said. I felt too surprised to be annoyed with him.

'That will make you think,' he remarked in triumph, 'unless I am an old Dutchman by profession and nationality.'

He put his little spear back on the shelf and looked at me crookedly from a sidewise angle with a certain quantity of what may be called *roi-s'amuse.*

'Maybe you can explain that?' he said.

'That is the limit,' I said wonderingly.

'It will take some analysis,' he said, 'intellectually.'

'Why did your spear sting when the point was half a foot away from where it made me bleed?'

'That spear' he answered quietly, 'is one of the first things I ever manufactured in my spare time. I think only a little of it now but the year I made it I was proud enough and would

69

not get up in the morning for any sergeant. There is no other spear like it in the length and breadth of Ireland and there is only one thing like it in Amurikey but I have not heard what it is. But I cannot get over the no-bicycle. Great Crikes!'

'But the spear,' I insisted, 'give me the gist of it like a good man and I will tell no one.'

'I will tell you because you are a confidential man,' he said, 'and a man that said something about bicycles that I never heard before. What you think is the point is not the point at all but only the beginning of the sharpness.'

'Very wonderful,' I said, 'but I do not understand you.'

'The point is seven inches long and it is so sharp and thin that you cannot see it with the old eye. The first half of the sharpness is thick and strong but you cannot see it either because the real sharpness runs into it and if you saw the one you could see the other or maybe you would notice the joint.'

'I suppose it is far thinner than a match?' I asked.

'There *is* a difference,' he said. 'Now the proper sharp part is so thin that nobody could see it no matter what light is on it or what eye is looking. About an inch from the end it is so sharp that sometimes — late at night or on a soft bad day especially — you cannot think of it or try to make it the subject of a little idea because you will hurt your box with the excruciation of it.'

I gave a frown and tried to make myself look like a



375

the excruciation of it.'

I gave a frown and tried to make myself look like a wise person who was trying to comprehend something that called for all his wisdom.

'You cannot have fire without bricks,' I said, nodding.

'Wisely said,' MacCruiskeen answered.

'It was sharp sure enough,' I conceded, 'it drew a little bulb of the red blood but I did not feel the pricking hardly at all. It must be very sharp to work like that.'

MacCruiskeen gave a laugh and sat down again at the table and started putting on his belt.

'You have not got the whole gist of it at all,' he smiled. 'Because what gave you the prick and brought the blood was not the point at all; it was the place I am talking about that

70

*Who could have imagined that those telephones would become equipped with lenses the size of a pea and record high-quality photographs that could be summoned at will from a vast but invisible library?*

*And in the early 1970s, who would have guessed that our telephones would communicate silently with other, yet-to-be-invented and unimaginable electronic devices, their conversations facilitated by an invisible, but allegedly blue, tooth?*

is a good inch from the reputed point of the article under our discussion.'

'And what is this inch that is left?' I asked. 'What in heaven's name would you call that?'

'That is the real point,' said MacCruiskeen, 'but it is so thin that it could go into your hand and out in the other extremity externally and you would not feel a bit of it and you would see nothing and hear nothing. It is so thin that maybe it does not exist at all and you could spend half an hour trying to think about it and you could put no thought around it in the end. The beginning part of the inch is thicker than the last part and is nearly there for a fact but I don't think it is if it is my private opinion that you are anxious to enlist.'

I fastened my fingers around my jaw and started to think

WORK

...I decided to stop using the word "work" as an experiment. It was very difficult! I had to compensate by substituting a more specific description of the activity. For example, instead of "I'm going to my studio to work," I'd have to say, "I'm going to make some drawings." Or instead of "I'm going to work around the house," I'd have to say, "I'm going to clean the kitchen and fold some laundry." I discovered that the absence of the word 'work' forced me to reconsider assumptions about leisure, because the idea of work implied its opposite. I let go of the notion that I deserved a certain amount of downtime from being productive or from being active. The labour/leisure dichotomy became uncoupled and then dissolved. I couldn't use labour to allay guilt or self-punish or feel superior. Work didn't exist, so all the psychological payoff of work for work's sake had nowhere to go.

WHAT IS AN ARTIST'S ACTIVITY IF IT'S NOT WORK?

I started to adjust my thinking about productivity so that it was no longer valued in and of itself. It strikes me as vulgar always to have to apply a cost/benefit analysis to days lived; it's like understanding an exchange of gifts only as barter. The work exercise made me feel as if I was awakening from one of the spells of capitalism. And there was more to it than that: I was able to begin the process of withdrawal from my culture's ideology around the instrumentality of time, i.e. that you can use time. I think the ability to withdraw from consensus reality is one of the most important skills for an artist to learn because it helps her to recognize invisible forces.

TIME AND INFORMATION MANAGEMENT

Your time is not a separate thing from you; it's not an instrument. Time is part of what you're made from. Emerson said, "A man is what he thinks about all day long." Everything that you do and think about is going to be in your artwork. The computer-science idea "garbage in, garbage out" applies to artists. This is something to consider when you're choosing your habitual activities. One question is, how do you create a way of being in the world that allows new things (ideas, information, people, places) into your life without letting everything in? I want to point out that your tolerance for media saturation might be lower than you realize. You need to conduct an open-ended search that doesn't overwhelm you with information and at the same time doesn't limit the search in a way that pre-determines your findings. That is a puzzle.

UNCENSORING

...Going back to school was great — after fourteen semesters off, I was ready. The worst part about being back in school was making art and having to explain it at the same time. It made it impossible for me to feel safe when experimenting. As a consequence of my profound self-doubt and insecurity, I was censoring what I really felt compelled to make, reasoning that since I was stupid, whatever I truly wanted to make would be stupid. I thought I would be better off faking it.
As soon as I got out of school, I was very curious to know what exactly it was that I was censoring, because the repression was so assiduous that I had absolutely no idea what it might be. I decided to try an experiment. I would make whatever I wanted for three months with the understanding that I would not show what I dredged up. Not to anyone. But I felt the need to discover my secret.
I can tell you now, since a lot of time has passed, that I discovered I wanted to draw portraits of pretty women. It seemed dumb at first, but I was patient and nonjudgmental and just let my desire take me wherever it wanted to go, and that's been my modus operandi ever since.
Creating a nonpurposive, free space in which to play and have fun is essential. You can tell when you're looking at art that was a drag to make: it's a drag to look at. On the other hand, it's thrilling to watch someone work through a problem that's exciting for him, even if the subject matter wouldn't normally move you.
I've watched kids playing with exciting, fun toys like bubble guns — they're good for ten minutes. But something like a doctor's kit that allows them to rehearse the drama of their lives is inexhaustibly interesting; they'll carry it everywhere for months. Your art should be like that kind of toy. It may be an

intellectual project, but it needs to be invested with your psychic life and driven by emotional necessity.

## RHYTHM OF WORKING

The format of school dictates a certain rhythm or pace of working. In the same way that in the Law and Order universe a murderer needs to be caught and brought to justice in roughly fifty minutes, artworks need to be completed and critiqued during the semester. I get the feeling that people set their speed in school and then it's reinforced by the art-fair schedule, and with the multiplying venues, our ability to fly cheaply and send high-res images instantly, everything is accelerating. But it's up to you to decide whether or not your work benefits from that pace. …

## MONEY

Becoming an artist is not a good business plan.

## GETTING A CAREER

I'm assuming you want to be an artist for life. I can see that people in their twenties have a lot of anxiety when their peers are showing and they're not, and I worried about that too. But I understand now that it's not a race and I wish I hadn't wasted all that energy worrying. In almost every instance I can think of, getting off to an early start hasn't been an advantage to artists' careers. You probably shouldn't even get serious about showing your work in a commercial context until you're close to thirty. Until then, it's best to observe. While you're learning how the art world works, keep the stakes low. That's to say, keep the career stakes low. It's never the wrong time to embrace psychological risk. I've just more or less equated selling with career, but those things are not equivalent and it's obviously more complicated than that. …

## HISTORY

You do need to know some art history. As a producer of art objects/gestures, the conventions you decide to ignore and the conventions you decide to repeat are as important, if not more so, than what you invent. If you're a total novice start with Cubism to Surrealism and then study 1945–75, then take it from there. …

## FINDING YOURSELF

Artwork comes from the total personality: ego, self, id, conscious and unconscious, transpersonal, linguistic and nonlinguistic, historically determined, sensual, emotional, physical, mental, ideological, and cultural. I believe that in order to make something that's meaningful you have to start by figuring yourself out psychologically. In order to figure myself out I've applied different modes of critique such as Marxism, feminist theory, psychoanalytic theory, history, ayurvedic principles, philosophy, Feldenkrais technique, anthropology, astrology, the physiology of perception, contemplating life as a caveman, health-food regimens, psychedelic experiences, reading self-help books, ebay, falling in love, practicing magical rites, teaching, the scientific method, psychotherapy, yoga, meditation, and dharmic traditions, fasting and other austerities, exercise, napping, resonance repatterning, literature and poetry, friendships, parenting, humour, and countless others. Artwork is self-expression, and clearly I'm talking about a notion of self that radiates far outside of one's body or even one's time.

## READING

1. Walter Benjamin's Illuminations
2. Julie Cameron's The Artist's Way; A Spiritual Path to Higher Creativity.
3. Timothy Ferris's The 4-Hour Workweek
4. Miwon Kwon's essay "Once Place after Another: Notes of Site Specificty"
5. Brian Wallis and Marcia Tuckers's Art After Modernism: Rethinking Representation
6. Fifteen-year-old art magazines.
Fifteen years is about half of a fashion cycle, so you see artowrks in their least flattering light.

## DOLPHINS – ON THE BRINK OF A DOUBLE-BUMMER
### St Ives Bay, Cornwall, Summer 1976

We were way out in the middle of the bay when the first dolphin broke the surface of the water. As he slid between us, my brother Joss stroked his tail and got dragged along and we were laughing and exhilarated. Then his mate came cruising and for a short while we were alone, the four of us under the sun.

God, some things are so incredible, but so unknown that they'll always be scary. These long suede submarines just below the surface of the water … It was a trip. And swimming in deep water is a trip too. I don't mean 20 or 30 feet, I mean right out in the middle of an Atlantic Ocean bay.

I spent a lot of time floating in St Ives Bay that summer. I was wondering what the hell was going on. This "A" level exam failure had spent the whole of his 18 years in Tamworth in the Midlands – it seemed like 18 years of faking it which were about to catch me up.

My parents had wanted me to go to Oxford University and become the new Charles Dickens. Anything less was inglorious failure. Anything at all, except maybe becoming Shakespeare. So I had wallowed in the vat of "potential" that all my teachers supposedly saw in me and hid that I wanted only to play music and hang around with the freaks. Earlier that summer, I'd walked into the kitchen to see my mother crying and saying to my father, "Oh, Alan … What are we going to do with him?"

Oh. My exam results must have arrived. God, these people drive me crazy. They brought me up on reason – that once you find the reason, you'll see clear round the world. Well, I tried to understand them. Even harder, to respect them. But something always hauled me back – and kicking kicking kicking.

And so that summer of 1976 ended. But St Ives Bay held my answer. My parents drove me crazy, but I saw clear round the world. And it wasn't me that found the reason. No, I was shown the reason. And swimming with the dolphins was swimming *next* to freedom…

Extract from Head-On, Julian Cope, 1999

A couple of years back I got mildly obsessed by English musician and eccentric Julian Cope. During this period I also read this Biography of his, "Head-On" (which is mostly about discovering LSD and making it "big" with The Teardrop Explodes), and his less entertaining follow-up "Repossessed" (which is mostly about watching TV in Tamworth and collecting toy cars). He apparently wrote it pretty much in one go, remembering everything with total recall, which is surprising considering the amount of acid the man has ingested. And so, this page is the first one of that first biography, and somehow it foreshadows the rest of his life story. I often find biographies reassuring, of course they often follow the cliché recipe of now famous people overcoming whatever adversity to finally come out on top and write about it. But they also have those moments of calm before the storm, of swimming with dolphins in St Ives Bay not knowing what fathoms of water lies beneath or what a massive chunk of life lies ahead.

I think that Julian here encapsulates the feeling of awe in one paragraph, a mix of fear and excitement of the unknown, he even starts off with "God" despite being a hardcore atheist, which is a word I myself tend to let slip in moments of shock and awe, despite my non-religousity. Also, swimming in open water terrifies me. Last summer me and two friends stayed for ten days at a cottage in Devon from where each day we tried to find new beaches and bays to explore. It was on one of those days that we made our way down a closed-off National Trust hike to Shipload Bay. From the beach we saw these two seals playing in the water, looking at us with curious seal eyes. Unfortunetly the tide was coming in and it was a bit too dangerous to swim. But it reminded me of Julian and his brother swimming next to the long suede submarines of freedom in Copes childhood.

A few years ago another great Englishman Stewart Lee interviewed Cope for The Guardian. Cope now lives inside (or close by? lets say inside) the massive stone circle in Avebury. For the interview he is dressed as what Lee describes as a mix of an "80s peace convoy anarchist and a WWII Nazi flying ace", he also has on a great NEU tank top and leather gauntlets supposedly made by a fan. Lee wonders how someone dressed in this way is treated in this rural land, Cope answers:

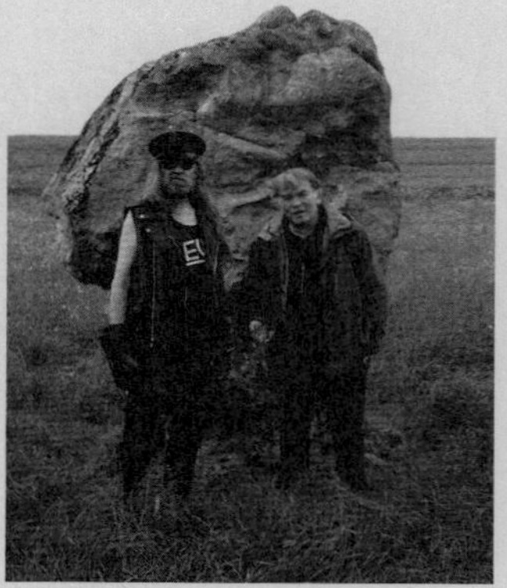

> *"...small communities have room for a local figure like this. All the old guys round here that come and do building and plumbing for our house saw Hendrix in Bath in 1967 and they've all got a crush on him. They don't see him as a guy, but as an exotic peacock creature. There's always room for one fucker. Everyone's got space in their hearts for one mad cunt."*

Amen!

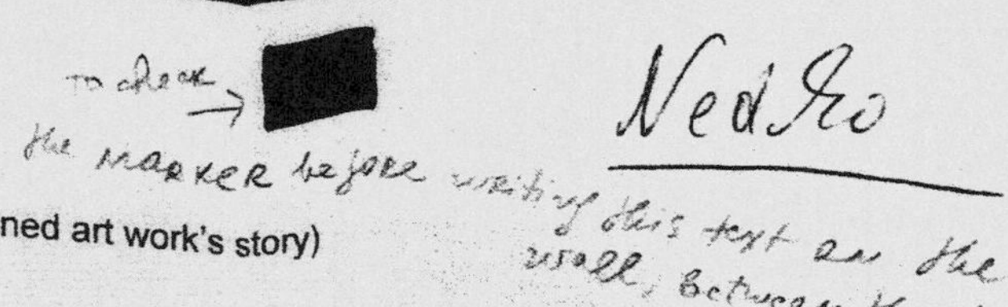


## The Passage (a commissioned art work's story)

I love Caravaggio. What I really like about his works is that most of his masterpieces are displayed in their original locations, in some of the most famous churches in Italy (and I fancy the idea that the visitors have to feed the semi-religious devices with coins to cast light on the Caravaggio paintings in those dark, narrow chapels). I also love his paintings when displayed in museums, too.

Sometimes, in order for the well-known masterpieces to be presented in a fresh way, special exhibitions are organized, combining them with more contemporary or modern classics. Recently, Caravaggio was remarkably paired with Francis Bacon (Caravaggio Bacon, Galleria Borghese, Rome, October 2, 2009 – January 24, 2010).

Then, in order for the exhibition's post-exhibition impact to be made more vivid to the audience, a still-living contemporary artist (me) was commissioned to do a project related to Caravaggio and Bacon at the Uccelliera, in the Galleria Borghese's secret garden. The invitation came jointly from Galleria Borghese, a powerful banking group (financially backing the project), and from the newly opened MAXXI, the Italian museum of contemporary art, which was supposed to receive – later, as a long term loan – the commissioned work.

I was very thrilled and excited...

I was very thrilled and excited, and even though the Caravaggio Bacon exhibition was yet to open when I visited the Galleria Borghese in September 2009, I immediately had an idea what to do in the Uccelliera, the charming space that used to accommodate birds (uccelli). I wanted to have two paintings on studio easels, placed on round plinths, situated harmoniously over the mosaic circles on the floor of the two rooms. On the left canvas, I wanted to have a painting of a man (or a woman), holding a walkie-talkie used by the gallery guards (or an audio guide for the visitors), painted in as Caravaggioesque a way as possible; on the right canvas I wanted to have a woman (or a man) holding an audio guide (or a guard's walkie-talkie), painted in a Baconesque manner. The idea remained in my mind for a long time.

Meanwhile, the Caravaggio Bacon exhibition was inaugurated and closed with great success. For some time there was no real communication among all the parties, which was acceptable for me because I was deeply involved in another matter – my dear father had passed away after suffering from cancer of his kidneys for two years. For 18 months he was relatively okay, treating it only with homeopathy, but in September 2009 (approximately the same time I was commissioned in Rome), he started to feel unwell, and even though he had no real pain, he felt extremely tired and weak, and on February 4th, 2010, at 10:40 p.m. he died in mine and my sister's hands (on the way to the bathroom of my old apartment in Sofia).

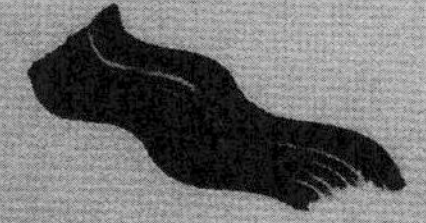

Understandably, the original idea to make those canvases a la Caravaggio and a la Bacon, using the walkie-talkie and the audio guide, wasn't appealing to me anymore. However, I did try to do something on the subject using two small MDF panels that were sent to me by the organizers as examples of the reddish color that was used to paint the walls of the Caravaggio Bacon show (you may still notice a bit of that color on the "Bacon panel"). As you can see, I didn't do well. At the same time, two 73 x 92 cm. white canvases (provided by one of the best art material shops in Europe, which supplies all the famous German painters) were waiting for me on the wall of my "dirty" Sofia studio (the one for making paintings, although the other, for making drawings – where I am writing this text right now – looks as much like an office as the "dirty" one). In a very natural way, I have decided to paint the famous tunnel – the one that a recently deceased person is supposed to appear in, the one leading to the eternal light. I still have and will treasure forever the feeling of holding my vanishing father and – believe me – it was not a bad feeling, there was so much quiet light in it. Here they are – the two tunnels, on your left and your right, facing each other, putting the visitor in the weird position of being in the darkness of his or her life between them, while still having the optimistic choice from which one to exit, if one day he/she decides to leave us.

However, as in some of my other spatial narratives, there will also be numerous little fellows, doodled *in situ*, living all over the two giant (for them) easels and grayish plinths, and probably they have to do the real job in this piece: to cheer you up and to neutralize any hint of unnecessary middle-aged man emotions. Luckily they will do so, because I will not tell them that they inhabit a commissioned art work, which, apparently, has failed to be a grand dedication to Caravaggio and Bacon (although the little ones can handle the situation even if I already told them about that failure).

Nedko Solakov

April, 2010


Edited by Christy Lange

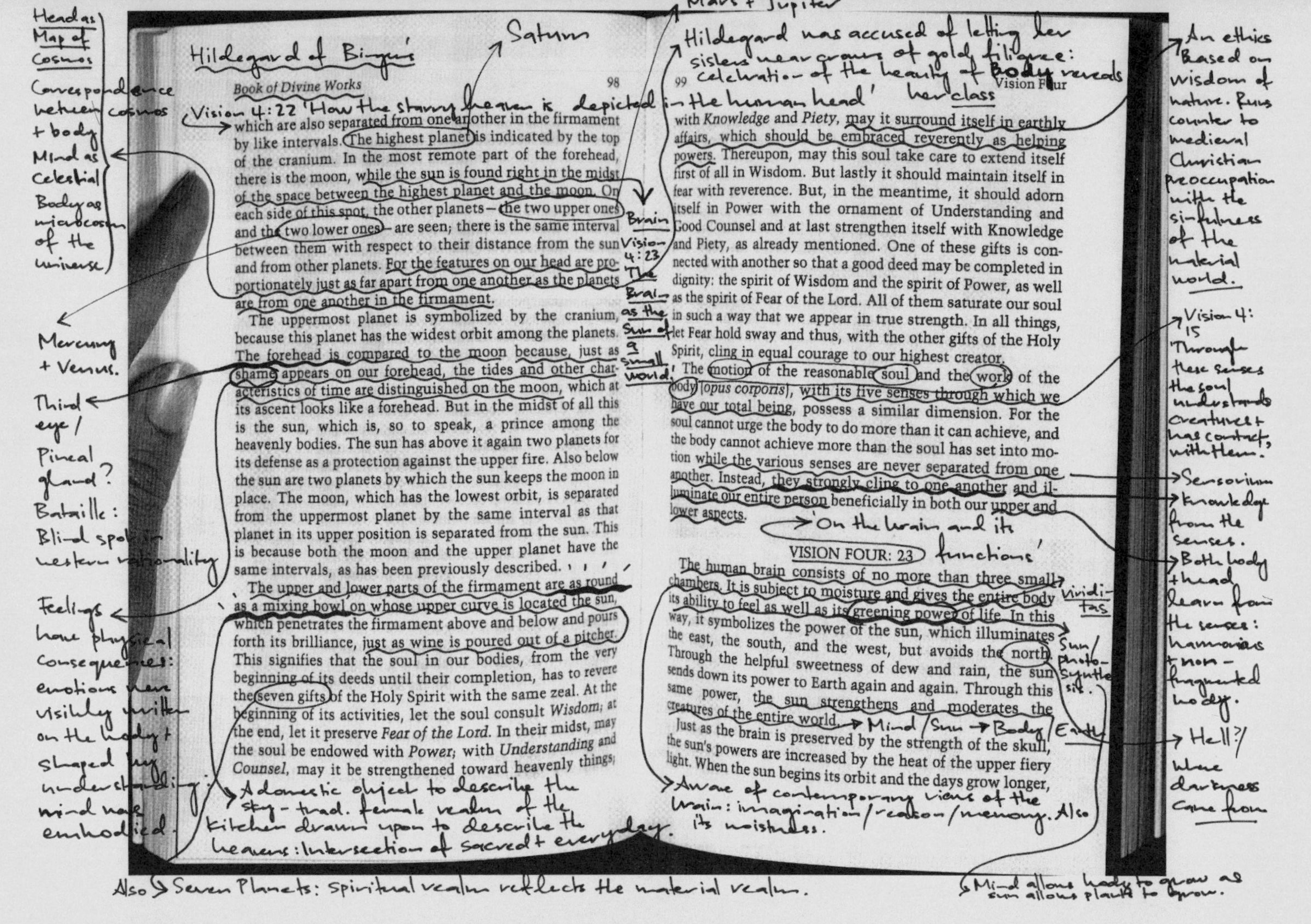


SRIWHANA SPONG ANNOTATED HILDEGARD OF BINGEN'S BOOK OF DIVINE WORKS, **1987**, ED. BY MATTHEW FOX

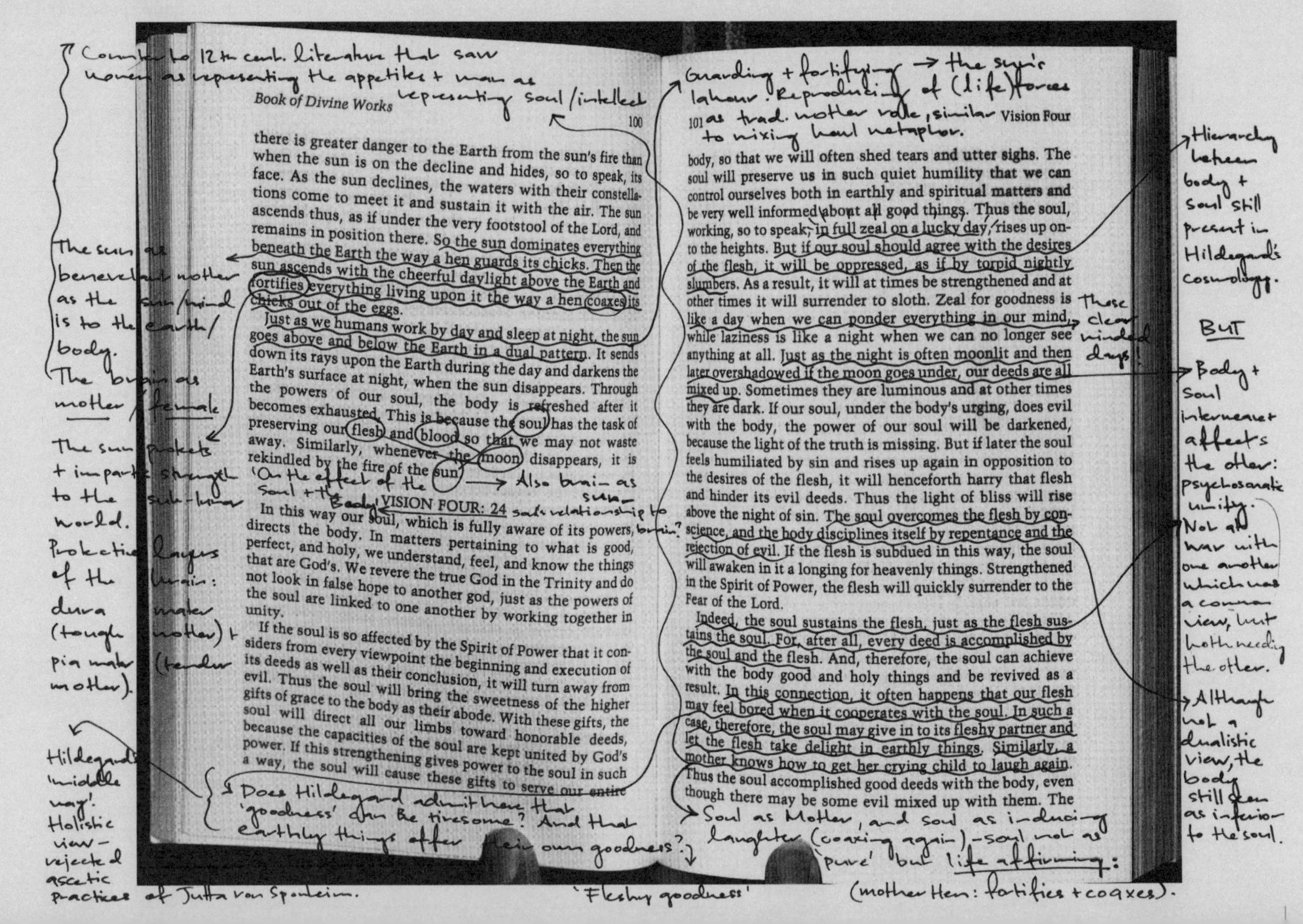



*Book of Divine Works*  100

there is greater danger to the Earth from the sun's fire than when the sun is on the decline and hides, so to speak, its face. As the sun declines, the waters with their constellations come to meet it and sustain it with the air. The sun ascends thus, as if under the very footstool of the Lord, and remains in position there. So the sun dominates everything beneath the Earth the way a hen guards its chicks. Then the sun ascends with the cheerful daylight above the Earth and fortifies everything living upon it the way a hen coaxes its chicks out of the eggs.

Just as we humans work by day and sleep at night, the sun goes above and below the Earth in a dual pattern. It sends down its rays upon the Earth during the day and darkens the Earth's surface at night, when the sun disappears. Through the powers of our soul, the body is refreshed after it becomes exhausted. This is because the soul has the task of preserving our flesh and blood so that we may not waste away. Similarly, whenever the moon disappears, it is rekindled by the fire of the sun.

VISION FOUR: 24

In this way our soul, which is fully aware of its powers, directs the body. In matters pertaining to what is good, perfect, and holy, we understand, feel, and know the things that are God's. We revere the true God in the Trinity and do not look in false hope to another god, just as the powers of the soul are linked to one another by working together in unity.

If the soul is so affected by the Spirit of Power that it considers from every viewpoint the beginning and execution of its deeds as well as their conclusion, it will turn away from evil. Thus the soul will bring the sweetness of the higher gifts of grace to the body as their abode. With these gifts, the soul will direct all our limbs toward honorable deeds, because the capacities of the soul are kept united by God's power. If this strengthening gives power to the soul in such a way, the soul will cause these gifts to serve our entire

101

body, so that we will often shed tears and utter sighs. The soul will preserve us in such quiet humility that we can control ourselves both in earthly and spiritual matters and be very well informed about all good things. Thus the soul, working, so to speak, in full zeal on a lucky day, rises up onto the heights. But if our soul should agree with the desires of the flesh, it will be oppressed, as if by torpid nightly slumbers. As a result, it will at times be strengthened and at other times it will surrender to sloth. Zeal for goodness is like a day when we can ponder everything in our mind, while laziness is like a night when we can no longer see anything at all. Just as the night is often moonlit and then later overshadowed if the moon goes under, our deeds are all mixed up. Sometimes they are luminous and at other times they are dark. If our soul, under the body's urging, does evil with the body, the power of our soul will be darkened, because the light of the truth is missing. But if later the soul feels humiliated by sin and rises up again in opposition to the desires of the flesh, it will henceforth harry that flesh and hinder its evil deeds. Thus the light of bliss will rise above the night of sin. The soul overcomes the flesh by conscience, and the body disciplines itself by repentance and the rejection of evil. If the flesh is subdued in this way, the soul will awaken in it a longing for heavenly things. Strengthened in the Spirit of Power, the flesh will quickly surrender to the Fear of the Lord.

Indeed, the soul sustains the flesh, just as the flesh sustains the soul. For, after all, every deed is accomplished by the soul and the flesh. And, therefore, the soul can achieve with the body good and holy things and be revived as a result. In this connection, it often happens that our flesh may feel bored when it cooperates with the soul. In such a case, therefore, the soul may give in to its fleshy partner and let the flesh take delight in earthly things. Similarly, a mother knows how to get her crying child to laugh again. Thus the soul accomplished good deeds with the body, even though there may be some evil mixed up with them. The

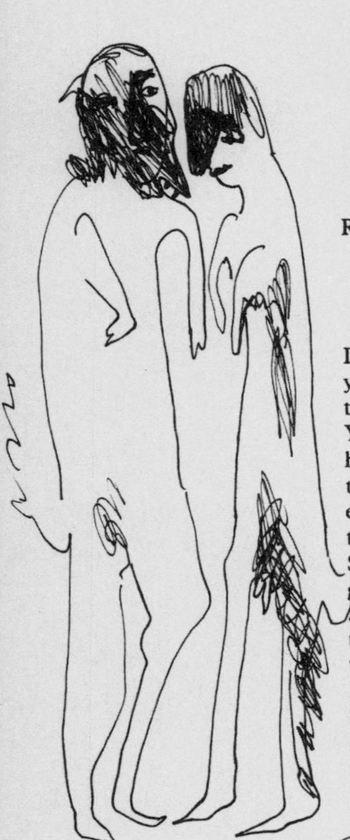

The Zanting Zigzag of language and quality of confusion, strucc with peircingness is perfect for Art making, paintings with stories in particular.

Roading with *Eusa* 7 in my mynd:

> 7. Thay dogs stud up on thear hyn legs & taukin lyk men.
> Folleree sed, Lukin for the 1 yu wil aul ways fyn thay 2.
> Folleroo sed, Thay 2 is 2ce as bad as the 1 . . .

I cud feal it in the guts and barrils of me. You try to make your self 1 with some thing or some body but try as you wil the 2ness of every thing is working agenst you all the way. You try to take holt of the 1ness and it comes in 2 in your hans. Jus the same as the Littl Shyning Man done when Eusa took holt of him. Orfingd said the Littl Shyning Man wer what ever cudnt never be put to gether and I wer beginning to think he wer right. And yet it lookit to me like the Littl Shyning Man wer jus and very what *wantit* to put its self to gether and trying its bes to do it. Not Goodparleys Littl Shyning Man that wer a nother thing and tirely. What I thot the Littl Shyning Man wer I thot he wer right doing. I thot the Littl Shyning Man wer what I ben putting to gether when I brung that yellerboy stoan to Belnot Phist and look what happent. If Id kep wide of him he myt stil be a live. Poor Belnot Phist parbly his hart give out on him. Hart of the Phist Hart of the Wud. I ben the 1 as made that happen and now I wer coming in 2 with it. Saying in my mynd over and over: Whatd I do whatd I do?

Now I wer trying to hol fas to being 1 with Lissener and I knowit wel the 2ness wer hot on my foller it wer out to get its teef in me and arga warga. That 2ness be come jus as real to me as if it ben a pack of dogs. I wer frendy with the dogs now but I dint know how to get frendy with the 2ness. Trying to

The Bewilderment in Riddleys voice so strong

The Way he speaks, is like a child, or like somebody after a break down — the whole word has had a break down — it is trying to puzzel and muddle it self into some kind of Cohesion.

The impossibility of holding true understandings with[149] other things — come apart —

Understandings are always imperfect We are all alone, at large — Making our way throgh things.

— There is a great ambivelnnce in book of Whenter it is a good thing to put things together or not — Can be a violent blundering

lissen in my mynd for Lissener but nothing come. My mynd wer all roylt and turbelt and muddy with every thing going roun in it. Trying to progam my self for Cambry yet at the same time trying not to get in front of my self.

Plus all the res of it it took me strange roading with them dogs by day pas all them lookouts be tween Widders Dump and Cambry. Dint realy matter nothing how many lookouts seen me dint matter nothing how many pigeons flew that message 1 form to the nex or to the Ram there wernt no body going to stop me longs the Pry Mincer wantit me luce and walking out my happenings. Stil and yet I dint want no 1 seeing me I wisht it wudve stayd nite. I dint want to be tol of every where. Riddley Walker the dog clevver or Riddley Walker running with the Black Pack. I kep out of site as wel as I cud but I knowit I wer seen time and agen becaws I wunt put no exter time nor faggers on to my road with going wide and slying roun I jus gone the straites way to Cambry trying to get to Lissener fas as I cud. Trying to get there befor the 2ness got me.

Coming in to Cambry outers and fealing the place rise up in me wylst I movit in to it. Jumbelt stoan and crummelt birk. Grean rot and number creaper. The old dry parcht smel and the wet grean smel to gether like in all the dead towns. No stilness like the other dead towns tho. Qwick it wer. All of it qwick and a qwickful hy moving coming up out of the groun and hyering hyering up thru the rain in to the dark what stans for ever on them broakin stoans with its hans over its face. Day time it wer then nor not raining but the rain wer in it and the dark is all ways there. The shape of the nite what beartht the day when Canterbury dyd. Hart of the Wud in the hart of the stoan. I cud feal that thing inside us how its afeart of

being beartht. I cud feal how every thing is every thing. I fealt like if I stampt my foot therewd come horns on my head and the Littl Shyning Man nekkit be twean them.

Thinking on the Littl Shyning Man he be come mixt to gether in my mynd with Belnot Phist. Poor old Belnot he bint pult in 2 acturel peaces and yet in a way of saying he ben pult a part and it wer the Power of the 2 as done it. Now that 2 wantit to be 1 agen and moving me I cud feal it strong that Big Power what ever it wer. Spirit of God may be that same what woosht roun the Power Ring time back way back. I wantit to be the happener for that Big Power. I wantit to happen that 1 Big 1. I thot of the yellerboy stoan ½ of it with me and ½ of it with Lissener. Reaching out then with my mynd I tryd to lissen him. Cudnt lissen nothing only jynt sylents there wernt nothing of him in it I wer all a loan. Eusas littl son nor cudnt fynd the other 1.

'Be your oan black dog and be your oan Ardship. Becaws you wont all ways have me.' Thats what hed said. Now I knowit why hed said it. Becaws he knowit time to come wewd go 2 diffrent ways. I wantit that Hy Power back agen and wooshing roun the Power Ring not jus the goast of it. I wantit that Spirit of God moving Inland frontwards agen. I wantit the same as Goodparley I wernt agenst him no mor and that wer the hart of the matter. Lissenerd lissent that and pult his mynd a way so I cudnt lissen him nor where he wer. Boath of us looking for that 1 Big 1 but we wernt on the same side no mor. Suddn it flasht in to my mynd may be he wer the Good Luck brother not me.

So sad I fealt then. Sad and emty with a crying in me. I fealt like that Other Voyce Owl of the Worl musve lissent the woal worl a way and every thing gone. Every thing emtyd out of the worl and out of me.

Funny fealing come on me then I fealt like that Power wer a Big Old Father I wantit it to do me like Granser done Goodparley I wantit it to come in to me hard and strong long and strong. Let me be your boy, I thot.

Stanning on them old broakin stoans I fealt like it *wer* coming in to me then and taking me strong. Fealt like it wer

158

# EMPEDOCLES'S RETURN

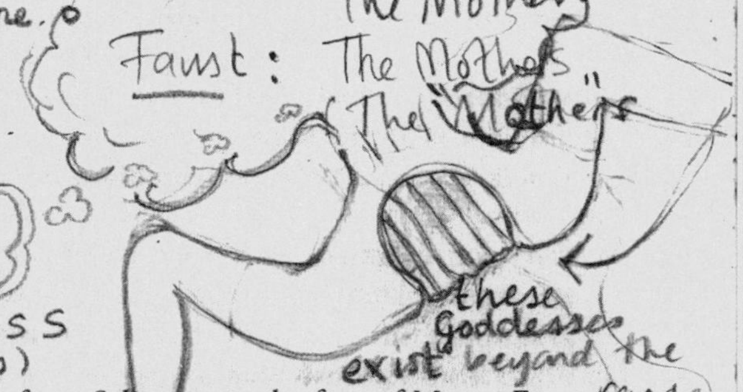

**Fire**

How he traversed the distance from Selinunte to the foot of Mount Etna, beneath the turbulent sky, the anxious nights, the dry wind, he would not have been able to say, blind to the hills on which the wheat was ripening, to the black olive trees tied to the slopes and to the cruel towns resting on the summits. However, he had passed through the center of the island, in the place called the navel, where Persephone, the priests said, was abducted and then dragged into the underworld. He had gone through the door of the world without realizing it.

One evening, he found himself in the talus scree. Walking became impossible. A recent eruption had spilled a large lava flow across the flows he recognized. It formed a field of ruins, of debris, black and discontinuous, marked with red and yellow traces. Cones, with their points downward, were collapsing; caverns were opening like hard and smooth arches crowned with ashy powder and let shafts be made out. Among the ejecta, rocks high as towers and other simple stones plagued the walker with obstacles and made him slip. Climbing straight up, he would immediately roll. The night added its shadow to the black sheet. To his right, already, a minor crater was burning. He received its acid smoke in waves; his eyes were tearing up. Sometimes, often, he fell to his knees under the too heavy weight and bled from his hands and feet.

He thought he heard clamors, the tumult of the wind and the furnace; was the ash slipping with a noise like falling water? The mountain at work was murmuring with its metamorphoses, cracking, rumbling, crackling, popping. He heard, all melted together, explosions and deflagrations of fire, muffled or loud, cave-ins, crashes and detonations of earth, heavy and deep, the lapping and bubbling, vibrant and rustling, of liquids, the

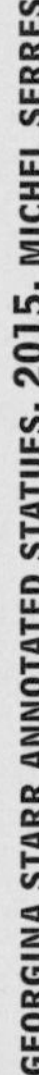

hissing and stridulations of the air, at the upper limits of the audible, like the tearing of a curtain. Under the turbulent black sky, amid the dark and moving lavas, the troubled murmur of things was raising its commotion. Hurricanes on the open sea, sandstorms in the desert, forest fires, water-spouts and lightning, he remembered all that, then, as almost simple components of this great random howling: here, the sum and product of all the world's noises, the great vortex. This high disordered, truncated cone solidified the turbulent form while leaving it changing and viscous. An interior turmoil that's come outside as an almost perfect excrescence, a hard fluid where multiple parts were born to unity, where unity was multiplied into its elements. The forces at work of union and dissociation in this thick magma seemed to be searching for a word across the scattered din.

For the first time the immense clamor of Love and Hate reached him. For Hate and Love rumble and wail, whereas, deaf to this racket, the vibrating strings of old Pythagoras sent out the world's first message, its first ordered signal. He passionately listened to the things panting beneath the acoustics, the disorder fidgeting before any type of sign; heard the primordial music, the buzzing of the burning chaos, the world's background noise. He knew then, personally and by hearsay, that his physics had touched the forces of origin, the shrill tearing of dissociation and the full and warm, harmonic and beating tonality of communion. Things speak, for a hurried listening, but rustle and babble for the profound ear. The craters, then, the flows, those collapsed sheets, those cliffs, those coombs appeared to him, in the black of meaning and under the teeming of the constellations, to be the great world organ, with lop-sided, twisted and divided up pipes, with disjointed stops, with scattered keyboards, roaring, under the vault of the sky, an aleatoric proto-music. Pythagoras had only known how to listen to the blacksmith at work, whereas he was hearing Hephaestus himself who, through fire, was filling space with mad tones. *Through his tenderness, he heard the primary Tenderness of things; through the hate that, in him, was twisting with bitterness, he heard the elementary and dark Hate.* The way, in the past, he had known the wind through the heady air that raised his chest, the devouring fire through the double furnace of the brain and the genitals, the waters through his secretions, the earth through the weight of his fatigue in the evening. The swirling noises of the world were reaching that internal ear that perceives the body's tumult. He too was a volcano; Hephaestus was forging in his own burning loins; Enceladus, beaten, crushed by the gods, was lying chained up in his belly, his liver, his thighs, from which he made plaintive and angry mutterings be heard, which came out of his own mouth in words of ash, cinder and smoke. The interminable war of the giants had

I was having a cup of tea with Takashi Okutani in Milan, during the
2005 Salone del Mobile, talking about projects underway with Muji
and describing to him the Alessi cutlery project and how I was feeling
this approach to design, of leaving out the design, seemed more
and more the way to go.

I mentioned having seen Naoto Fukasawa's aluminium stools for Magis
and how they seemed to have a special kind of normality about them,
and he added: "super normal". That was it, a name for what's been going
on, a perfect summary of what design should be, now more than ever.

A while ago I found some heavy old hand-blown wine glasses in
a junk shop. At first it was just their shape which attracted my attention,
but slowly, using them every day, they have become something more
than just nice shapes, and I notice their presence in other ways. If I use
a different type of glass, for example, I feel something missing in
the atmosphere of the table. When I use them the atmosphere returns,
and each sip of wine's a pleasure even if the wine is not. If I even catch
a look at them on the shelf they radiate something good. This quota
of atmospheric spirit is the most mysterious and elusive quality in objects.
How can it be that so many designs fail to have any real beneficial
effect on the atmosphere, and yet these glasses, made without much
design thought or any attempt to achieve anything other than a good
ordinary wine glass, happen to be successful? It's been puzzling me
for years and influencing my attitude to what constitutes a good design.
I've started to measure my own designs against objects like these
glasses, and not to care if the designs become less noticeable. In fact
a certain lack of noticeability has become a requirement.

Meanwhile design, which used to be almost unknown as a profession,
has become a major source of pollution. Encouraged by glossy lifestyle
magazines, and marketing departments, it's become a competition
to make things as noticeable as possible by means of colour, shape
and surprise. It's historic and idealistic purpose, to serve industry and
the happy consuming masses at the same time, of conceiving things
easier to make and better to live with, seems to have been side-tracked.
The virus has already infected the everyday environment. The need for

businesses to attract attention provides the perfect carrier for the disease. Design makes things seem special, and who wants normal if they can have special? And that's the problem. What has grown naturally and unselfconsciously over the years cannot easily be replaced. The normality of a street of shops which has developed over time, offering various products and trades, is a delicate organism. Not that old things shouldn't be replaced or that new things are bad, just that things which are designed to attract attention are usually unsatisfactory. There are better ways to design than putting a big effort into making something look special. Special is generally less useful than normal, and less rewarding in the long term. Special things demand attention for the wrong reasons, interrupting potentially good atmosphere with their awkward presence.

The wine glasses are a signpost to somewhere beyond normal, because they transcend normality. There's nothing wrong with normal of course, but normal was the product of an earlier, less self conscious age, and designers working at replacing old with new and hopefully better, are doing it without the benefit of innocence which normal demands. The wine glasses and other objects from the past reveal the existence of Super Normal, like spraying paint on a ghost. You may have a feeling it's there but it's difficult to see. The Super Normal object is the result of a long tradition of evolutionary advancement in the shape of everyday things, not attempting to break with the history of form but rather trying to summarise it, knowing its place in the society of things. Super Normal is the artificial replacement for normal, which with time and understanding may become grafted to everyday life.

Jasper Morrison

Re. The Crystal Goblet, Beatrice Warde

First Things First Manifesto, Ken Garland

Kenya Hara

Naoto Fukasawa

Bruno Munari: "To complicate is easy
To simplify is difficult".

# Obsidian

**There are many intriguing objects in the collection of the**
British Museum in London, but one of the most mysterious
has to be a thick, dark and highly polished disc with a
small, hooped handle. The Aztecs forged the mirror from
obsidian in honour of their god Tezcatlipoca (his name
means 'smoking mirror'), and it was brought over to the
Old World after Cortés's conquest of the region that is now
Mexico, in the mid-sixteenth century.[1] Obsidian, also
known as volcanic glass, is formed when molten lava,
erupting from the earth, comes into contact with ice or
snow, and cools very quickly.[2] It is very hard, glossy,
brittle and either black or a very dark bronze-green,
sometimes with a golden or iridescent sheen caused by
layers of tiny gas bubbles that become trapped in the
magma as it solidifies. Although there is some doubt about
this particular mirror's provenance, Sir Horace Walpole,
the British antiquarian who acquired it in 1771, was under
no doubt about its previous owner and what it had been
used for. On the label attached to the object's handle he
wrote a curious inscription: 'The Black Stone into which
Dr Dee used to call his spirits.'[3]

Dr John Dee was Elizabethan England's foremost
mathematician, astrologer and natural philosopher. He was
a Cambridge graduate, and the queen's philosopher and
advisor; he also spent many years talking to angels about
the natural order and the end of the world. These
conversations were held using his collection of 'shewstones'
– of which this mirror may have been one – and through
several mediums, most famously Edward Kelly. It is not
so remarkable that a man of Dee's intelligence believed
in the occult – most people did. Indeed, nearly a century
later one of the greatest scientific minds in history –
belonging to one Isaac Newton – expended the greater
part of its energy searching for the Philosopher's Stone.



AMY STEPHENS ANNOTATED OBSIDIAN, THE SECRET LIVES OF COLOUR, 2016, KASSIA ST CLAIR

# 8

## War Stories 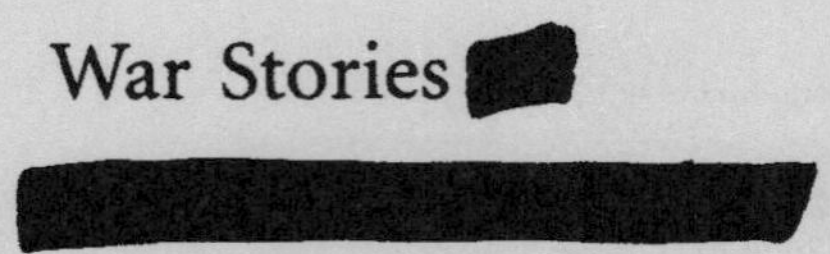

The use of war stories is a prominent feature of diagnosis among the technicians. These stories are anecdotes of experience, told with as much context and technical detail as seems appropriate to the situation of their telling. At a minimum they name the technician doing the work, the machine to which it was done, the problem, and its solution; in the majority of cases I observed, the technician telling the story is the one to whom it happened. The stories occur naturally in discourse among the technicians, either in diagnosis or in more purely social situations. There seems to be little question of gaining the right to tell stories (Sacks 1970, 1972, 1974); discourse among the technicians appears to presume that all competent members of the community will tell stories.

Telling stories in diagnostic contexts makes some of them extremely elliptical and barely recognizable to outsiders as stories. The ellipsis is permissible because the context will be used in interpretation to supply some of the missing detail, as will the common experience of teller and listeners, and because, in an interactive situation, the teller can count on the hearers to indicate if the ellipsis is too great. Such excessive ellipsis is easily corrected through normal conversational repair. This brevity is a matter of cultural propriety and competent practice; it would be inappropriate to waste everyone's time repeating the superfluous to make a well-structured story, particularly in the context of a ser-

125

vice call when the technicians' sense of their own professionalism requires a speedy resolution to the situation. It is also true that these elliptical stories provide all the essentials for those sufficiently versed in the world of service to fill in the rest.

Once war stories have been told, the stories are artifacts to circulate and preserve. Through them, experience becomes reproducible and reusable. At the same time, each retelling is, in a sense, a re-representation. The stories originate in problematic situations and are told or retold in diagnosis when the activity they represent becomes problematic again. They are retold in the consideration of a present problem, when the issue of comparability of context with some previous experience has arisen, and this renders the previous, completed episode once more problematic.

War stories are also told in pursuit of more purely social functions than diagnosis. They preserve and circulate hard-won information and are used to make claims of membership or seniority within the community. They also amuse, instruct, and celebrate the tellers' identity as technicians. Indeed, they are offered in response to questions from inquisitive ethnographers, whose questions may make the most mundane activity problematic. In more normal social discourse, the problematic quality that occasions the telling of the stories seems to stem primarily from a wide range of occasions on which technicians are called upon to account for their activities and secondarily from a need to represent themselves in a heroic or at least competent perspective. In these tellings, past problematic circumstances are made publicly and collaboratively inspectable by one's peers, and one's experience is made reproducible and reusable on subsequent occasions by others. Such tellings are also demonstrations of one's competence as a technician and therefore one's membership in the community.

War stories are told in diagnosis when no clear formulation of the problem is emerging from the welter of facts. Technicians may find with some problems that they know a great many things about the machine but that the facts do not add up to a clear picture of the problem. Telling stories of more or less similar experiences is a way of pushing the facts around, trying other perspectives to see if they suggest other interpretations. As discussed gues Borch-Jacobsen, nor the meaning or signified of the call (which has none of these). "'Guilty!' is the way in which you respond to the anguishing silence of the call, echoing it: guilty is the *Hören*, the hearing, that corresponds authentically to the call" (*E*, 97).

Your guilty conscience is a receptive spontaneity, as Heidegger elsewhere says regarding Kantian respect, engaging a contract and indebtedness. The other haunts hearing, even and especially if you hear no one, and it is toward him, toward her, or to you—you no longer know—that you are indebted, toward whom you are guilty and responsible. "When Heidegger, in §34 begins to trace the call of conscience, he demonstrates that the exchange of words presupposes a hearing and/or understanding of the Other, or more exactly, it presupposes communication (*Mitteilung*) as the sharing of Being-with (*Mitsein*), including everything that such 'sharing' implies concerning contractual agreements and indebtedness (the given and taken word, mutual recognition, answerability, etc.)" (*E*, 97).

Before speaking, before even hearing anything whatsoever or whomsoever, you hear this preparatory understanding: you are-with, you are shared, and sharing this share with the Other. "Being-with is in discourse 'expressly' shared (*geteilt*). Thus, hearing (*das Hören auf,* listening for), you are open (*offen*) to, upon, and for the Other. You receive him or it at your place (you receive the Other 'at home,' *tu le reçois* 'chez toi') and you 'share' yourself with him prior to any habitation, possession, or property, *owing* this hospitality prior to any contract, pact, or economical exchange. 'Receive the stranger': this ethical imperative that you would quickly oppose, and so easily, to the ontological solitude and egotism of Dasein. . . . Listen, therefore, and receive: listening for, **you already owe yourself to the Other**, having to respond to him/her and to render to him his due. . . . Listen again, you are not alone, your death is calling you—you owe it; your debt is outstanding: you are guilty" (*E*, 97–98). Both Borch-Jacobsen and Fynsk listen for the friend enigmatically mentioned by Heidegger—your most inner voice, familiarly Other, is that of the friend, therefore, whom you carry within you like a secret or a wound that is open or secret—perhaps like a crime. The voice of the absent friend, possibly dead: this contributes to making you Other, which is to say "with" or haunted. For no one speaks. Nobody's talking.

This kind of cryptological inflection—the effect of the phantom and the lodging of an undead Other will occupy our lines henceforth. In the meantime Heidegger's lines are tapped by the irreversible *Stimme des Freundes* which every Dasein carries within itself. Fynsk writes: "the voice of the friend is *always* there, just as Dasein itself is always there as thrown" (*SW*, 196). He

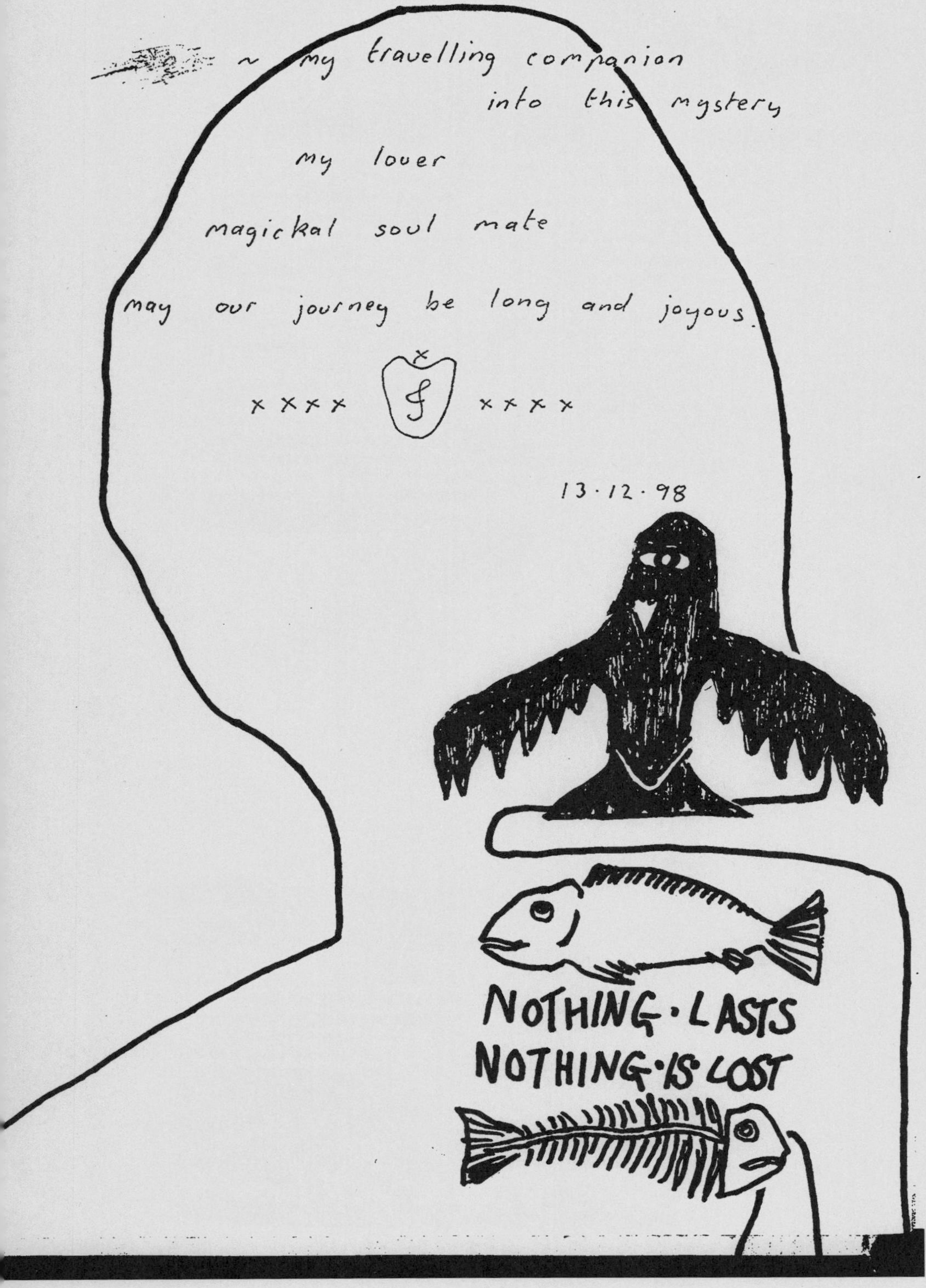

~ my travelling companion

into this mystery

my lover

magickal soul mate

may our journey be long and joyous.

x x x x  x x x x

13·12·98

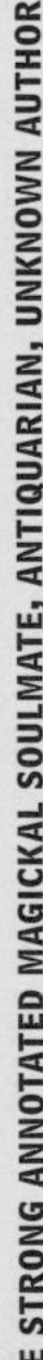



ALFIE STRONG ANNOTATED MAGICKAL SOULMATE, ANTIQUARIAN, UNKNOWN AUTHOR

# Grimes Graves

Far from the heartland of British megalithic culture, Grimes Graves are by far the largest flint mines in these islands. Set deep in the modern conifer plantations of Breckland, these 346 deep mine shafts have been discovered dug over a huge thirty-four acre area, representing many years of prehistoric work. The miners chose to ignore the average higher flint flakes and go deep to the best possible sources around fifty feet below the ground. Down at the chosen layer, a series of radiating galleries up to thirty feet long were dug into the flint, creating a wheel effect in the ground. Miners carried antler picks with which to prise the flint nodules out of the ground and lit their way with chalk-cup lamps. As nodules filled a bag, so it would be hauled up to the surface and immediately shaped into the specific tool it already resembled. All waste was used to fill up exhausted pits. The workers had extraordinary respect for their Mother Goddess. For it was here at Grimes Graves that archaeologists found a fertility shrine

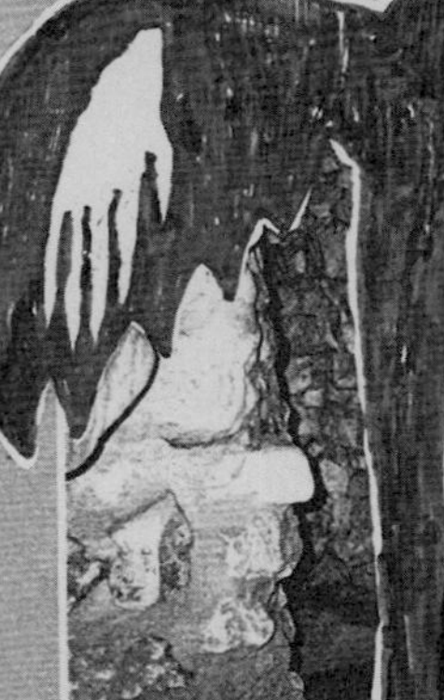

set up within a failed shaft, upon which was a chalk Goddess figurine, a carved chalk phallus balls, along with a spread of antler picks. This is somehow understandable in the powerful of Grimes Graves, for this is a place of the Goddess and the many months of work for the maticians claim that run Grimes Graves, who quarried and shaped. Those people considered this essential enough to travel many miles need for flint carried on into the pistols. Behind the Flint Knapper's Arms in the village of Brandon is a big pile of flints, for this dying art is still alive in the village. One shaft has been made open to public – it has a concrete roof and is entered down a thirty foot iron ladder. The chalk figurine is now in the British Museum.

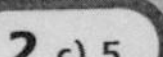

NOTES IN THE GLOAMING AT GRIMES GRAVES, NR THETFORD: 14TH OCTOBER 1997 CE

Crouching in this hole far below the ground, it is impossible not to wonder at the streams of consciousness that would have permeated these ancients as they toiled below ground. Four hundred such pits were dug here and each was then carefully infilled before the next was begun. Seven 'chambers' are arranged around the circular shaft, each in varying stages of excavation. This gives the effect of one of the Orcadian cairns, such as Quoyness[G]... or even the purposefulness of the Fairy Knowe[G]... The Greenwell Pit, named for Canon Greenwell

from the late 19th century, is not open to the public and is twenty feet deeper and equally more uncivilised. It is only possible to visit that pit with prior notice to English Heritage. It is such an important solitary experience that a visit to Grimes Graves should always be made out of season. Otherwise, 500 visitors per day will struggle past your meditating form. Now I shall leave, as the drips of water splash my neck and splatter my fieldnotes.

Top photo: © The British Museum

Drive south from Mundford on either the A1065 or the A134. Grimes Graves is clearly signposted from both roads, about the same distance along each. On most road atlases. Possible seasonal opening times – ring Thetford tourist information to be sure.

there is a distance in to which you'll forever fall

*Mutants And Mystics: Science Fiction, Superhero Comics And The Paranormal,*
Jeffrey J. Kripal, University of Chicago Press, 2011, 301-303.

Jamie Sutcliffe

Strieber, writing with sixty years of hindsight and a stunning array of personal experiences, adds further layers to Jung's original suggestions. He notes, for example, that a combination of the Cold War context of the original UFO sightings, the fact that fundamentalist Christians conditioned by simplistic Armageddon "cartoonlike" scenarios occupied many of the key positions in the military, and the production of dozens of really bad B-movies featuring evil invading aliens in the 1950s all came to-gether to more or less guarantee that the situation would be seriously misunderstood and grossly misread (B 230–32, 278; CON 256). It is precisely these sorts of military and religious distortions that Strieber's visitor corpus attempts to address and correct.

It would be tempting to read this corpus as an extension of Strieber's horror writing and suggest that it was his fiction background that allowed him to have such remarkable experiences, that his fiction perhaps even produced such impossible events. There is no doubt some truth to this, but not in the simplistic way that I have just stated it. Strieber himself makes the deeper connection when he notes that his earlier fiction had been orbiting around a hidden purpose in his life that he did not yet understand. In other words, exactly like we saw Philip K. Dick doing in our previous chapter, with all those 1960s novels featuring psychical powers and Martians lead-ing up to the metaphysical revelations of Valis in the winter of 1974, Strieber begins to read his life and work *backward*. He realizes, with more than a little concern, that "my whole life might have proceeded according to a hidden agenda," in effect a secret life that was leading up to *Communion* and all that it produced (COM 87). His entire corpus now appears as "some sort of attempt to cope with an enormous, hidden, and frightful reality" (B 125). Like Dick, he too was now a frightened knower of a secret. He too had become a Gnostic.

The works of fiction, Strieber now realized, were really about him struggling with repressed memories. *The Wolfen* was about "brilliant predators with huge, black visitor-like eyes." *The Hunger* was about "strange, immortal creatures that were very much like the tall, blond people I have occasionally glimpsed in my encounter experi-ences." And *Catmagic* was "about a fairy queen and a journey through the world of the dead and back again," another recurring theme of his visitor experiences. "In fact," Strieber confesses, "I believe my whole body of work—my whole life—has been an unconscious effort to somehow overcome my fears and reach back to the secret school" of his childhood occult encounters (SS xxi).

But the earlier horror fiction not only functioned as a kind of code for an emerg-ing hidden agenda. It also functioned to *close down* the experience. Thus at one point Strieber comes face to face with the visitors and decides that he cannot cross over to their dimension. Why? "Because I remembered the horror stories and I could not cross that threshold" (COM xvii). The poignant cries of the visitors that Strieber heard echo precisely those that Barry Smith heard when he too said no to the Endless Waves of Time.

So popular culture can open up. But, as we saw with the B-movies, it can also shut down and take us down some very misguided paths. Hence one of the more interesting suggestions Strieber has made, this time in person to a group of us discussing meta-physical film, is that he is absolutely certain that his visitor experiences appeared the way they did because of the sci-fi movies that he watched as a kid and young adult, and that if we could create more accurate metaphysical films ("manipulations of light," as he poetically calls them), future generations might have more accurate visitor experi-ences. In short, if we could recreate "the actual energy of the close encounter" on film, this would definitely advance both consciousness and culture, but only if we are willing to abandon our rational denials and current cultural beliefs about invading space aliens.

Queen Gertrude: More matter, with less art.

Lord Polonius: Madam, I swear I use no art at all.

The Tragedy of Hamlet, Prince of Denmark
(Act 2, Scene 2), William Shakespeare

## I swear I use no art at all

Whenever possible I avoid using CMYK in the graphic design of books. The techniques with which one can mix any colour with cyan, magenta, yellow and key black suggests reality can be simulated. I far prefer using a palette whereby the reader stays astutely aware of the fact that he is holding a printed reproduction in his hands. A palette of specific colours and inks which, in combination with the right type of paper, give the information its materiality. Ink will always be ink.

Nowadays almost everything is printed in full colour. CMYK has become a default. Nobody seems to spend much time looking for other methods simply because there doesn't seem to be a problem that needs solving. Travel guides from the 1950s and 60s, for instance, were generally printed in two colours, not the four available to us now. This meant a cartographer was faced with a host of challenges that were often solved graphically. The simplified colour palette meant that these guides had a strong graphic identity.

Architectural representation has always interested me more than the actual buildings. It is through representation that the architect's ambitions are articulated and show us who he considers to be his peers. Sketches, models and the way in which buildings are photographed or described all evoke the published collective memory of a profession. A London-based architect once told me how in the 1980s there weren't many commissions to go round. His firm focused on smaller projects such as interior design or putting in a new door, yet the representation of this work–through the cropping of a particular drawing or the choice of photographer–showed that architecture always lay at the root of their thinking.

In my final year studying architectural design I became occupied with multimedia. For me it offered an array of new techniques through which to present architecture,

SS: How is your book on book collecting doing?

JM: It's okay, it's getting there. Time is pressing so I'd better …

SS: Start focusing your thoughts …

JM: Before they float away.

SS: What do you think about book collecting? Are you recording this or making notes?

JM: I am trying to record this, but I'm not sure if it is working.

SS: Well why don't you play it back and see, it's your time – don't worry, it's my money!

JM: [Laughter] Let me see, wait a minute. Okay, it's working.

SS: We started off on a good track when we met in Berlin, if I remember.

JM: Yes, I don't know how we started, but it did appear to be heading in the right direction.

SS: We did not begin by talking about books, but I am not quite sure how we began; we just sort of zeroed in on book making, or maybe it was the publishing and the production side.

JM: We spoke about printing technology a little, and also distribution, and we talked a bit about how books are priced.

SS: Yes, apparently one of the things that did stick in your brain was the pric-ing of the Lawrence Weiner *Statements* and why it has a $1.95 printed on the cover. You suggested that it was the only book of the generation that actually had a fixed price. And I think, I am almost sure, it is because it was meant to be presented like a standard paperback book. The idea being in Lawrence's mind, and probably mine, that this kind of production could be seen as a kind of possible 'mass market literature': a popular book, something one could pick up in the train station to pass the time on a long journey somewhere, perhaps even on holiday.

JM: Do you think that actually happened?

SS: What it was intended to imply was that *Statements* could be bought at a mass-market news-stand in a train station, which is in itself, in fact, rather unlikely.

JM: Where was a book like that sold at the time?

SS: Actually, it was sold to very few people, but mostly given away: sold might be too big a word. Some were sold to some art bookstores. I don't think there were collectors of this kind of material at the time. Most of them were given away. There did not yet exist the right

57

I want to talk to you about "the work", art work.
I will speak of inspiration,

Art work is very important in the way that I will try to show when I speak about inspiration.
I have sometimes put myself ahead of my work in my mind and have suffered in consequence.

I thought I was important. I was taught to think that.

To think I am big is the work is big.
The position of pride is not possible.
And to think I am small and the work is small, the position of modesty, is not possible.
I will go on to inspiration and perhaps you will see what is possible.
As I describe inspiration I do not want you to think I am speaking of religion.
That which takes us by surprise — moments of happiness — that is inspiration.
Many people as adults are so startled by inspiration that they think they are unique in having had it. Nothing could be further from the truth.
Inspiration is there all the time.
For everyone whose mind is not clouded over with thoughts

Most people have no realization of the moments in which they are inspired.
Inspiration is pervasive but not a power.
It's a peaceful thing.
It is a consolation even to plants and animals.
Do not think that it is unique.
If it were unique no one would be able to respond to your work.
Do not think it is reserved for a few or anything like that.
It is an untroubled mind.
Of course we know that an untroubled state of mind cannot last. So we say that inspiration comes and goes but really it is there all the time waiting for us to be untroubled again. Young children are more untroubled than adults and have many more inspirations. All the moments of inspiration added together make what we call sensibility. The development of sensibility is the most important thing for children and adults but is much more possible in children. Some parents put the development of social mores ahead of aesthetic development. Small children are taken to the park for social play; But the little child sitting alone, perhaps even neglected and forgotten, is the one open to inspiration and the development of sensibility.

# Change



## The new master

For most of us, accepting change behavior as a new constant force is not an easy step. No matter that the subject rings in our ears and the highly tangible results of change constantly wear our elbows: this new reality is a hard lesson. Nevertheless, our culture shows all the signs of digesting ideas and producing new values at a dismayingly rapid rate. New music forms are innovated, adopted and rejected in a few months. Social evolution is bursting by all the old progress norms. Disorder is one of the signs of lag in change management.

The office as an institution will no longer be able to ignore the new master.

Curiously, it is the lack of mobility in our physical facilities that is the most stubborn laggard in offices. A great many of our irritations stem from services and facilities that respond too slowly, or not at all, to our new objectives and values. It is our buildings, furnishings and services that have to be revisualized and revitalized.

## A place for transacting abstractions

The office in its short evolution has adopted every kind of communication abstraction. Resultantly, we are concerned with reality simulation.

The management of symbolic representation of reality is the function of offices.

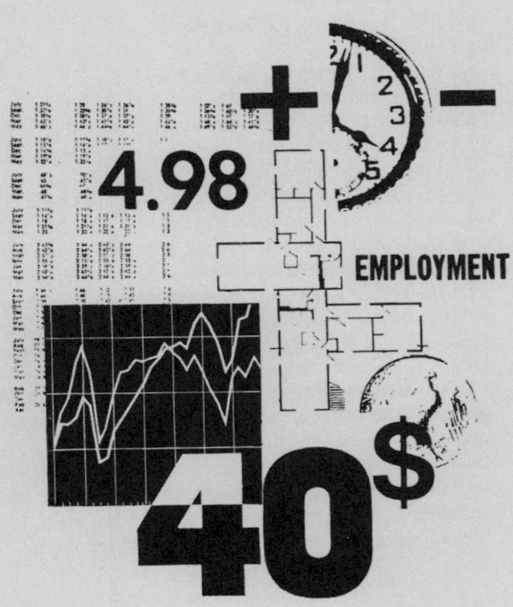


402

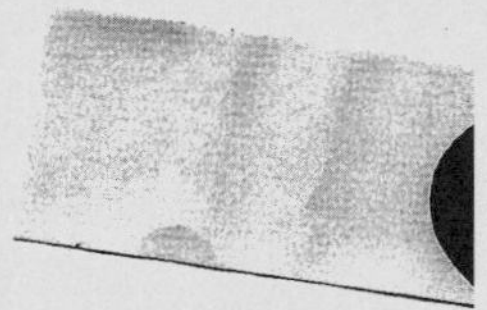

The office user seeks the answers. The answers lie in a concept that acts as an overview system, essentially the user's own; <u>an organizationally senior system that links shelter, services and human goals and objectives into a coherent effect.</u>

The Action Office II obeys the new rules. It is an implementing tool concept reconciling new software planning with the hardware of coordinated behavior. Its aim is to be responsive to the goals of the user. It aims at moderating the impact of diverse and competitive technology on the user.

It provides a combination of discipline and permissiveness in appropriate measure . . . <u>disciplined in that it limits and protects from chaotic, unregulated complexity . . . permissive in that it allows wide expression and re-expression for both the individual and the organization.</u>

Within this responsibility, three facility characteristics are paramount: the ability to forgive; the ability to change with grace; and the ability to do on-line planning and expression.

## Forgiving principle

We have an unfortunate heritage from our Victorian forefathers proposing that there is a kind of super vision that can place an organization in a perfectly planned facility in which we all live happily ever after. Such a thing never existed and now that the enormous complexity of organizational environment has received better definition, the humbling effect on planners should be considerable. This complexity coupled with the unpredictable course of future directions requires a *forgiving* behavior in facility design.

We must be allowed to change our minds. We must be allowed to respond to errors as they emerge. And this forgiving should not impose significant cost or delay on the user. Our design, manufacture and office services are obligated to make this a comfortable, legitimate objective.

## Grace with change

One of the objections to change is the kind of disruption it brings to our life. If change means a period of dust, confusion and loss of momentum, it is understandable why the cramped old shoe is lived in too long.

When we think of alternatives to ponderous change, we are worried about living a perpetually temporized life in jerry-built, junky facilities.

The requirement is to not only change with ease but to achieve a well appointed and resolved solution. . . . Grace with Change.

*RESPONSE:*   I have been thinking about what you said last time I saw you; about the potential of reading time. Or maybe you put it differently — durational judgement? This thing about time preoccupied me for the past weeks. I have as a consequence started to use my eyes less. It's not that I keep them closed. It's that I don't see like I used to see. I used to pretty much just look look and stay quiet. Doing those things simultaneously seemed a good way to inhabit the world. I mean, that's what it was; a way to be. Anyhow, things have changed and these days I seem to be having a more outspoken engagement. Different from the preceding one, this outspokenness feels to be of a critical nature. I doubt its potential, yet I am totally incapable of not doing it. I told you I have been using my eyes less. What I mean is; I have been using them differently. Say, the other day I spent five hours looking at dead matter, something that would have been totally out of my range six weeks ago. What happened was, I simply arrived, sat down and stared at this stubborn stuff. I didn't touch it, to check its flexibility, to see if it was alive. It seemed unnecessary. After those five hours my eyes were totally fucked. As a consequence I didn't use them for the rest of the day. In a dream that night I compiled a list of things I should reserve my sight for. It included: literature, faces especially when in conversation, scapes, ripe fruit and cultured phenomena in flight. I have since then regained control of my sight, or simply grown accustomed to this new way of using my eyes.

This morning I came across an image of an oyster. I have attached it. I thought you might find it of interest.

In the small hours, waiting for the morning train to Saxmundham, I would want the company of a friend. I would want a conversation of sorts. The title of this work by Jesper List Thomsen, RESPONSE, implies an existing dialogue. The continuation of a conversation that might have already begun. I know this text is intended to be performed, and familiar with Jesper's work, I would be comforted by the sound of his voice filling my head. I would welcome this exchange. Considering that Jesper reserves his sight for literature, faces, especially when in conversation, I think of a second hand citation from Luisa Muraro, via Franco 'Bifo' Berardi. Muraro links the learning of language to the affective relationship of the body of the learner to the body of the mother. Her point being that the double articulation of language (the voice and its delivery through the body) is reliant on the affective body to enforce the semiotics of language. When this process is reduced to a simplified exchange without the affective body (such as a tv, smart device), the delivery of language becomes an operational procedure and meaning simply exchanged as a set of instructions. Emphasis is on connecting through language and not connecting meaning in a real sense with our whole being.

I reserve my sight for these words, knowing this is not an exchange as instruction but a conversation without a face, I will think about cultured phenomena in flight and try to respond.

Art Behaviour Class
Dialectic Experience
Family Genius
Hegemony Industry
Jargon **Keywords**
Liberation Media
Naturalism Ordinary
Peasant Racial
Sex Tradition
Underprivileged
Violence Welfare
**Raymond Williams**
*A vocabulary of culture and society*

sufficiently strong for it to retain some normative quality; in this sense **civilization, a civilized way of life, the conditions of civilized society** may be seen as capable of being lost as well as gained.

See CITY, CULTURE, DEVELOPMENT, MODERN, SOCIETY, WESTERN

## CLASS

**Class** is an obviously difficult word, both in its range of meanings and in its complexity in that particular meaning where it describes a social division. The Latin word *classis*, a division according to property of the people of Rome, came into English in lC16 in its Latin form, with a plural *classes* or *classies*. There is a lC16 use (King, 1594) which sounds almost modern: 'all the classies and ranks of vanitie'. But **classis** was primarily used in explicit reference to Roman history, and was then extended, first as a term in church organization ('assemblies are either classes or synods', 1593) and later as a general term for a division or group ('the classis of Plants', 1664). It is worth noting that the derived Latin word *classicus*, coming into English in eC17 as **classic** from fw *classique*, F, had social implications before it took on its general meaning of a standard authority and then its particular meaning of belonging to Greek and Roman antiquity (now usually distinguished in the form **classical**, which at first alternated with *classic*). Gellius wrote: '*classicus . . . scriptor, non proletarius*'. But the form **class**, coming into English in C17, acquired a special association with education. Blount, glossing *classe* in 1656, included the still primarily Roman sense of 'an order or distribution of people according to their several Degrees' but added: 'in Schools (wherein this word is most used) a Form or Lecture restrained to a certain company of Scholars' – a use which has remained common in education. The development of **classic** and **classical** was strongly affected by this association with authoritative works for study.

From lC17 the use of **class** as a general word for a group or division became more and more common. What is then most difficult



is that **class** came to be used in this way about people as well as about plants and animals, but without social implications of the modern kind. (Cf. Steele, 1709: 'this Class of modern Wits'.) Development of **class** in its modern social sense, with relatively fixed names for particular classes (**lower class, middle class, upper class, working class** and so on), belongs essentially to the period between 1770 and 1840, which is also the period of the Industrial Revolution and its decisive reorganization of society. At the extremes it is not difficult to distinguish between (i) **class** as a general term for any grouping and (ii) **class** as a would-be specific description of a social formation. There is no difficulty in distinguishing between Steele's 'Class of modern Wits' and, say, the *Declaration* of the Birmingham Political Union (1830) 'that the rights and interests of the middle and lower classes of the people are not efficiently represented in the Commons House of Parliament'. But in the crucial period of transition, and indeed for some time before it, there is real difficulty in being sure whether a particular use is sense (i) or sense (ii). The earliest use that I know, which might be read in a modern sense, is Defoe's ' 'tis plain the dearness of wages forms our people into more classes than other nations can show' (*Review*, 14 April 1705). But this, even in an economic context, is far from certain. There must also be some doubt about Hanway's title of 1772: 'Observations on the Causes of the Dissoluteness which reigns among the lower classes of the people'. We can read this, as indeed we would read Defoe, in a strictly social sense, but there is enough overlap between sense (i) and sense (ii) to make us pause. The crucial context of this development is the alternative vocabulary for social divisions, and it is a fact that until lC18, and residually well into C19 and even C20, the most common words were *rank* and *order*, while *estate* and *degree* were still more common than **class**. *Estate*, *degree* and *order* had been widely used to describe social position from medieval times. *Rank* had been common from lC16. In virtually all contexts where we would now say **class** these other words were standard, and *lower order* and *lower orders* became especially common in C18.

The essential history of the introduction of **class**, as a word which would supersede older names for social divisions, relates to the increasing consciousness that social position is made rather than merely inherited. All the older words, with their essential metaphors of standing, stepping and arranging in rows, belong to a society in

Beckett to gloss — The music 'crowds in to the interstices of the text' 'as it were' ?

your head. The fleeting ground before your feet. From time to time. You do not count your steps any more. For the simple reason they number each day the same. Average day in day out the same. The way being always the same. You keep count of the days and every tenth day multiply. And add. Your father's shade is not with you any more. It fell out long ago. You do not hear your footfalls any more. Unhearing unseeing you go your way. Day after day. The same way. As if there were no other any more. For you there is no other any more. You used never to halt except to make your reckoning. So as to plod on from nought anew. This need removed as

50

we have seen there is none in theory to halt any more. Save perhaps a moment at the outermost point. To gather yourself together for the return. And yet you do. As never before. Not for tiredness. You are no more tired now than you always were. Not because of age. You are no older now than you always were. And yet you halt as never before. So that the same hundred yards you used to cover in a matter of three to four minutes may now take you anything from fifteen to twenty. The foot falls unbidden in midstep or next for lift cleaves to the ground bringing the body to a stand. Then a speechlessness whereof the gist, Can they go on? Or better, Shall they go

51

TING GROUND

MORE

MOTION

GRAMMAR OF
KING

RCEPTIBLE
EMENT
GHT DOWN
ET THE
TING GROUND
F FOCUS

D FROM SELF.

you he

last out
with clo
from yo
the snow

ACTION
①

with clos
as descri
out and
light. Yo
door pul
before th

ACTION
②

you are o
pasture a
and strew

ACTION
③

take the c
is a beeli
point in
western
entering

Two months have now passed. This conventional suburban villa is in fact the junction between our small illusory world and another larger and more real one. Miraculously, I have survived, though my last reserves of food were exhausted weeks ago. As I expected, Margaret paid a second and final visit. Still puzzled by my self-confidence and handsomely slimming figure, she told me that she would no longer be responsible for my mounting debts. I bade her farewell, and returned to my lunch of poodle pie.

The thought that I would never see Margaret again gave my modest meal an added relish, and afterwards I carefully set the dog-trap by the open door of the sitting room. The untended garden with its knee-deep grass has attracted my neighbours' pets, trusting beasts who trundle happily towards me as I sit smiling in the armchair, cleaver concealed within an inviting cushion. By the time their ever-hopeful owners call round a few days later I have safely consigned the bones to the space below the dining-room floorboards, a substantial ossuary that is the last resting-place of Bonzo, Major, Yorky and Mr Fred.

These dogs and cats, and the few birds I have been able to trap, soon formed my sole fare. However, it became clear that my neighbours were keeping a more careful eye on their pets, and I resigned myself to a diet of air. Fortunately, the television rental company intervened to provide a generous source of extra rations.

I remember the dour young man with the tool-kit who arrived to dismantle the attic aerial. He had made several earlier calls in the avenue, and had parked his van a hundred yards away. I followed him up the stairs, concerned that he too might lose his way among those vast rooms.

Sadly, my attempt to warn him came to nothing. As he stepped into the first of those white chambers, as large as aircraft hangars carved in the roof of an iceberg, he seemed to realise that he had entered a zone of danger. I grappled with him as we blundered through that white world, like arctic explorers losing all sense of distance within a few steps of their tent. An hour later, when I had calmed his fears and carried him down the staircase, he had sadly yielded to the terrors of light and space.

Three months – a period of continued discovery and few interruptions. The outside world has at last decided to leave me alone. I no longer answer the door, and there has been scarcely a caller, though threatening letters arrive from the local council, and from the water and electricity

companies. But an unshakable logic is at work, and I am confident that my project will be complete before the power and water supplies are disconnected.

The house enlarges itself around me. The invasion of light which revealed its true dimensions has now reached the ground floor. To keep my bearings I have been forced to retreat into the kitchen, where I have moved my mattress and blankets. Now and then I venture into the hall and search the looming perspectives. It amazes me that Margaret and I once lived in this vast pile and so reduced it in our minds.

Already I can feel the walls of the kitchen distancing themselves from me. I spend all day here, sitting on the floor against the freezer cabinet. The cooker, refrigerator and dishwasher have become anonymous objects in some remote department store display. How much longer can this expansion continue? Sooner or later the process will halt, at that moment revealing the true dimensions of the world we inhabit, and which the visual centres of our timid brains have concealed from us. I am on the verge of a unique revelation, the equal perhaps of Columbus's discovery of the new world. I can scarcely wait to bring the news to my neighbours – the modest villa which Mrs Johnson imagines herself to occupy is in fact an immense Versailles!

Nearby, the bones of the TV repairman lie on the yellow linoleum like the ribs and skull of a long-decayed desert traveller.


Somewhere a door is being forced. I listen to the grating of keys testing a lock, then the sound of heels on the patio steps before a second attempt to prise open the french window.

Rousing myself, I sway across the kitchen, trying to steady my arms against the faraway washing machine. A key turns, and a door opens somewhere beyond the great carpeted perspectives of the sitting room.

A young woman has entered the house. As she returns the keys to her handbag I recognise Brenda, my former secretary. She stares at the dismantled dog-traps beside the window and then peers around the room, at last seeing me as I watch her beside the door.

'Mr Ballantyne? I'm sorry to break in. I was worried that you might . . .' She smiles reassuringly and takes the keys from her handbag. 'Mrs Ballantyne said I could use the spare set. You haven't answered the phone, and we wondered if you'd fallen ill . . .'

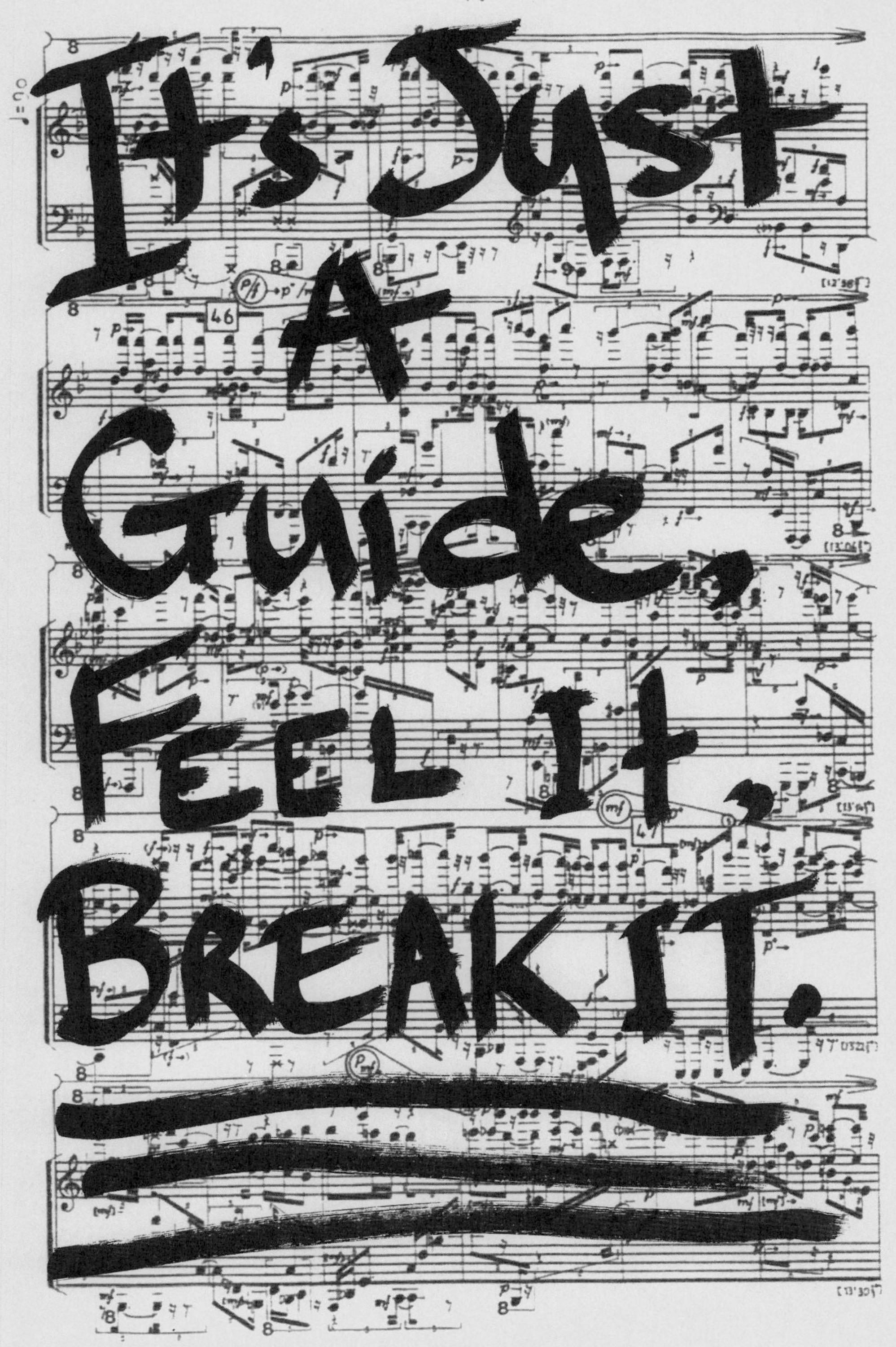
It's Just A Guide, Feel It. Break It.

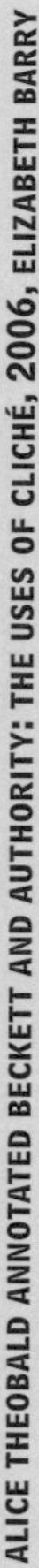

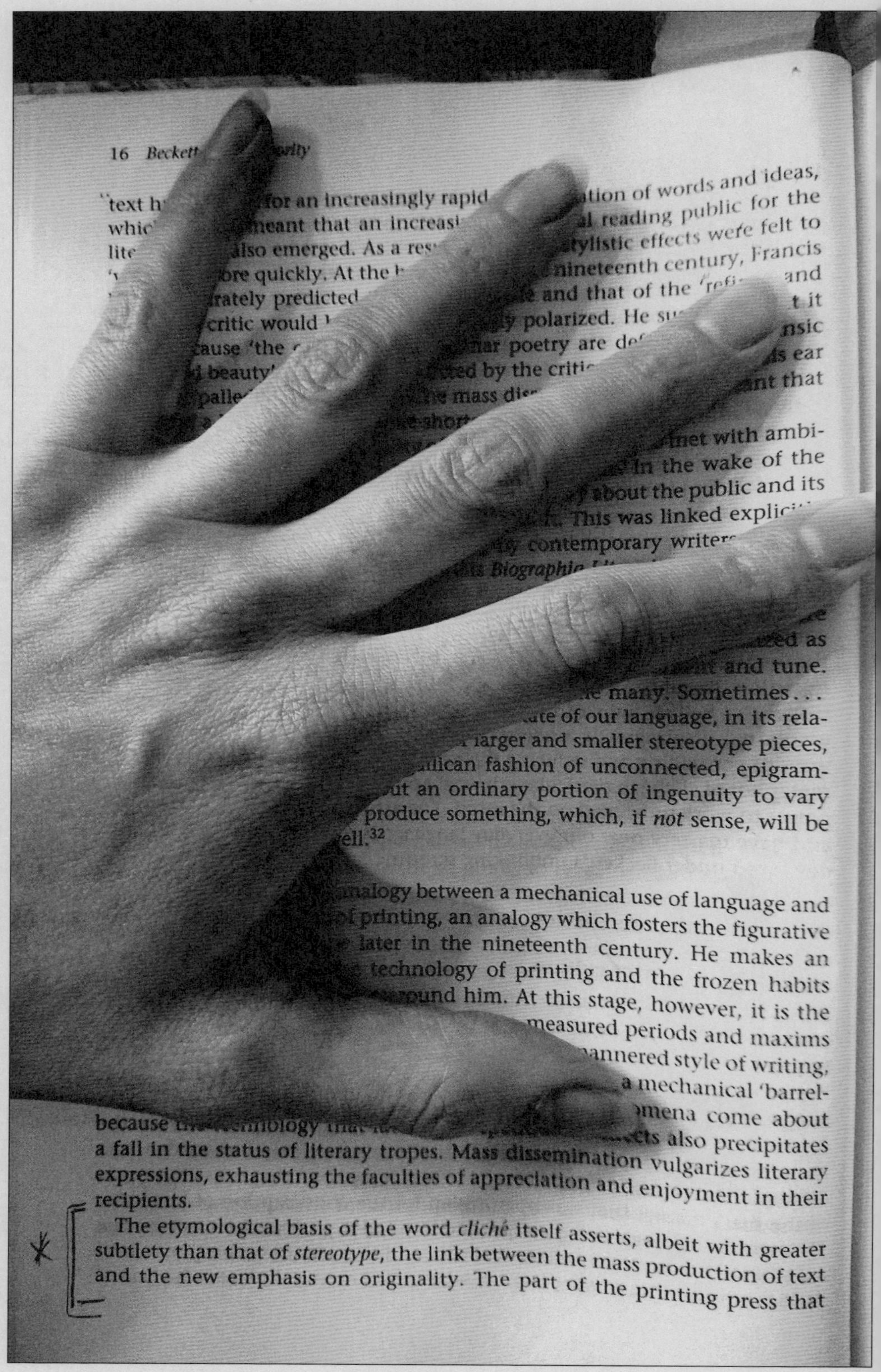

"text h... ...for an increasingly rapid ... ...tion of words and ideas,
whic... ...meant that an increasi... ...al reading public for the
lite... ...also emerged. As a res... ...tylistic effects were felt to
'... ...ore quickly. At the ... ...nineteenth century, Francis
... ...rately predicted ... ...e and that of the 'ref... ...and
...critic would ... ...y polarized. He su... ...nsic
...cause 'the ... ...nar poetry are de... ...s ear
...beauty' ... ...red by the criti... ...ant that
...palle... ...he mass dis... ...

...e short...

...net with ambi-
...In the wake of the
... about the public and its
... This was linked explici...
...y contemporary writers
...s *Biographia ...*

... ...ed as
... ...t and tune.
...e many. Sometimes...
...te of our language, in its rela-
...larger and smaller stereotype pieces,
...lican fashion of unconnected, epigram-
...ut an ordinary portion of ingenuity to vary
...produce something, which, if *not* sense, will be
...ell.³²

...nalogy between a mechanical use of language and
...printing, an analogy which fosters the figurative
...later in the nineteenth century. He makes an
...technology of printing and the frozen habits
...round him. At this stage, however, it is the
...measured periods and maxims
...annered style of writing,
...a mechanical 'barrel-
...mena come about
because th... ...nology that ... ...cts also precipitates
a fall in the status of literary tropes. Mass dissemination vulgarizes literary
expressions, exhausting the faculties of appreciation and enjoyment in their
recipients.

The etymological basis of the word *cliché* itself asserts, albeit with greater
subtlety than that of *stereotype*, the link between the mass production of text
and the new emphasis on originality. The part of the printing press that

allowed countless copies of a unit of text to be made was called in French the 'cliché', deriving from the clicking noise that the machine made. The term came to be used figuratively in the mid-nineteenth century to mean an idea or expression repeated countless times, and hence—the implication was— worn-out, its point blunted. The fear of cliché, then, emerges as the flip side of these developments in the production and reception of literature. The commonplace, once a neutral element of classical argumentation, became a derogatory label in the wake of the new demand for originality. If knowledge can be stored and retrieved easily, the reiteration of old forms of expression quickly becomes redundant as an aid to cognition, and is as quickly felt to be undesirable with respect to good taste.

The desire among Romantic artists such as Coleridge and Wordsworth for a rejuvenation ⟨of⟩ literary language in or⟨der⟩ to produce more emotive and enduring e⟨ffects⟩ ⟨itse⟩lf created the con⟨ditions⟩ for the idea of cliché to take hold of th⟨e⟩ ⟨poeti⟩c imagination. L⟨aurence L⟩erner has written on the significance of ⟨…⟩ a failed literary ⟨…⟩ excite or move; a fallen poetry, in sho⟨rt⟩. ⟨Clic⟩hé desires to ha⟨ve⟩ ⟨emot⟩ive effect on ⟨the⟩ hearer or ⟨re⟩ader, rather ⟨than sim⟩ply to instruct⟨…⟩ ⟨R⟩enaissance ⟨…⟩ ⟨ac⟩cording ⟨to⟩ Lerner, la⟨te⟩ ⟨com⟩monplaces i⟨n⟩ ⟨…or⟩dered p⟨…⟩ ⟨whe⟩reas the ⟨…⟩ Romanti⟨c⟩ ⟨ov⟩erreaches, eff⟨…⟩ ⟨g⟩ tipping ⟨…⟩ ⟨h⟩ysterical ⟨exaggeration⟩. ⟨…⟩ ⟨a⟩ttitudes to l⟨…⟩ ⟨b⟩efore cre⟨…⟩ ⟨po⟩ssibilities ⟨…⟩ failure ⟨…⟩ longer der⟨…⟩ ⟨…⟩ via a ra⟨…⟩ ⟨scient⟩ific purity ⟨…⟩langua⟨ge⟩ ⟨pri⟩nted som⟨e⟩ ⟨…⟩ as diffi⟨cult⟩ ⟨…ti⟩ve, the fluid ⟨…⟩'tensi⟨on⟩ ⟨…⟩ of meta⟨phor⟩ ⟨n⟩ew me⟨aning⟩ ⟨hel⟩d in tension ⟨wi⟩th old ⟨…⟩ ⟨w⟩ays of ⟨…⟩ ⟨blend⟩ed ⟨…⟩ ⟨Engli⟩sh w⟨…⟩ ⟨…⟩ng t⟨…⟩ ⟨th⟩e tension which ⟨…⟩ ⟨na⟩tion ⟨…⟩ ⟨…⟩ne ⟨…⟩ ⟨pur⟩ity on the other. ⟨…⟩ ⟨…o⟩ne in this respect. ⟨…⟩ in the idea of using ⟨…⟩ classical rhetoric had ⟨…⟩ ⟨thro⟩ugh shared ideas about ⟨…⟩ ⟨col⟩our, Romantic art had a ⟨…⟩. Wordsworth both relied ⟨…⟩ claims to universality and ⟨…⟩ ⟨na⟩ture (both human and non- ⟨…⟩ ⟨Col⟩eridge observed in *Biographia* ⟨…la⟩nguage was far away from its ⟨…⟩ himself expressed the dilemma ⟨…⟩ considered as *so* true, that they ⟨…⟩ lie bed-ridden in the ⟨…⟩ ⟨des⟩pised and explod⟨ed⟩ ⟨…⟩ from the 'imp⟨…⟩ ⟨…⟩ ⟨…⟩ance

THE I

'If Ducha
maybe t
like this r
immense
importan
but don't

But is it a
Mood is s
random b
mysteriou
up life.

Are
adju
pota
a na
nerv
chilc
eat
a re
and
are
you
doc
Co
on
res
ca

'Hypnot
Schehe

*[Handwritten annotation, left page:]* I had wanted to scan Elizabeth Hardwick's kind-of novel *Sleepless Nights* (1979), a collection of nocturnal wanderings, but I couldn't find it. Maybe I gave it away? Instead, the first pages of Padgett Powell's *The Interrogative Mood* which I had for the first time almost ten years ago but have skimmed through often, since then. A short book made up entirely of questions (its subtitle is *A Novel?*), it is the stuff of 3am musings.

*[Handwritten annotation, right page:]* Another question, asked by Hardwick's narrator towards the end of her reflections: "Why is it that we cannot keep the note of irony, the jangle of carelessness at a distance?"

**ARE YOUR EMOTIONS PURE?** Are your nerves adjustable? How do you stand in relation to the potato? Should it still be Constantinople? Does a nameless horse make you more nervous or less nervous than a named horse? In your view, do children smell good? If before you now, would you eat animal crackers? Could you lie down and take a rest on a sidewalk? Did you love your mother and father, and do Psalms do it for you? If you are relegated to last place in every category, are you bothered enough to struggle up? Does your doorbell ever ring? Is there sand in your craw? Could Mendeleyev place you correctly in a square on a chart of periodic identities, or would you resonate all over the board? How many push-ups can you do?

Are you inclined to favor the Windward Islands or the Leeward Islands? Does a man wearing hair

1

tonic and chewing gum suggest criminality, or are you drawn to his happy-go-lucky charm? Are you familiar with the religious positions taken regarding the various hooves of animals? Under what circumstance, or set of circumstances, might you noodle for a catfish? Will you spend more money for better terry cloth? Is sugar your thing? If a gentle specimen of livestock passed you by en route to its slaughter, would you palm its rump? Are you disturbed by overtechnical shoes? Are you much taken by jewelry? Do you recall the passion you had as an undergraduate for philosophy? Do you have a headache?

Why won't the aliens step forth to help us? Did you know that Native American mothers suckled their children to age five, merely bending at the waist to feed them afield? Have you ever witnessed the playing of shuffleboard at a nudist colony? If tennis courts could be of but one surface, which surface should that be? In your economics, are you, generally, laissez-faire or socialist? If you could design the flag for a nation, what color or colors would predominate?

Should a tree be pruned? Are you perplexed by what to do with underwear whose elastic is spent but which is oth___ ___good shape? Do you dance? Is

2



having collected Coke bottles for deposit money part of the fond stuff of your childhood? Have you inadvertently hurt, or killed, animals? Would you eat carrion? When it comes to pillows, are you a down man or feather? <u>Are you a man?</u> Will you place two hundred dollars in the traditional red envelope and give it to me? Have you ever had to concern yourself with the imminence of freezing water pipes or deal with frozen water pipes? How is your health? If it might be fairly said that you have hopes and fears, would you say you have more hopes than fears, or more fears than hopes? Are all of your affairs in order? Would you have the slightest idea, if we somehow started over, how to reinvent the radio or even the telephone? Do you recall the particular manila rubber buttons in the garters that held up ladies' hose before the invention of pantyhose? Who would you say is the best quarterback of all time? Between an automobile mechanic and a psychologist, which is worth more to you per hour?

Are you happy? Are you given to wondering if others are happy? Do you know the distinctions, empirical or theoretical, between moss and lichen? Have you seen an animal lighter on its feet than the sporty red fox? Do you cut slack for the crime of pas-

3

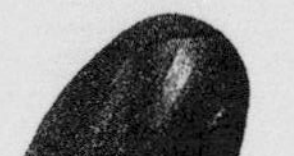

BLASÉ AIN'T YOU DADDY
YOU WHO SHOT YOUR SPERM
INTO ME
BUT NEVER SET ME FREE
THIS AIN'T A HATE THING
IT'S A LOVE THING
IF LOVERS EVER REALLY LOVE
THAT WAY
THE WAY THEY SAY
I GIVE YOU A LUMP OF SUGAR
YOU TILT MY WOMB TILL IT
RUNS
ALL OF ETHIOPIA AWAITS YOU
MY PRODIGAL SON
BLASÉ AIN'T YOU BIG DADDY
BUT MAMA LOVES YOU
ALWAYS HAS

*I always heard "womb" but I have found other transcripts that use the word "wound"*

But how can Daddy know if she loves him the way she says she does? There may be a difference between the way she says she loves him and the way she does or perhaps doesn't love him. There may be a difference between the way she tells him that she feels love for him and the way that she tells herself that she feels love for him. And the way that she tells both herself and Daddy that she loves him may be very different from the feeling of love itself which she might not have ever found quite the right words for, internally or externally.

This being a love thing rather than a hate thing seems to be contingent on Daddy's belief in this word "love" that she says to him. The word "love" meaning something specific to him from the way she spoke her declaration.

And the whole question of this encounter that may be to do with hate and may be to do with love, it is a thing. Or at least she seems to be telling him that it's not one thing to do with hate, but it is an equivalent thing to do with love. She says the word love to him in opposition to the word hate. She says the word love perhaps to frame her previous accusation as an utterance of transformation rather than a spoken wall, unyielding, that she might risk them crashing their bodies against.

Perhaps when she says the word love she attempts to persuade him of something that he may have persuaded her of before using that same word. Maybe that word is their legal tender. There seems to be a purpose for her in framing her previous affirma- tion about his shooting of sperm and withholding of her freedom as being conditioned by this word love rather than what she fears it may be assumed to be, conditioned by the word hate. Hate being a different word that may or may not have something to do with his casual indifference to the sperm and the restraining of her freedom.

She seems to sense that other lovers also use the word love to mask some of the things that they feel or do not feel. Perhaps the word love is a useful mask because it is already contained in their own name, as lovers that is. She insinuates that other lovers also run the risk of being mis-understood, of hiding what they don't understand, of not doing something the way they say something, of not saying something the way they do something. Perhaps the fact that those other lovers may not say what they do or do what they say makes her think that she can persuade or accuse him in relative safety. Maybe those other lovers give her the opportunity to tell him the truth, to use the word love to reconfigure the violence contained in her assertion. To let him know that her mirroring of his sperm and her lack of freedom back at him may contain a loving transformation for them both.

That is if she herself believes in the word love or the word hate.

both time and singularity) only after the fact. Flesh itself, in our ongoing cultural habituation to sight-able remains, supposedly cannot remain to signify "once" (upon a time). Even twice won't fit the constancy of cell replacing cell that is our everyday. Flesh, that slippery feminine subcutaneousness, is the tyrannical and oily, invisible-inked signature of the living. Flesh of my flesh of my flesh repeats, even as flesh is that which the archive presumes does not remain.

As Derrida notes, the archive is built on the domiciliation of this flesh with its feminine capacity to reproduce. The archive is built on "house arrest" – the solidification of value in ontology as retroactively secured in document, object, record. This retroaction is nevertheless a valorization of regular, necessary loss on (performative) display – with the document, the object, and the record being situated as survivor of time. Thus we have become increasingly comfortable in saying that the archivable object also becomes itself through disappearance – as it becomes the trace of that which remains when performance (the artist's action) disappears. This is trace-logic emphasizing loss – a loss that the archive can regulate, maintain, institutionalize – while forgetting that it is a loss that the archive produces. In the archive, bones are given not only to speak the disappearance of flesh, but to script that flesh as disappearing by disavowing recurrence or by marking the body always already "scandal."

An instituted loss that spells the failure of the bodily to remain is rife with a "patriarchal principle." No one, Derrida notes, has shown more ably than Freud how the archival drive, which he labels as a "paternal and patriarchic principle," is both patriarchal and parricidic. The archival drive

posited itself to repeat itself and returned to reposit itself only in parricide. It amounts to repressed or suppressed parricide, in the name of the father as dead father. The archontic is at best the takeover of the archive by the brothers. The equality and liberty of brothers. A certain, still vivacious idea of democracy.[31]

Ann Pellegrini has stated this Freudian schema succinctly: "[S]on fathers parent(s); pre-is heir to post-; and 'proper' gender identification and 'appropriate' object choices are secured backward" – a "retroaction of objects lost and subjects founded."[32]

Elsewhere I have discussed this parricidal impulse as productive of death in order to insure remains.[33] I have suggested that the increasing domain of remains in the West, the increased technologies of archiving, may be why the late twentieth-century has been both so enamored of performance and so replete with deaths: death of author, death of science, death of history, death of literature, death of character, death of the avant-garde, death of modernism, and even, in American playwright Suzan-Lori Parks' brilliant and ironic rendition, *Death of the Last Black Man in the Whole Entire World*.[34] Within a culture that privileges object remains as indices of and survivors of death, to produce such a panoply of deaths may be the only way to insure remains in the wake of modernity's crises of authority, "new" archiving is supposedly against loss, doesn't it institute more profoundly than anything the loss of a different approach to saving that is not invested in identicality? Doesn't it further undo an understanding of performance as remaining? Do not such practices buttress the phallocentric insistence of the ocularcentric assumption that if it is not visible, or given to documentation or sonic recording, or otherwise "houseable" within an archive, it is lost, disappeared?

It is interesting to take the example of battle reenactment into account and look at the particular case of Robert Lee Hodge – an avid Civil War enthusiast who participates in reenactments. As Marvin Carlson described him in an essay on theater and historical reenactment, Hodge has attained significant notoriety among reenactment communities for his "ability to fall to the ground and contort his body to simulate convincingly a bloated corpse."[26] The question is obvious: under what imaginable framework could we cite Hodge's actions as a viable mode of historical knowledge, or of remaining? Is Hodge's bloat not deeply problematic mimetic representation, and wildly bogus and indiscreet at that? Does Hodge, lying prone and fake-bloating in the sun, attempt to offer index of – as well as reference to – both the material photograph and the photographed material of Civil War corpses? Is the live bloater only offering a mimetic and perhaps even ludicrous copy of something only vaguely imagined as a bloated corpse? Yet, within the growing "living history" and reenactment movement, Hodge's bloating body is, for many enthusiasts, evidence of something that can touch the more distant historical record, if not evidence of something authentic itself.[27] In the often-ridiculed "popular" arena of reenactment, Hodge's bloat is a kind of affective remain – itself, in its performative repetition, a queer kind of evidence. If the living corpse is a remain of history, it is certainly revisited across a body that cannot pass as the corpse it recalls. If it cannot pass, what kind of claim to authenticity can such a faulty corpse demand?

I am reminded of Charles Ludlam's queer Theatre of the Ridiculous in which the replaying of classics or the "camp" reenactment of the folk art of "vulgar" commercial entertainment (such as B-movies) offers a different though perhaps related kind of "living history." Ludlam's parodic evenings offered a fractured re-entry of remainders – a history of identifications, of role-playing and its discontents. In Ludlam's theater, as Stefan Brecht described it in 1968,

> Removal of cadavers, necessitated by the high onstage death-rate, is done with exaggerated clumsiness, the corpse does not cooperate – but mostly the dead just sit up after a while, walk off, reparticipate in the action.[28]

When we approach performance not as that which disappears (as the archive expects), but as both the act of remaining and a means of re-appearance and "reparticipation" (though not a metaphysic of presence) we are almost immediately forced to admit that remains do not have to be isolated to the document, to the object, to bone versus flesh. Here the body – Hodge's bloated one – becomes a kind of archive and host to a collective memory that we might situate with Freud as symptomatic, with Cathy Caruth with Freud as the compulsory repetitions of a collective trauma, with Foucault with Nietzsche as "counter-memory," or

142

stellen kann, weil sie etwas ~~~~~~~~~~~ an sich haben.
Nichts ist poetisch an [der] Krankheit, und die großen Kranken von Dostojewskij bis Sylvia Plath wissen es, die Krankheit ist das schlechthin Entsetzliche, es ist etwas mit tödlichem Ausgang.

‹. . .›

Nun sollte sich Kritik auch fragen, wie schreibt Sylvia Plath, Stilfragen, Perspektiven, wie macht sie es.

Es ist aber die einzige Frage, die sich nie aufdrängt, denn wenn jemand etwas zu erzählen hat und so wenig Zeit hat, darüber nachzudenken, scheint es von selbst zu geraten, und der Dringlichkeit sind alle bloßen Kunstfragen untergeordnet, ohne daß [et]was andres würde als Kunst und nicht die Schablone des Kunstabenteuers, der Exhibition, des Verrats und des Selbstbetrugs, der fast alle neuen Romane »auszeichnet« und die Kritik immer [mehr] in die Enge treibt.

Es passiert sehr wenig Neues in der Literatur, ich glaube nicht, daß Sylvia Plath etwas Neues ist, sie hat weder die englische Sprache zertrümmert noch zum Auferstehen gebracht, noch etwas geleistet, was ihre Kritiker zu besonders hochtrabenden Einfällen veranlassen könnte.

Aber wie die Schriftsteller, die in der Hölle waren, wird sie unter den ersten sein, weil sie [unter] den letzten war. Und seit Malcolm Lowrys Nachlaß kenne ich nichts aus der englischen Literatur, das dieser Entgleisung fähig ist, und in dem es Stellen gibt, die den Verstand ebenso erschrek-

159

ken, wie sie [ihn] erschüttern. [— — —] ist, in dem die Feigen von dem Feigenbaum, von dem sie träumt, seltsamerweise doch gereift sind, nicht alle, aber die eine, für Esther heißt die »eine berühmte Dichterin« werden.
Und am Ende hat man auch den Titel vergessen, denn kein Buch und keine Person kann man sich weniger unter einer Glasglocke vorstellen als dieses über Esther.

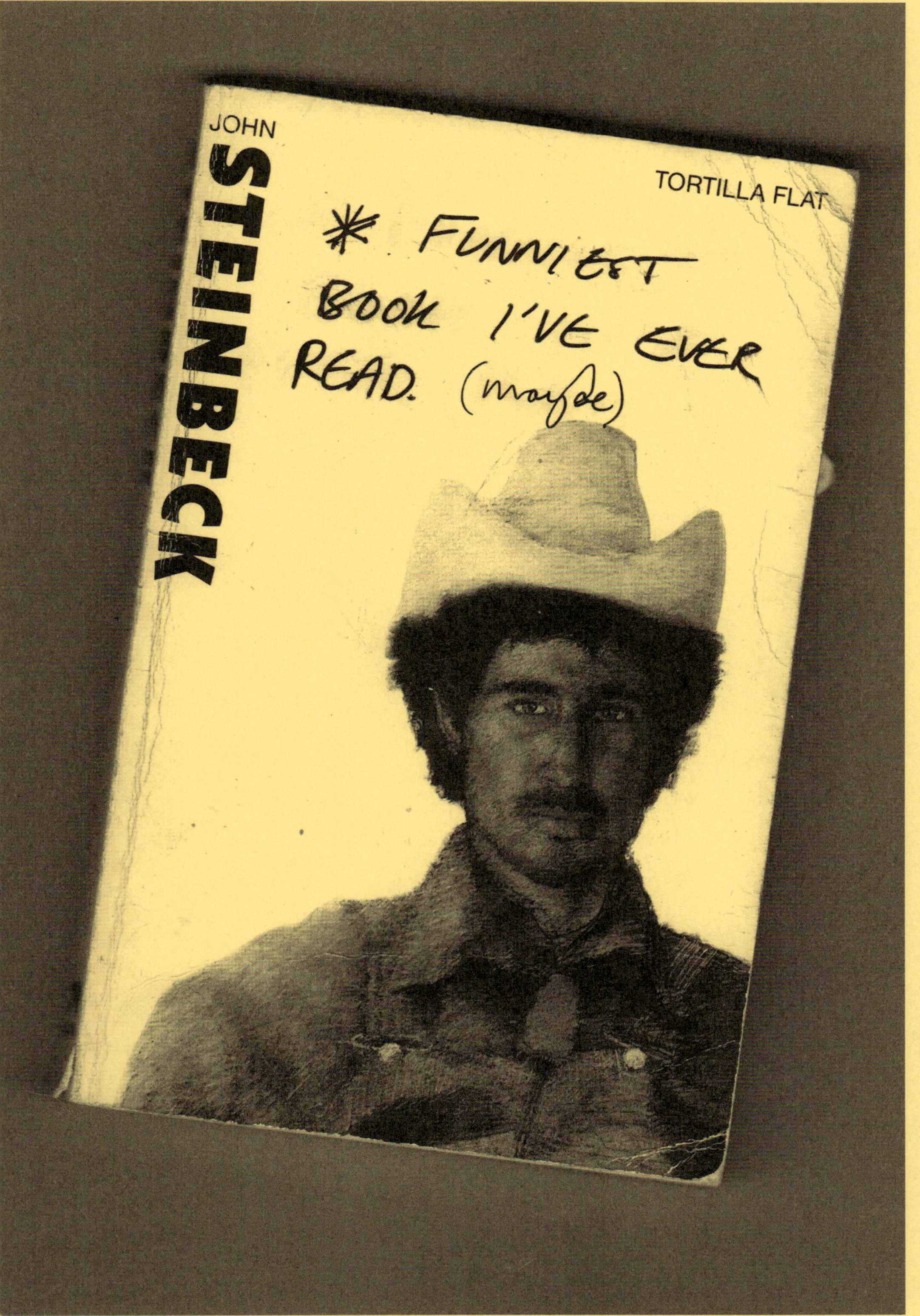


THOM TROJANOWSKI HOBSON ANNOTATED TORTILLA FLAT, 1935, JOHN STEINBECK

# 3  CLUB COUNTRY

The fault is, I can find no fault in you
Assault is say it or I'll say to you
If we stick around, we're sure to be looked down upon
What better way or should I say

Alive and kicking

Alive and kicking at the Country Club
We're always sickening at the Country Club
A drive from nowhere leaves you in the cold
Refrigeration keeps you young I'm told
Alive and kicking at the Country Club
We're always sickening at the Country Club
Your limitations are our every care
Every breath you breathe belongs to someone there

At all's two words, could they be soldered as one
Therein lies the pseudonym
You think you've learned to know someone and find
That you don't know; don't know all's at all

Alive and kicking

Alive and kicking at the Country Club
We're always sickening at the Country Club
A drive from nowhere leaves you in the cold
Refrigeration keeps you young I'm told
Alive and kicking at the Country Club
We're always sickening at the Country Club
Your limitations are our every care
Every breath you breathe belongs to someone there

Sad to see that you're suffering
Work hard at being a something
Sad to see that you're suffering
Work hard at being a something
Sad to see that you're suffering

Alive and kicking at the Country Club
We're always strychnine at the Country Club
A drive from nowhere leaves you in the cold
Refrigeration keeps you young I'm told
Alive and kicking at the Country Club
We're all receding at the Country Club
Your limitations are our every care
Every breath you breathe belongs to someone there

# 4  LOVE HANGOVER

ANONOTATE

THE ORIGINAL, BY DIANA ROSS,
WAS ONE OF THREE TRACKS
PLAYED AT THE CEREMONY OF
OUR WEDDING

thing. What is more, if it is not an intention of his, this will for the most part be clear without asking him.

Now it can easily seem that in general the question what a man's intentions are is only authoritatively settled by him. One reason for this is that in general we are interested, not just in a man's intention *of* doing what he does, but in his intention *in* doing it, and this can very often not be seen from seeing what he does. Another is that in general the question whether he intends to do what he does just does not arise (because the answer is obvious); while if it does arise, it is rather often settled by asking him. And, finally, a man can form an intention which he then does nothing to carry out, either because he is prevented or because he changes his mind: but the intention itself can be complete, although it remains a purely interior thing. All this conspires to make us think that if we want to know a man's intentions it is into the contents of his mind, and only into these, that we must enquire; and hence, that if we wish to understand what intention is, we must be investigating something whose existence is purely in the sphere of the mind; and that although intention issues in actions, and the way this happens also presents interesting questions, still what physically takes place, i.e. what a man actually does, is the very last thing we need consider in our enquiry. Whereas I wish to say that it is the first. With this preamble to go on to the second head of the division that I made in § 1 : intentional action.

5. What distinguishes actions which are intentional from those which are not? The answer that I shall suggest is that they are the actions to which a certain sense of the question 'Why?' is given application; the sense is of course that in which the answer, if positive, gives a reason for acting. But this is not a sufficient statement, because the question "What is the relevant sense of the question 'Why?'" and "What is meant by 'reason for acting'?" are one and the same.

To see the difficulties here, consider the question, 'Why did you knock the cup off the table?' answered by '<u>I thought I saw a face at the window and it made me jump</u>'. Now, so far I have only characterised reason for acting by opposing it to evidence for supposing the thing will take place—but the 'reason if you can do a favor for us, to release us from this prison, because we didn't do anything, we're just innocent people. You kill our hopes. We have families. We have friends, just like you. But there is not life for someone who is screaming. We know that you will not do it, but we want to deliver our message."

During the conversation, I felt sorry about the whole process and for being in prison; I have never been put in prison in my life because I have never broken the law. Unfortunately, I was put in prison this time because I was a refugee, but I did not know that being a refugee was a crime. I did not know how it looked like but what I heard and knew was that it was a place for criminals and people who commit crimes. I reiterated that many innocents are in prison and many criminals are walking free. الل

After a few days, the prison guards took Gofla, Keta, Ajab, and Abdu to another prison. I stayed with Filmon in room 6 for a while, then they sent us to other rooms. I was sent to room number 8 and again to room number 12. Filmon was sent to room number 7, then to room number 9, but we met every day during the break. After days, I was released and Filmon was sent to another prison.

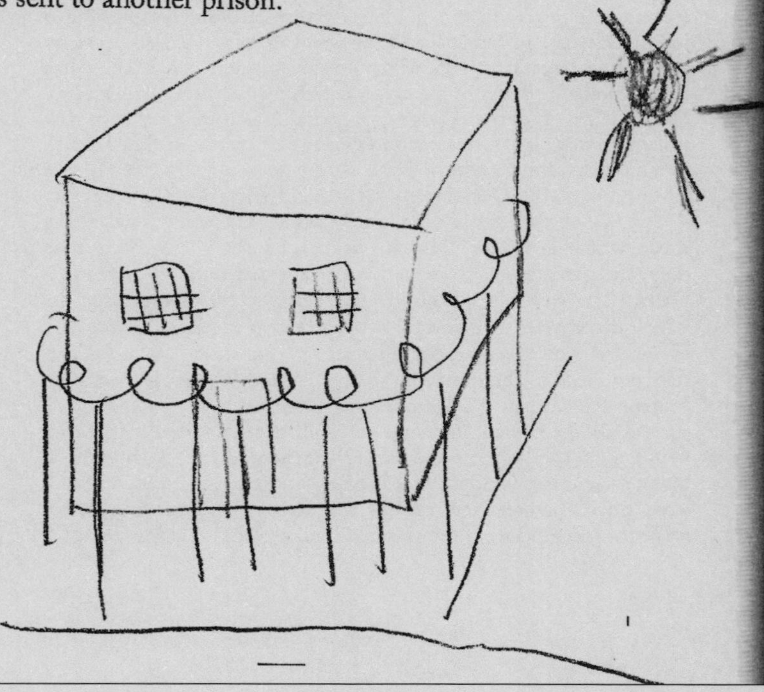

If I have felt obliged to give expression to my disagreement with Sartre regarding the points which bear on the philosophical fundaments of anthropology, I have only determined to do so after several readings of the work in question which occupied my pupils at the *Ecole des Hautes Etudes* and myself during many sessions of the year 1960–1. Over and above our inevitable divergences I hope that Sartre will recognize above all that a discussion to which so much care has been given constitutes on behalf of all of us a homage of admiration and respect.

I would like to express my warm thanks to my colleague, Jacques Bertin, professor at the *Ecole des Hautes Etudes* who was kind enough to make some of the diagrams for me in his laboratory; I. Chiva and J. Pouillon whose notes recalled to me some improvised points which were otherwise lost; Mme Edna H. Lemay who typed the manuscript; Mlle Nicole Belmont who helped me with the tasks of assembling the documentation and making the bibliography and the index; and my wife who aided me in rereading the text and correcting the proofs.



CHAPTER ONE

# THE SCIENCE OF THE CONCRETE

It has long been the fashion to invoke languages which lack the terms for expressing such a concept as 'tree' or 'anima' even though they contain all the words necessary for a detailed inventory of species and varieties. But, to begin with, while these cases are cited as evidence of the supposed ineptitude of 'primitive people' for abstract thought, other cases are at the same time ignored which make it plain that richness of abstract words is not a monopoly of civilized languages. In Chinook, a language widely spoken in the north-west of North America, to take one example, many properties and qualities are referred to by means of abstract words: 'This method', Boas says, 'is applied to a greater extent than in any other language I know.' The proposition 'The bad man killed the poor child' is rendered in Chinook: 'The man's badness killed the child's poverty'; and for 'The woman used too small a basket' they say: 'She put the potentilla-roots into the smallness of a clam basket' (Boas 2, pp. 657–8).

In every language, moreover, discourse and syntax supply indispensable means of supplementing deficiencies of vocabulary. And the tendentious character of the argument referred to in the last paragraph becomes very apparent when one observes that the opposite state of affairs, that is, where very general terms outweigh specific names, has also been exploited to prove the intellectual poverty of Savages:

Among plants and animals he [the Indian] designates by name only those which are useful or harmful, all others are included under the classification of bird, weed, etc. (Krause, p. 104).

A more recent observer seems in the same way to believe that the native gives names and forms concepts solely in accordance with his needs:

I well remember the hilarity of Marquesian friends . . . over the (to them) fatuous interest of the botanist of our expedition in 1921, who was collecting nameless ('useless') 'weeds' and asking their names (Handy and Pukui, Part VI, p. 127n).

However, Handy compares this indifference to that which specialists in our civilization show towards phenomena which have no immediate bearing on their own field. When his native collaborator stressed the fact that in Hawaii 'every botanical, zoological or inorganic form that is known to have been named (and personalized), was *some thing* . . . used', she is careful to add 'in some way'. She goes on to say that the reason why 'there was an infinite variety of living things in forest and sea, of meteorological or marine phenomena, which were unnamed' was that they were regarded as being of no 'use or interest' – terms which are not equivalent, as 'use' concerns practical, and 'interest' theoretical, matters. What follows confirms this by concentrating on the latter aspect at the expense of the former: 'Living was experience fraught with exact and definite significance' (id., p. 126–7).

In fact, the delimitation of concepts is different in every language, and, as the author of the article 'nom' in the *Encyclopédie* correctly observed in the eighteenth century, the use of more or less abstract terms is a function not of greater or lesser intellectual capacity, but of differences in the interests – in their intensity and attention to detail – of particular social groups within the national society: 'In an observatory a *star* is not simply a star but β of Capricorn or γ of Centaur or ζ of the Great Bear, etc. In stables every *horse* has a proper *name – Diamond, Sprite, Fiery,* etc.' Further, even if the observation about so-called primitive languages referred to at the beginning of the chapter could be accepted as it stands, one would not be able to conclude from this that such languages are deficient in general ideas. Words like 'oak', 'beech', 'birch', etc., are no less entitled to be considered as abstract word than the word 'tree'; and a language possessing only the word 'tree' would be, from this point of view less rich in concepts than one which lacked this term but contained dozens or hundreds for the individual species and varieties.

The proliferation of concepts, as in the case of technical languages, goes with more constant attention to properties of the world,





with an interest that is more alert to possible distinctions which can be introduced between them. This thirst for objective knowledge is one of the most neglected aspects of the thought of people we call 'primitive'. Even if it is rarely directed towards facts of the same level as those with which modern science is concerned, it implies comparable intellectual application and methods of observation. In both cases the universe is an object of thought at least as much as it is a means of satisfying needs.

Every civilization tends to overestimate the objective orientation of its thought and this tendency is never absent. When we make the mistake of thinking that the Savage is governed solely by organic or economic needs, we forget that he levels the same reproach at us, and that to him his own desires for knowledge seems more balanced than ours:

These native Hawaiians' utilization of their available natural assets was well-nigh complete – infinitely more so than that of the present commercial era which ruthlessly exploits the few things that are financially profitable for the time being, neglecting and often obliterating the rest (Handy and Pukui, Part VIII, p. 62).

Cash-crop agriculture is hardly to be confused with the science of the botanist. But, in ignoring the latter and taking only the former into account, the old Hawaiian aristocrat is simply repeating, and turning to the advantage of a native culture, a mistake of the same kind that Malinowski made when he claimed that primitive peoples' interest to totemic plants and animals was inspired by nothing but the rumbling of their stomachs.

Tessman (Vol. 2, p. 192) mentions 'the accuracy with which (the Fang of the Gabon) identify the slightest differences between species of the same genus'. The two authors quoted above make a similar observation about Oceania:

The acute faculties of this native folk noted with exactitude the generic characteristics of all species of terrestial and marine life, and the subtlest variations of natural phenomena such as winds, light and colour, ruffling of water and variation in surf, and the currents of water and air (Handy and Pukui, Part VI, p. 126).

Among the Hanunóo of the Philippines a custom as simple as that of betel chewing demands a knowledge of four varieties of areca nut and eight substitutes for them, and of five varieties of betel and five substitutes (Conklin, 3):

his income, his car or his house: these are merely amenities which make it possible for him to do his job. And if through them he enjoys a little more comfort than the average, it is still not a question of privilege, for certainly he has earned a right to that comfort.

He is privileged because of the way he can think and can talk. If the estimate of his privilege was strictly logical, it would include the fact of his education and his medical training. But that was a long time ago, whereas the evidence of the way he thinks – not purely medically but in general – is there every time he is there. It is why the villagers talk to him, why they tell him the local news, why they listen, why they wonder whether his unusual views are right, why some say 'He's a wonderful doctor but not what you'd expect', and why some middle-class neighbours call him a crack-pot.

The villagers do not consider him privileged because they find his thinking so impressive. It is the style of his thinking which they immediately recognize as different from theirs. They depend upon common-sense and he does not.

It is generally thought that common-sense is practical. It is practical only in a short-term view. Common-sense declares that it is foolish to bite the hand that feeds you. But it is foolish only up to the moment when you realize that you might be fed very much better. In the long-term view common-sense is passive because it is based on the acceptance of an outdated view of the possible. The body of common-sense has to accrue too slowly. All its propositions have to be proved so many times before they can become unquestionable, i.e. traditional. When they become traditional they gain oracular authority. Hence the strong element of *superstition* always evident in 'practical' common-sense.

Common-sense is part of the home-made ideology of those who have been deprived of fundamental learning, of those who have been kept ignorant. This ideology is compounded from different sources: items that have survived from religion, items of empirical knowledge, items of protective scepticism, items culled

## I. INTRODUCTION

This book is a resource manual. It is a reference book, not a curriculum, not a how-to-do-it book. Its projects represent different teaching styles and working methods, and vary in photographic sophistication. However, all the projects are linked by a common experimental attitude and it is hoped that the resource manual will be most valuable to the teacher who uses it as stimulation for meaningful experimentation, not just as a handy recipe book.

The manual is organized alphabetically, to encourage free exploration. Effort has been made to create provocative and meaningful juxtapositions between projects (such as "Old Age Looking In" and "Old Age Looking Out", which provide two contrasting methodological approaches to photographing the same subject). Whenever possible, projects have been organized to form a natural progression. The book's first three projects, for example, introduce photographic problems, varying in sophistication, to help reinforce specific language skills and concepts. Further relationships, progressions, and possible structures for organizing curriculum ideas may be found in the cross-referential index. This index includes major categories of general curriculum areas, such as math, reading, and art, and then diversifies to sub-categories of associative concepts, such as photo essay, role play, classification, and letter identification. Teachers are urged to become familiar enough with the material in the manual as a whole, to construct their own units, and thereby satisfy each program's individual needs.

This collection of photographic projects, compiled from the work of teachers and their students, came about in response to the need expressed by many educators for a sourcebook of ideas for using photography in the classroom. Although the value of integrating photography into the curriculum at many levels has been recognized — in the abstract — for 15 years, there is little practical information available for the teacher who wants to use the camera as a tool but who has been unable to discover a satisfying approach.

The projects presented in this book were possible because of the availability of Polaroid Land cameras and materials. Projects which use the final photograph as an integral step in a complex learning process require the simplicity, reliability and instant result of the Polaroid instant system. However, the very effortless quality associated with instant images can lead to a sloppy and uncaring attitude toward photographic activity. A thorough understanding of how the camera works seems to restore both the wonder and the seriousness of making pictures. Such an attitude starts with the teacher, who should explore and test the various parts of the camera to understand their roles in image formation, to then communicate this understanding to the student. Basic exploration, combined with a thorough reading of the instruction manual, will provide the confidence necessary for successful picture making.

Once mastered, the camera becomes a tool for both student and teacher. For students, Polaroid Land photography is magic, and the product remarkable. For their first experience with the camera, they can create something, capture something that is theirs to share. The power of that vision becomes increasingly clarified as the act of photographing is repeated. First, the student must see and select what to photograph, isolate that object with the camera's eye, then frame the object by cropping it or establishing a context in the picture frame which creates the intended image. A host of variables must be considered: – point of view, relative distance, camera angle, size, placement, exposure, proposed use, and accompanying text – so that the decisions governing their use determine the photograph's statement. A successful photographic statement demands skill and substantial thinking through, both before exposure and during the evaluation of the print. Beyond 'Is the picture in focus, too light, close enough?', must come other questions – 'Does this portray the subject's mood?' or 'What do I think and feel about this subject?' The immediacy of the instant process encourages students in problem solving until they feel satisfied with a photograph.

Involvement with these questions and the making of a successful photograph fosters a sense of competence in being able to control technology, self esteem at seeing one's own expression of imagination or beliefs, and self respect through presenting a statement that communicates with others.

A teacher's decision about how to use photography in the classroom will necessarily be determined by the amount of accessible equipment, budget, and scheduled time with students; however, the main criterion for planning a program must be its overall educational aims. The role of photography can be just a series of activities to complement the traditional academic disciplines, or it can be used as a catalyst, a tool for integrating and expanding the boundaries of the classroom. A primary distinction must be made between the teacher's use of photography for creation of special teaching materials not available commercially, and student use, in which the camera is a stimulant for expressive and investigative statements which document and introduce the outside world as a resource for the classroom.

No package of curriculum materials or ideas alone can make significant change in a classroom. Materials organized in a book cannot possibly provide the same experience as a workshop, where teachers together can explore materials and develop curriculum models. This manual is therefore a resource for ideas and a stimulus for dialogue. The following section, entitled "Strategies", is intended to initiate interaction through excerpted statements of teaching attitudes. The manual then proceeds to represent these styles with a range of projects. No single teaching method is recommended above another. Specific choice of direction must come from concrete situations which consider the teacher, students, school and community.

I wish to thank Dick Rogers for his inspiration and endless encouragement, Margie Praeger for her masterful editorial work, and Marcia Schiff, whose concern and commitment made this book possible. There is no way to thank Bill Field enough. And to all the teachers who have contributed their work, I am truly indebted. Finally, my one regret is that the children whose energy and enthusiasm were the essence of this creation remain anonymous. Hopefully they will not again be forgotten.

Susan Meiselas

der Kollision zwischen mythischer Satzung und Subjektivität, den Antagonismus zwischen der dem Schicksal verbündeten Herrschaft und der zur Mündigkeit erwachenden Humanität. Daß die geschichtsphilosophische Tendenz sowohl wie der Antagonismus zum Formapriori geworden sind, anstatt bloß stofflich behandelt zu werden, verleiht der Tragödie ihre gesellschaftliche Substantialität: Gesellschaft erscheint in ihr desto authentischer, je weniger sie intendiert wird. Die Parteiischkeit, welche die Tugend von Kunstwerken nicht weniger als von Menschen ist, lebt in der Tiefe, in der gesellschaftliche Antinomien zur Dialektik der Formen werden: indem Künstler ihnen durch die Synthesis des Gebildes zur Sprache verhelfen, tun sie gesellschaftlich das Ihre; selbst Lukács fühlte sich, in seiner Spätzeit, zu derlei Erwägungen genötigt. Gestaltung, welche die wortlosen und stummen Widersprüche artikuliert, hat dadurch Züge einer Praxis, die nicht nur vor der realen sich flüchtet; genügt dem Begriff von Kunst selbst als einer Verhaltensweise. Sie ist eine Gestalt von Praxis und muß nicht dafür sich entschuldigen, daß sie nicht direkt agiert: selbst dann vermöchte sie es nicht, wenn sie es wollte, die politische Wirkung auch der sogenannten engagierten ist höchst ungewiß. Die gesellschaftlichen Standpunkte der Künstler mögen ihre Funktion beim Einbruch ins konformierende Bewußtsein haben, in der Entfaltung der Werke treten sie zurück. Über den Wahrheitsgehalt Mozarts besagt es nichts, daß er beim Tod Voltaires abscheuliche Ansichten äußerte. Im Zeitalter ihres Erscheinens freilich ist von dem, was Kunstwerke wollen, auch nicht zu abstrahieren; wer Brecht einzig seiner künstlerischen Meriten wegen würdigt, verfehlt ihn nicht weniger, als wer über seine Bedeutung nach seinen Thesen urteilt. Die Immanenz der Gesellschaft im Werk ist das wesentliche gesellschaftliche Verhältnis der Kunst, nicht die Immanenz von Kunst in der Gesellschaft. Weil der gesellschaftliche Gehalt der Kunst nicht außerhalb ihres principium individuationis angesiedelt sondern in der Individuation beheimatet ist, ihrerseits einem Sozialen, ist der Kunst ihr eigenes gesellschaftliches Wesen verhüllt und erst von ihrer Interpretation zu ergreifen. Noch in Kunstwerken jedoch, die bis ins Innerste mit Ideologie versetzt sind, vermag der Wahrheitsgehalt sich zu behaupten.

345

Ideologie, als gesellschaftlich notwendiger Schein, ist in solcher Notwendigkeit stets auch die verzerrte Gestalt des Wahren. Es ist eine Schwelle des gesellschaftlichen Bewußtseins von Ästhetik gegen die Banausie, daß sie die gesellschaftliche Kritik am Ideologischen von Kunstwerken reflektiert, anstatt sie nachzubeten. Ein Modell des Wahrheitsgehalts eines in seinen Intentionen durchaus ideologischen œuvres ist Stifter. Ideologisch sind nicht nur die konservativ-restaurativ ausgewählten Stoffe und das fabula docet, sondern auch die objektivistische Formgebarung, welche mikrologisch zarte Empirie, ein sinnvoll richtiges Leben, von dem sich erzählen ließe, suggeriert. Darum wurde Stifter zum Abgott eines edel-retrospektiven Bürgertums. Die Schichten, die ihm seine halb esoterische Popularität verschafften, blättern ab. Damit jedoch ist nicht das letzte Wort über ihn gesagt, Versöhntheit und Versöhnlichkeit zumal seiner Spätphase sind outriert. Objektivität erstarrt zur Maske, beschworenes Leben wird zum abweisenden Ritual. Durch die Exzentrizität des Mittleren schimmert das verschwiegene und verleugnete Leid des entfremdeten Subjekts hindurch und die Unversöhntheit des Zustands. Blaß und fahl ist das Licht über seiner reifen Prosa, als wäre sie allergisch gegen das Glück der Farbe; sie wird gleichsam zur Graphik reduziert durch den Ausschluß des Störenden und Ungebärdigen einer sozialen Realität, die mit der Gesinnung des Dichters so unvereinbar ist wie mit dem epischen Apriori, das er krampfhaft von Goethe übernahm. Was gegen den Willen dieser Prosa durch die Diskrepanz ihrer Form und der bereits kapitalistischen Gesellschaft sich zuträgt, wächst ihrem Ausdruck zu. Ideologische Überspannung verleiht dem Werk mittelbar seinen unideologischen Wahrheitsgehalt, seine Überlegenheit über alle Literatur tröstenden Zuspruchs und beflissen landschaftlicher Geborgenheit und erwirbt ihm die authentische Qualität, die Nietzsche bewunderte. Er übrigens ist das Paradigma dafür, wie wenig dichterische Intention, sogar der von einem Kunstwerk unmittelbar verkörperte oder vertretene Sinn seinem objektiven Gehalt gleicht; bei ihm ist der Gehalt wahrhaft die Negation des Sinns, wäre aber nicht, ohne daß dieser vom Kunstwerk vermeint wäre und dann durch dessen eigene Komplexion aufgehoben. Affirmation wird zur Chiffre von Verzweiflung, und

346

die reinste Negativität des Gehalts enthält, wie bei Stifter, ein Gran von Affirmation. Der Glanz, den heute die alle Affirmation tabuierenden Kunstwerke ausstrahlen, ist die Erscheinung des affirmativen ineffabile, des Aufgangs eines Nichtseienden, als ob es doch wäre. Sein Anspruch zu sein erlischt im ästhetischen Schein, was nicht ist, wird jedoch dadurch, daß es erscheint, versprochen. Die Konstellation von Seiendem und Nichtseiendem ist die utopische Figur von Kunst. Während sie zur absoluten Negativität gedrängt wird, ist sie kraft eben jener Negativität kein absolut Negatives. Das antinomische Wesen des affirmativen Rests teilt sich den Kunstwerken keineswegs erst in ihrer Stellung zum Seienden als der Gesellschaft mit, sondern immanent, und verbreitet Zwielicht über sie. Keine Schönheit kann heute der Frage mehr ausweichen, ob sie denn auch schön sei und nicht durch prozeßlose Affirmation erschlichen. Der Widerwille gegen Kunstgewerbe ist, verschoben, das schlechte Gewissen von Kunst überhaupt, das sich beim Aufklingen eines jeglichen Akkords, im Angesicht einer jeglichen Farbe regt. Gesellschaftliche Kritik an Kunst braucht diese nicht erst von außen abzutasten: sie wird von den innerästhetischen Formationen gezeitigt. Die gesteigerte Empfindlichkeit des ästhetischen Sinnes nähert asymptotisch der gesellschaftlich motivierten gegen Kunst sich an. – Ideologie und Wahrheit der Kunst verhalten sich zueinander nicht wie Schafe und Böcke. Sie hat das eine nicht ohne das andere, solche Reziprozität lockt ihrerseits ebenso zum ideologischen Mißbrauch, wie sie zur summarischen Abfertigung im Kahlschlag-Stil ermuntert. Nur ein Schritt ist von der Utopie des sich selbst Gleichseins der Kunstwerke zum Gestank der himmlischen Rosen, welche die Kunst, wie nach Schillers Tirade die Frauen, ins irdische Leben streue. Je schamloser die Gesellschaft zu jener Totalität übergeht, in der sie wie allem auch der Kunst ihren Stellenwert zuweist, desto vollständiger polarisiert sie sich nach Ideologie und Protest; und diese Polarisierung gerät ihr schwerlich zum Guten. Der absolute Protest engt sie ein und springt um auf ihre eigene raison d'être, die Ideologie verdünnt sich zur armseligen und autoritären Kopie der Realität.

In der nach der Katastrophe auferstandenen Kultur vollends nimmt Kunst durch ihr schieres Dasein, vor allem Inhalt und



Gehalt, ein Ideologisches an. Ihr Mißverhältnis zu dem geschehenen und drohenden Grauen verdammt sie zum Zynismus; noch dort lenkt sie davon ab, wo sie ihm sich stellt. Ihre Objektivation impliziert Kälte der Realität gegenüber. Das degradiert sie zur Spießgesellin derselben Barbarei, der sie nicht minder verfällt, wo sie die Objektivation drangibt und unvermittelt, wäre es auch durchs polemische Engagement, mitspielt. Jedes Kunstwerk heute, auch das radikale, hat seinen konservativen Aspekt; seine Existenz hilft, die Sphären von Geist und Kultur zu befestigen, deren reale Ohnmacht und deren Komplizität mit dem Prinzip des Unheils nackt zutage treten. Aber dies Konservative, wider den Trend zur sozialen Integration stärker in den avanciertesten Gebilden als in den gemäßigten, ist nicht nur wert, daß es zugrunde geht. Einzig wofern Geist, in seiner fortgeschrittensten Gestalt, überlebt und weitertreibt, ist überhaupt Widerstand gegen die Allherrschaft der gesellschaftlichen Totale möglich. Eine Menschheit, der nicht der fortschreitende Geist übermachte, was sie zu liquidieren sich anschickt, versänke in jener Barbarei, die eine vernünftige Einrichtung der Gesellschaft verhindern soll. Kunst verkörpert noch als tolerierte in der verwalteten Welt, was nicht sich einrichten läßt und was die totale Einrichtung unterdrückt. Die neugriechischen Tyrannen wußten, warum sie Becketts Stücke verboten, in denen kein politisches Wort fällt. Asozialität wird zur sozialen Legitimation von Kunst. Um der Versöhnung willen müssen die authentischen Werke jede Erinnerungsspur von Versöhnung tilgen. Gleichwohl wäre die Einheit, der noch das Dissoziative nicht entrinnt, nicht ohne die alte Versöhnung. Kunstwerke sind a priori gesellschaftlich schuldig, während ein jedes, das den Namen verdient, seine Schuld zu büßen trachtet. Die Möglichkeit zu überleben haben sie daran, daß ihre Anstrengung zur Synthesis auch Unversöhnlichkeit ist. Ohne die Synthesis, welche das Kunstwerk als autonomes der Realität konfrontiert, wäre nichts außerhalb von deren Bann; das Prinzip der Abtrennung des Geistes, das den Bann um sich verbreitet, ist auch das, welches ihn durchbricht, indem es ihn bestimmt.

Daß die nominalistische Tendenz der Kunst im Extrem der Abschaffung vorgegebener Ordnungskategorien soziale Implikate

This is the introduction to photographer
Peter Hujar's book 'Portraits in Life
and Death' published ~~today~~ in 1976, written
by Susan Sontag. I wouldn't add or change
anything . . . .



## Introduction

Photographs turn the present into the past, make contingency into destiny. Whatever their degree of "realism," all photographs embody a "romantic" relation to reality.

I am thinking of how the poet Novalis defined Romanticism: to make the familiar appear strange, the marvelous appear commonplace. The camera's uncanny mechanical replication of persons and events performs a kind of magic, both creating and de-creating what is photographed. To take pictures is, simultaneously, to confer value and to render banal.

Photographs instigate, confirm, seal legends. Seen through photographs, people become icons of themselves. Photography converts the world itself into a department store or museum-without-walls in which every subject is depreciated into an article of consumption, promoted into an item for esthetic appreciation.

Photography also converts the whole world into a cemetery. Photographers, connoisseurs of beauty, are also — wittingly or unwittingly — the recording-angels of death. The photograph-as-photograph shows death. More than that, it shows the sex-appeal of death — another instance of the Surrealist "bad taste" that is the most persistent motif of good taste in photography. The intrusion of still photographs in that remarkable sequence in Robert Siodmak's film *Menschen am Sonntag* (1928) is like the intrusion of death. One minute we see ordinary folk milling, laughing, grimacing, yearning. The next moment — as, one by one, they step before the street photographer's black box—we see them frozen, embalmed in a "still." The photographs shock, in the flow of the movie. It's as if these vivacious people were already dead, and their paper photographs were cupped behind glass and affixed to tombstones, as is common practice in the cemeteries of Mediterranean countries.

* * *

"When one has a picture taken, the photographer says 'Perfect' Just as you are! That is death."

"Life is a movie. Death is a photograph."

I am quoting from my first novel, *The Benefactor* — from the conclusion of Professor Bulgaraux's lecture. The novel was published in 1963, which is also the year I met Peter Hujar. And the premonitory link between my sensibility and his that is suggested by this passage was transmuted into something much more concrete around 1966, when he showed me the extraordinary photographs he had taken in the Catacombs at Palermo. Readers of *Death Kit* will recognize how intimately the oneiric landscape of the final scene of my second novel — which came out in 1967 — is related to those photographs, the last in the present book.

In the first part of this selection of Peter Hujar's work, fleshed and moist-eyed friends and acquaintances stand, sit, slouch, mostly lie — and are made to appear to meditate on their own mortality. Do meditate, whether they — I — he (for the photographer is among his subjects) acknowledge it or not. We no longer study the art of dying, a regular discipline and hygiene in older cultures; but all eyes, at rest, contain that knowledge. The body knows. And the camera shows, inexorably. The Palermo photographs — which precede these portraits in time — complete them, comment upon them. Peter Hujar knows that portraits in life are always, also, portraits in death. I am moved by the purity and delicacy of his intentions. If a free human being can afford to think of nothing less than death, then these *memento mori* can exorcise morbidity as effectively as they evoke its sweet poetry and its panic.

— Susan Sontag



FRANCES VON HOFMANNSTHAL ANNOTATED INTRODUCTION BY SUSAN SONTAG, PORTRAITS IN LIFE AND DEATH, 1976, PETER HUJAR

Since feelings of pleasure or displeasure lie at the foundation of every aesthetic experience, the affective contradiction that zaniness exemplifies is one that goes straight to the heart of philosophical aesthetics. Could what keeps *The Gay Science* from embodying the kind of joyfully embodied philosophy Nietzsche so stridently calls for in it be in any way related to what makes the zany itself so anxiously shrill? Because the zany insists so strenuously on pleasure and more specifically on the pleasure of the activity of spontaneous, goalless play, the problem of art's "ever broken promise of happiness" seem more intensely concentrated in this aesthetic than in any other.[35] It therefore seems important to be as precise as we can about the reason for the zany's paradoxically entertaining failure to be joyful, or for why it becomes such a key example of the "euphoria in unhappiness" Herbert Marcuse finds endemic to the culture of advanced industrial societies.[36] What is eating the zany? Why is she so desperate and stressed out? And why have so many found this mix of desperation and playfulness so aesthetically appealing?

My simple answer to this question is that this playful, hypercharismatic aesthetic is really an aesthetic about work—and about a precariousness created specifically by the capitalist organization of work.[37] More specifically, as one might already discern from the strenuous performances of Lucy Ricardo (and their unique way of disclosing the artistry of Lucille Ball), zaniness speaks to a politically ambiguous erosion of the distinction between playing and working: from the exhausting pursuits of "fun while learning" in *Bouvard and Pécuchet* (a novel that for all its comedy has "nothing lighthearted about it," according to Raymond Queneau)[38] to the "raucous corporate culture" of Southwest Airlines personified in the "oddball ways" of its "colorful" CEO Gary Kelley (noted for convening meetings in which he addresses his employees in female drag).[39] In all its appearances across the *longue durée* of a modernity never entirely identical or reducible to capitalism but driven primarily by its contradictory logic of incessant expansion, and perhaps most conspicuously since the last half of the twentieth century, it is this cross-coupling of play and work—one marked by an increasing extraction of surplus value from affect and subjectivity, in particular—that provides the best explanation for the contradictory mix of affects that makes the zany what it is, and also such an interesting problem for philosophical aesthetics.

To describe the intensely affective/subjective style of zaniness as a style not just about work, but about the "putting to work" of affect and subjectivity for the generation of surplus value (as we will see in much more detail soon),[40] is to describe it as an aesthetic about production. But precisely insofar as our understanding of production—already a "certain mode of social cooperation and the application and development of a

certain body of social knowledge," as Raymond Williams reminds us— has widened over the course of the past half century to include surplus-value creating acts of working or performing not originally included in Marx's definition.[41] Increasingly—though for some Marxist economists, still not uncontroversially—acknowledged as leading to the creation of social/material wealth (and thus as "productive" in a specifically Marxist sense), these acts range from the caring and domestic work of waged and unwaged women (the culturally devalued "reproductive" labor brought to light by second-wave feminism) to the labor of teachers, artists, and information workers (the "immaterial" or "virtuosic" labor foregrounded by Italian neo-Marxism).[42] The kind of work zaniness indexes extends across both subcategories of labor (reproductive and immaterial). In addition to forcing us to revisit and think across this latest incarnation of the feminist/Marxist divide, the zany qua aesthetic of incessant doing, or of perpetual improvisation and adaptation to projects, also invites us to invert Bergson's famous thesis about comedy. If the "psychological calcifications which make an individual comical in an aesthetic sense . . . are bound up with his incapacity to cope with changing social situations,"[43] perhaps there is something fundamentally anticomical and even pathological—that is, something fundamentally zany—about those who do nothing else.

The unfunnyness of total or absolute adaptability, while arguably brought to a head by the flexible network capitalism of our current moment, goes a long way toward explaining the discomforting aspect of all of modernity's zanies. Far from being "divinely untroubled," zaniness projects the "personality pattern" of the subject wanting too much and trying too hard: the unhappily striving wannabe, poser, or arriviste.[44] The utter antithesis of ironic cool, the perspiring, overheated zany is a social loser not only in the vein of Bouvard and Pécuchet but also of Rameau's nephew, the "failed musician, frequenter of the drawing rooms of the not-so-great, immoralist, leech, and stupendously gifted mime" whom Diderot invents in his 1765 dialogue exploring the difference between modernity's genuine artists (Rameau himself, a brilliant musician) and its mediocre pedagogues (his nephew).[45]

As Joseph Roach argues, the "sweaty antics" of the nephew testify to the fact that his "entire nature is impromptu."[46] They also testify to his occupational überrole—one assumed due to economic necessity—of amusing/servicing/educating the rich. The nephew's "sycophantic visitations to the homes of his patrons" are thus directly correlated with his professional failure as an artist. Yet these visitations are also "minor masterpieces of instantaneous self-invention: he can burst like a thunderclap, whine like a lap dog, or whip up any buffoonery the lady of the house desires" (Roach, 123). A virtuosic performer in this feminized, less prestigious domain (the semiprivate drawing room, as opposed to the orchestra hall), Rameau's nephew performs with what would seem to be the detachment requisite for shifting so rapidly from one role to another. Yet he also seems to perform with not enough distance from his emotions, which are at once spontaneously generated and quite visibly put to work. There is perhaps no better index of this representation of affective spontaneity as effort than the nephew's perspiration, as singled out by his philosophical interlocutor and also by Roach: "The sweat, which, mixed with the powder in his hair, ran down the creases of his face was dripping and marking the upper part of his coat. What did he not attempt to show me? He wept, laughed, sighed, looked placid or melting or enraged. He was a woman in a spasm of grief, a wretched man sunk in despair, a temple being erected . . . a storm, a hurricane, the anguish of those about to die, mingled with the whistling of the wind and the noise of thunder."[47]

The wild seesawing of the nephew's actions in the story thus mirrors the discursive unevenness of his rhetorical style, remarked by the observer as "now elevated, now colloquial," in an informal genre whose own stylistic hybridity may have inspired that of the later Nietzsche (as Jacques Barzun notes, *Rameau's Nephew* is "part satire, part character sketch, part gossip column").[48] Diderot's zany passes out, foaming at the mouth, after this performative feat, which has followed an equally strenuous one in which he has pantomimed the sounds and movements of an entire opera, including the ballet, the choruses, all the individual instruments as well as the musicians playing them, the audience members, and, of course, the singers/characters/actors:

He jumbled together thirty different airs, French, Italian, comic, tragic—in every style. Now in a baritone voice he sank to the pit; then straining in falsetto he tore to shreds the upper notes of some air, imitating the while the stance, walk and gestures of the several characters; being in succession furious, mollified, lordly, sneering. First a damsel weeps and he reproduces her kittenish ways; next he is a priest, a king, a tyrant; he threatens, commands, rages. Now he is a slave, he obeys, calms down, is heartbroken, complains, laughs; never overstepping the proper tone, speech, or manner called for by the part. (67)

On regaining consciousness after his collapse from this succession of perfect imitations, the nephew has no real grasp of what he has done, suggesting that the performances are in control of the performer and not vice versa.[49] The very virtuosity of the nephew's performance thus paradoxically underscores his status as artistic failure:[50] "When I take my pen by myself, intending to write, I bite my nails and belabor my brow but—no



soap, the god is absent" (78). This dual status as virtuoso/loser recalls the nephew's simultaneously privileged and subservient position as entertainer in the drawing rooms of the wealthy: "I was their dear Rameau, pretty Rameau, *their* Rameau—the jester, the buffoon . . . the saucy rogue, the great greedy boob" (19). In a motif repeated throughout the dialogue, the multiple list of terms for "zany" here and elsewhere (jester, buffoon, rogue, boob) verbally echoes the succession of roles we see this zany repeatedly being asked to play. For if the nephew is a "bundle of charms," he is also, anticipating Bouvard and Pécuchet and also Lucy Ricardo, a bundle of what he calls "trade idioms": styles of occupational doing associated with "the financier, the judge, the soldier, the writer, the lawyer, the public prosecutor, the merchant, the banker, the workman, the singing teacher, the dancing master" (32). Yet the nephew links his remarkable fluency in the manners and mores of multiple professions to his own overarching "position" and thus to the economic necessity that mandates it: "The needy man doesn't walk like the rest, he skips, twists, cringes, crawls. He spends his life choosing and performing positions" (82).[51]

If Diderot's eighteenth-century pedagogue/imitator cuts a particularly memorable figure in the history of zaniness, so does the opera buffa character of Figaro, whose aria "Largo al factotum della città" from Rossini's *Barber of Seville* (based on Pierre Beaumarchais' 1775 stage comedy *Le Barbier de Séville* and first performed in Rome in 1816) has become the veritable theme song of zaniness. Well known to several generations in the late twentieth-century United States after unforgettable renditions by Bugs Bunny, Woody Woodpecker, Tom and Jerry, and other *Looney Tunes* characters, the aria with its 6/8 triplets, allegro vivace tempo, and alliterative, tongue-twisting lyrics is not just about work but also famously hard work to perform.[52] These formal features mirror the content of the lyrics, which testify not only to the factotum's "on standby" position and generalized relation to labor ("Pronto a far tutto / la notte e il giorno / sempre d'intorno in giro sta"; "Ready to do everything / Night and day / Always on the move"), but also to his accelerating state of "frenzy" ("Ahimè, che furia!") in attempting to meet all the demands of others ("Tutti mi chiedono, tutti mi vogliono, / donne, ragazzi, vecchi, fanciulle. . . . Pronto prontissimo son come il fulmine: sono il factotum della città"; "Everyone asks for me, everyone wants me / Ladies, young lads, old men, young girls. . . . Swifter and swifter, I'm like a thunderbolt: I'm the factotum of the city").[53] Although we first encounter Figaro working as "barber, wigmaker, surgeon, gardener, apothecary, vet—in short, Jack-of-all-trades" for Don Bartolo, his previous employment as a servant in the household of Count Almaviva is what inspires the count to ask him for help in his

Mary was the first to see the attackers coming, though she didn't know what they were.

It happened in midafternoon, when she was helping repair the roof of a hut. The *mulefa* only built one story high, because they were not climbers; but Mary was happy to clamber above the ground, and she could lay thatch and knot it in place with her two hands, once they had shown her the technique, much more quickly than they could.

So she was braced against the rafters of a house, catching the bundles of reeds thrown up to her, and enjoying the cool breeze from the water that was tempering the heat of the sun, when her eye was caught by a flash of white.

It came from that distant glitter she thought was the sea. She shaded her eyes and saw one—two—more, a fleet of tall white sails, emerging out of the heat haze, some way off but making with a silent grace for the river mouth.

*Mary!* called the *zalif* from below. *What are you seeing?*

She didn't know the word for *sail*, or *boat*, so she said *tall, white, many*.

At once the *zalif* gave a call of alarm, and everyone in earshot stopped work and sped to the center of the settlement, calling the young ones. Within a minute all the *mulefa* were ready to flee.

Atal, her friend, called: *Mary! Mary! Come! Tualapi! Tualapi!*

It had all happened so quickly that Mary had hardly moved. The white sails by this time had already entered the river, easily making headway against the current. Mary was impressed by the discipline of the sailors: they tacked so swiftly, the sails moving together like a flock of starlings, all changing direction simultaneously. And they were so beautiful, those snow white slender sails, bending and dipping and filling—

There were forty of them, at least, and they were coming upriver much more swiftly than she'd thought. But she saw no crew on board, and then she realized that they weren't boats at all: they were gigantic birds, and the sails were their wings, one fore and one aft, held upright and flexed and trimmed by the power of their own muscles.

There was no time to stop and study them, because they had already reached the bank, and were climbing out. They had necks like swans, and beaks as long as her forearm. Their wings were twice as tall as she was, and—she glanced back, frightened now, over her shoulder as she fled—they had powerful legs: no wonder they had moved so fast on the water.

She ran hard after the *mulefa*, who were calling her name as they streamed out of the settlement and onto the highway. She reached them just in time: her friend Atal was waiting, and as Mary scrambled on her back, Atal beat the road with her feet, speeding away up the slope after her companions.

The birds, who couldn't move as fast on land, soon gave up the chase and turned back to the settlement.

They tore open the food stores, snarling and growling and tossing their great cruel beaks high as they swallowed the dried meat and all the preserved fruit and grain. Everything edible was gone in under a minute.

And then the *tualapi* found the wheel store, and tried to smash open the great seedpods, but that was beyond them. Mary felt her friends tense with alarm all around her as they watched from the crest of the low hill and saw pod after pod hurled to the ground, kicked, rasped by the claws on the mighty legs, but of course no harm came to them from that. What worried the *mulefa* was that several of them were pushed and shoved and nudged toward the water, where they floated heavily downstream toward the sea.

Then the great snow-white birds set about demolishing everything they could see with brutal, raking blows of their feet and stabbing, smashing, shaking, tearing movements of their beaks. The *mulefa* around her were murmuring, almost crooning with sorrow.

*I help*, Mary said. *We make again*.

But the foul creatures hadn't finished yet; holding their beautiful wings high, they squatted among the devastation and voided their bowels. The smell drifted up the slope with the breeze; heaps and pools of green-black-brown-white dung lay among the broken beams, the scattered thatch. Then, their clumsy movement on land giving them a swaggering strut, the birds went back to the water and sailed away downstream toward the sea.

Only when the last white wing had vanished in the afternoon haze did the *mulefa* ride down the highway again. They were full of sorrow and anger, but mainly they were powerfully anxious about the seedpod store.

Out of the fifteen pods that had been there, only two were left. The rest had been pushed into the water and lost. But there was a sandbank in the next bend of the river, and Mary thought she could spot a wheel that was caught there; so to the *mulefa* 's surprise and alarm, she took off her clothes, wound a length of cord around her waist, and swam across to it. On the sandbank she found not one but five of the precious wheels, and passing the cord through their softening centers, she swam heavily back, pulling them behind her.

The *mulefa* were full of gratitude. They never entered the water themselves, and only fished from the bank, taking care to keep their feet and wheels dry. Mary felt she had done something useful for them at last.

(Extract from *The Amber Spyglass*, Philip Pullman, 2000)

Sort of embarrassed that this is not a more hi-brow source but this was the first thing that flashed up- and this stuck because of it the extended loopiness of it all. Remembering the vision of those sinister silent sails moving up a river in a regimented way, eventually becoming recognizable as huge terrifying birds. 2000 (along with 1994) seems like a mysterious and important year too. And a few years before this having a day off school (pretending to be sick) –perhaps it was 1997- watching *The Birds* on VHS from the library and literally trembling with fear.

The animals called *mulefa* move a bit like motorbikes, using these seedpods as wheels somehow held within their limbs. Extremely trippy also, this combination of vegetable and animal. And the character Mary is on some kind of mission to discover the nature of the material termed "dust", which is supposed to represent original sin? The religious elements (basically all of the book haha) was mostly lost on me. And she has some kind of assassin tracking her, a Father Gomez. All the characters have "dæmons" which are animals that embody your character or something, both little companions but also some kind of projection of yourself?

We live in a world of traces. Things leave traces. We must never try to make man believe that what is by definition constituted as a "trace," has indeed a different kind of reality—that of "object."

The emotion must never come, as it usually does, through our being convinced of the reality of the image or event presented, but only the ecstatic emotion of one's own seeing of things. Delight in one's own energy.

NEVER awe or delight in the "worshipful way" we feel emotion when we are awed or moved by the "other" which seems like an alien other in which we "wish" we could partake (all romantic art).

---

### Need for Confrontation

Art += to CONFRONT the object

Kitsch= atmosphere replaces object distance between you and object de-creased by atmosphere which makes you FEEL at one with the object because the atmosphere is felt to be that exuded by the object. But then object and you (feeling) are one and there is no ENCOUNTER, and no seeing. (To play the subtext, rather than the object, for instance.)

What is the object? The encountered object, encountered in making the work: the "real" chair, body, word, noise, etc.

The constructed object end with (art) is the we STRUCTURE of the articulating process. The MAKING A THING BE-THERE AS ITSELF (in its web of relations). Process.

The artist doesn't explain, analyze the object . . . but he sets it up so that one CONFRONTS in the realist fashion it's BEING-THERE which is a confrontation to your own BEING-THERE.

PARADOX
The way to confront the object is to allow it its own life—let it grow its own shoots in directions that do **not** re-inforce it's being-in-life for use as a tool,

PAINTINGS AS PROPS IN NARRATIVES



but that suggests a compositional scheme not centered on useful human expectations. So, let the chair that is for sitting have a string run from it to an orange, because if chair was just "chair for sitting" we would not "confront" as we not-confront in kitsch because we are too close to the chair, its meaning is too much OUR meaning; but now chair-connected-to-orange is an "alien" chair that we must CONFRONT.

(To reveal an object or act, gesture, emotion, idea, sound.
To make it seizable
To speak its name you must
make it part of a system not
its own. Involve it compositionally with
another realm, which is YOUR realm of pattern
making isomorphic with your
mind-process. THEN there is confrontation.)

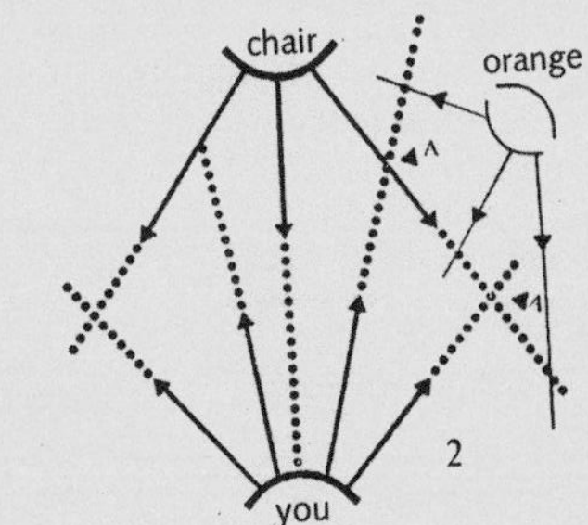


KITSCH
(and sleep) as
the moment of
contact between
you and object
is one dimensional
and you are
in a state of
identification
(hypnotized by)
with that face
of itself the
object presents
to you.

ART
(and awakedness)
as
the moment of
contact between
you and object
is multifaceted and
often "distant" (point A)
from the object.

also

in 2 (as opposed to 1)
your mind-pattern-
process is being as-it-is:

and THAT structure
inter-acts with the
object structure as-it-is.

In 1 the mind forgets
its own working and there
is no real meeting, only
a 1-dimensional (1 "presented"
face to another) moment of
"official" (cliched)
    "something"
that is too mindless: i.e. one dimensional
(lacking points "A" of 2)
to be a real encounter.

*Diagram 2 explains, once and for all, all of my plays!*

---

The message must be "To choose either turbulence or serenity is an error.
To choose either knowing or doing is an error." So…in the play…inject
disruption into knowing, and order into passion.

---

The play is a lecture in which you don't say "This is so…" but rather…
"This occurs to me and it occurs to me that the reason it occurs to me is this
act, which occurs to me," and so on and so on, deeper and deeper.

---

My message is "filling the space with the idea." Free play within the idea.
Ability to treat the "field" of the idea as an area for work and discovery.
Idea as a field…in which something that is not idea (but more physical,
sensual, ecstatic) can emerge.

---

I write to make life handle-able.

The deflection inherent in time. Space—
one makes art to be able to decide what goes into you
                    and what goes out of you.
        To be in control of what goes into you and out





of you is why you decide to make your own art.
Of course…as it goes in and out, space and time
give it an uncontrollable "twist."

---

Lived experience is a certain kind of focus. You focus on an aimed-at while
living, and because you are focused on that, you don't see your own
gestures. Art: is trying to see your own gestures. GESTURES!

My gesture has always been to pull away, to change what came into me, to
make something BETTER, that could then go into me instead of the thing
that did go into me. Hence, to find a way to make better FOOD for myself
than was provided by others. My art then (one's art) is a way of being-in-
the-world so that the INPUT is the best possible input…into me.
Journalism is trying to imitate life. Art is an amplification of the effects
encountered in trying to make art.

---

Art: a machine to effect input. To provide awakening, energy-giving discontinuities. To fight entropy. Art is NOT comment on life. It is fighting the
entropy of life-that-seeks equilibrium, that seeks-not-stress, which would
lead (as life does) to death. (Inject quantum shocks, discontinuities, to keep
twisting us away from sleep, death, into what is "artificially" sustained…
AWAKENED LIFE, CONSCIOUSNESS!

---

Form in art—form isn't a container (of content) but rather
    a rule for generating a possible "next move."
        That's where the subject is (in that next move, dictated or made
        possible by the form). The commonly-thought-of content or sub-
        ject is the pretext to set a process in operation, and that process is
        the real subject. KEEP THE PROCESS OPEN.
The text is me
It grows like I grow
It extends itself, falls, stumbles over…something.
    Recovers. It projects itself as it will. Encounters resistance of various
        sorts, but those resistances turn out to be steps affording a new advance
stretch   extension   twist
stage it: Try to make the compositional aspects be

Il écoute chanter leurs haleines craintives
Qui fleurent de longs miels végétaux et rosés
Et qu'interrompt parfois un sifflement, salives
Reprises sur la lèvre ou désirs de baisers.

Il entend leurs cils noirs battant sous les silences
Parfumés; et leurs doigts électriques et doux
Font crépiter parmi ses grises indolences
Sous leurs ongles royaux la mort des petits poux.

Voilà que monte en lui le vin de la Paresse,
Soupir d'harmonica qui pourrait délirer;
L'enfant se sent, selon la lenteur des caresses,
Sourdre et mourir sans cesse un désir de pleurer.

Voyelles

A noir, E blanc, I rouge, U vert, O bleu: voyelles,
Je dirai quelque jour vos naissances latentes:
A, noir corset velu des mouches éclatantes
Qui bombinent autour des puanteurs cruelles,

Golfes d'ombre; E, candeurs des vapeurs et des tentes,
Lances des glaciers fiers, rois blancs, frissons d'ombelles;
I, pourpres, sang craché, rire des lèvres belles
Dans la colère ou les ivresses pénitentes;

U, cycles, vibrements divins des mers virides,
Paix des pâtis semés d'animaux, paix des rides
Que l'alchimie imprime aux grands fronts studieux;

O, suprême Clairon plein des strideurs étranges,
Silences traversés des Mondes et des Anges:
– O l'Oméga, rayon violet de Ses Yeux!



He listens to their diffident, sing-song breath,
Smelling of elongated honey off the rose,
Broken now and then by a hiss: saliva sucked
Back from the lip, or a longing to be kissed.

He hears their dark eyelashes start in the sweet-
Smelling silence and, through his grey listlessness,
The crackle of small lice dying, beneath
The imperious nails of their soft, electric fingers.

The wine of Torpor wells up in him then
– Near on trance, a harmonica-sigh –
And in their slow caress he feels
The endless ebb and flow of a desire to cry.

Vowels

A black, E white, I red, U green, O blue: vowels,
I shall speak one day of your hidden origins:
A, black fur-corset of the dazzling flies
Buzzing round every cruel stink,

Gulfs of darkness; E, candour of vapour and tents,
Proud glacier shards; white kings; flicker of umbel;
I, purples; spat blood; full lips laughing
In anger or bouts of contrite ecstasy;

U, gyrations, divine shiver of viridian seas,
Peace of cattle-studded pastures, peace of the wrinkles
Carved by alchemy on a broad, studious forehead;

O, the Last Trumpet with its strange clangour,
Silent wastes of Worlds and Angels – traversed;
O, Omega, the violet gleam of Those Eyes!

**EVIE WARD ANNOTATED VOWELS, 1962, SELECTED POEMS AND LETTERS, 2004,
ARTHUR RIMBAUD, TRANSLATION BY JEREMY HARDING & JOHN STURROCK**

438

John Donne said that 'No man is an island ... Every man is a piece of the continent. IF a clod be washed away, Europe is less' - well, look how that turned out. Peter Sloterdijk is a German philosopher who writes about bubbles and stress and the aesthetic imperative in art. I don't understand a lot of it but he writes beautifully and wisely - as here in a book about the Japanese island of Naoshima - itself rejuvenated and brought back closer to the mainland through culture. I can't helping wondering what we will lose culturally now that we have decided to become 'more' island then ever before.

O.W. 12/6/18

bit personal, this →

# THE DRUNKEN ISLE

Peter Sloterdijk

*A fine intoxication urges me…*
Stephane Mallarmé, *Salut*

*On Shipwrecks and Evasions*

Do we know why "island" is the unconditional poetic word? It only needs be mentioned from afar and we mobilize everything in us that wishes to flee. From banality to entrancement, from worry to meditation, from *terra firma* to controlled waters. Before the bird, the angel, the demon, the island is the key term that describes the human essence. It speaks of space in the age of the amphibian kingdoms. He who speaks of the island conjures up an idea of something that is more intrinsic to the speaker than he is himself. The word evokes the notion of a place beyond the horizon that has been waiting since time immemorial for its rightful owner to visit it. Just as the soul is the possibility of an island, so the island is the possibility of a soul. A regular ferry is nowhere in sight. Where you expect to find a harbor, towering cliffs prevent you from landing. Only on the lee side is there an open beach, only ever reached by those who are almost drowned.

The ancient poets knew it, and modern writers have joined them: A shipwreck is the price you pay to arrive on

escape to where?

aka Han Solo

tea stain: or the mark of the British empire, learning to rule from an island by means of trade in opium, tea, and other goods.

for reals?

Brexit Britain!

33

stirring a personal memory. In other words, the mystery of the island lies in being a place that turns time into space. Anyone who has departed from the mainland and approaches the island also leaves all continental dimensions behind. On the island, the question of the possibility of a different beginning is omnipresent. It brings to mind the new beginning of Creation on smaller foundations. With its stones, its flora and fauna, it participates in the achievements of evolution that here has taken a special local tack. Its fascination derives from its ability to invite human visitors from remote continents to alight and dwell there. In that insular isolation from the continental continuum lies the opportunity to repeat the world experiment in a different place.

While the large continental expanses, especially those bifurcated by the great rivers, were home to high civilizations, from time immemorial islands have afforded man the opportunity of rejuvenating culture on a smaller scale. In literal terms, continents are nothing but containers, the greatest possible articulation of the idea of a vessel. They represent figures of encompassment, the boundaries of which provide succor for the existence of all organisms. Within their borders we find both indigenous and migrant life. Within their seemingly endless continuum, each species discovers the conditions for its survival and its preservation. Human life can follow its two innate impulses across the continental expanse, namely to live and to wander. On the continent it can combine its instinctual wish for vastness with its propensity for homelessness. In that immensity, humans can enjoy both adventure and security. The continental ground





underfoot grants human mobility an intimation of what immeasurability means. It seems to promise that there is more boundlessness and cohesion in the world than even the most restless of feet can pace out.

By leaping ashore on an island, mobile life finds a different footing. It moves from continental endlessness into confinement. It is this leap that quickens island mysteries. Whilst among men isolation is often just another word for misery, in the case of the island it designates the principle of being selected. Only by virtue of being isolated, does the island become itself. Since access to it is not granted by continental route, it is distanced in splendid inaccessibility. It is a queen whom the ocean serves as moat, the steep cliffs as the iron gate. Island existence entails sublime sequestration. The island makes no concessions whatsoever to those who are not at home on it. Insularity thus provides us with the model of all autarchy.

To live on an island means to face the task of finding the whole in an enclave. This is the natural location for the adventure of finitude. It is impossible to envision an island that is not likewise more than itself. As a biotope it is intrinsically animate; as a small world it is also the entire world. This underlies the philosophical rhyming of island and individual. Microcosms attract. If you let an island ask you a question, you will be brought up a mystic. One day it will come to pass that you walk along a beach before dawn's first light and pick up a seashell washed ashore during the night. You must change your life. Find out how you can pour the immeasurable into a finite vessel!

– by the many children and adults who have crossed these Gardens, then I believe this is the most precise and profound reason why they should exist.

A visit to the garden was almost always followed by a visit to the museum to contemplate the astonishing world of animals, laid out in charming order in glass cases, interspersed by *tableaux vivants* of animals in the forest. We'd end our day with a tour of Galleria Parmiggiani, to gaze upon art and history – leaving the city feeling as if we'd experienced the whole range of knowledge within a small, confined place (within a 500 meter radius).

It felt as if some invisible architect determined that at the centre of life, amongst the people, streets and universities, a garden should be found an extraordinary, mythical place, and also a model of absolute simplicity.

As a wise Chinese poet once said:

If you want to be happy for a day, spend it at the table with a friend.
If you want to be happy for a month, go on a journey.
If you want to be happy for a year, get married.
If you want to be happy all your life, plant a garden. — German.

*Il giardino di tutti* [*Everybody's Garden*]

Exhibition Catalogue, Reggio Emilia 1991

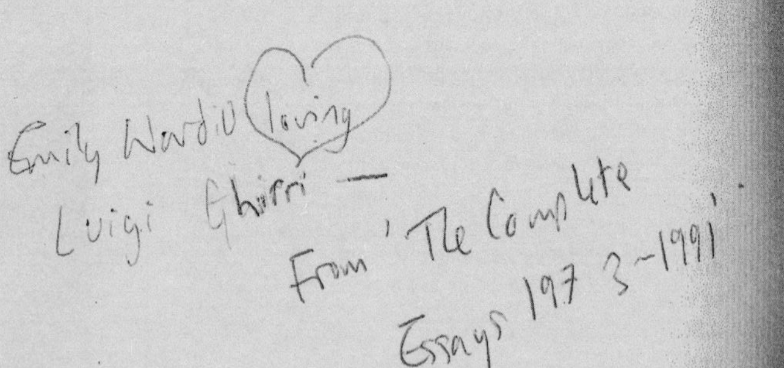

# The Sweet Letters

1991

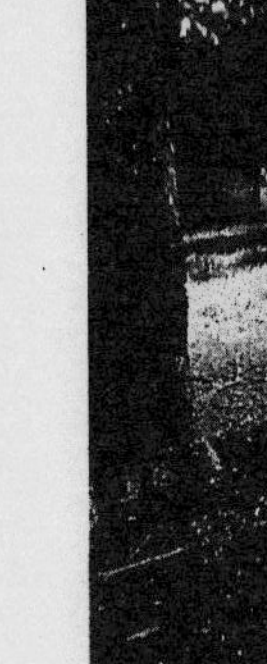

In one of his last interviews, the great American conductor Leonard Bernstein remembered how, as a child, he was introduced to reading by a particular Jewish custom. The teacher of the traditional Jewish primary school he attended would write the letters of the alphabet in honey on a slate, and have the children lick them, so that they would associate knowledge with something sweet and pleasant. As a consequence, the children associated letters of the alphabet with a pleasant taste, and following from this experience of pleasure, learning became an activity inextricably linked to a sense of serenity. I think this anecdote has something in common with the Public Gardens of Reggio Emilia, because these gardens – like the parks of any city around the world – are a bit like Bernstein's 'sweet letters'. There can be no other explanation for the sense of peace and serenity that can be felt when crossing the Garden, or just sitting down in them; it's something to do with a mysterious sweetness, unknown elsewhere. Many have written about the Garden, its origins, history, structure and evolution, and there is a great deal of scholarship far more precise than this short piece; but I believe the Garden's comforting aspect is its most important feature of all.

And so the Garden essentially becomes a 'sweet place' of nature, and it doesn't matter to what extent it's artificial or adulterated, circumscribed or domesticated, because whatever the reason, it still maintains a happy sense of belonging. For everyone, the Garden remains a primer, a sort of enormous ABC of nature, a sheltered part of the city where time and space, rationality and abstraction, are held together in mysterious suspension.

Ever since I was a child, when visiting the city on Sundays, I was enchanted by the enormous Lebanese cedars that line the avenues of the Gardens – even though I came from the countryside. I was captivated by the strange stone statues, the simple lawns and flower beds arranged so carefully, and even the kiosk selling barley water; sometimes I felt that this was the most beautiful place on earth.

Of course, the Gardens of Reggio Emilia are not that, but if this *feeling* of being in the most beautiful place in the world has been felt – even temporarily

# 2000s

34—

**Title:** Manifesto Contrasexual (excerpt)
**Author:** Paul B. Preciado
**Year:** 2002
**Publication:** *Manifesto Contrasexual*, Editorial Opera Prima, 2002.

, bod
or w
d the
others as speaking bodies. 1
for themselves the possibilit
all meaningful practices, as well
on, as s
ed as m
sequen
and na
y, but a
gain fr
naturalisation of the social, econ
and juridical effects of their mea

The heteronormative social technology… can be characterised as a machine of TECHNOlogical production that functions by means of the performative invocation of [the s]ubject as a sexed body.

Sexual identity is not the instinctive expression of the prediscursive truth of the flesh, but the effect of the reinscription of gender practices on the body.

[C]ountersexuality is also a theory of the [b]ody that situates itself outside the [o]ppositions of man/woman, masculine/[fe]minine, heterosexuality/homosexuality. [It] defines sexuality as technology and [co]nsiders that the different elements of [th]e system sex/gender denominated 'man', 'woman', 'homosexual', 'heterosexual', 'transsexual', as well as its practices and sexual identities, are nothing more than machines, products, instruments, apparatuses, tricks, prostheses, networks, applications, programs, connections, energy and information flows, interruptions and switches, keys, laws of circulation, borders, constraints, plans, logics, equipment, formats, accident, detritus, mechanisms, uses, detours…

Countersexuality affirms that

[…]

The architecture of the body is political.

[…]

The workers of the anus (e.g., those who practice fist-fucking) are the new proletarians of a possible countersexual revolution.

Sex, as organ and practice, is neither a precise biological place, nor a natural impulse. Sex is a technology of heterosocial domination that reduces the body to erogenous zones in function of an asymmetrical distribution of power between the genders (feminine/masculine), making coincide certain effects with certain organs, certain sensations with specific anatomical reactions.

Human nature is an effect of social technology that reproduces in bodies the spaces and the discourses of the equation nature=heterosexuality. The heterosexual system is a social apparatus for the production of femininity and masculinity that operates through the division and fragmentation of the body.

The sexual roles and practices that are naturally attributed to the masculine and feminine genders are an arbitrary conjunction of regulations inscribed in bodies that assure the material exploitation of one sex by another.

Cour
refe[r]ence t
[co]uld be found a lesbian heterotopia… that would be a kind of separatist radical feminist utopia. We do not need a pure origin of masculine and heterosexual domination to justify a radical transformation of the sexes and the genders.

[…]

Countersexuality plays on two temporalities. A slow temporality in which the sexual institutions seem to never have suffered any changes. In this temporality, the sexual technologies present themselves as fixed…This plane of fixed temporality is the metaphysical

Countersexuality is not the creation of a new nature, but rather the end of Nature as an order which legitimates the subjection of some bodies to others. Countersexuality is first a critical analysis of the difference of gender and sex, product of the heterocentric social contract, whose normative performances have been inscribed in bodies as biological truths. Secondly, countersexuality points to a substation of this social contract which we call Natural by a countersexual contract. Within the framework of the countersexual contract, bodies recognise themselves not as men or women but as spe... others for the all mea...

> Gender is not simply performative... It is before all else prosthetic, that is, it is not given except in the materiality of bodies. It is purely constructed and at the same time entirely organic. It escapes the false metaphysical dichotomies between body and soul, form and matter. Gender is like the dildo, because they are both more than imitation. Its carnal plasticity destabilises the distinction between the imitated and the imitator, between truth and representation of the truth, between reference and the referent, between nature and the artificial, between the sexual organs and the practices of sex. Gender could result from a sophisticated technology that manufactures sexual bodies.

It is time to stop studying and describing sex as part of the natural history of human societies. The 'history of humanity' would benefit if it were to re-baptise itself as the 'history of technologies' with sex and gender being apparatuses inscribed in a complex technological system. This 'history of technologies' is nothing but the effect of the permanent negotiation of the borders between human and animal, body and machine (Donna Haraway), but also between organ and plasticity.

[...]

The sex-gender system is also system of writing.

[...]

**ARE NOTHING MORE THAN** ... temporality, the sexual technologies present themselves as fixed... This plane of fixed temporality is the metaphysical foundation of all sexual technology. All the work of countersexuality is directed against, operates and intervenes in this temporal sphere. There is also however a temporality of the event in which each fact escapes linear causality. A fractal temporality constituted of multiple 'times' that cannot be the simple effects of the natural truth of sexual identity or of a symbolic order.

Countersexuality is also... body that situates itsel... oppositions of man/wo... feminine, heterosexual... It defines sexuality as t... considers that the diffe... the system sex/gender... ...xual', ...ell as ...ies, a ...oduc ...ks, pr applications, programs energy and information interruptions and switc circulation, borders, co logics, equipment, form detritus, mechanisms,

...system of representation of SEX/gender. The recuperation of the ANUS as a centre of countersexual pleasure has moments in common with the LOGIC of the dildo: each location on the BODY is not only ...ential plane across which the dildo may move, but also an ORIFICE entry, a point of escape, a centre of discharge, an axis of action-passion.

ἐλθάτω ἡ βασιλεία σου

*Thy Kingdom Come.* This concerns something to be achieved, something not yet here. The Kingdom ~~of God~~ means the complete filling of the entire soul of intelligent creatures ~~with the Holy Spirit~~. The Spirit bloweth where they listeth? We can only invite them. We must not even try to invitethemin a definite and special way to visit us or anyone else in particular, or even everybody in general; we must just invite them purely and simply, so that our thought of them is an invitation, a longing cry. It is as when one is in extreme thirst, ill with thirst; then one no longer thinks of the act of drinking in relation to oneself, or even of the act of drinking in a general way. One merely thinks of water, actual water itself, but the image of water is like a cry from our whole being.

*I know that Alfred Appel — a writer I love, whose Art of Celebration I reviewed glowingly for The New York Times, wrote an annotated Lolita. But I have not read it. I recently came across this incredible text from Lolita for an article I was writing about tennis in American fiction —*

*Nabokov changed this word forever.*

She was more of a nymphet than ever, with her apricot-colored
limbs, in her sub-teen tennis togs! … the white wide little-boy
shirts, the slender waist, the apricot midriff, the white breast-
kerchief whose ribbons went up and encircled her neck to end
behind in a dangling knot leaving bare her gaspingly young and
adorable apricot shoulder blades with that pubescence and those
lovely gentle bones, and the smooth downward-tapering back. Her
cap had a white peak. Her racket had cost me a small fortune! …

*great word, always*

*so much better than "teenager".*

*when he repeats, it is poetic*

*again! like a musical motif*

*echo down as anomal'so*

*How reductive he makes that out!!*

*I love his becoming an old penny-pinching grouch, with a) practical mind, in*

She would wait and relax for a bar or two of white-lined time
before going into the act of serving, and often bounced the ball
once or twice, or pawed the ground a little, always at ease, always
rather vague about the score, always cheerful as she seldom was in
the dark life she led at home. Her tennis was the highest point to
which I can imagine a young creature bringing the art of make-
believe. … *and more of the same here.*

*V.N. knows the sport — the tennis serve. Surrounds the conversation ...*

The exquisite clarity of all her movements had its auditory
counterpart in the pure ringing sound of her every stroke. The ball
when it entered her aura of control became somehow whiter, its
resilience somehow richer, and the instrument of precision she
used upon it seemed inordinately prehensile and deliberate at the
moment of clinging contact. Her form was, indeed, an absolutely
perfect imitation of absolutely top-notch tennis.… My Lolita had a
way of raising her bent left knee at the ample and springy start of
the service cycle when there would develop and hang in the sun for
a second a vital web of balance between toed foot, pristine armpit,

*I can't yet own it.*

*Brilliant, including the hint of fuzz*

*the middle of his crazy obsession*

*I could read this sentence as many times as true as great groundstrokes when Nadal plays Del Potro.*

*Does anyone else use language the way he does? So playful*

burnished arm and far back-flung racket, as she smiled up with gleaming teeth at the small globe suspended so high in the zenith of the powerful and graceful cosmos she had created for the express purpose of falling upon it with a clean resounding crack of her golden whip.

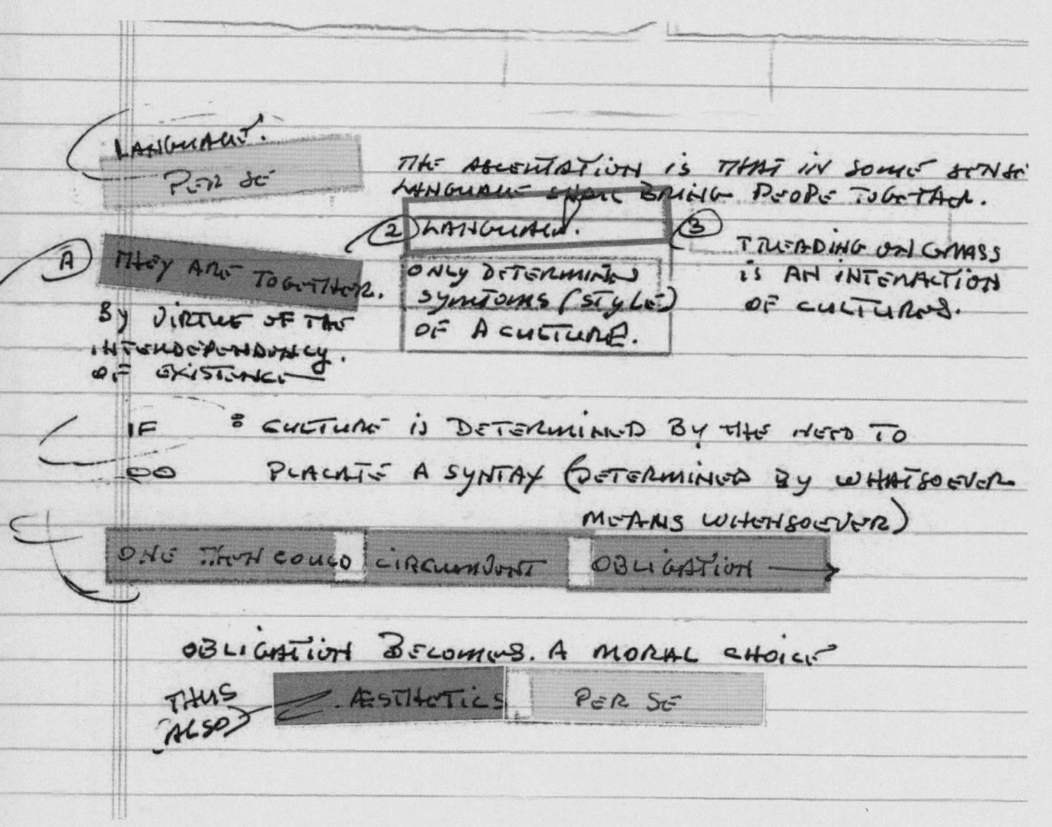

LANGUAGE.
PER SE
THE ASSERTATION IS THAT IN SOME SENSE
LANGUAGE SHALL BRING PEOPLE TOGETHER.
(A) THEY ARE TOGETHER.
BY VIRTUE OF THE
INTERDEPENDENCY.
OF EXISTENCE
(2) LANGUAGE.
ONLY DETERMINES
SYNTOMS (STYLE)
OF A CULTURE.
(3) TREADING ON GRASS
IS AN INTERACTION
OF CULTURES.
IF   CULTURE IS DETERMINED BY THE NEED TO
    PLACATE A SYNTAX (DETERMINED BY WHATSOEVER
                MEANS WHENSOEVER)
ONE THEN COULD CIRCUMVENT OBLIGATION →
OBLIGATION BECOMES. A MORAL CHOICE
THUS          . AESTHETICS   PER SE
(ALSO)

447

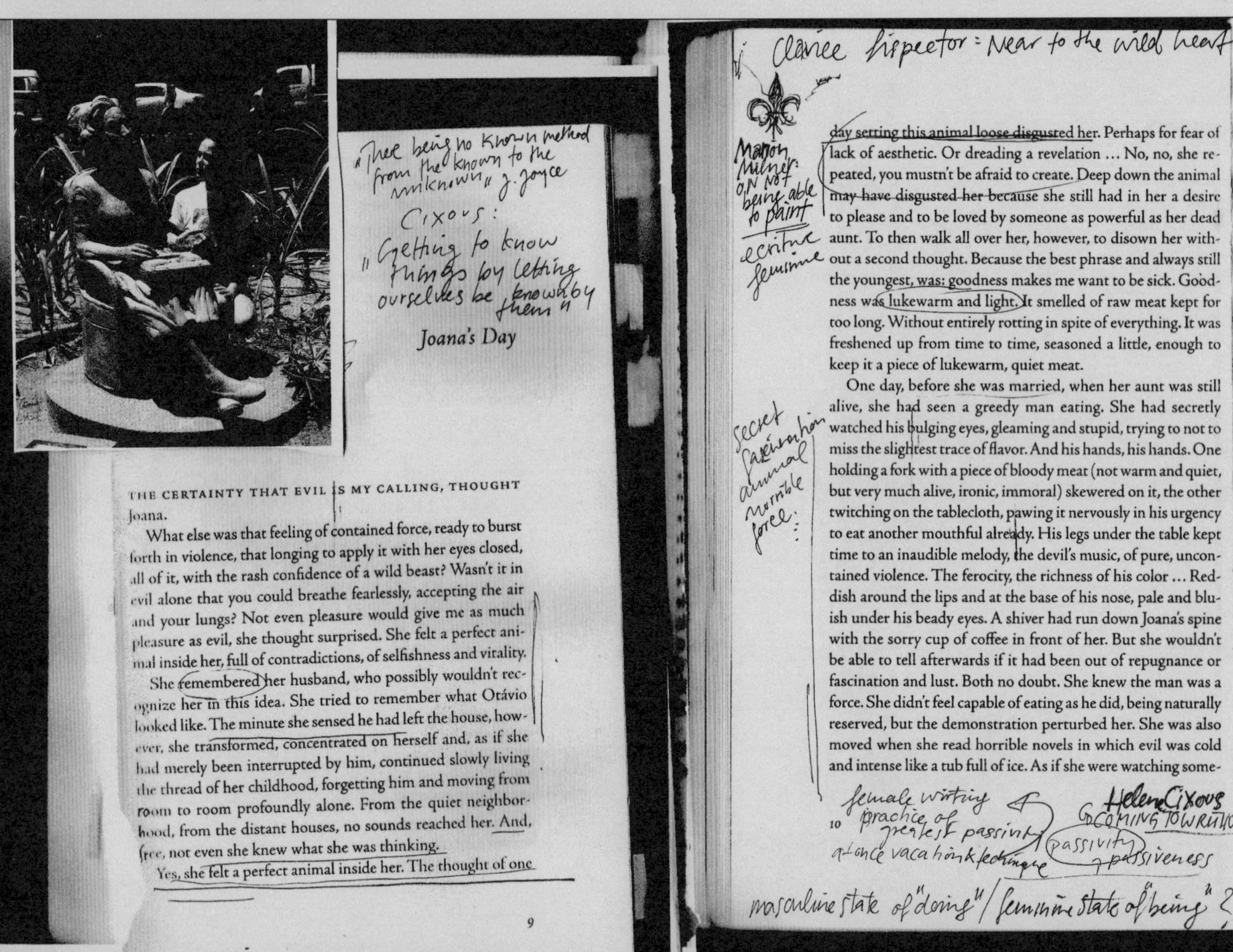



Joana's Day

THE CERTAINTY THAT EVIL IS MY CALLING, THOUGHT Joana.

What else was that feeling of contained force, ready to burst forth in violence, that longing to apply it with her eyes closed, all of it, with the rash confidence of a wild beast? Wasn't it in evil alone that you could breathe fearlessly, accepting the air and your lungs? Not even pleasure would give me as much pleasure as evil, she thought surprised. She felt a perfect animal inside her, full of contradictions, of selfishness and vitality.

She remembered her husband, who possibly wouldn't recognize her in this idea. She tried to remember what Otávio looked like. The minute she sensed he had left the house, however, she transformed, concentrated on herself and, as if she had merely been interrupted by him, continued slowly living the thread of her childhood, forgetting him and moving from room to room profoundly alone. From the quiet neighborhood, from the distant houses, no sounds reached her. And, free, not even she knew what she was thinking.

Yes, she felt a perfect animal inside her. The thought of one

9

day setting this animal loose disgusted her. Perhaps for fear of lack of aesthetic. Or dreading a revelation … No, no, she repeated, you mustn't be afraid to create. Deep down the animal may have disgusted her because she still had in her a desire to please and to be loved by someone as powerful as her dead aunt. To then walk all over her, however, to disown her without a second thought. Because the best phrase and always still the youngest, was: goodness makes me want to be sick. Goodness was lukewarm and light. It smelled of raw meat kept for too long. Without entirely rotting in spite of everything. It was freshened up from time to time, seasoned a little, enough to keep it a piece of lukewarm, quiet meat.

One day, before she was married, when her aunt was still alive, she had seen a greedy man eating. She had secretly watched his bulging eyes, gleaming and stupid, trying to not to miss the slightest trace of flavor. And his hands, his hands. One holding a fork with a piece of bloody meat (not warm and quiet, but very much alive, ironic, immoral) skewered on it, the other twitching on the tablecloth, pawing it nervously in his urgency to eat another mouthful already. His legs under the table kept time to an inaudible melody, the devil's music, of pure, uncontained violence. The ferocity, the richness of his color … Reddish around the lips and at the base of his nose, pale and bluish under his beady eyes. A shiver had run down Joana's spine with the sorry cup of coffee in front of her. But she wouldn't be able to tell afterwards if it had been out of repugnance or fascination and lust. Both no doubt. She knew the man was a force. She didn't feel capable of eating as he did, being naturally reserved, but the demonstration perturbed her. She was also moved when she read horrible novels in which evil was cold and intense like a tub full of ice. As if she were watching some-

Clarice Inspector: Agua Viva     I AM
Bilder schreiben, writing images

Today I finished the canvas I told you about: curves that intersect in fine black lines, and you, with your habit of wanting to know why—I'm not interested in that, the cause is past matter—will ask me why the fine black lines? because of the same secret that now makes me write as if to you, writing something round and rolled up and warm, but sometimes cold as the fresh instants, the water of an ever-trembling stream. Can what I painted on this canvas be put into words? Just as the silent word can be suggested by a musical sound.

I see that I've never told you how I listen to music—I gently rest my hand on the record player and my hand vibrates, sending waves through my whole body: and so I listen to the electricity of the vibrations, the last substratum of reality's realm, and the world trembles inside my hands.
*writing through the body*

And so I realize that I want the vibrating substratum of the repeated word sung in Gregorian chant. I'm aware that I can't say everything I know, I only know when painting or pronouncing, syllables blind of meaning. And if here I must use words, they must bear an almost merely bodily meaning. I'm struggling with the last vibration. To tell you of my substratum I make a sentence of words made only from instants-now. Read, therefore, my invention as pure vibration with no meaning beyond each whistling syllable, read this: "with the passing of the centuries I lost the secret of Egypt, when I moved in longitudes, latitudes, and altitudes with the energetic action of electrons, protons, and neutrons, under the spell of the word and its shadow." What I wrote you here is an electronic drawing without past or future: it is simply now.

H. Cixous: 'to live the orange'
" a woman's voice came to me from far away (…)
(…) a writing came to me with gleaming hands in the darkness, when I no longer dared to help myself, (…) a writing found me when I was unfindable to myself"

page 5

fragments, instants, Hallelujahs, plasma
leaving behind rational discourse : exploring unknown

C. Lisp.                    so…
                ›Écriture feminine ‹

fear. All that's guiding me is a sense of discovery. Beyond what's beyond thought.

Following myself along is really what I'm doing when writing to you and now: following myself without knowing where it will lead me. Sometimes it's so hard to follow myself along. Because I'm following something that's still nothing more than a nebula. Sometimes I end up giving up.

Shhh… Now I'm afraid. Because I'm going to tell you something. Wait until the fear passes.

It passed. It's this: dissonance is harmonious to me. Melody sometimes wears me out. And also the so-called "leitmotif." I want in music and in what I write to you and in what I paint, I want geometric streaks that cross in the air and form a disharmony that I understand. Pure *it*. My being is completely absorbed and grows slightly intoxicated. What I'm telling you is very important. And I work while I sleep: because that is when I move inside the mystery.

Today is Sunday morning. On this Sunday of sun and Jupiter I am alone in the house. I suddenly doubled over as if in the deep pain of childbirth—and saw that the girl in me was dying. I shall never forget that bloody Sunday. It will take time for the wound to heal. And here I am tough and silent and heroic. Without a girl inside me. All lives are heroic lives.

Creation escapes me. And I don't even want to know so much. That my heart beats in my breast is enough. The impossible living of the *it* is enough.

→ 'to live the orange' by
Cixous : "the living text"
   - active reading -
  I experience the text
     Meditation - work of Art - a text - a canvas

page 59

Agua Viva - Clarice Lispector

449

# CONTENTS

*SUBJECT*



*CRAFTS / TRADES*

# Biophilia hypothesis

From Wikipedia, the free encyclopedia
 (Redirected from Biophilia)

The **biophilia hypothesis** suggests that there is an instinctive bond between human beings and other living systems. Edward O. Wilson introduced and popularized the hypothesis in his book entitled *Biophilia*.[1]

## Contents

- 1 Love of living systems
- 2 Product of biological evolution
- 3 Selfish genes
- 4 Development
- 5 References
- 6 See also
- 7 External links

## Love of living systems

The term "biophilia" literally means "love of life or living systems." It was first used by Erich Fromm to describe a psychological orientation of being attracted to all that is alive and vital.[2] Wilson uses the term in the same sense when he suggests that biophilia describes "the connections that human beings subconsciously seek with the rest of life." He proposed the possibility that the deep affiliations humans have with nature are rooted in our biology. Unlike phobias, which are the aversions and fears that people have of things in the natural world, philias are the attractions and positive feelings that people have toward certain habitats, activities, and objects in their natural surroundings.

## Product of biological evolution

Human preferences toward things in nature, while refined through experience and culture, are hypothetically the product of biological evolution. For example, adult mammals (esp. humans) are generally attracted to baby mammal faces and find them appealing across species. The large eyes and small features of any young mammal face are far more appealing than those of the mature adults. The biophilia hypothesis suggests that the positive emotional response that adult mammals have toward baby mammals across species helps increase the survival rates of all mammals.

Similarly, the hypothesis helps explain why ordinary people care for and sometimes risk their lives to save domestic and wild animals, and keep plants and flowers in and around their homes. In other words, our natural love for life helps sustain life.

## Selfish genes

Richard Dawkins proposed the hypothesis of Selfish genes and The Extended Phenotype. Selfish gene theory suggests that genes evolve primarily through natural selection due to their replication capabilities being enhanced. According to this particular view, the Biophilia hypothesis would need to explain why living organisms help other living organisms which do not contain their DNA. Domestic animals and plants can evolve genes which make humans want to care for them and protect them. However some evolutionary biologists believe this can be explained by reputation-based models, which demonstrate an individual's genetic quality by his ability to not only look after himself, but others as well. Helping others at a small cost to yourself is an honest signal of genetic quality because it is costly to maintain, and only high quality individuals can afford the cost. It should also be noted, that the tendency to care for animals and plants could be a byproduct of our development of agriculture and domesticated animals. Although purely hypothetical, these behavioral attributes could have

# INTRODUCTION

*(REVOLUTION AT POINT ZERO - SILVIA FEDERICI)*

+ MARLOW MOSS
UK
1889 - 1958
WWI + WW II
LESBIAN
CHANGED TO ANDROGYNOUS NAME
WORE JODHPURS + SUITS

+ GRACE CROWLEY
AUS
1890 - 1979
WWI + WWII
SINGLE / BISEXUAL RUPE [SPECULATION]
(CONSIDERED USING MALE NAME FOR PAINTINGS
TEACHER / FOUNDER SCHOOL

} ALL FEMALE
ABSTRACT ARTIST + 1 MUSICIAN
MOSS, CROWLEY + CHOUCAIR STUDIED AT ACADÉMIE MODERNE PAR

+ SALOUA RAOUDA CHOUCAIR
LBN
1916 - 2017
WWI (DAD DIES) + LEBANESE CIVIL WAR
MARRIED + DAUGHTER

+ ETEL ADNAN
LBN + US
1925
ALGERIAN WAR OF INDEPENDENCE
VIETNAM WAR

+ PAULINE OLIVEROS
US
1932 - 2016
VIETNAM WAR

ABSTRACT (ART)
WAR ____/ LANGUAGE
| FEMALE POSITION |

+ ERGONOMICAL HOUSEHOLD OBJECT → PLACE OF KNOWLEDGE
TRANSFER → CAN INFLUENCE SOCIETY + HISTORY
+ ABSTRACTION / MODERNISM 1920s → ORGANI IDEAS AND THEORIES ON
ABSTRACTION HAVE BEEN APPLIED INTO THE DOMESTIC SPACE AND LIVING ORGANISATION

I have hesitated in the past to publish a volume of essays concerned exclusively with the question of "reproduction" as it seemed an artificial abstraction from the varieties of issues and struggles to which I have dedicated my work over many years. There is, however, a logic behind the concentration of writings in this collection: the question of reproduction, intended as the complex of activities and relations by which our life and labor are daily reconstituted, has been a thread that has run through all my writing and political activism.

The confrontation with "reproductive work"—understood, at first, as housework, domestic labor—was the defining factor for many women of my generation, who came of age in the aftermath of World War II. For after two world wars that in a space of three decades decimated more than seventy million people, the lures of domesticity and the prospect of sacrificing our lives to produce more workers and soldiers for the state had no hold on our imagination. Indeed, even more than the experience of self-reliance that the war bestowed on many women—symbolized in the United States by the iconic image of Rosie the Riveter—what shaped our relation to reproduction in the postwar period, especially in Europe, was the memory of the carnage into which we had been born. This is a chapter in the history of the international feminist movement still to be written.[1] Yet, in recalling the visits that as school children in Italy we made to exhibits on the concentration camps, and the tales told around the dinner table of the many times we barely escaped being killed by bombs, running through the night searching for safety under a blazing sky, I cannot help wondering how much those experiences weighed on my and other women's decisions not to have children and not to become housewives.

# WAGES AGAINST HOUSEWORK (1975)

*They say it is love. We say it is unwaged work.*
*They call it frigidity. We call it absenteeism.*
*Every miscarriage is a work accident.*
*Homosexuality and heterosexuality are both working conditions . . . but homosexuality is workers' control of production, not the end of work.*
*More smiles? More money. Nothing will be so powerful in destroying the healing virtues of a smile.*
*Neuroses, suicides, desexualization: occupational diseases of the housewife.*

**M**any times the difficulties and ambiguities that women express in discussing wages for housework stem from the fact that they reduce wages for housework to a thing, a lump of money, instead of viewing it as a political perspective. The difference between these two standpoints is enormous. To view wages for housework as a thing rather than a perspective is to detach the end result of our struggle from the struggle itself and to miss its significance in demystifying and subverting the role to which women have been confined in capitalist society.

When we view wages for housework in this reductive way we start asking ourselves: what difference could more money make to our lives? We might even agree that for a lot of women who do not have any choice except for housework and marriage, it would indeed make a lot of difference. But for those of us who seem to have other choices—professional work, an enlightened husband, a communal way of life, gay relations or a combination of these—it would not make much of a difference. For us there are supposedly other ways of achieving economic independence, and the last thing we want is to get it by identifying ourselves as housewives, a fate that we all agree is, so to speak, worse than death. The problem with this position is that in our imagination we usually add a bit of money to the wretched lives we have now and then ask "so what?" on the false premise that we could ever get that money without at the same time revolutionizing—in the process of struggling for it—all our family and social relations. But if we take wages for housework as a political

OR MIDDLE CLASS FAMIL THAT SUPPOR WITH AN ALLOWANCE

perspective, we can see that struggling for it is going to produce a revolution in our lives and in our social power as women. It is also clear that if we think we do not need that money, it is because we have accepted the particular forms of prostitution of body and mind by which we get the money to hide that need. As I will try to show, not only is wages for housework a revolutionary perspective, but it is the only revolutionary perspective from a feminist viewpoint.

### "A Labor of Love"

It is important to recognize that when we speak of housework we are not speaking of a job like other jobs, but we are speaking of the most pervasive manipulation, and the subtlest violence that capitalism has ever perpetrated against any section of the working class. True, under capitalism every worker is manipulated and exploited and his or her relation to capital is totally mystified. The wage gives the impression of a fair deal: you work and you get paid, hence you and your boss each get what's owed; while in reality the wage, rather than paying for the work you do, hides all the unpaid work that goes into profit. But the wage at least recognizes that you are a worker, and you can bargain and struggle around and against the terms and the quantity of that wage, the terms and the quantity of that work. To have a wage means to be part of a social contract, and there is no doubt concerning its meaning: you work, not because you like it, or because it comes naturally to you, but because it is the only condition under which you are allowed to live. Exploited as you might be, you are not that work. Today you are a postman, tomorrow a cabdriver. All that matters is how much of that work you have to do and how much of that money you can get.

The difference with housework lies in the fact that not only has it been imposed on women, but it has been transformed into a natural attribute of our female physique and personality, an internal need, an aspiration, supposedly coming from the depth of our female character. Housework was transformed into a natural attribute, rather than being recognized as work, because it was destined to be unwaged. Capital had to convince us that it is a natural, unavoidable, and even fulfilling activity to make us accept working without a wage. In turn, the unwaged condition of housework has been the most powerful weapon in reinforcing the common assumption that housework is not work, thus preventing women from struggling against it, except in the privatized kitchen-bedroom quarrel that all society agrees to ridicule, thereby further reducing the protagonist of a struggle. We are seen as nagging bitches, not as workers in struggle.

— FIGHTING FOR WAGES IS FIGHTING FOR A TOOL TO FIGHT WITH —



Yet, how natural it is to be a housewife is shown by the fact that it takes at least twenty years of socialization, day-to-day training, performed by an unwaged mother, to prepare a woman for this role, to convince her that children and husband are the best that she can expect from life. Even so, it hardly succeeds. No matter how well trained we are, few women do not feel cheated when the bride's day is over and they find themselves in front of a dirty sink. Many of us still have the illusion that we marry for love. A lot of us recognize that we marry for money and security; but it is time to make it clear that while the love or money involved is very little, the work that awaits us is enormous. This is why older women always tell us, "Enjoy your freedom while you can, buy whatever you want now." But unfortunately it is almost impossible to enjoy any freedom if, from the earliest days of your life, you are trained to be docile, subservient, dependent and, most importantly, to sacrifice yourself and even to get pleasure from it. If you don't like it, it is your problem, your failure, your guilt, and your abnormality.

We must admit that capital has been very successful in hiding our work. It has created a true masterpiece at the expense of women. By denying housework a wage and transforming it into an act of love, capital has killed many birds with one stone. First of all, it has gotten a hell of a lot of work almost for free, and it has made sure that women, far from struggling against it, would seek that work as the best thing in life (the magic words: "Yes, darling, you are a real woman"). At the same time, it has also disciplined the male worker, by making "his" woman dependent on his work and his wage, and trapped him in this discipline by giving him a servant after he himself has done so much serving at the factory or the office. In fact, our role as women is to be the unwaged but happy and most of all loving servants of the "working class," i.e., those strata of the proletariat to which capital was forced to grant more social power. In the same way as god created Eve to give pleasure to Adam, so did capital create the housewife to service the male worker physically, emotionally, and sexually, to raise his children, mend his socks, patch up his ego when it is crushed by the work and the social relations (which are relations of loneliness) that capital has reserved for him. It is precisely this peculiar combination of physical, emotional and sexual services that are involved in the role women must perform for capital that creates the specific character of that servant which is the housewife, that makes her work so burdensome and at the same time so invisible. It is not an accident, then, if most men start thinking of getting married as soon as they get their first job. This is not only because now they can afford it, but also because having somebody at home who takes care of you is the only condition of not going crazy after a day spent on an assembly line or at a desk. Every woman knows

# Designer Communism: non-places as utopia

Mark Fisher

When we are told that we must knuckle down and prepare ourselves for a period of austerity, we might be forgiven if we are bewildered. For hasn't the period we've just lived through been marked by a certain austerity? As Franco Berardi has argued, the neoliberal moment was governed by a very restricted definition of wealth – "a projection of time aimed at gaining power through acquisition and consumption". The alternative model of wealth that Berardi proposes – "the simple capacity to enjoy the world available in terms of time, concentration, and freedom" – has become impossible for precarious workers endlessly harried by always-on digital communications equipment. There is no time to linger; any time not spent hustling (for sales, for work, for opportunities) is time wasted. But perhaps this other kind of wealth is just as inaccessible to the super-rich, too, who take their laptops and smartphones on holiday with them, who are never free from the pull of email, who are only as good as their last deal, and whose ceaseless agitation operates as a Stakhanovite example that the rest of us are supposed to follow.

For Berardi, the consequence of all this infernal inertia is a reduction in eroticism, where eroticism is understood not just in the narrow sense of sexual contact, but in the broader sense of the art of enjoyment. For the super-rich, money possesses no use-value (and, at any rate, they have no time to spend the money they have accumulated). Their massive salaries function as signs: a multi-million dollar bonus can seem like a humiliation if it less than what a rival receives. Similarly, the houses of the super-rich are not intended to be lived in; they are objects for display, in which wealth is signalled by the conspicuous wastage of space.

As a major generator of sign value, design has been crucial to all this, and we shouldn't underestimate the role that the co-option of design played in the success of neoliberalism. The prefix *designer* is now synonymous with hyper-capitalist, whereas anything anti- or non-capitalist is deemed to be drab, functional. The sarcastic coinage of the concept of *designer socialism* in the 1980s was meant to suggest that the 'designer' and the 'socialist' were incompatible: a designer socialist was someone who espoused left-wing principles but who consumed like a capitalist. Owen Hatherley has worked tirelessly to overturn these clichés. From Hatherley's perspective, design is a prisoner of capitalism rather than as its willing servant. While neoliberalism presents us with a situation in which the rich retreat into heavily protected compounds and invite us to admire their interior designs, the "militant modernism" that Hatherley excavates and reconstitutes involves extravagant visions of public space: "Imagine if … the paragon of the Twentieth Century's inorganic desires was a Delirious Moscow rather than New York".

Designing capitalist realism

The destruction – both physical and conceptual – of public space has been central to the neoliberal world's libidinal austerity. Steven Spielberg's seemingly anodyne 2004 tragicomedy, *The Terminal*, provides us with a vision of this degraded public space. Loosely based on the real-life case of Mehran Karimi Nasseri, who spent eighteen years at Charles de Gaulle airport in Paris, the film stars Tom Hanks as Viktor Navorski, a citizen of the fictional Eastern European country of Krakozhia. While Navorski is flying to the United States, Krakozhia becomes embroiled in a revolution. By the time he lands at JFK airport in New York, the United States no longer recognises Krakozhia, and Navorski is not permitted to enter America. Navorski is plunged into a state of suspension – Spielberg doing a kind of Kafka-lite – in which the ratification of his status as an authorised person is perpetually postponed.

The significance of *The Terminal* is the fantasy that underlies it – the idea that, beyond the airport, there is a 'real' United States that can be distinguished from the 'artificiality' of the airport terminal, a promised land which Navorski is prevented from entering. But what could be a more authentic introduction to United States culture than Spielberg's hypercommercialised terminal, crowded with franchise retail outlets and all of the semiotic paraphernalia of multinational corporations? The terminal fulfils a similar function for the United States that, according to Baudrillard, Disneyland once did. Baudrillard famously argued that Disneyland was presented as imaginary in order to make us believe in the reality of the rest of the United States; in the same way, Spielberg's airport is presented as inauthentic, as a (non)place of waiting and suspension, in order to secure the authenticity of the America outside the terminal.

The Baudrillardian resonances multiply when we reflect on the terminal building itself. As the film's title suggests, it is the terminal that is the real star of the movie. The auteur behind *The Terminal* would then be Spielberg's production designer, Alex McDowell. The construction of the terminal was a considerable design feat, as architecture critic Hugh Pearman explains:

> Spielberg's JFK is not the real place or even a close replica of one of the terminals there, but a set built at huge expense in a hangar in Palmdale, California. Production designer Alex McDowell produced a full-size, fully operational terminal derived from a selection of American and European airports. It is deliberately made just slightly more terminalistic than the real thing. Its surfaces are just a bit shinier and more brittle, there are more escalators and flight-information screens, a state-of-the-art Dutch-designed airport signage system, a veritable casbah of familiar shops and cafes, and of course there is the inevitable section undergoing rebuilding, a parallel universe for the characters who inhabit the place.

> The interesting thing about Spielberg's terminal is that – in order to function convincingly – it had to be built as a real, three-storey building rather than as a flimsy set. Complete with 60,000 feet of granite floors and 35 familiar retailers, some with real Starbucks-style staff, it took 20 weeks and 200 workers to build. No virtual reality for Spielberg here: what you see, apart from spliced-in scenes of planes pulling up outside, is physical actuality. As love interest Catherine Zeta-Jones remarked: "It even smelled like an airport."

Pearman's account of the design and building of Spielberg's terminal is a parable for Baudrillard's much misunderstood concept of the hyperreal. Rather than being defined by the disappearance of reality, as is sometimes misleadingly claimed, the hyperreal is instead characterised by a claustrophobic excess of reality. Change can be imagined, but only as a metastatic expansion of that which already exists. Just as Spielberg's terminal is "slightly more terminalistic than

A New Career in a New Town, David Bowie / Hit the North (Part 1), The Fall / Alone, The Cry / Halah, Mazzy Star / Night Walk, Dirty Beaches / Like A Swp, Faster T.L. Barrett & the Youth for Christ choir / Oh Sinnerman, Black Diamond Heavies / Guess I'm Dumb, Glen Campbell / Moving, Suede /

LILLIAN WILKIE ANNOTATED DESIGNER COMMUNISM: NON-PLACES AS UTOPIA, PROGRAM, MARK FISHER, THE PRODUCTION LINE OF HAPPINESS, 2013, CHRISTOPHER WILLIAMS

The Platters / Isi, NEU! / Planet Caravan, Black Sabbath /

the real thing", so the hyperreal is *more real than real*. Pearman is quite right when he observes that Spielberg's JFK is "not even close" to the actual JFK. In fact, the differences between the airport and Spielberg's simulation are striking. Whereas practically every frame of Spielberg's film features a conspicuous corporate logo, the actual JFK is surprisingly spartan, with only a modest selection of retail outlets. But in order for Spielberg's composite-simulation to seem *realistic*, it was necessary for it to include *far more* multinational retail spaces than are at JFK. *The Terminal* is therefore an exemplary case of what I have elsewhere called *capitalist realism*[5]: a worldview which assumes that there are no plausible – or even imaginable – alternatives to capitalism. The appearance of brands in *The Terminal* is not only a matter of representation – in much the same way that the film's retailers were populated by "real Starbucks-style staff", so the corporate logos are, naturally, real logos. Criticising Spielberg for facilitating the intrusion of corporations into culture misses the obvious point that the culture which Spielberg is depicting is already saturated with corporate signifiers. In such a situation, product placement becomes a technique of realism, and realism necessarily becomes advertising.

The dialectics of the non-place
The fact that Navorski comes from Eastern Europe is of course crucial. Despite being annexed by capitalism over two decades ago, Eastern Europe still carries with it a residual sense of being outside capitalism – in the Hollywood imagination at least. Navorski's wandering around the retail arcades of the airport therefore suggests a total subsumption by the homogenous spaces of global capitalism; now, even the ghost of an outside is absorbed. The disappearance of Krakozhia stands in for the disappearance of all localities, of all places. In addition to being a parable about the hyperreal, *The Terminal* also seems to exemplify Marc Augé's discussion of the non-place. Augé draws a well-known distinction between the anthropological place – small towns with market squares; villages with greens – and non-places – zones of transit such as retail parks, hotels, and of course, airports. The fact that such spaces are increasingly interchangeable – and, after all, Spielberg's airport terminal is nothing if not a multi-levelled retail park – seems to reinforce Augé's point.

Yet we should resist any reactionary take on Augé's typology, not only because appeals to tradition and to the local have an intrinsically reactionary tenor, but also because anti-capitalism will continue to fail if it does not reckon with the libidinal pull of the non-place. J. G. Ballard understood the appeal of the non-place very well. His "favourite building in London was Michael Manser's 1992 Hilton hotel at Heathrow airport – a slab of international style with a dizzying glass atrium. 'Sitting in its atrium one becomes, briefly, a more advanced kind of human being,' he told Hans Ulrich Obrist in 2003, echoing Marc Augé's message that antiseptic non-places, in particular hotels and airports, give us a glimpse of an anonymous future city-world. … In in-between spaces and non-places, Ballard saw an architecture that appealed to the immediate here and now, the instant, as opposed to bowing towards some abstract posterity or an idea of taste. We are at our most free in the non-place, the atrium, the departure lounge, on the motorway."[6]

Ballard's intuition that we are most free in the non-place echoes the views of none other than L. M. Sabsovich, one of the early Soviet planners, who imagined the future communist society as a series of non-places:

> In Sabsovich's vision, communal life replaces the wasteful and deadening private household, a "scourge that deforms the lives of adults and children alike" …
>
> The aims of communalism? To free all workers (especially women) from responsibility for the provision of daily needs and from the private obligation of child-rearing and education, to make woman equal to man by opening the doors of her domestic jail, to release

energies for the fulfillment of individual needs and collective life, to enhance the health of children, to raise the cultural level of all people, and to end the distinction between hand and brain labor. The means? The "industrialization" of all tasks previously performed, separately and wastefully, inside the "petty bourgeois" home. Building on the whole tradition of socialist dreams of household collectivism, Sabsovich imagined the coordination of all food producing operations in order to transform raw food products into complete meals, deliverable to the population in urban cafeterias, communal dining rooms, and the workplace in ready-to-eat form by means of thermos containers. No food shopping, no cooking, no home meals, no kitchens. Similar industrialization of laundering, tailoring, repair, and even house cleaning (with electrical appliances) would allow each person a sleeping-living room, free of all maintenance cares. *Russia would in fact become a vast free-of-charge hotel chain.*[7]

If we adopt Sabsovich's perspective for a moment, we can see late capitalism, with its shoddy ready meals, dreary franchise coffee bars, inadequate and expensive childcare arrangements, and disintegrating family units, as a blind and flailing attempt to attain what Sabsovich planned. In the spirit of Fredric Jameson's startling suggestion that there are utopian possibilities to be found in something as super-capitalist as Wal-Mart[8], it's possible to argue that, far from signalling the ultimate triumph of corporate capitalism, the success of something like Starbucks – which has proliferated through high streets and retail parks with all the implacability of a commercial super-virus – is testament to a thwarted desire for communism. It's striking, in fact, how much the clichéd attacks on Starbucks echo the caricatures of communism: both are condemned for their homogeneity, for their generic replicability. What if the desires that Starbucks caters for were nothing other than the desires for a public space that neoliberalism has dismantled at the level of ideology but which capitalism is now forced to reconstruct in a disavowed form? After all, what is sought out in Starbucks has little to do with capitalism or consumerism: the pleasures here are to do with the predictability and anonymity of standardised spaces. Many, in fact, go to Starbucks because of its public toilets – and it can't be an accident that Starbucks has risen to popularity in the wake of the decline of public amenities under neoliberalism.

In conditions where the world is increasingly dominated by the same few multinational chains, it is hard to argue that capitalism is delivering the diversity or choice that it promises. But the poverty of experiences in such spaces actually make the task of revivifying public space seem like an surprisingly easy one. The very homogeneity of corporate chain space compels us to imagine a superior form of homogeneity: one designed for public enjoyment rather than corporate profit. Surely it is possible to envisage standardised spaces – public non-places – that are far better designed than the ones we currently endure? In any case, this is the project that designer communism must undertake.


1 Ivor Southwood, *Non-Stop Inertia* (Alresford, United Kingdom: Zer0 books, 2011), p. 15.
2 Franco Berardi, *The Soul At Work: From Alienation To Autonomy* (Los Angeles: Semiotext(e), 2009), p. 61.
3 Owen Hatherley, *Militant Modernism* (Alresford, United Kingdom: Zer0 books, 2008), p. 61.
4 Hugh Pearman, "The Terminal: not just a movie but architecture at extremes", http://www.hughpearman.com/articles5/airports2.html.
5 See Mark Fisher, *Capitalist Realism: Is there no alternative?* (Alresford, United Kingdom: Zer0 books, 2009).
6 William Wiles, "JG Ballard", *ICON* (July 2009), online at http://www.iconeye.com/index.php?option=com_content&view=article&id=4052:jg-ballard.
7 Richard Stites, *Revolutionary Dreams: Utopian Vision and Experimental Life in the Russian Revolution* (Oxford: Oxford University Press, 1989), p. 12 [emphasis added].
8 See "Utopia as Replication" in Jameson's *Valences of the Dialectic* (London: Verso, 2010).


Christopher Williams

9, Föllakzoid / Still As The Night, Sanford Clark /

Thomas / Interzone, Joy Division / Cut and Run, Electrelane / The Great Pretender,

Here on my own, U.N.P.O.C. / The Coldest Days of my life, Timmy

# TOO CLOSE TO SEE:
# NOTES ON FRIENDSHIP,
# A CONVERSATION WITH
# JOHAN FREDERIK HARTLE

Céline Condorelli

The following text addresses the practice of friendship as a specific entry in relation to the large question of how to live and work together towards change, as a way of acting in the world. Being a friend entails a commitment, a decision, and encompasses the implied positioning that any cultural activity requires. In the context of self-organisation, friendship is perhaps at its most evident in relation to a labour process, in *how we work together*.

I have been engaging with what I call *support*, which I consider essential to cultural production, for some time.[1] Friendship is a fundamental aspect of personal support, a condition of doing things together that deserves substantial attention, and is in many ways the missing chapter to my book *Support Structures*.[2] Friendship, like support, is considered here as an essentially political relationship of allegiance and responsibility. One of the best definitions of cultural production is perhaps that of 'making things public': the process of connecting things, establishing relationships, which in many ways means befriending issues, people, contexts. Friendship in this way is both a set-up for working and a dimension of production. In addition, working together can start from as well as create forms of solidarity and friendship, which are then to be pursued as both condition and intent, motivating actions taken and allowing work undertaken. The line of thought that threads through the following text therefore, is that of friendship as a form of solidarity: friends in action.

It seems appropriate to tackle friendship, itself a relation-ship, in the format of a dialogue, here taking place between philosopher Johan Frederik Hartle and myself. A chance encounter led us to develop an unexpected conversation on the subject over several months, mostly via email, which forms the basis of this text. While philosophy is the field in which friendship appears as a subject, it also holds the word friend (philía) in its very name, so the two are intimately and inextricably linked. The conversation, however, is articulated from our particular respective positions, that of an artist and that of a philosopher, between two practices that produce in different registers, even though they might sometimes share similar concerns. Our practices are usually differentiated between making and thinking, while making is also a form of thinking, and thinking is, undeniably, a way of making. These two positions produce

1. See the long-term project *Support Structure* with Gavin Wade, from 2003 to 2009, www.supportstructure.org.
2. Céline Condorelli, *Support Structures*, Sternberg Press, 2009.

different questions, and, of course, answers, that open up friendship as a productive concept and proactively ask the question: what can friends do?

There are many ways of working together, and it is important to put one's own practice in a constant relation to acting in public in the world at large.

My practice, like that of many others, often involves putting fragments in relationship to each other, so that the cumulative sum of these things – words, ideas – somehow proposes something that each part alone could not; through this I speak, not so much through an individual authorial voice, but through a multiplicity of voices. I find my position by collecting and navigating through material, and I try to make work that speaks in the same way, that works by articulating a complexity of material, explicitly in both form and content.

Perhaps this is a way of working that creates close ties and connections between things, people, and myself, and more often than not this feels like a friendship of sorts. I work by spending time with things I have collected, with the references that I carry along, with the numerous voices – of friends, acquaintances and peers – that are part of the process of developing work, which also include the essential voices of inspirational thinkers from the past that populate our thoughts and conversations and are thus also present. Friendship, then, is perhaps a condition of work. It might never be the actual subject of the work – however close it is to a long-term object of my practice, support – but it is a formative, operational condition that works on multiple, simultaneous levels.

With this particular awareness in mind, I recently started visiting the small, but rich philosophical discourse on friendship – through Aristotle, Montaigne, Derrida, Agamben and Blanchot – and found it is a discourse on friendship among men. Derrida addresses this problem in one chapter of *The Politics of Friendship*, and yet the issue remains: no female philosophers have written about friendship, to the best of my knowledge, and, more crucially, there seems to be something inherently patriarchal, perhaps fratriarchal about these constructions of friendship. They are closely linked to notions of freedom and democracy that come from the idea of nations of brothers (and the terrifying consequence that we can only live together because we are the same, we share the same land, the same birth, the same blood, the same language). Simple, haunting questions emerge from this: can I use a discourse that excludes

me, and, if so, how?[3] Should I produce my own? And how would a discourse on friendship that includes women be structured?

*Your observation on the patriarchal dimension of the traditional philosophy of friendship is striking. Why would friendship be fratriarchal? It is true that, more often than not, friends are conceived of as men among themselves, in their controlled and rational manliness, as colleagues and comrades. Fraternity – an equality of bodies, styles, culture and size – keeps others out. The archetypal depiction of the concord of male friends is in official or public dress, with all heads appearing on one level, in such a way that the signs of accord are all formal. Legitimate friends are rational citizens who agree on basic public issues: this is the liberalist construction that has dominated political discourse ever since the 1789 declaration of human rights.[4] This construction of political rationality is exclusive and I think that it appears in depictions of friendship too; while representations of male concord are inclusive and open to some extent, certain qualities seem to be required to be worthy a friend.*

*I suspect this may have something to do with the stabilising function of 'good affections'. Friendship seems to describe a connection undisturbed by desire, predominantly understood as a connection between mature subjects. It is, of course, affectionate, but these affections are, by definition, not threatening: friendship is an art of life, a form of the everyday. It is a confirmation of what we already are, rather than its interference.*

*In this sense friendship is reduced to a public agreement in line with liberal, contractual ideas. Should we understand it as a contract on agreed upon terms, or is it by definition in excess of any such rigid forms of agreement? 'In friendship and in politics', the German philosopher Hauke Brunkhorst writes, 'the citizens must, in a double sense, be free. They must find one another of their own free will, and they must be just as free from the cares of daily survival – thus, from labour – as they are from the will and commands of a master. Therefore, they can be neither slaves*

3. See also Svetlana Boym, 'Scenography of Friendship', *Cabinet Magazine*. No. 36, winter 2009-10, pp. 88-94.

4. Ideal *citoyens* [citizens], as opposed to socially concrete *hommes* [men].

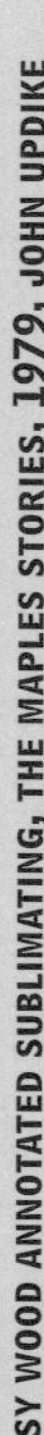

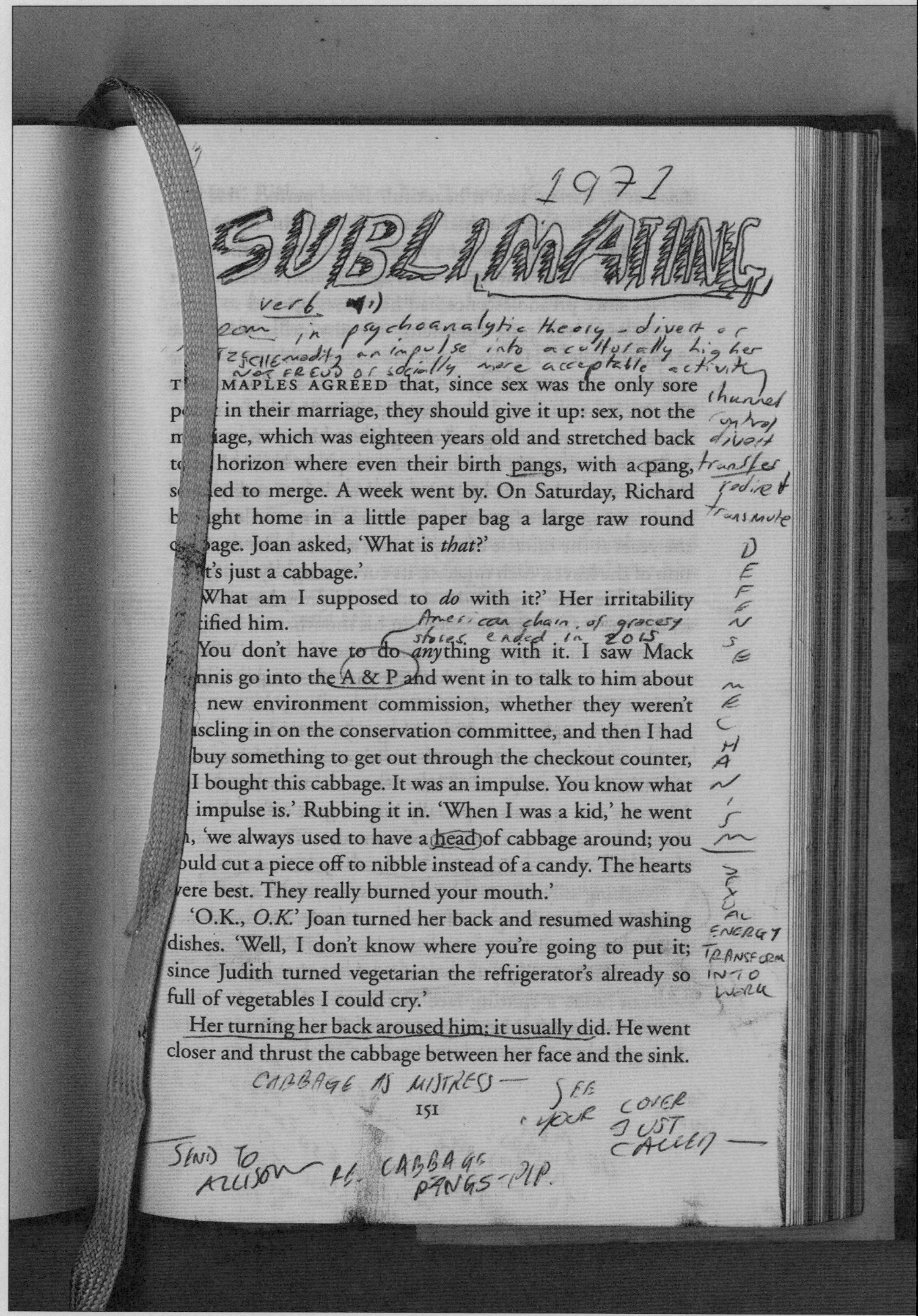

*1971*

# SUBLIMATING

*verb* ◄))

*in psychoanalytic theory – divert or
redirect (an impulse) into a culturally higher
or socially more acceptable activity*
*not Freud*

THE MAPLES AGREED that, since sex was the only sore
point in their marriage, they should give it up: sex, not the
marriage, which was eighteen years old and stretched back
to a horizon where even their birth pangs, with a pang,
seemed to merge. A week went by. On Saturday, Richard
brought home in a little paper bag a large raw round
cabbage. Joan asked, 'What is *that*?'

'It's just a cabbage.'

'What am I supposed to *do* with it?' Her irritability
gratified him.

'You don't have to do anything with it. I saw Mack
Dennis go into the A & P and went in to talk to him about
the new environment commission, whether they weren't
muscling in on the conservation committee, and then I had
to buy something to get out through the checkout counter,
so I bought this cabbage. It was an impulse. You know what
an impulse is.' Rubbing it in. 'When I was a kid,' he went
on, 'we always used to have a head of cabbage around; you
could cut a piece off to nibble instead of a candy. The hearts
were best. They really burned your mouth.'

'O.K., *O.K.*' Joan turned her back and resumed washing
dishes. 'Well, I don't know where you're going to put it;
since Judith turned vegetarian the refrigerator's already so
full of vegetables I could cry.'

Her turning her back aroused him; it usually did. He went
closer and thrust the cabbage between her face and the sink.

151

*Look* at it, darley. Isn't it beautiful? It's so perfect.' He was only partly teasing; he had found himself, in the A & P, ravished by the glory of the pyramided cabbages, the mute and glossy beauty that had waited ages for him to rediscover it. Not since preadolescence had his senses opened so innocently wide; the pure sphericity, the shy cellar odor, the cannonball heft. He chose, not the largest cabbage, but the roundest, the most ideal, and carried it naked in his hand to the checkout counter, where the girl, with a flicker of surprise, dressed it in a paper bag and charged him thirty-three cents. As he drove the mile home, the secret sphere beside him in the seat seemed a hole he had drilled back into reality. And now, cutting a slice from one pale cheek, he marvelled across the years at the miracle of the wound, at the tender compaction of the leaves, each tuned to its curve as tightly as a guitar string. The taste was blander than his childhood memory of it, but the texture was delicious in his mouth.

Bean, their baby, ten, came into the kitchen. 'What is Daddy eating?' she asked, looking into the empty bag for cookies. She knew Daddy as a snack-sneaker.

'Daddy bought himself a cabbage,' Joan told her.

The child looked at her father with eyes in which amusement had been prepared. There was a serious warmth that Mommy and animals, especially horses, gave off, and everything else had the coolness of comedy. 'That was silly,' she said.

'Nothing silly about it,' Richard said. 'Have a bite.' He offered her the cabbage as if it were an apple. He envisioned inside her round head leaves and leaves of female psychology, packed so snugly the wrinkles dovetailed.

Bean made a spitting face and harshly laughed. 'That's nasty,' she said. Bolder, brighter-eyed, flirting: *You're* nasty.' Trying it out.

152

# It'll Be Me

Jerry Lee Lewis

Well, if you hear somebody knocking on your door
If you see something crawling across the floor
Baby, it'll be me and I'll be looking for you

If you see a head a-peeping from a crawdad hole
If you see somebody climbing up a telephone pole
Baby, it'll be me and I'll be looking for you

I'm gonna look on the mountain and in the deep blue
sea
Gonna search all the forests and look and look in
every tree

Well, if you feel something heavy on your fishing hook
If you see a funny face in your comic book
Baby, it'll be me and I'll be looking for you

If you hear a thought calling out in the night
If you see somebody hanging from a lamp post bright
Baby, it'll be me and I'll be looking for you

Well if you see somebody looking in all the cars
If you see a rocket ship on its way to Mars
Baby, it'll be me and I'll be looking for you

Gonna look in the city where the lights are blue
Gonna search the countryside and all the haystacks,
too

We'll, if you see a new face on a totem pole
If you find a lump in your sugar bowl
Baby, it'll be me and I'll be looking for you

Songwriters: Jack Clement

# of future releases from Unit Core

announcements

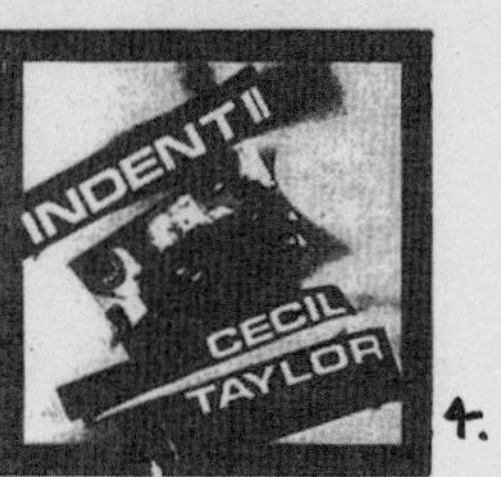


Cecil Taylor has prepared a series of recordings and books for release in early 1974 the first of these, "Spring of Two Blue—J's," can be ordered from Unit Core at $6.00 including postage. Please fill in the form to be informed of their availability.

3. INDENT (Mysteries) was released in August, 1973, the first production of Cecil Taylor's own label Unit Core

INDENT II is the next three movements or "layers" from the same concert recorded at Antioch College while Mr. Taylor was Artist-and-Composer-in-Residence.
His first entire solo piano recording, INDENT, received the highest critical recognition. A quote from a five-star review printed in Downbeat, October 25, 1973, "To describe Taylor's music in terms other than those of total amazement would do it a disservice. And to refer to him as less than one of the world's few musical geniuses would be to show a complete disregard for the music of the last half-century. Some have referred to his music as somewhat inaccessible. They should be surprised with INDENT. It's all here—the Taylor of thunder and the Taylor of almost pastoral grace. If you miss it, you're missing an important facet of the artistic climate of the universe."

**Cecil Taylor Unit Core Ensemble**
A double album of music recorded at Antioch College and performed by twenty-five musicians who were participants in the Cecil Taylor Program in Yellow Springs, Ohio. The first release of Mr. Taylor's composition for large ensemble makes this an historic event. It is music of tremendous scope, epic in qualities expressing spontaneous energies and meditative pathos. Such powerful artistry will startle some but stand as a contribution to the expansion of the musical vocabulary of the twentieth century.

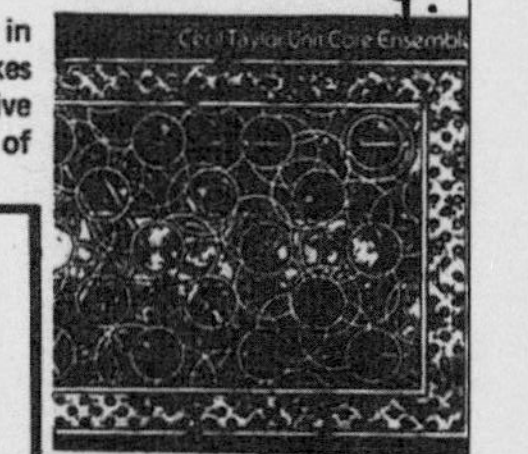


Word Placement is a volume of poetry by Cecil Taylor. The liner notes to "Spring of Two Blue—J's" are an excerpt from this volume, and are presented in the form of a holograph (literary term for a manuscript written in the artist's own hand). Cecil Taylor has other annotated holographs available. Publication of both books has been made possible in part by a Guggenheim Fellowship.

Word Placement
WORD PLACEMENT
Placement
Word
Placement
Word
Placement

Cecil Taylor

The manuscript included in this album is an adjunct chapter to Mysteries "an investigation into methodological concepts of black music." It sets forth the aesthetic theory of one of the foremost single influences in the development of the so-called "new music," Cecil Taylor. The concepts are the basis of the courses Mr. Taylor taught on the aesthetics of music as Artist-and-Composer-in-Residence at The University of Wisconsin and Antioch College (1969—73).

MYST-
ERIES

CECIL
TAYLOR

To be informed of other Unit Core releases as they are released check off the items you are interested in and you will be notified by mail. "Spring of Two Blue—J's" is only production available as of Feb., 1974 and is $6.00 postage paid.

As soon as available, notify me of the following:

1 ☐ INDENT II, solo piano
2 ☐ Cecil Taylor Unit Core Ensemble
3 ☐ Mysteries, an investigation into methodological concepts of black music.
4 ☐ Word Placement, poetry by Cecil Taylor
5 ☐ Holographs (manuscripts in artist's hand), signed in limited edition.

UNIT CORE
P.O. BOX 3041
NYC, NY 10001

Name . . . . . . . . . . . . . . . . . . . . . . . . . . Address . . . . . . . . . . . . . . . . . . . . . . . . . . . . . . . .

City, State, Zip . . . . . . . . . . . . . . . . . . . . . . . . . . . . . . . . . . . . . . . . . . . . . . . . . . . .

1. Lost? to-be-imagined? to-be-[re]now-released?
2. How ready were these?
   (why did they not emerge?)
3. How did Indent III/unit Core Ensemble sound?
4. Is this the cover? Was the design all done? Pattern/montage?
   'Placement'? Texts with these two?
   [cf. Spring of Two Blue-J's + Indent stuff]
5. Who? (Exactly who?)
6. Locate? Imagine?
7. Imagine these courses? Take these courses? (Re-)run these courses?
8. How?
9. These?
10. Find? Imagine? Publish?
*. who wrote this announcement?

In 2002, Berssenbrugge stated straightforwardly, "I cherish the label 'Asian American poet' because I identify with other Americans who come from China, and with other Asian Americans."[10] What is one to do with such a quote? It seems shockingly unfashionable and out of step—not to mention rare—in this "post-race" era for a poet of color who has finally scaled the walls of the avant-garde inner sanctum to make such an identity claim. Why do avant-garde poetics seem so at odds with (self-)identification as a minority American poet? What are the underlying assumptions and categories that critics bring to the discourse and debates about poetry today?

Both sets of critics—on opposite poles of the aesthetic/poetic ideological spectrum but not the social/racial ideological one (they often share a certain familiar type of white liberalism)—fail to recognize how racial subjectivity can make itself felt *in* and *as* language and in what is not said or said obliquely. The imbrication of "form" and "content" is complex and subtle. Both groups of critics take at face value what appears on the page as thematic "content": for critics of more traditional ethnic poetry, everything is reducible to ethnic themes; for critics of avant-garde minority poetry, a lack of overt racial content in the poetry is proof of the irrelevance of race in the work. Both groups of critics in their treatment of minority poets also exhibit the liberal tendency to treat these writers as tokens of diversity.

But Mei-mei Berssenbrugge does not want to be thought of as *either* an identity poet *or* an avant-garde poet who has disavowed her Asian American "identity."

In another poem, "Forms of Politeness," also from *Empathy* (and included in *I Love Artists*), the speaker says:

> Because it's not possible to absorb more than one insight at a time, there seems to be
> a contradiction between the visual or space, and the context or meaning.
> She felt deep uneasiness with the image of this sunset of unnatural energy, its
> sinister expression
> of an order of impossible beauty we thought we lost, accounting for the intensity of
> yellow light on the hill,
> which is not a thing, *and* it is not a metaphor, the way your life is not a metaphor to
> her. . . . (original emphasis; 55)

This idea of something's occupying a state of being that is "not a thing" and "not a metaphor"—in this case, "yellow light"[23]—is an important idea in Berssenbrugge's work.

She rejects the seeming contradiction: the false binary of abstract versus concrete, metaphor versus thing. It is not that Berssenbrugge rejects either metaphors[24] or things; she rejects the false binary. The multiple and shifting pronouns in this passage—"she," "we," "your"—could indicate different persons, but they could also be read as referring to the same person. The "she" is part of the "our"; the "your" could also be an address to the she's self, the she's "I."

Indeed, pronouns work at the level of both content and form. They refer to antecedents, yet, as Roman Jakobson says, they are "purely grammatical . . . units."[25] They shimmer, without forcing us to have to choose between content *or* form. In this respect, Berssenbrugge's use of pronouns reflects her belief that identity—including poetic identity—is not an either-or choice. Berssenbrugge does not want to have to choose between being either an Asian American poet, who is read by critics as operating only at the level of content, or a "formally innovative" poet, who supposedly operates only at the level of "form" or language.

In proceeding through Berssenbrugge's poems, I want to temporarily set aside the question of her identity as Asian American poet or an Asian American experimental poet and, instead, begin by approaching her poetry from a broader perspective. I do so because I immediately recognize the difficulty in trying to talk about the link between the body of her work and her formation (and self-identification) as an Asian American poet. Trying to make an argument about the relationship between a poet's experiences, history, and formation, on the one hand, and her words on the page, on the other, is a difficult—some might say impossible—task for all critics. "No one can describe the relation between an experience / that needs to be communicated and the form of communication," says the speaker in section 5 of Berssenbrugge's poem "Irises" from her 1998 volume *Four Year Old Girl*.[20] The relation between "experiences" and poems is arguably most difficult to articulate in the case of avant-garde or experimental poetry, where mimetic representation is usually refused and language and meaning are stretched to their limits.

In the second example, the speaker understands that she can see only certain parts of other people's bodies, while other parts are hidden in fog—itself both visible and invisible—a state that is like ("as if") a hypothetical state of muffled sounds. So two sensory states, seeing and hearing, are brought into comparison without contradiction. As we have seen in earlier examples, human perception and the external world of natural phenomena are brought in contiguity (is the fog actual or metaphorical?). When speaking of "parts of the people," the poetic speaker is referring both to physical parts of their bodies and parts of their being or identity. The notion of visibility holds particular import, of course, for people of color, whose visible "parts"—skin color, the shape of a nose or an eye—are often read as metonyms *and* metaphors for some sort of racialized essence, while "other parts rest in folds," invisible to the eye. The line preceding this quote reads, "This is a realm or field in which other people exist in subtler forms than the body in daylight" (42).

In the third example, two states of the natural world—or rather, two phases of the same natural phenomenon—day and night, become merged by means of the speaker's perception; the diurnal and nocturnal become, in a manner of speaking, inseparable from the speaker's consciousness. Because she can see as if it were day, she has converted night into day by her perception of the landscape.

The natural phenomenon of fog exemplifies the simultaneous states of being material and immaterial, embodied and disembodied ("Though it is visible, it is not a concrete substance"). Water itself is one substance that can change quickly from one form to another or occupy two or even three states at once: "Fog is a kind of grounded cloud composed like any cloud of tiny drops of water or of ice crystals, forming / an ice fog" (38). At the same time, "fog" is a metaphor for human states of being or identity. The phrase "as if" opens the door to these other worlds, revealing to us the instability of knowing and of being—in other words, epistemological and ontological contingency, both of natural phenomena and of human states of being in the world.

If natural and human states of being (what we label the "self") are not fixed, then the representation of those states, the rendering of them into words, must be approached with great care. Berssenbrugge is acutely aware of the poet's task:

> You could try to make some fog into a piece of white cloth. This is impossible. Though it is visible, it is not a concrete substance. She tried to make a delicate cloud into a cloth.... ("Fog," section 6, 43)

> Anything with limits can be imagined, correctly or incorrectly, as an object. ("Empathy," 50)

Making something as amorphous as "fog" into a piece of cloth, an object, is not unlike the act of making a poem from the ephemerality of human and natural life. The end products are concrete things, a piece of cloth, words, which cannot possibly capture in full that fog —or a life.[50] It is in the *trying* to make, the act of making, that something from that cloud or the fog, even if only a color or a memory or a texture, necessarily finds its way into the cloth—or the poem. The critic's task is as delicate as the poet's and as weighty: "How you look into . . . lit and unlit complexities . . . / is the complicated question of looking" ("Honeymoon," 63).

DANA GIOIA

## Notes on the New Formalism

1

Twenty years ago it was a truth universally acknowledged that a young poet in possession of a good ear would want to write free verse. Today one faces more complex and problematic choices. While the overwhelming majority of new poetry published in the U.S. continues to be in "open" form, for the first time in two generations there is a major revival of formal verse among young poets. The first signs of this revival emerged at the tail end of the seventies long after the more knowing critics had declared rhyme and meter permanently defunct. First a few good formal books by young poets like Charles Martin's *Room For Error* (1978) and Timothy Steele's *Uncertainties and Rest* (1979) appeared but went almost completely unreviewed. Then magazines like *Paris Review* which hadn't published a rhyming poem in anyone's memory, suddenly began featuring sonnets, villanelles, and syllabics. Changes in literary taste make good copy, and the sharper reviewers quickly took note. Soon some of the most lavishly praised debuts like Brad Leithauser's *Hundreds of Fireflies* (1982) and Vikram Seth's *The Golden Gate* (1986) were by poets working entirely in form.

Literature not only changes; it must change to keep its force and vitality. There will always be groups advocating new types of poetry, some of it genuine, just as there will always be conservative opposing forces trying to maintain the conventional models. But the revival of rhyme and meter among some young poets creates an unprecedented situation in American poetry. The new formalists put free verse poets in the ironic and unprepared position of being the status quo. Free verse, the creation of an older literary revolution, is now the long-established, ruling orthodoxy; formal poetry the unexpected challenge.

There is currently a great deal of private controversy about these new formalists, some of which occasionally spills over into print. Significantly, these discussions often contain many odd misconceptions about poetic form, most of them threadbare clichés which somehow still survive from the sixties. Form, we are told authoritatively, is artificial, elitist, retrogressive, right-wing, and (my favorite) un-American. None of these arguments can withstand critical scrutiny, but nevertheless, they continue to be made so regularly that one can only assume they provide some emotional comfort to their advocates. Obviously, for many writers the discussion of formal and free verse has become an encoded political debate.

When the language of poetic criticism has become so distorted, one needs to make some fundamental distinctions. Formal verse, like free verse, is neither intrinsically bad nor good. The terms are strictly descriptive not evaluative. They define distinct sets of metrical technique rather than rank the quality or nature of poetic performance. Nor do these techniques automatically carry with them social, political, or even, in most cases, aesthetic values. (It would, for example, be very easy for a poet to do automatic writing in meter. One might even argue that surrealism is best realized in formal verse since the regular rhythms of the words in meter hypnotically release the unconscious.) However obvious these distinctions should be, few poets or critics seem to be making them. Is it any wonder then that so much current writing on poetry is either opaque or irrelevant? What serious discussion can develop when such primary critical definitions fail to be made with accuracy?

2

Meter is an ancient, indeed primitive, technique that marks the beginning of literature in virtually every culture. It dates back to a time, so different from our specialized modern era, when there was little, if any, distinction between poetry, religion, history, music, and magic. All were performed in a sacred, ritual language separated from everyday speech by its incantatory metrical form. Meter is also essentially a pre-literate technology, a way of making language memorable before the invention of writing. Trained poet-singers took the events ing in the world. Failing is something queers do and have always done ceptionally well; for queers failure can be a style, to cite Quentin Crisp, r a way of life, to cite Foucault, and it can stand in contrast to the grim scenarios of success that depend upon "trying and trying again." In fact if success requires so much effort, then maybe failure is easier in the long run and offers different rewards.

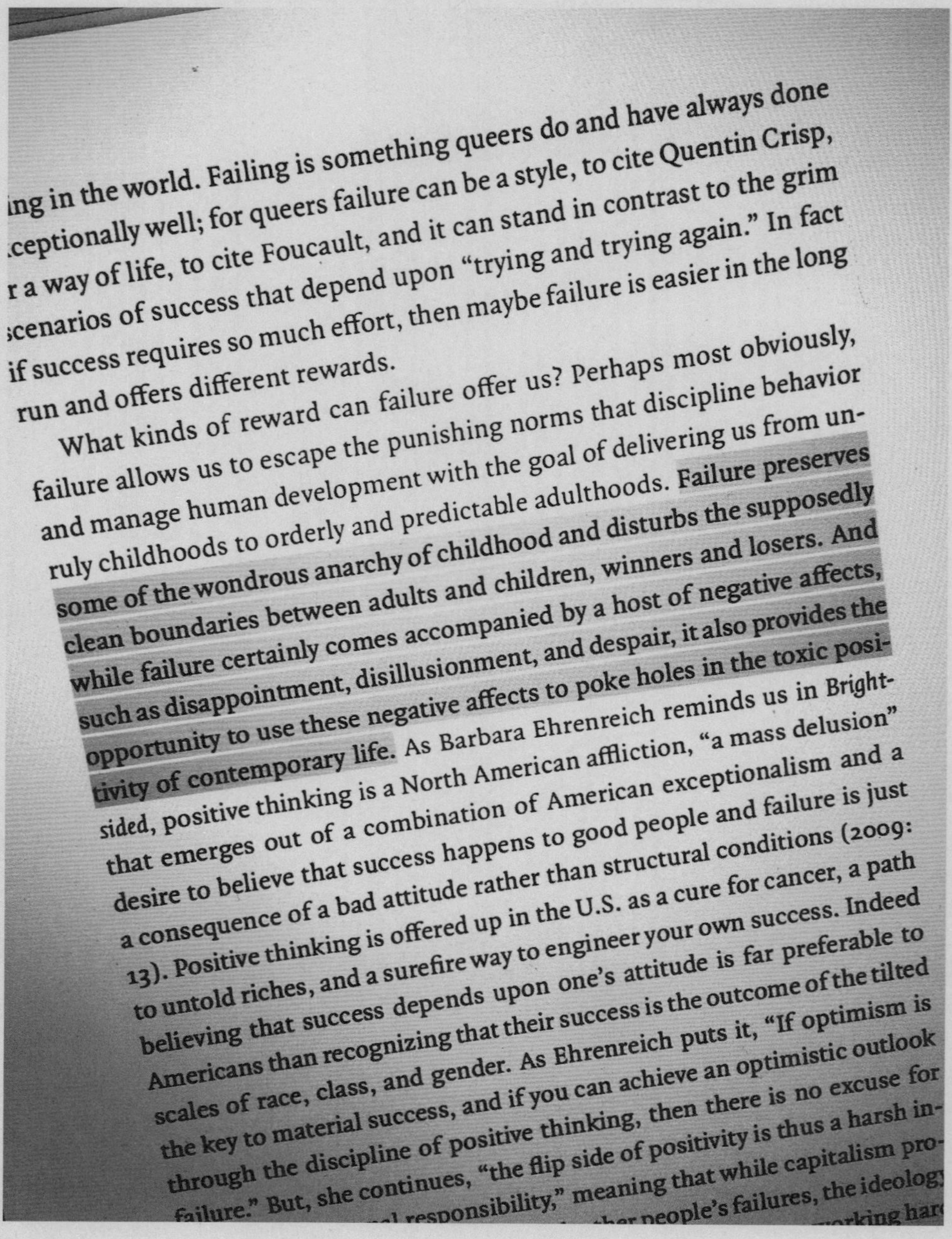

What kinds of reward can failure offer us? Perhaps most obviously, failure allows us to escape the punishing norms that discipline behavior and manage human development with the goal of delivering us from un-truly childhoods to orderly and predictable adulthoods. Failure preserves some of the wondrous anarchy of childhood and disturbs the supposedly clean boundaries between adults and children, winners and losers. And while failure certainly comes accompanied by a host of negative affects, such as disappointment, disillusionment, and despair, it also provides the opportunity to use these negative affects to poke holes in the toxic positivity of contemporary life. As Barbara Ehrenreich reminds us in Bright-sided, positive thinking is a North American affliction, "a mass delusion" that emerges out of a combination of American exceptionalism and a desire to believe that success happens to good people and failure is just a consequence of a bad attitude rather than structural conditions (2009: 13). Positive thinking is offered up in the U.S. as a cure for cancer, a path to untold riches, and a surefire way to engineer your own success. Indeed believing that success depends upon one's attitude is far preferable to Americans than recognizing that their success is the outcome of the tilted scales of race, class, and gender. As Ehrenreich puts it, "If optimism is the key to material success, and if you can achieve an optimistic outlook through the discipline of positive thinking, then there is no excuse for failure." But, she continues, "the flip side of positivity is thus a harsh in- ... responsibility," meaning that while capitalism pro- ... ther people's failures, the ideolog ... working har

**never forgive**

ses to the banality of straig
aginativeness of heteronormativity. The second aren
ore in keeping with the undisciplined kinds of responses that Leo
ani at least seems to associate with sex and queer culture, and it is
e that the promise of self-shattering, loss of mastery and meaning,
regulated speech and desire are unloosed. Dyke anger, anticolonial de-
pair, racial rage, counterhegemonic violence, punk pugilism—these are
he bleak and angry territories of the antisocial turn; these are the jagged
zones within which not only self-shattering (the opposite of narcissism
in a way) but other-shattering occurs. If we want to make the antisocial
turn in queer theory we must be willing to turn away from the comfort
zone of polite exchange in order to embrace a truly political negativity,
one that promises, this time, to fail, to make a mess, to fuck shit up, to
be loud, unruly, impolite, to breed resentment, to bash back, to speak up
and out, to disrupt, assassinate, shock, and annihilate.

"If at first you don't succeed," wrote Quentin Crisp, "failure may be
your style." The style of failure is better modeled by my list of antisocial
dignitaries. It is quite possibly a lesbian style rather than a gay style (since
very often gay style is style writ large), and it lives in the life and works of
Patricia Highsmith, for example, who wrote hateful letters to her mother
and in her notebooks scribbled of her strong desire to be disinvited to
friends' dinner parties.[4] I will return to the archive of antisocial feminism later in the book, but for now, in relation to the art of failure, I turn
to queer artwork preoccupied with emptiness, a sense of abandonment.
The queer collaborative Spanish artists Cabello/Carceller link queerness
to a mode of negativity that lays claim to rather than rejects concepts
like emptiness, futility, limitation, ineffectiveness, sterility, unproductiveness. In
this work a queer aesthetic is activated through the function of negation
rather than in the mode of positivity; in other words, the works strive to
establish queerness as a mode of critique rather than as a new investment

OUTSOURCING CRIME

Its old demons are catching up with it, and the masks are falling off. But it is still breathing. It hasn't succeeded in conquering my territory yet, thank God. I am not looking for an escape. Of course, the encounter with the great South terrifies me, but I surrender. I don't flee the undocumented worker's gaze and I don't avert my own from the starving Harraga who wash up on our shores, dead or alive. I would rather come clean. I am a criminal. But an extremely sophisticated one. I don't have any blood on my hands. That would be too vulgar. No justice system in the world would drag me to court. I outsource my crime. Between my crime and I, there's the bomb. I own nuclear fire. My bomb threatens all *métèques*[23] and protects my interests. Between my crime and I, first there is geographic distance and then geopolitical distance. But there are also great international bodies: the UN, the IMF, NATO, multinationals, the banking system. Between my crime and I, there are national bodies: democracy, the rule of law, the Republic, the elections. Between my crime and I, there are beautiful ideas: human rights, universalism, freedom, humanism, secularism, the memory of the Shoah, feminism, Marxism, Third Worldism. And even suitcase carriers. They stand at the pinnacle of white heroism. I respect them though. I wish I could respect them more, but they are already hostages of good conscience. The foils of the white

Left. Between my crime and I, there is the renewal and metamorphosis of great ideas, should the "beautiful soul" come to expire: fair trade, ecology, organic commerce.

Between me and my crime, there is my father's sweat and salary, social welfare, paid leave, labor law, school holidays, summer camp, hot water, heat, public transportation, my passport…. I am detached from my victim—and from my crime—by an insurmountable distance. This distance stretches. European check points have moved south. Fifty years after the independence movements, North Africa is the one subduing its own citizens and black Africans. I was going to say "my African brothers." But I no longer dare to, now that I have admitted my crime. Farewell Bandung. Sometimes the distance between my crime and I shrinks. Bombs explode in the subway. Towers are struck by airplanes and collapse like a house of cards. The journalists of a famous magazine are decimated. But immediately, good conscience does its work. "We are all American!" "We are all Charlie." This is the democrats' rallying cry. The sacred union. They are all American. They are all Charlie. They are all white.

If I were judged for my crime, I wouldn't claim my innocence. But I would plead extenuating circumstances. I am not exactly white. I am whitened. I am here because I was thrown up by

# The Metaphysics of Youth

## The Conversation

Where are you, Youth, that always wakes me
Promptly in the morning? Where are you, Light?
—Friedrich Hölderlin, "The Blind Singer"

### I

Daily we use unmeasured energies as if in our sleep. What we do and think is filled with the being of our fathers and ancestors. An uncomprehended symbolism enslaves us without ceremony.—Sometimes, on awakening, we recall a dream. In this way rare shafts of insight illuminate the ruins of our energies that time has passed by. We were accustomed to spirit [*Geist*] just as we are accustomed to the heartbeat that enables us to lift loads and digest our food.

Every conversation deals with knowledge of the past as that of our youth, and with horror at the sight of the spiritual masses of the rubble fields. We never saw the site of the primal struggle our egos waged with our fathers. Now we can see what we have unwittingly destroyed and created. Conversation laments lost greatness.

### II

Conversation strives toward silence, and the listener is really the silent partner. The speaker receives meaning from him; the silent one is the unappropriated source of meaning. The conversation raises words to his lips as do vessels, jugs. The speaker immerses the memory of his strength in words and seeks forms in which the listener can reveal himself. For the speaker speaks in order to let himself be converted. He understands the listener despite the flow of his own speech; he realizes that he is addressing someone whose features are inexhaustibly earnest and good, whereas he, the speaker, blasphemes against language.

(continued on back flap)

Well, after *that* had been straightened out . . .

"Pooh!" he cried. "There's something climbing up your back."

"I thought there was," said Pooh.

"It's Small!" cried Piglet.

Those who do things by the Pooh Way find this sort of thing happening to them all the time. It's hard to explain, except by example, but it works. Things just happen in the right way, at the right time. At least they do when you *let* them, when you work *with* circumstances instead of saying, "This isn't supposed to be happening this way," and trying hard to make it happen some other way. If you're in tune with The Way Things Work, then they work the way they need to, no matter what you may think about it at the time. Later on, you can look back and say, "Oh, now I understand. That had to happen so that *those* could happen, and those had to happen in order for *this* to happen. . . ." Then you realize that even if you'd tried to make it all turn out perfectly, you couldn't have done better, and if you'd *really* tried, you would have made a mess of the whole thing.

Let's take another example of Things Work Out: Eeyore's birthday party, as arranged by Pooh and Piglet.

… maintenant, parvenu à la vieillesse, il avait devant
lui la tranquillité, un empire dont les Anciens avaient
rêvé mais qu'ils n'avaient jamais pu constituer, les
bateaux allant de la Crimée à Barcelone, tout ce
domaine ne faisant qu'un, avec la même monnaie, la
même langue, le même drapeau. Le grand Union Jack
flottant du soleil levant au couchant ; elle avait fini par
se réaliser, cette union du soleil et du drapeau.

… avait-il vraiment parcouru les rues aux voitures
silencieuses, par ce paisible dimanche matin sur le Tier-
garten, il y a si longtemps ? Une autre vie. La crème gla-
cée, un goût qui pouvait n'avoir jamais existé. À
présent ils faisaient bouillir des orties et ils étaient bien
contents d'en avoir. Dieu ! s'écriait-il. Ne pouvaient-ils pas
s'arrêter ? Les énormes chars anglais s'avançaient.
Encore un immeuble, il avait pu être une maison de
rapport, un magasin, une école, un building de
bureaux ; il ne pouvait dire, les parois s'écroulaient se
réduisaient en fragments. Dans les décombres, en des-
sous, étaient ensevelis des survivants – une poignée – et
l'on n'entendait même pas le bruit de la mort. La mort
s'étendait partout, également sur les vivants entas-
sés, les cadavres en couches superposées qui com-
mençaient déjà à sentir. Le cadavre frissonnant, puant
de Berlin, les tourelles sans yeux encore sorties, s'affais-
sant sans protestation comme cet édifice sans âme
qu'un homme avait un jour érigé avec fierté.
Le garçon remarqua ses bras ; ils étaient couverts
d'une pellicule grise – la cendre en partie minérale,
mais composée en outre de matière organique, brûlée,
réduite en poudre. Tout cela était mélangé. Le garçon
s'essuyait sans aller plus loin. Une autre pensée
s'emparait de son esprit au moment où il croyait qu'il
allait y passer, dans le hurlement et le foum foum des
obus. La faim. Depuis six jours il ne mangeait que des
orties, et à présent il n'y en avait même plus. La prairie
de mauvaises herbes avait disparu, il n'y avait à cette
place qu'un vaste entonnoir. D'autres silhouettes
efflanquées, à peine visibles, s'étaient montrées sur le
bord, comme le jeune garçon, étaient restées là silencieuses, puis s'étaient éloignées. Une vieille mère avec
une baboushka nouée autour de sa tête grisonnante,
un panier – vide – au bras. Un manchot, aux yeux
aussi vides que le panier. Une jeune fille. Disparus
dans l'amoncellement d'arbres abattus où Eric, le
jeune garçon, s'était caché, lui aussi. Et le serpent
approchait.
Cela finirait-il un jour ? demanda le jeune garçon sans
s'adresser à personne. Et si cela doit finir, quand ?
Rempliront-ils leur ventre, ces…

… en silence, Karl contemplait le cercueil recouvert
d'un drapeau. Il gisait là, et maintenant il s'en était
allé, vraiment. Même les puissances inspirées par le
démon étaient incapables de le faire revenir. L'homme
– ou bien était-il après tout Übermensch ? – que Karl
avait suivi aveuglément, adoré… même jusqu'au bord
de la tombe. Adolf Hitler n'était plus, mais Karl se
cramponnait à la vie. Je ne le suivrai pas, murmurait
Karl dans le fond de lui-même. Je continuerai à vivre.
Et je reconstruirai. Et nous reconstruirons tous. Nous
le devons.

ZBIGNIEW ZUŁAWSKI & LPPL ANNOTATED  LE POIDS DE LA SAUTERELLE, 1960 HAWTHORNE ABENDSEN

# END NOTES

The text I have chosen to annotate is an essay entitled *The Morality Issue of "Contemporary" Critics* (*Dangdai pipingjia de daode wenti* 《"当代"批评家的道德问题》). This essay was written by Chinese literary historian Hong Zicheng in 2011. I read it as one of the collection of essays included in his book *Materials and Annotations*, published in 2016. In my view, *Materials and Annotations* is by far the most important volume in the prolific oeuvre of this professor of contemporary literature. This collection of essays lays out excerpts of primary documents of Chinese contemporary literature from 1950s to 1970s, an era of frequent political movements in Chinese history. These documents consisted mostly of various accounts and records provided by different parties or by the same person at various times, under various circumstances, but relating to the same period of time, the same historical event or issue. Their juxtapositions turn them into points of references and partners of conversations for each other, revealing the multifaceted nature and complexity of histories.

*The Morality Issue of "Contemporary" Critics* helped resolve some of my perplexity in terms of understanding the self-positioning of contemporary art and artists towards the political establishment. My recent practice has been revolving around a study of the legacy of Socialist Realism in the historical formation, process and practice of contemporary art in China. In this research, I set out to understand the complex relationship between individual artists, art practitioners and the ideological machine, the political life in contemporary China. This essay gave examples of political struggles of the 1950s and 1960s, in which moral judgment of character played a primary role in condemnation of political enemies, to such an extent that morality-based criticism was the most destructive weapon exercised by many high-ranking party officials and intellectuals, towards their political rivals. Hong Zicheng traced the origin of such a phenomenon to the internal logic of China's 20th century Socialist movement, in which intense clashes existed between orthodoxy and heterodoxy, trueness and falseness. He considered the relevance of the structure and operation of power to the limitation of space for "internal exile" and the dependence on moral judgment. Everyone was forced into taking sides and no one could remain silent. As contemporary China promoted a kind of "pan-moralized" political practice since 1949, many revolutionary writers and critics tended to acquire the role of moralist in terms of distinguishing the real and the false and appear correct and fierce in guarding what they consider the truth. But as the documents revealed, the moralists also resorted to dishonest and hypocritical methods to make accusations of their rivals. The accusers and the accused often exchanged positions under changing political circumstances.

This piece of sophisticated writing sheds light on contemporary conditions in China. It relieves some of the anxiety one experiences

when realizing the gaps, contradictions, inconsistency and sense of
uncertainty within oneself. The political structure that gave rise to the
prevalence of moralists in the 1950s to 1970s remains in firm place
today. As Hong pointed out, it's the transformation, split, inconsistency
that has the potential to escape visible and invisible constraints, to
realize the vitality of discovery and innovation.

**AMIR GEORGE**

**JONATHAN KEMP**

Text compiled from pieces of articles and film reviews.

Text reads:
1. In normalising radiation the states de-facto geo-logic means
our bodies become its site, in a form of sokushinbutsu devoid of
enlightenment. If the historical performance of different knowledge
regimes have effected distributions of the 'real' and 'unreal' they have
been complicit in sedimenting action and non-action.

2. In any non-muddy episteme there's always a containment at work:
avoiding the recursion of explaining its means of description (such as
'the sun will rise tomorrow' as in a smuggled inductive reasoning); and
that any 'excess' of description will always be erased or put on hold as
a carry-out or 'undecideable'...

3. Such a geo-logic oozes the confluence of the ancient and geo-
mythical with the technological, industrial, as resonant vectors,
contingent and conspiratorial crisscrossing to ever shift our impression
of the earth...

4. How to halt the forkbomb of the temporary temporary
temporariness?

**MIDORI MATSUI**

Quotation and commentary by Midori Matsui

1. Children never stop talking about what they are doing or trying to
do: exploring milieus, by means of dynamic trajectories, and drawing
up maps of them. The maps of these trajectories are essential to
psychic activity. Little Hans wants to leave his family's apartment to
spend the night at the little girl's downstairs and return in the morning—
the apartment building as a milieu....(ellipsis mine)

But a milieu is made up of qualities, substances, powers and events:
the street, for example, with its materials (paving stones), its noises
(the cries of merchants), its animals (harnessed horses) or its dramas (a
horse slips, a horse falls down a horse beaten...) the trajectory merges
not only with the subjectivity of those who travel through a milieu, but
also with the subjectivity of the milieu itself, insofar as it is reflected
in those who travel through it. The map expresses the identity of the
journey and what one journeys through. It merges with its object, when
the object itself is movement. (p. 61)

2. The libido does not undergo metamorphoses, but follows world-
historical trajectories. From this point of view, it does not seem that the
real and the imaginary form a pertinent distinction. A real voyage, by
itself, lacks the force necessary to be reflected in the imagination; the
imaginary voyage, by itself, does not have the force, as Proust says,
to be verified in the real. This is why the imaginary and the real must
be, rather, like two juxtaposable or superimposable parts of a single
trajectory, two faces that ceaselessly interchange with one another, a
mobile mirror. Thus the Australian Aborigines' link nomadic itineraries
to dream voyages, which together compose "an interstitching of
routes," "in an immense cut-out [decoupe]]of space and time that must
be read like a map." At the limit, the imaginary is a virtual image that

**180**

**228**

**274**

**474**

is interfused with the real object, and vice versa, thereby constituting
a crystal of the unconscious. It is not enough for the real object or the
real landscape to evoke similar or related images; it must disengage
its own virtual image at the same time that the latter, as an imaginary
landscape, makes its entry into the real, following a circuit where each
of the two product of this doubling or splitting in two (*doublement
ou dedoublement*), this coalescence. It is in such crystals of the
unconscious that the trajectories of the libido are made visible.

A cartographic conception is very distinct from the archaeological
conception of psychoanalysis. The latter establishes a profound
link between the unconscious and memory; it is a memorial,
commemorative, or monumental conception that pertains to persons
and objects, the milieus being nothing more than terrains capable of
conserving, identifying, or authenticating them. From such a point
of view, the superimposition of layers is necessarily traversed by a
shaft that goes from top to bottom, and it is always a question of
penetration. Maps, on the contrary, are superimposed in such a
way that each map finds itself modified in the following map, rather
than finding its origin in the preceding one; from one map to the
next, it is not a matter of searching for an origin, but of evaluating
displacements. Every map is a redistribution of impasses and
breakthroughs, of thresholds and enclosures, which necessarily go
from bottom to top. There is not only a reversal of directions, but
also a difference in nature: the unconscious no longer deals with
persons and objects, but with trajectories and becomings; it is no
longer an unconscious of commemoration but one of mobilization, an
unconscious whose objects take flight rather than remaining buried in
the ground. (pp.62-3)

3. Maps should not be understood only in extension, in relation to a
space constituted by trajectories. There are also maps of intensity, of
density, that are concerned with what fills space, what subtends the
trajectory. Little Hans defines a horse by making out a list of its affects,
both active and passive: having a big widdler, hauling heavy loads,
having blinkers, biting, falling down, being whipped, making a row
with its feet. It is this distribution of affects (with the widdler playing
the transformer or converter) that constitutes a map of intensity. It is
always an affective constellation. Here again, it would be abusive to
see this as a simple deviation from the father-mother, as does Freud—
as if the "vision" of the street, so frequent at the time (a horse falls
down, is whipped, struggles) were incapable of affecting the libido
directly, and had to recall a lovemaking scene between the parents...
Identifying the horse with the father borders on the grotesque and
entails a misunderstanding of all the unconscious's relations with
animal forces. And just as the map of movements or intensities was not
a derivation from or extension of the father-mother, the map of forces
or intensities is not a derivation from the body, an extension of a prior
image, or a supplement or afterward. Pollack and Sivadon have made
a profound analysis of the cartographic activity of the unconscious;
perhaps their sole ambiguity lies in seeing it as a continuation of the
image of the body. On the contrary, it is the map of intensity that
distributes the affects, and it is their links and valences that constitute
the image of the body in each case — an image that can always be
modified or transformed depending on the affective constellations that
determine it.

A list or constellation of affects, an intensive map, is a becoming: Little
Hans does not form an unconscious representation of the father with
the horse, but is drawn into a becoming-horse to which his parents

are opposed. It is the same with little Arpad and his becoming-cock:
in each case, psychoanalysis misconstrues the relationship of the
unconscious with forces. The image is not only the trajectory, but
also a becoming. Becoming is what subtends the trajectory, just as
intensive forces subtend motor forces. Hans's becoming-horse refers to
a trajectory, from the apartment house to the warehouse. The passage
along side the warehouse, or even the visit to the henhouse, may be
customary trajectories, but they are not innocent promenades. We see
clearly why the real and the imaginary were led to exceed themselves,
or even to interchange with each other: a becoming is not imaginary,
any more than a voyage is real. It is becoming that turns the most
negligible of trajectories, or even a fixed mobility, into a voyage; and
it is the trajectory that turns the imaginary into a becoming. Each of the
two types of maps, those of trajectories and those of affects, refers to
the other.

What concerns the libido, what the libido invests, presents itself with
an indefinite article, or rather is presented by the indefinite article:
an animal as a qualification of a becoming or the specification of
a trajectory (a horse, a chicken); a body or an organ as the power
to affect and to be affected (a stomach, some eyes); and even the
characters that obstruct a pathway and inhibit affects, or on the
contrary that further them (a father, some people). Children express
themselves in this manner — a father, a body, a horse. These intensities
often seem to result from a lack of determination due to the defenses
of consciousness. For psychoanalysis, it is always a question of
my father, me, my body. It has a mania for the possessive and the
personal. And interpretation consists in recovering persons and
possessions. "A child is being beaten" must signify "I am being beaten
by my father," even if this transformation remains abstract; and
"a horse falls down and kicks about with its legs" means that my father
makes love with my mother. Yet the indefinite lacks nothing; above all,
it does not lack determination. It is the determination of a becoming,
its characteristic power, the power of an impersonal that is not a
generality but a singularity at its highest point. For example, I do not
play the horse, any more than I imitate this or that horse, but I become
a horse, by reaching a zone of proximity where I can no longer be
distinguished from what I am becoming.

Art also attains this celestial state that no longer retains anything of
the personal or rational. In its own way, art says what children say. It
is made up of trajectories and becoming, and it too make maps, both
extensive and intensive (pp.64–66).

Commentaries:
"What Children Say" presents a special way of comprehending the
world shared by children, Aborigines and artists. It argues that they
create their unique map of the phenomenological world through
"trajectories" and "intensities," redistributing "milieus" and "affects."

Trajectory is a path of doing something, often following one's libidinal
drive; it involves, on the way, external things — "qualities, substances,
powers and events: the street, for example, with its materials (paving
stones), its noises (the cries of merchants), its animals (harnessed horses)
or its dramas (a horse slips, …)"(ellipsis mine); the states of things and
the dramas that happen to them inevitably evoke the subject's emotional
or conceptual responses, creating a specific "milieu."

Deleuze describes, for example, a visit, at night, of little Hans, the
protagonist of Freud's case study "Analysis of a Phobia in a Five-year-

*old Boy"*(1909), to a little girl who lives downstairs of his apartment, as an occasion that makes his apartment a "milieu." But, Deleuze argues, the "milieu, " or the trajectory, should not be limited to the boy's relationship with his father or mother. As opposed to the symbolism that reduces facts to symptoms, according to the authoritative dictates of psychoanalysis, "trajectories" never follow any external doctrines; instead of binding an event to an origin or a goal, trajectories are spontaneously projected, only to displace the former ones, letting a shape of desire emerge through the traces of such displacements.

The milieu, or trajectory, is neither completely a product of the subjective reflections of the actor, nor mere facts; it is always the combination of both, having the force to intervene in reality as well as the ability to give an internal meaning to an action. Deleuze discusses the drawing of autistic children and dream vision of the Australian Aborigines as perfect examples of the map of trajectories. The Aborigines intuitively understand the meaning of their wandering by accompanying it with the vision of a dream voyage; the moment a dream vision is created through the transformation of facts by imagination marks the point of an encounter ("overlapping") of the actor's inner world and the external facts. The imaginary vision also transmits (shows in the clairvoyant's crystal) the work of the unconscious, which turns the amorphous stream of desire into visible forms.

There is also a map of intensities or affects, as another way of knowing the world directly. Affects is the physical and psychological influences of something on the human body and mind; for example, Little Hans understands the horse through its attributes —"having a big widdler, hauling heavy loads, having blinkers, biting, falling down, being whipped...." (ellipsis mine) He understands the horse's unique being through his empathy with its states and dramas, in a sense, "becoming a horse." It is a dynamic, if animistic, way of knowing the unique being of something.

A creature or a phenomenon thus understood no longer belongs to an abstract or general category, but it becomes a singular entity, and, at the same time, a palpable evidence of the subject's physical and psychological understanding of the phenomenological world. The knowledge fortifies the sense of one's singular positioning in the world, giving one a definite sense of being uniquely connected with a certain moment, place, and event, which is the perception of one's becoming.

I learned from this essay the following:

1. The map of trajectories and intensities helped my appreciation of the Art Brut type of drawing without a center and peripheries, having, instead, details develop out of other details, as if from bottom to top, following libidinal drives, or chain of associations.

2. It presented an idea of the unconscious not as a storage of memories, but as an active mechanism producing new images by transforming (displacing) external facts with imaginary visions that reflect libidinal activities.

3. It defined the essential power of art as the force of affecting, making the spectators find their own internal paths of understanding. Although Deleuze describes, as a "cartographical" art, a post-Minimalist type of sculptural installation that lays out, not a finished monument, but tentative "paths" for the spectators to use in realizing their own unique ways of approaching the work, finding their own angles to look at it,

he also reassures that the same experience can be found in "any kind of art, even in music." A focus on the affective elements in painting, for example, opens up a unique horizon of appreciating painting as an experiential medium.

4. It presented a method of understanding the phenomenological world through "sense," which signifies my perception of physical impacts of things and my mind's responses to them. This method makes me aware of my own unique positioning in the phenomenological world. If I keep making this sort of perceptual entry into the world, I would naturally comprehend the uniqueness of my own being as an event, or a "becoming," without referring to any predetermined epistemological systems. I would always know the singularity of my positioning in a spontaneous relation to the other things' unique modes of being; this would make the most anonymous, or incidental, detail and action of my everyday life an illumination of a truth; the thinking model makes my idea of subject more flexible, dynamic, and yet concrete.

5. If one compares the map of trajectories and affects to the "longitude and latitude" of the plane of immanence, which signifies the determination of the unique being of living creatures, through the speed and slowness of bodies in motion and rest, and the capacity of affecting and being affected, presented in Deleuze's other book, *Spinoza: Practical Philosophy*, one would realize his consistent emphasis on the pragmatic determination of an individual through a sense of "becoming" as a dynamic process of affective identification and imaginative displacement.

This essay should be read entirely as an integral discussion.

Due to the word limit, and also for the sake of highlighting Deleuze's insights about "milieu," the flight of the unconscious, the distribution of affects in the formation of one's unique being as "becoming," I quoted the above sections and underlined the sentences which seem to communicate his points explicitly.

<table>
<tr><td>NIALL MCCLELLAND</td><td>The physical lyric sheet was Jeremy Jansen's when his band was doing a cover of the song.</td><td>276</td></tr>
<tr><td>GIORGIO SADOTTI</td><td>These words jumped out at me from any sentence in any book that contained the word ME, so it's hard to pin down a specific instance. They are universally seen words that come at you from anywhere.</td><td>353</td></tr>
<tr><td>MIRIAM VISACZKI</td><td>English translation by Robert Hullot-Kentor, 1997 for *Ästhetische Theorie*, 1973, Theodor W. Adorno.<br>Source: https://archive.org/stream/theodor-w-adorno-aesthetic-theory-1997/theodor-w-adorno-aesthetic-theory-1997_djvu.txt</td><td>429</td></tr>
</table>

Yet even in artworks that are to their very core ideological, truth content can assert itself. Ideology, socially necessary semblance, is by this same necessity also the distorted image of the true. A threshold that divides the social consciousness of aesthetics from the philistine is that aesthetics reflects the social critique of the ideological in artworks, rather than mechanically reiterating it. Stifter provides a model of the truth content of an oeuvre that is undoubtedly ideological in its intentions. Not only the conservative-restorative choice of thematic material and the fabula docet are ideological, but so is the objective deportment of the form, which suggests a micrologically tender world, a meaningfully correct life that lends itself to narration. This is why Stifter became the idol of a retrospectively noble bourgeoisie. Yet

the layers of his work that once provided him with his half esoteric
popularity have with time peeled away and vanished. This, however,
is not the last word on Stifter, for the reconciling, conciliatory aspects,
especially in his last works, are exaggerated. Here objectivity
hardens into a mask and the life evoked becomes a defensive ritual.
Shimmering through the eccentricity of the average is the secret and
denied suffering of the alienated subject and an unreconciled life.
The light that falls over his mature prose is drained and bleak, as if
it were allergic to the happiness of color; it is, as it were, reduced to
a pencil sketch by the exclusion of everything unruly and disturbing
to a social reality that was as incompatible with the mentality of the
poet as with the epic apriori that he took from Goethe and clung
to. What transpires, in opposition to the will of his prose, through
the discrepancy between its form and the already capitalist society
devolves upon its expression; ideological exaggeration endows
his work mediately with its nonideological truth content, with its
superiority over all consoling, assiduously pastoral literature, and
it won for it that authentic quality that Nietzsche admired. Stifter is
the pardigm of how little poetic intention, even that meaning that is
directly embodied or represented in an artwork, approximates its
objective content; in his work the content is truly the negation of the
meaning, yet this content would not exist if the meaning were not
intended by the work and then canceled and transformed by the
work's own complexion. Affirmation becomes the cipher of despair
and the purest negativity of content contains, as in Stifter, a grain
of affirmation. The iridescence that emanates from artworks, which
today taboo all affirmation, is the appearance of the affirmative
ineffable, the emergence of the nonexisting as if it did exist. Its claim
to existence flickers out in aesthetic semblance; yet what does not
exist, by appearing, is promised. The constellation of the existing and
nonexisting is the utopic figure of art. Although it is compelled toward
absolute negativity, it is precisely by virtue of this negativity that it is
not absolutely negative. By no means do artworks primarily develop
this inwardly antinomical affirmative element as a result of their
external attitude to what exists, that is, to society; rather, it develops
immanently in them and immerses them in twilight.

No beauty today can evade the question whether it is actually
beautiful and not instead surreptitiously acquired by static affirmation.
The antipathy toward applied arts is, indirectly, the bad conscience
of art as a whole, which makes itself felt at the sound of every musical
chord and at the sight of every color. There is no need for social
criticism of art to investigate this externally: It emerges from the
inner-aesthetic formations themselves. The heightened sensitivity of
the aesthetic sensorium converges asymptotically with the socially
motivated irritability toward art. In art, ideology and truth cannot be
neatly distinguished from each other. Art cannot have one without
the other, and this reciprocity in turn is an enticement toward the
ideological misuse of art as much as it is an enticement toward
summarily finishing it off. It is only a step from the utopia of the self-
likeness of artworks to the stink of the heavenly roses that art scatters
here below as do the women in Schiller's tirade. The more brazenly
society is transformed into a totality in which it assigns everything,
including art, to its place, the more completely does art polarize
into ideology and protest; and this polarization is hardly to art's
advantage. Absolute protest constrains it and carries over to its own
raison d'etre; ideology thins out to an impoverished and authoritarian
copy of reality.

In the culture resurrected after the catastrophe, art — regardless of
its content and substance [Inhalt and Gehalt] has even taken on an
ideological aspect by its mere existence. In its disproportion to the
horror that has transpired and threatens, it is condemned to cynicism;
even where it directly faces the horror, it diverts attention from it.
Its objectivation implies insensitivity to reality. This degrades art to
an accomplice of the barbarism to which it sucumbs no less when
it renounces objectivation and directly plays along, even when this
takes the form of polemical commitment. Every artwork today, the
radical ones included, has its conservative aspect; its existence helps
to secure the spheres of spirit and culture, whose real powerlessness
and complicity with the principle of disaster becomes plainly evident.
But this conservative element — which, contrary to the trend toward
social integration, is stronger in advanced works than in the more
moderate ones — does not simply deserve oblivion. Only insofar
as spirit, in its most advanced form, survives and perseveres is any
opposition to the total domination of the social totality possible. A
humanity to which progressive spirit fails to bequeath what humanity is
poised to liquidate would disappear in a barbarism that a reasonable
social order should prevent. Art, even as something tolerated in
the administered world, embodies what does not allow itself to be
managed and what total management suppresses.